# THE RULE OF LAW UNDER PRESSURE

*The Rule of Law under Pressure* provides readers with an accessible and richly detailed assessment of recent challenges to the rule of law. The rule of law is closely tied to both democracy and human rights. The erosion of the rule of law, within a rising number of countries and in international relations, places populations under increasingly authoritarian and rights-abusing governments and threatens to destabilize peaceful relations among states. The book brings conceptual clarity to this complex and multidimensional topic and assesses recent trends in the rule of law at both national and international levels. The opening chapter clearly sets out the key concepts and evaluates broad transnational trends in the rule of law. Succeeding chapters assess rule-of-law developments at the international level and within key countries around the world. This title is also available as Open Access on Cambridge Core.

GREGORY SHAFFER is the Scott K. Ginsburg Professor of International Law at Georgetown University Law Center and a former president of the American Society of International Law. The award-winning author of *Emerging Powers* and *The World Trade System*, Shaffer is the author of eleven books.

WAYNE SANDHOLTZ is a political scientist specializing in international law, international courts, and human rights. Since 2012 he has held the John A. McCone Chair in International Relations at the University of Southern California. His most recent books include *Prohibiting Plunder: How Norms Change* (2007) and *Research Handbook on the Politics of International Law* (2017, coeditor).

# THE RULE OF LAW UNDER PRESSURE

## A Transnational Challenge


Edited by

GREGORY SHAFFER

*Georgetown University*

WAYNE SANDHOLTZ

*University of Southern California*



CAMBRIDGE
UNIVERSITY PRESS

CAMBRIDGE
UNIVERSITY PRESS

Shaftesbury Road, Cambridge CB2 8EA, United Kingdom

One Liberty Plaza, 20th Floor, New York, NY 10006, USA

477 Williamstown Road, Port Melbourne, VIC 3207, Australia

314–321, 3rd Floor, Plot 3, Splendor Forum, Jasola District Centre, New Delhi – 110025, India

103 Penang Road, #05–06/07, Visioncrest Commercial, Singapore 238467

Cambridge University Press is part of Cambridge University Press & Assessment, a department of the University of Cambridge.

We share the University's mission to contribute to society through the pursuit of education, learning and research at the highest international levels of excellence.

www.cambridge.org
Information on this title: www.cambridge.org/9781009460248

DOI: 10.1017/9781009460286



First published 2025

*A catalogue record for this publication is available from the British Library*

*Library of Congress Cataloging-in-Publication Data*
Names: Shaffer, Gregory, editor. | Sandholtz, Wayne, editor.
Title: The rule of law under pressure : a transnational challenge / edited by Gregory Shaffer, Georgetown University, Washington DC; Wayne Sandholtz, University of Southern California.
Description: Cambridge, United Kingdom ; New York, NY : Cambridge University Press, 2025. | Includes bibliographical references and index.
Identifiers: LCCN 2024029008 | ISBN 9781009460248 (hardback) | ISBN 9781009460255 (paperback) | ISBN 9781009460286 (ebook)
Subjects: LCSH: Rule of law – International cooperation. | International law and human rights.
Classification: LCC K3171 .R8569 2025 | DDC 340/.11–dc23/eng/20240626
LC record available at https://lccn.loc.gov/2024029008

ISBN 978-1-009-46024-8 Hardback
ISBN 978-1-009-46025-5 Paperback

# CONTENTS

# CONTRIBUTORS

OLABISI D. AKINKUGBE, Associate Professor, Viscount Bennett Professor of Law, Schulich School of Law, Dalhousie University

JEREMY FARRALL, Professor, Australian National University College of Law and Adjunct Professor, University of Tasmania Faculty of Law

TOM GINSBURG, Leo Spitz Distinguished Service Professor of International Law and Ludwig and Hilde Wolf Research Scholar, University of Chicago Law School

TYRELL HABERKORN, Professor, Department of Asian Languages and Cultures, University of Wisconsin – Madison

TERENCE C. HALLIDAY, Research Professor Emeritus, American Bar Foundation and Honorary Professor in the School of Regulation and Global Governance (REGNET), Australian National University

JEFFREY KAHN, University Distinguished Professor, Altshuler Distinguished Teaching Professor and Professor of Law, Dedman School of Law, Southern Methodist University

MARTIN KRYGIER, Gordon Samuels Professor of Law and Social Theory, School of Global and Public Law, University of New South Wales and Senior Research Fellow, Rule of Law Program, Central European Democracy Institute

DILEK KURBAN, Visiting Researcher, Berlin Social Science Center (WZB)

JI LI, John and Marilyn Long Professor of US–China Business and Law, University of California, Irvine School of Law

ANA MARÍA MONTOYA, Director of Data Analytics, World Justice Project

ANNE PETERS, Director, Max Planck Institute for Comparative Public Law and International Law

ALEJANDRO PONCE, Chief Research Officer, World Justice Project

FRANCISCA POU GIMÉNEZ, Senior Researcher, Institute for Legal Research, National Autonomous University of Mexico (UNAM)

WAYNE SANDHOLTZ, John A. McCone Chair in International Relations and Professor of International Relations and Law, University of Southern California

KIM LANE SCHEPPELE, Laurance S. Rockefeller Professor of Sociology and International Affairs, Princeton School of Public and International Affairs and the University Center for Human Values, Princeton University

CHRISTOPH SCHOPPE, Willkie Farr & Gallagher LLP (Frankfurt/ Hamburg)

GREGORY SHAFFER, Scott K. Ginsburg Professor of International Law, Georgetown University Law Center, former president of the American Society of International Law

BRIAN TAMANAHA, John S. Lehmann University Professor, School of Law, Washington University in Saint Louis

# PREFACE

The rule of law has been eroding for more than a decade in every region of the world. This transnational phenomenon is visible "in both established democracies like the United States, and in entrenched autocracies, from Russia to China to Venezuela."[1] In Latin America, observers note "a dire, real challenge to the rule of law."[2] In Africa, "the last decade has seen this commitment [to the rule of law] steadily weaken."[3] More broadly, the globe is undergoing "a rule of law recession characterized by executive overreach, curtailing of human rights, and justice systems that are failing to meet people's needs."[4] In short, "[t]here is a global crisis of the rule of law."[5]

At the international level, events have likewise raised concerns about the continued vigor of rules that have stabilized world politics for decades. Russia's invasion of Ukraine, including the removal of some 19,000 children to Russia and the intense bombardment of Ukrainian cities, is a frontal assault on rules that prohibit the use of force in relations among states. China's establishment of military bases on artificial islands in the western Pacific Ocean, and its claims over the surrounding seas, raise

[1] Ted Piccone, *The Rule of Law Is Under Duress Everywhere*, BROOKINGS (Mar. 17, 2020), www.brookings.edu/articles/the-rule-of-law-is-under-duress-everywhere/. See also Ted Piccone, *The Compounding Rule of Law Crisis*, BROOKINGS (Nov. 10, 2023), www.brookings.edu/articles/the-compounding-rule-of-law-crisis/.

[2] Catalina Botero, *The Rule of Law in Latin America: From Constitutionalism to Political Uncertainty*, DIALOGUE: LEADERSHIP FOR THE AMERICAS (Mar. 4, 2019), https://tinyurl.com/y72vpt5n.

[3] Charles Manga Forbad, *An Overview of the Crisis of the Rule of Law in Africa*, 18 AFR. HUM. RTS. L.J. 213 (2018).

[4] *Over 6 Billion People Live in a Country Where the Rule of Law Is Declining*, WORLD JUST. PROJECT (Oct. 25, 2023), https://worldjusticeproject.org/news/wjp-rule-law-index-2023-global-press-release.

[5] Irene Khan, Director-General of the International Development Law Organization, Statement at the High-Level Meeting on the Rule of Law at the National and International Levels (Sept. 24, 2012), www.un.org/ruleoflaw/wp-content/uploads/2017/05/Statement-by-IDLO.pdf.

further concern over the status of international rules governing territorial boundaries. When the Permanent Court of Arbitration ruled against China's claims over maritime areas within its so-called nine-dash line, China rejected the decision.[6] The United States, in parallel, undermined the dispute resolution system of the World Trade Organization when it blocked the appointment of judges to fill vacancies on the WTO's Appellate Body. Under the Trump administration, it withdrew from multiple treaties in order to reduce international scrutiny and accountability over its actions.

The rule of law constrains the arbitrary exercise of power. Its decline means that governments become less restrained by legal norms that temper and channel power's exercise. The waning of the rule of law also entails the erosion of democracy and human rights since both depend on respect of legal rules and institutions that support them. In this book, contributors assess rule-of-law trends at the domestic and international levels affecting all the world's regions.

The contributions in Part I provide the conceptual and empirical foundations for the volume. In Chapter 1, which frames the book, we define core concepts, assess the relationship between national and international law and institutions implicating the rule of law transnationally, and show how rule-of-law practices are shifting in parallel at the domestic and international levels. We formulate a teleological conception of the rule of law in terms of the goal of constraining power's arbitrary exercise, which, in turn, calls for an assessment of institutional mechanisms to advance this goal given varying social conditions and contexts. We examine the ways in which international law and institutions are important for rule-of-law ends, as well as their potential pathologies since power also is exercised beyond the state in an interconnected world. The chapter next examines empirical indicators of the decline of the rule of law at the national and international levels. We conclude by assessing what might be done in response to the decline of rule-of-law protections.

Brian Tamanaha, in Chapter 2, addresses why sovereigns are entitled to the benefit of the international rule of law. He critically responds to arguments advanced by Jeremy Waldron in concluding that sovereign states are not entitled to the benefits of the international rule of law. Waldron's conclusion follows from his assertions that the purpose of the rule of law is to protect individual liberty, and the purpose of

6 South China Sea Arbitration (Phil. v. China), Case No. 2013-19, Award (Perm. Ct. Arb. 2016).

international law is to protect individuals. Tamanaha argues that legal relations in the international community of states constitute the horizontal dimension of the rule of law, which Waldron overlooked. Focusing on horizontal rule-of-law functions, he provides descriptive, theoretical, and normative reasons why states are, and should be, entitled to the benefits of the rule of law.

Ana María Montoya and Alejandro Ponce, in Chapter 3 on rule-of-law backsliding, present quantitative evidence from the World Justice Project on the deterioration of the rule of law at the transnational level and on how this phenomenon has transpired. They find that the rule of law has deteriorated in recent years around the world. They differentiate three groups of countries. The first group is composed of countries that have experienced a deterioration in all indicators, but most notably as regards limits to state power, open government, and respect for human rights. The second group is composed of countries where overall rule-of-law trends have declined slightly. The third group is composed of countries where most indicators have experienced slight improvements. As limits on the exercise of state power have weakened, rule-of-law protections have declined. Montoya and Ponce find that retrogressions in the rule of law appear to be associated, in part, with an increase in authoritarian tendencies in existing authoritarian regimes and, in part, with the rise of anti-pluralist and populist leaders.

In Part II, contributors evaluate the role of international institutions in interacting with national ones in supporting the rule of law. Anne Peters, in Chapter 4 on international organizations as constitution-shapers, evaluates the efforts of international organizations in issuing recommendations and prescriptions for constitution-making and reform. She finds that such constitution-shaping activities by European and universal organizations, notably the United Nations (UN), have generally not led to improvements in the rule of law on the ground. Peters maintains that international organizations' constitution-shaping efforts should address postcolonial concerns, which include respect for local rule-of-law cultures flowing from non-European constitutional thought and the inclusion of a much deeper social agenda. Thus revamped, international organizations' constitution-shaping role could be reinvigorated to support rule-of-law protections at the domestic level, thereby contributing to more legitimate and effective transnational legal ordering and global constitutionalism.

In Chapter 5 on international measures to support the rule of law, Tom Ginsburg and Christoph Schoppe assess efforts by regional courts and organizations to uphold the rule of law. While not originally the primary focus of regional human rights and trade systems, these institutions have provided a thicker set of obligations toward protecting the rule of law, along with democracy and other related goals. Supranational and international organizations, as a result, have become important actors confronting real-world threats to the rule of law. The chapter compares developments in Europe, Africa, and Latin America.

Jeremy Farrall and Terence Halliday, in Chapter 6 entitled *Transnational Legal Order through Rule of Law?*, deploy the book's framework to address two central questions in global governance. First, what are the prospects and limits of the power of the UN Security Council (UNSC) in promoting rule-of-law goals? And second, can rule-of-law norms constrain UNSC powers? The chapter sketches an interpretive narrative of UNSC engagement with the rule of law from the early 1990s to the present in three areas of UNSC action: peacekeeping, sanctions, and use of force. Conceptually, Farrall and Halliday propose that the rule of law in the UNSC manifests itself in three dimensions: discourse, procedure (or rules), and structures. These dimensions play out internally, within the UNSC itself, and externally, with respect to rule-of-law institution-building in and between states, as well as in post-conflict zones, with a rather gray area between (such as when UN peacekeeping missions are themselves subject to rule-of-law oversight for the behavior of their personnel). They examine the emergence of micro transnational legal orders under construction within the UNSC itself. The chapter concludes by considering the potential for elected members of the UNSC and weaker states in the UN to press for rule-of-law constraints on the UNSC.

Part III of the book evaluates rule-of-law developments in national and regional contexts, with chapters that address each region of the world. Chapter 7, *The Rule of Law Writ Large: The European Union and Its Rogue Member States* by Kim Lane Scheppele, assesses the rule of law in transnational context. Virtually all philosophical discussions of the rule of law's meaning, she notes, assume that the proper horizon of the concept is the national legal system, or what she calls "the rule of law writ small." But governments are bound by a web of transnational legal obligations that should also be considered part of the rule of law's scope. Analyzing whether the rule of law is honored against the backdrop of both national and transnational law gives us "the rule of law writ large." This concept has force in the context of both backsliding and democracy-restoring governments – that is, both when autocrats first pull their governments away from transnational rule-of-law norms and when newly elected democrats seek to restore compliance with those norms. While both sorts of governments may change domestic law, pack political institutions with those who share their values, and fire those who get in their way, only the democracy restorers can be said to be honoring the rule of law writ large. Scheppele applies her analysis to developments in Hungary and Poland.

In Chapter 8, Jeffrey Kahn examines how the Council of Europe sought to promote the rule of law in Russia after the collapse of the Soviet Union. Soviet president Mikhail Gorbachev called for the construction of "a Common European Home" that included Russia, which would be pursued in concert with European states and international organizations.[7] Russian president Boris Yeltsin and, initially, his successor Vladimir Putin appeared to pursue this ambition. But after roughly a decade of reforms, that effort foundered, reversed, and then collapsed. Russia descended again into authoritarianism and, shortly after its full-scale invasion of Ukraine, Russia was expelled from the Council of Europe. The chapter shows how the dynamics of Russia's pursuit and rocky course of membership of the Council of Europe affected both the Russian state and the Council of Europe itself.

Dilek Kurban evaluates the experience of Turkey in Chapter 9. She argues that under President Recep Tayyip Erdoğan Turkey has become an autocratic regime. The Turkish case raises questions about how international organizations tasked with upholding the rule of law are able not only to permit illiberal states to violate rule-of-law norms but also to undermine those principles themselves. Conceptually, she argues, the rule-of-law/rule-by-law binary fails to account fully for authoritarian contexts. If the rule of law constitutes one end of the analytical spectrum, the other end is "lawless rule," not rule by law, with the "dual state" lying somewhere between. Her chapter analyzes the case law of the European Court of Human Rights (ECtHR) concerning Erdoğan's resort to the law to consolidate his power ("rule by law") and his utter disregard of legal rules in repressing democratic dissent and engaging in state violence ("lawlessness"). Her analysis assesses not only ECtHR judgments but also inadmissibility decisions and strike-out rulings that have enabled lawlessness in Turkey.

In Chapter 10, Francisca Pou Giménez asks whether the institutional solutions typically embraced by contemporary Latin American constitutions

[7] Speech by Mr. Mikhail Gorbachev Before the Parliamentary Assembly of the Council of Europe (July 6, 1989), Council of Europe Information Department, D(89)36.

make a difference in fighting contemporary patterns of rule-of-law violations. She advances the preliminary hypothesis that Latin American last-wave constitutions have made a positive difference. After recalling historic trends with regard to democracy and the rule of law in Latin America and providing an overview of the standard institutional tools contained in Latin American constitutions, she assesses patterns that undermine the rule of law in Mexico. Although actors have used the Mexican constitution successfully to resist erosion of the rule of law, she finds that these efforts excessively rely on *ex post* responses to executive actions and overburden the courts.

Chapter 11, by Olabisi D. Akinkugbe, examines how military coups have returned in a number of states in the western, central, and Sahel regions of Africa. The rule of law and democratic governance correspondingly are under significant stress. A confluence of events – colonial legacies, uprisings, regional conflicts, term elongation, challenges to the dynastic style of leadership, and the rising incidence of coups – challenge the entrenchment of the rule of law in contemporary Africa. Focusing on the period between 2020 and 2023, the chapter assesses whether the decline of the rule of law and democratic governance in sub-Saharan Africa as a region is overstated, given that the coups are concentrated in francophone West and the Central Africa. Akinkugbe asks how we should think of the role of geopolitical contestations and colonial linkages in unsettling democratic regimes and eroding the rule of law in Africa.

Tyrell Haberkorn, in Chapter 12 on the criminalization of dissent, examines the largest democracy movement in a generation that emerged in Thailand in June 2020. The movement began with three demands: the current prime minister must resign, a new constitution must be drafted, and the state must stop threatening dissidents. In August 2020, activists added a fourth demand: the monarchy must be reformed. This demand was potentially transformative, but it triggered a swift crackdown involving police violence and prosecutions. The government wielded law to criminalize peaceful dissent. Haberkorn shows how the Thai regime deploys repressive power to dominate the polity and the use of law within it.

In Chapter 13, Ji Li evaluates the evolving rule of law with Chinese characteristics and its impacts on the international legal order. He notes that Chairman Xi Jinping and the leaders of the Chinese Communist Party have pledged to build a "rule of law" country. But when the ruling elites of a one-party authoritarian state allege commitment to the rule of law, what do they mean? Li assesses how the current model in China differs from Western concepts of the rule of law, especially "thick" versions of it that have been closely tied to liberal democratic values. The chapter investigates the key features of the "rule of law with Chinese characteristics." Li traces the development of the Chinese legal system and evolving rule-of-law debates in China, and then examines how China might impact the international legal order.

In conclusion, Chapter 14 by Martin Krygier reflects upon the book's findings from the perspective of the book's two central distinguishing themes. First, he endorses and explores the implications of understanding the rule of law in terms of a central aspiration or goal – reduction of the possibilities of the arbitrary exercise of power – rather than any purported checklist of legal instruments said to embody it. Second, he discusses the distinctive implications of examining the rule of law in a transnational, and not merely a national, context. The chapter examines the geopolitical sources of transnational enthusiasms for the rule of law, and the implications of geopolitical changes that might lead to the exhaustion or extinction of such enthusiasms. Krygier suggests that optimists might curb their constructivist enthusiasms, and pessimists might acknowledge that speed bumps are not necessarily the end of the road, if both were to reflect on how long securing the rule of law has taken and can be expected to take.

# ACKNOWLEDGMENTS

We thank the University of California Irvine School of Law, Georgetown University Law Center, and the University of Southern California for supporting this project. Wayne Sandholtz is grateful to the Berlin–Potsdam Research Group "The International Rule of Law – Rise or Decline?" at Humboldt University in Berlin, where he was a senior fellow and where he conducted the initial research that informed his contributions to this book. The Group's codirectors – Georg Nolte, Heike Krieger, and Andreas Zimmermann – provided constructive insights and suggestions. The authors also thank Sarah Gansen and Madeline Owens for outstanding research assistance.

# PART I

# Introduction: Concepts and Empirics

# 1

# The Rule of Law under Pressure

## The Enmeshment of National and International Trends

GREGORY SHAFFER AND WAYNE SANDHOLTZ

> *The legal theory of post-war German counter-revolutionists was decisively influenced by international events and the concept which permitted an unlimited sovereignty to ignore international law is the source of the theory that political activity is not subject to legal regulation. This was the presupposition for the theory of the Prerogative State.*
>
> —Ernst Fraenkel, *The Dual State: A Contribution to the Theory of Dictatorship*[1]

> *War is no longer declared*
> *but rather continued. The outrageous*
> *has become the everyday. The hero*
> *is absent from the battle. The weak*
> *are moved into the firing zone.*
>
> —Ingeborg Bachmann, "Every Day"[2]

These are difficult times. Populist and authoritarian leaders are dismantling rule-of-law norms domestically, and they are working to do so internationally. Although political actors increasingly deploy rule-of-law discourse, they frequently abuse it to legitimate authoritarian rule, often in the name of law and order. How to measure these shifts is a challenge given the variety of institutional means to advance or undermine the rule of law, yet both qualitative and quantitative analyses

We thank participants at workshops at Georgetown University Law Center, the University of California, Irvine, the University of Pennsylvania, Utrecht University School of Law, Vanderbilt University, and the 2022 Law and Society Association conference in Lisbon for their comments.

[1] Ernst Fraenkel, The Dual State: A Contribution to the Theory of Dictatorship 66 (Oxford Univ. Press 2017) (1941).

[2] Ingeborg Bachmann, *Every Day*, *in* Darkness Spoken 39 (Peter Filkins trans., Zephyr Press 2006) (1953).

indicate overall declines in rule-of-law protections transnationally, which are essential for individuals to lead lives not subject to domination.

We conceive of the rule of law as an ideal – or meta-principle – under which individuals are not to be subject to the arbitrary exercise of power. We examine the interaction of domestic and international factors in eroding the rule of law, including the rise of populist, authoritarian leaders in traditionally democratic countries, the intensification of repression in existing authoritarian regimes, and the relative decline of Europe and the United States in relation to an authoritarian China and other emerging powers. These shifts weaken the diffusion and settling of rule-of-law norms within states, which, in turn, affects normative development and institutional practice internationally. They also are generating robust responses that we evaluate.

Challenges to the rule of law raise a series of conceptual and empirical questions that are transnational in their scope and implications. This introductory chapter is in five parts. Part I explains our conceptualization of the rule of law, necessary for the orientation of empirical study and policy responses. Following Martin Krygier, we formulate a teleological conception of the rule of law in terms of goals and practices, which, in turn, calls for an assessment of institutional mechanisms to advance these goals given varying social conditions and contexts. Part II sets forth the ways in which international law and institutions are important for rule-of-law ends, as well as their pathologies, since power also is exercised beyond the state in an interconnected world. Part III examines empirical indicators of the decline of the rule of law at the national and international levels. It notes factors that explain such decline, and why such factors appear to be transnationally and recursively linked. Part IV discusses what might be done given these shifts in rule-of-law protections. It responds to the Biden administration's rallying of a coalition of democracies to combat authoritarian trends at home and internationally, and it assesses tensions between political and economic liberalism. We then conclude in Part V, noting the implications of viewing the rule of law in transnational context for conceptual theory, empirical study, and policy response.

## I Conceptualizing the Rule of Law: What's the Point?

We develop concepts because they are useful for understanding the world and intervening within it. The starting point for developing the concept of the rule of law is to assess what is at stake for individuals and the communities of which they form part – that is, what is the problem that the rule of law aims to address. We start with Krygier's conception of the rule of law in terms of social goals and practices, after which we turn to different normative and institutional means to advance these goals. It is both the ends and the means that can – and must – be assessed empirically to inform any effective response.

We posit that the rule of law is a normative ideal that should be viewed teleologically in terms of its ends. The goal of the rule of law is *to oppose the arbitrary exercise of power by setting boundaries on, and channeling, power's exercise through known legal rules and institutions that apply to all.*[3] The rule of law aims to limit, through legal rules and institutionalized practices, the exercise of power by some persons over others. Arbitrary power can be terrorizing. People internalize its threat.[4] Through self-suppression and self-protective collaboration, individual freedom and civil society wither. The goal is thus to create restraints on government, as well as private power, together with channels for cooperative and coordinative activities,[5] which provide security and predictability so that people can plan and organize their pursuits and do so without fear. Power can be used for good or ill. For us, as for theorists ranging from Judith Shklar in the last century to Montesquieu earlier, "the fear of violence and the threat of arbitrary government provide an essential context in which the rule of law takes its meaning."[6] As a goal, the rule of law is best viewed as a principle and

[3] Martin Krygier, *The Rule of Law: Legality, Teleology, Sociology*, *in* RELOCATING THE RULE OF LAW 45, 60 (Gianluigi Palombella & Neil Walker eds., 2009). In the larger rule-of-law tradition, power is predominantly viewed in relational/agentic terms and not in constitutive terms. For multifaceted conceptions of power, at times referenced in terms of the four faces of power, see, for example, Michael Barnett & Raymond Duvall, *Power in Global Governance*, *in* POWER IN GLOBAL GOVERNANCE 1 (Michael Barnett & Raymond Duvall eds., 2005); Peter Digeser, *The Fourth Face of Power*, 54 J. POL. 977, 980 (1992); DENNIS WRONG, POWER: ITS FORMS, BASES, AND USES (3d ed. 2002). Whatever conception of power one adopts, or on which one focuses, there will be variation in practice, and one should assess imperfect institutional alternatives for tempering power through "criteria for distinguishing better from worse forms of power relations, or, more specifically, relations that promote participants' political freedom – that is, their capacity to act in ways that affect norms and other political mechanisms defining the field of the possible – from those that approximate states of domination." CLARISSA RILE HAYWARD, DE-FACING POWER 7 (2000).

[4] HANNA ARENDT, THE ORIGINS OF TOTALITARIANISM 325 (1951) (conceptualizing "totalitarianism" as "a means of dominating and terrorizing human beings from within").

[5] On law's channeling effects, see, for example, Lon Fuller, *Consideration and Form*, 41 COLUM. L. REV. 799, 799–824 (1941).

[6] Leslie Green, *Law's Rule*, 24 OSGOODE HALL L.J. 1023, 1026 (1986) (referencing Montesquieu); Judith Shklar, *Political Theory and the Rule of Law*, *in* POLITICAL

not simply as a set of rules, because rules can be manipulated to subvert goals.[7] As an ideal, the rule of law will never be fully attained given human failings, but that does not make the principle any less important. In this chapter, we focus predominantly on public power, while noting that effective state power also is required to temper the arbitrary exercise of private power, particularly as states delegate and outsource traditional public tasks to private actors.[8]

Ultimately, for the rule of law to become effective, it must be institutionalized as part of a culture of conduct. It must become a *practice*.[9] It is for this reason that we apply a broader conception of law that includes institutionalized practice.[10] From a socio-legal perspective, the rule of law provides restraints on arbitrary state and private behavior through norms that enable people to reasonably know what is required of them, what is prohibited, what they may do, and what can be done to them, combined

Thought and Political Thinkers 21, 24 (Stanley Hoffmann ed., 1998) ("freedom from fear").

[7] John Braithwaite, *Rules and Principles: A Theory of Legal Certainty*, 27 Austl. J. Leg. Phil. 47 (2002).

[8] *See* Elizabeth Anderson, Private Government: How Employers Rule Our Lives (and Why We Don't Talk about It) (2017); Philip Selznick, Law, Society, and Industrial Justice (1969); Martin Krygier, *The Ideal of the Rule of Law and Private Power, in* Research Handbook on the Politics of Constitutional Law 14 (Mark Tushnet & Dimitry Kochenov eds., 2023). On the outsourcing of public tasks, see Jody Freeman & Martha Minow, Government by Contract: Outsourcing and American Democracy (2009).

[9] In this vein, Tamanaha defines the rule of law to mean that "government officials and citizens are bound by and abide by the law." Brian Tamanaha, *The History and Elements of the Rule of Law*, Sing. J. Legal Stud. 232, 233 (2012). As Gerald Postema writes, "law can rule only if a certain *ethos* takes root in the political community .... [T]he rule of law is robust in a polity only where its members, legal officials and legal subjects alike, take responsibility for holding each other to account under the law." Gerald J. Postema, Law's Rule: The Nature, Value, and Viability of the Rule of Law 20 (2022).

[10] Halliday and Shaffer stipulate a meaning of law in processual terms that includes "soft law" and practice in Terence C. Halliday & Gregory Shaffer, *Transnational Legal Orders, in* Transnational Legal Orders 1, 6–14 (Terence C. Halliday & Gregory Shaffer eds., 2015) (defining a "transnational legal order" as "a collection of formalized legal norms and associated organizations and actors that authoritatively order the understanding and practice of law across national jurisdictions"). From this perspective, law includes legislation, judicial decisions, and the practices of officials. Grattet et al. exemplify this approach in studying hate crimes, involving not only the diffusion of state legislation but also the conduct of police officers and prosecutors. Ryken Grattet, Valerie Jenness & Theodore R. Curry, *The Homogenization and Differentiation of Hate Crime Law in the United States, 1978 to 1995*, 63 Am. Socio. Rev. 286 (1998). In a related vein, see the legal realist Karl Llewellyn, *The Normative, the Legal, and the Law-Jobs: The Problem of Juristic Method*, 49 Yale L.J. 1355, 1357 (1940) (referring to "law-ways").

with the institutionalization of these norms so that they "count as a source of restraint and a normative resource."[11] These restraints facilitate the advancement of multiple social goals.[12] Where institutionalized, the rule of law becomes a habit or routine.[13]

A teleological perspective reasons both forward in terms of an ideal, and backward in light of experience. It is the history of the arbitrary exercise of power, the real experience of abuse, that inspires conceptualization, empirical study, and social intervention. Our study of the rule of law is a legal-realist one, grounded in practice and experience and not in deductive reasoning.[14] Pragmatically, we know the value of the rule of law through historical and contemporary experiences of the arbitrary exercise of power. But our study is also based on a goal and purpose, or – to use the terminology of the pragmatist John Dewey – an "end in view."[15]

Before developing our argument regarding the rule of law from a transnational perspective, some caveats are in order. First, the rule of law is obviously not enough by itself and needs to be understood in relation to other social and institutional goals and practices. People and societies pursue multiple "goods," including the satisfaction of basic human needs to enhance individual autonomy to make choices. As Michael Oakeshott writes, the rule of law "bakes no bread, it is unable to distribute loaves or fishes."[16] Yet, the rule-of-law conception used in this chapter has powerful ties to theories of liberty based on furthering people's real-life capacities. It contributes to a vision (in Amartya Sen's

[11] Krygier, *supra* note 3, at 60.

[12] Tamanaha highlights five "manifest functions" of the rule of law: personal and collective security and trust; the integration of society; legal restrictions on officials; individual liberty; and economic development. Brian Tamanaha, *The Functions of the Rule of Law, in* THE CAMBRIDGE COMPANION TO THE RULE OF LAW 221, 221–32 (Jens Meierhenrich & Martin Loughlin eds., 2021). For a parallel functionalist account of the international rule of law, see Simon Chesterman, *An International Rule of Law?*, 56 AM. J. COMP. L. 331 (2008) ("tool with which to protect human rights, promote development, and sustain peace").

[13] FRANCIS A. ALLEN, THE HABITS OF LEGALITY: CRIMINAL JUSTICE AND RULE OF LAW (1996); Halliday & Shaffer, *supra* note 10, at 42–44 (on normative settlement).

[14] Karl N. Llewellyn, *Some Realism About Realism: Responding to Dean Pound*, 44 HARV. L. REV. 1222, 1236 (1931) (viewing "law as a means to social ends and not as an end in itself; so that any part needs constantly to be examined for its purposes, and for its effect, and to be judged in the light of both and of their relation to each other").

[15] John Dewey, *Valuation and Experimental Knowledge*, 31 PHIL. REV. 325 (1922); John Dewey, *Theory of Valuation*, 6 PHIL. SCI. 490 (1940).

[16] MICHAEL OAKESHOTT, *The Rule of Law, in* ON HISTORY AND OTHER ESSAYS 164 (1999).

terms) of "expanding the real freedoms that people enjoy," thereby expanding their capacity to make choices in furtherance of what they value.[17] People are thus better situated to resist domination, from a republican perspective, and protect their autonomy from the arbitrary exercise of power.[18] The rule of law, in this sense, can be viewed as a complement to other (nonlegal) means of tempering power, and thus as supportive of this broader ideal.

Second, from a critical perspective, the pursuit of the rule of law is also linked to the substance of law. When only the powerful determine law's substance, adherence to rules is less a matter of choice and more a reflection of power relations. Democratic participation in the determination of law's substance is thus a necessary complement to rule-of-law ideals.[19] Contestation over the content of rules is a critical dimension of a robust, inclusive society protected by the rule of law.[20] The relation of

[17] Sen and Martha Nussbaum define liberty in terms of "capabilities," such that government has a role in furthering them. For Sen, a person's capability reflects their "ability to achieve valuable functionings and well-being." Amartya Sen, *Freedom of Choice: Concept and Content*, 32 Eur. Econ. Rev. 269, 278 (1988); Amartya Sen, Development as Freedom 3 (1999); Martha C. Nussbaum, Women and Human Development: The Capabilities Approach 4–15 (2000) (providing an overview of the capabilities approach in general and of the philosophy of Sen and Nussbaum); Amartya Sen, Commodities and Capabilities (1985); Iris Marion Young, Justice and the Politics of Difference 39 (1990) ("Justice should refer not only to distribution, but also to the institutional conditions necessary for the development and exercise of individual capacities and collective communication and cooperation.").

[18] Philip Pettit, Republicanism: A Theory of Freedom and Government (1997).

[19] We conceptualize the rule of law and democracy as complements, while recognizing their overlaps when democracy is conceptualized in constitutional terms. Some theorists incorporate the rule of law in conceptualizing constitutional democracy. *See, e.g.*, Aziz Huq & Tom Ginsburg, How to Save a Constitutional Democracy 10 (2018) (defining liberal constitutional democracy in terms of three elements: free and fair elections; core rights related to those elections; and the bureaucratic rule of law, involving independent courts and agencies, particularly as relates to democratic governance). Others incorporate democracy in conceptualizing the rule of law. *See, e.g.*, Mattias Kumm, *Global Constitutionalism and Rule of Law*, *in* Handbook on Global Constitutionalism 197, 203 (Anthony Lang & Antje Wiener eds., 2017) (representative institutions under free elections); Roberto Gargarella, *Constitutionalism and the Rule of Law*, *in* The Cambridge Companion to the Rule of Law, *supra* note 12, at 425.

[20] Antje Wiener, *The Rule of Law in Inter-National Relations: Contestation Despite Diffusion – Diffusion Through Contestation*, in Handbook on the Rule of Law 109 (Christopher May & Adam Winchester eds., 2018).

the rule of law to democracy is complex.[21] Rule-of-law norms can be, and have been, advanced outside of democratic governance to different degrees in certain areas,[22] and democratic governments can exercise arbitrary power and claim democratic legitimation to do so. Illiberal democracies have proliferated, as illiberal governments borrow from each other's playbooks to exercise power arbitrarily.[23] Their aim is to use rule-of-law language for their own illiberal ends.

The principles of democracy and the rule of law respond to different but interrelated questions and social problems. The issue of democratic governance poses the question of *who* exercises power. Rule-of-law concerns examine the question of *how* power is exercised.[24] Democracy and the rule of law nonetheless are related – even though, at times, in tension – since the rule of law provides a check and counterbalance to the unbridled exercise of power through majority rule. To start, the rule of law is a necessary condition for democracy. It is needed to assure that officials impartially conduct elections and count votes. In addition, the rule of law protects individual autonomy from domination so that citizens may freely participate in public processes that, in turn, affect them. As Jürgen Habermas writes, "on the one hand, citizens can make adequate use of their public autonomy only if, on the basis of their equally

21 *Cf.* TOM GINSBURG, DEMOCRACIES AND INTERNATIONAL LAW 21 (2021) (defining the rule of law in bureaucratic administration, focusing on the running of elections, as a component of democracy); Martin Krygier, *Tempering Power*, *in* CONSTITUTIONALISM AND THE RULE OF LAW: BRIDGING IDEALISM AND REALISM 34, 37 (Maurice Adams, Anne Meuswese & Ernst Hirsch Ballin eds., 2017) (would treat the rule of law as the broader concern and address constitutional concerns as falling within it); Corey Brettschneider, *A Substantive Conception of the Rule of Law: Non-Arbitrary Treatment and the Limits of Procedure*, 50 NOMOS: AM. SOC'Y POL. & LEGAL PHIL. 52, 57–61 (2011) (commenting on Waldron and conceptually differentiating participation under the rule of law, in terms of reason-giving consistent with citizens' equal status, from participation under democracy).

22 Take, for example, England at the time of the enclosure laws, as captured in E.P. THOMPSON, OF WHIGS AND HUNTERS: THE ORIGIN OF THE BLACK ACT 258–69 (1975), and Singapore today, as captured in JOTHIE RAJAH, AUTHORITARIAN RULE OF LAW: LEGISLATION, DISCOURSE AND LEGITIMACY IN SINGAPORE (2012).

23 Fareed Zakaria, *Illiberal Democracy*, 76 FOREIGN AFFS. 22 (Nov./Dec. 1997); Kim L. Scheppele, *Autocratic Legalism*, 85 U. CHI. L. REV. 545 (2018); David Landau, *Democratic Erosion and Constitution-Making Moments: The Role of Transnational Legal Norms*, *in* CONSTITUTION-MAKING AND TRANSNATIONAL LEGAL ORDER 234 (Gregory Shaffer, Tom Ginsburg & Terence C. Halliday eds., 2019); ROSALIND DIXON & DAVID LANDAU, ABUSIVE CONSTITUTIONAL BORROWING: LEGAL GLOBALIZATION AND THE SUBVERSION OF LIBERAL DEMOCRACY (2021); Alvin Cheung, *Legal Gaslighting*, 72 U. TORONTO L. REV. 50 (2022).

24 Martin Krygier, *Democracy and the Rule of Law*, *in* THE CAMBRIDGE COMPANION TO THE RULE OF LAW, *supra* note 12, at 406.

protected private autonomy, they are sufficiently independent," and "on the other hand, they can arrive at a consensual regulation of their private autonomy only if they make adequate use of the political autonomy as enfranchised citizens."[25] Both constitutional democracy and the rule of law provide institutional checks as moderating mechanisms that disincentivize the exercise of arbitrary power.[26] Because they serve as complements, they often rise and decline in parallel, as Part III shows.

Third, there is a long tradition of socio-legal and critical scholarship assessing the role of capital, class, race, and other attributes where law helps to constitute unequal social relations. As Robert Gordon writes, "legal relations . . . don't simply condition how the people relate to each other but to an important extent define the constitutive terms of the relationship, relations such as lord and peasant, master and slave, employer and employee."[27] For many scholars who criticize the liberal tradition, the rule of law is viewed more in terms of establishing "order" through the legitimating mechanism of law and legal institutions than "justice" in any substantive sense.[28] They are rightly wary of how law can mask, normalize, legitimate, and maintain unjust social relations. Within democracies such as the United States, minorities have been systematically subject to greater rule-of-law violations, whether formally under slavery and Jim Crow laws in the eighteenth, nineteenth, and twentieth centuries, or in institutional practices today in criminal, immigration, public health, and other areas of law.[29] Similarly, at the international

[25] Jürgen Habermas, *On the Internal Relation Between Rule of Law and Democracy*, 3 Eur. J. Phil. 12, 17–18 (1995). *See also* Jürgen Habermas, Between Facts and Norms: Contributions to a Discourse Theory of Law and Democracy 453 (William Rehg trans., 1996) (legitimacy as "procedural rationality"). In this vein, Kumm writes: "In the constitutionalist tradition, law actually has the legitimate authority it claims if, and only if, both in terms of the procedure used and results reached it is justifiable in terms of public reasons that those over whom laws claim authority might reasonably accept as free and equals." Kumm, *supra* note 19, at 202.

[26] On the role of incentives, see, for example, Barry Weingast, *The Political Foundations of Democracy and the Rule of Law*, 91 Am. Pol. Sci. Rev. 245 (1997).

[27] Robert W. Gordon, *Critical Legal Histories*, 36 Stan. L. Rev. 57, 103 (1984). Gordon focuses on law as power in a constitutive sense. For a related approach regarding economic ordering, see Katerina Pistor, The Code of Capital: How the Law Creates Wealth and Inequality (2019).

[28] As Tamanaha notes, in the process these ordering mechanisms also empower and enrich lawyers. Tamanaha, *supra* note 12, at 233–34.

[29] Eric Foner, Reconstruction: America's Unfinished Revolution, 1863–1877 (1988); Margaret Burnham, By Hands Now Known: Jim Crow's Legal Executioners (2022); Michelle Alexander, The New Jim Crow: Mass Incarceration in the Age of Colorblindness (2010); Michele Goodwin, *The*

level, critical scholars assess much of international law as a remnant of colonialism and imperialism.[30] Historical studies depict how colonizers exercised power under law to establish order and legitimate rule,[31] although clearly in violation of this book's conception of the rule of law.[32] Those in power in postcolonial states likewise can deploy colonial forms of state control in the name of the rule of law to dominate their populations.[33]

These critiques support conceptualizing the rule of law in terms of its *goals* – its point – and differentiating the ends from any particular formal and substantive *means* to attain it. It is thus important to distinguish the "rule of law" from "rule by law" and not collapse them into a single formal concept of "legality." Governments around the world embrace rule-of-law rhetoric while instantiating a "rule of some groups over others *by* and through the law."[34] "Rule by law" implies that those

*Thirteenth Amendment: Modern Slavery, Capitalism, and Mass Incarceration*, 104 Cornell L. Rev. 899 (2019); Michele Goodwin, Policing the Womb: Invisible Women and The Criminalization of Motherhood (2020); Dorothy Roberts, Torn Apart: How the Child Welfare System Destroys Black Families – and How Abolition Can Build a Safer World (2022).

30 Sundhya Pahuja, Decolonizing International Law: Development, Economic Growth and the Politics of Universality (2011); Antony Angie, Imperialism, Sovereignty, and the Making of International Law (2005). As E.H. Carr earlier wrote, "When modern writers on international politics find the highest moral good in the rule of law, we are equally entitled to ask, What law? and Whose law?" E.H. Carr, The Twenty Years' Crisis, 1919–1939, at 179 (2d ed. 2001).

31 *See, e.g.*, Lauren Benton & Lisa Ford, Rage for Order: The British Empire and the Origins of International Law, 1800–1850 (2018); Jennifer Pitts, Boundaries of the International: Law and Empire (2018).

32 Lisa Ford notes the link between the logic of colonial peacekeeping and domestic rule-of-law violations, in line with this introduction's central thesis. She writes: "The license of colonial peacekeeping also helped to produce Carl Schmitt's conviction that the essence of modern sovereignty is the state of exception – the sovereign's power to exceed and suspend the rule of law." Lisa Ford, The King's Peace: Law and Order in the British Empire 22 (2022). *See also* Caroline Elkins, Legacy of Violence: A History of the British Empire 140 (2022) (calling the array of decrees that justified martial law, detention without trial, and collective punishment in the colonies "legalized lawlessness," using the term "to describe the incremental legalizing, bureaucratizing, and legitimating of exceptional state-directed violence when ordinary laws proved insufficient for maintaining order and control").

33 Nick Cheesman, *Rule-of-Law Ethnography*, 14 Ann. Rev. L. Soc. Sci. 167, 171 (2018); Rajah, *supra* note 22, at 26, 43.

34 Brian Z. Tamanaha, Law as a Means to an End: Threat to the Rule of Law 225 (2006) (emphasis in original); Brian Z. Tamanaha, On the Rule of Law: History, Politics, Theory 96 (2004). For empirical illustrations, see Rule by

holding the power to make and enforce legal norms do so to regulate and control the population, while those who govern are not themselves subject to the rules that they impose. The rule of law requires that both the governed and those who govern are subject to the same rules so that all are protected from the arbitrary exercise of power. It is distinguished from rule by law both in terms of purpose and consequence. Conceptualizing the rule of law in this way, and differentiating it from rule by law, clarifies how law – whether local, national, or international – can be used for good or ill, can curtail and temper, or support and legitimate, the arbitrary exercise of power.

The rule of law and rule by law are ideal-type constructs. In reality, "arbitrariness comes in degrees," and practices vary along a continuum.[35] State practices vary across issue areas and as regards different populations. Singapore operates as a "dual state," Jothie Rajah writes, "in that it matches the 'law' of the liberal 'West' in the commercial arena while repressing civil and political individual rights."[36] In this regard, Singapore, given its economic success, can serve as a model for other authoritarian regimes that wish to attract domestic and transnational investment. Relatedly, Tamir Moustafa and others theorize how authoritarian regimes often provide for pockets of judicial independence for different functional reasons, including for controlling administrative agents.[37] The rule of law also can be applied variably to different populations. Michael McCann and Filiz Kahraman document how the US legal system has long operated as a "dual state" for Blacks and other

LAW: THE POLITICS OF COURTS IN AUTHORITARIAN REGIMES (Tom Ginsburg & Tamir Moustafa eds., 2008).

35 Martin Krygier, *The Rule of Law: Pasts, Presents and Two Possible Futures*, 12 ANN. REV. L. SOC. SCI. 199, 204 (2016).

36 RAJAH, *supra* note 22, at 23. The conception of the dual state begins with Ernst Fraenkel's work on law in Nazi Germany. Fraenkel writes: "The courts are responsible for seeing that the principles of the capitalist order are maintained – even though the Prerogative State occasionally exercises its right to deal with individual cases in the light of expedience and the special nature of the case at hand." FRAENKEL, *supra* note 1, at 73.

37 Tamir Moustafa, *Law and Courts in Authoritarian Regimes*, 10 ANN. REV. L. & SOC. SCI. 281 (2014); RULE BY LAW: THE POLITICS OF COURTS IN AUTHORITARIAN REGIMES, *supra* note 34; Melissa Curley, Bjorn Dressel & Stephen McCarthy, *Competing Visions of the Rule of Law in Southeast Asia: Power, Rhetoric and Governance*, 42 ASIAN STUD. REV. 192 (2018); Mark Jia, *Special Courts, Global China*, 62 VA. J. INT'L L. 559, 566 (2022) (noting special courts for intellectual property, finance, internet, and international commercial law, showing how "China's legal system can be increasingly professional in some ways while remaining lawless in others").

minorities,[38] while Eric Foner describes the United States in the Jim Crow South as "a quasi-fascist polity . . . embedded within a purported democracy."[39] Ji Li similarly assesses variation in rule-of-law protections in China as a function of the issue and parties in a dispute.[40]

A central reason to define the rule of law in terms of goals and practices is the risk of creating formulaic checklists based on specified, formal characteristics. Authoritarians have become proficient in adopting formal institutions deemed important for the rule of law, but which – in practice – serve to subvert it, and replace it with the rule of a particular party, faction, or person that rules by law. Many scholars, moreover, tend to derive these checklists parochially from their own legal traditions – particularly European legal traditions – and not others. Countries can produce quite different sets of rules for regulating social life in furtherance of rule-of-law principles. As Laurence Rosen writes regarding Islamic conceptions of the rule of law: "One need not, therefore, be an unrepentant relativist or a claimant of universal values to nevertheless respect the organizing principles by which others place limits on power and treat one another with that degree of consideration to which they would expect any valid system of law to treat them as well."[41] Similarly, Makau Mutua stresses that Western concepts should not be simply transplanted to Africa, but rather varying cultural traditions and contexts must be recognized.[42] There are, in other words, a variety of means to advance rule-of-law goals, adapted to local traditions and conditions.

In practice, one must advance beyond goals to address means. It is at this stage, we maintain, that the concept of the rule of law becomes more contested.[43] One way to understand perennial debates over whether to adopt a "thin" or a "thick" concept of the rule of

[38] Michael McCann & Filiz Kahraman, *On the Interdependence of Liberal and Illiberal/Authoritarian Legal Forms in Racial Capitalist Regimes . . . The Case of the United States*, 17 Ann. Rev. L. & Soc. Sci. 483, 483–503 (2021).

[39] Eric Foner, *A Regional Reign of Terror*, N.Y. Rev. of Books, Apr. 26, 2023, at 63, 64 (reviewing Margaret Burnham, By Hands Now Known: Jim Crow's Legal Executioners (2022)).

[40] Ji Li, *The Power Logic of Justice in China*, 6 Am. J. Comp. L. 95 (2017).

[41] Lawrence Rosen, *Islamic Conceptions of the Rule of Law*, *in* The Cambridge Companion to the Rule of Law, *supra* note 12, at 86.

[42] Makau Mutua, *Africa and the Rule of Law*, 23 Sur – Int'l J. on Hum Rts. 159, 170 (2016) ("these core norms must grapple with Africa's unique history and be adopted to its historical circumstances to achieve cultural legitimacy").

[43] Jeremy Waldron, *Is the Rule of Law an Essentially Contested Concept (in Florida)?*, 21 L. & Phil. 137, 138–44 (2002); Shklar, *supra* note 6.

law is that scholars turn to different *means* for the protection of the goal of the rule of law. Proponents contend that these thin and thick conceptions provide particular "promise" for attaining rule-of-law ends.[44] Specifying different means is necessary, but they must be empirically evaluated with the end always in view, and they must be adapted to fit different social conditions and contexts that will vary over time and place.

Many focus on, and argue for, a "thin" concept of the rule of law that views it only in procedural terms. Many legal theorists adopt formal conceptions, such as the law's generality, equality of application, and certainty. Lon Fuller notably advanced eight elements that constitute conditions for the rule of law (or, in his terms, "excellence toward which a system of rules may strive"). Law should be "general, publicized, prospective, clear, non-contradictory, compliable, consistently applied, and reasonably stable."[45] Joseph Raz specified similar principles and divided them into two groups, the first focused on formal standards that provide certainty and predictability to guide action, and the second focused on legal machinery to make the first effective.[46] These proponents highlight the coordinative and channeling functions of legal norms in providing a framework through which individuals and organizations might orient action, interact, and plan.[47] They stress, in the words of Raz, that the rule of law's value lies in "curtailing arbitrary power, and in securing a well ordered society, subject to accountable, principled government."[48] The checklists, however, should not define what the rule of law *is*. They rather incorporate important means to achieve

[44] *Compare* Jorgen Moller, *The Advantages of a Thin View*, *in* Handbook on the Rule of Law, *supra* note 20, at 21, *with* Adriaan Bedner, *The Promise of a Thick View*, *in* Handbook on the Rule of Law, *supra* note 20, at 34, *and* Tom Bingham, The Rule of Law (2010) (including human rights).

[45] Lon L. Fuller, The Morality of Law (rev. ed. 1969). Fuller defends, in his words, a "procedural version of natural law." *Id.* at 96–97. The succinct, quoted summary of Fuller is taken from Charles Sampford, *Reconceiving the Rule of Law for a Globalizing World*, *in* Globalization and the Rule of Law 9, 14 (Spencer Zifcak ed., 2005).

[46] *See* Joseph Raz, The Authority of Law: Essays on Law and Morality 214–19 (1979) (listing eight principles). In a related vein, Chesterman views the rule of law in terms of three essential components: (1) the powers of government can only be exercised through law, (2) the law applies to the state and its officials, and (3) the law must apply equally to all. Chesterman, *supra* note 12.

[47] Jeremy Waldron, *The Concept and the Rule of Law*, 43 Ga. L. Rev. 1, 48 (2008) ("Law in the first sense requires the existence of certain general norms that serve as a basis of orientation for people's behavior, as well as a basis for decision by the courts."). *Cf.* Friedrich Hayek, The Constitution of Liberty (1960).

[48] Joseph Raz, *The Politics of the Rule of Law*, 2 Indian J. Const. L. 1, 8 (2008).

rule-of-law goals because, as we argue below, they address key sources of arbitrariness.

It is when the conception of the rule of law includes substantive norms and goals, such as a democratic form of government, participation, deliberation, and individual rights, that it becomes more contested. Leading philosophers and social theorists advance thicker conceptions of the rule of law that vary in their inclusion of substantive issues, such as participatory rights and human rights.[49] As Gianluigi Palombella puts it, the rule of law cannot "coincide with the mere existence of a legal order."[50] Theorists such as Ronald Dworkin, Jeremy Waldron, Jürgen Habermas, and Philip Selznick all incorporate a discursive quality of reason-giving and argumentative justification in their conception of the rule of law.[51] Proponents likewise advance these attributes as important checks on arbitrariness. Indeed, the lack of reason-giving constitutes an important source of arbitrariness, as we explain below.

Going further, Palombella insists that the rule of law requires democracy "paired with fundamental rights."[52] Terry Nardin similarly argues that the rule of law should not be confused with the mere existence of laws: "The expression 'rule of law' does no intellectual work if any effective system of enacted rules must be counted as law, no matter what its moral qualities."[53] These moral qualities, he insists, must include rights: "The expression 'rule of law' … should be used only to designate a kind of legal order in which law both constrains decision-making *and protects the moral rights of*

[49] RONALD DWORKIN, A MATTER OF PRINCIPLE 259 (1985) (proposing the ideal of rule as a public conception of individual rights).

[50] Gianluigi Palombella, *The Rule of Law Beyond the State: Failures, Promises, and Theory*, 7 INT'L J. CONST. L. 442, 454 (2009).

[51] Jeremy Waldron, *The Rule of Law and the Importance of Procedure*, 50 NOMOS: AM. SOC'Y POL. & LEGAL PHIL. 1, 23 (2011) ("the Rule of Law rests upon: respect for the freedom and dignity of each person as an active intelligence"); Waldron, *supra* note 47, at 58–59 (concept "should emphasize … the procedural and argumentative aspects of legal practice"); JÜRGEN HABERMAS, BETWEEN FACTS AND NORMS: CONTRIBUTIONS TO A DISCOURSE THEORY OF LAW AND DEMOCRACY 453 (William Rehg trans., 1996) (legitimacy as "procedural rationality"); P. PHILIP SELZNICK, PHILIPPE NONET & HOWARD M. VOLLMER, LAW, SOCIETY AND INDUSTRIAL JUSTICE 253 (1969) ("Procedure cannot be 'due' if it does not conform to the canons of rational discourse.").

[52] Palombella, *supra* note 50 at 461.

[53] Terry Nardin, *Theorising the International Rule of Law*, 34 REV. INT'L STUD. 385, 394 (2008). *Cf.* Kumm conceptualizing in proceduralist terms "rights enabling individuals to contest" as unjustifiable any infringements of liberty and equality, as well as "the absence of meaningful possibilities to exercise … social and economic rights." Kumm, *supra* note 19, at 203.

*those who come within its jurisdiction.*"[54] United Nations reports on the rule of law similarly incorporate substantive conceptions, including consistency with "international human rights norms and standards."[55]

More controversially, some World Bank reports have offered definitions of the rule of law that support market-oriented development policies grounded in property rights and contract enforcement.[56] Secure property and contract rights can be important means to advance the rule of law in that they provide for certainty and predictability and thus protection from power's arbitrary exercise. However, democratically governed societies will differ in how they define property and contract rights. It is important not to tether the concept of the rule of law to a particular form of political or economic ordering, such as a neoliberal model.[57]

Whether one takes a thinner or thicker view of the means to advance the rule of law, the common goal among these conceptions is to oppose arbitrariness. Although we do not incorporate human rights within the definition of the rule of law, there are clear overlaps – such as regards due

[54] Nardin, *supra* note 53, at 397 (emphasis added). *Cf.* PAUL GOWDER, THE RULE OF LAW IN THE REAL WORLD (2016) (conceptualizing the rule of law in terms of social equality).

[55] *See, e.g.*, U.N. Secretary-General, The Rule of Law and Transitional Justice in Conflict and Post-Conflict Societies, ¶ 6, U.N. Doc. S/2004/616 (Aug. 23, 2004) (rule of law as a "principle of governance in which all persons, institutions, and entities, public and private, including the State itself, are accountable to laws that are publicly promulgated, equally enforced and independently adjudicated, and which are consistent with international human rights norms and standards").

[56] *See* Erik Jensen, *The Rule of Law and Judicial Reform: The Political Economy of Diverse Institutional Patterns and Reformers' Responses*, *in* BEYOND COMMON KNOWLEDGE: EMPIRICAL APPROACHES TO THE RULE OF LAW 336 (Eric Jensen & Thomas Heller eds., 2003); Kathryn Hendley, *The Rule of Law and Economic Development in a Global Era*, *in* THE BLACKWELL COMPANION TO LAW AND SOCIETY 605 (Austin Sarat ed., 2004); Patrick McAuslan, *Law, Governance and the Development of the Market: Practical Problems and Possible Solutions*, *in* GOOD GOVERNMENT AND LAW: LEGAL AND INSTITUTIONAL REFORM IN DEVELOPING COUNTRIES 25, 42 (Julio Faundez ed., 1997) ("[In] World Bank publications . . . the rule of law . . . is being redefined to emphasize its role in facilitating the enforcement of private contracts so that law reform to advance the rule of law is the same as law reform to advance the market economy."). Ironically, Chinese conceptions of the rule of law in terms of a private law variant involving the enforcement of contracts and dispute settlement for business sectors resonates with this conception. Karen Alter & Ji Li, *Chinese and Western Perspectives on the Rule of Law and Their International Implications*, *in* CAMBRIDGE HANDBOOK ON CHINA AND INTERNATIONAL LAW 94 (Ignacio de la Rasilla & Cai Congyan eds., 2024).

[57] Brian Z. Tamanaha, *The Dark Side of the Relationship Between the Rule of Law and Liberalism*, 3 N.Y.U. J.L. & LIBERTY 516 (2008) (tracing classical liberal and neoliberal use of rule-of-law rhetoric to challenge state legislation, from Dicey to Hayek to the World Bank); William C. Whitford, *The Rule of Law*, 2000 WIS. L. REV. 723, 723 ("phrase has been a slogan used for many political purposes").

process rights – and the two are intertwined and complementary in protecting individuals from power's unbridled exercise.[58] Critically, the rule of law is a necessary condition and prerequisite for the protection of human rights, just as it is for democracy. If one can persecute individuals with impunity to stay in power, then formal rights lack bite.

From a socio-legal perspective, the ultimate challenge is implementation in practice (the law-in-action), which will be mediated by social institutions and legal culture. Because law is frequently ambiguous, involving the interplay of standards, rules, and exceptions, the application of the rule of law will always be contested. No legal process is "discretion-free" because law's meaning is mediated through the operation of institutions and interactions involving people.[59] The rule of law thus should not be confused with the rule of courts or any other institutional means. It is an end that must be pursued through some form of institutionalization, of which courts can be an important exemplar. But any institutional means can be co-opted, abused, and subverted in practice. It is thus essential to keep the end always in view, and never confuse the existence of a particular institutional apparatus with the rule of law.

To develop appropriate means to protect rule-of-law goals, it is best to start with the source (or sources) of the problem – the different sources of arbitrariness.[60] Theorists define arbitrary power in slightly different ways, but the term generally refers to power that is subject to no constraints and, in particular, is not made to take account of the interests of those subject to it.[61] In this vein, Philipp Pettit writes that an arbitrary act is one that "is chosen or

[58] We do not include human rights and democracy per se in the definition of the rule of law because we think it mistaken to load the concept with too many substantive requirements in a complex, pluralistic world. Nonetheless, we also conceive of human rights and democracy as important complementary means to temper the arbitrary exercise of power. We thus agree with the Venice Commission of the Council of Europe that the rule of law, democracy, and human rights are "three intertwined and partly overlapping core principles." COUNCIL OF EUR. VENICE COMM'N, RULE OF LAW CHECKLIST (2016), www.venice.coe.int/images/SITE%20IMAGES/Publications/Rule_of_Law_Check_List.pdf; *see also* POSTEMA, *supra* note 9, at 106 ("The two [rule of law and human rights] are interdependent, each having its own nature and function, as it were, but depending on the other to fulfill that function adequately.").

[59] *See, e.g.*, Duncan Kennedy, *Form and Substance in Private Law Adjudication*, 89 HARV. L. REV. 1685 (1976).

[60] Krygier, *supra* note 35, at 203–05; Martin Krygier, *Tempering Power* (on file with author).

[61] For different conceptions of arbitrariness, see, for example, Samuel Arnold & John R. Harris, *What Is Arbitrary Power?*, 10 J. POL. POWER 1 (2017) (assessing three conceptual formations of arbitrariness, and advocating the latter: (i) power as arbitrary insofar as it is unconstrained; (ii) power as arbitrary insofar as it is uncontrolled by those subject to it; and (iii) power as arbitrary insofar as it is not forced to track the interests of those subject to it).

not chosen at the agent's pleasure. And in particular ... it is chosen or rejected without reference to the interests, or the opinions, of those affected."[62] For a dictionary-oriented, legal definition, the tribunal in the case of *Siemens v. Argentina* cites *Black's Law Dictionary* and defines arbitrariness as follows: "In its ordinary meaning, 'arbitrary' means 'derived from mere opinion,' 'capricious,' 'unrestrained,' 'despotic.' *Black's Law Dictionary* defines this term as 'fixed or done capriciously or at pleasure; without adequate determining principle,' 'depending on the will alone,' 'without cause based upon the law.'"[63]

Building from Krygier, we note five sources of arbitrariness to which different rule-of-law prescriptions respond.[64] A first, primordial concern is where the wielder of power is not subject, in practice, to the law, its controls and limits.[65] Authoritarian governments, in particular, violate this first and most critical dimension. They may pack institutions with their friends, or institutional decision-makers will decide in their favor out of fear. Democratic governments can as well, as illustrated by the 2024 US Supreme Court decision in *Trump v. United States*, where the Court granted "absolute" and "presumptive immunity" to the President, respectively for "core constitutional powers" and "official acts."[66] When

[62] PHILIP PETTIT, REPUBLICANISM: A THEORY OF FREEDOM AND GOVERNMENT 55 (1997) (developing a republican theory of nondomination).

[63] Siemens A.G. v. Argentina, ICSID Case No. ARB/02/08, Award, ¶ 318 (Feb. 6, 2007) (also citing *The Oxford English Dictionary*). The word "arbitrary" derives from the Latin phrase "ad arbitrium," or "at will." *See* PHILIP PETTIT, ON THE PEOPLE'S TERMS: A REPUBLICAN THEORY AND MODEL OF DEMOCRACY 58 (2012) (distinguishing the republican conception of arbitrariness from legality, or mere conformity to rules). The International Court of Justice, in its opinion in *ELSI*, wrote: "Arbitrariness is not so much something opposed to a rule of law, as something opposed to the rule of law .... It is a wilful disregard of due process of law, an act which shocks, or at least surprises, a sense of judicial propriety." *See* Elettronica Sicula S.p.A. (ELSI) (U.S. v. It.), Judgment, 1989 I.C.J. 15, ¶ 128 (July 20).

[64] As we noted earlier, proponents of democracy and human rights also respond to concerns over arbitrariness, which aim to create checks on political decision-makers. The former (democracy) implicates *who* exercises power; and the latter (human rights) creates substantive limits on state prerogatives. We focus on a conception of the rule of law that addresses *how* power is exercised. Together, the three provide complementary means to temper the exercise of unbridled power.

[65] A polity subject to the rule of law is one where, in Plato's words, "law is master over rulers, and the rulers are slaves to the law." PLATO, THE LAWS 156 (Malcolm Schofield ed., Tom Griffith trans., 2016). In contrast, President Richard Nixon infamously stated, "when the president does it ... that means that it is not illegal." *Transcript of David Frost's Interview with Richard Nixon* (1977), TEACHING AM. HISTORY, https://tinyurl.com/5n7dfycj (last visited Aug. 21, 2024).

[66] The US Supreme Court held that a President has "absolute immunity" from criminal prosecution for acts, however criminal, when conducted within his "core constitutional

the law does not apply to those who rule, autocrats can attack opponents with impunity. When this dimension is lacking, the rule of law cannot guarantee fair elections and democratic government. The separation of powers and systems of institutional checks and balances are important means to hold rulers to account in support of rule-of-law goals and practices, but they too may be insufficient.[67]

A second source of arbitrariness is where individuals are unable to know and predict how power will be wielded over them. It is because of these risks that many theorists define the rule of law in terms of known, nondiscriminatory, relatively stable, prospective, consistently applied rules. These attributes are important for all areas of law, but they are particularly important for criminal law and the application of sanctions. Individuals then can plan their lives with reasonable certainty and predictability regarding the law, and thus be less subject to coercion. It is this source of arbitrariness that inspired theorists such as Hayek, Fuller, and Raz, as well as the broader *Rechtsstaat* tradition.[68] These attributes contribute to greater social trust, facilitating cooperation.

A third source of arbitrariness is where individuals have no place to be heard, inform, question, or respond to how power is exercised over them. Due process assured by impartial institutions is critical for the protection of the rule of law. Raz highlights the importance of institutional machinery, and Waldron the need for contestation, to ensure the rule of law. If citizens have no place to contest decision-making and no institutional mechanism to access justice, the exercise of public power becomes less

powers," and "presumptive immunity" for all other "official act(s)." Trump v. United States, 144 S. Ct. 2312, 2327, 2331 (2024). As Justice Sotomayor wrote in dissent: "The Court effectively creates a law-free zone around the President . . . . In every use of official power, the President is now a king above the law." Trump v. United States, 144 S. Ct. 2312, 2731 (2024) (Sotomayor, J., dissenting). In a related vein, Trump himself wrote: "I have the absolute right to PARDON myself." Jeannie Suk Gersen, *The Dangerous Possibilities of Trump's Pardon Power*, New Yorker (Dec. 3, 2020), www.newyorker.com/news/our-columnists/the-dangerous-possibilities-of-trumps-pardon-power.

67 Justice Brandeis wrote in dissent regarding the President's removal power: "The doctrine of the separation of powers was adopted by the Convention of 1787, not to promote efficiency but to preclude the exercise of arbitrary power." Myers v. United States, 272 U.S. 52, 293 (1926).

68 Carl Schmitt, in contrast, theorized law in terms of "who decides on the exception." Since the exception is always available, law is without normative constraint, and the concept of the rule of law is illusory, a mask for the "will to power." William E. Scheuerman, Carl Schmitt: The End of Law 34 (1999).

subject to controls, and decision-makers face fewer incentives to act in a nonarbitrary manner.[69]

A fourth source of arbitrariness, articulated by Habermas and Selznick among others, is where authorities do not engage in public reason-giving in issuing their decisions, which reasons then can be contested, including before judicial, political, and administrative processes. One may, and indeed will, often disagree with the reasons given, but the very practice of public reasoning can provide important constraints on power's arbitrary exercise. Under the rule of law, in Justice Brandeis's words, "deliberative forces prevail over the arbitrary."[70]

A fifth source of arbitrariness is the proportionality of any measure in terms of the reasonable relationship of means and ends.[71] Decision-makers may create clear rules and provide access to courts but apply sanctions that are clearly disproportionate to the offense. Any restrictive measure should be grounded and justified as regards its proportionate relation to a public goal.

These five sources of arbitrariness all call for institutional checks. Different "thin" and "thick" conceptions of the rule of law respond to these concerns. These conceptions have given rise to numerous rule-of-law "checklists,"[72] which are important, but only provided that the focus remains on the goal and actual practices. In this chapter, we thus conceptualize legal and institutional attributes advanced by theorists as important *means* to respond to the above sources of arbitrariness, as opposed to the definition of the rule of law itself.

Because sources of arbitrariness differ, rule-of-law protections can decline or improve along different dimensions in different substantive areas, as documented in the literature on dual states. For example, many authoritarian regimes create rule-of-law protections in commercial and administrative law to attract investment and spur economic growth. In contrast, they do not subject themselves to the law when that would threaten their hold on power. A key test for the rule of law thus lies in the

[69] Governments may attempt to create "legal black holes" to avoid public scrutiny of their actions, such as the United States in detaining without trial "enemy combatants" offshore in Guantanamo Bay. *See* David Dyzenhaus, The Constitution of Law: Legality in the Time of Emergency 1–3 (2006).

[70] Whitney v. California, 274 U.S. 357, 375 (Brandeis, J., concurring).

[71] Alec Stone Sweet & Jud Mathews, *Proportionality, Balancing, and Global Constitutionalism*, 47 Colum. J. Transnat'l L. 72 (2008).

[72] *See, e.g.*, Council of Eur. Venice Comm'n, *supra* note 58.

civic and political domains to constrain governments from engaging in repression to maintain power.

In the end, any meaningful understanding of the rule of law must be based on cultures of practice embedded in rule-governed institutions. To quote Nicholas Barber, "the rule of law amounts to a normative demand, a requirement that a certain set of mechanisms for the coercion and regulation of law is desirable."[73] Implementing this goal will give rise to variation, in reflection of different traditions, circumstances, and ideologies.[74] In this vein, Fuller rightly maintained that pursuit of the rule of law is ultimately a "practical art" of developing institutions.[75] We thus must turn from the question of goals to the question of means. We must address the question of *how to* – or, as Nicola Lacey writes, "how to develop legal arrangements capable of constraining abuses of power and of addressing such abuses."[76] The means entail different forms of checks on power's uncontrolled exercise.

## II The International Rule of Law from a Transnational Perspective

Many are skeptical about transporting the rule-of-law concept to international law. To start, many note the relatively "primitive" nature of international law in international relations, especially given the lack of institutions to enforce compliance.[77] Simon Chesterman, for example, cites the early rule-of-law theorist Dicey, who suggests international law is "miscalled" law and rather involves "rules of public ethics."[78] International relations realists continue in this vein, arguing that international law is epiphenomenal and reflects the interests of powerful states. From this vantage, international law still can be useful for purposes

[73] Nicholas Barber, The Principles of Constitutionalism 85 (2018).

[74] Taking a pluralist approach, Meierhenrich calls them "social imaginaries" that vary as a function of time and place. Jens Meierhenrich, *What the Rule of Law Is . . . and Is Not*, *in* The Cambridge Companion to the Rule of Law, *supra* note 12, at 569.

[75] Fuller, *supra* note 45, at 91. *Cf.* Philippe Nonet & Philip Selznick, Law and Society in Transition: Toward Responsive Law 53 (2017) ("The rule of law is better understood as a distinctive institutional system than as an abstract ideal.").

[76] Nicola Lacey, *Philosophy, Political Morality and History: Explaining the Enduring Resonance of the Hart-Fuller Debate*, 83 N.Y.U. L. Rev. 1059, 1072 (2008).

[77] *See, e.g.*, H.L.A. Hart, The Concept of Law 227 (2d ed. 2012) (1961). Rawls takes this approach in applying his theory of justice at the international level. John Rawls, The Law of Peoples (1999).

[78] Chesterman, *supra* note 12, at 358 (citing Dicey).

of interstate coordination and cooperation, but powerful states will ignore it when it does not advance their interests.[79]

The political scientist Ian Hurd maintains that one can still conceptualize the international rule of law from an international relations perspective, but one must do so distinctly in terms of the role of "law talk." For Hurd, international law involves a practice of argumentation in which actors use international law strategically to justify state behavior, which he calls "lawfare."[80] Powerful states "have the greatest influence over the design of international rules and the greatest capacity to both deploy and evade them."[81] They seek to justify their conduct by offering self-serving interpretations of international law, and those interpretations shape "future readings of the law."[82] For these reasons, third world approaches to international law (TWAIL) point to the biases in international law structures and practices that advantage powerful states and powerful constituencies within them.[83] They nonetheless stress the need and potential for international law.[84]

We see no reason to create a distinct conception of the "international rule of law." Rather, we maintain that the concept of the rule of law ultimately addresses the relation of authorities to individuals,[85] but that

79 Jack Goldsmith & Eric Posner, The Limits of International Law (2005).

80 The term "lawfare" was prominently used in response to those contesting the George W. Bush administration's policies following the September 11, 2001, terror attacks. For an early use of the term, see, for example, Charles Dunlap, Law and Military Interventions: Preserving Humanitarian Values in 21st Century Conflicts (2001).

81 Ian Hurd, How to Do Things with International Law 11 (2017).

82 *Id.* at 52.

83 B.S. Chimni, *Legitimating the International Rule of Law*, *in* The Cambridge Companion to International Law 290 (James Crawford & Martti Koskenniemi eds., 2015).

84 James Gathii, *The Promise of International Law: A Third World View*, 36 Am. U. Int'l L. Rev. 378 (2021).

85 *Cf.* Jeremy Waldron, *Are Sovereigns Entitled to the Benefit of the International Rule of Law?*, 22 Eur. J. Int'l L. 315, 341 (2011) (rule of law "requirements apply to the state for the sake of the well-being, liberty, and dignity of individuals"); Carmen Pavel, *The International Rule of Law*, 23 Crit. Rev. Int'l Soc. & Pol. Phil. 332, 334–47 (2020) (contending that the goal of an international rule of law is "the protection of individual and state autonomy," but viewing state autonomy as "valuable to the extent it protects individual autonomy"). Brian Tamanaha conceptualizes the rule of law in terms of legality, "*when government officials and legal subjects are bound by and abide by law*," and he thus maintains that the concept applies to interstate relations. *See* Chapter 2. We do not adopt a conception of the rule of law in terms of legality in light of the history of law's deployment for purposes of domination, as in the history of colonialism and slavery. Nonetheless, we concur with Tamanaha on international law's importance

international law's horizontal dimension of governing interstate relations is critical directly and indirectly for protecting individuals from power's arbitrary exercise. We thus retain our conception of the rule of law in terms of goals – to protect individuals from arbitrary power through legal rules and institutionalized practices, while providing channels for cooperative and coordinative activities. We nonetheless contend that international law is critical for advancing the rule of law in multiple direct and indirect ways that affect individuals and societies. At a minimum, the recognition of state boundaries and prohibition of the use of force except in self-defense helps ensure international peace and reduce the violence of war, thus protecting individuals and communities from power's arbitrary exercise in war. Going further, states can be viewed as agents or trustees in advancing rule-of-law goals, and not simply as subjects and beneficiaries of international law. International law creates norms, institutions, and mechanisms that aim to protect individuals from arbitrary power, whether directly or indirectly. At the same time, international institutions, multinational companies, and foreign states can wield power arbitrarily in ways that affect individuals. International law is thus critical for tempering their unbridled exercise of power as well.

Our assessment of the role of international law and institutions in advancing rule-of-law goals and practices is a *transnational* one. It incorporates international law and institutions within dynamic processes that implicate rule-of-law concerns within and across states, affecting individuals and societies. From a transnational perspective, we contend that international norms and institutions are important for protecting individuals from the arbitrary exercise of power. However, they also can advance the rule of the powerful by and through law. They thus also must be subject to critical scrutiny and transnational checks.

We build a socio-legal theory of the relation of international law and institutions to the rule of law conceptually and apply it empirically. As we will see in Part III, in an interconnected world trends regarding rule-of-law protections are transnational in scope. They involve shifting norms,

from a rule-of-law perspective in terms of the indirect and direct protections of individuals from power's arbitrary exercise that it can provide. In this vein, Tamanaha writes: "Protections for state sovereigns . . . are and should be included within the benefits of the international rule of law *for the good of individuals* in societies around the world." *Id.* We agree and use similar examples as Tamanaha to make our point, such as Russia's violation of basic norms in invading Ukraine and its implications for individuals and communities.

institutions, and practices at the local, national, and international levels. These developments are often enmeshed; they interact and recursively implicate international law and institutions, and, in turn, are implicated by them. Following World War II, and, more saliently, following the collapse of the Soviet Union and the end of the Cold War in the early 1990s, international law shifted from "classical Charter-based international law with its emphasis on state-oriented principles and underdeveloped human rights obligations towards a more value-based order which is actually capable of protecting and serving individuals," including from the arbitrary exercise of power.[86] Rule-of-law norms and institutions became more salient around the globe, both in discourse and in actual practices.[87] The empirical question arises as to whether these trends are now in reverse, such that there are cycles in which rule-of-law norms advance and retreat at both the national and international levels.

To assess these trends, one should place international and national law and institutions within a single analytic frame in dynamic relationship with each other. Halliday and Shaffer conceptualize these processes in terms of "transnational legal ordering" that can give rise to the settlement and unsettlement of legal norms as part of "transnational legal orders" (TLOs) in different substantive domains.[88] TLOs are normative orders that implicate law and legal practice across and within multiple national boundaries. They consist of working equilibria of relatively settled legal norms and practices that can vary in their substantive and geographic reach. Halliday and Shaffer define them as "a collection of formalized legal norms and associated organizations and actors that authoritatively order the understanding and practice of law across national jurisdictions."

Transnational legal ordering arises out of the transnational framing and understanding of a social problem, which catalyzes actors to seek a resolution through law. Such problems affect all areas of social life and range from global warming to a lack of capital for economic development

[86] Heike Krieger & Georg Nolte, *The International Rule of Law – Rise or Decline? – Approaching Current Foundational Challenges*, *in* THE INTERNATIONAL RULE OF LAW: RISE OR DECLINE? 3, 12 (Heike Krieger, Georg Nolte & Andreas Zimmermann eds., 2019). *Cf.* ANNE PETERS, BEYOND HUMAN RIGHTS: THE LEGAL STATUS OF THE INDIVIDUAL IN INTERNATIONAL LAW 8 (2016) ("The individual has become a primary subject (person) of international law.").

[87] *See, e.g.*, Chapters 3 (on global trends over time), 10, and 13.

[88] *See generally* TRANSNATIONAL LEGAL ORDERS, *supra* note 10.

to the exercise of arbitrary state power. TLO theory thus concords with viewing the rule of law as a solution concept – as a response to a problem, the problem of the arbitrary exercise of power.

Transnational legal ordering entails dynamic processes that lead to the settlement and unsettlement of legal norms. Various facilitating circumstances and precipitating events catalyze lawmaking and changing practices at different levels of social organization, which, in turn, interact in a recursive manner over time. Different factors drive these processes at the transnational, national, and local levels. These factors include diagnostic struggles over the nature of the problem, actor mismatch between the codifiers and implementers of legal norms, indeterminacies in the law, and ideological tensions and contradictions within the norms.[89] Where certain mechanisms are ineffective, actors may develop new tools. Where new tools are operationalized, actors may seek new ways to harness or thwart them. Through these processes, transnational legal orders can become more or less settled and institutionalized, varying in their geographic and substantive scope, including but not limited to regions. These legal orders also can vary in their alignment with an underlying problem, whether addressing it directly or only tangentially, or addressing all or only a part of it.[90] For example, the legal order could address a broad definition of the problem (climate change) or narrower ones (such as the regulation of air transport, cargo ships, or energy infrastructure). Legal orders also may overlap and be in competition, as illustrated by advocates contesting the primacy of intellectual property and public health legal orders regarding access to medicines, or of antiterrorism and national security law in light of due process requirements. Over time, transnational legal orders may rise, transform, and fall as legal norms settle and unsettle transnationally.

[89] Terence C. Halliday & Bruce G. Carruthers, *The Recursivity of Law: Global Norm Making and National Lawmaking in the Globalization of Corporate Insolvency Regimes*, 112 AM. J. SOCIO. 1135 (2007) (on the concept of recursivity of law and practice); Halliday & Shaffer, *supra* note 10, at 37–42. The argument that international law is not a fixed set of rules but rather a recursive process echoes Sandholtz, who foregrounds the inherent dynamism of international norm systems. International law constantly evolves as "[a]ctors argue about which norms apply and what the norms require or permit." WAYNE SANDHOLTZ, PROHIBITING PLUNDER: HOW NORMS CHANGE 10 (2007); *see also* Wayne Sandholtz, *Explaining International Norm Change*, *in* INTERNATIONAL NORMS AND CYCLES OF CHANGE 1, 13–15 (Wayne Sandholtz & Kendall Stiles eds., 2009).

[90] Halliday & Shaffer, *supra* note 10.

Our use of TLO theory in this book departs slightly from the way we have deployed it in the past. In the past, Halliday, Shaffer, and their collaborators viewed legal concepts in terms of how actors at different levels of social organization – ranging from the international to the national and local – framed problems and gave legal concepts meaning through recursive processes. In this way, they examined how legal norms develop, settle, unsettle, and change transnationally, such that their substantive meaning may alter, obscure, or become taken for granted. For example, Shaffer earlier conceptualized "transnational law" from a socio-legal perspective in terms of the "transnational construction and flow of legal norms," "in which transnational actors, be they transnational institutions or transnational networks of public or private actors, play a role in constructing and diffusing legal norms, even if the legal norm is taken in large part from a national legal model."[91]

Had we taken this approach, we would study how the meaning of the "rule of law" changes over time transnationally, settling and unsettling in practice in ways that transcend national boundaries. Such an approach would have applied a "phenomenological" conception of the rule of law, as developed elsewhere by Jens Meierhenrich[92] and applied by Jothie Rajah, who examined different transnational rule-of-law scripts developed by the World Bank, United Nations, and World Justice Project.[93] In this introductory chapter, in contrast, we define the rule of law as a principle and practice (*constraints on the arbitrary exercise of power by setting boundaries on, and channeling, power's exercise*), and we then assess the extent to which the principle and practice are under serious challenge today. This principle (or meta-principle) implicates law's practice across substantive domains. We still assess changes in legal practice transnationally, but here we do so in light of a principle that we define in terms of goals and practices in response to different sources of arbitrariness. Both approaches (phenomenological and normative) are important for empirical investigation, critique, and policy responsiveness to different social and political contexts.

91 Gregory Shaffer, *Transnational Legal Process and State Change*, 37 L. & Soc. Inquiry 229, 235 (2012).

92 Meierhenrich, *supra* note 74, at 494–512 (citing UNCTAD, World Investment Report 2018, at 95 (2018)).

93 Jothie Rajah, *"Rule of Law" as Transnational Legal Order, in* Transnational Legal Orders, *supra* note 10, at 340; Terence C. Halliday & Gregory Shaffer, *Researching Transnational Legal Orders, in* Transnational Legal Orders, *supra* note 10, at 475, 494–95.

In this Part II, we assess the direct and indirect relation of international law and institutions to rule-of law goals and practices as we have defined them. We contend that, in an interconnected world, the rule of law should be viewed as a normative social order that involves the horizontal, vertical, and transversal interaction of domestic and international law, which, in turn, reciprocally affect each other.[94] Any equilibrium at the international, national, or local level will be subject to influence by norms that are conveyed, settle, and unsettle transnationally.

International law and institutions implicate rule-of-law protections for individuals in the following three ways. First, from a minimalist perspective, international law and institutions can help to secure international peace, which ultimately affects individuals and societies. Second, international law and institutions can indirectly affect domestic rule-of-law practices in relation to individuals. National law often incorporates international law; national courts and other bodies may reference it; and national actors may otherwise harness it, including to protect rule-of-law concerns. Third, international law and institutions can directly grant rights to individuals and impose duties on national governments, international institutions, and private actors.

In each case, we note how international law can either support rule-of-law practices or undermine them. As law generally, it can validate practices of freedom or of domination, which is why it is important to differentiate the concept of rule of law from that of rule by law. Because international law is part of larger, transnational, norm-making processes, one should assess interactions between international, national, and local norms, institutions, and practices that implicate the rule of law. Figure 1.1 captures these processes of interaction as regards anti-terrorism and due process norms at different levels of social organization, which we further address below.

[94] Halliday & Shaffer, *supra* note 93. For an assessment of such interactions from a legal perspective, in complement to this book's socio-legal one, see THE RULE OF LAW AT THE NATIONAL AND INTERNATIONAL LEVELS: CONTESTATIONS AND DEFERENCE (Machiko Kanetake & Andre Nollkaemper eds., 2016). On the transnational interaction of global and regional human rights bodies, see Yuval Shany, *The Interplay Between the Global and the Regional*, *in* OXFORD HANDBOOK ON COMPARATIVE HUMAN RIGHTS LAW (Neha Jain & Mila Versteeg eds., forthcoming).

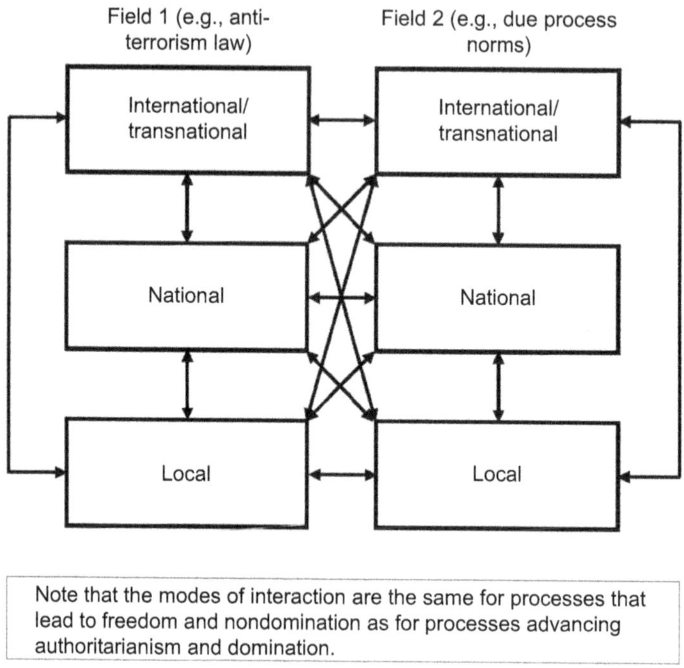


**Figure 1.1** The transnational web of rule-of-law interactions.

## 1 *Minimalist Perspective of Rule of Law for Nonviolence, Peace, and Public Order*

The rule of law links analytically with the concept of peace by stressing the use of law to resolve conflicts in lieu of unbridled coercion and violence. At the international level of interstate relations, one of the core features of a "liberal international order" is the creation of multilateral institutions for the resolution of disputes under international law, thereby enhancing the security of states and their constituents.[95] There is no greater risk of arbitrary power exercised over individuals than the violence of war. As the philosopher Bernard Williams writes, the "Hobbesian question" of securing "order, protection, safety, trust, and the conditions of cooperation" is the "first" political question: "[S]olving it is the condition of solving, indeed posing, any others."[96] It is for this reason that Steven Ratner prioritizes international law's

[95] David A. Lake, Lisa L. Martin & Thomas Risse, *Challenges to the Liberal Order: Reflections on* International Organization, 75 INT'L ORG. 225, 225–57 (2021).

[96] Bernard Williams, *Realism and Moralism in Political Theory*, *in* IN THE BEGINNING WAS THE DEED: REALISM AND MORALISM IN POLITICAL ARGUMENT 3 (Geoffrey Hawthorn ed., 2005).

potential in providing a "pillar of peace" as a core aspect of theorizing international law in terms of justice.[97] The same is true as regards the rule of law. In a "thin" sense, international law is foundational to political order. It supports the maintenance of secure political communities and thus enhances the prospects of rule-of-law protections for these communities' members.[98] Simply put, war and the immediate threat of war subject individuals and communities to increased risks of coercion and violence, whether by a foreign state, their own state, or nonstate actors. Practically, international law can protect, and has protected, individuals and communities from power's arbitrary exercise.[99]

Relatedly, from a transnational perspective, democratic peace theory provides powerful evidence that democracies grounded in the rule of law are less likely to go to war against each other than are authoritarian states, the latter being more likely to go to war against both each other and democratic states.[100] Where democratic norms grounded in the rule of law diffuse transnationally, the prospect of peace should increase, giving rise to "security communities."[101] These communities may be tied together through shared norms and broader legal orders that become institutionalized, particularly at the regional level.[102] These two

[97] Steven R. Ratner, The Thin Justice of International Law: A Moral Reckoning of the Law of Nations (2015) (focusing first on the "pillar of peace" in terms of the absence of armed conflict); Hersch Lauterpacht, The Function of Law in the International Community 440 (2011) (international rule of law as an "instrument of preserving peace").

[98] As Postema writes, "In the modern world, states are the sites of more or less integrated political communities, and well-ordered political communities realize to varying extents the value of membership .... [T]ransnational peace and security and international cooperation among states ... are important for rule of law purposes because they also underwrite and secure the efforts of political communities to provide the good of membership." Postema, *supra* note 9, at 329.

[99] Oona A. Hathaway & Scott Shapiro, The Internationalists: How a Radical Plan to Outlaw Ward Remade the World (2017).

[100] *See, e.g.*, Bruce Russett & John R. Oneal, Triangulating Peace: Democracy, Interdependence, and International Organizations (2000); Michael Doyle, Liberal Peace: Selected Essays 4 (2012) (referring to states "founded on such individual rights as equality before the law, free speech and other civil liberties, private property, and elected representation" and notably "freedom from arbitrary authority"). For a precursor, see Immanuel Kant, Perpetual Peace: A Philosophical Sketch (1795). *Cf.* Christopher Layne, *Kant or Cant: The Myth of the Democratic Peace*, 19 Int'l Security 5 (1994).

[101] Emmanuel Adler & Michael Barnett, Security Communities (1998) (writing from a constructivist perspective).

[102] International organizations with mostly democratic member states are significantly more likely to contribute to the peaceful resolution of disputes than those with fewer

perspectives – democratic peace theory and transnational diffusion of norms – can be combined to show how rule-of-law norms at the national and international levels mutually and recursively support each other to enhance the prospects of peace and nonviolence, and thus reduce the likelihood of arbitrary power inflicted on individuals.

The international institutions created in the decades after World War II, at a minimum, provided rules for governing interstate relations and reducing the risk of armed conflict. One of the goals of promoters of the United Nations and its family of specialized international organizations was to ensure peace among states. The UN Charter prohibits the use of force – and thus war – to settle international disputes other than for self-defense against an armed attack (Article 51) or when authorized by the UN Security Council (Article 42). Regional regimes developed in parallel, with the aim of not only preserving peace within the region but also promoting nonviolent, law-governed, democratic transitions within states. After the end of the Cold War, international institutions grew in prominence. The UN Security Council has never lived up to its purpose under the UN Charter of ensuring "the maintenance of international peace and security." Following the end of the Cold War, it reached consensus in a few prominent cases, giving rise to interventions, including to promote peace and security in post-conflict settings. Most notably, the Security Council authorized interventions in Iraq in 1991 following Iraq's invasion of Kuwait (Resolution 688), in Bosnia in 1992 (Resolution 770), in Somalia in 1992 (Resolution 794), in Haiti in 1994 (Resolution 940), and in Afghanistan in 2001 (Resolution 1386). Regional organizations in Africa – ECOWAS and the African Union – even acquired the authority to intervene militarily in their member states to uphold law-governed, democratic transitions.

Among the core aims of international courts and other institutions is the peaceful resolution of disputes. The International Court of Justice (ICJ) offers a general-purpose mechanism for resolving disputes when states grant it jurisdiction. Counterfactually, without the ICJ and other international tribunals, it would be more difficult for states to peacefully resolve disputes.[103] Take, for example, international boundary disputes. The ICJ has been particularly effective in peacefully resolving disputes in this area, complemented by the Permanent Court of Arbitration (PCA)

democracies. John Pevehouse & Bruce Russett, *Democratic International Governmental Organizations Promote Peace*, 60 INT'L ORG. 969 (2006).

103 Tom Ginsburg & Richard H. McAdams, *Adjudicating in Anarchy: An Expressive Theory of International Dispute Resolution*, 45 WM. & MARY L. REV. 1229 (2004).

Table 1.1 *Compliance with international court decisions on land and sea borders*

| | Compliance | Partial compliance | Noncompliance | Total cases |
|---|---|---|---|---|
| ICJ | 26 | 7 | 4 | 37 |
| PCA | 7 | 0 | 4 | 13 |
| ITLOS | 3 | 0 | 0 | 3 |
| Total | 38 | 7 | 8 | 53 |

and the International Tribunal for the Law of the Sea (ITLOS). From 1951 to 2021, there were 53 boundary disputes decided by international tribunals, comprising 22 land boundary disputes, 19 maritime boundary disputes, and 12 disputes involving land and sea questions. As shown in Table 1.1, the ICJ decided 37, the PCA 13, and ITLOS 3 in total.[104] Overall, states complied either fully or partially with 45 (around 85 percent) of these judgments.

The ICJ is complemented by other general purpose and specialized international tribunals. For example, the World Trade Organization (WTO) provides a legalized system for resolving trade disputes. Without it, trade wars are much more difficult to restrain, since tit-for-tat retaliation can lead to greater distrust and conflict, as evidenced both by the tariff and currency wars of the 1930s and the US–China trade war launched by the Trump administration in 2018 as the United States blocked appointments to the WTO's Appellate Body. Indeed, US Secretary of State Cordell Hull believed that "economic blocs of the 1930s, practiced by Germany and Japan but also Britain, were the root cause of the instability of the period and the onset of the war."[105] Among the aims of international investment arbitration is to resolve disputes over the treatment of aliens and their property that earlier had led to

104 Authors' count from the databases of the three tribunals and a review of post-judgment responses. In addition, there were two PCA cases, one in 1909 and the other in 1914, but we do not include these in the table given our focus on the legal order that arose after World War II. The ICJ was created in 1945, succeeding the earlier Permanent Court of International Justice, and it heard its first case, *Corfu Channel*, in 1947, issuing its decision on the merits in 1949. For earlier work, see *id.*

105 John Ikenberry, After Victory: Institutions, Strategic Restraint, and the Rebuilding of Order after Major Wars 176–77 (2000); 1 Cordell Hull, The Memoirs of Cordell Hull 81 (1948) ("unhampered trade dovetailed with peace; high tariffs, trade barriers, and unfair economic competition, with war").

armed interventions. Although the investment law regime is subject to significant critique from a rule-of-law perspective, the illegality of the use of force to protect citizens' property claims abroad represents, at a minimum, a significant advance.

Other international and regional fora provide jurisdiction for a range of disputes within their competence. The European Union (EU) provides a regional model. In this case, the EU and its predecessor organizations, starting with the European Coal and Steel Community, tied a powerful state (Germany) to a regional economic integration project with the aim of ensuring peace within Europe. Alec Stone Sweet analogously conceptualizes the European Court of Human Rights (ECtHR) under the Council of Europe as a Kantian "cosmopolitan legal order" advancing "Kant's blueprint for achieving Perpetual Peace."[106] These international institutions provide settings in which states can air their differences and resolve them through law and third-party institutions.

Global threats other than war affect the security of borders. Most saliently, there are the increasing risks posed by climate change, which have led to severe droughts and storms, cataclysmic fires and flooding. These threats can spur new interstate conflicts, whether over access to scarce water from shared lakes and river systems or because internal upheaval spills over borders, increasing the risks of power's arbitrary exercise. International cooperation is required to address the underlying causes of climate change, since one state's efforts go to naught if greenhouse gas-intensive production shifts elsewhere and other states take no action. International law and institutions can facilitate such cooperation, such as through binding rules, reciprocal pledges, and the generation of funding to address climate change risks. As with international law aimed at reducing the risks of war, international law and institutions addressing climate change also can indirectly support rule-of-law goals by reducing the underlying risks of power's arbitrary exercise.

Yet, international law and institutions also can support invasions and facilitate domination by powerful states over others. The 1884–85 Berlin Conference carved up Africa, which authorized King Leopold's brutal exploitation of the Congo. The League of Nations' and United Nations' mandate and trusteeship systems served to legitimate Western nations' continued rule over their colonies, with the UN Trusteeship Council

[106] Alec Stone Sweet & Clare Ryan, A Cosmopolitan Legal Order: Kant, Constitutional Justice and the European Convention on Human Rights (2018). *See also* Harold Koh, *The Trump Administration and International Law*, 56 Washburn L.J. 413, 467 (2017) (referencing a "Kantian postwar system").

continuing to operate until 1994 when the last trusteeship territory, the island of Palau, became independent from the United States. Powerful states remain dominant in shaping and enforcing international law today, as reflected in the veto powers of the five permanent members of the UN Security Council. The fact that these nations can block the application of any measure as applied to themselves when they violate the UN Charter and invade other countries undermines the rule of law – the first source of arbitrariness discussed earlier. Moreover, when the Security Council authorizes action, there is no international court or other institution to hold it, or countries acting under its authorization, accountable. For example, US and NATO excesses in enforcing a Security Council resolution for a "no-fly zone" in Libya in 2011 led to the overthrow of the Qaddafi regime, and increased insecurity, suffering, and mass violence in that country.[107] In theory, interventions authorized by international institutions or referencing international law can reduce violence and conflict, but they also can worsen situations, rendering individuals more vulnerable to violence and arbitrary power.[108] Rule-of-law norms thus must apply to international institutions themselves.[109]

Powerful actors also reference international law to authorize invasions that can lead to increased violence. For example, human rights claims helped frame the creation of a "responsibility to protect" doctrine, which can serve to justify "humanitarian interventions" and thus armed conflict in the name of human rights enforcement.[110] President Putin's rhetoric to legitimize Russia's 2022 invasion of Ukraine in the name of "humanitarian intervention" illustrates how powerful actors deploy humanitarian rhetoric and international law for self-interested reasons. Russia's veto of a Security Council resolution calling on it to halt its attacks and withdraw

[107] Phyllis Bennis, *Lessons from NATO's Last No-Fly Zone*, Foreign Pol'y in Focus (Mar. 29, 2022), https://fpif.org/lessons-from-natos-last-no-fly-zone/; Alan J. Kuperman, *A Model Humanitarian Intervention? Reassessing NATO's Libya Campaign*, 38 Int'l Security 105 (2013) ("The intervention extended the war's duration about sixfold; increased its death toll approximately seven to ten times; and exacerbated human rights abuses, humanitarian suffering, Islamic radicalism, and weapons proliferation in Libya and its neighbors.").

[108] Simon Chesterman, Just War or Just Peace? Humanitarian Intervention and International Law (2001); Tom Ginsburg, *In Defense of Imperialism? The Rule of Law and the State-Building Project*, *in* Getting to the Rule of Law 224 (James Fleming ed., 2011). UN peacekeepers are to step in when states "fail." In these cases, they directly assume rule-of-law responsibilities.

[109] *See* Chapter 6.

[110] Mark Mazower, Governing the World: The History of an Idea: 1815 to the Present ch. 13 (2012).

from Ukraine illustrates how the Council's permanent members block the application of international law against themselves.

### 2 *Indirect Processual Links Supporting Rule-of-Law Practices within States*

International institutions and international law are important for norm-making, oversight, assessment, and funding of rule-of-law initiatives that indirectly affect institutional practices within states.[111] They are best viewed as part of larger transnational normative processes involving the conveyance of norms, which ultimately are applied within states toward individuals. Since World War II, international institutions have aimed to delimit state prerogatives affecting the rights of all persons, for which the rule of law is fundamental. They create focal points for transnational networks of civil society groups that can help to embolden and empower those advancing rule-of-law goals domestically. Domestic groups can use reporting, peer review, and judicial or other transnational mechanisms to enhance their positions in domestic political, judicial, and administrative institutions and processes, potentially "locking in" domestic rule-of-law reforms.[112]

One way that scholars have framed the so-called liberal international order in the post-World War II era is to view states as agents of higher-order international rules for the protection of human rights, for which the rule of law provides a foundation. Political scientists Tanja Börzel and Michael Zürn labeled this a "postnational liberal international order" in that it comprised conditionally sovereign states, which gained legitimacy by enforcing and guaranteeing liberal rights, rules, and decisions implicating the rule of law.[113] The Universal Declaration of Human Rights sets out fundamental individual rights that states are obligated to respect

[111] For a sample of work on the indirect impact of international institutions, see Geoff Dancy & Kathryn Sikkink, *Ratification and Human Rights Prosecutions: Toward a Transnational Theory of Treaty Compliance*, 44 NYU J. INT'L L. & POL. 751 (2011); Xinjuan Dai, *Why Comply? The Domestic Constituency Mechanism*, 59 INT'L ORG. 363 (2005); SALLY ENGLE MERRY, HUMAN RIGHTS AND GENDER VIOLENCE: TRANSLATING INTERNATIONAL LAW INTO LOCAL JUSTICE (2006); BETH SIMMONS, MOBILIZING FOR HUMAN RIGHTS: INTERNATIONAL LAW IN DOMESTIC POLITICS (2009).

[112] Tom Ginsburg, *Locking in Democracy: Constitutions, Commitment, and International Law*, 38 N.Y.U. J. INT'L L. & POL. 707 (2006).

[113] Tanja A. Börzel & Michael Zürn, *Contestations of the Liberal International Order: From Liberal Multilateralism to Postnational Liberalism*, 75 INT'L ORG. 282, 282–305 (2021).

through "the rule of law."[114] The International Covenant on Civil and Political Rights (ICCPR) and the International Covenant on Economic, Cultural and Social Rights, together with other global and regional treaties, elaborate these rights and create international mechanisms to oversee their application. Over time, these treaties' membership, scope of coverage, and enforcement mechanisms have expanded.

We conceptualize the protection of human rights, as noted in Part I, as important means that complement and overlap with the rule of law in advancing rule-of-law goals. These rights are almost universally recognized in national constitutions,[115] which, in turn, reflect transnational processes of constitution-making and constitutional practice.[116] To be a modern state is to have a constitution, and increasingly since 1945 national constitutions define individual rights and obligate the state to respect and protect them through institutionalized means founded on the rule of law.[117] The Universal Declaration of Human Rights has been particularly influential in shaping rights provisions in national constitutions.[118] Such rights are developed recursively in international and domestic law and institutions through transnational processes.[119] In the words of the late ICJ judge James Crawford, one of the main roles "of international law is to reinforce, and on occasions to institute, the rule of law internally."[120] In this vein, in 2004 UN Secretary-General Kofi Annan stressed:

114 The Declaration's preamble provides, "Whereas it is essential, if man is not to be compelled to have recourse, as a last resort, to rebellion against tyranny and oppression, that human rights should be protected by *the rule of law*." G.A. Res. 217 (III) A, Universal Declaration of Human Rights (Dec. 10, 1948) (emphasis added). In addition, various provisions directly address rule-of-law concerns. To give two examples, Article 7 of the Universal Declaration provides that "[a]ll are equal before the law and are entitled without any discrimination to equal protection of the law," and Article 11 prohibits ex post facto penal laws. *Id.*

115 David Sloss & Wayne Sandholtz, *Universal Human Rights and Constitutional Change*, 27 Wm. & Mary Bill Rts. J. 1183 (2019).

116 Constitution-Making and Transnational Legal Order, *supra* note 23.

117 Colin J. Beck et al., *Constitutions in World Society: A New Measure of Human Rights, in* Constitution-Making and Transnational Legal Order, *supra* note 23, at 85, 95; Zachary Elkins, Tom Ginsburg & Beth Simmons, *Getting to Rights: Treaty Ratification, Constitutional Convergence, and Human Rights Practice*, 54 Harv. Int'l L.J. 61 (2013).

118 Zackary Elkins & Tom Ginsburg, *Imagining a World Without the Universal Declaration of Human Rights*, 74 World Pol. 327 (2022).

119 Engle Merry, *supra* note 111; Halliday & Shaffer, *supra* note 10, at 37–42.

120 James Crawford, *International Law and the Rule of Law*, 24 Adel. L. Rev. 3, 8 (2003). Crawford also writes that "it is better to see the present system of public order at the international level . . . as an interpenetration of legal orders." *Id.* at 10.

> States are now widely understood to be instruments at the service of their peoples, and not vice versa. At the same time individual sovereignty – by which I mean the fundamental freedom of each individual, enshrined in the charter of the UN and subsequent international treaties – has been enhanced by a renewed and spreading consciousness of individual rights. When we read the charter today, we are more than ever conscious that its aim is to protect individual human beings, not to protect those who abuse them.[121]

These protections are contingent on the rule of law.

The protection of individual rights against the arbitrary exercise of power is part of the mission of a range of international and regional institutions. Eight of the principal international human rights treaties include provisions that allow the relevant treaty bodies to receive individual communications alleging violations. The Human Rights Committee, for example, established under the ICCPR, can receive and decide on individual claims of ICCPR rights violations by the 106 states that have accepted the First Optional Protocol to the ICCPR.[122] The Human Rights Committee lacks power to enforce these rights directly, but states are obliged to respond to its findings. In 2022, for example, it found that Australia had arbitrarily interfered with the rights of indigenous Torres Strait Islanders by failing to protect them adequately from the effects of climate change.[123]

This is just one part of the architecture of international human rights institutions, which include the UN Human Rights Council, the Office of the High Commissioner for Human Rights under the UN Secretary-General, the committees created to oversee the other international human rights treaties, and various reporting and investigative bodies, such as the system of UN special rapporteurs. States are accountable to these bodies, and constituents within states can reference and appeal to their work to advance rule-of-law goals. For example, under the UN Paris Principles, over one hundred countries created national human rights institutions, which generated a transgovernmental system of monitoring that facilitates norm diffusion.[124] Similarly, more reporting mechanisms

[121] Kofi Annan, *Two Concepts of Sovereignty*, ECONOMIST, Sept. 18, 1999, at 49.

[122] Hum. Rts. Committee, *Introduction to the Committee*, UNITED NATIONS (2022), www.ohchr.org/en/treaty-bodies/ccpr/introduction-committee.

[123] Kristen Lyons, *Australia Violated the Rights of Torres Strait Islanders by Failing to Act on Climate Change, the UN Says. Here's What That Means*, CONVERSATION (Sept. 25, 2022, 4:41 AM), https://tinyurl.com/serrdsej.

[124] Katerina Linos & Tom Pegram, *Architects of Their Own Making*, 38 HUM. RTS. Q. 1109, 1110 (2016) ("International endorsement has since triggered a norm cascade on a global

can have catalytic impacts within countries through media coverage, nongovernmental advocacy, legislative references, and administrative follow-up.[125]

Regional bodies are particularly important for overseeing and monitoring human rights protections implicating rule-of law goals.[126] The European Union established conditions for membership under which state institutions must guarantee democracy, the rule of law, and human rights (the "Copenhagen criteria" of 1993). It also established a mechanism for holding states accountable for violations of rights contained in the EU's Charter of Fundamental Rights (CFR). National judges can hear individual complaints regarding violations of the Charter, and, where there is uncertainty, they can seek interpretive guidance from the Court of Justice of the European Union.[127] The Court of Justice has found that Article 2 of the Treaty of the European Union "contains values [including the rule of law] which … are an integral part of the very identity of the European Union as a common legal order, values which are given concrete expression in principles containing legally binding obligations for the Member States."[128] It has applied the value of the "rule of law" embedded in Article 2 to require member states to maintain an independent judiciary, which is a major concern in Hungary and Poland.[129] In parallel, the European Commission for Democracy and Law (the "Venice Commission"), within the Council of Europe, is charged with helping states that wish "to bring their legal and institutional structures into line with European standards and international experience in the fields of democracy, human rights and the rule of law."[130] These regional bodies can contribute to the formation of regional legal orders, although these too

scale, with NHRIs increasing from twenty such structures before 1990 to approximately 130 NHRIs in 2015."); Luka Glušac, *Universal Periodic Review and Policy Change: The Case of National Human Rights Institutions*, J. Hum. Rts. Prac. 1, 2 (2022) ("Today more than a hundred countries have established NHRIs, of which more than 85 are accredited with the highest A status by GANHRI, in a process facilitated and approved by the United Nations – proving that they are fully compliant with the Paris Principles.").

125 *See, e.g.*, Cosette Creamer & Beth Simmons, *The Dynamic Impact of Periodic Review of Women's Rights*, 81 L. & Contemp. Probs. 31 (2018).

126 Governance Transfer by Regional Organizations: Patching Together a Global Script (Tanja Börzel & Vera Van Jullen eds., 2015).

127 *How to Report a Breach of Your Rights*, Eur. Comm'n (Dec. 7, 2021), https://tinyurl.com/4prmka52.

128 Case C-156/21, Hungary v. Parliament & Council (Conditionality Regulation), EU:C:2022:97 (Feb. 16, 2022).

129 Kim Lane Scheppele, *Restoring Democracy Through International Law*, Am. U. J. Int'l L. (forthcoming).

130 *For Democracy Through Law*, Council of Eur. Venice Comm'n, www.venice.coe.int/WebForms/pages/?p=01_Presentation&lang=EN (last visited Aug. 21, 2024).

will show internal variation in terms of the concordance of regional, national, and local practice.[131] Variation among regional legal orders can reflect different regional traditions and transnational borrowings among neighboring countries.[132]

International human rights law and institutions arguably are most powerful when national institutions, such as national courts, reference and enforce international norms within national systems.[133] This transnational framing of international law resonates with Kim Lane Scheppele's assessment of international courts in "three-dimensional space." As she maintains, international courts should not be viewed hierarchically as super appeals courts or primarily as "back stops" to national courts, but rather as part of broader normative orders that horizontally among themselves and vertically in relation to national courts affect institutional practices, particularly for the protection of the rule of law.[134] All members of the Council of Europe must incorporate the European Convention on Human Rights into national law, and national judges in these countries reference the Convention in applying national law.[135] The UK Human Rights Act, for example, requires that UK judges interpret statutes, so far as possible, in ways that are compatible with the UK's international human rights commitments.[136] In Germany, courts generally are obliged "to take note of and consider the relevant case law of the international courts with jurisdiction for Germany."[137]

131 On variations in patterns of concordance, see Halliday & Shaffer, *supra* note 10, at 44–46.

132 *See, e.g.*, Melissa Curley, Bjorn Dressel & Stephen McCarthy, *Competing Visions of the Rule of Law in Southeast Asia: Power, Rhetoric and Governance*, 42 Asian Stud. Rev. 192 (2018).

133 Simmons, *supra* note 111.

134 Kim Lane Scheppele, *The Constitutional Role of Transnational Courts: Principled Legal Ideas in Three-Dimensional Political Space*, 28 Penn. St. Int'l L. Rev. 451 (2010). *See also* Chapters 7 and 11.

135 See, for example., the "Border Guard" case where the German court appeals to the norms of international law. Rudolf Geiger, *The German Border Guard Cases and International Human Rights*, 9 Eur. J. Int'l L. 540, 546 (1998). *Cf.* S. Afr. Const, 1996, § 233 ("When interpreting any legislation, every court must prefer any reasonable interpretation of the legislation that is consistent with international law over any alternative interpretation that is inconsistent with international law.").

136 Human Rights Act 1998, c. 42, § 3 (UK), www.legislation.gov.uk/ukpga/1998/42/section/3.

137 BVerfGK 9, 174 (2006) (First Chamber of the Second Senate), 2 BvR 2115/01, 2 BvR 2132/01, 2 BvR 348/032010, of 19 Sept. 2006, para. 53 (cited in Peters, *supra* note 86, at 485).

Direct decisions of a human rights court against one state can have effects in other states, illustrating transnational processes at work. Laurence Helfer and Eric Voeten, for example, provide evidence that ECtHR decisions against one country substantially increase the probability of national-level policy change across Europe, such as in the area of the protection of LGBT equality.[138] Relatedly, within many Latin American countries one cannot meaningfully study constitutional law developments without incorporating their relation to the inter-American human rights system and changes in legal culture regarding the rule of law.[139] These bodies generate interpretations that courts outside of their regions reference, including other regional courts and other national courts (such as in the United States and India).[140]

Courts also frequently apply or otherwise consider international law in interpreting national law.[141] In doing so, they participate in, and are critical to, international law's implementation, development, and practice. As the Supreme Court of Canada stated in the case Nevsun Resources Ltd. v. Araya et al., "Canadian courts, like all courts, play an important role in the ongoing development of international law."[142] They are important not only in "implementing" international law, but also in "advancing" it. In that way, they "contribute . . . to the 'choir' of domestic court judgments around the world shaping the 'substance of international law.'"[143] The opinion affirmatively cites former member of the Canadian Supreme Court Gérard La Forest, who writes, "our

[138] Laurence Helfer & Erik Voeten, *International Courts as Agents of Legal Change: Evidence from LGBT Rights in Europe*, 68 Int'l Org. 77 (2014).

[139] Javier Couso, Alexandra Huneeus & Rachel Sieder, Cultures of Legality: Judicialization and Political Activism in Latin America 112 (2010); *see also* Chapter 10.

[140] *See, e.g.*, Alec Stone Sweet, Wayne Sandholtz & Mads Andenas, *The Failure to Destroy the Authority of the European Court of Human Rights: 2010–2018*, 21 Law & Prac. Int'l Cts. & Tribunals 244 (2022) ("The Inter-American Court of Human Rights and the various African regional courts virtually never issue an important judgment without consulting the relevant rulings of the European Court."); Lawrence v. Texas, 539 U.S. 558 (2003) (referencing a decision of the ECtHR); Khosla Madhav, *Inclusive Constitutional Comparison: Reflections on India's Sodomy Decision*, 59 Am. J. Comp. L. 909 (2011).

[141] See, for example, the "Charming Betsy" canon of interpretation in the United States, which derives from Justice John Marshall's statement that "an act of Congress ought never to be construed to violate the law of nations if any other possible construction remains." Murray v. The Schooner Charming Betsy, 6. U.S. 64 (1804).

[142] Nevsun Resources Ltd. v. Araya [2020] 1 S.C.R. 166, para. 70 (Can.).

[143] *Id.* paras. 71–72.

courts – and many other national courts – are truly becoming international courts in many areas involving the rule of law."[144]

Many international organizations have incorporated and promoted rule-of-law norms in their rules and jurisprudence. For example, WTO panels have found that a central goal of the WTO legal system is to provide individual traders with certainty and predictability from the arbitrary action of other governments. In the *United States – Section 301* case, the European Union challenged US unilateral legislation used to threaten US sanctions against it before the WTO dispute settlement system had completed its review. The panel found that such legislation could be challenged "as such" given its "'chilling effects' on the economic activities of individuals." The panel stressed, "it would be entirely wrong to consider that the position of individuals is of no relevance to the GATT/WTO legal matrix .... The multilateral trading system is, per force, composed not only of States but also, indeed mostly, of individual economic operators. The lack of security and predictability affects mostly these individual operators."[145]

Relatedly, in the United States – Shrimp case, a group of south and southeast Asian nations challenged a US ban on shrimp imports from countries that did not require certain shrimp trawling practices to protect endangered sea turtles. The Appellate Body found that, although the US objective was legitimate, the United States had failed to provide "due process" rights to the other countries to defend themselves and adapt to the new measure. It found that the application of the US measure was "arbitrary" in that the certification process was not "transparent" or "predictable," did not provide any "formal opportunity for an applicant country to be heard or to respond to any arguments that may be made against it," did not result in a "formal written, reasoned decision," and offered "no procedure for review of, or appeal from, a denial of an application."[146] The Appellate Body focused, in particular, on the transparency obligations set forth in Article X of the GATT, pursuant to which WTO members are to publicize their laws and regulations so as to give

[144] Gérard La Forest, *The Expanding Role of the Supreme Court of Canada in International Law Issues*, 34 CAN. Y.B. INT'L L. 89, 100–01 (1996) (cited in *Nevsun*, para. 70).

[145] Panel Report, *United States – Sections 301–310 of the Trade Act of 1974*, ¶¶ 7.73, 7.76, 7.81, WTO Doc. WT/DS152/R (adopted Jan. 25, 2000). The GATT is the General Agreement on Tariffs and Trade, which went into effect in 1948 and was incorporated as a WTO-covered agreement in 1995.

[146] Appellate Body Report, *United States – Import Prohibition of Certain Shrimp and Shrimp Products*, ¶ 180, WTO Doc. WT/DS58/AB/R (adopted Oct. 12, 1998).

foreign traders proper notice.[147] These requirements respond to two of the sources of arbitrariness we foregrounded in Part I – the provision of transparent, published rules, and of an impartial tribunal where persons can respond to and challenge an authority's decisions against them.

The United Nations, World Bank, and other organizations, including regional and national agencies, have created a rule-of-law industry of consultants giving technical advice, which intensified in the 1990s and 2000s.[148] Discourse on the rule of law proliferated in Security Council resolutions, in Secretary-General reports, and in other UN groups, particularly as relates to UN peacebuilding and rule-of-law assistance in post-conflict settings.[149] Some of these processes focused on legal empowerment to support civil society and grassroots organizations within states.[150] As one UN document declares, the rule of law is a concept "at the very heart of the UN mission," which is "interlinked and mutually reinforcing" with human rights and democracy.[151] In parallel, rule-of-law promotion became central within the World Bank and other development agencies.[152]

147 *Id.* ¶¶ 182–83.

148 Veronica Taylor, *Big Rule of Law*, *in* STRENGTHENING THE RULE OF LAW THROUGH THE UN SECURITY COUNCIL 27 (Jeremy Farrall & Hillary Charlesworth eds., 2016); Kristen Boon, *"Open for Business": International Financial Institutions, Post-conflict Economic Reform, and the Rule of Law*, 39 N.Y.U. J. INT'L L. & POL. 513, 572 (2007).

149 *See* Chapter 6. Between 1998 and 2006, the phrase "rule of law" appeared in at least sixty-nine Security Council resolutions. JEREMY FARREL, UNITED NATIONS SANCTIONS AND THE RULE OF LAW 22 (2007). A Security Council resolution first used the words "rule of law" in 1996 regarding the Secretary-General's efforts in Burundi. S.C. Res. 1040, ¶ 2 (Jan. 29, 1996). In 2011, the UN published its *Rule of Law Indicators: Implementation Guide and Project Tools*, which focused on criminal justice institutions, and in particular on police, the judicial system, and prisons.

150 Stephen Golub, *The Legal Empowerment Alternative*, *in* PROMOTING THE RULE OF LAW ABROAD: IN SEARCH OF KNOWLEDGE 161 (Thomas Carothers ed., 2006); U.N. Secretary-General, *Guidance Note of the Secretary-General: UN Approach to Rule of Law Assistance* (Apr. 14, 2008) ("meaningful ownership requires the legal empowerment of all segments of society").

151 UNITED NATIONS, NEW VOICES: NATIONAL PERSPECTIVES ON RULE OF LAW ASSISTANCE 8 (2011); *see also* G.A. Res., Declaration of the High-level Meeting of the General Assembly on the Rule of Law at the National and International Levels, U.N. Doc. A/RES/67/1 (Nov. 30, 2012). For a list and brief overview of relevant UN documents, see Leander Beinlich & Anne Peters, *An International Rule of Law*, OXFORD BIBLIOGRAPHIES (2021), https://tinyurl.com/b4a3t6dw.

152 David Trubek, *The "Rule of Law" in Development Assistance: Past, Present, and Future*, *in* THE NEW LAW AND ECONOMIC DEVELOPMENT: A CRITICAL APPRAISAL 74 (David Trubek & Alvaro Santos eds., 2006); *see, e.g.*, WORLD BANK, WORLD DEVELOPMENT REPORT 2017: GOVERNANCE AND THE LAW (2017).

International and transnational processes are also critical for targeting the practices of nonstate entities, such as multinational corporations that operate in countries with few rule-of-law protections. The United Nations developed Guiding Principles on Business and Human Rights in 2011, to which multinational corporations agree to adhere.[153] Private organizations and national regulatory agencies have promoted reporting on adherence to legal norms involving expanded environmental, social, and governance practices (ESG), as under the Global Reporting Initiative[154] and the Equator Principles.[155] At times, different public and private initiatives combine in complex ways to bolster rule-of-law protections, such as in the industrial workplaces of global supply chains.[156]

However, just as international law and institutions can support rule-of-law processes, they also can undermine them. The turn to securitization after the September 11, 2001, terrorist attacks offers a powerful example. The UN Security Council created an Al-Qaida and Taliban sanctions regime in which a sanctions committee, mirroring the composition of the Security Council, could require the global freezing of an individual's assets with no transparency or due process. Following the Security Council's lead, countries around the world passed anti-terrorism laws that governments then used in repressive ways.[157] Some human rights and other regional courts responded to these developments, most notably in the European Union in the *Kadi* case. There, the European Court of Justice voided an EU regulation implementing UN Security Council mandates to freeze the assets of suspected terrorists and their

[153] United Nations, Guiding Principles on Business and Human Rights: Implementing the United Nations "Protect, Respect and Remedy" Framework (2011).

[154] Cynthia Williams, *The Global Reporting Initiative, Transnational Corporate Accountability, and Global Regulatory Counter-Currents*, 1 U.C. Irvine J. Int'l Transnat'l Comp. L. 67 (2016).

[155] John M. Conley & Cynthia A. Williams, *Global Banks as Global Sustainability Regulators?: The Equator Principles*, 33 Law & Pol'y 542 (2011).

[156] Larry Cata Backer, *Are Supply Chains Transnational Legal Orders? What We Can Learn from the Rana Plaza Factory Building Collapse*, 1 U.C. Irvine J. Int'l Transnat'l Comp. L. 11 (2016).

[157] Kim Lane Scheppele, *The International Standardization of National Security Law*, 4 J. Nat'l Security L. Pol'y 437 (2010); Kim Lane Scheppele, *The Migration of Anti-Constitutional Ideas: The Post-9/11 Globalization of Public Law and the International State of Emergency*, *in* The Migration of Constitutional Ideas 347 (Sujit Choudhry ed., 2007).

financiers on the grounds that it violated the accused's due process rights.[158] Other courts followed suit.[159] This response catalyzed some Security Council reforms, notably the creation of an Office of the Ombudsperson, although its powers were limited.[160]

Private actors, such as multinational companies, also harness rule-of-law rhetoric to advance their material interests. Public and private actors have developed different indicators to measure the rule of law, some of which reflect a neoliberal tilt that can favor foreign capital.[161] The Heritage Foundation's rule-of-law index, for example, focuses on the security of property rights.[162] Bilateral investment treaties and investor–state arbitration highlight how businesses may use international law to challenge government regulations that, investors contend, undermine certainty and predictability under the rule of law. The *Tecmed* arbitration, for example, recalling Hayek's attack on social welfare legislation, set a standard for "fair and equitable treatment" under which "the foreign investor expects the host State to act in a consistent manner, free from ambiguity and totally transparently in its relations with the foreign investor so that it may know beforehand any and all rules and regulations that will govern its investments."[163] Because democratic political processes legitimately change environmental, labor, and other regulations over time, the *Tecmed* standard of fixing all rules and regulations in advance could be highly constraining. Business can use it not only to sue states for billions of dollars when new regulations violate business

[158] Grainne de Burca, *The European Court of Justice and the International Legal Order After* Kadi, 51 HARV. INT'L L.J. 1 (2009).

[159] Machiko Kanetake, *The Interfaces Between the National and International Rule of Law: The Case of UN Targeted Sanctions*, 9 INT'L ORGS. L. REV. 267 (2012); Erika de Wet, *Judicial Challenges to the Security Council's Use of Sanctions*, *in* STRENGTHENING THE RULE OF LAW THROUGH THE UN SECURITY COUNCIL, *supra* note 148, at 193; *see, e.g.*, Nada v. Switzerland, App. No. 10593/08 (Sept. 12, 2012), https://hudoc.echr.coe.int/eng?i=001-113118.

[160] Kimberly Prost, *The Office of the Ombudsperson: A Case for Fair Process*, *in* STRENGTHENING THE RULE OF LAW THROUGH THE UN SECURITY COUNCIL, *supra* note 148, at 181.

[161] Rajah, *supra* note 93.

[162] Tom Ginsburg & Mila Versteeg, *Rule of Law Measurement*, *in* THE CAMBRIDGE COMPANION TO THE RULE OF LAW, *supra* note 12, at 494, 498.

[163] Técnicas Medioambientales Tecmed SA v. United Mexican States, ICSID Case No. ARB(AF)/00/2, Award, ¶ 154 (May 29, 2003), 8 ICSID Rep. 130 (2006). *Cf.* FRIEDRICH A. HAYEK, THE ROAD TO SERFDOM 80 (1994) (defining the rule of law as where "the government in all its actions is bound by rules fixed and announced beforehand" – i.e., private planning is protected from democratic, legislative intervention).

"expectations."[164] They also can chill regulation by threatening legal claims.[165] Yet, domestic institutions often operate corruptly and arbitrarily, which is a central reason to create international institutional complements. It is thus critical to retain focus not only on rule-of-law goals but also on institutional alternatives to pursue them, all of which will be imperfect, but where some will be better or worse in different contexts.[166]

### 3 *Direct Links between International Institutions and Individuals*

International law also, in some cases, provides direct legal protections and legal accountability for individuals in support of the rule of law. It can do so in jurisdictions where international law is directly applicable as a cause of action before national courts, and under treaties granting individuals the right to bring direct claims against states before regional courts. The most active regional human rights court is the ECtHR, followed by the Inter-American Court of Human Rights (IACtHR), and the African Court on Human and Peoples' Rights. These regional human rights courts receive and adjudicate individual claims of state violations of the relevant regional treaties.

In these cases, international law and institutions serve, in part, as a backstop to protect the rule of law, while also potentially shaping the normative field transnationally. International human rights courts, like the ECtHR and the IACtHR, can accept jurisdiction over a petition only after all domestic legal recourse has been sought and exhausted. In those cases, where domestic courts are to enforce rights under the convention but fail to do so, individuals retain the right to bring claims directly to the regional court in question. Stone Sweet labels such tribunals "trustee courts," since they are charged not with advancing state purposes but rather with holding states accountable for violations of treaty-based

164 "In cases decided in favor of the investor, the average amount claimed was US$1.3 billion and the average amount awarded was US$504 million." Anne Orford, *A Global Rule of Law*, *in* The Cambridge Companion to the Rule of Law, *supra* note 12, at 538 (citing UNCTAD, World Investment Report 2018, at 95).

165 Tarald Laudal Berge & Axel Berger, *Do Investor–State Settlement Cases Influence Domestic Environmental Regulation? The Role of Respondent State Bureaucratic Capacity*, 12 J. Int'l Disp. Settlement 1 (2021); Kyla Tienhaara, *Regulatory Chill in a Warming World: The Threat to Climate Policy Posed by Investor–State Dispute Settlement*, 7 Transnat'l Env't L. 229 (2018).

166 Sergio Puig & Gregory Shaffer, *Imperfect Alternatives: Institutional Choice and the Reform of Investment Law*, 112 Am. J. Int'l L. 361 (2018) (evaluating alternative institutional mechanisms for resolving investment disputes in light of the rule of law).

rights against those within the state's jurisdiction.[167] As regards criminal law, international criminal law and courts primarily serve to establish responsibility for international crimes when domestic institutions are incapable of, or prevented from, doing so. The International Criminal Court (ICC) was designed to provide for legal accountability when state institutions fail. The ICC Office of the Prosecutor prosecutes genocide, crimes against humanity, war crimes, and the crime of aggression only when states are unwilling or unable to do so. In practice, it has catalyzed national investigations and some prosecutions for atrocity claims, and it can have other indirect effects.[168] Likewise, in investment law, under the World Bank's Convention on the Settlement of Investment Disputes, a "Contracting State may require the exhaustion of local administrative or judicial remedies as a condition of its consent to arbitration under this Convention," although this requirement often is not applied in practice.[169]

These complementarity mechanisms prioritize legal decision-making within domestic jurisdictions. They recognize domestic authorities as the primary guardians of the rule of law, but subject to an international accountability mechanism. In the process, they can enhance legal certainty and equal application of the law. By empowering domestic courts to oversee compliance with legal obligations (which directly or indirectly reflect international law), complementarity mechanisms can broaden international law's reach within states.[170] There is some (preliminary)

167 Alec Stone Sweet & Clare Ryan, A Cosmopolitan Legal Order 102 (2018).

168 James Stromseth, *Is the ICC Making a Difference?* Just Security (Dec. 6, 2017), www.justsecurity.org/47717/icc-making-difference/. For a case study, see William Burke-White, *Complementarity in Practice: The International Criminal Court as Part of a System of Multi-level Governance in the Democratic Republic of Congo*, 18 Leiden J. Int'l L. 557 (2005). *Cf.* Leigh Payne, *The Justice Paradox?: Transnational Legal Orders and Accountability for Past Human Rights Violations*, *in* Transnational Legal Orders, *supra* note 10, at 439 (noting how processes can also be abused to target the opposition).

169 Convention on the Settlement of Investment Disputes Between States and Nationals of Other States, art. 26, Mar. 18, 1966, 575 U.N.T.S. 159.

170 For example, Anne Van Aaken maintains that "[i]f investment law is a kind of international administrative law, a harmonious combination and an alignment of the internationalized system of state liability and the national systems seems desirable." Anne Van Aaken, *Primary and Secondary Remedies in Investment Arbitration and State Liability: A Functional and Comparative View*, *in* International Investment Law and Comparative Public Law 721, 754 (Stephan Schill ed., 2010); *see also* Richard C. Chen, *Bilateral Investment Treaties and Domestic Institutional Reform*, 55 Colum. J. Transnat'l L. 547 (2017).

empirical evidence that they may do so better than the alternative of using international tribunals as substitutes for domestic courts.[171]

In practice, international institutions are both promoters (on the offensive) and subjects (on the defensive) of the rule of law. Although there is no centralized public power at the international level, international and regional institutions began to exercise increasing authority directly over individuals following the collapse of the Soviet Union and the end of the Cold War, particularly in relation to peacekeeping operations, sanctions, the use of force, and the US-pronounced "war on terror." Given its new regulatory roles, the United Nations' adherence to the rule of law has been seriously challenged. While the UN established thirteen peacekeeping operations between 1946 and 1988, with constrained roles that were primarily tasked with monitoring ceasefire lines, the UN Security Council has created fifty-eight additional operations around the globe since 1988, whose operational scope significantly expanded, including the provision of basic policing functions.[172] The Security Council authorized peacekeeping and rule-of-law-building mandates in Afghanistan, Iraq, Haiti, Sierra Leone, and Timor Leste, as have NATO and the European Union in Kosovo and the African Union in Somalia. When UN personnel were accused of murder, rape, torture, corruption, and other tortious acts, the United Nations claimed immunity, in violation of fundamental rule-of-law accountability norms, spurring protestations against UN practices.[173] Similarly, while the Security Council applied only two sanctions regimes in its first forty-three years (against the racist, white minority regimes of Rhodesia and South Africa), since 1989 it has imposed thirty-two additional ones.[174] The Security Council also increasingly authorized the use of force in its resolutions,

[171] *See* Chapter 5. *See also* Jennifer L. Tobin & Susan Rose-Ackerman, *When BITs Have Some Bite: The Political-Economic Environment for Bilateral Investment Treaties*, 6 REV. INT'L ORGS. 1, 5 (2011) (providing empirical evidence that international dispute settlement mechanisms have more impact when they complement an existing set of effective domestic institutions); Tom Ginsburg, *International Substitutes for Domestic Institutions: Bilateral Investment Treaties and Governance*, 25 INT'L REV. L. & ECON. 107, 119 (2005) (providing empirical evidence that investor–state dispute settlement may "reduce courts' incentives to improve performance by depriving key actors from a need to invest in institutional improvement").

[172] *See* Chapter 6.

[173] Jeni Whalan, *Strengthening the Local Accountability of UN Peacekeeping*, *in* STRENGTHENING THE RULE OF LAW THROUGH THE UN SECURITY COUNCIL, *supra* note 148, at 135, 139; *see also* Jose Alvarez, *The United Nations in the Time of Cholera*, 108 AJIL UNBOUND 22 (2017).

[174] Whalan, *supra* note 173.

rising from one extraordinary instance during the Cold War (in Korea when the Soviet Union briefly absented itself from the Security Council) to forty-eight resolutions between 1990 and 2014.[175]

The Security Council has been particularly challenged for exercising legislative and administrative power to combat "terrorism." After the September 11, 2001, terror attacks, the Security Council issued a series of resolutions, most notably Resolution 1373 which, among other matters, required states to criminalize terrorism in domestic law and freeze assets of individuals and groups that the Security Council blacklists.[176] Anti-terrorism laws proliferated globally, and government officials used them to advance their own agendas, including to criminalize dissent.[177] The Security Council ordered the seizure of an accused's assets with little to no due process, as noted in Section 2. As Scheppele writes, "for states whose commitment to international law is part of their own deep devotion to the rule of law as a basic principle of state legitimacy, new draconian anti-terrorism laws could be portrayed as necessary in order to comply with international law," regardless of the lack of due process.[178]

From the vantage of TLO theory, national and regional courts can intervene to protect rule-of-law concerns involving international institutions, just as international institutions have done regarding national practices.[179] They are part of a broader transnational legal process. As we have seen, some regional and national courts responded by constraining compliance with Security Council asset seizure orders where they were deemed to violate rule-of-law requirements within regional and national legal orders, as in the *Kadi* case.[180] The Security Council responded in 2009 by creating the Office of the Ombudsperson, empowered to investigate and make "delisting"

175 *Id.*

176 S.C. Res. 1373, U.N. Doc. S/RES/1373 (Sept. 28, 2001).

177 Kim Lane Scheppele, *The Empire of Security and the Security of Empire*, 27 TEMPLE INT'L COMPAR. L.J. 241 (2013).

178 *Id.* at 248.

179 Each involves a form of *Solange* reasoning, where courts at the national or international level, as the case may be, will not intervene so long as rule-of-law protections are observed at the other level. *Solange* refers to jurisprudence of the German constitutional court regarding the enforcement of judgments of the Court of Justice of the European Union. Alec Stone Sweet, *The Structure of Constitutional Pluralism: Review of Nico Krisch, "Beyond Constitutionalism: The Pluralist Structure of Post-National Law,"* 11 INT'L J. CONST. L. 491 (2013).

180 Machiko Kanetake, *The Interfaces Between the National and International Rule of Law: The Case of UN Targeted Sanctions*, 9 INT'L ORGS. L. REV. 267 (2012); STRENGTHENING THE RULE OF LAW THROUGH THE UN SECURITY COUNCIL, *supra* note 148.

recommendations. In this transnational sense, the late judge James Crawford was not wholly correct when he wrote that only when the International Court of Justice has "clear jurisdiction judicially to review action of all United Nations political agencies, including the Security Council . . . could the rule of law be said to extend to international political life."[181] Nonetheless, serious challenges remain, illustrated by the ombudsperson's resignation in 2021 on rule-of-law grounds, including the lack of institutional independence of the Office of the Ombudsperson, the Security Council's extensive reliance on confidential evidence, and a refusal to permit petitioners to examine the reasons for their inclusion on the sanctions list.[182] These ongoing challenges continue to catalyze responses and reform proposals from within and outside the Security Council by state and nonstate actors.[183]

Because international law and institutions not only support rule-of-law protections but also affect individuals directly in ways that implicate the rule of law, scholars have turned to analytic frames borrowed from constitutional and administrative law for assessing and constraining international institutions. Global administrative law theorists foreground tools of accountability, transparency, and reason-giving as checks on international and domestic institutions.[184] Other scholars have developed global constitutionalist frames,[185] transnational pluralist ones,[186] and constitutional pluralist hybrids,[187] for reconceptualizing international law in ways that place greater focus on the individual and individual rights.[188] These normative projects aim, in different ways, to advance rule-of-law concerns globally, including in response to the enhanced role and authority of international institutions since the 1990s. These conceptions of

181 James Crawford & Susan Marks, *The Global Democracy Deficit: An Essay in International Law and Its Limits*, *in* Re-Imagining Political Community 72, 84 (Daniele Archibugi, David Held & Martin Kohler eds., 1998).

182 Colum Lynch, *How a Dream Job Became a Bureaucratic Nightmare for a Top U.N. Lawyer*, Foreign Pol'y (July 27, 2021, 12:50 PM), https://tinyurl.com/3d7nr8a7. *See generally* Fiona de Londras, The Practice and Problems of Transnational Counter-Terrorism (2022).

183 *See* Chapter 6.

184 Benedict Kingsbury, Nico Krisch & Richard Stewart, *The Emergence of Global Administrative Law*, 68 L. & Contemp. Probs. 15 (2005).

185 *See, e.g.*, Alec Stone Sweet & Jud Mathews, Proportionality, Balancing and Constitutional Governance: A Comparative and Global Approach ch. 6 (2019).

186 *See, e.g.*, Nico Krisch, Beyond Constitutionalism: The Pluralist Structure of Postnational Law (2010).

187 *See, e.g.*, Neil Walker, *The Idea of Constitutional Pluralism*, 65 Mod. L. Rev. 317 (2002).

188 Jan Klabbers, Anne Peters & Geir Ulfstein, The Constitutionalization of International Law (2009); Kumm, *supra* note 19; Peters, *supra* note 86.

international law are components of viewing the rule of law within a broader transnational context involving transnational legal ordering.[189]

## III Empirical Trends in Transnational Context

International and national law and practice interact to shape norms across substantive fields. These interactions are recursive in that developments in one site can have intended and unintended effects in others, which in turn can spur new normative development and institutional change. For example, national legal norms, especially those of powerful states, often shape international ones, but the norms may be revised and recalibrated in the process. In turn, international legal norms and institutions provide normative resources for actors at the national and local levels, new strategies of justification and argument, and new alternatives for social action. These processes also can catalyze national and local resistance that spurs new institutional strategies and normative change.

In this Part III, we first lay out our argument that the world risks a deepening negative cycle of overall decline in rule-of-law protections at the national and international levels (Section 1). After addressing the challenge of measuring rule-of-law practices (Section 2), we then examine existing evidence of national (Section 3) and international (Section 4) trends. We conclude by appraising possible explanatory factors for the parallel decline of multiple rule-of-law indicators (Section 5).

### *1 Our Argument*

From a transnational perspective, this volume assesses whether there might be common trends regarding rule-of-law protections at the national and international levels, involving cycles of settlement and unsettlement of rule-of-law norms and practices. We ask: Do rule-of-law norms and practices shift at the national and international levels in parallel? Our working hypothesis is that they do, although with variation across and within regions. Given the transnational enmeshment of national and international norm-making and practice, we contend that developments at one level can have reinforcing – and subverting – effects on the other in a recursive manner. These trends can give rise to virtuous and vicious cycles. Where national rule-of-law practices erode, especially in powerful states, and where authoritarian states become more powerful globally, we

189 Transnational Legal Orders, *supra* note 10; Shaffer, *supra* note 91.

expect that such erosion and power shifts will implicate international law and practice. Where international rule-of-law norms and monitoring and enforcement institutions weaken, national and local actors will have fewer institutional and normative resources available to protect the rule of law.

To flesh out our claim, we note that rule-of-law promotion proliferated as part of transnational legal ordering processes after the collapse of the Soviet Union in 1990.[190] Liberal norms diffused transnationally, backed by significant economic incentives, such as the carrot of joining the European Union, spurring studies of "the global diffusion of markets and democracy."[191] The wave of democratization and transnational constitutional processes, in turn, spurred greater openness of state legal systems toward international law.[192] At the time, as former Soviet bloc states gained independence, they joined the key international institutions at the core of an international order grounded in law: the European Union, the European Convention on Human Rights under the Council of Europe, the World Trade Organization, and the various specialized organizations of the United Nations system. International courts and cases before them proliferated beyond Europe. As captured by the Project on International Courts and Tribunals, the number of international courts rose from six to over two dozen between 1989 and 2014, which collectively issued over 37,000 binding legal rulings.[193] In parallel, states adopted new constitutions and institutions that created new resources and mechanisms for national and local actors to enhance rule-of-law protections. These constitutions incorporated international norms and created new institutional oversight and enforcement processes. During this period, indicators on the rule of law and neighboring concepts such as democracy reached their peaks.[194] There were, of course, severe challenges in advancing the rule of law in many jurisdictions, especially

[190] Rajah, *supra* note 93; Halliday & Shaffer, *supra* note 93, at 494–95.

[191] Beth A. Simmons, Frank Dobbin & Geoffrey Garrett, *Introduction: The Diffusion of Liberalization*, *in* The Global Diffusion of Markets and Democracy 1 (Beth A. Simmons, Frank Dobbin & Geoffrey Garrett eds., 2008).

[192] Kevin Cope, Pierre-Hugues Verdier & Mila Versteeg, *The Global Evolution of Foreign Relations Law*, 116 Am. J. Int'l L. 1, 48–53 (2022).

[193] Karen Alter, The New Terrain of International Law (2014); Ruth Mackenzie et al., The Manual on International Courts and Tribunals (2d ed. 2010).

[194] Larry Diamond, Ill Winds: Saving Democracy from Russian Rage, Chinese Ambition, and American Complacency (2019).

those with weak institutions.[195] Nonetheless, the overall trends were positive, captured in Kathryn Sikkink's claim of a transnational "justice cascade."[196]

In the last decade, by contrast, indicators measuring the rule of law, together with complementary concepts such as democracy, have declined, while national demands for greater autonomy from regional and multilateral institutions and their normative constraints have increased. Overall, we appear to be moving from what Thomas Carothers characterized as a "rule-of-law revival"[197] in the 1980s to what can be characterized as authoritarian relapse and rule-of-law decline today.[198] In an interconnected world, we have turned from a period characterized by the development of institutions and transnational processes promoting "transitional justice," as reflected in a profuse literature,[199] to processes consolidating what can be viewed as "gradual autocratization."[200] In this shift, authoritarian regimes do not simply terminate institutions developed during the rule-of law-revival. Rather, having inherited them, they mimic and harness formally liberal mechanisms for authoritarian ends.[201] Witness Victor Orbán referencing other countries' institutional mechanisms while adapting them in new ways to defend his authoritarian, anti-liberal aims.[202] Anti-liberal movements learn from and adapt these processes for similar authoritarian purposes.[203] These strategies illustrate the risks of focusing exclusively on rule-of-law checklists as opposed to goals and practices. As

195 PROMOTING THE RULE OF LAW ABROAD: IN SEARCH OF KNOWLEDGE, *supra* note 150.

196 *Compare* KATHRYN SIKKINK, EVIDENCE FOR HOPE: MAKING HUMAN RIGHTS WORK IN THE 21st CENTURY (2017), *with* TRICIA D. OLSEN, LEIGH A. PAYNE & ANDREW G. REITER, TRANSNATIONAL JUSTICE IN BALANCE: COMPARING PROCESSES, WEIGHING EFFICACY (2010).

197 Thomas Carothers, *The Rule-of-Law Revival*, FOREIGN AFFS., Mar./Apr. 1998. By the early 2000s, however, Carothers already had written of the "end of the transition paradigm." Thomas Carothers, *The End of the Transition Paradigm*, 13 J. DEMOCRACY 5 (2002).

198 For a current example, see Chapter 12.

199 *See, e.g.*, RUTI TEITEL, TRANSITIONAL JUSTICE (2000).

200 Anna Luhrmann & Staffan Linderg, *A Third Wave of Autocratization Is Here: What Is New About It?*, 26 DEMOCRATIZATION 1095, 1107 (2019).

201 *See, e.g.*, Kim Lane Scheppele, *Autocracy Under Cover of the Transnational Legal Order*, *in* CONSTITUTION-MAKING AND TRANSNATIONAL LEGAL ORDER, *supra* note 23, at 188.

202 *Id.*

203 S.G.F. Hall & T. Ambrosio, *Authoritarian Learning: A Conceptual Overview*, 33 E. EUR. POL. 143 (2017); Scheppele, *supra* note 201.

David Law writes, the role of law and courts in authoritarian regimes "deserves attention for the insights that it contains into the biases and vulnerabilities concealed within the structure of our own judicial institutions."[204] One can add the vulnerabilities contained within our executive, legislative, and administrative institutions as well.

There can be considerable resistance to these developments, so that change will be neither linear nor determined. Challenges to the rule of law in Hungary and Poland, for example, have catalyzed responses from the European Union, as well as from internal groups.[205] Yet, there are also powerful forces aimed at constraining regional oversight, whether through exit (such as Brexit) or voice, which will weaken regional institutions, their influence, and the resources they provide to local actors (say, following the election of Georgia Meloni in Italy or if Marie Le Pen were to triumph in France). Other international shifts will affect these internal regional developments, such as resurgent nationalism and coercive geopolitics in powerful states such as China, Russia, and the United States. Sections 3, 4, and 5 provide empirical evidence and explanations regarding enmeshed trends at the international and national levels, and the cycles they represent.

## 2 *The Challenge of Measurement*

Before discussing the empirical evidence, we stress both the challenge of measuring trends in rule-of-law protections and the importance of doing so. Given different conceptions of what constitutes the rule of law and the means to achieve it, different indicators measure different things. Measurements use different sources of information, which raises challenges regarding validity, reliability, and bias in the data, especially as regards uneven cross-country data. Moreover, even where common trends are identified regarding rule-of-law practices, it is very difficult to establish the causal forces behind these trends.[206]

A number of indexes purport to measure the rule of law, but they measure different things, highlighting certain goals and means over

[204] David Law, *How to Rig the Federal Courts*, 99 Geo. L. Rev. 779, 835 (2010).

[205] Antoine Buyse et al., *The Rule of Law from Below: A Concept Under Development*, 17 Utrecht L. Rev. 1 (2021).

[206] Tamanaha, *supra* note 12, at 231–32 (noting the problem of establishing causation and causal direction); Tom Ginsburg, *Pitfalls of Measuring the Rule of Law*, 3 Hague J. on Rule L. 269 (2011); Stephan Haggard et al., *The Rule of Law and Economic Development*, 11 Ann. Rev. Pol. Sci. 205 (2008).

others. Mila Versteeg and Tom Ginsburg examined rule-of-law indicators developed by the World Bank, the Heritage Foundation, Freedom House, and the World Justice Project, assessing their different focuses and their overlaps.[207] These indexes differ in emphases, with the Heritage Foundation focused to a greater extent on property rights and Freedom House more on human rights, while the World Bank and World Justice Project examine broader ranges of issues. One might thus expect these indicators to be weakly correlated.

Despite the use of different component measurements, Versteeg and Ginsburg find "the four indicators . . . to be remarkably similar."[208] They show that the measurement of "corruption," which – like the rule of law – encompasses the goal of "government impartiality," closely correlates with all four rule-of-law indicators.[209] The correlation of these measurements could suggest that they indeed capture something broadly about empirical trends. Corruption, for example, affects each of the five sources of arbitrariness noted in Part I, as it leads to non-transparency, inconsistency, partiality, and a lack of proportionality, which the powerful can harness for authoritarian ends.

Versteeg and Ginsburg nonetheless raise caution. In particular, they question the extent to which convergences in measurement may reflect a common reliance on expert perceptions and information constraints given the challenges of gathering data. They also note that, by combining multiple factors into a single ordinal number, indexes will conflate different aspects of the rule of law and the means to attain it.[210] They thus applaud the World Justice Project's index for being modular, so that researchers can use the database to focus on particular aspects (or sources of arbitrariness),[211] which then can be assessed in different contexts.

Lon Fuller long ago wrote that we need "standards against which the degree of attainment of a condition of legality could be evaluated."[212]

207 Ginsburg & Versteeg, *supra* note 162, at 494–512.

208 *Id.* at 502.

209 *Id.* at 504–05

210 *See also* SALLY ENGLE MERRY, THE SEDUCTIONS OF QUANTIFICATION: GLOBAL GOVERNANCE, HUMAN RIGHTS, AND THE RISE OF INDICATOR CULTURE (2016).

211 Ginsburg & Versteeg, *supra* note 162; *see also* Rachel Kleinfeld, *Competing Definitions of the Rule of Law*, *in* PROMOTING THE RULE OF LAW ABROAD: IN SEARCH OF KNOWLEDGE, *supra* note 150, at 31, 63 (on disaggregation); Jerg Gutmann & Stefan Voigt, *The Rule of Law: Measurement and Deep Roots*, 54 EUR. J. POL. ECON. 68 (2018).

212 Kristen Rundle, *The Morality of the Rule of Law: Lon L. Fuller*, *in* THE CAMBRIDGE COMPANION TO THE RULE OF LAW, *supra* note 12, at 186.

Developing and revising such standards, nonetheless, should always focus on the ends of the rule of law and not be fixed on particular institutional mechanisms. Given differences in social, cultural, and institutional contexts and heritages around the world, as well as the role of informal institutions, there is no one means to advance the rule of law. Since advancing the rule of law will take different forms in different contexts, the promotion of the rule of law will always bedevil advocates and institutions.[213]

Despite these challenges, we contend that empirical study is crucial, and quantitative and qualitative data and studies are improving thanks to sustained efforts, ranging from ethnographies to large-n statistical analyses. The large-n studies tend to rely on surveys and thus assess perceptions within countries. The World Justice Project has developed extensive surveys, which it uses to assess the perceptions of lawyers and lay persons within countries.[214] These perceptions are important from the perspective of TLO theory, since the law in action depends on the mentalities of actors, what they take as norms for appropriate behavior, affecting social expectations, communication, and behavior.[215] To assess social context and institutional behavior, one needs empirical study, which calls for the integration of law and the social sciences.[216] If our argument is correct, then such empirical work must engage with transnational processes to assess how national and international trends interact.

## 3 *National Rule-of-Law trends*

The past decade has witnessed a worrisome decline in the rule of law at the domestic level across a range of countries, on a variety of measures. In this

[213] Thomas Carothers, *The Problem of Knowledge*, *in* PROMOTING THE RULE OF LAW ABROAD: IN SEARCH OF KNOWLEDGE, *supra* note 150, at 15, 21 (2006) ("Rule-of-law practitioners have been following an institutional approach, concentrating on judiciaries, more out of instinct than well-researched knowledge."); Haggard et al., *supra* note 206, at 221 (there are a variety of formal and informal institutions that make up a "rule of law complex").

[214] *See* Chapter 3.

[215] Halliday & Shaffer, *supra* note 10; NIKLAS LUHMANN, A SOCIOLOGICAL THEORY OF LAW 105 (1985) ("Law is essential as structure, because people cannot orient themselves towards others or expect their expectations without the congruent generalization of behavioral expectations.").

[216] Daniel Abebe, Adam Chilton & Tom Ginsburg, *The Social Science Approach to International Law*, 22 CHI. J. INT'L L. 1 (2021); Terence C. Halliday & Gregory Shaffer, *International Law and Transnational Legal Orders: Permeating Boundaries and Extending Social Science Encounters*, 22 CHI. J. INT'L L. 168 (2021).

section, we look at several of those indicators.[217] Each of them relies on a different set of observable features of governments – features that plausibly capture key behavioral implications of our conception of the rule of law (legal rules that set limits on the arbitrary exercise of power by some persons over others) in light of different sources of arbitrariness.[218] Each set shows overall declines in the rule of law within both democracies and authoritarian regimes. These declines generally do not reflect sudden transitions, such as following a military coup, but rather are gradual declines in the degree of rule-of-law protections within countries at different starting points.

According to World Justice Project (WJP) data (Figure 1.2),[219] over the past eight years forty-three states show a significant decrease in the rule of law, whereas only three show a significant improvement.[220] Table 1.2 lists the states with the largest declines. Most of the states with a drop in the rule of law started from a relatively low point, though two (Poland and the Republic of Korea) began with scores above 0.70 (on a scale of 0–1).[221] For those distrustful of quantitative indicators, the list of states – which includes Brazil, Egypt, Hungary, Poland, the Philippines, Turkey, and Venezuela – resonates, in our view, with common understandings. Overall, the WJP reports that in every year since 2015 the rule of law diminished in about 60 percent of countries, with a peak of 74 percent of countries showing a decline in 2020.[222]

217 As Versteeg and Ginsburg have noted, the various indicators developed to assess the rule of law status of states "build significantly different substantive values into their definitions of the RoL" and deploy varying measurement strategies. Mila Versteeg & Tom Ginsburg, *Measuring the Rule of Law: A Comparison of Indicators*, 42 L. & Soc. Inquiry 100, 101 (2017). The four indicators (including those produced by the World Justice Project and Freedom House) examined by Versteeg and Ginsburg are nevertheless highly correlated. *Id.* at 102. The question of how adequately the indicators capture the underlying concept (rule of law) is beyond the scope of this study; we therefore report rule-of-law data and readers can take into account the challenges inherent in empirically measuring the concept.

218 The rule of law indicators that we review here all claim to be based on rule-of-law practices, not on formal law.

219 WJP data, unlike other measures, relies on both country experts and citizen surveys.

220 To exclude minor shifts in the rule of law score, we counted only those states that experienced a change of more than one standard deviation in the *WJP Rule of Law Index*.

221 For comparison, ten countries scored 0.80 or higher in the *WJP Rule of Law Index* in 2021 (Austria, Canada, Denmark, Estonia, Finland, Germany, Netherlands, New Zealand, Norway, and Sweden).

222 *WJP Rule of Law Index*, World Just. Project, https://worldjusticeproject.org/rule-of-law-index/insights (last visited Aug. 21, 2024). Those 74 percent of countries, moreover, represented 85 percent of the world's population.

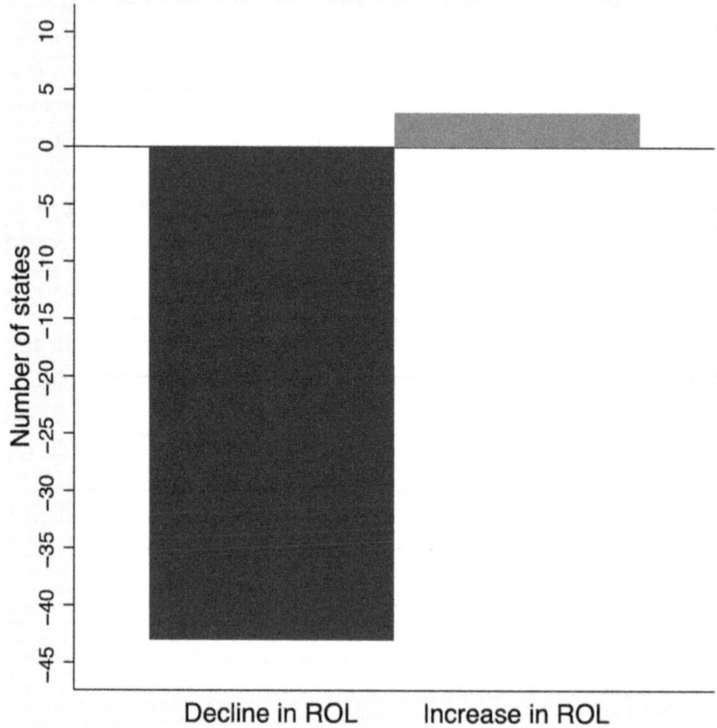


**Figure 1.2** Changes in the rule of law, 2015–23, World Justice Project.

When we disaggregate the WJP data in terms of those indicators most directly tied to the five sources of arbitrariness that we identified in Part I, we find similar declines, as captured in Table 1.3. Using WJP data, we constructed indicators for three of the five sources of arbitrariness.[223] We then compared countries' performance on these measures in 2015 and 2023.

[223] The *WJP Rule of Law Index* is composed of forty-four component indicators. We devised indicators of the *sources of arbitrariness* reported in Table 1.3 with selected *WJP Rule of Law Index* components. The WJP data did not include suitable measures of the fourth and fifth sources of arbitrariness (authorities do not engage in reason-giving, such as regards proportionality, in issuing their decisions). The measures reported in Table 1.3 were constructed using the following WJP indicators:

**For 1, first source of arbitrariness (The wielder of power is not subject to controls, limits, or accountability mechanisms):** 1.1 Government powers are effectively limited by the legislature; 1.2 Government powers are effectively limited by the judiciary; 1.3 Government powers are effectively limited by independent auditing and review; 1.4 Government officials are sanctioned for misconduct; 1.5 Government powers are subject to nongovernmental checks; 1.6 Transition of power is subject to the law.

Table 1.2 *World Justice Project: largest declines in rule of law, 2015/16 to 2023*

| Country | WJP 2015/2016 | WJP 2023 | Change |
|---|---|---|---|
| Belarus | 0.53 | 0.45 | −0.08 |
| Egypt | 0.43 | 0.35 | −0.08 |
| Poland | 0.72 | 0.64 | −0.08 |
| Hungary | 0.58 | 0.51 | −0.07 |
| Mexico | 0.48 | 0.42 | −0.07 |
| Nicaragua | 0.42 | 0.35 | −0.07 |
| Brazil | 0.55 | 0.49 | −0.06 |
| El Salvador | 0.51 | 0.45 | −0.06 |
| Georgia | 0.66 | 0.60 | −0.06 |
| Grenada | 0.66 | 0.60 | −0.06 |
| Myanmar | 0.41 | 0.35 | −0.06 |
| Philippines | 0.52 | 0.46 | −0.06 |
| Bosnia and Herzegovina | 0.56 | 0.51 | −0.05 |
| Ghana | 0.60 | 0.55 | −0.05 |
| Iran | 0.44 | 0.39 | −0.05 |
| Republic of Korea | 0.79 | 0.74 | −0.05 |
| Trinidad and Tobago | 0.57 | 0.52 | −0.05 |
| Turkey | 0.46 | 0.41 | −0.05 |
| Venezuela | 0.31 | 0.26 | −0.05 |

*Note:* World Justice Project, *WJP Rule of Law Index* (2023). World Justice Project scores range from 0 to 1. The table shows the nineteen largest declines. An additional eleven countries had a decline of 0.04. For most countries, the first year included in the data is 2015; for two countries in the table (Grenada, Trinidad and Tobago) it is 2016.

**For 2, second source of arbitrariness (Individuals are unable to know and predict how power may be wielded over them):** 3.1 Publicized laws and government data; 3.2 Right to information; 3.3 Civic participation.

**For 3, third source of arbitrariness (Individuals have no place to be heard, inform, question, or respond to how power is exercised over them):** 3.4 Complaint mechanisms; 4.3 Due process of the law and rights of the accused; 4.4 Freedom of opinion and expression is effectively guaranteed; 4.7 Freedom of assembly and association is effectively guaranteed; 6.4 Due process is respected in administrative proceedings; 7.1 People can access and afford civil justice. Interestingly, for this third source, indicators have declined significantly regarding freedom of expression and of assembly, but not regarding the other indicators.

*See* WORLD JUST. PROJECT, THE GLOBAL RULE OF LAW RECESSION CONTINUES (2023), https://worldjusticeproject.org/rule-of-law-index/ (last visited Aug. 21, 2024).

Table 1.3 *Changes in the sources of arbitrariness, 2015–2023*

| | Number of countries | |
|---|---|---|
| Sources | Less arbitrariness | More arbitrariness |
| 1. Wielder of power is not subject to controls, limits, or accountability mechanisms. | 35 | 78 |
| 2. Individuals unable to know how power may be wielded over them. | 24 | 89 |
| 3. Individuals have no place to question or respond to how power is exercised over them. | 33 | 80 |

N = 113 countries. Eleven countries lacked data for 2015; for those countries we used 2016 data.

Strikingly, for all three sources of arbitrariness, far more countries underwent an increase in arbitrariness than experienced a decline, as shown in Table 1.3. It is also telling that 58 countries showed greater arbitrariness on all three counts in 2023. Out of 113 countries for which we have data, 88 showed an increase in two or more of the sources of arbitrariness.

Figure 1.3 charts the number of countries showing an increase and the number undergoing a decline in the Freedom House rule-of-law indicator. Strikingly, in no year since 2005 has the number of countries showing an increase in the rule of law exceeded the number suffering a decline. Since 2017, the number of countries expanding the rule of law has dropped dramatically, while the number with a declining rule of law has remained high. Rule of law scores from the Varieties of Democracy project depict a similar trend. Rule of law scores began a steady rise after the 1990 collapse of the Soviet Union. From 1990 until 2012, states showing increases outnumbered states undergoing declines in all but two years. By contrast, from 2013 through 2021, declines were more numerous than increases in all but two years.[224]

In some instances, autocratic governments expanded their powers (as in Niger and Belarus). In others, elected governments eroded the

[224] Michael Coppedge et al., *V-Dem Codebook v11.1*, VARIETIES OF DEMOCRACY (V-DEM) PROJECT (2021), www.v-dem.net/static/website/img/refs/codebookv111.pdf.

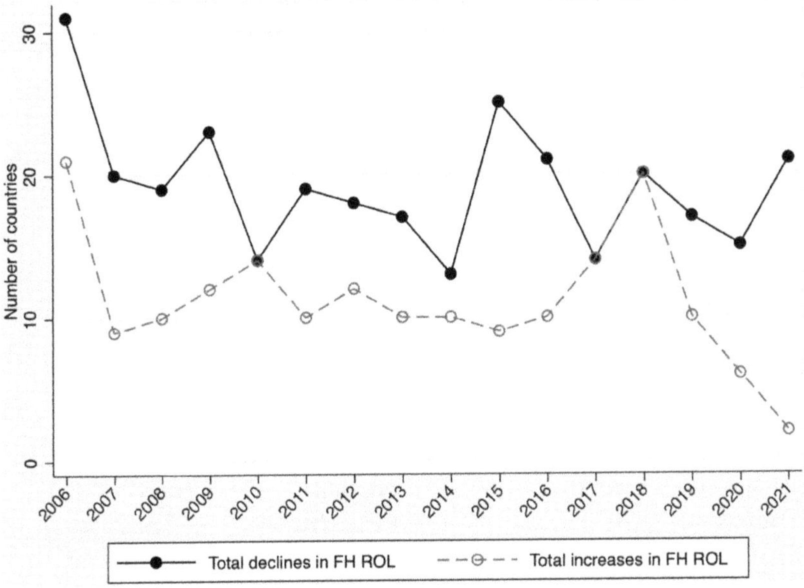


**Figure 1.3** Freedom House rule of law index.

rule of law by bringing formerly independent regulatory bodies under executive control and replacing judges on supreme courts (as in Hungary and Poland). Table 1.4 lists the twenty countries with the largest declines in the rule of law under two measures (V-Dem and Freedom House). Turkey has undergone an especially striking retreat. Notably, Freedom House lists the same democracies that display declines in the V-Dem rule-of-law indicator, but it also includes the United States.

Democracy and the rule of law are tightly interlinked. On the one hand, the rule of law is an essential prerequisite of democracy, since people cannot freely participate if they fear being subject to the arbitrary exercise of power, and election results can be manipulated without a trustworthy, independent, and institutionalized election system. On the other hand, strong democratic institutions can serve as an important bulwark of the rule of law, tempering the exercise of power (although not necessarily, as Hungary and Poland demonstrate). Measures of democracy show striking declines over the past decade. Figure 1.4 shows the net change in the level of democracy in the world according to two V-Dem indicators. The first measures the extent to which countries meet the criteria of *polyarchy*. It captures the "electoral principle of democracy," which, through free and

Table 1.4 *Decline in the rule of law, 2011–2020*

| V-Dem | | Freedom House | |
|---|---|---|---|
| Country | Decrease (on a scale of 0–1) | Country | Decrease (on a scale of 0–16) |
| Turkey | −0.43 | Turkey | −5 |
| Zambia | −0.30 | Nicaragua | −4 |
| Thailand | −0.20 | Rwanda | −4 |
| Comoros | −0.14 | Tanzania | −4 |
| El Salvador | −0.14 | Ukraine | −4 |
| Ivory Coast | −0.14 | Venezuela | −4 |
| Poland | −0.14 | Azerbaijan | −3 |
| Brazil | −0.13 | Bosnia and Herzegovina | −3 |
| Philippines | −0.13 | Burundi | −3 |
| Belarus | −0.11 | Central African Republic | −3 |
| Bosnia and Herzegovina | −0.11 | Gabon | −3 |
| Hungary | −0.11 | Hungary | −3 |
| Mauritius | −0.11 | Lesotho | −3 |
| Niger | −0.11 | Philippines | −3 |
| Mauritania | −0.10 | Tajikistan | −3 |
| Nicaragua | −0.10 | United States of America | −3 |
| Serbia | −0.10 | Indonesia | −2 |
| Moldova | −0.09 | Moldova | −2 |
| Slovenia | −0.08 | Poland | −2 |
| Togo | −0.08 | Yemen | −2 |

*Note:* The V-Dem rule-of-law variable (v2x_rule) has a range of 0 to 1. The Freedom House rule-of-law indicator ranges from 0 to 16.

fair electoral competition, makes "rulers responsive to citizens."[225] The second, *liberal democracy*, "emphasizes the importance of protecting individual and minority rights against the tyranny of the state and the tyranny of the majority," in addition to free elections.[226] The graphs indicate the balance between the number of states showing an increase in

[225] *Id.* at 43.
[226] *Id.* at 44.

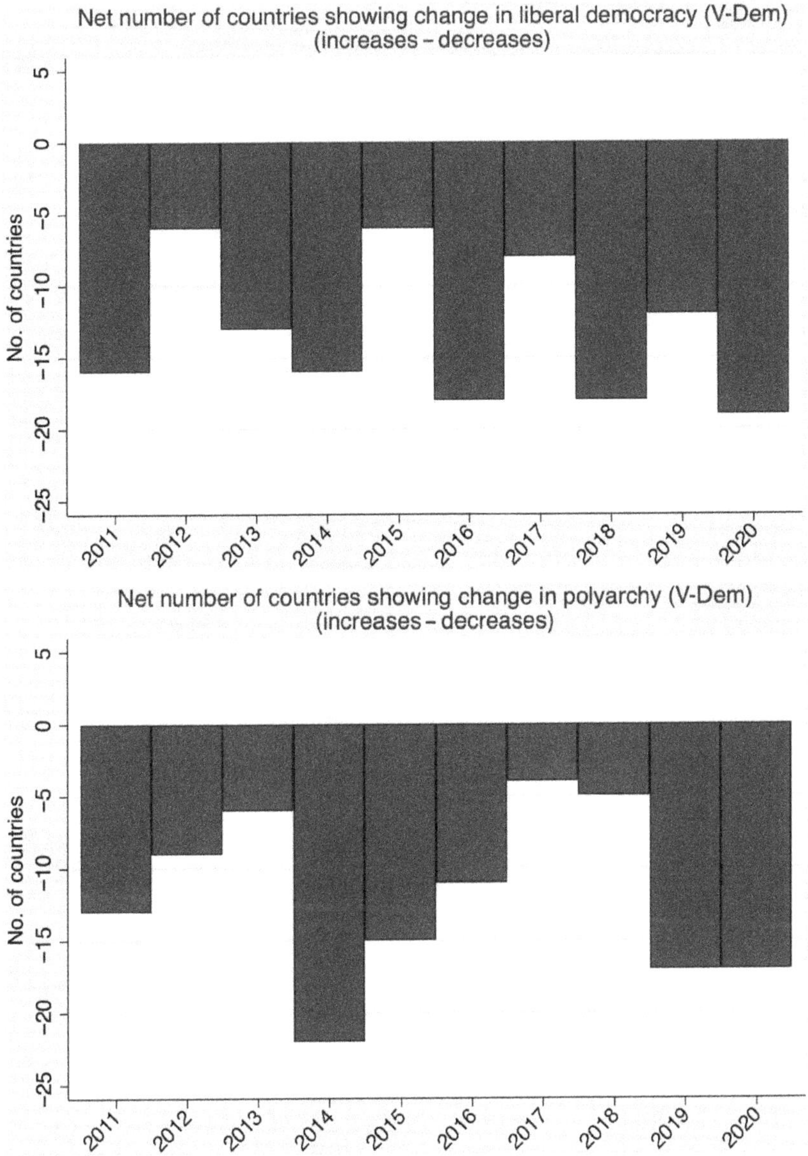


**Figure 1.4** Decline in democracy indicators.

a given indicator (greater democracy) and the number of states exhibiting a decrease (diminished democracy). For each of the last ten years, declines have been more numerous, sometimes dramatically so.

Table 1.5 *Decline in democracy, 2011–2020*

| V-Dem polyarchy | | V-Dem liberal democracy | |
|---|---|---|---|
| Country | Decrease | Country | Decrease |
| Bolivia | −0.36 | Poland | −0.34 |
| Hungary | −0.32 | Hungary | −0.29 |
| Serbia | −0.27 | Brazil | −0.28 |
| Poland | −0.26 | Turkey | −0.28 |
| Thailand | −0.26 | Serbia | −0.25 |
| Turkey | −0.26 | India | −0.23 |
| India | −0.25 | Mauritius | −0.23 |
| Yemen | −0.22 | Benin | −0.22 |
| Nicaragua | −0.21 | Thailand | −0.21 |
| Venezuela | −0.21 | Bolivia | −0.18 |
| Brazil | −0.20 | Comoros | −0.17 |
| Comoros | −0.20 | Philippines | −0.16 |
| Mauritius | −0.20 | Zambia | −0.16 |
| Benin | −0.19 | Botswana | −0.15 |
| Zambia | −0.19 | Nicaragua | −0.15 |
| Bangladesh | −0.17 | Moldova | −0.14 |
| Mali | −0.14 | Slovenia | −0.14 |
| Botswana | −0.13 | United States of America | −0.12 |
| Burundi | −0.13 | Czech Republic | −0.11 |
| Philippines | −0.12 | Mali | −0.11 |

*Note:* The V-Dem polyarchy variable captures the extent to which "the ideal of electoral democracy" is "in its fullest sense achieved." The V-Dem liberal democracy variable captures the extent to which the "liberal principle of democracy" – including protection of individual and minority rights – is achieved. Both variables range from 0 to 1 (V-Dem Codebook 2021, 43–44).

Table 1.5 lists the countries showing the greatest declines in both measures. Many of the same democracies that suffered drops in measures of the rule of law (Brazil, Hungary, Philippines, Poland, Turkey, United States) also show declines in measures of democracy. India appears in both lists as well. In parallel, the Economist Intelligence Unit downgraded Japan, South Korea, and the United States from "Full Democracies" to "Flawed Democracies" between 2014 and 2019. For the first time in three decades, it found that over half of the world's countries, governing over half of world population, are neither "Full" nor "Flawed Democracies."[227] Similarly, in its *Freedom in the World 2021* report, Freedom House warned that 2020 "marked the 15th consecutive year of decline in global freedom. The countries experiencing deterioration outnumbered those with improvements by the largest margin recorded since the negative trend began in 2006."[228] In other words, three complementary mechanisms for tempering the arbitrary exercise of power (rule of law, democracy, and civil and political rights) declined in parallel.

Sandholtz examines three key indicators of decline that implicate the rule of law: judicial independence, independent media, and civil society.[229] Civil society organizations are key compliance constituencies needed to keep governments and other powerful actors accountable, and independent media and independent courts provide important support for their efforts. These institutional actors help protect the rule of law by casting light on and countering power's arbitrary exercise, and all three are under attack. Judicial independence has declined globally through the purging and intimidation of judges and the packing of courts with government loyalists, as illustrated by authoritarian strategies in Hungary and Poland.[230] The Hungarian government even passed legislation voiding the entire jurisprudence of the country's constitutional court in order to thwart institutional checks on its power.[231] Freedom House documents, in parallel, continuous attacks on and deterioration of media independence around the world over a decade, "with new forms of repression taking hold in open societies and authoritarian states alike."[232] Governments in traditional democracies have increasingly cracked down on independent media, with many launching tax and other civil and criminal investigations in retaliation for adverse coverage. Reporters

227 Economist Intelligence Unit, Democracy Index 2022: Frontline Democracy and the Battle for Ukraine 3 (2023).

228 Sarah Repucci & Amy Slipowitz, *Freedom in the World 2021: Democracy Under Siege*, Freedom House (2022), https://freedomhouse.org/report/freedom-world/2021/democracy-under-siege.

229 Wayne Sandholtz, *Resurgent Authoritarianism and the International Rule of Law*, 28 Sw. J. Int'l L. 209 (2023).

230 *Id.*; R. Daniel Keleman, *The Assault on Poland's Judiciary*, Foreign Affs. (July 26, 2017), www.foreignaffairs.com/poland/assault-polands-judiciary.

231 Scheppele, *supra* note 23, at 550–53.

232 Sarah Repucci, *Freedom of the Media: A Downward Spiral*, Freedom House (2019), https://freedomhouse.org/report/freedom-and-media/2019/media-freedom-downward-spiral.

Without Borders dropped Japan to 71st in "world press freedom rankings," while India, under President Modi, fell to 150th.[233] UNESCO's 2022 report finds that "[o]ver the past five years, approximately eighty-five percent of the world's population experienced a decline in press freedom in their country."[234] Governments, in addition, increasingly repress civil society organizations, including by cutting off financial support from foreign sources.[235] Following the lead of China and Russia, dozens of countries have adopted new restrictions on foreign funding of nongovernmental organizations, and many have prohibited such funding.[236] UN High Commissioner for Human Rights Michelle Bachelet rebuked Israel, for example, when it not only cracked down on civil society groups but, in December 2021, designated without substantiation as "terrorist organizations" six Palestinian civil society groups that had long defended human rights and delivered humanitarian aid.[237] These trends bode ill for the rule of law.

## 4 *International Trends*

There is parallel evidence of decline in international law and institutions, which some now call a "crisis," a decline that implicates rule-of-law protections.[238] The evidence that we present is largely of a qualitative nature. It concerns challenges to, and constraints placed on, international courts, a turn away from treaties to informal agreements and understandings, the

[233] *Index*, Reporters Without Borders (2022), https://rsf.org/en/index; *India: Media Freedom Under Threat*, Reporters Without Borders (May 3, 2022), https://rsf.org/en/india-media-freedom-under-threat.

[234] UNESCO, Journalism Is a Public Good: World Trends in Freedom of Expression and Media Development, Global Report 2021–2022 (2022) (on file with authors).

[235] U.N. Secretary-General, *Rep. of the Special Rapporteur on the Rights to Freedom of Peaceful Assembly and Association*, U.N. Doc. A/74/349 (Sept. 11, 2019) ("there continues to be a worrying trend of closing civic space in many countries across the world").

[236] Darin Christensen & Jeremy M. Weinstein, *Defunding Dissent: Restrictions on Aid to NGOs*, 24 J. Democracy 77, 80 (2013); Saskia Brechenmacher, *Repression and Responses: Cross-Cutting Themes*, in Civil Society Under Assault: Repression and Responses in Russia, Egypt, and Ethiopia 91 (2017), https://tinyurl.com/3h4typ7z; Chrystie F. Swiney, *The Counter-Associational Revolution: The Rise, Spread, and Contagion of Restrictive Civil Society Laws in the World's Strongest Democratic States*, 43 Fordham Int'l L.J. 399 (2019).

[237] Press Release, United Nations, Outraged over Israel's Designation of Six Civil Society Groups as Terrorists, U.N. Doc. GA/PAL/1443 (Dec. 7, 2021), /www.un.org/press/en/2021/gapal1443.doc.htm.

[238] Krieger & Nolte, *supra* note 86, at 4.

neutering of international institutional scrutiny of human rights and rule-of-law violations, and the distortion and harnessing of international law to support repression, such as in the name of suppressing "terrorism," "separatism," and "extremism" to maintain "public order."

First, states have negatively responded to international judicial oversight over the last decade, and in particular by international human rights courts.[239] To start, there has been considerable backlash against the flagship human rights court, the ECtHR, which addresses the "rule of law" in its jurisprudence, building on the preamble to the European Convention on Human Rights.[240] States have done so through threats of withdrawal, pressures for greater accommodation through the principles of subsidiarity and the margin of appreciation, reduced support from national courts, and executive neglect of the Court's rulings. It was the rising number of claims – and their increased political and economic stakes – that triggered state responses. For example, the number of individual applications charging Russia with human rights violations nearly doubled from 1999 to 2001, and they rose to 12,328 in 2013. Following the ECtHR judgment in *Yukos v. Russia*, which ordered 2.51 billion dollars in compensation to Yukos shareholders for unfair tax proceedings,[241] President Putin signed a law that gave the Constitutional Court of Russia the authority to decide whether to comply with ECtHR judgments.[242] Following its invasion of the Ukraine in 2022, Russia was expelled from the Council of Europe and ceased being a party to the European Convention on Human Rights on September 16, 2022.[243]

239 Erik Voeten, *Populism and Backlashes Against International Courts*, 18 PERSPS. ON POL. 407, 408 (2020) ("[B]acklashes against international courts are not just about sovereignty. Populist attacks on international courts often closely track efforts to curb domestic courts . . . ."); Wayne Sandholtz, Yining Bei & Kayla Caldwell, *Backlash and International Human Rights Courts, in* CONTRACTING HUMAN RIGHTS: CRISIS, ACCOUNTABILITY, AND OPPORTUNITY 159 (Alison Brysk & Michael Stohl eds., 2018); Mikael Madsen, Pola Cebulak & Micha Wiebusch, *Backlash Against International Courts: Explaining the Forms and Patterns*, 14 INT'L J.L. CONTEXT 197 (2018).

240 Mario Oetheimer & Guillem Cano Palomares, *European Court of Human Rights (ECtHR)*, MAX PLANCK ENCYCLOPEDIA OF PUBLIC INTERNATIONAL LAW ¶ 71 (2020) ("The Court has used concepts such as the rule of law and 'democracy', two fundamental values underlying the whole ECHR system and the COE, as interpretative tools for the development of the rights set forth in the ECHR.").

241 Lukas L. Alpert, *Russia Must Compensate Yukos Shareholders, European Court Rules*, WALL ST. J. (July 28, 2014), https://tinyurl.com/uhssz97p.

242 Alexandra Sims, *Vladimir Putin Just Signed a Law Allowing Russia to Ignore International Human Rights*, INDEPENDENT (Dec. 15, 2015), https://tinyurl.com/5n7bv8z2.

243 *See* Chapter 8.

Long-standing democracies also challenged the Court, including Denmark, Switzerland, and the United Kingdom. The United Kingdom, for instance, had generally shown a high rate of compliance with ECtHR judgments, but a pair of cases – one involving prison inmates' right to vote and another involving the deportation of a Muslim cleric to Jordan – raised the British government's ire and fueled a rise in public opinion favorable to withdrawing from the Court. At the 2012 Brighton ministerial conference on the future of the ECtHR, the British government sought to trim the Court's powers,[244] a project that so far has failed.[245] However, Conservative governments in power until mid 2024 considered withdrawing from the Convention and replacing the Human Rights Act so that the Convention is no longer incorporated into UK law.

There has been similar backlash against other regional human rights courts, as well as the International Criminal Court. In the Americas, after a series of rulings by the IACtHR against Venezuela, the Constitutional Chamber of the country's Supreme Tribunal of Justice blocked six IACtHR judgments from being applied. President Hugo Chávez then withdrew Venezuela from the Inter-American Convention on Human Rights in 2012, following Trinidad and Tobago earlier. After the IACtHR ruled in 2014 that the government of the Dominican Republic violated the Inter-American Convention on Human Rights by denying identity documents and Dominican nationality to Haitian immigrants and their descendants, and detaining and expelling them, the Dominican Constitutional Tribunal issued a decision that appeared to nullify the country's IACtHR membership and remove it from the IACtHR's jurisdiction.[246] In April 2019, Argentina, Brazil, Chile, Colombia, and Paraguay issued a joint declaration to the Inter-American Commission on Human Rights calling for greater national "autonomy," signaling that the inter-American human rights system had become too intrusive in challenging state failures to respect individual rights. The African Court on Human and Peoples' Rights has faced similar pressures, with only eight states currently permitting nationals to bring cases to the Court, after four states – Rwanda, Tanzania, Benin, and Côte d'Ivoire – withdrew their permission for direct access, following

[244] Lawrence R. Helfer, *The Benefits and Burdens of Brighton*, ESIL Reflections (June 8, 2012), https://esil-sedi.eu/the-burdens-and-benefits-of-brighton/.

[245] Stone Sweet, Sandholtz & Andenas, *supra* note 140.

[246] Expelled Dominicans and Haitians v. Dominican Republic, Merits, Reparations, and Costs, Judgment, Inter-Am. Ct. H.R. (ser. C) No. 282 (Aug. 28, 2014); Press Release, Organization of American States, IACHR Condemns Judgment of the Constitutional Court of the Dominican Republic, O.A.S. Press Release No. 130/14 (Nov. 6, 2014).

decisions against them.[247] Similarly, Burundi and the Philippines have withdrawn from the International Criminal Court, and other states have threatened to follow suit.[248]

The backlash is not limited to human rights courts. China rejected a ruling of the Permanent Court of Arbitration against its claims in the South China Sea, calling the decision "wastepaper."[249] The United States neutered the Appellate Body of the World Trade Organization by blocking the appointment of new members after existing members' terms expired, a tactic that Zimbabwe (under President Mugabe) earlier used against the South African Development Community Tribunal following unfavorable rulings regarding its land seizures.[250] The United States then increasingly deployed its economic power unilaterally to challenge foreign practices it did not like, in violation of WTO law, a tactic that China also adopted. Similarly, a number of states terminated (or allowed to expire) bilateral investment treaties instituting investor–state dispute settlement (including India, Indonesia, South Africa, and the United States regarding NAFTA's investment chapter), and some withdrew from the International Centre for Settlement of Investment Disputes, which provides a procedural framework for such arbitrations. Investor–state arbitral tribunals themselves have raised rule-of-law challenges given their asymmetric nature, where only investors can bring claims and investors appoint one of the three arbitrators. Still, if the goal is enhanced rule-of-law protections within states, the better institutional alternative will vary with different contexts, which alternatives should include international venues, especially when national rule-of-law indicators decline.[251]

Second, in addition to challenges to international courts, states have turned away from treaty-making and increasingly made use of informal, nonbinding mechanisms.[252] Since the early 2000s, there has been

247 *Declarations*, AFR. CT. ON HUM. & PEOPLES' RTS., www.african-court.org/wpafc/declarations/ (last visited Aug. 21, 2024).

248 Jason Guttierez, *Philippines Officially Leaves the International Criminal Court*, N.Y. TIMES (Mar. 17, 2019), www.nytimes.com/2019/03/17/world/asia/philippines-international-criminal-court.html.

249 Jane Perlez, *Tribunal Rejects Beijing's Claims in South China Sea*, N.Y. TIMES (July 12, 2016), www.nytimes.com/2016/07/13/world/asia/south-china-sea-hague-ruling-philippines.html.

250 Karen Alter, James Gathii & Laurence Helfer, *Backlash Against International Courts in West, East and Southern Africa: Causes and Consequences*, 27 EUR. J. INT'L L. 293 (2016).

251 Puig & Shaffer, *supra* note 166.

252 INTERNATIONAL LAWMAKING (Joost Pauwelyn, Ramses Wessel & Jan Wouters eds., 2012).

a quantitative decline in new treaties, and the International Law Commission's work has ceased giving rise to treaties.[253] Nonbinding international norms – sometimes referred to as "soft law" – can exercise normative influence in support of problem-solving, and thus help develop international law and enhance its effectiveness and legitimacy.[254] The turn to less formal mechanisms thus should not necessarily worsen rule-of-law protections.[255] Nonetheless, the move away from multilateral treaties and from publicized written commitments monitored by third-party institutions reflects systemic changes that are worrisome, especially with the rise in power of authoritarian states and heightened geopolitical competition and conflict. As geopolitics and security become more pervasive concerns and more issues are viewed in zero-sum terms, states use less formal and less transparent means to govern their relations. These shifts toward informal, nontransparent mechanisms reduce accountability and enhance the ability of powerful states to deploy coercive leverage to advance their interests. For example, China's Belt and Road Initiative illustrates the use of informal mechanisms, such as memoranda of understanding and undisclosed contracts, through which ruling elites form economic and political ties. Deploying these mechanisms, China is well positioned to exercise leverage as it works to create a China-centric economic order.[256] Given a lack of public scrutiny, these types of arrangements, in turn, raise corruption concerns, which is a key source of arbitrariness and thus an indicator of the undermining of the rule of law.[257] Authoritarian governments are likely to rely on these types of less formal arrangements, which provide fewer specific legal commitments backed by third-party dispute settlement.[258]

253 Jan Wouters, *International Law, Informal Law-Making and Global Governance in Times of Anti-Globalism and Populism*, *in* THE INTERNATIONAL RULE OF LAW: RISE OR DECLINE?, *supra* note 86, at 242, 251–52.

254 DINAH SHELTON, COMMITMENT AND COMPLIANCE: THE ROLE OF NON-BINDING NORMS IN THE INTERNATIONAL LEGAL SYSTEM (2000); Gregory Shaffer & Mark A. Pollack, *Hard and Soft Law*, *in* INTERDISCIPLINARY PERSPECTIVES ON INTERNATIONAL LAW AND INTERNATIONAL RELATIONS: THE STATE OF THE ART 197 (Jeffrey L. Dunoff & Mark A. Pollack eds., 2012).

255 Sanderijn Duquet et al., *Upholding the Rule of Law in Informal International Lawmaking Processes*, 6 HAGUE J. ON RULE L. 75 (2014).

256 Gregory Shaffer & Henry Gao, *A New Chinese Economic Order?*, 23 J. INT'L ECON. L. 607 (2020).

257 See Ginsburg & Versteeg, *supra* note 162, at 504–05.

258 Tom Ginsburg, *Authoritarian International Law?*, 114 AM. J. INT'L L. 221 (2020).

Third, authoritarian governments, in parallel, have worked to neutralize existing international institutions' scrutiny of human rights practices, while developing and harnessing international norms to enhance state control. China's and Russia's leaders have viewed international civil and political rights in support of rule-of-law norms as a tool used by the West to weaken their governments' standing internationally and to destabilize their governments internally. In response, they aim to reshape international law to protect their hold on power, whether by curtailing existing institutions' oversight of compliance with international law commitments, or by creating new institutions and new legal norms.[259]

These governments use different forms of leverage to curtail international scrutiny of their internal practices by engaging, as Ginsburg writes, in a "concerted effort to neutralize multilateral forums as vehicles for democracy promotion," human rights, and the rule of law.[260] China has a seat on the Human Rights Council, where (for the 2020 Council session), nearly half of the membership (21 out of 47 countries) consisted of autocracies,[261] despite the formal requirement that members of the Council have a strong record of respecting human rights. Following the issuance of a report by the Office of the United Nations High Commissioner for Human Rights in August 2022, which found that China's human rights violations in Xinjiang could amount to crimes against humanity, China called the Office a "thug and accomplice of the US and the West."[262] China then won a vote in the Human Rights Council to block further scrutiny of the report's findings, defeating a US proposal.[263] In parallel, China has attempted to defund human rights promotion in UN peacekeeping operations, block the accreditation of civil society groups before the UN, and curtail the role of UN Special Rapporteurs.[264] The result could be a decline in human rights

[259] Tom Ginsburg, *Authoritarian International Law, in* Democracies and International Law 186 (2021).

[260] Ginsburg, *supra* note 258, at 255.

[261] Wayne Sandholtz, *Authoritarianism, International Human Rights, and Legal Change, in* Is the International Legal Order Unraveling? (David Sloss ed., 2022). Russia held a seat until it was suspended in 2022 following its invasion of Ukraine.

[262] Michele Bachelet, the UN High Commissioner for Human Rights, released the report minutes before her term ended. China had placed considerable pressure on her to not release it. Jan van der Made, *Beijing Furious over Damning UN Rights Report on Uyghurs in Xinjiang*, RFI (Sept. 1, 2022, 16:59), https://tinyurl.com/mfah6urh.

[263] Nick Cumming-Bruce, *China Turns Back Move for U.N. Debate on Abuse of Uyghurs*, N. Y. Times (Oct. 6, 2022), www.nytimes.com/2022/10/06/world/asia/china-un-xinjiang-uyghurs.html (vote of 19–17, with 11 abstentions).

[264] Nicholas Bequelin, *China's Crimes in Xinjiang Cannot Go Unpunished*, N.Y. Times, Oct. 3, 2022, at A22.

monitoring and enforcement and, more generally, a reduced use of third-party institutions, including international courts.[265]

Fourth, authoritarian governments aim to reshape the content of international law in ways that they can deploy domestically to support their hold on power. They do so, in part, through increasing their participation and leadership roles within international organizations in order to exercise influence. China, for example, has successfully pursued leadership roles for Chinese nationals. In 2020, Chinese nationals headed four of the UN's fifteen agencies; no other country's nationals led more than one.[266] Chinese nationals led the Food and Agricultural Organization (FAO), critical for issues of food security and standard setting; the UN Industrial Development Organization (UNIDO), which has praised and supported China's Belt and Road Initiative; the International Civil Aviation Organization (ICAO), which controversially worked to isolate Taiwan; and the International Telecommunications Union (ITU), which helps shape the governance of information and communications technologies, implicating government controls. In addition, a Chinese national almost became Director General of the World Intellectual Property Organization (WIPO) in 2020, losing only after concerted US and European lobbying for an alternative candidate from Singapore.[267] In parallel, China has dramatically increased its leadership positions in international standard-setting bodies across councils, technical management boards, technical committees, subcommittees, and working groups. Such standards are crucial for infrastructure projects, including for telecommunications, where Chinese companies are among the world's leaders. China regularly volunteers to host standards meetings and provide secretariat services. Chinese nationals held the presidencies of the International Standardization Organization (ISO) from 2015 to 2017, and of the International Electrotechnical Committee (IEC) from 2020 to 2022. A Chinese national also presided over Interpol, the

[265] John Fisher, *Human Rights Council Membership Has Its Consequences*, HUM. RTS. WATCH (Jan. 14, 2019, 9:11 AM), www.hrw.org/news/2019/01/14/human-rights-council-membership-has-its-consequences; Ginsburg, *supra* note 258.

[266] Courtney J. Fung & Shing-Hon Lam, *China Already Leads 4 of the 15 U.N. Specialized Agencies – and Is aiming for a 5th*, WASH. POST (Mar. 3, 2020, 6:00 AM), https://tinyurl.com/y37xde4z.

[267] Michael McCaul, *The United States Can't Cede the U.N. to China*, FOREIGN POL'Y (Sept. 24, 2019, 12:32 PM), https://foreignpolicy.com/2019/09/24/the-united-states-cant-cede-the-u-n-to-china/. The United States organized a campaign to block China's candidate to lead WIPO. Nick Cumming-Bruce, *U.S.-Backed Candidate for Global Tech Post Beats China's Nominee*, N.Y. TIMES (Mar. 4, 2020), https://tinyurl.com/5n9y2acs.

International Criminal Police Organization, until (ironically) China arrested him on a trip home in 2018, in the middle of his term, on charges of corruption and bribery.

Through enhancing their engagement in international institutions, authoritarian governments can reshape, develop, and then harness international norms for authoritarian ends at home. China and other authoritarian states have promoted international law norms of sovereignty and noninterference in a state's internal affairs. In this way, China hopes to counter the individualist turn of international law, with its increased emphasis on human rights, which the United States and Europe championed during the Cold War, and which became more institutionalized after the Soviet Union's collapse. China and other authoritarian states, in particular, have championed the development of international norms and mechanisms that they can use for repressive purposes. China, for example, has worked within the International Telecommunications Union to develop a new internet infrastructure that facilitates state control. It successfully supported a UN General Assembly resolution on "Countering the Use of Information and Communications Technologies for Criminal Purposes" that it and others can reference to justify internal suppressive measures. It also promulgates regional norms that it can use to repress internal dissent and counter foreign critique, such as regards China's suppression of Uyghurs, Tibetans, and the people of Hong Kong. Through the Shanghai Cooperation Organization, China cooperates with neighboring countries to combat the "three evils" of "terrorism, separatism, and extremism," including through international extradition agreements.[268] These agreements serve to legitimize China's targeting of human rights and democracy activists, including their lawyers, and its suppression of free expression and the free flow of information on national security grounds. Russia and other states have followed its lead. The result of these shifts could be the recasting of international law and institutions to better serve authoritarian interests, leading to an "authoritarian international law."[269]

One should be careful not to idealize the turn to international law and institutions in the 1990s and 2000s given the exercise of Western hegemony.[270] At the same time, one should assess the implications of existing trends for the rule of law from a comparative institutional perspective. That is, one should ask whether the rising challenges to

[268] Shanghai Coop. Org., Shanghai Convention on Combating Terrorism, Separatism, and Extremism (2011).

[269] Ginsburg, *supra* note 258.

[270] Detlev Vagts, *Hegemonic International Law*, 95 Am. J. Int'l L. 843 (2001).

international institutions and law will advance or undermine rule-of-law goals. The evidence presented above indicates that domestic rule-of-law protections are declining overall, and that they parallel challenges to international law and institutions. These dual challenges to rule-of-law goals at the domestic and international levels, we contend, are part of a broader, transnational, interactive, negative cycle.

## 5 *The Enmeshment of National and International Trends*

Rule-of-law norms are part of a liberal tradition that can have quite radical political implications.[271] They are increasingly contested through a combination of illiberal *domestic* developments within traditional democracies (including in the United States) and shifts in *international* power with China's rise as an authoritarian state. *Internally*, a populist, anti-globalist backlash against the international order has upended domestic politics in many countries. President Donald Trump's "America First" attacks on the international legal order, which the United States had predominantly forged, illustrate the links between national processes and international institutional checks. The Trump administration and its allies within the United States promoted and forged new ties with nationalist and authoritarian parties and leaders abroad while attacking, neutering, and withdrawing from international institutions and treaties, from the UN Human Rights Council to the International Criminal Court and its Office of the Prosecutor. *Externally*, international anti-terrorism norms and institutions promoted by the United States in the early 2000s already had created new institutional and normative resources for authoritarian governments.[272] These authoritarian governments, most notably China, rose as global economic powers, creating new challenges for international institutions, and particularly international courts. The result could be the "dejudicialization of international politics."[273]

The upsurge of illiberalism and economic nationalism within the United States undercut the liberal international order from within, as the United States under the Trump administration paradoxically became

[271] Nick Cheesman, Opposing the Rule of Law: How Myanmar's Courts Make Law and Order 263 (2016) ("The rule-of-law ideal is not a conservative doctrine but a radical one: a doctrine going to the radix, or root, of political power. It is an idea that fundamentally challenges how power has been and continues to be exercised.").

[272] Scheppele, *The Migration of Anti-Constitutional Ideas*, *supra* note 157.

[273] Daniel Abebe & Tom Ginsburg, *The Dejudicialization of International Politics?*, 63 Int'l Stud. Q. 521 (2019).

a revisionist power. Europe has faced parallel internal contestations, illustrated by Brexit, the rise of illiberal parties within member states, especially but not only within Central and Eastern Europe,[274] and an increasingly aggressive Russia. Externally, an authoritarian China now vies for regional and global leadership to shape international norms and institutions, and its repressive politics are fundamentally at odds with liberal values. These domestic and international developments interrelate, and they pose severe challenges to the advancement of rule-of-law goals and practices.

The transnational development and conveyance of norms occur through different mechanisms, including through coercion, reciprocity, socialization, and modeling.[275] In parallel, iterative transnational processes of norm development are driven by the indeterminacy of legal texts, ideological tensions and contradictions within texts, diagnostic struggles over the nature of the problem (including as contexts change), and actor mismatch between those that adopt norms and those that implement them in practice.[276] For example, the term "rule of law" is vague and its meaning contested, reflecting a degree of indeterminacy. To the extent that actors view the rule of law in terms of legality or as defined by checklists, authoritarians can deploy rule-of-law rhetoric and adapt formal measures in ways that advance authoritarian ends.[277] International norms, in turn, often reflect compromises that incorporate ideological tensions and contradictions. For example, take the tensions between international law norms for the suppression of terrorism and norms to ensure due process and proportionality. Authoritarian governments can advance one aspect (suppressing terrorism) while ignoring the other (ensuring due process and proportionality).[278] Relatedly, there will be ongoing tensions concerning the conceptualization of problems, which implicates legal responses. For example, the governing norms of the trade regime are being redefined in national security terms, and they have moved away from concerns about nondiscrimination and fairness toward nonnationals.[279] Finally, there are always mismatches between

[274] IVAN KRASTEV & STEPHEN HOLMES, THE LIGHT THAT FAILED: A RECKONING (2019).

[275] JOHN BRAITHWAITE & PETER DRAHOS, GLOBAL BUSINESS REGULATION 17 (2000); Simmons, Dobbin & Garrett, *supra* note 191.

[276] Halliday & Carruthers, *supra* note 89; Halliday & Shaffer, *supra* note 10, at 37–42.

[277] *See, e.g.*, Scheppele, *supra* note 201.

[278] GINSBURG, *supra* note 259.

[279] *Cf.* Appellate Body Report, *United States – Import Prohibition of Certain Shrimp and Shrimp Products*, ¶ 180, WTO Doc. WT/DS58/AB/R (adopted Oct. 12, 1998);

those who negotiate and enact international legal norms and those who implement them. Implementing institutions and officials at the state and substate levels shape the law in action.

From the perspective of transnational legal ordering, the question becomes, What are the facilitating circumstances and precipitating conditions that give rise not only to a transnational legal order but also to its decline, including through the formation of rival transnational legal orders?[280] There have been a number of facilitating circumstances over the last decade, including power shifts, unintended consequences, legitimacy challenges, effectiveness concerns, and a reconceptualization of problems. There has been a shift in global power with the economic and political rise of China and the relative decline of the United States and Europe. These shifts have increased China's leverage over others while decreasing those of the United States and European Union. China's economic rise was, in part, an unintended consequence of the legal architecture for economic globalization that the United States had erected. After China joined the WTO, foreign capital invested massively in China, as well as in global supply chains linked to new Chinese manufacturing. This legal architecture also favored transnational capital over domestic labor, since capital was free to invest elsewhere and use that leverage in labor–capital relations. The result was a significant rise in income for capitalists, high-level management, and many professionals, accompanied by stagnant income for most Americans, which drove income inequality to levels not seen in the United States since the 1920s.[281] These developments undercut a sense of the legitimacy and effectiveness of the trade regime. They triggered a growing invocation of national security exceptions that enhance executive power at the expense of legislative and judicial

Anthea Roberts, Henrique Choer Moraes & Victor Ferguson, *Toward a Geoeconomic Order in Trade and Investment*, 22 J. Int'l Econ. L. 655 (2019).

280 Halliday & Shaffer, *supra* note 93, at 507–11, 524 (setting forth a series of hypotheses that come out of the book's case studies, including power shifts, legitimacy deficits, changed contexts, inflexibility, internal contradictions, distributive bias, and ineffectiveness); Halliday & Shaffer, *supra* note 10, at 32–37 (on facilitating circumstances and precipitating conditions).

281 Emmanuel Saez & Gabriel Zucman, The Triumph of Injustice (2019); U.S. Int'l Trade Comm'n, Distributional Effects of Trade and Trade Policy on U.S. Workers 18–19 (2022) (based on the existing literature, which needs further development, finding reduced employment for low-skill manufacturing workers, reduced earnings for non-college-educated workers or those previously employed in manufacturing jobs, and a disproportionate effect on wages of minority workers).

oversight.[282] They help explain why, paradoxically, the United States (as the incumbent power) and not China (the emerging power) has become revisionist in upending the regime.[283]

China's emergence as a regional and global power, and rising concerns about inequality, in turn, catalyzed a shift in the conceptualization of international "problems" within US and European policy circles, spurring a rethinking of international law and institutions' role. In international economic law, there has been a shift toward a focus on geopolitics, national security, supply chain resiliency, and social inclusion, away from one on economic efficiency, which had been foundational for an international legal system supportive of economic globalization. As a result, national security bureaucracies' power has risen both in the United States and China at the expense of trade ministries.

These facilitating circumstances create the conditions for precipitating events that implicate rule-of-law practices. For example, the North Atlantic financial crisis of 2008 helped accelerate China's gains in economic power, called into question the superiority of the US economic model in relation to China's state-driven alternative, and further contributed to economic precarity for working-class Americans.[284] The combination of facilitating circumstances and precipitating conditions catalyzed backlash against the international economic order and helped empower populist, economic nationalist leaders within countries.[285] Ongoing crises could further these trends, including ecological crises driven by climate change,[286] which, in turn, exacerbate "migration crises" that populist leaders can harness.

282 Kristen Eichensehr & Cathy Hwang, *National Security Creep in Corporate Transactions*, 123 COLUM. L. REV. 549 (2023).

283 GREGORY SHAFFER, EMERGING POWERS AND THE WORLD TRADING SYSTEM: THE PAST AND FUTURE OF INTERNATIONAL ECONOMIC LAW (2021). *Cf.* JOHN IKENBERRY, AFTER VICTORY: INSTITUTIONS, STRATEGIC RESTRAINT, AND THE REBUILDING OF ORDER AFTER MAJOR WARS (2000).

284 ADAM TOOZE, CRASHED: HOW A DECADE OF FINANCIAL CRISES CHANGED THE WORLD (2018). The US-led invasions of Iraq and Afghan and its "war on terror" following the September 11, 2001, attacks also contributed to China's relative rise and US decline, creating groundwork for populist leaders that would challenge rule-of-law norms. *See* SPENCER ACKERMAN, REIGN OF TERROR: HOW THE 9/11 ERA DESTABILIZED AMERICA AND PRODUCED TRUMP xvii (2021) ("The mortar of birtherism was the War on Terror . . . .").

285 David H. Autor et al., *Importing Political Polarization? The Electoral Consequences of Rising Trade Exposure*, 110 AM. ECON. REV. 3139 (2020).

286 EVE DARIAN-SMITH, GLOBAL BURNING: RISING ANTIDEMOCRACY AND THE CLIMATE CRISIS (2022).

Leaders around the globe – from Modi in India, Duterte and then Marcos in the Philippines, Orbán in Hungary, Erdogan in Turkey, and (when in power) Trump in the United States – embrace a populism, which, following Jan Werner Müller, we conceptualize as a combination of anti-elitism and moralized anti-pluralism.[287] Anti-elitism justifies populist challenges to institutional constraints since institutions – whether they be independent courts, agencies, the civil service, or media – allegedly have been populated and controlled by elites.[288] A moralized anti-pluralism differentiates the "real people" from others, who tend to be minorities, migrants, and political opponents. Populists cast these "others" as immoral, disloyal, and corrupt.[289] International institutions and civil society organizations are dismissed and attacked as foreign or "foreign agents." The exclusionary politics of "Us" (the "real people") versus "Them" (not "Us") – with opponents and critics labeled as "enemies of the people" – puts serious strains on rule-of law norms. "For my friends, everything; for my enemies, the law," becomes the norm.[290] Populist, nativist parties have shaped public agendas even when they are not elected to power, especially as regards migrants and policing.[291] The global COVID pandemic appears to have further emboldened many national governments to expand their powers relative to civil society[292] – a creeping authoritarianism that bodes further ill for rule-of-law protections. Montoya and Ponce show a strong statistical

[287] Jan Werner Müller, What is Populism? (2016); *see also* Pippa Norris & Ronald Inglehart, Cultural Backlash: Trump, Brexit, and Authoritarian Populism (2019).

[288] A "main institutional aspect of populism under this account is a frontal assault upon the separation of powers." Wojciech Sadurski, A Pandemic of Populists 16 (2022).

[289] *Id.*

[290] O'Donnell attributes this quote to Brazilian populist Getulio Dornelles Vargas. Guillermo O'Donnell, *Why the Rule of Law Matters*, 15 J. Democracy 32, 40 (2004). Others, however, attribute it to Oscar Benavides, president of Peru from 1933 to 1939.

[291] Nicola Lacey, *Populism and the Rule of Law*, *in* The Cambridge Companion to the Rule of Law, *supra* note 12, at 458, 465.

[292] Ted Piccone, *Rule of Law Takes a Big Hit During COVID-19*, Brookings (Oct. 18, 2021), https://tinyurl.com/46ktu3av; Frances Z. Brown, Saskia Brechenmacher & Thomas Carothers, *How Will the Coronavirus Reshape Democracy and Governance Globally?*, Carnegie Endowment for Int'l Peace (Apr. 6, 2020), https://tinyurl.com/mwtpjucw; Selam Gebrekidan, *For Autocrats, and Others, Coronavirus Is a Chance to Grab Even More Power*, N.Y. Times (Mar. 30, 2020), https://tinyurl.com/4fntber9. There is a clear distinction between responsible governments taking discretionary action to protect people from the risks of contagion, on the one hand, and the harnessing of the pandemic for self-serving authoritarian ends, on the other.

correlation between populist, anti-pluralist platforms and declines in the rule of law.[293]

The rise of populism and erosion of democracy within countries correlates with increased challenges to international institutions.[294] For instance, US president Trump drove a populist, nativist agenda in which he undermined US governance norms, expressed admiration for authoritarian leaders and disdain for democratic ones, and sought repeatedly to block the transfer of power, including through pressuring election officials to "find" him enough votes, scheming to create fake, pro-Trump electors, and then rallying an attack on the US capitol, all as part of an attempted coup.[295] In parallel, in line with his "America First" policies, Trump undercut international institutions and agreements. He withdrew the United States from the Paris Agreement on climate change, the Trans-Pacific Partnership, the Iran nuclear deal, the Open Skies Treaty, the Intermediate Nuclear Forces Treaty, and the Optional Protocol to the Vienna Convention on Diplomatic Relations, and he withdrew US participation in the Global Compact on Migration.[296] He likewise withdrew, or initiated withdrawal, of the United States from the UN Human Rights Council, the World Health Organization, and the UN Economic, Social, and Cultural Organization (UNESCO), while neutering the World Trade Organization's dispute settlement system, challenging and threatening to withdraw from NATO and the WTO, and sanctioning the Prosecutor for the International Criminal Court as if she were a terrorist threat.[297] Similarly, within Europe, authoritarian regimes in Hungary and Poland took advantage of the consensual decision-making processes in the

[293] *See* Chapter 3.

[294] Voeten finds that populist governments were responsible for eighteen of twenty-eight state backlashes against international courts that he traces. Voeten, *supra* note 239.

[295] Michael D. Shear & Stephanie Saul, *Trump, in Taped Call, Pressured Georgia Official to 'Find' Votes to Overturn Election*, N.Y. Times (Jan. 3, 2021), www.nytimes.com/2021/01/03/us/politics/trump-raffensperger-call-georgia.html; Luke Broadwater & Alan Feuer, *Panel Ties Trump to Fake Elector Plan, Mapping His Attack on Democracy*, N.Y. Times (June 21, 2022), www.nytimes.com/2022/06/21/us/politics/trump-pressure-state-officials.html.

[296] Oona A. Hathaway, *Reengaging on Treaties and Other International Agreements (Part I): President Donald Trump's Rejection of International Law*, Just Security (Oct. 2, 2020), https://tinyurl.com/7zs5pue3; Richard Haass, Opinion, *Trump's Foreign Policy Doctrine? The Withdrawal Doctrine*, Wash. Post (May 27, 2020, 12:10 PM), https://tinyurl.com/3pdr9fsx.

[297] Hylke Dijkstra et al., *Donald Trump and the Survival Strategies of International Organisations: When Can Institutional Actors Counter Existential Challenges?*, Cambridge Rev. Int'l Affs. 1, 1 (2022), www.tandfonline.com/doi/full/10.1080/09557571.2022.2136566.

European Union to bring some EU actions to a virtual halt.[298] More generally, populism has led to reduced references in domestic courts to international law, further limiting international law's reach, such as its ability to provide normative resources for protecting minorities.[299]

Authoritarian leaders in Russia and China also have moved in totalitarian directions that have implications for international law and the normative resources that it provides. Xi Jinping has clamped down on independent voices in China and is extending his rule well into the future. In parallel, because China is the world's largest trading nation and provider of development finance, it exercises significant leverage over countries that are dependent on it for trade, investment, and finance to curtail international scrutiny and support of rule-of-law practices, while developing and harnessing international norms, such as those of anti-terrorism, for illiberal ends. Russia further illustrates the enmeshment of national and international developments for the rule of law. Its internal autocratic turn and its war of aggression against Ukraine interrelate. President Putin's fear of an internal threat to his rule helped spur his war on Ukraine, since Ukraine's democratization and ties with Europe facilitated the conveyance of liberal norms. In his televised address announcing Russia's invasion of Ukraine, for example, Putin blamed "the West" for its attack on Russia's traditional values, including through imposing attitudes that "are contrary to human nature" – referencing the extension of legal rights and cultural acceptance of LGBTQI peoples.[300] Putin since has used the Ukraine war to shut down independent Russian media and "self-cleanse" Russia of opposition to his rule – labeling opponents "scum and traitors" that should be "spit out like a midge."[301] One of the fallouts of the Ukraine war is Russia's departure from the Council of Europe and withdrawal from the European Convention on Human Rights, curtailing the normative resources and international oversight they provide. In the process, Putin has upended European security and the settlement of Europe's borders.

[298] Robert Csehi & Edit Zgut, *"We Won't Let Brussels Dictate Us": Eurosceptic Populism in Hungary and Poland*, 22 Eur. Pol. & Soc'y 53 (2021); Yasmeen Serhan, *The Other Threat to Democracy in Europe*, Atlantic (Apr. 11, 2022), https://tinyurl.com/bdfnmmmv.

[299] Tamar Hosovsky Brandes, *International Law in Domestic Courts in an Era of Populism*, 17 Int'l J. Const. L. 576 (2019).

[300] *Transcript of Vladimir Putin's Speech Announcing "Special Military Operation" in Ukraine*, Sydney Morning Herald (Feb. 24, 2022), https://tinyurl.com/3r6hu6k5.

[301] *Putin Vows to Rid Russia of 'Traitors' While Waging Ukraine War*, Bloomberg (Mar. 16, 2022), https://tinyurl.com/5n6h4sbs.

Overall, the combination and enmeshment of populist, authoritarian trends within states and shifts in global power toward authoritarian states will reshape international law and institutions, which, in turn, could further support authoritarian practices within states. In his foundational work on multilateralism, John Ruggie stressed the importance of a "permissive domestic environment" for multilateral cooperation.[302] He argued that the "post-World War II situation" reflected "less the fact of American *hegemony*," than "of *American* hegemony." He maintained, in turn, that "the durability of multilateral arrangements … is also a function of domestic environments."[303] In short, a decline of multilateralism and international promotion of the rule of law will echo changes in the domestic environment of powerful states, including within the United States. To play off the title of Ruggie's book, *transnationalism matters.*[304] It is the interaction of domestic and international factors that give rise to positive and negative cycles for the rule of law.

## IV What Might Be Done?

At the national level, institutions can have resilience. Although we assessed challenges to the rule of law in Part III, these challenges are occurring within the context of transnational rule-of-law institutional developments over the last three decades that provide normative resources to those resisting authoritarian trends. Pou Giménez, for example, notes the importance of constitutional developments in Mexico and elsewhere in Latin America over the last three decades that gave rise to new institutions providing fora for professional and activist networks to resist executive encroachments on rule-of-law protections.[305] In the United States, there was considerable resistance to the Trump administration's decrees, including from civil servants within the executive branch.[306] The American Civil Liberties Union alone filed over four hundred lawsuits against the administration, ranging from its ban on Muslims entering the United States to its separation of migrant children from their parents and placing them in cages.[307]

302 JOHN RUGGIE, *Multilateralism: The Anatomy of an Institution*, in MULTILATERALISM MATTERS: THE THEORY AND PRACTICE OF AN INSTITUTIONAL FORM 8 (1993).
303 *Id.* at 33.
304 The title of Ruggie's book is *Multilateralism Matters.*
305 *See* Chapter 10.
306 Jennifer Nou, *Civil Servant Disobedience*, 94 CHI.-KENT L. REV. 349 (2019).
307 *ACLU Has Filed 400 Legal Actions Against Trump Administration*, ACLU (Aug. 17, 2020), https://tinyurl.com/y54r8s7h.

International institutions also have resilience, and many of them support rule-of law norms and practices.[308] For example, the most active regional human rights courts – the ECtHR and the IACtHR – so far have withstood efforts by states to curtail their formal authority. Moreover, when international institutions have become complicit in rule-of-law violations, they have spurred regional, state, and civil society responses, as reflected in the *Kadi* line of cases and efforts to reform Security Council procedures.[309] Nonetheless, the erosion of rule-of-law and democratic norms within states, combined with the economic and political rise of powerful authoritarian states, pose considerable challenges. What might be done to return to a virtuous transnational cycle that advances rule-of-law goals?

First, because national and international norms regarding the rule of law recursively interact, responses to the current negative cycle must occur at multiple levels, including domestically, regionally, and globally. Developments elsewhere matter for rule-of-law developments at home, as illustrated by the vicious and virtuous cycles of rule-of-law developments that this introductory chapter and the volume as a whole document. As Kwame Anthony Appiah writes, "[while] populist demagogues around the world exploit the churn of economic discontent, the danger is that the politics of engagement could give way to the politics of withdrawal." Forgetting that "we are all citizens of the world – a small, warming, intensely vulnerable world – would be a reckless relaxation of vigilance."[310] "Elsewhere," Appiah stresses, "has never been more important."[311]

The Biden administration actively reengaged the United States at the international level. It rejoined the UN Human Rights Council, UNESCO, the Paris Agreement on climate change, and the Migration Compact, among other organizations and treaties. In 2021, it hosted a "Summit for Democracy" to address the authoritarian challenge.[312] In parallel, it

[308] Scheppele illustrates the potential of the European Union, the European Convention on Human Rights, and the Venice Commission as checks against authoritarian developments in Hungary and Poland. *See* Chapter 7. *See also* Nicole Deitelhoff & Lisbeth Zimmermann, *Norms Under Challenge: Unpacking the Dynamics of Norm Robustness*, 4 J. GLOB. SEC. STUD. 2 (2019); Wayne Sandholtz, *Norm Contestation, Robustness, and Replacement*, 4 J. GLOB. SEC. STUD. 139 (2019); Madsen, Cebulak & Wiebusch, *supra* note 239, at 217.

[309] *See* Chapter 6.

[310] Kwame Anthony Appiah, *The Importance of Elsewhere: In Defense of Cosmopolitanism*, FOREIGN AFFS. (Feb. 12, 2019), www.foreignaffairs.com/world/importance-elsewhere-cosmopolitanism-appiah.

[311] *Id.*

[312] Edward Wong, *Biden Puts Defense of Democracy at Center of Agenda, at Home and Abroad*, N.Y. TIMES (Sept. 6, 2022), www.nytimes.com/2022/09/06/us/politics/biden-democracy-threat.html.

launched a new Joint Transatlantic Agenda with the European Union that aimed to reinvigorate transatlantic cooperation and to counter China and Russia.[313] Russia's invasion of the Ukraine spurred transatlantic cooperation to levels not seen since the end of the Cold War. This new transatlantic agenda linked with the administration's efforts to develop a new transpacific governance framework with allies in Asia through an "Indo-Pacific Economic Framework."[314] Both involve predominantly soft law, in contrast to the Obama administration's earlier proposals for a Transatlantic Trade and Investment Partnership and a Trans-Pacific Partnership, which were to create a broad array of new binding rules backed by third-party dispute settlement. These initiatives are admirable in rallying governments to defend and promote democratic, rule-of-law values through bolstering old alliances and developing and engaging new ones.

Nonetheless, the administration's rhetoric and strategic initiatives pose risks. They could deepen nationalist reactions domestically in China and elsewhere and, in the process, empower authoritarian leaders who, viewing such alliances as threats, expand their powers in defense of "national security." They also risk dividing the world into opposing blocs, catalyzing new authoritarian alliances, such as between Russia and China. They thus could threaten the underlying Hobbesian task of securing order, trust, and peace through providing the conditions for cooperation.[315]

Balancing the creation and invigoration of organized clubs of like-minded, democratic states as part of broader security alliances, on the one hand, with commitments to multilateral institutions and bilateral mechanisms to defuse conflicts and respond to global challenges, on the other hand, will be a key challenge for the future.[316] The United States needs to engage with China in and through international institutions and bilateral processes to address global and transnational risks, reduce conflict, and resolve disputes peacefully. Shaffer elsewhere proposed a framework for governing US–China relations in this vein across the three dimensions of economic relations, national security, and concerns

313 Mark Pollack & Gregory Shaffer, *A New Transatlantic Agenda: A Defensive Turn*, MEDIUM (July 19, 2021), https://tinyurl.com/yv4453pt.

314 Ana Swanson, *Biden Administration Outlines Scope of Asian Economic Pact*, N.Y. TIMES (Sept. 9, 2022), www.nytimes.com/2022/09/09/business/ipef-framework-asia-trade .html.

315 Gregory Shaffer, *The Risks of an "Alliance of Democracies,"* MEDIUM (July 12, 2021), https://tinyurl.com/5n92kwn7.

316 William Burke-White, *A Strategic Roadmap for Reentry: 2021 and Beyond*, BROOKINGS (Feb. 2021), www.brookings.edu/articles/a-strategic-roadmap-for-reentry-2021-and-beyond/.

over human rights, which will be necessary to manage and defuse conflict and create conditions for cooperation, especially when crises arise.[317] It provides a contrasting template to that pursued by the Trump and Biden administrations vis-à-vis China, although the Biden administration recognized the need to manage the US economic relationship with China in more tailored ways.[318]

Second, much analysis of international law and institutions has focused on their relation to state practices because states are most frequently the direct subjects of international law. However, given the ability of transnational capital to exercise arbitrary power, and given that state and private power interact (including through the regulation, or lack of regulation, of private power), it is mistaken to assess international law and international rule-of-law concerns as only regarding states. Globalization processes arguably need to be reined in to equalize the bargaining power of transnational capital and labor, which raises the issue of arbitrary power exercised by corporations over workers. Before the industrial revolution, in the age of Adam Smith and his advocacy of free trade to enhance the wealth of nations, political theorists had better grounds to view market capitalism and trade liberalization as means to dismantle hierarchies and advance egalitarian prospects.[319] In contrast, the contemporary age of mega-oligopolists, billionaire capitalists, and precarious working conditions for mass labor call for new forms of regulation.[320] Otherwise, there will be fertile ground for populist, exclusionary forces that challenge fundamental rule-of-law norms. The Biden administration's proclamation of a "worker-centered trade policy," its reframing of trade relations in terms of "resilience, sustainability, and inclusion," and its aim to coordinate tax policies to preserve the ability of states to tax high-wealth individuals and corporations and thus fund domestic policies to redress gaping inequalities need to be worked out.[321] Yet,

[317] Gregory Shaffer, *Governing the Interface of U.S.-China Relations*, 115 Am. J. Int'l L. 622 (2021).

[318] *See, e.g.*, Dani Rodrik, *Don't Let Geopolitics Kill the World Economy*, Project Syndicate (Nov. 10, 2022), https://tinyurl.com/4peddur8; *Remarks by National Security Advisor Jake Sullivan on Renewing American Economic Leadership at the Brookings Institution*, White House (Apr. 27, 2023), https://tinyurl.com/dfd2xdut.

[319] Anderson, *supra* note 8, ch. 1.

[320] *Id.* at 65–71 (noting the need for exit rights, rule-of-law constraints, constitutional rights, and enhanced worker voice within the workplace).

[321] U.S. Trade Representative, 2022 Trade Policy Agenda & 2021 Annual Report (2022), https://tinyurl.com/42w56max.

they reflect real concerns about the impact of market processes on society.

Democracies need to address tensions within liberalism, both at home and in international agreements, and, in particular, between political and economic liberalism.[322] In earlier theorizing, Hayek and others promoted international norms of economic liberalization to constrain national democratic choices regarding economic regulation.[323] In contrast, more recently, following Karl Polanyi's classic account,[324] the economist Dani Rodrik has stressed the trade-offs among economic globalization, national sovereignty, and democracy in terms of a "trilemma" – one could have any two of them but not all three, he contended.[325] Rodrik stressed that "we need to place the requirements of liberal democracy ahead of those of international trade and investment," as trade and investment policy can undermine domestic social bargains and increase inequality.[326] We agree with Rodrik in this regard. There is evidence that increased economic integration under a neoliberal economic model helped spur the rising inequality and job precarity that sparked populist and nationalist reactions.[327] Studies show a correlation of higher inequality with acceptance of authoritarianism, as struggles over economic distribution become more salient.[328]

To respond to these challenges within liberalism, global governance institutions and norms should be recalibrated to facilitate greater protection for domestic economic policy space. The application of international economic law norms should be revisited to provide greater room for countries to ensure social inclusion, and thus preserve

[322] *See, e.g.*, ISAIAH BERLIN, LIBERTY 216 (Henry Hardy ed., 2002); T.M. SCANLON, WHAT WE OWE EACH OTHER 78–107 (1998) (discussing the interaction of values, including liberty and equality).

[323] FRIEDRICH HAYEK, THE ROAD TO SERFDOM (1944); QUINN SLOBODIAN, GLOBALISTS: THE END OF EMPIRE AND THE BIRTH OF NEOLIBERALISM (2018).

[324] KARL POLANYI, THE GREAT TRANSFORMATION: THE POLITICAL AND ECONOMIC ORIGINS OF OUR TIME (1944).

[325] DANI RODRIK, STRAIGHT TALK ON TRADE: IDEAS FOR A SANE WORLD ECONOMY (2017).

[326] *Id.* at 12.

[327] David H. Autor, David Dorn & Gordon H. Hanson, *The China Shock: Learning from Labor Market Adjustment to Large Changes in Trade*, 8 ANN. REV. ECON. 205 (2016); Autor et al., *supra* note 285; JACOB HACKER, THE GREAT RISK SHIFT: THE NEW ECONOMIC INSECURITY AND THE DECLINE OF THE AMERICAN DREAM (2014).

[328] Adam Przeworski, *The Poor and the Viability of Democracy*, *in* POVERTY, PARTICIPATION, AND DEMOCRACY: A GLOBAL PERSPECTIVE 125, 125–134 (Anirudh Krishna ed., 2008).

economic liberalism from the risks of overreach. Domestic social welfare policies can be combined with policies that combat harmful tax avoidance and deter social dumping through trade.[329] In this way, governments would enhance their ability to fund domestic initiatives, and capital would have greater incentives to work with domestic labor representatives and not move or threaten to move offshore to jurisdictions without protections. Such a shift does not signify a return to sovereignty-based norms, as advocated by economic nationalists, populists, and authoritarians. Transnational processes will remain critical for the advancement of economic and social rights, the coordination of policies to combat tax evasion and avoidance, and the bolstering of economic resilience and sustainability. These policies should be viewed as part of a broader complementary package in support of rule-of-law goals.

Finally, the rising challenges to democracy and the rule of law are more than economic. They also reflect cultural backlash against the relative success of liberal, pluralist norms from those who feel a loss of status or a sense that their ways of life are under threat.[330] Immigration becomes an easy target, reflecting rising social cleavages in the United States and Europe.[331] Norms of social community, solidarity, and cooperation decline.[332] Minorities and foreigners become scapegoats, creating social conditions ripe for authoritarianism. Hannah Arendt's analysis of the rise of totalitarianism in the twentieth century is chillingly foreboding:

> The preparation has succeeded when people have lost contact with their fellow men as well as the reality around them; for together with these contacts, men lose the capacity of both experience and thought. The ideal subject of totalitarian rule is not the convinced Nazi or the convinced Communist, but people for whom the distinction between fact and fiction (i.e., the reality of experience) and the distinction between true and false (i.e., the standards of thought) no longer exist . . . . It [totalitarianism] bases itself on loneliness, on the experience of not belonging to the world at all, which is among the most radical and desperate experiences of man.[333]

329 Gregory Shaffer, *Retooling Trade Agreements for Social Inclusion*, 2019 Ill. L. Rev. 1.

330 Pippa Norris & Ronald Inglehart, Cultural Backlash: Trump, Brexit, and Authoritarian Populism 14 (2019).

331 *Id.* at 18.

332 Robert D. Putnam, Bowling Alone: The Collapse and Revival of American Community (2001).

333 Arendt, *supra* note 4, at 474–75.

Today, populist, nativist politicians and partisan media capitalize on and stoke anxieties through a politics of fear, anger, and resentment,[334] giving rise to Schmittian friend–enemy politics of social identity.[335] Climate change, political repression, war, and other crises will spur further migration, potentially heightening social conflict.[336] The policy implications are challenging. Economists generally maintain that societies economically benefit from increased migration, but the domestic politics continue to raise barriers, indeed physical walls.[337] To start, policies addressing rising economic inequality and social precarity could help stem such cultural backlash. Yet, those policy changes also face political blockages.

It is not for this chapter to provide definitive responses to the rise of populism and the decline of the rule of law around the world. Our central aim is to show how international norms and institutions interact with domestic ones, and how they can do so in positive as well as in unintended and negative ways, including by exacerbating inequality, empowering populists, and thereby undermining rule-of-law goals. Policies to counter existing trends need to be adopted at both the domestic and international levels to advance rule-of-law objectives. At the national level, they need to be responsive to and calibrated for local contexts to ensure social and economic inclusion, local engagement, and thus legitimacy.

## V Conclusion

History is not linear. It involves cycles of advances and retrenchments in light of ongoing struggles. Rule-of-law protections that temper the arbitrary exercise of power are under challenge globally. In contrast, rule by law – the deploying of legal rules to serve the interests of autocratic power-holders – is on the rise. One of the critical challenges is how to stabilize and then revitalize rule-of-law principles and institutions within countries where they are under assault. An interlinked challenge is to

334 Jean L. Cohen, *Populism and the Politics of Resentment*, 1 Jus Cogens 5 (2019).

335 Theda Skocpol & Vanessa Williamson, The Tea Party and the Remaking of the Republican Party 54–74 (2016). *See* Carl Schmitt, The Concept of the Political (1932) (defining the political in terms of the distinction of friend and enemy).

336 Gaia Vince, Nomad Century: How Climate Migration Will Reshape Our World (2022).

337 Beth Simmons & Michael Kenwick, *Border Orientation in a Globalizing World*, 66 Am. J. Pol. Sci. 853 (2021).

reinforce and recalibrate regional and international legal norms and institutions, which are also under stress, in order to support the rule of law domestically.

To address these challenges, we must conceptualize and empirically study the rule of law in transnational context. Most rule-of-law scholarship does not engage transnational processes. The analytic framework of transnational legal ordering and transnational legal orders, in contrast, foregrounds them. The rule of law affects all substantive areas implicated by these processes, shaping legal practice and its consequences.

Although the concept of the rule of law applies ultimately to the protection of individuals from the arbitrary exercise of power, and thus is not focused on interstate relations per se, international law and international institutions are critical in an interconnected world. They directly and indirectly implicate rule-of-law practices in light of the normative and material resources that they provide. Challenges to the rule of law are part of broader domestic and international contests over governing norms and institutions, which have transnational implications. This book makes the case that trends at the national and international levels enmesh, and they can reinforce a turn toward or away from rule-of-law goals and practices. By expanding our understanding of these transnational dynamics, we hope to contribute to the assessment and recalibration of means to advance rule-of-law goals.

# 2

# Why Sovereigns Are Entitled to (Horizontal) Benefits of the International Rule of Law

BRIAN Z. TAMANAHA

## I Introduction

A decade ago, Jeremy Waldron published an influential article arguing that sovereign states are not entitled to the benefits of the rule of law. Pared to the core, his argument is: (1) "the point of the ROL [rule of law] is to protect individual values like liberty, dignity, etc.";[1] (2) "the 'true' subjects of IL [international law] are really human individuals (billions of them)";[2] (3) in domestic legal systems, government officials and agencies are not entitled to rule-of-law protections like private individuals;[3] (4) sovereign states should be seen as "officials" or "agents" of the international law system rather than as subjects;[4] and (5) "then maybe it is inappropriate to think that sovereign states are entitled to the same ROL protections at the international level as individuals are entitled to at the municipal level."[5] This narrow construction, I argue in this chapter, is an unwarranted and undesirable theoretical limitation of the benefits of national and international rule of law.

A few words about the current Russian invasion of Ukraine will help set up this argument. Russian president Vladimir Putin justified the invasion as necessary to protect Russian-speaking residents of the Donbas region (who he claims want to be part of Russia) from genocide

For very helpful critical comments on earlier drafts, I thank Gregory Shaffer, Wayne Sandholtz, Tom Ginsburg, and participants at the University of California, Irvine School of Law symposium on the rule of law in transnational context.

1 Jeremy Waldron, *Are Sovereigns Entitled to the Benefit of the International Rule of Law?*, 22 Eur. J. Int'l L. 315, 322 (2011).

2 *Id.* at 315.

3 *Id.* at 322–23.

4 *Id.* at 327–32.

5 *Id.* at 315.

by Ukraine; he claimed that Ukraine is not a genuine state but a historic part of greater Russia, and that NATO's expansion into Eastern Europe is a threat to Russia's security.[6] The UN General Assembly voted overwhelmingly to condemn Russia's invasion as a violation of Article 2(4) of the UN Charter prohibiting the use of force against the territorial integrity and political independence of another state.[7] The first line of the resolution states: "Reaffirming the paramount importance of the Charter of the United Nations *in the promotion of the rule of law among nations.*"[8] Ukraine filed a complaint against Russia at the International Court of Justice (ICJ), arguing that Russia falsely claimed Ukraine was committing genocide as a pretext for its invasion. By a vote of 13 to 2 (the dissenting judges were from Russia and China), the ICJ ordered that "[t]he Russian Federation shall immediately suspend the military operations."[9] Russia has ignored this order. After holding a "referendum" in areas under its occupation, Putin signed a law annexing nearly 20 percent of Ukrainian territory, proclaiming it part of Russia.[10] The UN General Assembly rejected this purported annexation as illegal under international law by a vote of 143 to 4 (with 35 abstentions).[11]

Waldron is likely aghast at the murderous and horrifically destructive Russian invasion of Ukraine. Still, those who argue that sovereign states are not subjects entitled to the benefits of the international rule of law should be given pause by this latest reminder of the danger that states pose to one another and their populaces. They should consider why states view actions like this as a violation of the rule of law, and consider whether granting states the benefits of the rule of law has important positive consequences.

On descriptive, theoretical, and normative grounds, I argue that sovereign states, along with all persons and entities, should be regarded as subjects fully entitled to all benefits of international rule of law. Part II

[6] *See Extracts from Putin's Speech on Ukraine*, Reuters (Feb. 21, 2022, 12:39 PM), www.reuters.com/world/europe/extracts-putins-speech-ukraine-2022-02-21/.

[7] G.A. Res. A/ES-11/L.1 (Mar. 1, 2022).

[8] *Id.* at 1 (emphasis added).

[9] Press Release, Allegations of Genocide Under the Convention on the Prevention and Punishment of the Crime of Genocide (Ukr. v. Russ. Fed'n), I.C.J. Unofficial Press Release No. 2022/11 (Mar. 16, 2022), www.icj-cij.org/public/files/case-related/182/182-20220316-PRE-01-00-EN.pdf.

[10] Jonathan Landay & Felix Hoske, *Putin Finalises 'Annexation' in Ukraine Even as Troops Flee Front*, Reuters (Oct. 5, 2022, 6:37 PM), https://tinyurl.com/2cvhf2c9.

[11] Bill Chappell, *Only 4 Countries Side with Russia as UN Rejects Annexations in Ukraine*, NPR (Oct. 13, 2022, 9:49 AM), www.npr.org/2022/10/13/1128642820/un-rejects-russian-annexations-ukraine.

elaborates the fundamental international law principle of sovereign autonomy, comprising a nested arrangement that protects both states and individuals. Depicting the rule of law as the ideal of a legally ordered community, Part III shows that the rule of law advances several vertical and horizontal functions – not only individual liberty. Part IV reveals that Waldron overlooked the horizontal rule of law treatment of government within domestic legal systems. Articulating the international rule of law as the ideal of the legal ordering of the international community, Part V argues that sovereign states already are, and should be, entitled to the benefits of the international rule of law. Part VI closes the chapter with brief comments about how this understanding is well suited to addressing the emerging transnational legal order. In the course of this critical engagement with Waldron's position, I lay out a broad understanding of the rule of law that applies within states and the international community.

## II International Law's Nested Dualism of States and Individuals

"The *real* purpose of IL and, in my view, of the ROL in the international realm is not the protection of sovereign states but the protection of the populations committed to their charge,"[12] Waldron asserts. This stance, however, tends to erase the pivotal role international law accords to states, protecting state autonomy as well as individuals in a nested arrangement.[13] Respect for state sovereignty, noninterference, and sovereign equality are fundamental principles of international law that enable states to serve their responsibilities to their populations. Primary responsibility for the protection of individuals in this arrangement is accorded to the nation-state, while direct protection for individuals under international law is largely limited to human rights.

This nested arrangement has long been a staple of international law. Samuel Pufendorf articulated a view variously expressed by many theorists in the past four centuries during the consolidation of the state system: "[T]he over-riding purpose of states is that, by mutual cooperation and assistance, men may be safe from the losses and injuries which they may and often do inflict on each other."[14] Emer de Vattel, an influential early

[12] Waldron, *supra* note 1, at 325 (emphasis added).

[13] *See* Carmen E. Pavel, *The International Rule of Law*, 23 Critical Rev. Int'l Soc. & Pol. Phil. 332 (2019) (arguing that international law protects individuals and the autonomy of states).

[14] Samuel Pufendorf, On the Duty of Man and Citizen According to Natural Law 139 (Michael Silverthorne trans., Cambridge Univ. Press 1991) (1673).

international law writer, similarly held that nations are "societies of men united together for the purpose of promoting their mutual safety and advantage by the joint efforts of their combined strength."[15] The duty of the state is to ensure the safety and welfare of the populace.[16] "States are now widely understood to be instruments at the service of their peoples, and not vice versa," observed UN secretary-general Kofi Annan.[17]

Sovereign states discharge this duty through the right and power to act on behalf of their populace both internally and externally. "It is an evident consequence of the liberty and independence of nations, that all have a right to be governed as they think proper, and that no state has the smallest right to interfere with the government of another," Vattel observed.[18] "The sovereign is he to whom the nation has entrusted the empire and the care of the government," he continued. "It does not then belong to any foreign power to take cognizance of the administration of that sovereign, to set himself up for a judge of his conduct, and to oblige him to alter it."[19] Immanuel Kant's fifth article for peace among nations declares: "No state shall violently interfere with the constitution and administration of another."[20] Article 2(4) of the UN Charter codifies this position: "All Members shall refrain in their international relations from the threat or use of force against the territorial integrity or political independence of any state, or in any other manner inconsistent with the Purposes of the United Nations." Consistent with this position, the ICJ asserted: "Every State possesses a fundamental right to choose and implement its own political, economic and social systems."[21]

The right of sovereign states to noninterference is upheld, not out of a naive faith in states or misplaced dedication to sovereignty as an abstract notion, but because it serves several crucial purposes. A major impetus in the development of international law was to diminish incessant wars in Europe and the carnage they wrought on civilian populations. Wars of aggression occur when a state (or coalition of states) seeks to expand its territory or access to resources by conquering or

[15] Emer de Vattel, The Law of Nations 67 (Béla Kapossy & Richard Whatmore eds., Liberty Fund 2008) (1797).

[16] Pufendorf, *supra* note 14, at 151; Vattel, *supra* note 15, at 97.

[17] *See* Chapter 1.

[18] Vattel, *supra* note 15, at 289.

[19] *Id.* at 290.

[20] Immanuel Kant, Perpetual Peace: A Philosophical Essay 112 (M. Campbell Smith trans., George Allen & Unwin 1903) (1795).

[21] Military and Paramilitary Activities in and Against Nicaragua (Nicar. v. U.S.), Judgment, 1986 I.C.J. Rep. 14, ¶ 131 (June 27).

absorbing or controlling another state or its territory; and also when a governing regime feels its internal hold on power is threatened by rising internal discontent or by aggression from another state, which it attacks to rally the populace and to reduce the perceived external threat. Respect for sovereignty and noninterference protects individuals by dampening wars.

Nonetheless, many international law scholars (particularly from Western societies) disfavor sovereignty[22] – a shield behind which states all too often abuse their own citizens – and insist that the *primary* objective of international law is to protect individuals. Carmen Pavel argues that state autonomy has no intrinsic value of its own: "State autonomy is valuable to the extent it protects individual autonomy."[23] This position links state sovereignty to a deeper ultimate purpose that provides a critical standard and justification for outsiders coercively penetrating state autonomy when necessary to protect citizens from bad actions by their own governing regime.

Owing to conflicting interests, mutual distrust, nationalist sentiments, global pluralism of values, and the prioritization of peace, however, it is not acceptable to penetrate state sovereignty for other than the most blatant violations of human rights. States are not in a position to determine in an unbiased way – one not colored by their own interests and values – whether or when other states are in fact serving or harming their citizens. The leaders of every state are skeptical and critical of the actions of other states (including allies), while at the same time they reject criticisms from others of their own conduct. Officials in the United States, Germany, and Japan, no less than officials in Russia and China, and every other country, insist that they, and they alone, are in the best position to recognize and advance the interests of their populace. All states legislate morality, set up economic and political systems, specify the status of religion, impose criminal law and taxation, create and utilize coercive policing, restrict political opposition within certain parameters, and limit protests by citizens, in certain states suppressing the press (through criminal or civil sanctions) or using brutal crackdowns in the name of maintaining public security and order. In these and other matters states make choices and take actions that other states do differently. Self-determination and political and moral pluralism – which give

[22] Brad Roth, Sovereign Equality and Moral Disagreement: Premises of a Pluralist Legal Order 3 (2011).

[23] Pavel, *supra* note 13.

rise to contrasting views of substantive justice and the common good within societies – are moral considerations that underlie sovereign autonomy.[24] Finally, coercively penetrating sovereignty may provoke a violent backlash by the governing regime, leading to further abuses and possibly outright war.

State sovereignty and noninterference have become entrenched in the primary international law principle of sovereign equality: all states must be treated equally in their capacity to act on behalf of their respective populations (self-determination) and all states enjoy the same legal rights as sovereigns within international law.[25] What sovereign equality means, Arthur Watts wrote, "is that since all States are sovereign, they are thus neither subject to any external authority nor themselves possessors of authority or pre-eminence over other States, and are accordingly in those respects in principle legally equal with one another as members of the international community."[26] Sovereign equality is especially necessary to protect weak states against the coercive intrusions of powerful states.[27] The 2012 declaration of the high-level meeting of the UN General Assembly on the rule of law emphasized: "We rededicate ourselves to support all efforts to uphold the sovereign equality of all states, to respect their territorial integrity and political independence . . . ."[28] A country-by-country study by Noora Arajarvi found that nonaligned countries (120 in total) collectively and individually have "consistently demanded that the international rule of law must be anchored in the principle of sovereign equality."[29]

Russia and China have affirmed the principle of "sovereign equality," which includes that "[s]tates enjoy their rights on the basis of independence and on an equal footing" along with "the principle of non-intervention in the internal or external affairs of States."[30] A joint statement they issued three weeks before Russia's invasion of Ukraine states:

[24] For an account, see ROTH, *supra* note 22.

[25] *See* Stéphane Beaulac, *The Rule of Law in International Law Today*, *in* RELOCATING THE RULE OF LAW 197, 209–12 (Gianluigi Palombella & Neil Walker eds., 2009).

[26] Arthur Watts, *The International Rule of Law*, 36 GER. Y.B. INT'L L. 15, 31 (1993).

[27] ROTH, *supra* note 22, at 13–15.

[28] G.A. Res. A/67/L.1, ¶ 3 (Sept. 19, 2012) [hereinafter Rule of Law Declaration]. *See also* Part V.

[29] Noora Arajarvi, *The Core Requirements of the International Rule of Law in the Practice of States*, 13 HAGUE J. ON RULE L. 173, 183 (2021).

[30] *See* Kenneth Anderson, *Text of Russia–China Joint Declaration Promotion and Principles of International Law*, LAWFARE (July 7, 2016, 7:18 AM), https://tinyurl.com/5eu4sfv8; *see also* Joint Statement of the Russian Federation and the People's Republic of China on the International Relations Entering a New Era and the Global Sustainable Development,

> The sides [Russia and China] believe that the advocacy of democracy and human rights must not be used to put pressure on other countries. They oppose the abuse of democratic values and interference in the internal affairs of sovereign states under the pretext of protecting democracy and human rights, and any attempts to incite divisions and confrontation in the world. The sides call on the international community to respect cultural and civilizational diversity and the rights of peoples of different countries to self-determination.
>
> The sides [Russia and China] note that the Charter of the United Nations and the Universal Declaration of Human Rights set noble goals in the area of universal human rights, set forth fundamental principles, which all the States must comply with and observe in deeds. At the same time, as every nation has its own unique national features, history, culture, social system and level of social and economic development, universal nature of human rights should be seen through the prism of the real situation in every particular country, and human rights should be protected in accordance with the specific situation in each country and the needs of its population.[31]

Significantly, Russia and China affirm their commitment to international law and human rights, as well as their obligation to serve their populace; they also support democracy, tailored to the conditions of each society. Russia contends that its conduct in Ukraine is justified under international law, as described at the outset. On its treatment of Uyghurs, which has received international condemnation, China denies that it has mass imprisonment camps and insists that the Uyghurs who have been detained have engaged in terroristic acts. Their joint statement contends that foreign critics are imposing their own values and agenda, failing to respect the unique cultural, social, economic, political, and legal circumstances of Russia and China.

Skepticism about Western motives has ample grounds. Many examples of uses and abuses of international law by Western countries to bludgeon other societies can be cited, from Western colonization of large parts of the globe, to the United States invasion of Iraq to topple Saddam Hussein, to torture of detainees by the Bush administration.[32] The Chinese no doubt recall the Opium War, in which Britain seized control of Hong Kong and, in the name of international law and free trade, forced China to allow in opium brought by the British East India Company.[33] International law was

Official Internet Res. of the President of Russia (Feb. 4, 2022), http://en.kremlin.ru/supplement/5770 [hereinafter Joint Statement].

31 Joint Statement, *supra* note 30, § III.

32 *See* Ian Hurd, *The International Rule of Law: Law and the Limits of Politics*, 28 Ethics & Int'l Affs. 39, 48 (2014).

33 *See* C.A. Bayly, The Birth of the Modern World 1780–1914: Global Connections and Comparisons 137–38 (2004).

born of European notions and practices that were applied as standards to adjudge other nations.[34] As Terry Nardin describes, this "generated a bifurcated international order: an egalitarian horizontal international law for relations between European states and a hierarchical imperial law for relations between European and non-European peoples."[35] International lawyers may insist (exasperatedly) that this is all in the past and not relevant today, but the invasion of Iraq is a recent event, not to mention ongoing US drone strikes in other nations without their permission.[36] In an article on the international rule of law, James Crawford, a prominent international lawyer who subsequently served on the ICJ, wryly commented: "The United States these days appears to apply the policy: international law for others and not for itself."[37]

Past and present illegal actions by Western states, of course, do not absolve Russia and China of their own violations of international law. States regularly make factual claims and offer legal justifications for their actions that are not true or not consistent with international law. The factual premises of the US invasion of Iraq were false, and its overthrow of the government and subsequent occupation violated Iraq's sovereignty, resulting in the deaths of several hundred thousand Iraqi civilians from war-related causes.[38] Russia's invasion and attempted annexation of eastern and southern Ukraine patently violates the territorial integrity of Ukraine, and its deliberate attacks on civilians are war crimes;[39] and strong evidence has been compiled that China is violating the human rights of Uyghurs.[40]

[34] *See* Brian Z. Tamanaha, *What Is International Law?*, *in* A Realistic Theory of Law 151 (2017).

[35] Terry Nardin, *Theorising the International Rule of Law*, 34 Rev. Int'l Stud. 385, 388 (2008).

[36] Peter Baker et. al., *U.S. Drone Strike Kills Ayman al-Zawahri, Top Qaeda Leader*, N.Y. Times (Aug. 1, 2022), www.nytimes.com/2022/08/01/us/politics/al-qaeda-strike-afghanistan.html.

[37] James Crawford, *International Law and the Rule of Law*, 24 Adel. L. Rev. 3, 8 (2003).

[38] *See* Philip Bump, *15 Years After the Iraq War Began, the Death Toll Is Still Murky*, Wash. Post (Mar. 20, 2018), https://tinyurl.com/eyju4827.

[39] *See* Missy Ryan et al., *Russia Strikes Kyiv and Cities Across Ukraine After Crimea Bridge Attack*, Wash. Post (Oct. 10, 2022), www.washingtonpost.com/world/2022/10/10/kyiv-missile-strikes-russia-ukraine-war/; Masha Gessen, *The Prosecution of Russian War Crimes in Ukraine*, New Yorker (Aug. 8, 2022), www.newyorker.com/magazine/2022/08/08/the-prosecution-of-russian-war-crimes-in-ukraine.

[40] Off. of the High Comm'r for Hum. Rts., OHCHR Assessment of Human Rights Concerns in the Xinjiang Uyghur Autonomous Region, People's Republic of China (Aug. 31, 2022), https://tinyurl.com/ywkenkvs.

The point of this discussion is that, owing to well-founded concerns about wars, conflicting interests, a mutual lack of trust, nationalism, contrasting political and moral values, and the depredations of powerful states on weak states, international law constructs a nested dual arrangement in which states have the primary duty to protect their populace and are shielded from coercive foreign interference in their treatment of their own citizens (except when this treatment rises to the level of flagrant and extreme human rights violations, and even then with great reluctance). This arrangement gives a state regime great scope to harm its populace – a sadly common occurrence but no other approach is currently viable. For these reasons, the preservation of state autonomy within a community of states is a direct objective of international law, even as it strives to protect individuals.

Waldron may be correct that "*ultimately*, international law is oriented to the well-being of human individuals, rather than the freedom of states."[41] But international law serves this goal via protections for state autonomy and equal sovereignty to act on behalf of citizens. Protections for state sovereigns, I argue below, are and should be included within the benefits of the international rule of law *for the good of individuals* in societies around the world.

## III Horizontal and Vertical Functions of the Rule of Law

Disagreement over what the rule of law means and its defining features, requirements, and purposes is endemic.[42] Even greater disagreement exists over the rule of law in the international context – including doubts about whether the rule of law applies beyond the nation-state.[43] Given this pervasive state of disagreement, declarations about the rule of law should be taken, not as generally agreed-upon descriptive or conceptual

[41] Jeremy Waldron, *The Rule of International Law*, 30 HARV. J.L. & PUB. POL'Y 15, 25 (2006) (emphasis added).

[42] *See generally* BRIAN Z. TAMANAHA, ON THE RULE OF LAW: HISTORY, POLITICS, THEORY (2004).

[43] The literature on international rule of law has ballooned in recent decades. *See* Leander Beinlich & Anne Peters, *An International Rule of Law*, OXFORD BIBLIOGRAPHIES (Aug. 25, 2021), https://tinyurl.com/35kaavma. Along with other articles on the topic cited in this chapter, illuminating recent articles include Robert McCorquodale, *Defining the International Rule of Law: Defying Gravity?*, 65 INT'L & COMP. L.Q. 277 (2016); Ian Hurd, *The International Rule of Law and the Domestic Analogy*, 4 GLOB. CONST. 365 (2015); Simon Chesterman, *An International Rule of Law?*, 56 AM. J. COMP. L. 331 (2008); Paul Burgess, *Deriving the International Rule of Law: An Unnecessary, Impractical, and Unhelpful Exercise*, 10 TRANSNAT'L LEGAL THEORY 65 (2019); Richard Collins, *Two Idea(l)s of the International Rule of Law*, 8 GLOB. CONST. 191 (2019); Nardin, *supra* note 35.

claims, but as arguments offered by theorists to persuade others about how the rule of law *should* be understood.

When evaluating these arguments, one must be wary of shifts from conditional assertions to unconditional assertions. Early in his essay, Waldron states: "We usually say that the point of the ROL is to protect individual values like liberty, dignity etc."[44] ("Usually" is a conditional assertion.) It is true that many theorists highlight liberty and dignity – Waldron calls it "Hayekian freedom"[45] – though there is no consensus that this is *the* point. Later in the essay, Waldron puts it in stronger terms: "[T]he *whole point* of the ROL is to secure individual freedom . . . . To eliminate uncertainty in the interests of freedom and to furnish an environment conducive to the exercise of individual autonomy – that is the *raison d'etre* of the ROL."[46] But this statement is too unequivocal for a concept that Waldron himself famously called "essentially contested."[47] And this assertion carries much of his argument. Once he identifies *the* point of the rule of law as advancing individual autonomy, and *the* purpose of international law as being to protect individuals, it all but follows that states are not entitled to the benefits of international rule of law – since states are not individuals and, Waldron emphasizes, "are not the bearers of ultimate value."[48]

Martin Krygier, another influential rule-of-law theorist, recognizes that "many problems have been identified for the rule of law to solve."[49] "And in truth, all sorts of goods are today claimed to flow from it – e.g., economic development, human rights, and democracy."[50] While rule of law is linked to various benefits and solutions to various problems, he writes: "Rule of law traditions have particularly focused on arbitrary exercise of power, often using precisely that word, as the antihero in the rule of law story."[51] Krygier identifies the *telos* of the rule of law as restraining the arbitrary exercise of power, and he analyzes various implications of seeing the rule of law in terms of this end.[52]

[44] Waldron, *supra* note 1, at 322.
[45] *Id.* at 339; *see also id.* at 338 n.71.
[46] *Id.* at 338 (emphasis added).
[47] Jeremy Waldron, *Is the Rule of Law an Essentially Contested Concept (in Florida)?*, 21 L. & PHIL. 137 (2002).
[48] Waldron, *supra* note 41, at 24.
[49] Martin Krygier, *The Rule of Law: Pasts, Presents, and Two Possible Futures*, 12 ANN. REV. L. & SOC. SCI. 199, 203 (2016).
[50] *Id.* at 215.
[51] *Id.* at 203.
[52] *See also* Martin Krygier, *The Rule of Law: Legality, Teleology, Sociology*, *in* RELOCATING THE RULE OF LAW, *supra* note 25, at 45.

Presenting the rule of law in terms of a *singular* purpose or point or end is problematic for several reasons. To start with, various purposes have been identified by theorists, including Waldron and Krygier, who correctly assert that theories about the rule of law have often referred to the (different) purpose each highlights. But centering on liberty produces different emphases and implications for the rule of law than centering on restraining the arbitrary exercise of power. Why pick one as *the* end when both have been identified for sound reasons? Furthermore, the assertion that the rule of law serves a specific purpose (*telos*) that explains its existence (*raison d'etre*) fits uneasily with how the rule of law has come about. The rule of law (whatever it means) was not designed or created by anyone for a particular purpose, but rather evolved over centuries owing to a confluence of beliefs, motivations, circumstances, and institutional developments in connection with cultural, religious, economic, political, legal, and other factors.[53] Every rule-of-law society has a unique history, institutional arrangement, and set of consequences. Assertions about *the* purpose is a projection by given theorists based on their particular priorities. For instance, consistent with his liberal commitment to economic liberty and his antagonism to the social welfare state, Hayek proclaimed that the rule of law is about individual freedom.[54] Another objection to claims about *the* purpose or point is that that social institutions commonly have multiple uses and do various things, so selecting one downplays or obscures others that may also be significant. Encompassing various functions provides a fuller understanding and appreciation of the rule of law at the national and international levels. In a study of historical and conceptual discussions of the rule of law, Richard Fallon gleans three purposes: "to protect against anarchy and establish a scheme of public order, to allow people to plan their affairs with advance knowledge of the legal consequences, and to protect against at least some types of official arbitrariness."[55]

Rather than project a single purpose, let us instead focus on function, understood in terms of what the rule of law does (its effects). Bypassing the theoretical impasse over definition and elements, my starting point is a basic proposition about when the rule of law exists: *the rule of law exists*

[53] *See* TAMANAHA, *supra* note 42.

[54] *Id.* at 65–71.

[55] Richard H. Fallon, *"The Rule of Law" as a Concept in Constitutional Discourse*, 97 COLUM. L. REV. 1, 42–43 (1997).

*in a society when government officials and legal subjects are bound by and abide by law.* "Legal subject" includes people as well as entities with legal personality (i.e., corporations, organizations, states, etc.) that engage in actions addressed by the law. The rule of law, then, is an *ideal* that strives to achieve an *effective legal ordering within a community.* As I show, this conception of the rule of law applies within states as well as at the international level.

This formulation does not reduce the rule of law to simply following the law. It is the ideal of a legally ordered community. Law does not address all actions and no society is completely legally ordered – matters not regulated by law always exist and legal violations always occur. This ideal is actualized as a matter of degree; its degree of achievement varies across locations as well as across areas of legal regulation (economic transactions, criminal conduct, government actions, etc.); and it is achieved to a greater extent in rule-of-law societies than at the international level.

Now let me summarily identify five major functions of an effective legal ordering within a community grounded in the ideal of universally binding law (others functions may exist as well).[56] The first two functions, as Waldon and Krygier respectively assert, is that the rule of law *enhances individual freedom and dignity*, and *restrains the arbitrary exercise of power.*[57] A third crucial function the rule of law provides is overall *security* and *trust* that one is protected from intentional and negligent injuries by others, that one's property is protected, that economic exchanges will be effective, that the government will carry out its duties, and so forth, allowing actors to rely upon the presence of legal rules and institutions that protect, enable, and stand behind their activities in case something goes wrong.[58] A fourth function is that rule of law in modern society gives rise to (*constructs* or *constitutes*) a multitude of institutions and relationships in society – from the creation of corporations, to property ownership and contractual relations, to business transactions, to employment relations, to the creation and operation of government and private organizations, and vastly more. Fifth, drawing on the preceding functions, the rule of law *enhances economic development.*

All five functions matter greatly. Personal liberty is important, to be sure, but theorists inclined to prioritize individual liberty among these various benefits should recognize that not all cultures and circumstances

[56] *See* Brian Z. Tamanaha, *Functions of the Rule of Law, in* THE CAMBRIDGE COMPANION TO THE RULE OF LAW 221 (Jens Meierhenrich & Marttin Loughlin eds., 2021).

[57] *Id.*

[58] *Id.* at 222–23.

share this priority, nor is it obviously the most fundamental. Protection from arbitrary government power is essential, though other threats and concerns exist. If a pervasive lack of security and trust prevails, social interaction would be limited and productive activities would freeze. Large scale societies function vastly more effectively thanks to the constitutive power of law. Economic development provides basics like food, water, clothes, shelter, sanitation, medical care, and education, which are prerequisites to exercising freedom.

For the purposes of analysis, it is useful to subdivide these functions into two perspectives on the rule of law: *vertical* and *horizontal*. The vertical perspective emphasizes coercive government treatment of citizens, whereas the horizontal perspective emphasizes actions and intercourse within society. The first two functions identified above – enhancing liberty and restraining arbitrary power – are based on the vertical perspective, derived from liberalism's concerns about government tyranny and individual liberty.[59] The other three functions – bringing security and trust, constituting relations and institutions, and enhancing economic development – are based on the horizontal perspective that encompasses the benefits of the rule of law within society generally.[60] The horizontal benefits of the rule of law are enjoyed by *all* actors within society, including the state, and, as explained shortly, they have particular relevance to the international rule of law.

## IV What Waldron Overlooked When Excluding Sovereigns

Waldron's argument that states are not subjects entitled to the benefit of the rule of law is sophisticated and lengthy, so only a summary of his core points can be provided here. As mentioned, he identifies *the* purpose of the rule of law as enhancing individual freedom, and *the* purpose of international law as protecting individuals.[61] He points out that since the rule of law is about placing legal restraints on government in furtherance of individual liberty, its primary thrust is to constrain the liberty of government. "Governmental freedom is not the *raison d'etre* of the

[59] For a discussion of liberal understandings of the rule of law, see BRIAN Z. TAMANAHA, *Liberalism*, *in* ON THE RULE OF LAW: HISTORY, POLITICS, THEORY, *supra* note 42, at 32.

[60] To be illustrated and supported by the author's article "Vertical and Horizontal Dimensions of the Rule of Law," in progress as of this writing.

[61] Waldron, *supra* note 1, at 322–24.

ROL."[62] Waldron challenges the conventional analogy between states in the international community under international law and the position of individuals within society under domestic law. This analogy is misleading, he contends, for "it must be understood that the state is not *just* a subject of international law; it is additionally both a *source* and an *official* of international law."[63] So "regulating a sovereign state in international law is more like regulating a law-maker in municipal law than like regulating a private individual."[64] Sovereign states at the international level have the same potential for governmental abuse that the domestic rule of law guards against.[65]

> The governmental character of the nation-state does not evaporate when we move up a level to the international realm. It remains a governmental entity the dangerousness of which continues to generate ROL concerns. We may also have ROL concerns about IL and international institutions apart from nation-states, but most of those ROL concerns will be motivated by our interest in the well-being, liberty, and dignity of natural human individuals, who are vulnerable directly or indirectly to IL in various ways, not by our interest in the freedom of action of natural sovereigns.[66]

It follows, therefore, that sovereigns are not entitled to the benefits of the rule of law.

A notable feature of Waldron's analysis is the determinative weight he places on the domestic rule of law in his analysis of the international rule of law. He does not seriously contemplate whether or how the rule of law in such different arenas can be understood on their own terms.[67] Before suggesting an alternative starting point for the international rule of law in Part V, this discussion identifies an aspect of domestic rule of law that Waldron overlooked, tied to the horizontal benefits of the rule of law identified above.

Waldron overlooks that a comparable coexistence of official capacity and legal subject also holds in the national context: government entities operate in public roles while exercising rights as legal subjects in their various activities. At the domestic level, recognition that government officials are limited by law, as the rule of law holds, does not diminish or

[62] *Id.* at 339.
[63] Waldron, *supra* note 41, at 23.
[64] *Id.*
[65] *See id.* at 20–26; Waldron, *supra* note 1, at 327–37.
[66] Waldron, *supra* note 1, at 342.
[67] For an argument that the domestic understanding of the rule of law does not fit the international arena, see Hurd, *supra* note 43.

detract from the benefits the government obtains through the rule of law in its activities like any other actor within a legally ordered society. To put this point in terms of the preceding discussion, Waldron's conception of government in the national context was limited to the vertical dimension of the rule of law that emphasizes legal limits on government actions against the populace, but he ignored the horizontal dimension of the rule of law in which government benefits from the rule of law. Within domestic legal systems, the horizontal dimension operates vis-à-vis private actors (people and entities), and vis-à-vis other government entities.

In its interaction with private actors, the government itself relies heavily on, and benefits from, a legally bound order because many of its daily activities are legally constituted and arranged. Think of government contracts with employees, suppliers of goods and services, banks for loans and bond issues, landlords for rental property rented for government use, and in other ways, utilizing law in its undertakings; ordinary tort law, property law, and criminal law also apply to and protect governmental activities and assets. The government benefits from the predictability, certainty, security, trust, and constitutive aspects achieved by an effective legal order. In myriad contexts when carrying out its public role, the government holds, utilizes, and exercises the same legal status and rights as all actors in society.

Governments also rely on and benefit from the legal ordering in their relations with other governmental entities in the furtherance of their public responsibilities. In the United States, individual states have sued other states on a variety of matters, including boundary disputes, distribution of water rights from shared rivers, harm from pollution, contract claims, acquisition of property from people who die without heirs, disputes over domicile for tax purposes.[68] Individual states have also brought suits against the federal government as well as against federal agencies in support of "the State's sovereign interest in the continued enforceability of state law."[69] And the United States has sued states on a variety of federal matters.[70]

Consider the situation as a coexisting bifurcation of governmental roles. In domestic rule-of-law systems, on the one hand, government officials are subject to legal restraints in their actions directed at citizens

[68] For lists of cases and claims, see *Controversies Between Two or More States*, Legal Info. Inst., https://tinyurl.com/y96sx5m7; *Suits Between Two or More States*, Justia, https://law.justia.com/constitution/us/article-3/29-suits-between-two-or-more-states.html.

[69] Tara Leigh Grove, *When Can a State Sue the United States?*, 101 Cornell L. Rev. 851, 865 (2016).

[70] *See Suits Against States*, Legal Info. Inst., www.law.cornell.edu/constitution-conan/article-3/section-2/clause-1/suits-against-states.

and entities (vertical dimension), and, on the other hand, governments are legal subjects with enforceable powers and rights like all actors (private and public) within a legally ordered community (horizontal dimension). The fact that we want government to be limited by law does not erase the fact that the government has rights as a legal subject entitled to equal treatment under law, to predictability and certainty, to the application of public, prospective rules, to an unbiased judge, and to all other aspects of the rule of law. Which aspect of this bifurcation matters in a given instance depends on what is at issue in that situation. This same coexisting bifurcation holds in the international arena.

## V Why International Rule of Law Does Benefit Sovereigns

A great deal of sophisticated theoretical analysis has been written on the international rule of law. Disagreement prevails. Every account of the rule of law – including the one I sketch here – is proffered by theorists in the conviction that their particular articulation is descriptively, theoretically, and/or normatively useful. Remember that political and legal theorists do not have exclusive or final authority over what the rule of law means. Many theoretical analyses are grounded on what theorists (Dicey, Hayek, Raz, Waldron, and others) have said about the rule of law, but it is an ideal shaped by how people collectively understand the rule of law. When states and other international actors repeatedly express their desire for and commitment to an international rule of law, it makes sense to try to discern what they mean by this, and in what sense it is achievable and desirable.

Waldron's position is substantially weakened by the fact that it contradicts past and recent pronouncements about the rule of law by actors on the international level, and is inconsistent with international law treatment of states. The UN General Assembly condemned Russia's aggression against Ukraine as a breach of "the rule of law among nations," in contravention of international law prohibitions against "the threat or use of force against the territorial integrity or political independence of any state."[71] The clear import of these statements is that Ukraine – in its status as sovereign state – is entitled to the benefits of the rule of law.

The unanimously adopted 2012 Declaration of the High-Level Meeting of the General Assembly on the Rule of Law at the National and International Levels expressed agreement in being "guided by the rule of law, as it is the *foundation of friendly and*

[71] G.A. Res. A/ES-11/L.1, at 1 (Mar. 1, 2022).

*equitable relations between States* and the basis on which just and fair societies are built."[72] Paragraph 2 specifies who is subject to, as well as benefits from, the rule of law:

> We recognize that the rule of law applies to all States equally, and to international organizations, including the United Nations and its principal organs, and that respect for and promotion of the rule of law and justice should guide all of their activities and accord predictability and legitimacy to their actions. We also recognize that *all persons, institutions and entities, public and private, including the State itself, are accountable* to just, fair and equitable laws *and are entitled without any discrimination to equal protection of the law.*[73]

Subsequent paragraphs reaffirm a commitment, consistent with the rule of law, to "all efforts to uphold sovereign equality of all States";[74] to respect for "territorial integrity and political independence";[75] to "non-interference in the internal affairs of states";[76] to refraining from the use of force against other states;[77] to the duty to peacefully settle disputes;[78] to the universal value of human rights and democracy;[79] to the belief that "the rule of law and development are strongly interrelated and mutually reinforcing" and necessary to eradicate poverty;[80] to recognizing "fair, stable and predictable legal frameworks" as necessary for international trade;[81] to the importance of international cooperation in combating transnational criminal networks (trafficking in drugs, money laundering, arms, people, terrorism);[82] and much more.

Three seminal points about the international rule of law stand out from these passages. First, they portray the rule of law as the basis for friendly and equitable relations among the international community of states. That is consistent with my characterization of the rule of law as an *ideal* that strives

72 Rule of Law Declaration, *supra* note 28, pmbl. (emphasis added). For a detailed look at the Declaration, noting that it followed extensive high-level discussions and was unanimously adopted, see Clemens A. Feinaugle, *The UN Declaration on the Rule of Law and the Application of the Rule of Law to the UN: A Reconstruction from an International Public Authority Perspective*, 7 GOETTINGEN J. INT'L L. 157 (2016).

73 Rule of Law Declaration, *supra* note 28, ¶ 2 (emphasis added).

74 *Id.* ¶ 3.

75 *Id.*

76 *Id.*

77 *Id.*

78 *Id.*

79 *Id.* ¶ 5.

80 *Id.* ¶ 7.

81 *Id.* ¶ 8.

82 *Id.* ¶¶ 24, 26.

to achieve an *effective legal ordering within a community*. Second, they state that *all* persons and entities in the international arena, explicitly including the state, are *bound by* law and also *entitled to* the protection of law. Under this formulation, the state is not treated differently from any other person or entity within the community, which is consistent with my earlier description of legal "subject" as covering both people and entities with legal personality (corporations, organizations, states, etc.) that engage in actions addressed by the law. Third, consistent with the expressed desire for friendly and equitable relations within the international community, the bulk of matters mentioned relate to the horizontal dimension of the rule of law. The passages emphasize respecting sovereignty in order to generate mutual security and trust, creating certainty and predictability for economic exchanges and development, and cooperating to fight crime and terrorism and control money flows – all of which are about the benefits of the rule of law to nations and international society. This account encompasses a number of rule-of-law benefits beyond enhancing individual freedom.

In fairness to Waldron, the Declaration was issued a year after his article, but this perspective on the international rule of law is not a recent development. Under the heading "Rule of Law," the 2005 UN World Summit Outcome stated:

> Recognizing the need for universal adherence to and implementation of the rule of law at both the national and international levels, we:
>
> (a) Reaffirm our commitment to the purposes and principles of the Charter and international law and to an international order based on the rule of law and international law, which is essential for peaceful coexistence and cooperation among States.[83]

Again, the rule of law is presented as the (horizontal) ordering of the community of states under international law. In 1970, a UN Declaration on Principles of International Law adopted by the General Assembly cited "the paramount importance of the Charter of the United Nations in the promotion of the rule of law among nations."[84] Commenting on this and similar statements, three decades ago, Arthur Watts observed that the international rule of law must be understood as "legal ordering of affairs within [the international] community."[85]

83 G.A. Res. 60/1, 2005 World Summit Outcome ¶ 134 (Oct. 24, 2005).

84 G.A. Res. 2625 (XXV) (Oct. 24, 1970), *quoted in* Watts, *supra* note 26, at 25.

85 Watts, *supra* note 26, at 25. Robert McCorquodale likewise defines the rule of law in terms of legal ordering, though he incorporates additional factors. McCorquodale, *supra* note 43, at 296.

"International society is a society of states; international law seeks to achieve the goals and values of that society; it does so primarily by regulating states," Anne-Marie Slaughter declared.[86] The vision of international law as a society of states subject to legal regulations matches Kant's celebrated outline of the conditions for perpetual peace:

> Nations, as states, may be judged like individuals who, living in the natural state of society – that is to say, uncontrolled by external law – injure one another through their very proximity. Every state, for the sake of its own security, may – and ought to – demand that its neighbour should submit itself to conditions, similar to those of civil society where the right of every individual is guaranteed.
>
> . . .
>
> For states, in their relation to one another, there can be, according to reason, no other way of advancing from that lawless condition which unceasing war implies, than by giving up their savage lawless freedom, just as individual men have done, and yielding to the coercion of public laws.[87]

In an article on international rule of law, Terry Nardin recognizes that "states can be subjects of law – 'legal persons' with rights and duties under international law. International law makes that assumption by treating states as artificial persons who associate, like citizens, on the basis of law."[88] The international rule-of-law ideal entails a legally ordered international community of states and other actors.

Waldron argues that it is wrong to see the international community of states as analogous to individuals within society.[89] But this analogy is ingrained within international law, and it is an apt depiction of the international situation. Interpersonal violence and abuse of power within society – say, when a powerful person or gang attacks a weaker person to injure them and seize their assets – is directly analogous to when a strong state or coalition attacks or seizes the territory of a weaker state. Both contexts involve the lawless, violent, arbitrary abuse of power, antithetical to the (horizontal) rule of law. When a few states are militarily and economically strong, while many states are weak, Arthur Watts wrote,

86 Anne-Marie Slaughter, *A Liberal Theory of International Law*, 94 PROC. ANN. MEETING 240, 242 (2000).
87 KANT, *supra* note 20, at 128, 136.
88 Nardin, *supra* note 35, at 398.
89 Waldron, *supra* note 41, at 20–26.

only through international legal ordering "can the conditions be established for increased *prosperity and security*, whether of individual States or of the international community as a whole."[90]

Russia illegally and arbitrarily utilized its superior military might against the government, territory, and citizens of Ukraine, killing and maiming people and causing millions to flee, disrupting the functioning of government, destroying their collective security, trust, and economy. The United States also inflicted grievous harm on the state and populace when it illegally invaded Iraq. The respective actions of Russia and the United States, in turn, had severe regional and global consequences that harmed people in many societies around the globe. To vindicate their sovereign equality and repair their governments and the lives of their people, Ukraine and Iraq should be entitled to access legal tribunals and remedies for these violations of international law. The geopolitical reality that great powers cannot be forced to acknowledge and rectify their illegal wrongdoings does not mean international law is weak or not law – no legal system successfully holds all law violators (particularly powerful ones) accountable. Rather, their lawless conduct is exposed as all the more reprehensible by its very abuse of power, flouting the rule of law of international ordering with devastating consequences, while shamelessly claiming legal justifications for their actions.

There are multiple examples, beyond wars and invasions, where international law secures the benefits of the rule of law for sovereign states and their populace. Treaties and international agreements between states cover trade, aviation, communications, intellectual property, climate change, and numerous other matters. International and transnational laws and regulations combat illegal drug trade and terrorism, secure borders, manage cross-border financial flows, limit nuclear weapons and waste, biohazards, and so forth.

It is true that sovereign states act as officials and agencies with the power to create law at the international level, as Waldron points out, but they are also legal subjects with enforceable legal rights and powers. Only states can bring cases before the ICJ for violations of international law, and only states can file complaints with the World Trade Organization's Dispute Settlement Body against other states for violating trade agreements. The vast majority of cases at the International Tribunal of the Law of the Sea involve conflicts between states over violations of national maritime rights. European nations have brought

[90] Watts, *supra* note 26, at 24 (emphasis added).

actions in the European Court of Justice against another European nation for breach of EU law.[91] Sovereign states also have enforceable rights in the courts of other nations that provide for such suits. For instance, foreign states have filed over 300 suits in US courts against private parties as well as government defendants, raising commercial claims, treaty violations, and other legal claims.[92] In many of these suits the sovereign state is defending its own powers and rights (the state's trade agreement, the state's territory, the state's maritime border, etc.), while in others it is acting to vindicate the rights and interests of its citizens or private companies.

The common treatment of sovereign states as legal subjects with enforceable rights in both national and international contexts requires Waldron to draw a tenuous line: although states are subjects with enforceable legal rights, nonetheless they are not beneficiaries of the rule of law. This stance works only if one accepts that the *only* benefit of the rule of law is individual freedom and *only* the vertical dimension of the rule of law matters.

It is plain, however, that legal principles, rules, and regulations at the international level constitute relations and institutions, and provide and enhance certainty, predictability, security, trust, and economic development within the international community, which are important benefits of the rule of law. These benefits accrue to *all* legal subjects with rights and obligations, including individuals, corporations, international organizations and agencies, sovereign states, and other entities in the international arena, consistent with the 2012 Declaration's affirmation that sovereign states (like all other entities) are "without discrimination entitled to equal protection of the law."[93]

In debates about how the rule of law should be understood, one must consider whether particular accounts are descriptively apt, theoretically sound, and normatively beneficial – the latter considering whether desirable consequences follow therefrom. The ideal of an international rule of law as the basis for the legal ordering of friendly and equitable relations that benefits individuals, states, and all other legal subjects, fits international law principles and matches the expressed understanding and desires of international actors. It is a theoretically sound way of seeing the benefits of the rule of law in holistic terms within a legally ordered

[91] *See, e.g.*, Case C-457/18, Slovenia v. Croatia, ECLI: EU:C:2020:65 (Jan. 31, 2020).

[92] *See* Hannah L. Buxbaum, *Foreign Governments as Plaintiffs in U.S. Court and the Case Against "Judicial Imperialism,"* 73 Wash. & Lee L. Rev. 653, 656 (2016).

[93] Rule of Law Declaration, *supra* note 28.

society. As a pragmatic matter, furthermore, states will see it as being in their self-interest to commit to the international rule of law if they stand to benefit therefrom, which will help bring about a more effective legal ordering. Ian Hurd remarks: "The international rule of law refers to the intellectual and political commitment . . . to the idea that all state behaviour should conform to whatever international legal obligations relate to it and that the result of executing this commitment faithfully is a well-ordered international space."[94] Individuals around the globe – and every sovereign state – would be better off if this ideal was substantially realized at the international level.

## VI The Emerging Transnational Legal Ordering

The discussion thus far has been framed in terms of the international rule of law – with an emphasis on international law, to comport with Waldron's framework – but my analysis applies more generally to the emerging transnational legal ordering of the international community.[95] Transnational legal ordering encompasses all forms of law and regulation that address matters between and across states, a great deal of which is outside of international law proper. This includes local, national, and international law and regulations and it involves public and private actors, organizations, and tribunals. It addresses cross-border matters like trade in goods and services; migration; money flows and banking; pollution control and environmental regulation; regulation and taxation of multinational corporations; shipping, rail, and air travel; telecommunications and the internet; terrorism; global health matters like pandemics; intellectual property; and much more. Much of this regulatory activity has been prompted by the expansion and intensification of capitalism around the globe and technological advances in telecommunications and transportation. All nations are now mutually intertwined in multiple ways with other nations that require coordination and regulation. This ongoing proliferation of law and regulatory regimes and institutions constitutes an extension and thickening of legal ordering in connection with activities and consequences that cross state borders. Absent world-devastating man-made or natural catastrophes – looming possibilities in an age of nuclear weapons and rapid global warming – the

[94] Hurd, *supra* note 43, at 391.

[95] For an overview, see Gregory Shaffer, *Theorizing Transnational Legal Ordering*, 12 ANN. REV. L. & SOC. SCI. 231 (2016); TAMANAHA, *supra* note 34.

extension and thickening of law addressing these matters appears likely to continue.

A substantial portion of intercourse between and across nations involves commercial activities, which have beneficial consequences beyond merely economic ones. Montesquieu observed over two-and-a-half centuries ago: "The natural effect of commerce is to lead to peace. Two nations that trade with each other are reciprocally dependent."[96] (Think of China and the United States today.) Kant made the same point: "The commercial spirit cannot co-exist with war, and sooner or later it takes possession of every nation."[97] Commerce at a distance is facilitated by legal rules, regulations, and tribunals.[98] The European Union is a nonpareil, economically based transnational legal ordering built on the ideal of the rule of law. National, bilateral, regional, and global regulatory regimes dealing with transnational economic activities (not to mention private elements like arbitration, model contract terms, commercial usages, and so forth) are abundant and increasing.[99] One commentator on transnational economic law estimated that "90 percent of international law work is in reality international economic law in some form or another."[100]

Many actors operate within and utilize the transnational legal ordering of the international community: individuals, municipalities, state agencies, private corporations, public corporations, NGOs, regional and international organizations (United Nations, World Trade Organization, World Bank, International Monetary Fund, and a multitude more), sovereign states, and others. Rule-of-law theorists who emphasize individual freedom and preventing governmental abuse of power should bear in mind that states are not the only actors who pose dangers to individuals. International organizations like the UN Security Council and the World Bank have enormous power; transnational corporations rival states in wealth and influence;[101] and both have the capacities to coerce states (particularly weak states) and harm their populaces. Seeing the rule of

96 Charles Louis de Secondat, Baron de La Brède et de Montesquieu, The Spirit of the Laws 338 (Anne M. Cohler, Basia C. Miller & Harold S. Stone eds., Cambridge Univ. Press 1989) (1748).

97 Kant, *supra* note 20, at 56.

98 *See* Tamanaha, *supra* note 34, at 167–78.

99 For a broad account of transnational economic regulatory regimes, see Joel P. Trachtman, *The International Economic Law Revolution*, 17 U. Pa. J. Int'l Econ. L. 33 (1996).

100 John H. Jackson, *Global Economics and International Economic Law*, 1 J. Int'l Econ. L. 1, 8 (1998).

101 *See* Tamanaha, *supra* note 34, at 171–72.

law as an ideal of effective legal ordering within, between, and across nations in the international community that restrains *and* benefits *all* actors provides the most adequate way to address the global situation.

Let me close with a note of optimism, albeit not easy to hold on to with so many dire events occurring in the world today. Over centuries of gradual development, the rule of law emerged within societies that embraced the rule-of-law ideal that everyone – people and corporate entities, rich and poor, government officials, monarchs – is bound by and should abide by law. Indications of this ideal taking hold on the international level are evident, at least in word if not always in deed. Keep in mind that when the domestic rule of law developed, sovereigns routinely swore oaths to abide by the law, which they nonetheless violated when it suited their interests, although they endeavored to justify their actions as consistent with law. This pattern of conduct is being repeated on the international level today, as sovereign states, transnational corporations, international organizations, and everyone else, increasingly claim to uphold the rule of law. The universal avowal of this ideal is a necessary step on the path to achieving the national and international rule of law, though there is a long way to go.

# 3

# Rule-of-Law Backsliding

## Where, How, and Why

ANA MARÍA MONTOYA AND ALEJANDRO PONCE

## I Introduction

The rule of law – understood as a societal equilibrium in which state and society are bound by law, and in which the state provides an enabling environment for people to enjoy their rights – is considered an essential element to guarantee the development of modern societies. Around the world, however, strengthening the rule of law remains a pending task. Despite the democratizing waves that emerged after the Cold War and multiple advances in the areas of transparency and justice, the world seems to have entered a stage of institutional stagnation and democratic backsliding. In 2019, more than 5 billion people lacked access to justice,[1] and few countries made significant progress against corruption in the last decade.[2] Moreover, democracy has been in decline worldwide. In 2021, Freedom House reported the sixteenth consecutive year of democratic erosion and the Varieties of Democracy (V-Dem) institute reported that the level of democracy enjoyed by the average global citizen in 2021 fell to 1989 levels[3], which means that the advances of the third wave of democratization have receded.

In response to this crisis, scholars have recently turned their attention to documenting these trends and to examining why democracies are

We thank Wayne Sandholtz and Gregory Shaffer for comments, and Santiago Pardo and Carlos Toruño for excellent research assistance.

[1] World Just. Project, Measuring the Justice Gap: A People-Centered Assessment of Unmet Justice Needs Around the World (2019), https://tinyurl.com/yuajbx57.

[2] Transparency Int'l, Global Corruption Barometer Latin America and the Caribbean 2019: Citizens' Views and Experiences of Corruption (2019), https://tinyurl.com/2u5599ka.

[3] Sebastian Hellmeier et al., *State of the World 2020: Autocratization Turns Viral*, 28 Democratization 1053 (2021).

breaking down[4]. These studies have focused on democratic backsliding but have neglected to study rule-of-law backsliding. There are virtually no empirical studies examining this issue, and the existing theoretical sources that discuss it only do so in reference to the European Union.[5] Although the principles of democracy and the rule of law are closely related, they are not the same. As stated by Shaffer and Sandholtz in Chapter 1, "The issue of democratic governance poses the question of *who* exercises power. Rule-of-law-concerns examine the question of *how*' power is exercised." More specifically, definitions of democracy are typically centered on free and fair elections (electoral democracy) and on the provision of civil liberties and political rights (liberal democracy). In contrast, definitions of the rule of law focus on compliance with and enforcement of the law, and the imposition of limits on the exercise of power, although there is no consensus on the specific elements to be included in a universal definition. Rule of law is therefore a broader concept than democratic governance and demands a more comprehensive analysis.

In this chapter, we explore whether the rule of law has deteriorated around the world in recent years, and if so, how this shift has occurred and where. We generate indicators using various conceptualizations of the rule of law, including some focused on the imposition of limits on the arbitrary use of power by agents of the state – such as proposed by Shaffer and Sandholtz in Chapter 1 – as well as thicker conceptualizations that

[4] Nancy Bermeo, *On Democratic Backsliding*, 27 J. DEMOCRACY 5 (2016); STEVEN LEVITSKY & DANIEL ZIBLATT, HOW DEMOCRACIES DIE (2018); RONALD INGLEHART & PIPPA NORRIS, CULTURAL BACKLASH: TRUMP, BREXIT, AND AUTHORITARIAN (2019); Milan W. Svolik, *Polarization versus Democracy*, 30 J. DEMOCRACY 20 (2019); Stephen Haggard & Robert Kaufman, *The Anatomy of Democratic Backsliding*, 32 J. DEMOCRACY 27 (2021).

[5] The expression "rule-of-law backsliding" emerged from the periphery of the European Union. *See* Dimitry Kochenov & Petra Bárd, *Rule of Law Crisis in the New Member States of the EU: The Pitfalls of Overemphasizing Enforcement* (Reconnect Working Paper No. 1, 2018), https://papers.ssrn.com/sol3/papers.cfm?abstract_id=3221240. Some scholars have frequently used the expression to denote the pervasive effect of a ruling party's attack on judicial autonomy, independent media, and minorities. According to Peche and Scheppele, rule-of-law backsliding is a "process through which elected public authorities deliberately implement governmental blueprints which aim to systematically weaken, annihilate or capture internal checks on power with the view of dismantling the liberal democratic state and entrenching the long-term rule of the dominant party." Laurent Pech & Kim Lane Scheppele, *Illiberalism Within: Rule of Law Backsliding in the EU*, 19 CAMBRIDGE Y.B. EUR. LEGAL STUD. 3, 8 (2017); *see also* Tom Theuns, *Containing Populism at the Cost of Democracy? Political vs. Economic Responses to Democratic Backsliding in the EU*, 12 GLOB. JUST.: THEORY, PRAC., RHETORIC 141 (2020).

include not only the imposition of limits on executive discretion but also the creation of an enabling environment where citizens can enjoy their rights. We then examine the variations in these indicators with a view to unpacking the sources of the rule-of-law backsliding. We also explore whether such backsliding has occurred in countries with high or lower levels of rule of law, and whether this trend is associated with the recent rise to power of leaders with populist or antipluralist tendencies.

It is clear to see that authoritarian leaders may seek to dismantle institutional checks and balances – or dismantle the "guardrails of democracy" mentioned by Levitsky and Zibblat[6] – in order to restrict fundamental freedoms and weaken transparency and accountability. However, it is not obvious that authoritarian leaders are interested in encouraging particularism and corruption[7] or in causing a deterioration in administrative agencies or security and justice systems. Indeed, autocratic leaders have mixed incentives to develop state capacity. On the one hand, state-building can help address citizens' demands and strengthen the control apparatus. On the other hand, state-building can generate resistance – for example, through the strengthening of bureaucracy – and fuel collective demands for the right to participate in the decision-making process.[8]

To explore these questions, we use data from the World Justice Project's *WJP Rule of Law Index* covering more than 100 countries from 2015 to 2022. This dataset contains indicators on various dimensions of the rule of law, including those that capture the limits on the exercise of power by state agents and the limits imposed by the state on the actions of members of society. These indicators' scores are generated from assessments by the general public and in-country legal practitioners and range from 0 to 1, with 1 representing strongest adherence to the rule of law.

We find that the rule of law has indeed deteriorated in recent years around the world. Aggregate *WJP Rule of Law Index* scores, which capture perceptions about the functioning of the state and institutional checks and balances, fell in 74 percent of countries between 2015 and 2022, with the decline averaging −3.1 percent This fall, however, has not

[6] Levitsky & Ziblatt, *supra* note 4.

[7] On the one hand, government accountability – which tends to be lower in autocratic regimes – reduces corrupt practices. Alícia Adserà et al., *Are You Being Served? Political Accountability and Quality of Government*, 19 J.L. Econ. & Org. 445 (2003). On the other hand, state control – which tends to be greater in autocratic regimes – facilitates the ability of political leaders to control the behavior of lower-level officials. Andrei Shleifer & Robert W. Vishny, *Corruption*, 108 Q.J. Econ. 599 (1993).

[8] Sebastián L. Mazzuca & Gerardo L. Munck, *State or Democracy First? Alternative Perspectives on the State-Democracy Nexus*, 21 Democratization 1221 (2014).

been homogeneous across indicators. The indicators of fundamental rights and constraints on government powers fell during this period in 76 percent and 68 percent of countries and by an average of −6.7% and −5.1%, respectively. Other indicators' scores, constructed from disaggregated *WJP Rule of Law Index* data, tell a similar story. The scores of the indicators capturing the sources of arbitrariness proposed by Shaffer and Sandholtz fell in more than 60 percent of countries. Similarly, scores measuring anti-authoritarianism fell in 68 percent of countries by an average of −5.5%. In contrast, scores under the state capacity indicator, which capture perceptions of the functioning of the regulatory, security, and justice systems, fell in only 56 percent of countries and by an average of only −0.3%. To further investigate the backsliding and examine the countries in which it has occurred, we use cluster analysis of the change over time in the main indicators of the *WJP Rule of Law Index.* We identify three groups of countries. The first is composed of countries that have experienced a deterioration in all indicators, but most notably in those measuring limits to state power, open government, and respect for human rights, and that already had low rule-of-law levels in 2015. The second group is composed of countries where overall rule-of-law trends have also declined, but less severely. These countries had different levels of rule of law in 2015, although higher than the levels of the first group, and have also experienced considerable declines in the indicators measuring limits to state power and respect for human rights. The third group is composed of countries where most indicators have experienced slight improvements. This group is composed of countries in transition, such as Kazakhstan, and countries with high levels of rule of law located mainly in the European Union.

These results suggest that the rule-of law-backsliding has been incremental and driven by the weakening of limits on state power, as measured by the governmental and nongovernmental checks and balances and the protection of fundamental rights and freedoms, rather than by an acute deterioration in the application or enforcement of the law or in access to justice (except in those cases that have experienced a sharp decline). Furthermore, although significant, backsliding in most countries has been less pronounced, probably due to less severe shocks, greater institutional strength[9],

[9] M. Steven Fish, *The Dynamics of Democratic Erosion, in* Post-communism and the Theory of Democracy 54 (Richard Anderson et al. eds., 2001); Miguel Carreras, *The Rise of Outsiders in Latin America, 1980–2010: An Institutionalist Perspective*, 45 Compar. Pol. Stud. 1451 (2012); Aníbal Pérez-Liñán & Scott Mainwaring, *Regime Legacies and Levels of Democracy: Evidence from Latin America*, 45 Compar. Pol. 379 (2013).

economic development[10], state capacity[11], developed bureaucracy, effective opposition[12], free and critical press and civil society, or changes in administration during the period. Overall, our results indicate that the weakening of the rule of law appears to be associated, in part, with an increase in the authoritarian tendencies of certain regimes and, in part, with the rise of antipluralist and populist leaders. Our analysis is limited to the years 2015 to 2022, as the data for previous years is not comparable. Nonetheless, other data sources show improvements in the earlier periods, which may indicate a wave effect, rising in the preceding three decades and then falling more recently.

Our contribution to the literature is threefold. First, our chapter is the first to analyze empirically the issue of rule-of-law backsliding at the transnational level, approaching it from a broad perspective bearing in mind that there is no consensus about the meaning of this concept. Second, our chapter contributes to the debate on the way in which the ascension of antidemocratic leaders affects various dimensions of the rule of raw and, more broadly, to the literature on democratic decline. Finally, methodologically, very few studies have applied cluster analysis to analyze and group different trends across countries. In this regard, our work is closely related to the "democracy cluster classification" index developed by Ristei and Centellas, where the authors use hierarchical cluster algorithms to classify countries according to their regime types and trends in democratic governance.[13] Our work has several limitations. Our analysis is mostly descriptive and does not explore the causes of the rule-of-law backsliding or the different institutional structures that might explain the cross-country variations. The analysis focuses on national trends and omits subnational variations, which can be important in federalist and decentralized countries. Our analysis is also limited to recent years and uses perception data. In spite of this, the analysis is useful for laying the groundwork for in-depth comparative analysis and case studies.

10 Milan Svolik, *Authoritarian Reversals and Democratic Consolidation*, 102 AM. POL. SCI. REV. 153 (2008).

11 STEVEN LEVITSKY & LUCAN WAY, COMPETITIVE AUTHORITARIANISM: HYBRID REGIMES AFTER THE COLD WAR (2010); Larry Diamond, *Facing Up to the Democratic Recession*, 26 J. DEMOCRACY 141 (2015); Michael W. Bauer & Stefan Becker, *Democratic Backsliding, Populism, and Public Administration*, 3 PERSPS. ON PUB. MGMT. GOVERNANCE 19 (2020).

12 Laura Gamboa, *Opposition at the Margins: Strategies Against the Erosion of Democracy in Colombia and Venezuela*, 49 COMPAR. POL. 457 (2017).

13 Mihaiela Ristei Gugiu & Miguel Centellas, *The Democracy Cluster Classification Index*, 21 POL. ANALYSIS 334 (2013).

The rest of this chapter proceeds as follows. In Part II, we explore the concept of the rule of law. In Part III, we describe the data. In Part IV, we develop our analysis. Finally, in Part V, we conclude.

## II The Rule-of-Law Concept

The first step in determining whether the rule of law has deteriorated in recent years is to define the concept. Although the rule of law is considered central to achieving a wide variety of social goals –such as promoting peace, justice, and economic development – there is little consensus on what it means, and little literature exploring the notion of rule-of law-backsliding, its sources, or how the rule of law emerges or recovers in environments where it has deteriorated or does not exist.[14]

Across the literature, it is possible to identify two principal conceptions of the term: a formalist, or "thin," definition and a substantive, or "thick," definition. Formalist definitions of the rule of law do not make a judgment about the legitimacy or justness of the laws themselves. Instead, they focus on procedure. They focus on whether rules exist and scrutinize whether those rules are followed by all, including the sovereign: "Stripped of all technicalities this means that government in all its actions is bound by rules fixed and announced beforehand."[15]. In contrast, substantive or "thick" definitions take into consideration certain rights that are seen to be fundamental to the rule of law and incorporate adherence to normative standards of rights, fairness, and equity.[16]

A central element in most of these conceptualizations is that the law imposes limits on the arbitrary exercise of power by the government and

[14] Guillermo O'Donnell, *Why the Rule of Law Matters*, 15 J. DEMOCRACY 32 (2004); BRIAN Z. TAMANAHA, ON THE RULE OF LAW: HISTORY, POLITICS, THEORY (2004); PROMOTING THE RULE OF LAW ABROAD: IN SEARCH OF KNOWLEDGE (Thomas Carothers, ed. 2006) [hereinafter PROMOTING THE RULE OF LAW ABROAD]; Thomas Carothers, *Rule of Law Temptations*, 33 FLETCHER F. WORLD AFFS. 49 (2009), https://dl.tufts.edu/concern/pdfs/8k71nv35v; Daniel M. Brinks, From Legal Poverty to Legal Agency: Establishing the Rule of Law in Latin America (Mar. 2009), https://tinyurl.com/2suv45hk; AŠHRAF ĠANI & CLARE LOCKHART, FIXING FAILED STATES: A FRAMEWORK FOR REBUILDING A FRACTURED WORLD (2009); Michael Zürn, Andre Nollkaemper & Randall Peerenboom, *Rule of Law Dynamics in an Era of International and Transnational Governance* (Amsterdam L. Sch. Res. Paper No. 2011-28, 2011), https://papers.ssrn.com/sol3/papers.cfm?abstract_id=1933701; Gillian K. Hadfield & Barry R. Weingast, *Microfoundations of the Rule of Law*, 17 ANN. REV. POL. SCI. 21 (2014).

[15] F.A. HAYEK, *Planning and the Rule of Law*, *in* THE ROAD TO SERFDOM 75 (1944).

[16] PROMOTING THE RULE OF LAW ABROAD, *supra* note 14; Carothers, *supra* note 14.

other social actors, although the emphasis is usually put on the restraints imposed on the ruler. This approach can be found, for instance, in the working definition offered by the European Commission in 2014 in a communication titled *A New EU Framework to Strengthen the Rule of Law*, where it distinguished six core components based on various rulings by the Court of Justice of the European Union (CJEU): legality; legal certainty; prohibition of arbitrariness on the part of executive powers; independent and impartial courts; effective judicial review including respect for fundamental rights; and equality before the law. Subsequently, this definition was slightly refined in a 2019 communication, *Further Strengthening the Rule of Law Within the Union: State of Play and Possible Next Steps*, in which the Commission observed: "Under the rule of law, all public powers always act within the constraints set out by law, in accordance with the values of democracy and fundamental rights, and under the control of independent and impartial courts." Shaffer and Sandholtz similarly refer to some of these elements in their discussion of sources of arbitrariness and attendant rule-of-law definitions – i.e., application of law to rules, predictability of published rules, fora for bringing challenges, proportionality of means to ends, and reason-giving.[17]

Other conceptualizations have gone beyond this narrow formulation – protection from the sovereign or from each other – to include additional organizational features of a society, such as the existence of an environment in which people can enjoy their rights, use the law proactively to pursue their goals, and secure redress when those rights are violated. This is captured, for instance, in the definition proposed by the United Nations: "The rule of law … refers to a principle of governance in which all persons, institutions and entities, public and private, including the State itself, are accountable to laws that are publicly promulgated, equally enforced and independently adjudicated, and which are consistent with international human rights norms and standards."[18] A similar approach can be found in the definition used by the World Justice Project (WJP):

> The rule of law is a durable system of laws, institutions, norms, and community commitment that delivers four universal principles: accountability, just law, open government, and accessible and impartial justice.

[17] See Chapter 1.

[18] U.N. Secretary-General, *The Rule of Law and Transitional Justice in Conflict and Post-Conflict Societies*, U.N. Doc. S/2004/616 (Aug. 23, 2004).

> **Accountability**
> The government as well as private actors are accountable under the law.
>
> **Just Law**
> The law is clear, publicized, and stable and is applied evenly. It ensures human rights as well as property, contract, and procedural rights.
>
> **Open Government**
> The processes by which the law is adopted, administered, adjudicated, and enforced are accessible, fair, and efficient.
>
> **Accessible and Impartial Justice**
> Justice is delivered timely by competent, ethical, and independent representatives and neutrals who are accessible, have adequate resources, and reflect the makeup of the communities they serve.[19]

These various definitions all consider the rule of law in terms of its goals or outcomes, as opposed to means (or inputs), which is important as it allows "rule of law" to be distinguished from "rule by law" and for different types of institutional arrangements to be used to attain them.

In this chapter, we distance ourselves from questions about how legal orders arise, or how various conceptualizations differ, and instead follow a practical approach to operationalize some of these definitions. We use the indicators of the *WJP Rule of Law Index* as a starting point. Taken together, these indicators capture the idea of the rule of law as a societal equilibrium in which the state and members of society are bound by law,[20] and in which the state limits the actions of members of society and provides an enabling environment so that the public interest is served, people enjoy their rights and are protected from violence, and all members of society have access to dispute settlement and grievance mechanisms. This approach has three advantages. First, it looks at the rule of law not only as an ideal of societal coexistence but also as an equilibrium arising from the interaction of institutions and beliefs that shape the behavior and collective actions of members of society. This equilibrium varies depending on the sphere of action of the law and, more

[19] *What is the Rule of Law?*, World Just. Project, https://tinyurl.com/3v6fj5w6 (last visited Aug. 22, 2024).

[20] Another way to describe this first element of the definition is to say that authorities and citizens comply systematically with laws that are consistent with a democratic regime and with the protection of fundamental rights, or alternatively, that the law (and the agents in charge of enforcing it) imposes limits on the exercise of power by state and nonstate actors.

importantly, the functioning of the legal and institutional frameworks, the relative power of the agents to whom they apply, and the role of social norms and voluntary compliance. In particular, the normative frameworks, which range from the constitution to secondary laws, executive regulations, and public policies, and the way in which the state agencies in charge of interpreting, enforcing, or making use of them function (congresses, judicial system, police, government agencies, etc.) shape agents' behavior and beliefs and generate different types of incentives and equilibria.[21] These institutional frameworks reflect the fundamental patterns of social organization and power distribution in society and are shaped by the agents through institutional and political processes. Second, this approach is consistent with the definitions in the literature and envisages the rule of law comprehensively, incorporating classic guidelines on the exercise of power by the state as propounded in Hobbesian and Madisonian thinking.[22] It is state-centered and focuses on how governments perform – that is, how they exercise authority and how they administer and enforce laws. Thirdly, our approach is tailored to the data, allowing us to empirically assess the status and evolution of various rule-of-law outcomes and to dissect the factors contributing to the backsliding.

## III Data

In this chapter, we explore three hypotheses: (1) The rule of law has deteriorated around the world in recent years. (2) This deterioration has manifested itself through a weakening of the limits on state power (i.e., the weakening of institutional checks and balances and a deterioration in civil liberties reflected in escalating authoritarian behaviors and legal, organizational, administrative, or budgetary changes (the first element of our definition)). In contrast, regressions in the rule of law have not been

[21] Ponce, A. J. Rios & D. Brinks, The Rule of Law in Latin America (2022) (unpublished paper prepared for UNDP and the Yale Center for the Study of Globalization).

[22] According to Hobbes, the state must be able to enforce the law effectively, systematically, and impersonally to generate peaceful cooperation between citizens, avoiding depredations of one citizen against another. The state must control the use of violence, provide public security, provide effective and accessible mechanisms to resolve conflicts between citizens, and ensure the protection of rights. According to Madison, the exercise of power by the state must be governed by democratic principles to avoid the arbitrary use of power. The state must abide by the law and must enforce it on state agents or persons related to them, when necessary. This presupposes mutual and effective supervision between the executive, legislative, and judicial powers, as well as the existence of regulatory bodies.

characterized by increased particularism or a deterioration in the functioning of state agencies in charge of interpreting, applying, administering, or enforcing the law (i.e., police, prosecutors, courts, ombudsmen, anticorruption agencies, regulatory bodies, etc.). (3) This backsliding has been brought about, in part, by a deterioration in institutional checks in authoritarian countries and, in part, by the rise, through relatively democratic processes, of leaders with antipluralist and populist tendencies during this period.

Through the lens of these hypotheses, we examine a selection of annual country indicators that measure different dimensions of the rule of law in a large number of countries around the world. Over the last ten years, the World Justice Project has been collecting information from citizens and legal practitioners in the countries surveyed in order to measure adherence to the rule of law in practice and comprehensively. This information, which forms the basis of the *WJP Rule of Law Index*, is structured around forty-four outcome indicators (or subfactors) and eight dimensions (or factors): constraints on government powers, absence of corruption, open government, fundamental rights, order and security, regulatory enforcement, civil justice, and criminal justice. These dimensions incorporate the two elements that characterize various rule-of-law definitions – constraints on executive discretion and an enabling legal environment that provides justice for the people. The scores under the eight factors and forty-four subfactors of the index are drawn from surveys of the general public and legal practitioners, experts, and academics with expertise in civil and commercial law, constitutional law, civil liberties, criminal law labor law and public health in the countries concerned. These data sources capture citizens' and professionals' experiences and perceptions of the performance of the state and its agents and the operation of the legal framework in their respective countries or jurisdictions. Therefore, these data capture the situations perceived within countries and do not touch on transnational institutions. The scores in the 2022 edition of the *WJP Rule of Law Index* were derived from more than 150,000 household surveys and 3,600 legal practitioner and expert surveys in 140 countries and jurisdictions.

In our analysis, we use aggregate index scores, the scores of the index's eight factors, and composite indicators constructed from combinations of the index factors and subfactors. The indicators use a scale of 0 to 1, where 1 signifies higher adherence to the rule of law. The data in our sample covers 102 countries and the following years:2015, 2016, 2017–18, 2019, 2020, 2020, 2021, 2022. This selection of years is for two reasons: First, it was in 2015 that the concept of rule of law began to have greater visibility. Figure 3.1 shows

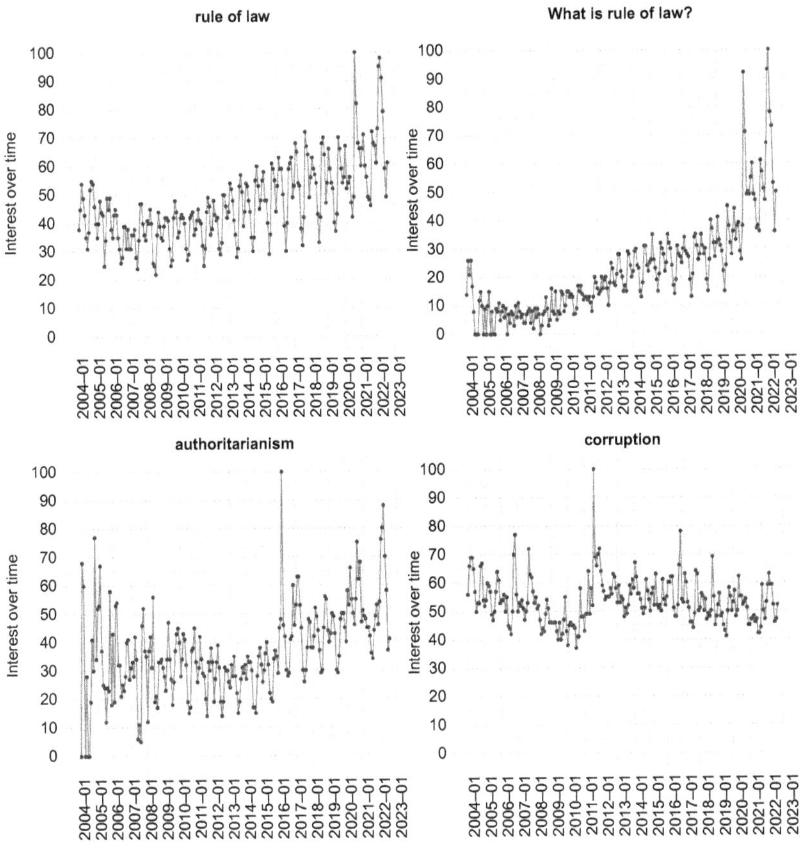


**Figure 3.1** Google trends of selected terms over time.
Source: Google

the relative importance in Google of various terms related to rule of law and authoritarianism, as well as some controls (such as corruption). In these graphs, the positive trend in recent years starts in 2015. These patterns are confirmed in longitudinal cross-country data sources measuring various governance aspects over a longer time frame, such as V-Dem (see Figure 3.2). The second reason is practical: the WJP data is not comparable to data published before 2015 due to the addition of new countries, changes in the methodologies of normalization, and the addition of concepts and questions from that year onwards. Our final data comprises 714 country–year observations (102 countries and 7 years of data).

The main advantage of the WJP data is that it is multidimensional, which allows us to explore variations across the different dimensions of

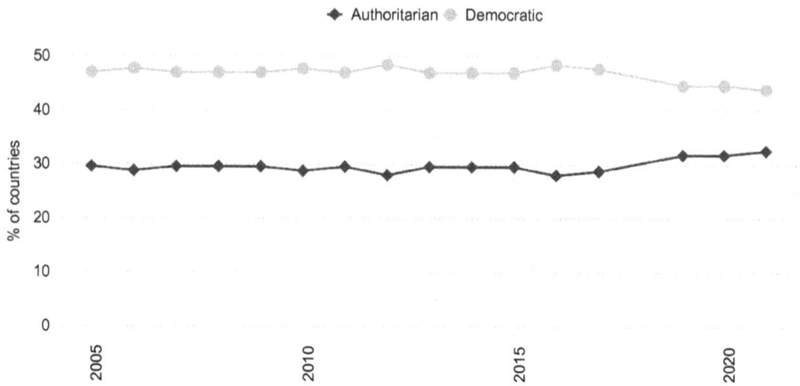


**Figure 3.2** Percentage of democratic vs. authoritarian regimes (2005–21).
Source: V-Dem

the rule of law and not just variations in aggregate scores. The underlying data captures information not only on respect of the law by state agents (or on the functioning of institutional checks and balances) but also on the state's effectiveness in ensuring that citizens respect the law, enjoy their rights, and obtain access to justice. The data can be reorganized to form new indicators that approximate concepts used in different definitions, including those proposed by Shaffer and Sandholtz.[23] A further advantage is the data's numerical nature, which allows us to calculate changes in the different indicators in percentage instead of ordinal terms, and to construct scores from a large number of variables that cover multiple facets of the concepts evaluated. The main disadvantage is that the time frame is relatively short. Nevertheless, the data covers the period of interest. Additionally, the data is based on perceptions and may not reflect the true underlying situation. However, perceptions are important to legal orders as they shape the behavior and beliefs of actors.[24] To test our third hypothesis, we supplement the WJP data with the V-Party dataset. The latter allows us to construct variables on countries' exposure to authoritarian regimes over the years. Specifically, we use the V-Party dataset to construct two variables on the political party platforms of candidates coming to power (i.e., antipluralism and populism).

In the analysis, we focus on the percentage changes in the various indicators of the dataset between 2015 and 2022. We use four sets of indicators. The first two are from the WJP: its aggregate rule-of-law

[23] See Chapter 1.
[24] Transnational Legal Orders (Terrence C. Halliday & Gregory Shaffer eds., 2015).

indicator, which is an unweighted average of the eight factors that make up the WJP index, and the eight factors of its index. Third, we indicators to approximate the sources of arbitrariness described by Shaffer and Sandholtz. We construct these indicators using the factors and subfactors of the WJP index; however, the matching between the concepts behind the sources of arbitrariness and the data is not very close, as the index indicators come from a different conceptual framework. Fourth, we approximate the indicator of application of law to rulers to the indicator of constraints on government powers of the WJP index (factor 1). This indicator measures the functioning of checks and balances, including legislative constraints, judicial constraints, auditing and review, sanctions, nongovernmental checks, and legally compliant power transitions.

The indicator of predictability of published rules is equivalent to the open government indicator (factor 3). This indicator measures the openness of government defined as "the extent to which a government shares information, empowers people with tools to hold the government accountable, and fosters citizen participation in public policy deliberations."[25] The indicator of fora for challenges is equivalent to the civil justice indicator (factor 7), which measures "whether ordinary people can resolve their grievances peacefully and effectively through the civil justice system,"[26] and the indicator of proportionate link of means to end and reason-giving is the average of the indicators of judicial constraints (subfactor 1.2) and the absence of improper government influence in civil and criminal justice (subfactors 7.4 and 8.6, respectively). Finally, we also use indicators to capture the concept of control of authoritarianism (or anti-authoritarianism), control of particularism (or anti-particularism), and state capacity. We constructed the anti-authoritarianism indicator using the average of the scores of the indicators of constraints on government powers (factor 1), fundamental rights (factor 4), open government (factor 3) and absence of improper government influence in civil and criminal justice (average of sub-factor 7.4 and 8.6). The anti-particularism indicator is equal to the absence of corruption indicator (factor 2), while the state capacity indicator is the average of the indicators of absence of crime (subfactor 5.1), regulatory enforcement (factor 6), and civil justice and criminal justice (factors 7 and 8). We focus on changes over the last seven years because in most countries changes in the rule of law from one

[25] *Open Government*, World Just. Project, https://worldjusticeproject.org/rule-of-law-index/factors/2023/Open%20Government.

[26] *Civil Justice*, World Just. Project, https://worldjusticeproject.org/rule-of-law-index/factors/2023/Civil%20Justice/.

year to the next remain relatively small. In part of our analysis we nonetheless show changes over different time periods in order to encompass variations in indicators when a new administration takes over. Table 3.1 describes the factors used as measures in the *WJP Rule of Law Index.*

Table 3.1 *WJP rule-of-law factors*

| Factor | Concepts measured |
|---|---|
| 1. Constraints on government powers | Factor 1 measures the extent to which those who govern are bound by law. It covers the means, both constitutional and institutional, by which the powers of the government and its officials and agents are limited and held accountable under the law. It also includes nongovernmental checks on the government's power, such as a free and independent press. This indicator addresses the effectiveness of the institutional checks on government power by the legislature (1.1), the judiciary (1.2), and independent auditing and review agencies (1.3), as well as the effectiveness of nongovernmental oversight by the media and civil society (1.5), which play an important role in monitoring government actions and holding officials accountable. The extent to which transitions of power occur in accordance with the law is also examined (1.6). In addition to these checks, this factor also measures the extent to which government officials are held accountable for official misconduct (1.4). |
| 2. Absence of corruption | Factor 2 measures the absence of corruption in a number of government agencies. The factor considers three forms of corruption: bribery, improper influence by public or private interests, and misappropriation of public funds or other resources. These three forms of corruption are examined with respect to government officers in the executive branch (2.1), the judiciary (2.2), the military and police (2.3), and the legislature (2.4), and encompass a wide range of possible situations in which corruption – from petty bribery to major kinds of fraud – can occur. |
| 3. Open government | Factor 3 measures open government defined as a government that shares information, empowers people with tools to hold the government accountable, and fosters citizen participation in public policy deliberations. The factor measures whether basic laws and information on legal rights are publicized and evaluates the quality of |

Table 3.1 (*cont.*)

| | |
|---|---|
| | information published by the government (3.1). It also measures whether requests for information held by a government agency are properly granted (3.2). Finally, it assesses the effectiveness of civic participation mechanisms – including the protection of freedoms of opinion and expression, assembly and association, and the right to petition (3.3), and whether people can bring specific complaints to the government (3.4). |
| 4. Fundamental rights | Factor 4 measures the protection of fundamental human rights. It encompasses adherence to the following fundamental rights: effective enforcement of laws that ensure equal protection (4.1), the right to life and security of the person (4.2), due process of law and the rights of the accused (4.3), freedom of opinion and expression (4.4), freedom of belief and religion (4.5), the right to privacy (4.6), freedom of assembly and association (4.7), and fundamental labor rights, including the right to collective bargaining, the prohibition of forced and child labor, and the elimination of discrimination (4.8). |
| 5. Order and Security | Factor 5 measures how well a society ensures the security of persons and property. Security is a defining aspect of any rule of law society and a fundamental function of the state. It is also a precondition for the realization of the rights and freedoms that the rule of law seeks to advance. This factor encompasses the effectiveness in controlling crime (5.1), the limitation of civil conflict (5.2), and the prevention of resorting to violence to redress personal grievances (5.3). |
| 6. Regulatory enforcement | Factor 6 measures the extent to which regulations are fairly and effectively implemented and enforced. Regulations, both legal and administrative, structure behaviors within and outside of the government. Strong rule of law requires that these regulations and administrative provisions are enforced effectively (6.1) and are applied and enforced without improper influence by public officials or private interests (6.2). Additionally, strong rule of law requires that administrative proceedings are conducted timely, without unreasonable delays (6.4), that due process is respected in administrative proceedings (6.3), and that there is no expropriation of private property without adequate compensation (6.5). |

Table 3.1 (*cont.*)

| | |
|---|---|
| 7. Civil justice | Factor 7 measures whether ordinary people can resolve their grievances peacefully and effectively through the civil justice system. The delivery of effective civil justice requires that the system be accessible and affordable (7.1), free of discrimination (7.2), free of corruption (7.3), and without improper influence by public officials (7.4). The delivery of effective civil justice also presupposes that court proceedings are conducted in a timely manner and are not subject to unreasonable delays (7.5). Finally, recognizing the value of alternative dispute resolution (ADR) mechanisms, this factor also measures the accessibility, impartiality, and efficiency of mediation and arbitration systems that enable parties to resolve civil disputes (7.7). |
| 8. Criminal justice | Factor 8 evaluates the criminal justice system. An effective criminal justice system is a key aspect of the rule of law, as it constitutes the conventional mechanism for redressing grievances and bringing action against individuals for offenses against society. Effective criminal justice systems are capable of investigating and adjudicating criminal offenses successfully and in a timely manner (8.1 and 8.2), through a system that is impartial and nondiscriminatory (8.4), as well as free of corruption and improper government influence (8.5 and 8.6), all while ensuring that the rights of both victims and the accused are effectively protected (8.7). The delivery of effective criminal justice also needs correctional systems that effectively reduce criminal behavior (8.3). Accordingly, an assessment of the delivery of criminal justice should take into consideration the entire system, including the police, lawyers, prosecutors, judges, and prison officers. |

*Source:* World Justice Project

## IV Empirical Analysis

### 1 *Is the Rule of Law in Decline?*

We first explore the hypothesis that the rule of law has been in decline around the world since 2015 and identify the types of countries in which it has regressed. Table 3.2 shows the percentage changes in the rule-of-law

Table 3.2 *Annual percentage changes in rule-of-law scores*

| **Backsliding** | | | | | | | |
|---|---|---|---|---|---|---|---|
| **Country** | **Δ15–16** | **Δ16–17** | **Δ17–19** | **Δ19–20** | **Δ20–21** | **Δ21–22** | **Δ15–22** |
| Egypt, Arab Rep. | −16.7% | −1.0% | −1.1% | 0.1% | −2.8% | −3.7% | −23.5% |
| Cambodia | −12.2% | −1.1% | 0.5% | 0.7% | −2.3% | −2.3% | −16.1% |
| Venezuela, RB | −13.7% | 4.0% | −3.5% | −2.6% | −1.5% | 3.0% | −14.4% |
| Nicaragua | −1.1% | 3.2% | −6.9% | −2.6% | −3.7% | −3.0% | −13.6% |
| Myanmar | 4.0% | −3.2% | −0.5% | 0.0% | −6.3% | −6.6% | −12.3% |
| Belarus | 1.4% | −4.6% | 0.8% | −0.5% | −7.5% | −2.2% | −12.2% |
| Bolivia | −2.7% | −5.2% | 0.0% | 0.3% | 0.9% | −5.0% | −11.4% |
| Philippines | −3.6% | −7.7% | 0.4% | 0.8% | −2.9% | 1.7% | −11.0% |
| El Salvador | −3.2% | −2.8% | −0.4% | 3.2% | −3.3% | −4.1% | −10.3% |
| Poland | −0.2% | −5.8% | −0.9% | −1.1% | −2.4% | 0.2% | −9.9% |
| Turkey | −7.2% | −3.1% | 2.7% | 0.3% | −2.5% | −0.3% | −9.9% |
| Mexico | −1.7% | −0.7% | −0.2% | −2.8% | −2.9% | −1.8% | −9.8% |
| Cameroon | −8.0% | −0.1% | 2.8% | −4.4% | −2.1% | 2.1% | −9.7% |
| Hungary | −1.3% | −3.9% | −2.2% | −1.1% | −1.4% | 0.8% | −8.8% |
| Georgia | −0.2% | −6.7% | −0.2% | −1.1% | 0.5% | −0.9% | −8.3% |
| Ghana | −3.7% | 2.4% | −2.5% | −1.9% | −2.2% | −0.5% | −8.2% |
| Bosnia and Herzegovina | −1.7% | −4.9% | −0.2% | −1.4% | −0.8% | 0.9% | −8.0% |
| Brazil | 2.9% | −3.1% | −1.2% | −2.9% | −2.9% | −0.5% | −7.6% |
| Iran, Islamic Rep. | 7.5% | 1.8% | −6.2% | −4.2% | −2.3% | −3.1% | −6.9% |
| Cote d'Ivoire | −1.4% | 1.4% | −1.3% | −0.4% | −3.4% | −1.2% | −6.1% |
| Albania | −3.2% | 0.8% | −0.3% | −1.2% | −1.7% | −0.6% | −6.1% |
| Bangladesh | −2.1% | 0.2% | 1.4% | −1.6% | −2.8% | −0.1% | −4.9% |
| China | 0.3% | 3.8% | −2.7% | −1.5% | −1.9% | −0.8% | −2.9% |
| Tanzania | −1.4% | 0.2% | −0.3% | 0.5% | −1.1% | −0.1% | −2.1% |
| *Average* | *−2.9%* | *−1.5%* | *−0.9%* | *−1.1%* | *−2.5%* | *−1.2%* | *−9.7%* |
| **Neutral** | | | | | | | |
| **Country** | **Δ15–16** | **Δ16–17** | **Δ17–19** | **Δ19–20** | **Δ20–21** | **Δ21–22** | **Δ15–22** |
| Korea, Republic of | −7.7% | −1.0% | 1.7% | 0.0% | 0.4% | −0.4% | −7.0% |
| Botswana | −9.9% | 1.3% | 1.3% | 1.7% | −1.5% | 0.7% | −6.9% |
| Morocco | 1.4% | −3.4% | −1.2% | −0.5% | −2.6% | −0.2% | −6.4% |
| Zambia | 0.5% | −0.8% | −1.2% | −2.6% | −2.3% | 0.0% | −6.4% |
| Honduras | −0.5% | −3.9% | −0.3% | 0.2% | −2.2% | 0.2% | −6.3% |
| Tunisia | −4.6% | 0.3% | −0.2% | 0.7% | −1.5% | −0.8% | −6.0% |
| Lebanon | −5.4% | 2.7% | 0.2% | −3.3% | −0.9% | 1.0% | −5.8% |
| Uganda | −4.1% | 2.6% | 0.6% | −1.8% | −0.9% | −0.7% | −4.3% |

Table 3.2 (*cont.*)

| | | | | | | | |
|---|---|---|---|---|---|---|---|
| Russian Federation | −4.1% | 3.2% | 1.0% | −1.4% | −0.7% | −2.0% | −4.1% |
| Hong Kong SAR, China | 1.3% | −0.4% | −0.2% | −0.4% | −2.0% | −2.3% | −4.1% |
| Singapore | 1.0% | −2.6% | 0.0% | −0.9% | −1.0% | −0.6% | −4.0% |
| Colombia | 1.2% | −0.4% | −1.4% | 0.8% | −2.2% | −2.0% | −4.0% |
| North Macedonia | −1.7% | −2.3% | 1.8% | −0.9% | −0.3% | −0.2% | −3.6% |
| Thailand | −0.3% | −1.8% | −0.4% | 0.9% | −2.2% | 0.1% | −3.6% |
| United States | 1.4% | −1.1% | −1.5% | −0.6% | −2.9% | 1.2% | −3.6% |
| United Arab Emirates | −2.1% | −1.5% | −0.7% | 0.6% | −0.9% | 1.2% | −3.6% |
| Liberia | 0.1% | 1.2% | 1.4% | −1.3% | −2.6% | −2.0% | −3.3% |
| Panama | −1.9% | −0.3% | −0.2% | 0.5% | −0.7% | −0.7% | −3.2% |
| Jordan | 4.1% | 1.5% | −4.8% | −0.1% | −3.0% | −0.6% | −3.2% |
| Madagascar | 0.6% | −3.9% | −1.4% | 2.4% | −0.6% | −0.1% | −3.2% |
| Peru | 3.1% | 1.7% | −2.9% | −1.5% | −2.0% | −0.8% | −2.6% |
| Vietnam | 2.9% | −2.1% | −2.4% | 0.6% | −0.6% | −0.7% | −2.3% |
| Austria | 1.3% | −2.4% | 1.0% | −0.6% | −0.6% | −1.0% | −2.3% |
| Chile | 0.8% | −2.4% | 1.5% | −0.9% | −0.8% | −0.2% | −2.0% |
| Portugal | 1.7% | 0.9% | −0.8% | −1.1% | −0.6% | −2.0% | −1.9% |
| Australia | 0.5% | 0.2% | −0.4% | −0.3% | −1.2% | 0.1% | −1.2% |
| India | 1.4% | 0.9% | −1.2% | −0.5% | −1.9% | 0.3% | −1.0% |
| France | −2.9% | 2.8% | 0.0% | −1.3% | −0.9% | 1.6% | −0.8% |
| New Zealand | 0.0% | −0.3% | −0.5% | 0.3% | 0.7% | −0.6% | −0.4% |
| Costa Rica | 0.4% | −0.1% | 0.3% | −0.5% | −0.8% | 0.4% | −0.2% |
| Japan | −0.8% | 1.1% | −0.8% | 0.0% | 0.8% | 0.0% | 0.3% |
| United Kingdom | 3.0% | −0.1% | −0.7% | −1.7% | −0.4% | 0.3% | 0.4% |
| Netherlands | 3.4% | −0.7% | −1.5% | −0.5% | −0.5% | 0.2% | 0.4% |
| South Africa | 1.7% | 0.3% | −1.6% | 1.4% | −0.4% | −1.0% | 0.4% |
| Guatemala | −0.1% | 0.1% | 4.6% | −2.3% | −1.2% | −0.6% | 0.4% |
| Sri Lanka | 0.6% | 2.8% | −0.9% | −0.2% | −3.0% | 1.2% | 0.4% |
| Uruguay | 1.9% | −1.9% | −0.6% | 0.7% | 0.6% | 0.0% | 0.5% |
| Sweden | 1.3% | 0.2% | −0.4% | 0.2% | 0.0% | −0.5% | 0.8% |
| Dominican Republic | −3.4% | −0.4% | −0.4% | 3.1% | 0.0% | 2.1% | 0.9% |
| Pakistan | 1.1% | 1.9% | −0.2% | −0.7% | −0.4% | −0.6% | 1.0% |
| Belize | −2.8% | −0.2% | 0.8% | 0.1% | 0.0% | 3.6% | 1.3% |
| Nigeria | 9.0% | −1.2% | −1.0% | −0.9% | −3.7% | −0.2% | 1.5% |
| Croatia | 1.0% | 1.0% | −0.6% | 1.1% | −1.0% | 0.7% | 2.3% |
| Norway | 1.7% | 0.8% | 0.7% | 0.1% | 0.5% | −1.5% | 2.3% |
| Romania | 6.6% | −0.7% | −1.9% | −1.5% | −0.8% | 0.9% | 2.4% |
| Canada | 3.8% | 0.3% | −0.1% | −0.2% | −1.0% | 0.1% | 2.9% |
| Slovenia | 1.9% | −0.3% | 0.5% | 1.7% | −0.4% | −0.4% | 3.0% |
| *Average* | *0.2%* | *−0.2%* | *−0.3%* | *−0.2%* | *−1.1%* | *−0.1%* | *−1.8%* |

Table 3.2 (*cont.*)

| | **Improving** | | | | | | |
|---|---|---|---|---|---|---|---|
| **Country** | **Δ15-16** | **Δ16-17** | **Δ17-19** | **Δ19-20** | **Δ20-21** | **Δ21-22** | **Δ15-22** |
| Ethiopia | −9.4% | −0.8% | 3.3% | 5.6% | −1.0% | −2.7% | −5.6% |
| Serbia | −0.7% | −0.3% | 0.1% | 0.6% | −1.8% | −0.9% | −3.0% |
| Afghanistan | −2.2% | −0.3% | 0.9% | 4.3% | −2.7% | −2.8% | −2.8% |
| Nepal | −2.2% | 1.1% | 0.8% | −0.7% | −1.1% | 0.5% | −1.7% |
| Kyrgyz Republic | −0.7% | 0.7% | 0.9% | 1.4% | −3.7% | −0.2% | −1.7% |
| Malaysia | −5.2% | −0.5% | 3.6% | 5.1% | −1.4% | −2.4% | −1.1% |
| Bulgaria | −0.8% | −2.4% | 2.4% | 0.5% | −1.0% | 0.8% | −0.6% |
| Senegal | 0.8% | −4.0% | 0.3% | −0.1% | 0.5% | 2.7% | 0.2% |
| Mongolia | 1.1% | 0.8% | 0.3% | −2.2% | 2.0% | −1.7% | 0.3% |
| Ecuador | −3.4% | 3.7% | 1.2% | 2.0% | −0.1% | −2.5% | 0.7% |
| Kenya | −3.5% | 4.0% | 0.5% | −0.2% | −0.9% | 1.0% | 0.7% |
| Indonesia | −0.1% | −0.9% | 0.9% | 1.3% | −1.0% | 1.2% | 1.3% |
| Czech Republic | 4.1% | −1.2% | −1.4% | 0.6% | −0.4% | 0.5% | 2.1% |
| Germany | 2.7% | 0.0% | 0.0% | 0.1% | 0.4% | −1.0% | 2.3% |
| Finland | 3.0% | −0.3% | 0.6% | −0.1% | 0.4% | −0.9% | 2.6% |
| Sierra Leone | | | 0.1% | −0.9% | −1.5% | 1.3% | 2.8% |
| Jamaica | 1.5% | 0.7% | −2.0% | 0.8% | 0.4% | 1.4% | 2.8% |
| Greece | −0.2% | 0.5% | 2.3% | −0.9% | −0.5% | 1.9% | 3.1% |
| Belgium | 2.8% | −2.0% | 2.4% | −0.5% | 0.6% | −0.1% | 3.1% |
| Denmark | 1.9% | 0.6% | 0.8% | 0.0% | 0.0% | 0.3% | 3.6% |
| Malawi | 0.7% | 0.6% | 0.8% | 0.7% | 1.0% | 0.2% | 4.0% |
| Italy | 0.1% | 0.6% | 0.9% | 0.5% | 0.2% | 1.6% | 4.1% |
| Ukraine | 1.9% | 1.6% | 1.0% | 0.8% | 0.6% | −1.3% | 4.7% |
| Kazakhstan | 1.3% | 2.2% | 0.9% | 0.9% | 0.3% | −0.9% | 4.9% |
| Argentina | 6.7% | 5.0% | 0.1% | −0.5% | −3.7% | −1.9% | 5.4% |
| Burkina Faso | 3.1% | 4.8% | 0.5% | −0.1% | −0.9% | −1.4% | 6.1% |
| Estonia | 1.8% | 1.2% | 1.3% | 0.0% | −0.1% | 1.7% | 6.2% |
| Spain | 2.0% | 0.9% | 2.4% | 1.3% | 0.1% | −0.2% | 6.6% |
| Zimbabwe | 0.8% | 0.6% | 7.1% | −1.5% | 0.0% | 0.7% | 7.7% |
| Moldova | 2.4% | −0.5% | −1.0% | 2.2% | 3.2% | 1.9% | 8.6% |
| Uzbekistan | −1.4% | 1.9% | 1.0% | 1.7% | 4.1% | 1.4% | 8.9% |
| *Average* | *0.3%* | *0.6%* | *1.1%* | *0.7%* | *−0.3%* | *0.0%* | *2.5%* |

scores for the 102 countries analyzed between 2015 and 2022. Three facts stand out. First, the aggregate rule-of-law score has dropped over time. The average percentage change revealed by this indicator during the period of analysis was −3.1 percent. Approximately 74 percent of countries

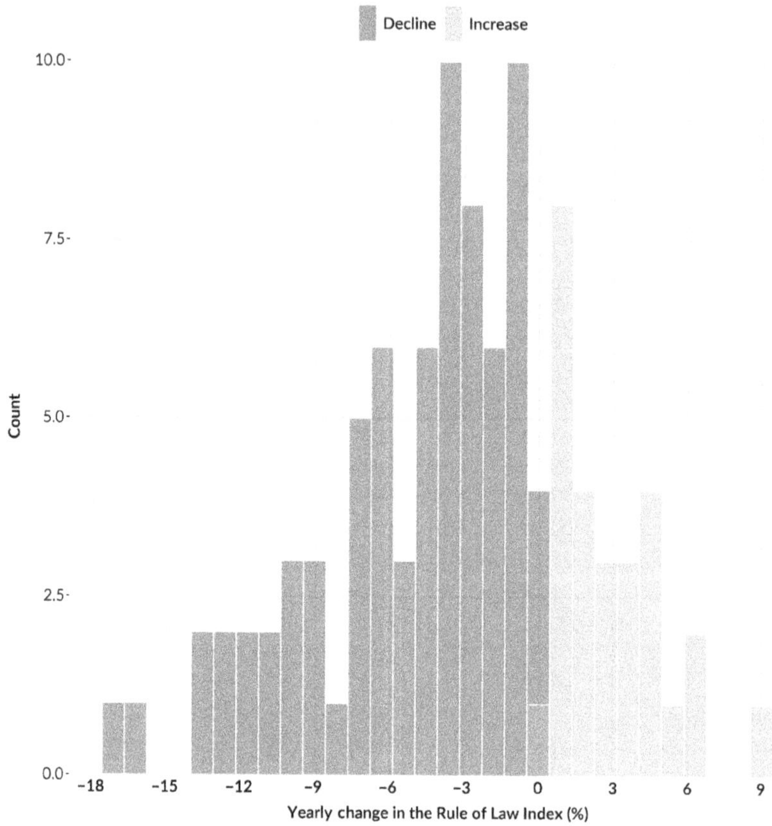


**Figure 3.3** Distribution of year-to-year changes in rule-of-law scores (2015 to 2022).
Source: World Justice Project

experienced a decline during these years, in some cases of significant magnitude, and only a few experienced improvements. Those that experienced a decline represent 69 percent of the world's population. Figure 3.3 presents these changes in the form of a histogram. Moreover, the decline has affected all regions of the world, but particularly the Middle East and North Africa, Latin America, and East Asia and the Pacific.

Second, rule-of-law backsliding has been more pronounced in countries that were already authoritarian and where the rule of law was already weak (i.e., Belarus, Cambodia, Nicaragua, and Venezuela) or in countries that have been exposed to emerging leaders with authoritarian tendencies (i.e., Brazil, El Salvador, Hungary, Poland, Philippines, Turkey). The average rule-of-law score for the ten countries in which the decline was steepest is

0.48, while the score for the remaining countries with negative changes is 0.58. In contrast, countries that experienced moderate declines between 0 and −5 percent during the study period (42 percent of the countries) are found across the entire rule-of-law spectrum. Countries that experienced improvements during these years comprise those that underwent ambitious reform processes (i.e., Kazakhstan, Moldova, and Uzbekistan), regime changes (Zimbabwe), changes of administration with ups and downs (i.e., Argentina and Burkina Faso), or minor improvements over the years (countries in the European Union). Finally, with the exception of countries that have experienced significant deterioration, in most countries the rule of law has waxed and waned over the years. In some cases, the rule of law strengthened at the beginning of the period and has weakened in recent years (i.e., Nigeria, Morocco, and Peru). In others, changes have occurred intermittently throughout the period (i.e., United Kingdom and South Africa). Interestingly, in some cases, year-to-year changes in the *rate* of changes – particularly when downwards – or changes from positive to negative, or vice versa, appear to be associated with changes in administration (i.e., Philippines in 2016, and the United States in 2016 and 2020). In other cases, however, they reflect small changes in the course of an administration (i.e., France since 2017). The greatest overall deterioration occurred notably during the COVID-19 pandemic.

Next, we explore changes in the index components and other indicators developed from the disaggregated data. Table 3.3 presents the descriptive statistics. In comparison with the overall rule-of-law scores, the scores for institutional checks on executive discretion, particularly factors 1 (constraints on government powers) and 4 (fundamental rights), have shown a much more pronounced deterioration during this period, both in terms of magnitude and number of countries. Factor 1 declines were experienced in 64 percent of countries and factor 4 declines in 76 percent of countries. The average percentage change for these indicators was −4.8 percent and −6.7 percent. The scores of other indicators constructed from the disaggregated data show similar trends. Scores for the sources of arbitrariness fell in more than 60 percent of countries, while those measuring anti-authoritarianism fell in 68 percent of countries (i.e., authoritarianism *increased* in 68 percent of countries), with the drop averaging −5.5 percent. In contrast, the indicators that measure the functioning of the legal system and, more broadly, the application of the law by state agents – i.e., security, regulatory enforcement, civil justice, and criminal justice – fell relatively little. Scores for the state capacity indicator fell in only 56 percent of countries, by an average of −0.3 percent.

Table 3.3 *Summary statistics based on the* WJP Rule of Law Index

| | Scores | | | Changes over time | | |
|---|---|---|---|---|---|---|
| | Average score in 2015 | Average score in 2022 | Δ 2015–22 | Proportion of countries that improved | Proportion of countries that declined | Δ 2019–22 |
| Rule-of-law score | 0.57 | 0.55 | -2.4% | 40% | 60% | −1.4% |
| F1. Constraints on government powers | 0.58 | 0.55 | -4.8% | 36% | 64% | −2.2% |
| F2. Absence of corruption | 0.52 | 0.51 | -0.9% | 40% | 60% | −1.9% |
| F3. Open government | 0.55 | 0.53 | -2.6% | 48% | 62% | −0.5% |
| F4. Fundamental rights | 0.60 | 0.57 | -6.3% | 24% | 76% | −2.7% |
| F5. Order and security | 0.73 | 0.73 | 0.0% | 44% | 66% | −0.3% |
| F6. Regulatory enforcement | 0.54 | 0.54 | 0.9% | 60% | 40% | −1.0% |
| F7. Civil justice | 0.55 | 0.54 | -1.1% | 46% | 54% | −1.2% |
| F8. Criminal justice | 0.49 | 0.48 | -1.8% | 44% | 56% | −1.2% |

*Source:* World Justice Project

## 2 *Unpacking the Backsliding: Country Groupings*

These findings suggest that the rule of law has indeed weakened worldwide, and this drop appears to have been caused by a weakening of limitations on the exercise of state power and a deterioration in fundamental rights (including the closure of civic space). In this section, we explore this hypothesis and unpack the backsliding of the rule of law. Given the slight variation in the aggregate scores, our analysis is based on variations over time in the different dimensions (or factors) of the *WJP Rule of Law Index*. We use cluster analysis to group countries according to how far each country lies from the others in terms of the overall change in factor scores between 2015 and 2022. To use the maximum possible variations, our main analysis focuses on the percentage change in the factor scores of the index. Later, we perform a similar analysis using the percentage change in the scores of the other two sets of indicators to classify countries. This numerical method allows us to organize the information efficiently and assign labels that provide a concise description of patterns of similarities and differences in rule-of law-trends. Once the information is organized, we can explore (a) the variations in the rule of law over time for the different countries, (b) the characteristics of the countries that have experienced declines, (c) the variations in the components of the index that explain the movements in the rule of law for different countries, and (d) factors that could be associated with the declines and, more broadly, with variations in the rule of law over time. Since the number of groups to classify is unknown, we use hierarchical clustering techniques.[27]

In our analysis, we identify three clusters. The dendrogram in Figure 3.4 shows the distribution of countries in each of these clusters. The first cluster comprises seventeen countries, the second sixty-two countries, and the third twenty-three countries. These groups show clear differences in rule-of-law trends. The panels of Table 3.2 present the cluster in which each country is located: backsliding, neutral, or improving. Although there are some exceptions, the clusters closely resemble the patterns identified in this table showing the aggregate scores. Figure 3.5 shows the changes in the aggregate rule-of-law indicator for the countries in each of the three groups.

[27] This method partitions a set of N observations into K groups in which each observation belongs to the group whose mean value is closest. In other words, the process minimizes the distance between each computed change through iterations that combine the most similar observations until they converge to form a given group. This method works better with homogeneous data, such as the change rate of the *WJP Rule of Rule of Law Index*.

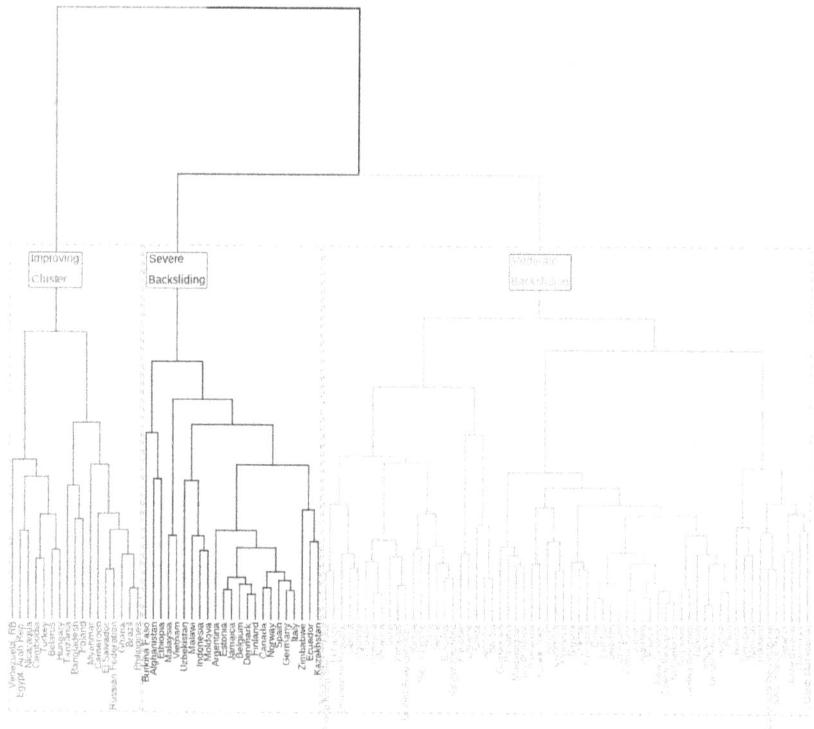


**Figure 3.4** Distribution of countries by cluster.

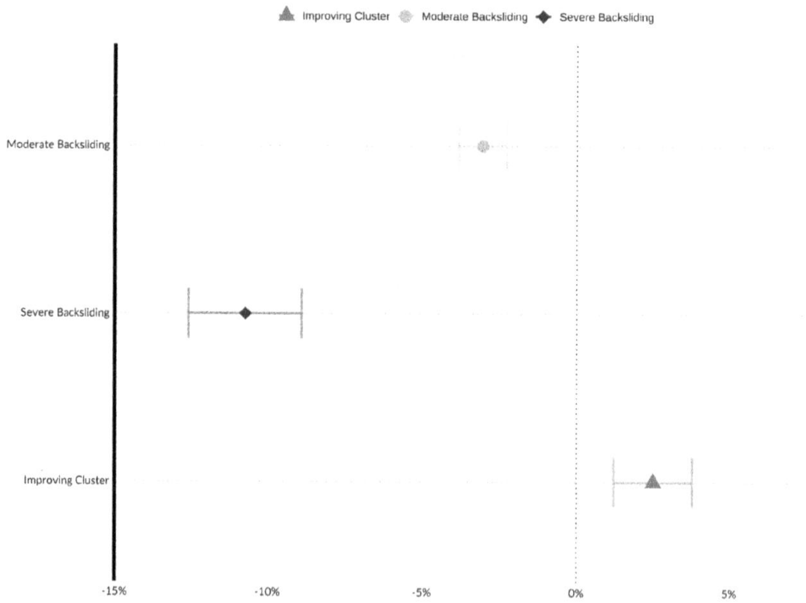


**Figure 3.5** Percentage changes in rule-of-law scores between 2015 and 2022, by clusters.

The countries in the first cluster experienced a drop in the rule-of-law score of –9.7 percent during the period. We label this group the "severe backsliding" cluster. Countries in the second group underwent a decline, but not as severe, with an average change of –3 percent. We call this group the "moderate backsliding" cluster. In contrast, the countries in the third cluster slightly improved their scores during the period, with an average change of 2.5 percent. We call this group the "improving" cluster. The difference between the three groups is statistically significant at the 5 percent level.

Table 3.4 shows additional statistics for the countries in the three clusters. The first section (A) presents the distribution of the clusters by region, the second (B) by income level, and the third (C) by socioeconomic characteristics. The fourth section (D) shows the rule of law scores at the beginning of the period. Three points deserve attention. First, as shown in Table 3.3, backsliding occurred in all regions of the world. Second, severe backsliding occurred mainly in middle-income countries, while moderate backsliding occurred mainly in high- and middle-income countries. Finally, countries in the backsliding cluster had lower scores than the other countries in 2015. Figure 3.6 is a scatter plot showing changes in the *WJP Rule of Law Index* between 2015 and 2022 and the levels of the rule of law in 2015 for the three groups of countries. Countries in the first group tend to have lower levels of rule of law, with the exception of Poland, while those in the second and third groups are spread across the entire rule-of-law spectrum.

## 3 *Drivers of the Decline*

We next examine the main drivers of these rule-of-law patterns. Figure 3.7 shows the average change in the indicators (factors) of the *WJP Rule of Law Index* over the 2015–22 period for the countries in each of the three clusters. Three findings stand out. First, the indicators in each of the groups tend to move in the same direction. The countries in the severe backsliding cluster show a statistically significant drop in almost all indicators. The indicators in the moderate backsliding group experienced statistically significant declines in almost all indicators, albeit of lesser magnitude, while the indicators in the third group experienced improvements in most indicators. Second, the indicators that fell most in the severe backsliding cluster are those measuring constraints on government powers, fundamental rights, criminal justice, and open government, which fell by 20 percent, 21 percent, 17 percent and 13 percent respectively. The indicators measuring constraints on government powers and fundamental rights

Table 3.4 *Country characteristics, by cluster*

| | Average for all countries | Backsliding | Neutral | Improving |
|---|---|---|---|---|
| | | *A. Distribution across regions* | | |
| EU, EFTA, and North America | 24% | 8% | 26% | 32% |
| East Asia and Pacific | 15% | 17% | 17% | 10% |
| Eastern Europe and Central Asia | 13% | 21% | 4% | 20% |
| Latin America and Caribbean | 19% | 25% | 21% | 10% |
| Middle East and North Africa | 7% | 8% | 11% | 0% |
| South Asia | 6% | 4% | 6% | 6% |
| Sub-Saharan Africa | 18% | 17% | 15% | 22% |
| | | *B. Distribution across income groups* | | |
| High | 32% | 8% | 47% | 29% |
| Upper-middle | 30% | 42% | 28% | 26% |
| Lower-middle | 29% | 50% | 19% | 29% |
| Low | 8% | 0% | 6% | 16% |
| | | *C. Socioeconomic characteristics* | | |
| Δ% GDP per capita (2015–22) | 1.13% | 0.57% | 2.15% | 1.24% |
| Unemployment rate (2015) | 7.46% | 7.35% | 7.31% | 7.74% |
| Share of world population (2021) | - | 37% | 48% | 15% |
| | | *D.: Rule of law* | | |
| Rule-of-law score in 2015 | 0.57 | 0.48 | 0.61 | 0.56 |

also fell in the moderate backsliding group and in some countries in the improving cluster. Figure 3.8, a scatter plot showing the percentage changes in these two indicators, confirms the clear differences that exist in these areas between the three groups of countries. The chart also reveals a clear link between checks and balances and the protection of individual rights. Finally, the indicators measuring corruption, order and security, regulatory enforcement, and civil justice fell much less in the countries in the severe backsliding cluster, declined slightly or remained unchanged in those in the moderate backsliding cluster, and improved in the third cluster countries.

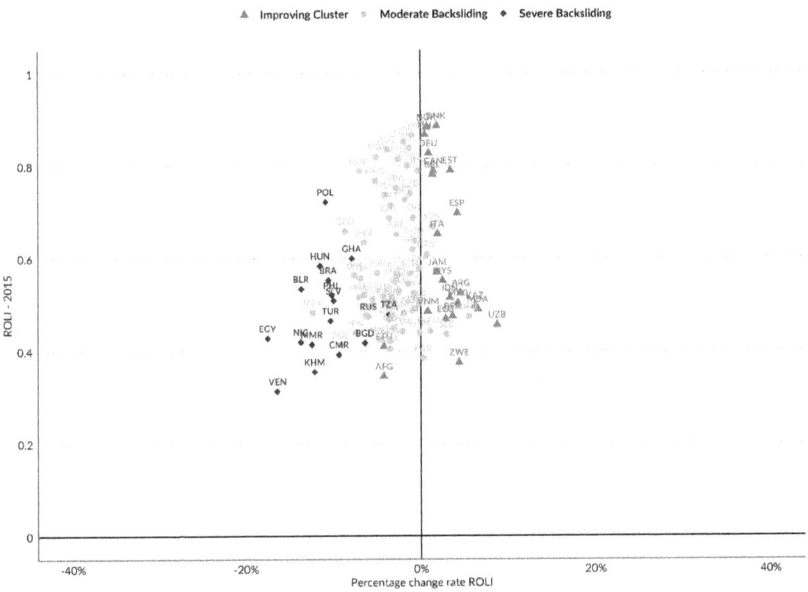


Figure 3.6 Rule-of-law changes and levels, by clusters.

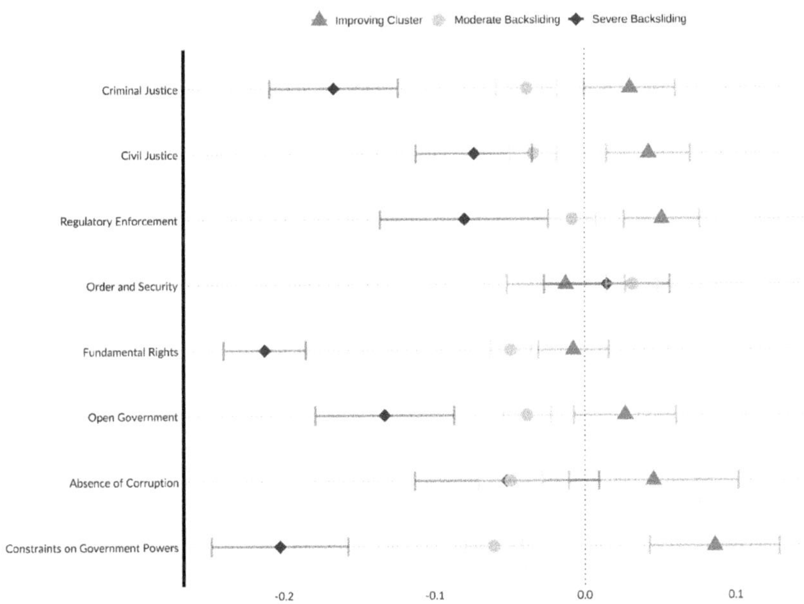


**Figure 3.7** Percentage changes in rule-of-law factor scores between 2015 and 2022, by clusters.

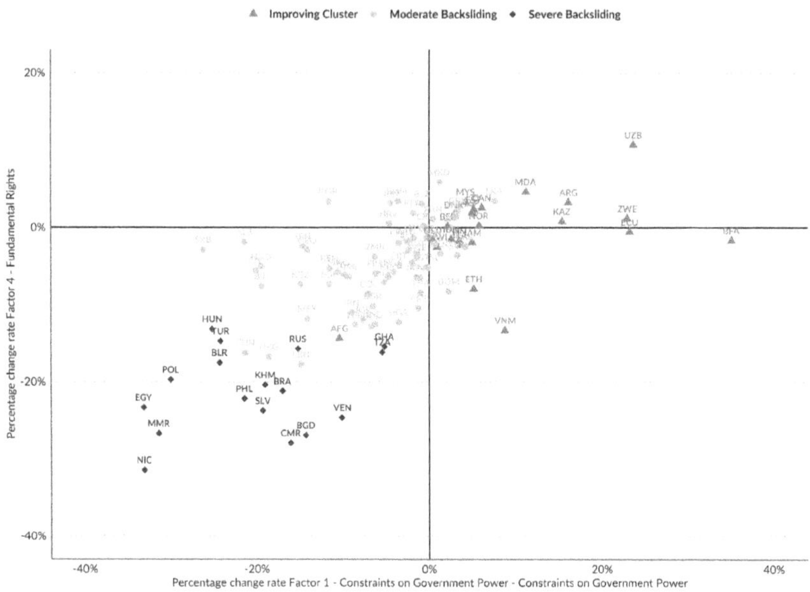


**Figure 3.8** Percentage changes in scores for constraints on government powers and fundamental rights between 2015 and 2022, by clusters.

These differences between clusters are robust to different rule-of-law definitions. Figures 3.9 and 3.10 show the changes over time in different rule-of law-indicators for the three groups of countries. Figure 3.9 shows the average change in the indicators proposed by Shaffer and Sandholtz over the 2015–22 period for the countries in each of the three clusters. These indicators focus on the imposition of limits on the exercise of power. Countries in the first group (severe backsliding) suffered declines under all indicators, with more pronounced declines under those measuring application of the law to rulers and proportionate link of means to end and reason-giving. The countries in the second group (moderate backsliding) also worsened under all indicators, although to a lesser extent and in a more homogeneous manner. Finally, the indicators in the third group showed improvements in all areas. Figure 3.10 shows the average changes for the indicators measuring control of authoritarianism (anti-authoritarianism), control of particularism (anti-particularism) and state capacity. The results confirm the above patterns. Countries in the first group suffered significant declines according to the indicators measuring control of authoritarianism, and more moderate declines according to the other two indicators. The countries in the second

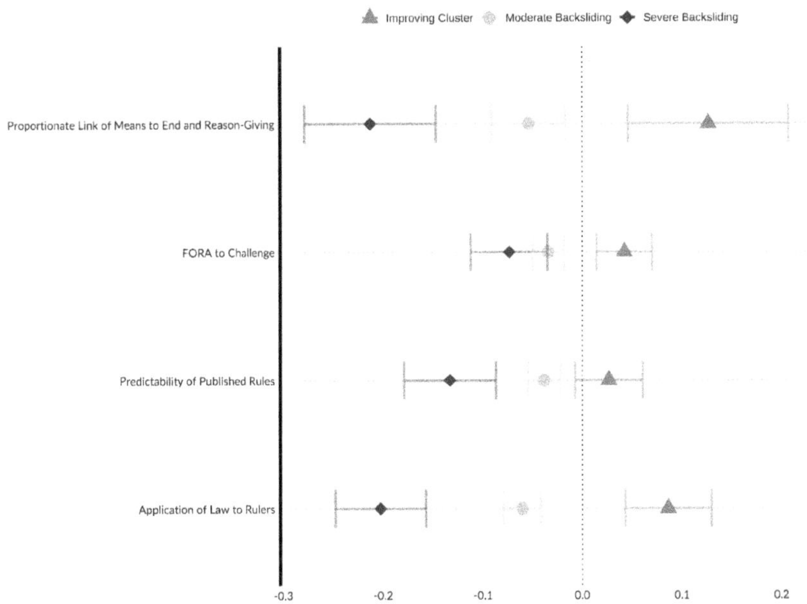


**Figure 3.9** Percentage changes in the scores under indicators measuring sources of arbitrariness between 2015 and 2022, by clusters.

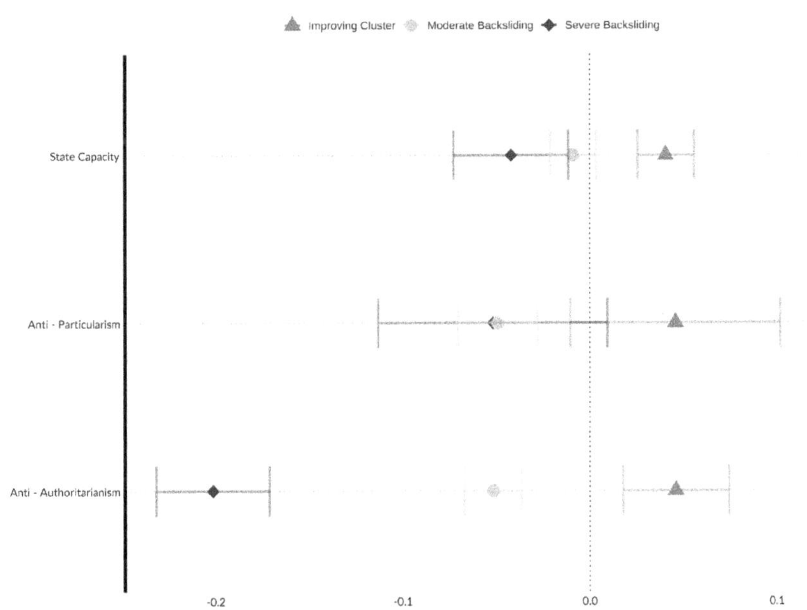


**Figure 3.10** Percentage changes in the anti-authoritarianism, anti-particularism and state capacity scores between 2015 and 2022, by clusters.

group (moderate backsliding) suffered similar declines in all areas and of lesser magnitude. Countries in the third group improved in all areas.

To explore the type of countries found in each of the groups, Figure 3.11 shows the percentage changes in different indicators over the study period and their levels in 2015. Consistent with the results in Table 3.2, rule-of-law backsliding has been more pronounced in authoritarian countries that began with weak rule of law. Countries with a less severe decline in the rule of law constitute a mixed group, some of them having strong institutions and higher levels of rule of law (France, Korea, Portugal), and others weak institutions and low levels of rule of law (India). Countries that have improved are either countries in transition, with weak rule of law, or countries with strong rule of law producing marginal changes. Although there is no single pattern, these results support the idea that the level of deterioration in the rule of law depends on the strength of institutions. Leaders of states with weak institutions have fewer constraints and can accelerate autocratization. In contrast, leaders of states with stronger institutions face greater constraints and checks, which serve as a buffer against backsliding. The source of these checks can be varied, and may include stronger legal and institutional frameworks, a developed bureaucracy, an effective opposition, a critical and free civil society and press, or free elections and democratic processes that allow for change of government.

The clustering of countries may vary due to year-to-year variations in the different indicators or to different ways of organizing the rule-of-law data. To check the robustness of our results, we performed two exercises. First, we repeated the cluster analysis by changing the starting periods. We found that 47 percent of the countries in the 2015–22 severe backsliding cluster remained in this group in three of the five exercises conducted for the different study periods. This figure rose to 65 percent when we considered the countries in the severe and moderate backsliding groups. In contrast, many countries in the improving group moved after changing the initial periods.

These results make sense. The countries in the severe backsliding group have experienced a significant and steady deterioration in the rule of law, measured through declines in all or almost all of the index indicators/factors. In contrast, countries in the other groups have suffered less severe downturns, or even experienced improvements, but these have been of lesser intensity, shorter, and linked to changes in administrations throughout the study period. At the same time, these countries have made little progress in improving regulatory enforcement, fighting corruption, or advancing justice, their scores for the other index

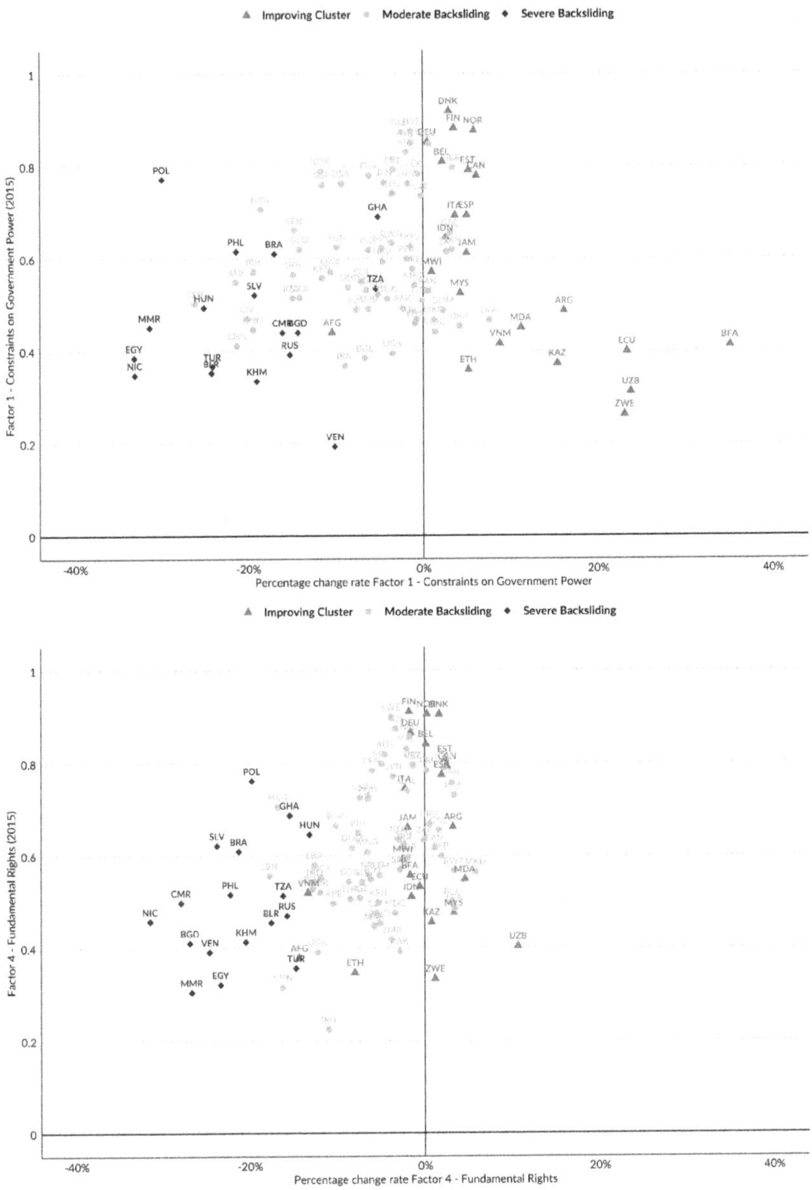


**Figure 3.11** Percentage changes (2015–22) and levels in 2015 for the indicators measuring constraints on government powers and fundamental rights, by clusters.

factors having changed (positively or negatively) to a lesser extent depending on the period of analysis. Second, we performed cluster analyses for the two groups of indicators explored above. In both cases, the classification yields three groups, one with severe declines and two other groups that are quite similar and less susceptible to change over the time period, in part because these exercises rely on fewer indicators. In spite of this, 82 percent of the countries in our original severe backsliding cluster fall into the clusters grouping countries with largest deteriorations resulting from the exercises involving the other two sets of indicators. In addition, we performed a cluster analysis on changes in index factors between 2015 and 2022 and the respective levels of these indicators in 2015. This analysis yielded a different classification comprising three groups: one similar to the severe backsliding cluster, another consisting of countries with high levels of rule of law, and a residual group containing the remaining countries.

Taken together, these results confirm the initial data trends. Of the countries in which the rule-of-law scores fell, 87 percent experienced a decline in the scores for constraints on government powers and 85 percent a decline in the scores for fundamental rights. In 79 percent of countries, both indicators fell. Similarly, 90 percent of countries in which the rules of law fell experienced a decline in the scores for freedom of opinion and expression or freedom of association, which are a proxy for civic space. These results lend support to our hypothesis that the deterioration in the rule of law is the result of a weakening of limitations on state power and a deterioration in fundamental rights, not the result of an increase in the level of particularism (or a rise in corruption) or a deterioration in the functioning of the legal system (i.e., law enforcement agencies, regulatory agencies, or judicial actors).

We now turn from manifestations of the decline trends in the rule of law to focus on political factors that could explain these trends. As we saw in Table 3.2, in many countries the rule of law moves in cycles – that is, an abrupt trend change between two years led to a situation that lasted several years until another abrupt trend change occurred. The length and extent of these cycles vary from country to country, which suggests that rule-of-law changes may be linked to changes in political leadership, and thus in the structure of government. Recent literature has shown that populism and antipluralistic trends are dangerous for the rule of law. According to the literature, populist and antipluralistic leaders rise to power because of the failure of governments, elites, and institutions to meet citizens' growing demands. Such leaders use narratives centered on people and antigroups, often the political elite (antiestablishment). These narratives change little when the leaders come to power; on the contrary, they expand to include democratic institutions, media, and civil society. Bugaric and Kuhelj assert that the surge of populism and authoritarian populism in countries whose core principles no longer enjoy democratic support put the rule of law and liberal institutions in danger, largely because populist leaders have the legitimacy to change laws and even constitutions – as in Hungary – that protect minorities, limit discretion, and give voice to different political groups.[28] Sato and Arce argue that populist and antipluralistic leaders could be associated with democratic backsliding.[29] They found that the exclusionary rhetoric of populist leaders in some countries in Latin America and their attack on existing democratic norms have been used as a tool to win elections. In other cases, backsliding occurs through participatory processes, such as referendums or assemblies.[30]

We examine this hypothesis using the V-Party dataset to construct a measure of exposure to authoritarian platforms. More specifically, we use two composite annual indicators based on the platforms and speeches of the political parties that have come to power in each country between 2015 and 2019:[31] (a) an antipluralism index that measures the extent to which representatives of a given party show a lack of commitment to democratic norms prior to elections; and (b) a populism index that measures the extent to which representatives of a given party use a populist rhetoric. The first indicator is an aggregate score that a group of experts assign to a political party based on the treatment of political opponents and minority groups by its leaders or the respect they show for free and fair elections or political freedoms, among other aspects. The second indicator is an aggregate score that a group of experts assign to a political party based on the use of antielite rhetoric or the frequency with which they glorify ordinary people and identify with them, among other aspects. We use these indices to define two binary variables that equal one if the head of government resulting from the election belongs to a political party whose antipluralism or populist index is above the

[28] Bojan Bugaric & Alenka Kuhelj, *Varieties of Populism in Europe: Is the Rule of Law in Danger?*, 10 HAGUE J. ON RULE L. 21 (2018).

[29] Yuko Sato & Moisés Arce, *Resistance to Populism*, 29 DEMOCRATIZATION 1137 (2022).

[30] ANTHONY W. PEREIRA, POLITICAL (IN)JUSTICE: AUTHORITARIANISM AND THE RULE OF LAW IN BRAZIL, CHILE, AND ARGENTINA (2005); Nancy Bermeo, *On Democratic Backsliding*, 27 J. DEMOCRACY 5 (2016).

[31] The indicators are annual and cover up to 2019.

seventieth percentile of the value for all parties recorded between 2015 and 2019. We say that a country experienced a change of party administration to an antidemocratic platform if at least one of these two variables is equal to one. Conversely, we say that a country experienced a change of party administration to a democratic platform if both these variables are equal to zero.

Table 3.5 shows the change in the rule of law between 2015 and 2022 for each of the countries in the three clusters, together with categorical variables indicating whether, during the 2015–19 period, there was a regime change in which the winning party used an antipluralist or populist (antidemocratic) platform, whether there was a regime change in which the winning party did not use either of these platforms (democratic), whether there was no platform change (although there may have been a change of party), or whether there were both democratic and antidemocratic changes in the country during the period of analysis. Although the data does not indicate whether the parties that came to power in 2019 were still in power in 2022 or whether there was a platform change after 2019, it reveals some interesting patterns. First, the vast majority of countries did not experience regime changes with different political platforms, which may simply reflect the shortness of the time frame. Despite this, the rule of law fell in many of them. Second, most of the countries listed as backsliding did not experience a regime change. This makes sense since many of those countries are autocracies, which supports the idea that a weakening of the rule of law, checks and balances, and accountability mechanisms tends to lead to a weakening of democratic processes. Nevertheless, several countries, including Poland, Turkey, Mexico, Brazil, Iran, and Côte d'Ivoire, did experience power changes and new leaders rising to power on antipluralist or populist platforms. On average, the rule of law in countries with no regime change and those with regime changes to antidemocratic platforms deteriorated by approximately the same amount within the backsliding cluster. Third, in general, the rule of law improved (or deteriorated less) in countries where leaders came to power on pluralist and nonpopulist (what we call democratic) platforms, compared to countries where the leaders used antipluralist or populist platforms.

Taken together, these results show that the rule of law has indeed deteriorated in most countries around the world. In some countries, this deterioration has been continuous; in others, it has varied over the years. The deterioration in the rule of law is associated with a weakening of limitations on state power, as measured by governmental and

Table 3.5 *Rule-of-law backsliding and regime change*

| | Backsliding | |
|---|---|---|
| **Country** | **Δ2015–22** | **Regime change** |
| Egypt | −23.5% | No change |
| Cambodia | −16.1% | No change |
| Venezuela | −14.4% | No change |
| Nicaragua | −13.6% | No change |
| Myanmar | −12.3% | Democratic to antidemocratic |
| Belarus | −12.2% | No change |
| Bolivia | −11.4% | No change |
| Philippines | −11.0% | No change |
| El Salvador | −10.3% | No change |
| Poland | −9.9% | Change to antidemocratic |
| Turkey | −9.9% | Antidemocratic |
| Mexico | −9.8% | Antidemocratic |
| Cameroon | −9.7% | No change |
| Hungary | −8.8% | No change |
| Georgia | −8.3% | No change |
| Ghana | −8.2% | No change |
| Bosnia and Herzegovina | −8.0% | Democratic/antidemocratic |
| Brazil | −7.6% | Antidemocratic |
| Iran | −6.9% | Antidemocratic |
| Côte d'Ivoire | −6.1% | Antidemocratic |
| Albania | −6.1% | No change |
| Bangladesh | −4.9% | No change |
| China | −2.9% | No change |
| Tanzania | −2.1% | No change |
| *No change* | *−10.2%* | *16* |
| *Antidemocratic* | *−8.4%* | *6* |
| *Democratic* | - | *0* |
| *Democratic to antidemocratic* | *−10.2%* | *2* |
| | **Neutral** | |
| **Country** | **Δ2015–22** | **Regime change** |
| Korea, Republic of | −7.0% | Democratic |
| Botswana | −6.9% | No change |
| Morocco | −6.4% | No change |
| Zambia | −6.4% | No change |
| Honduras | −6.3% | No change |
| Tunisia | −6.0% | No change |
| Lebanon | −5.8% | No change |
| Uganda | −4.3% | No change |
| Russian Federation | −4.1% | No change |

Table 3.5 (*cont.*)

| | **Backsliding** | |
|---|---|---|
| Hong Kong SAR, China | −4.1% | No change |
| Singapore | −4.0% | No change |
| Colombia | −4.0% | Antidemocratic |
| Thailand | −3.6% | Democratic |
| Thailand | −3.6% | Antidemocratic |
| United States | −3.6% | Antidemocratic |
| United Arab Emirates | −3.6% | No change |
| Liberia | −3.3% | No change |
| Panama | −3.2% | Antidemocratic |
| Jordan | −3.2% | No change |
| Madagascar | −3.2% | No change |
| Peru | −2.6% | Democratic |
| Vietnam | −2.3% | No change |
| Austria | −2.3% | Democratic |
| Chile | −2.0% | Democratic |
| Portugal | −1.9% | Democratic |
| Australia | −1.2% | Democratic |
| India | −1.0% | Antidemocratic |
| France | −0.8% | Democratic |
| New Zealand | −0.4% | Democratic |
| Costa Rica | −0.2% | Antidemocratic |
| Japan | 0.3% | No change |
| United Kingdom | 0.4% | No change |
| Netherlands | 0.4% | No change |
| South Africa | 0.4% | No change |
| Guatemala | 0.4% | Democratic/antidemocratic |
| Sri Lanka | 0.4% | Anti-democratic |
| Uruguay | 0.5% | Democratic |
| Sweden | 0.8% | Democratic |
| Dominican Republic | 0.9% | No change |
| Pakistan | 1.0% | Antidemocratic |
| Belize | 1.3% | No change |
| Nigeria | 1.5% | Antidemocratic |
| Croatia | 2.3% | Democratic |
| Norway | 2.3% | Democratic |
| Romania | 2.4% | No change |
| Canada | 2.9% | Democratic |

Table 3.5 (*cont.*)

| | **Backsliding** | |
|---|---|---|
| Slovenia | 3.0% | Democratic |
| *No change* | *−2.9%* | *22* |
| *Antidemocratic* | *−1.4%* | *9* |
| *Democratic* | *−0.7%* | *15* |
| *Democratic/antidemocratic* | *0.4%* | *1* |
| **Country** | **Improving Δ2015–22** | **Regime change** |
| Ethiopia | −5.6% | No change |
| Serbia | −3.0% | Anti-democratic |
| Afghanistan | −2.8% | No change |
| Kyrgyz Republic | −1.7% | No change |
| Malaysia | −1.1% | Antidemocratic |
| Senegal | 0.2% | No change |
| Mongolia | 0.3% | Antidemocratic |
| Ecuador | 0.7% | No change |
| Kenya | 0.7% | Democratic/antidemocratic |
| Indonesia | 1.3% | Antidemocratic |
| Czech Republic | 2.1% | Democratic/antidemocratic |
| Germany | 2.3% | No change |
| Finland | 2.6% | Democratic |
| Greece | 3.1% | Democratic |
| Greece | 3.1% | Antidemocratic |
| Belgium | 3.1% | Democratic |
| Denmark | 3.6% | Democratic |
| Malawi | 4.0% | No change |
| Italy | 4.1% | Democratic |
| Ukraine | 4.7% | Antidemocratic |
| Kazakhstan | 4.9% | No change |
| Argentina | 5.4% | Democratic/antidemocratic |
| Burkina Faso | 6.1% | Democratic/antidemocratic |
| Estonia | 6.2% | Democratic |
| Spain | 6.6% | Democratic |
| Zimbabwe | 7.7% | No change |
| Moldova | 8.6% | Antidemocratic |
| Uzbekistan | 8.9% | No change |
| *No change* | *1.9%* | *10* |
| *Antidemocratic* | *2.0%* | *7* |
| *Democratic* | *4.2%* | *7* |
| *Democratic To antidemocratic* | *3.6%* | *4* |

nongovernmental checks and balances and the protection of fundamental rights and freedoms. Except in those cases that have experienced a sharp decline, the weakening of the rule of law is not associated with an acute deterioration in the application or enforcement of the law or diminished access to justice. These indicators, however, have shown little improvement in recent years. The weakening of the rule of law appears to be associated, in part, with an increase in the authoritarian tendencies of already authoritarian regimes and, in part, with the rise of antipluralist and populist leaders. In general, the rule of law has strengthened in most high-income countries (although the United States is a noteworthy exception), which reveals an emerging global divergence between high-rule-of-law countries (liberal democracies) and low-rule-of-law countries (autocracies).

## V Conclusion

In this chapter we have presented evidence of the backsliding in the rule of law around the world. This deterioration has been caused by the weakening of institutional checks and balances and the closing of civic space, and has not been homogeneous around the world. This backsliding of the rule of law raises important challenges.

From an academic point of view, there are questions that require immediate attention. For example, what are the mechanisms that have led to rule-of law-backsliding? What factors explain this deterioration over time? What institutional or social safeguards are most effective in preventing this erosion? Is it possible to reverse these trends? How does this type of backsliding impact other rule-of-law outcomes? How does it affect other socioeconomic outcomes? Answering these questions requires detailed cross-country datasets that go beyond perceptions, case studies, and the segmentation of the problems analyzed. More importantly, it calls for the rule of law to be understood as the result of interplay between a multiplicity of institutions and actors, each with differing degrees of power and incentives.

From a practical point of view, the deterioration of the rule of law can have an enormous social impact. The weakening of institutional checks and balances – by restricting the independence and autonomy of democratic institutions and closing civic spaces – reduces government accountability and the incentives of state agents to deliver results or improve their performance, as well as the ability of citizens to exert pressure or seek change through the ballot box. This is particularly worrisome, given other shortcomings in the rule of law that afflict people around the world – i.e., corruption, violence, legal marginalization, and lack of access to justice. Meanwhile, this deterioration continues to expand across the apparatus of government and the legal system, becoming all the harder to reverse.

Combating these tendencies is a complicated political problem, given the lack of incentives for authoritarian leaders and power groups to accept being bound by certain rules and the citizens' growing disaffection with existing institutions and the establishment that populist and anti-pluralist leaders have been quick to exploit. That said, the fact that rule-of-law backsliding is often gradual means that it potentially can be reversed if a new administration that is more committed to the rule of law takes office.

# PART II

## International Organizations and Transnational Legal Ordering of the Rule of Law

# 4

# International Organizations as Constitution-Shapers

## Promoting or Undermining a Transnational Rule of Law?

ANNE PETERS

## I Introduction

The United Nations Assistance Mission in Afghanistan (UNAMA) had been mandated by the UN Security Council to "support the efforts of the Government of Afghanistan in fulfilling its commitments to improve governance and the rule of law."[1] In hindsight, after the irregular seizure of power by the Taliban government on August 15, 2021, this reads as being, misguided and naive. After all, the twenty-year-long, UN-led rule-of-law process in Afghanistan, including the adoption of a liberal constitution with intense UN (and US) involvement,[2] seems to have been annihilated.

UNAMA is only one example of the widespread rule-of-law-related activities by a range of international organizations at different places on the globe. This chapter spotlights their recommendations and prescriptions on *constitution-making and reform* – which involve the rule of law as a constitutional principle.[3] The explanation for focusing on constitution-making and reform is that the rule of law seems to be better protected when a given polity possesses a constitution. The UN

[1] S.C. Res. 2543, ¶ 6(h) (Sept. 15, 2020). This Res. is no longer cited in current S.C. Res. 2727 (March 15, 2024).

[2] CONSTITUTION (Jan. 3, 2004) (Afg.). On the UN engagement, see Zaid Al-Ali, *Constitutional Drafting and External Influence*, *in* COMPARATIVE CONSTITUTIONAL LAW 77, 80–82 (Tom Ginsburg & Rosalind Dixon eds., 2011); Tanya Domenica Bosi, *Post-Conflict Reconstruction: The United Nations' Involvement in Afghanistan*, 19 N.Y. L. SCH. J. HUM. RTS. 819 (2003).

[3] This chapter thus zooms in on one form of the "indirect processual links supporting rule-of-law practices within states" discussed by Gregory Shaffer and Wayne Sandholtz in Chapter 1. I use material from Anne Peters, *International Organizations as Constitution-Shapers: Lawful but Sometimes Illegitimate, and Often Futile*, 8 U.C. IRVINE J. INT'L TRANSNAT'L & COMP. L. 61 (2023).

Secretary-General's 2008 Guidance Note on the Rule of Law posits as a "framework for strengthening the rule of law" a "Constitution or equivalent, which, as the highest law of the land," must also possess certain ingredients, ranging from the incorporation of international human rights guarantees to upholding an independent judiciary.[4]

The constitution-shaping activity of international organizations involves other constitutional principles besides the rule of law, notably human rights and democracy.[5] Depending on how it is conceptualized, the rule of law encompasses or complements these ideas.[6] Importantly, UN member states have embraced the rule of law as a lead concept for *both* domestic and international law:[7] the key General Assembly resolution expressly stipulates that "the rule of law applies *to all states* equally *and to international organizations*, including the United Nations and its principal organs."[8] This statement indicates that the rule of law has a transnational or multilevel quality.[9]

The chapter proceeds as follows: Part II gives some examples of how, since 1989, international organizations have sought to shape state constitutions and thereby the domestic rule of law. Part III briefly shows that, for the most part, these activities have not led to better operation of the rule of law on the ground. Next, in Part IV, the main critiques against constitutional assistance and advice by international organizations are listed. My response is that, in order to become more legitimate (which might then also improve effectiveness) constitution-shaping by international organizations needs to absorb postcolonial concerns and must be complemented by a much deeper social agenda with a global ambition (Part V). Thus revamped, international organizations' constitution-shaping role could be reinvigorated so as to sustain the rule of law on the domestic level (Part VI).

[4] UN Secretary-General, *United Nations Approach to Rule of Law Assistance*, Guidance Note of the Secretary General, at 4–5 (Apr. 14, 2008), https://digitallibrary.un.org/record/4024519?v=pdf [hereinafter *UN Approach*] (emphasis added).

[5] On the promotion of democracy by international organizations, see Jon C. Pevehouse, Democracy from Above: Regional Organizations and Democratization 204 (2005); Paul Poast & Johannes Urpelainen, *How International Organizations Support Democratization: Preventing Authoritarian Reversals or Promoting Consolidation?*, 67 World Pols. 72, 107 (2015).

[6] *See* Chapter 1.

[7] G.A. Res. 67/1, Declaration of the High-Level Meeting of the General Assembly on the Rule of Law at the National and International Levels (Nov. 30, 2012).

[8] *Id.* ¶ 2 (emphasis added).

[9] On the transnational perspective, see Chapter 1 (Part II).

## II Constitution-Shaping in Various Guises

### *1 Membership Conditions*

Since 1989, organizations such as the European Union (EU), the Council of Europe (CoE), and the North Atlantic Treaty Organization (NATO) have stimulated serious constitutional reforms in those Eastern and Central European states that sought to accede. As a condition for membership, deep rule-of-law-related reforms had to be undertaken.

The most influential organization has probably been the EU. Twelve Central and Eastern European candidate states acceded to the EU in two main waves, in 2004 and 2007.[10] When the first Central Eastern enlargement was under discussion, the European Community, as the organization was then called (under the broader 'roof' of the European Union), did not yet possess substantive accession criteria in its primary law. Rather, the accession criteria were spelled out in the Presidency Conclusions issued at the European Council's Copenhagen meeting in 1993 in which it was stated:

> Membership requires that the candidate country has achieved stability of institutions guaranteeing democracy, the *rule of law*, human rights and respect for and protection of minorities, the existence of a functioning market economy as well as the capacity to cope with competitive pressure and market forces within the Union. Membership presupposes the candidate's ability to take on the obligations of membership including adherence to the aims of political, economic and monetary union.[11]

Later, these so-called Copenhagen criteria for accession were written into the 2007 Lisbon version of the Treaty on European Union in Article 49, read in conjunction with the clause on the Union's "values" in Article 2. These "values" include the rule of law.[12] As a result, accession of the new Central and Eastern European states to the EU implied transformations that affected "the very structure of the constitution" of those states.[13]

[10] In 2004, ten states acceded to the EU: Cyprus, Czech Republic, Estonia, Hungary, Latvia, Lithuania, Malta, Poland, Slovakia, and Slovenia. In 2007, Bulgaria and Romania became EU members.

[11] Council, Conclusions of the Presidency 13 (European Council in Copenhagen, June 21–22, 1993) (emphasis added).

[12] Consider the parallelism between internal and "outbound" principles in Treaty on European Union art. 21, Dec. 13, 2007, 2008 O.J. (C 115) 13.

[13] Luis López Guerra, *The Challenges to Candidate States*, *in* CONSTITUTIONAL IMPLICATIONS OF ACCESSION TO THE EUROPEAN UNION 21, 27 (Eur. Comm'n for Democracy through Law ed., 2002).

Similarly, the CoE requested rule-of-law reforms. The accession standards are laid down in Article 3 of the organization's founding treaty (the Statute of the CoE) and in secondary law. Article 3 requires acceptance of "the principles of the rule of law." In accession practice, this provision has been interpreted as requiring ratification of the European Convention on Human Rights (ECHR) and the establishment of a pluralist parliamentary democracy.[14] Membership is strictly conditioned upon having a liberal and democratic constitution that endorses the trinity of rule of law, human rights, and democracy.[15]

Admission to the World Trade Organization (WTO) also had repercussions for the rule of law. The requirements for WTO membership are laid down in so-called accession protocols, which differ from one candidate state to another. A famous case was China's accession to the WTO in 2001. In its accession protocol, China notably committed itself to transparency and judicial review.[16] Transparency and judicial review are key components of the rule of law. These principles must now be observed by China in trade and economic policy, because the state would otherwise not be fulfilling its treaty obligations.

These examples illustrate how the prospects of accession to various international and regional organizations have functioned as incentives for domestic constitutional reforms, including the improvement of rule-of-law-related institutions.

### 2 *Conditionalities, Indicators, Benchmarking, Advice*

Further and subsequent to preaccession incentives, the activity of international organizations has the potential to directly or indirectly shape the constitutions of states, which in turn has repercussions on the national

[14] On democracy as the only political model compatible with the ECHR, see Zdanoka v. Latvia, App. No. 58278/00, ¶ 98 (Mar. 16, 2006), https://hudoc.echr.coe.int/?i=001-72794.

[15] On the demands that the CoE, in particular its Parliamentary Assembly, brought to bear on new postcommunist constitutions, see Heinrich Klebes & Despina Chatzivassiliou, *Problèmes d'ordre constitutionnel dans le processus d'adhésion d'États de l'Europe centrale et orientale au Conseil de l'Europe*, 8 REVUE UNIVERSELLE DES DROITS DE L'HOMME 269 (1996); Jean-François Flauss, *Les conditions d'admission des pays d'Europe centrale et orientale au sein du Conseil de l'Europe*, 5 EUR. J. INT'L L. 401 (1994); Heinrich Klebes, *Membership in International Organizations and National Constitutional Law: A Case Study of the Law and Practice of the Council of Europe*, 69 ST. LOUIS-WARSAW TRANSATLANTIC L.J. 69 (1999).

[16] World Trade Organization, *Accession of the People's Republic of China*, WTO Doc. WT/L/423, at 34 (2001).

rule of law. Rule-of-law promotion by international organizations that calls for constitutional reform often overlaps with other activity that does not directly address or imply specifically *constitutional* law. A famous example is the Venice Commission's *Rule of Law Checklist* of 2016.[17] Also the UN Secretary-General has defined the rule of law in the context of transitional justice.[18]

This chapter leaves aside those rule-of-law activities by international organizations that pertain to specific fields such as fighting impunity. Also, it leaves out the work of universal human rights bodies and regional human courts, although, as part of their human rights monitoring, they occasionally recommend or request not only individual measures toward specific victims or legislative reforms but also *constitutional* reforms to remedy human rights violations. A recent example is the response to the ongoing rule-of-law crisis in Hungary and Poland. Here, European courts have derived the states' obligations to restore an independent judiciary from human rights obligations.[19] Another example of explicit and broad rule-of-law requests by a human rights body is the work of the Inter-American Commission concerning corruption – corruption (the rule of money) being the antithesis of the rule of law.[20]

International financial institutions (IFIs), especially, have exercised pressure to reform state constitutions. Their activity (of both benchmarking[21] and outright conditionalities) has included a focus on explicit requests for rule-of-law-related reforms, which in turn imply constitutional reform. For example, the worldwide governance indicators created by the World Bank and the Brookings Institution have always invoked the rule of law. And the World Bank country policy and institutional assessments (CPIA), which since 2005 have been made public, rate

[17] Eur. Comm'n for Democracy Through Law (Venice Comm'n), Rule of Law Checklist, 106th Sess., Study No. 711/2013, CDL-AD(2016)007-e (2016), www.venice.coe.int/webforms/documents/default.aspx?pdffile=CDL-AD(2016)007-e.

[18] UN Secretary-General, *The Rule of Law and Transitional Justice in Conflict and Post-conflict Societies*, ¶ 6, UN Doc. S/2004/616 (Aug. 23, 2004) [hereinafter *The Rule of Law and Transitional Justice*].

[19] Gręda v. Poland, App. No. 43572/18, ¶ 323 (Mar. 15, 2022), https://hudoc.echr.coe.int/?i=001-216400.

[20] INTER-AM COMM'N H.R., CORRUPTION AND HUMAN RIGHTS IN THE AMERICAS: INTER-AMERICAN STANDARDS (Dec. 6, 2019).

[21] *E.g.*, World Bank Group's Ease of Doing Business rankings, https://data.worldbank.org/indicator/IC.BUS.EASE.XQ; OECD's FDI Regulatory Restrictiveness Index, www.oecd-ilibrary.org/finance-and-investment/data/oecd-international-direct-investment-statistics/oecd-fdi-regulatory-restrictiveness-index-edition-2021_2a305f32-en.

the recipient countries according to various criteria such as "property rights and rule-based governance" and "transparency, accountability, and corruption in the public sector."[22]

The next most relevant constitutional dimension affected by IFIs' activities concerns the welfare and social provisions of state constitutions. World Bank and IMF policies, programs, and rules of the game, notably the conditionalities, may affect the recipient states' bureaucracy and influence public spending (e.g., on state education).[23] As part of adjustment programs set up by IFIs, states have enacted legal reforms that have negatively affected the enjoyment of constitutionally (and internationally) guaranteed human rights, such as entitlements to pensions protected as property, the right to social security, the right to health, and the right to education. These rights form part of a "thick" and "social" vision of the rule of law.[24]

Another "defender of the rule of law" (to use the word of its former Director and Secretary Thomas Markert) is the Venice Commission.[25] This is a body operating within the framework of the CoE.[26] Since its creation in 1990, the Venice Commission has been heavily involved in constitution-making and constitutional reform, always upon a request from a member state, a body of the CoE such as the Committee of Ministers or the Parliamentary Assembly, or from an international organization such as the EU. The Venice Commission has issued opinions that concern the drafting of entire constitutions or significant parts of them, has provided assistance for constitutional reforms, and has made pronouncements on legislative projects that flesh out constitutional provisions in numerous cases. The Commission notably gives regular advice on the organization of the judiciary and on electoral law. Although the latter group of opinions formally rank as provisions of

[22] World Bank Group, CPIA Africa: Assessing Africa's Policies and Institutions, at 62 (August 2020) ("Cluster D").

[23] Thomas Stubbs et al., *How to Evaluate the Effects of IMF Conditionality: An Extension of Quantitative Approaches and an Empirical Application to Public Education Spending*, 15 Rev. Int'l. Org. 29 (2020).

[24] *Id.*

[25] Thomas Markert, *Die Venedig-Kommission des Europarats: Vom Beratungsgremium zum Akteur der Verteidigung von Rechtsstaat und Demokratie (1990–2022)*, 49 Europäische Grundrechte-Zeitschrift 608 (2022).

[26] Eur. Comm'n for Democracy through Law (Venice Comm'n), CM Res. (2002)3, Revised Statute of the European Commission for Democracy through Law, art. 3(2), CDL (2002) 27 (2002).

ordinary statutory law, they are eminently important for the practical functioning of the rule of law in the states concerned.[27]

Outside Europe, regional organizations have been working to support the establishment, consolidation, and protection of democratic systems of government, and concomitantly the rule of law. The Organization of American States adopted the Inter-American Democratic Charter on the very day of the September 11, 2001 terrorist attacks. Article 2 of the Charter states that "[t]he effective exercise of representative democracy is *the basis for the rule of law* and of the constitutional regimes of the member states of the Organization of American States."[28]

In 2007, the African Union adopted the African Charter on Democracy, Elections and Governance.[29] Under this instrument, which entered into force in 2012, the Peace and Security Council (PSC) of the African Union can suspend governments that have come to power through an unconstitutional change in government. Such suspensions have most recently been put in place against Mali, Guinea, Sudan, and Burkina Faso after military coups in those states.[30]

Given that many other rule-of-law-related activities of international organizations also, to a lesser or greater extent, involve state constitutions, the examples given in this section are incomplete. They must suffice to illustrate the claim that international and regional organizations have a track record of attempting to improve the "domestic" rule of law by shaping the constitutions of their member states. The intensity of their engagement has varied greatly, however, across the different regions of the world.

[27] Paul Craig, *Transnational Constitution-Making: The Contribution of the Venice Commission on Law and Democracy*, *in* CONSTITUTION-MAKING AND TRANSNATIONAL LEGAL ORDER 156, 156–87 (Gregory Shaffer et al. eds., 2019).

[28] Org. of Am. States, Assembly Res. AG/Res. 1 (XXVIII-E/01), Inter-American Democratic Charter (2001) (emphasis added), https://tinyurl.com/yrs26fte.

[29] African Charter on Democracy, Elections and Governance, Jan. 30, 2007, U.N.T.S. No. 55377. By March 3, 2022, thirty-eight of the fifty-five member states of the African Union had ratified, and a further forty-six have signed, the Charter. *See List of Countries Which Have Signed, Ratified/Acceded to the African Charter on Democracy, Elections and Governance* (Feb. 14, 2022), https://tinyurl.com/ymx34j7v.

[30] *See, e.g.*, Peace and Security Council, African Union, *Communiqué on the Situation in Burkina Faso*, PSC/PR/COMM.1/1062(2022) (Jan. 31, 2022), https://tinyurl.com/5433ky3b. *See generally* Erika de Wet, *The African Union's Struggle Against "Unconstitutional Change of Government": From a Moral Prescription to a Requirement Under International Law?*, 32 EUR. J. INT'L L. 199 (2021).

### 3 *Constitution-Shaping by the United Nations*

A special case is UN assistance in constitution-making and constitutional reform processes in the Global South (Africa, Latin America, the Near East, and Asia).[31] Since 1989, albeit with different degrees of intensity, the United Nations has been involved in constitutional processes in at least nine states, ranging from Yemen in 1991[32] to the Central African Republic in 2016.[33] The list includes Cambodia (1993),[34] Guinea-Bissau (substantial constitutional revision in 1996),[35] Afghanistan (2004),[36] Libya (2011),[37] and Côte d'Ivoire (2016).[38] The UN has also participated in the creation of two new states and their constitutions (East Timor (2002) and South Sudan (2011)).

#### a Constitution-Making as Peacemaking

All these constitution-shaping activities were set in the context of peace processes. The United Nations' involvement was based on the understanding that peacemaking requires (inter alia) the creation of a state constitution which in turn implements the rule of law.[39] In 1992, the UN Secretary-General had already asserted that there was "an *obvious connection* between democratic practices – such as the *rule of law* and transparency in decision-making – and the achievement of true *peace and security* in any new and stable political order." Once such a link is presumed, the United Nations are not only authorized by its membership but even "have an obligation" to provide "technical assistance" and give

[31] On these processes, see Manon Bonnet, *The Legitimacy of Internationally Imposed Constitution-Making in the Context of State Building*, *in* The Law and Legitimacy of Imposed Constitutions 208, 208–26 (Richard Albert et al. eds., 2019).

[32] Constitution of the Republic of Yemen, May 16, 1991.

[33] Constitution of the Central African Republic, March 27, 2016, Decree 160218.

[34] Constitution of the Kingdom of Cambodia, Sept. 21, 1993. On the UN engagement, see Lucy Keller, *UNTAC in Cambodia: From Occupation, Genocide and Civil War to Peace*, 9 Max Planck Y.B. U.N. L. 127 (2005).

[35] Constitution of Guinea-Bissau, Dec. 4, 1996.

[36] Constitution of Afghanistan, Jan. 3, 2004.

[37] An interim constitutional declaration was issued by the National Transitional Council on August 3, 2011. A draft constitution was drawn up in 2017 but never adopted.

[38] Constitution de la République de Côte d'Ivoire [Constitution] Nov. 8, 2016. On UN involvement, see Dorina A. Bekoe, *The United Nations Operation in Côte d'Ivoire: How a Certified Election Still Turned Violent*, 25 Int'l Peacekeeping 1, 128 (2018).

[39] The UN Secretary General placed constitutional reform squarely in the context of peace and security in his guidance note *UN Approach*, *supra* note 4, ¶ 65.

"support for the transformation of deficient national structures and capabilities, and for the strengthening of new democratic institutions."[40]

Next, in the 1996 Agenda for Democratization, Secretary-General Boutros Boutros-Ghali stressed a new, constitution-shaping role for peace missions: "The peace-keeping mandates entrusted to the United Nations now often include both the restoration of democracy and the protection of human rights. United Nations departments, agencies and programmes have been called upon to help States draft constitutions . . . ."[41] In 2001, the Secretary-General ascribed even a conflict-preventing role to the rule of law: "An essential aspect of conflict prevention is the strengthening of the *rule of law,* and within that the protection of women's human rights achieved through a focus on gender equality in constitutional, legislative, judicial and electoral reform."[42]

In his annual report for 2005, under the heading "Achieving peace and security," the UN Secretary-General made a point of mentioning rule-of-law promotion as a task of the peace missions:

> The United Nations worked tirelessly around the globe throughout the year to prevent and resolve conflicts and to consolidate peace. . . . Peacekeepers deployed to conflict zones in record numbers and in complex multidimensional operations, working . . . to help war-torn countries, *write constitutions*, hold elections *and strengthen* human rights and *the rule of law*. United Nations agencies, funds and programmes tailored their assistance to the special needs of post-conflict societies.[43]

In his 2006 progress report on conflict prevention, under the heading "Strengthening norms and institutions for peace," the UN Secretary-General mentioned that "the United Nations and its partners offer a variety of important services, at the request of Member States. These include electoral assistance, constitutional assistance, human rights capacity-building," and more. These important services are intended to help individual governments " find their own path to democracy."[44]

40 UN Secretary-General, *An Agenda for Peace: Preventive Diplomacy, Peacemaking and Peace-Keeping*, U.N. Doc. A/47/227-S/2411 (June 17, 1992).

41 UN Secretary-General, *Supplement to Reports on Democratization*, ¶ 5, U.N. Doc. A/51/761 (1996).

42 UN Secretary-General, *Prevention of Armed Conflict*, U.N. Doc. A/55/985-S/2001/574, ¶ 132 (June 7, 2001) (emphasis added).

43 UN Secretary-General, *Report on the Work of the Organization*, U.N. Doc. A/60/1, ¶ 10 (2005) (emphases added).

44 UN Secretary-General, *Progress Report on the Prevention of Armed Conflict*, U.N. Doc. A/60/891, ¶ 46 (July 18, 2006).

In all instances, the United Nations had established peace missions on the ground, sometimes in collaboration with regional organizations. The transitional processes, including constitution-making, frequently involved those missions. In sum, the UN has consistently depicted its rule-of-law activities as a contribution to peace (broadly conceived) and as being instrumental not only in managing and terminating armed conflict but even preventing such conflict.

### b UN Guidance on Constitutional Process and Substance

It took the United Nations several years of action on the ground to develop guidance notes for the processes of constitution-making and for the substance of the new or reformed constitutions. Building on the 2008 guidance note on the UN approach to rule of law assistance,[45] a specific guidance note on constitution-making processes was issued by the UN Secretary-General in 2009. In its own words:

> The note sets out a policy framework for UN assistance to constitution-making processes derived from lessons learned from constitution-making experiences and from UN engagement in these processes. It is *informed by the Guidance Note of the Secretary-General on United Nations Approach to Rule of Law Assistance*. It outlines the components of a constitution-making process and identifies the expertise the UN will require to provide effective assistance.[46]

As far as the constitutional *processes* are concerned, the 2009 note lists the following guiding principles:

1. Seize the opportunity for peacebuilding
2. Encourage compliance with international norms and standards
3. Ensure national ownership
4. Support inclusivity, participation and transparency
5. Mobilize and coordinate a wide range of expertise
6. Promote adequate follow-up.[47]

In contrast to these procedural steps, the 2009 guidance note does not prescribe particular *substance* for the (new or amended) state constitution. The premium placed on "national ownership" gives the target state leeway in that regard. But this leeway is not boundless, because not only

[45] *See supra* note 4.

[46] UN Secretary-General, *United Nations Assistance to Constitution-Making Processes*, Guidance Note of the Secretary General, at 2 (Apr. 2009) (emphasis added), www.refworld.org/policy/legalguidance/unsecgen/2009/en/71419 [hereinafter *UN Assistance*].

[47] *Id.*

the constitutional process but also its substance need to satisfy "compliance with international norms and standards."[48] Moreover, the earlier 2008 guidance note on the UN approach to the rule of law even refers to specific constitutional content: It quite precisely describes the principles and ingredients that a state constitution needs to display in order to conform to the rule-of-law ideal as defined by the UN. They range from the incorporation of international human rights treaties, to nondiscrimination and gender equality, to institutions based on and limited by law, to an impartial judiciary.[49]

### c Involvement of the Security Council

The Security Council, in particular, has placed normative demands on states. Security Council resolutions, sometimes adopted under Chapter VII of the UN Charter, have reiterated the principles of constitution-making, both with respect to process and constitutional substance. This activity overlaps with the Security Council's rule-of-law agenda.[50] Importantly, China and Russia – to mention but these two powers with a right of veto – have regularly voted in favor of these resolutions. This practice shows that something like a transnational rule-of-law consensus is still alive – at least when the interests of the two anti-liberal powers, China and Russia, are not directly affected.

With regard to constitutional *process*, the Security Council has restated principles of "national ownership."[51] Frequently, the Security Council has urged free and fair elections as part of a transition and reconciliation process (such as for Cambodia in 1992,[52] East Timor in 2001,[53] Afghanistan in 2005,[54] Libya (most recently in 2020),[55] Yemen,[56] South Sudan,[57] and the Central African Republic (CAR)).[58]

48 *Id.* at 4.
49 *UN Approach*, *supra* note 4, at 4–5.
50 For a comprehensive overview, see NUSCHA WIECZOREK, THE SECURITY COUNCIL'S CONTRIBUTION TO A GLOBAL CONCEPT OF THE RULE OF LAW 137–319 (2020).
51 S.C. Res. 1996, ¶ 3(c) (July 8, 2011); S.C. Res. 2542, ¶ 1 (Sept. 15, 2020).
52 S.C. Res. 745, pmbl. ¶ 5 (Feb. 28, 1992).
53 S.C. Res. 1338, pmbl. ¶ 5 (Jan. 21, 2001).
54 S.C. Res. 1589, ¶ 3 (Mar., 24, 2005).
55 S.C. Res. 2009, ¶ 5(c) (Sept. 16, 2011); S.C. Res. 2486, pmbl. ¶ 8, ¶ 1(v) (Sept. 12, 2019); S.C. Res, 2542, ¶ 1(v) (Sept. 15, 2020).
56 S.C. Res. 2051, ¶ 3(d) (June 12, 2012).
57 S.C. Res. 1996, ¶ 3(a)(ii) (July 8, 2011) (adopted under Chapter VII).
58 S.C. Res. 2149, ¶ 30(b)(v) (Apr. 10, 2014) (adopted under Chapter VII).

Many more Security Council resolutions imply the need to organize elections or a referendum, such as in Somalia in 2012, where the UN mission was tasked with giving strategic policy advice on peacebuilding and state-building, including a "referendum on the constitution; and preparations for elections."[59] This is not a phenomenon of the past but is ongoing. The Security Council asked the Integration Peacebuilding Office in Guinea-Bissau and the special representative to "support, through good offices," democratic elections in Guinea-Bissau in 2019.[60] In the same year, the Security Council asked the UN Secretary-General to establish in Haiti a UN office whose key tasks was to include assisting the government to "plan and execute free, fair, and transparent elections."[61]

The Security Council has also – and this is related to the democratic principle – encouraged "inclusive" and participatory processes of constitution-making and constitutional reform (for South Sudan in 2011,[62] Libya in 2011,[63] Yemen in 2012,[64] and Guinea-Bissau in 2019[65]). It also asked for transparent procedure (for example, in Yemen[66]). Finally, the Security Council has frequently and explicitly voiced its expectation that women participate in the constitutional process, such as in South Sudan 2011,[67] the Central African Republic

59 S.C. Res. 2102, ¶ 2(b)(iii) (May 2, 2013).

60 S.C. Res. 2458, ¶ 5(b) (Feb. 28, 2019).

61 S.C. Res. 2476, ¶ 1(b)(i) (June 25, 2019).

62 S.C. Res. 1996, ¶ 3 (July 8, 2011) (adopted under Chapter VII) (Security Council "authorizes UNMISS [United Nations Mission in the Republic of Sudan] to perform the following tasks; (a) … (ii) Promoting popular participation in political processes, including through advising and supporting the Government of the Republic of South Sudan on an inclusive constitutional process …").

63 S.C. Res. 2009, ¶ 5 (Sept. 16, 2011) (adopted under Chapter VII) (Security Council "[e]ncourages the National Transitional Council to implement its plans to … (c) ensure a consultative, inclusive political process with a view to agreement on a constitution and the holding of free and fair elections").

64 S.C. Res. 2051, ¶ 5 (June 12, 2012) (not adopted under Chapter VII) (Security Council "[e]mphasizes the importance of conducting a fully-inclusive, participatory, transparent and meaningful National Dialogue Conference including with the youth and women's groups and calls upon all stakeholders in Yemen to participate actively and constructively in this process").

65 S.C. Res. 2458, ¶ 5(d) (Feb. 28, 2019) (not adopted under Chapter VII) (Security Council requests United Nations Integration Peacebuilding Office in Guinea-Bissau (UNIOGBIS) to "[s]upport, through good offices the electoral process to ensure *inclusive, free and credible legislative elections*" (emphasis added)).

66 S.C. Res. 2051, ¶ 5.

67 S.C. Res. 1996, ¶ 3 (authorising UNMISS to ensure the participation of women in decision-making forums).

in 2014,[68] Guinea-Bissau in 2019,[69] Haiti in 2019,[70] and Libya in 2020.[71]

Another set of Security Council propositions concerns the *substance* of the constitution. The normative advice covers all three limbs of constitutionalism's trinity. First of all, the Security Council inevitably required the new constitution to be built on the *rule of law*, as it did for Afghanistan in 2011,[72] Somalia in 2013,[73] and Mali in 2013.[74] With regard to the constitution of Guinea-Bissau, the Security Council asked for the separation of powers and access to the judiciary (2019).[75] Second, the Security Council has often suggested that the new constitution must be democratic, such as in East Timor in 2001,[76] Afghanistan in

[68] S.C. Res. 2149, ¶ 30 (Apr. 10, 2014) (mandating the UN Multidimensional Integrated Stabilization Mission in the Central African Republic (MINUSCA) to "devise, facilitate and provide technical assistance to the electoral process . . . for the holding of free, fair, transparent and inclusive elections, including the full and effective participation of women at all levels").

[69] S.C. Res. 2458, ¶ 6(d) (Feb. 28, 2019) (not adopted under Chapter VII) (UNIOGBIS's work to include "[p]roviding support to the Government of Guinea-Bissau . . . to ensure the involvement, representation and participation of women at all levels").

[70] S.C. Res. 2476, ¶ 3 (June 25, 2019) (not under Chapter VII) ("requests that BINUH . . . assist the Government of Haiti in ensuring the full, meaningful, and effective participation and involvement and representation of women at all levels").

[71] S.C. Res. 2542, (Sept. 15, 2020) ("Urging the parties to ensure the full, equal, effective and meaningful participation of women in all activities and decision-making relating to democratic transition . . ." (pmbl. ¶ 9); and "Requests UNSMIL [United Nations Support Mission in Libya] . . . to assist the GNA [Government of National Accord] in ensuring the full, effective and meaningful participation and leadership of women in the democratic transition, reconciliation efforts . . ." (operative ¶ 8)).

[72] S.C. Res. 1974, ¶¶ 24, 31–32 (Mar. 22, 2011) (not under Chapter VII) (reiterating the importance of ensuring the rule of law throughout the country.).

[73] S.C. Res. 2102, ¶ 2 (May 2, 2013) (not under Chapter VII) ("Decides that the mandate of UNSOM [UN Assistance Mission in Somalia] shall be as follows: . . . (b) To support the Federal Government of Somalia, and AMISOM [African Union Mission in Somalia] as appropriate, by providing strategic policy advice on peacebuilding and statebuilding, including on: . . . (ii) security sector reform, rule of law . . .").

[74] S.C. Res. 2100, ¶ 16 (April 25, 2013) ("Decides that the mandate of MINUSMA shall be . . . (a) . . . (iii) To support national and international efforts towards rebuilding the Malian security sector . . . as well as the rule of law and justice sectors . . .").

[75] S.C. Res. 2458, ¶ 25 (Feb. 28, 2019) (not under Chapter VII) ("Calls upon the authorities of Guinea-Bissau to continue to actively reform and strengthen the judicial system, while ensuring the separation of powers and access to justice for all citizens").

[76] S.C. Res. 1338, pmbl. (Jan. 31, 2001) (not adopted under Chapter VII) ("Expressing support for the steps taken by [the UN Transitional Administration in East Timor] to strengthen the involvement and direct participation of the East Timorese people in the administration of their territory").

2005,[77] Libya in 2011,[78] South Sudan in 2011,[79] and Mali in 2013.[80] Third, human rights protection has been explicitly required, as for Afghanistan.[81] Finally, the Security Council recommended a federal system for Somalia in 2013.[82]

The Security Council's intense engagement with the rule of law (broadly conceived) is tempered by the fact that of the resolutions mentioned only four were adopted under Chapter VII.[83] Of those, to the best of my knowledge, only Resolution 2149 (2014), on technical assistance to elections in the Central African Republic, employs mandatory language.[84]

77 S.C. Res. 1589 (Mar. 24, 2005) (not adopted under Chapter VII) ("pledging its continued support thereafter for the Government and people of Afghanistan as they rebuild their country, strengthen the foundations of a constitutional democracy . . ." (pmbl. ¶ 5); and "Welcomes the international efforts to assist in setting up the new Afghan Parliament and ensure its efficient functioning, which will be critical to the political future of Afghanistan and the steps towards a free and *democratic Afghanistan*" (operative ¶ 5) (emphasis added)).

78 S.C. Res. 2009, ¶ 5 (Sept. 16, 2011) (adopted under Chapter VII) "Encourages the National Transitional Council to implement its plans to . . . (c) ensure a consultative, inclusive political process with a view to agreement on a constitution and the holding of free and fair elections").

79 S.C. Res. 1996, ¶ 3 (July 8, 2011) (adopted under Chapter VII) ("Decides that the mandate of UNMISS shall be to consolidate peace and security, and to help establish the conditions for development in the Republic of South Sudan, with a view to strengthening the capacity of the Government of the Republic of South Sudan to govern effectively and *democratically* and . . . authorizes UNMISS to perform the following tasks; (a) . . . (ii) Promoting popular participation in political processes, including through advising and supporting the Government of the Republic of South Sudan on an inclusive constitutional process; the holding of elections in accordance with the constitution; . . ." (emphasis added)).

80 S.C. Res. 2100, pmbl. (April 25, 2013) ("Stressing the need to work expeditiously toward the restoration of democratic governance and constitutional order, including through the holding of free, fair, transparent and inclusive presidential and legislative elections").

81 S.C. Res. 1589, ¶ 10 (March 24, 2005) (not adopted under Chapter VII) ("Calls for full respect for human rights and international humanitarian law throughout Afghanistan and, in this regard, requests UNAMA, with the support of the Office of the United Nations High Commissioner for Human Rights, to continue to assist in the full implementation of the human rights provisions of the new Afghan constitution").

82 S.C. Res. 2102, ¶ 2 (May 2, 2013) (not adopted under Chapter VII) ("Decides that the mandate of UNSOM shall be as follows: . . . (b) To support the Federal Government of Somalia, and AMISOM as appropriate, by providing strategic policy advice on peacebuilding and statebuilding, including on: . . . (iii) the development of a federal system; the constitutional review process and subsequent referendum on the constitution; and preparations for elections in 2016").

83 S.C. Res. 1996 (July 8, 2011) (on South Sudan); S.C. Res. 2009 (Sept. 16, 2011) (on Libya); S.C. Res. 2100 (Apr. 25, 2013) (on Mali); S.C. Res. 2149 (Apr. 10, 2014) (on the Central African Republic).

84 S.C. Res. 2149, ¶ 30 (Apr. 10, 2014) ("Decides that the mandate of MINUSCA *shall* initially focus on the following priority tasks . . ." (emphasis added)).

The other resolutions, even if the resolutions as such were based on Chapter VII, couch the principles on process and substance of constitution-making in soft language, often placed in the resolutions' preambles. Most resolutions were based on Chapter VI. These, like the majority of the Chapter VII resolutions, merely "stress" the importance of constitutional principles, and they "encourage", "support", and "assist" the states concerned, but do not "request" or "impose" anything.

## III Have International Constitution-Shaping Efforts Led to Domestic Rule-of-Law Improvements?

Part II has shown that the rule of law has been espoused and disseminated through the constitution-shaping activities of international organizations in all regions of the world. The rule of law has thereby become part and parcel of the web of international norms and standards that forms a benchmark for state constitutions. It has become a global principle of constitutionalism, or a principle of transnational ordering – at least on paper. However, the real effects of international organizations' constitution-shaping so that the rule of law benefits people on the ground are very difficult to measure.[85] The situation is further obscured by the continued tendency of recipient states to point to international organizations as convenient scapegoats in order to hide their own policy choices. The question of effects and limits can therefore not be answered in a definitive way. We can only take snapshots.

### 1 *Universal Organizations*

With regard to international financial institutions, their impact on recipient states' tax revenues, public sector wages, and the like has been corroborated by recent studies.[86] This impact partly concerns the states' constitutions and the domestic rule of law. However, it has mostly been evaluated as being negative for the concerned populations.[87]

The effects of accession to the WTO on the Chinese constitution and rule of law have been variously assessed. Eight years after accession,

[85] On the challenge of measurement, see Chapter 1 (Part III.2).

[86] Bernhard Reinsberg et al., *The World System and the Hollowing Out of State Capacity: How Structural Adjustment Programs Affect Bureaucratic Quality in Developing Countries*, 124 Am. J. Socio. 1222 (2019); André Broome et al., *Bad Science: International Organizations and the Indirect Power of Global Benchmarking*, 24 Eur. J. Int'l Rel. 514, 514 (2018).

[87] *See* Part IV.

Esther Lam found that the WTO requirements formed an important model for further changes in non-WTO-related areas "such as uniformity of laws and legal administration, non-discrimination, transparency, and impartial mechanisms for challenging government decisions and actions."[88] Lam also claimed that "[a]lthough the enforcement of laws remains weak, legal rules are assuming an unprecedented level of prescriptive power in post-WTO accession China."[89] According to Lam, the result was, inter alia, "legal guarantees to individual freedom of actions and the right to trade, and it [the enhanced role of law] restricts political power from arbitrarily encroaching onto spheres where law does not prescribe it to do so."[90] In contrast, more recent studies have downplayed or denied the impact of WTO membership on China's rule of law.[91]

## 2 *European Organizations*

The constitution-shaping by the two European regional organizations – the EU and the CoE – has only in part produced deep and lasting effects. Political scientists found that the EU's political accession conditionalities had a "tremendous impact" on what they called the "Europeanization" of Central and Eastern Europe.[92] It has also been said that "[h]uman rights, liberal democracy, and the rule of law are the fundamental rules of legitimate statehood in the European Union."[93]

However, the EU's preaccession "pull" toward the rule of law is by no means guaranteed. Since Croatia's accession to the EU in 2013, other Eastern European states (Albania, Bosnia and Herzegovina, Kosovo, Montenegro, North Macedonia, and Serbia) have not moved closer to accession. Montenegro and Serbia have been conducting accession talks since 2012 and 2014, respectively, but the prospect of accession does not

88 Esther Lam, China and the WTO: A Long March Towards the Rule of Law 115 (2009).

89 *Id.* at 149.

90 *Id.*

91 Liao Li & Yu Minyou, *Impact of the WTO on China's Rule of Law in Trade: Twentieth Anniversary of the WTO*, 49 J. World Trade 837 (2015); Nga Kit Tang, *The WTO's Impact on China: A Battle of Administrative Review Settings Between Internal and External Regulatory Frameworks*, 10 Vienna J. on Int'l Const. L. 251 (2016); Henry Gao, *The WTO's Transparency Obligations and China*, 12 J. Comp. L. 329 (2017).

92 Frank Schimmelfennig & Ulrich Sedelmeier, *Conclusions: The Impact of the EU on the Accession Countries*, *in* The Europeanization of Central and Eastern Europe 210, 226 (Frank Schimmelfennig & Ulrich Sedelmeier eds., 2005).

93 Frank Schimmelfennig et al., *The Impact of EU Political Conditionality*, *in* The Europeanization of Central and Eastern Europe, *supra* note 92, at 29, 29.

seem to have initiated a further dynamic of constitutional reform in those states.

With regard to the actual constitutional reforms triggered by accession to the EU, Anneli Albi found that the constitutional amendments in Central and Eastern European countries "remained relatively minimal" – often contrary to initial enthusiast rhetoric.[94] From the outset, "international socialization" through the EU (and the CoE) did not work in those states that had been clearly antiliberal, such as Belarus, Ukraine, Serbia, or Russia.[95] For those states that had already been on the path to liberalism before the accession to the CoE (Estonia, the Czech Republic, Hungary, Latvia, Lithuania, Poland, and Slovenia), it first looked as if the liberal constitutional principles required by both organizations for membership would work well. But thirty years later, some of these states have turned away from the international standards and are becoming illiberal democracies, such as Hungary and Poland.

Current events in the EU seem to confirm that once a state has been admitted to the international organization, there is no longer any leverage to press for reforms, as the carrot of membership that was the incentive for reform has gone. This then leads to a loss of effectiveness of any further constitutional intervention. Whether new tools such as the EU's so-called rule-of-law mechanism can bring illiberal member states back in line and up to constitutionalist standards is unknown for the time being.[96]

For the CoE, it is obvious that the actual application and implementation of these imperative constitutional principles on the ground have been only weakly monitored. Russia, which was excluded from the Council in March 2022, is an example – the organization had arguably not properly responded to Russia's continual disregard of the rule of law until it turned into extreme violation when Russia invaded Ukraine in February 2022.

[94] Anneli Albi, EU Enlargement and the Constitutions of Central and Eastern Europe 111 (2005).

[95] Frank Schimmelfennig, *Strategic Calculation and International Socialisation: Membership Initiatives, Party Constellations, and Sustained Compliance in Central and Eastern Europe*, 59 Int'l Org. 827 (2005).

[96] *See* Communication from the Commission to the European Parliament, the Council, the European Economic and Social Committee and the Committee of the Regions, 2022 Rule of Law Report: The Rule of Law Situation in the European Union, COM (2022) 500 (July 13, 2022).

All this suggests that the European organizations' impact on strengthening the rule of law in accession candidates and member states has been uneven.

### 3 *UN Impact on Constitutions in the Global South*

The lack of effectiveness of rule-of-law building through constitutional assistance is especially palpable in the Global South. Once the constitution is made, with international assistance and following international standards, it needs to be put to work by domestic actors. But this generally does not function well. The lofty constitutional principles adopted under the influence of the United Nations or other foreign actors have frequently not been translated into concrete rules that are followed by state officials.

Take the constitutions of Cambodia (1993, as amended up to 2008), South Sudan (2011), and the Central African Republic (2016), to name but three constitutions that were recently adopted with UN and other international actors' assistance. They all contain catalogues of fundamental rights that on the whole faithfully mirror international human rights standards and are complemented by features specific to each region.[97] However, constitutional rights are hardly applied on the ground due to a lack of infrastructure, impunity of violators, dictatorship (as in Cambodia), and armed conflict (as in the Central African Republic).[98] In extreme cases, constitutional rights exist only on paper. In all cases, a gap of greater or lesser glaringness persists between the constitutional document and its effects on the political, legal, and administrative practice of public institutions.[99]

### 4 *Observations*

In conclusion, both in Europe and in the Global South, the external constitutional assistance lent by international organizations has

[97] CONSTITUTION OF THE KINGDOM OF CAMBODIA art. 31-50; CONSTITUTION OF SOUTHERN SUDAN art. 9-34; CONSTITUTION OF CENTRAL AFRICAN REPUBLIC, art. 1-23.

[98] HUMAN RIGHTS WATCH, WORLD REPORT 2021: EVENTS OF 2020, at 129, 149, 611 (2021).

[99] Cheryl Saunders, *Global Constitutionalism: Myth and Reality*, *in* THE FRONTIERS OF PUBLIC LAW 19, 28–29 (Jason N. E. Varuhas & Shona Wilson Stark eds., 2020).

produced only moderate positive effects – if any at all – for the functioning of the rule of law.

Already in 2011, a consultative process on rule-of-law assistance organised by the UN found that rule-of-law assistance was "too often executed in an ad hoc manner, designed without proper consultations with national stakeholders, and absent exacting standards of evaluation." It inquired how "rule of law assistance can be better channelled to deliver results."[100]

Probably, the advising and accompanying organizations would need to pay much more attention to the matter of practical application and transposition of constitutional and rule-of-law principles into (ordinary) domestic law. It has been asserted that in recent instances of UN constitutional assistance, the question of implementation was barely touched on at the stage of constitutional negotiations.[101]

However, implementation depends first of all on the states themselves. A chief reason for the constitutions having little impact is probably the fragility of the institutions in the states concerned. Many factors contributing to this fragility are (and properly so) beyond the reach of the international organizations.

Also, it is unlikely (although – as a counterfactual – not verifiable by empirical investigation) that the constitutions would work better in practice had they been adopted without any external assistance. It must remain a matter of speculation whether purely home-grown constitutions in those countries would be (or have been) more socially acceptable because of a stronger sense of ownership and because of a better fit to local norms. Social acceptance normally leads to better compliance. But the price to pay might be deficiencies in substance and an even larger distance from the constitutional ideal of the rule of law.

## IV Critiques

"[O]n the whole," external influence (including, but not limited to, that of international organizations) on constitution-making and -shaping processes is said to have been "enormously useful in the development of constitutional law in countless countries in recent decades."[102] At the same time, the sentiment lingers that international organizations' various

[100] United Nations and the Rule of Law, New Voices: National Perspectives on Rule of Law Assistance, 5 (Apr. 6, 2011), https://tinyurl.com/bddx666b.

[101] Al-Ali, *supra* note 2, at 84.

[102] *Id.* at 77.

techniques of cajoling, persuading, and motivating states to adopt constitutions that embody the rule of law constitute an unlawful intervention into the domestic affairs of the receiving states, a risk of infringement of state sovereignty and national self-determination, or simply unfairness and normative inappropriateness due inter alia to selectivity and hypocrisy. Accordingly, constitution-shaping and other forms of rule-of-law promotion by various international organizations have been denounced as an illegitimate exercise;[103] they have been condemned as "evangelization,"[104] "meddling,"[105] and legal imperialism.[106]

In the context of the reception of European human rights standards disseminated by the EU and the CoE in Central and Eastern European states, Romanian scholar Alexandra Iancu, already in 2014, diagnosed a prevailing "double standard sentiment" that held a "backlash potential."[107] This potential seems now to have become fully realized.[108] All international organizations, and especially IFIs, have come under heavy fire for pursuing neoliberal policies that manifest the preferences and interests of the states of the North at the expense of the Global South.[109]

Vijayashri Sripati criticizes especially the United Nations' constitutional assistance from the perspective of Third World Approaches to International Law (TWAIL).[110] She perceives a historical continuity in constitutional assistance from colonialism to the post-1945 involvement of the UN Trusteeship Council in nonsovereign territories and to the revival of constitutional assistance after 1989, offered to formally sovereign states.[111] Sripati's key claim is that a kind of internationalization of state constitutions has been brought about through the combined

[103] *Cf.* Mark Brown, *"An Unqualified Human Good"? On Rule of Law, Globalization, and Imperialism*, 43 L. & Soc. Inquiry 1391 (2018).

[104] Vijayashri Sripati, Constitution-Making Under UN Auspices 12 (2020).

[105] Bonnet, *supra* note 31, at 225.

[106] Brown, *supra* note 103.

[107] Alexandra Iancu, *"Europeanization" versus "New Localism" in Shaping Fundamental Rights: "Free Speech" Definitions, Limitations, and Deadlocks in New Democracies, in* Europeanization and Judicial Culture in Contemporary Democracies 148, 155 (Manuel Gutan & Bianca Selejan Gutan eds., 2014).

[108] *See* Chapters 1 and 7.

[109] Ngaire Woods, The Globalizers: The IMF, the World Bank and Their Borrowers (2006); Jean Ziegler, Les nouveaux maîtres du monde: Et ceux qui leur résistent (2002); Broome et al., *supra* note 86, at 514.

[110] Sripati, *supra* note 104.

[111] Sripati sees this sequence interrupted only by a short period of rejection of UN assistance by the newly independent states in the 1960s. *Id.* at 153.

interventions of the United Nations and international financial institutions (World Bank and International Monetary Fund) against the background of poverty and high indebtedness of the receiving states. According to Sripati, the underlying political and economic agenda is to create a constitutional environment that is favorable to the West (and to investors). Ultimately, Sripati claims, "powerful Western states create within developing states constitutional regimes that have the effect of throwing open the latter's resources for the transnational capitalist class (TCC), that is, the banks, investors, corporations, and geopolitical/imperialist strategists."[112] The reproach is that the international organizations themselves are captured by global capitalist interests. Moreover, this strategy of "creating within developing states a constitutional environment that is not inimical to the West, but officially explaining it as being intended to modernize the former – is reminiscent of the imperial civilizing mission."[113] The receiving states are, once again, "entrapped in an imperial relationship, although this time they are ostensibly sovereign."[114] The constitutional assistance extended by the United Nations, in tandem with the Bretton Woods institutions, is thus a form of "legal imperialism."[115]

Another source of illegitimacy concerning the constitutional interventions of international organizations might be the *cultural inaptness and lack of local roots* of the rule of law and other constitutional principles. The shallowness of the normative consensus on constitutional substance might also explain the deficient implementation of constitutional law in receiving countries. With regard to human rights, it has been argued that domestic and external actors have often agreed only on a narrow set of rights, leaving out other matters. Inaptness might also arise in relation to further constitutional features such as the separation of powers or the independence of the judiciary.

Alexandra Iancu, who examined the Europeanization of human rights protection in the Eastern and Central European countries in the post-accession period, painted a gloomy picture of "limited substantial transformations,"[116] "shallow Europeanization,"[117] and "post-accession decline … reversing or distorting the very essence of newly created

[112] *Id.* at 8, also 202.
[113] *Id.* at 4.
[114] *Id.* at 185.
[115] *Id.* at 221.
[116] Iancu, *supra* note 107, at 149.
[117] *Id.*

institutions."[118] She pointed out that the Europeanization process "failed in producing the cultural background of the law providing the proper meaning of new provisions."[119] She also deplored that European norms had been imposed "with no reference to value-systems, traditions, or practices" in the region of Central and Eastern Europe.[120] This situation, she wrote, is "conducive to a polarization of the national legal culture and a legalistic Babel in which each side selectively quotes European standards or the ECHR jurisprudence."[121]

Another set of critiques against constitution-shaping by international organizations points out that it has neglected the necessities of *economic development* in the target countries. It highlights that the institutions which must implement the rule of law (a functioning administration, courts, democratic electoral system, and so on) expend resources that should first be used for the economic development of a state. A related point is that the *actual enjoyment* of the supposed benefits of the rule of law (ranging from the exercise of political and civil rights to informed participation in elections) presupposes a certain level of economic development and material security for the population. According to the critique, these material factors are neglected or even worsened by the international organizations.

## V Responses

The critical assessment of international organizations' constitution-shaping is timely and necessary. However, it needs to be nuanced. An accusation that all constitution-shaping exercises serve only the global capitalist class yet again presents a master narrative explaining the world. Ultimately, it is as simplistic as the story of the selfless and humanitarian promotion of the rule of law for the benefit of the local population that it seeks to dispel.

### 1 *Respecting State Sovereignty*

Constitutional assistance by international organizations would violate the principle of non-intervention if the organizations intruded upon the *domaine réservé* of the target state and, additionally, the means of

[118] *Id.*
[119] *Id.* at 150 (internal references omitted).
[120] *Id.* at 151.
[121] *Id.* at 176–77.

interference amounted to "coercion." However, the rule of law no longer pertains to the *domaine réservé*. Rather, like human rights and democracy, it has become a familiar topos in international legal discourse – not the least through the constitutional assistance of international organizations. The approval and continuity of such practices has created a loop by which these issues (respect for the rule of law, human rights, and democratic processes) have been lifted out of the *domaine réservé* of states – they have been transnationalized.[122] Although somewhat circular, this process now means that the constitutional assistance afforded by international organizations can no longer be categorically dismissed as unlawful intervention. Rather, the practice has created the space for examining the extent to which the objectives of constitutional assistance justify the *means* employed by the organizations, and whether the means–ends relationship is proportionate.

The second prong of a prohibited intervention (coercion) is not an all-or-nothing concept. Only when interference in state affairs reaches a certain intensity or "magnitude"[123] will it leave the realm of lawful pressure and cross the threshold of "coercion."[124] This threshold is defined by relying on reasonableness[125] or through balancing: the interference amounts to an unlawful intervention when either the means or the ends are per se unlawful, or when means and ends in combination become unlawful, notably because the means–ends relationship is not appropriate (i.e., disproportionate).[126] Factors to take into account are the depth of the interference with interests of the target state, the breadth (effects on third states), the duration of the measure, and the objectives of the interference.[127] It is often stated that the aim of bringing about a regime change is "the most coercive form of political interference."[128] The adoption of a new constitution, especially when combined with elections, can be seen as a regime change, and therefore could be accused of having crossed the red line to become unjustified intervention.

122 *See* Chapter 1 (Part II).

123 Maziar Jamnejad & Michael Wood, *The Principle of Non-Intervention*, 22 LEIDEN J. INT'L L. 345, 348 (2009).

124 Florian Kriener, Intervention, Prohibition of, in: Max Planck Encyclopedia of International Law, Anne Peters and Rüdiger Wolfrum (eds), OUP 2024, paras 20, 49–50.

125 Jamnejad & Wood, *supra* note 123, at 348.

126 MARCO ATHEN, DER TATBESTAND DES VÖLKERRECHTLICHEN INTERVENTIONSVERBOTS 236–37 (2017).

127 *Id.* at 284–85.

128 Jamnejad & Wood, *supra* note 123, at 368.

However, in formal terms, constitutional assistance by international organizations is generally not coercively imposed. Constitution-making assistance has been offered only on request. For example, the 2009 UN guidance note on constitution-making emphasizes that UN assistance will be offered only "when requested by national authorities." In line with this, UN bodies should "recognize constitution-making as a sovereign national process, which, to be legitimate and successful, must be nationally owned and led."[129]

Coercion may nevertheless be present informally, due to economic dependency. The formal voluntariness of consenting to constitutional assistance, and especially to austerity programs with constitutional repercussions, might only be a sham. With regard to UN assistance, Vijayashri Sripati has argued that receiving states consent only "technically speaking" to the adoption of a new constitution. In reality, they are faced with no choice because they are "groaning under mountains of debt."[130] Their consent is therefore, according to Sripati, "utterly compromised."[131]

In a similar way, the acceptance of pre- or postaccession conditions for membership of a given organization, and the signing of memorandums with international financial institutions might be made de facto inevitable by economic and political circumstances. Formally, states *apply* to the World Bank for project financing, and they *ask* the international monetary fund for a credit. States *wish* to join the EU – they could also stay out. However, strong factual constraints push the states to apply "voluntarily."

Do these constraints lead to "imposition" by the international organizations? I submit that this is not the case as long as the pressure does not amount to coercion or military threat. Relevant legal thresholds have been developed in practice and in scholarship regarding "coercion," not only for the definition of "intervention,"[132] but also in the context of the conclusion of treaties (Articles 51 and 52 of the Vienna Convention on the Law of Treaties)[133] and the use of force prohibited by Article 2(4) of

[129] *UN Assistance*, *supra* note 46, at 2.

[130] Sripati, *supra* note 104, at 442.

[131] *Id.*

[132] Military and Paramilitary Activities in and Against Nicaragua (Nicar. v. U.S.), Judgment, 1986 I.C.J. 14, ¶ 250 (June 27).

[133] *See* UN Conference on the Law of Treaties, *Final Act of the United Nations Conference on the Law of Treaties*, at 285, UN Doc. A/CONF.39/26 (1969).

the UN Charter. Although the thresholds differ in detail, they all convey the legal message that constraints resulting from an unfavorable economic and political position, weak bargaining power, and even a situation perceived by a state as leaving it with no choice do not undermine the state's "free" decision. These thresholds and delimitations can also be applied to situations where constitutional assistance is invited. It is "free" and "voluntary" in the eyes of international law as long as the inviting state has not been pressured by military threats.

However, this answer of international law is formalistic and reflects the interests of the most powerful states of the North. Therefore, the assessment of lawfulness does not obviate the need to examine the broader issues of legitimacy.

### 2 *Respecting Local Rule-of-Law Cultures*

The critiques mentioned above suggest that when constitutional assistance is provided by international organizations care needs to be taken to avoid legal imperialism, double standards, capitalist capture, and cultural imposition. At this point, we need to distinguish between radical repudiation of the rule of law as such and the less profound problem of a lack of culture-specific adaptations. While a radical repudiation of the rule of law is nowhere to be found, assistance that is applied schematically and without adequate consideration of the need for local adaptations in the rule of law seem to be real issues.

As far as UN activity is concerned, after some years of experimenting with transitional justice, the UN Secretary-General admitted: "Unfortunately, the international community has not always provided rule of law assistance that is appropriate to the country context. Too often, the emphasis has been on foreign experts, foreign models and foreign-conceived solutions . . . ."[134] He continued that "we have learned" that the transitional justice processes need to be based on a thorough analysis of the local situation, based preferably on "expertise resident in the country," and that the processes must be based on "active and meaningful participation of national stakeholders ... while leaving process leadership and decision-making to the national stakeholders."[135] "Pre-packaged solutions are ill-advised. Instead, experiences from other places should simply be used as a starting point for local

[134] *The Rule of Law and Transitional Justice*, *supra* note 18, ¶ 15.
[135] *Id.*

debates and decisions."[136] Although these "lessons learned" pertained to transitional justice processes, they would seem equally to apply *mutatis mutandis* to constitutional assistance.

Because law is a product of culture and society, difficulties arising from deep differences in legal culture (and culture more generally) are serious. The identification of the problem, the "lesson" drawn, is only the first analytical step, and in no way guarantees that a remedy is at all possible. We need to acknowledge that the rule of law is so abstract that it cannot "deliver" anything in and of itself.[137] The tension between the vagueness of the rule of law and the fact that it is contingent on concrete and context-dependent, bottom-up action on the ground remains irresolvable.

The next big problem is the rule of law's Eurocentric and colonial baggage. In order to overcome this, the international organizations need to take up the ideas flowing from non-European constitutionalist thought.[138] For example, the Latin American concept of a "social rule of law" could be inspiring.[139]

## 3 *A More "Social" Rule of Law*

The aforementioned idea of a "social rule of law" underlines the spreading insight that the neoliberal constitutional frame that has been pursued by a number of international organizations is not enough. A key problem in constitution-shaping has been the neglect of the social dimension of constitutionalism, in line with an exclusively formal conception of the rule of law. However, this neoliberal tilt – especially when it comes to

[136] *Id.* ¶ 16.

[137] Brian Tamanaha, *The Failures of Law and Development*, 44 CORNELL INT'L L.J. 209, 237, 246–47 (2011).

[138] *See generally* ROBERTO GARGARELLA, LATIN AMERICAN CONSTITUTIONALISM, 1810–2010: THE ENGINE ROOM OF THE CONSTITUTION 4–7 (2013); BERIHUN GEBEYE, A THEORY OF AFRICAN CONSTITUTIONALISM 1–3 (2021); Daniel Bonilla Maldonado, *Introduction*, *in* CONSTITUTIONALISM OF THE GLOBAL SOUTH: THE ACTIVIST TRIBUNALS OF INDIA, SOUTH AFRICA, AND COLOMBIA 1, 31 (2013); THE GLOBAL SOUTH AND COMPARATIVE CONSTITUTIONAL LAW (Philipp Dann, Michael Riegner & Maxim Bönnemann eds., 2020).

[139] This principle coevolved at the beginning of the twentieth century with the German principle of the *Sozialstaat*. *See, e.g.*, Carlos Andrés Pérez-Garzón, *Unveiling the Meaning of Social Justice in Colombia*, 10 MEXICAN L. REV. 27, 39–40 (2018).

IFIs – is not inevitable and not historically entrenched.[140] The IFIs' policies could change (and are arguably in the process of doing so).[141] In the face of rising material inequality in wealth and income that is exploited by populist and authoritarian leaders, it is no longer sufficient to wait for the developmental benefits of a formal and "thin" rule of law.

International organizations – at least since the 1990s – have insisted on the *positive* feedback loop (as opposed to antagonism) between economic/social development and constitutionalism/rule of law.[142] This can be seen from the World Summit Outcome Document of 2005 stating that "rule of law at the national and international levels [is] essential for sustained economic growth, sustainable development and the eradication of poverty and hunger."[143] Accordingly, the UN General Assembly Agenda 2030 (adopted in 2015) deals with development but embraces a strong rule-of-law component: "The new Agenda recognizes the need to build peaceful, just and inclusive societies that provide equal access to justice and that are based on respect for human rights (including the right to development), *on effective rule of law* and good governance at all levels and on transparent, effective and accountable institutions."[144]

This passage and Sustainable Development Goal 16 advocating for rule of law were controversial and one of the "hotly debated topics" in the process of adopting Agenda 2030.[145] The outcome has been called a "sea change"[146] in the area of law and development. Goal 16 seeks to "promote peaceful and inclusive societies for sustainable development, provide access to justice for all and build effective, accountable and inclusive institutions at all levels." More specifically, subgoal 16.3 seeks to "promote the rule of law at the national and international levels and ensure

140 *See generally* ERIC HELLEINER, FORGOTTEN FOUNDATIONS OF BRETTON WOODS: INTERNATIONAL DEVELOPMENT AND THE MAKING OF THE POSTWAR ORDER 258 (2014).

141 Anne Peters, *Constitutional Theories of International Organizations: Beyond the West*, 20 CHINESE J. INT'L L. 649, 697 (2022).

142 The World Bank shuns the expression "rule of law" in order to avoid any interference in the political affairs of any member, which is prohibited by Article IV, section 10, of the Articles of Agreement. Instead, the Bank coined the term "good governance," which inter alia covers the rule of law. Edith Brown Weiss & Ahila Sornarajah, *Good Governance*, *in* MAX PLANCK ENCYCLOPEDIA OF PUBLIC INTERNATIONAL LAW 3, 14 (Anne Peters & Rüdiger Wolfrum eds., 2021).

143 G.A. Res. 60/1, ¶ 11 (Sept. 16, 2005).

144 G.A. Res. 70/1, Declaration ¶ 35 (Sept. 25, 2015) (emphasis added).

145 Irene Khan, *Shifting the Paradigm: Rule of Law and the 2030 Agenda for Sustainable Development*, 7 WORLD BANK LEGAL REV. 221, 221 (2016).

146 *Id.* at 238.

equal access to justice for all." A Washington-based think tank has written: "Global declarations and persuasive research demonstrate that there is a connection between the rule of law and sustainable development. Some have questioned both the strength and the causal direction of this connection. But the correlation between a society's adherence to the rule of law and its progress toward stability and development is beyond question."[147]

Contrary to what the think-tank wrote, the alleged correlation between the rule of law and economic growth does continue to be questioned.[148] Skeptics are probably right in asking for incremental improvement of developmental governance capabilities on a small scale (by experimentation and trial and error), taking into full account the political, economic, and institutional conditions in each country.[149]

A different story is that the fixation on economic growth is not sustainable and might need to be complemented or replaced by more ecology- and climate-friendly strategies of development such as "degrowth." In the end, the economic problems point to the limits of the law as a factor of order, less powerful than economic factors. A moderate capacity to shape reality attaches to the law in general, to constitutional law in particular, and to the rule of law as a principle, too.

## VI Conclusions

The current backlash against the "international liberal order" with the rule of law at its core[150] must be taken seriously. In this constellation, international organizations' constitution-shaping requires "[a]n effort for 'being earnest'" imposing "the need to recognize the political dimension of this agenda *and its limits*."[151] This remark by Valentina Volpe on democracy-promotion applies equally to rule-of-law promotion by international organizations.

147 James Michel, The Rule of Law and Sustainable Development 2 (Ctr. for Strategic & Int'l Stud. Rep., 2020).

148 Mushtaq Khan, *Beyond Good Governance: An Agenda for Developmental Governance*, *in* Is Good Governance Good for Development? 151 (Jomo Kwame Sundaram & Anis Chowdhury eds., 2012).

149 *Id.* at 179.

150 *See* David A. Lake, Lisa L. Martin & Thomas Risse, *Challenges to the Liberal Order: Reflections on International Organization*, 75 Int'l Org. 225, 225 (2021).

151 Valentina Volpe, *The Importance of Being Earnest: The United Nations and Democracy-Promotion*, *in* Mentoring Comparative Lawyers: Methods, Times, and Places 219, 232 (Francesca Fiorentini & Marta Infantino eds., 2020) (emphasis added).

It is, at this juncture, not sufficient to point to the fact that the rule-of-law standards used by international organizations as benchmarks derive their legitimacy from state consent and ultimately from state sovereignty. Indeed, the international organizations' constitutional assistance has not been formally imposed or coerced. However, once a state has decided to take advice, the "national owners" must then comply with the international standards.[152] This pathway often fuels a sentiment of loss of control that risks backfiring. Therefore, the international organizations' constitution-shaping activity must pay attention to deeper issues of legitimacy, and must interrogate also the substance and scope of the transnationalized rule of law *à fond*.

One possible strategy would be to cut back the work of international organizations to the so-called "classic" interstate principles, such as territorial integrity and military security, and leave aside all work on the rule of law (including democracy and human rights). However, this option is not viable, as the Russian invasion of Ukraine shows. Had the rule of law (including protection of fundamental rights, free elections, and proper dealing with crimes of the past) been guaranteed in Russia, that state would most likely not have engaged in a blatant violation of international law. A transnational rule of law, cutting across the "levels" of governance (entailing both domestic and international law), thus remains a *necessary* legal principle in order to safeguard international peace and security in their most basic form. For this reason, the constitution-shaping rule-of-law agenda pursued by international organizations should not be abandoned.

However, it needs to be revamped. For the constitution-shaping (and probably all other forms of rule-of-law assistance) to become more legitimate, all international organizations (and their member states) need to avoid the pitfalls of lopsided political human-rightism, abandon double standards, and pursue a much deeper global social agenda. Only then will respect for the rule of law (including access to justice) help with realizing development objectives. Only then will international organizations be able to respond to the current postcolonial sensibility and convince non-Western participants in the transnational ordering process that, indeed, "international law can be transformed into a means by which the marginalized may be empowered" and that "law can play its ideal role in limiting and resisting power."[153]

[152] Saunders, *supra* note 99, at 31.

[153] ANTONY ANGHIE, IMPERIALISM, SOVEREIGNTY AND THE MAKING OF INTERNATIONAL LAW 318 (2005).

5

# International Measures to Support the Rule of Law

TOM GINSBURG AND CHRISTOPH SCHOPPE

## I Introduction

The rule of law is a core concept of modern governance, central to discourses of constitutionalism, good governance, and democracy. It is also increasingly the subject of a transnational discourse, and a "transnational legal order" (TLO) has emerged around the issue, promoting it in national discourse as well as supranational contexts.[1] The "international rule of law" transposes the idea to the international legal system.[2] We thus have an ideal, operating at multiple levels of law that interact in complex ways. Enmeshment can take various forms. As regional and international institutions play a greater role in supporting the rule of law on the national plane, the different levels of legal order can be complements to each other toward advancing rule-of-law values. But they might, in some instances, also be institutional substitutes for each other.[3] This might occur when rule-of-law practices at one level undermine those at another level.

In this chapter we examine efforts to uphold the rule of law by transnational authorities tasked with protecting it. This reflects the general orientation of this collective socio-legal project toward institutional instantiations of the rule of law, rather than pure philosophical definitions.[4] How, exactly, is the rule of law defended at the international

[1] TRANSNATIONAL LEGAL ORDERS (Terence C. Halliday & Gregory Shaffer eds., 2015).

[2] On the international rule of law, see Chapters 2 and 4; Leander Beinlich & Anne Peters, *An International Rule of Law*, *in* OXFORD BIBLIOGRAPHIES (2021); THE INTERNATIONAL RULE OF LAW: RISE OR DECLINE? (Heike Krieger, Georg Nolte, & Andreas Zimmermann eds., 2019.)

[3] *See* Tom Ginsburg, *International Substitutes for Domestic Institutions*, 25 INT'L REV. L. & ECON. 107 (2005).

[4] *See* Chapter 1.

or transnational level, and are these efforts substitutes for or complementary to domestic efforts?

To answer this question, we examine the practices of regional courts and organizations. Regional trade regimes and human rights systems were initially set up with specific goals in mind, for which the rule of law was an implicit requirement but not explicitly stated. Rule-of-law norms crept in through the back door, as it were. But in the past two decades, regional organizations in Africa, Latin America, and Europe have taken on a thicker set of obligations toward protecting the rule of law (along with democracy and other related concepts.) The result is that supranational and international organizations have institutions – courts, commissions, bureaucracies – confronting real-world threats to the rule of law. It is the institutional work that gives actual content to rule-of-law values, and so an appropriate place to look for data on how the concept operates.

The chapter is organized as follows. We briefly sketch definitions. We then briefly survey the use of the rule of the law in the normative architecture and actual case law of major regional organizations, beginning with Latin America, moving to Europe and then Africa. This sequence is determined by the age of the relevant regional system rather than any sense of ontological priority. (We do not devote a separate section to Asia, which is a region notable for its absence of any kind of enforceable framework outside the level of the nation-state. The Charter of the Association of Southeast Asian Nations does mention strengthening the rule of law as part of its object and purpose,[5] but there has self-consciously been little effort to develop any deeper structure at the regional level.[6])

We conclude with some reflections on what is learned through the exercise. Courts and other bodies outside the state, in following their own rules, will sometimes find themselves butting up against national-level authorities that are following the dictates of the rule of law according to their own conception, whether or not in good faith. Some tension is to be expected, especially when international regimes are powerful. When one level exercises sufficient power to have an impact on others, it can serve as a substitute or complement in buttressing the rule of law, but interactions can create dynamics that can change the relationship. The region with the

[5] ASEAN Charter art. 1(7).

[6] Joel Ng, *Rule of Law as a Framework Within the ASEAN Community*, *in* ASEAN INTERNATIONAL LAW 161 (Eric Yong Joong Lee ed., 2021).

least powerful and effective institutions, Africa, is one in which the tensions between the two levels are also absent. This suggests that while harmonious relations across levels of legal order seems intuitively desirable on the surface, such harmony might actually indicate a situation in which the substantive values underpinning the rule of law are too weakly enforced to generate tension.

## II The Rule of Law: Trans-, Supra-, Inter-, and National

Definitions of the rule of law are varied, as it is something of an "essentially contested concept."[7] Definitions tend to be categorized in relatively thinner, procedural versions and thicker substantive versions. We follow Sandholtz and Shaffer in adopting Krygier's general conception of the rule of law, whose purpose is to "oppose the 'arbitrary exercise of power' by setting boundaries on, and channeling, power's exercise through known legal rules and institutions that apply to all."[8] This ideal can be applied to any exercise of power, including by, most obviously, national-level authorities that must abide by the constitution, but also those authorities operating at the supra- and international levels. We can characterize as international or supranational rule of law the idea that authorities above the level of the nation-state must themselves be bound by rule-of-law principles. National rule of law refers to domestic authority; supranational refers to regional institutions; international to international or global ones.

Complicating this framework is the transnational dimension. The "rule of law revival" of the past two decades has created another phenomenon: a transnational movement to promote the rule of law at the national level.[9] This movement is best understood as a TLO in Shaffer and Halliday's terms.[10] It has normative content, institutional manifestations, and is articulated in a decentralized network that involves actors below, inside, and above the state. Examples include "law and

[7] Jeremy Waldron, *The Rule of Law as an Essentially Contested Concept*, *in* THE CAMBRIDGE COMPANION TO THE RULE OF LAW 121 (Jens Meierhenrich & Martin Loughlin eds., 2021).

[8] *See* Chapter 1; Martin Krygier, *The Rule of Law: Legality, Teleology, Sociology*, *in* RELOCATING THE RULE OF LAW 45, 60 (Gianluigi Palombella & Neil Walker eds., 2009).

[9] Thomas Carothers, *The Rule of Law Revival*, 77 FOREIGN AFFS. 95 (1998); Stephen Humphreys, *An "International Rule of Law Movement"?*, *in* THE CAMBRIDGE COMPANION TO THE RULE OF LAW, *supra* note 7, at 474.

[10] Jothie Rajah, *"Rule of Law" as Transnational Legal Order*, *in* TRANSNATIONAL LEGAL ORDERS, *supra* note 1, at 340.

development" work, funded by foreign donors or regional development banks, to build up domestic legal institutions; the World Justice Project's effort to incentivize improvements through ratings; and transnational movements of judges and lawyers, such as the International Commission of Jurists. These projects seek to bolster and improve the rule of law at the domestic level, playing a complementary role.

Yet another transnational manifestation is the way in which international investment arbitration enforces norms of legality and antiarbitrariness against national authorities. International investment regimes also can require the exhaustion of domestic remedies before seeking international relief. Here, we see the logic of complementarity at first glance: the pressure from outside the country is designed to improve local performance, while deferring in the first instance to national authorities. Of course, the empirical effects are not always so straightforward, and scholars have identified a "substitution effect" from bilateral investment treaties, as they can reduce domestic pressure for reform or provoke backlash.[11] A transnational rule of law, in this example, might actually undermine domestic rule of law.

When international legal institutions themselves slip from rule-of-law values, supranational or national institutions may be playing the role of buttressing and complementing. For example, in the *Kadi* line of cases, the European Court of Justice found that fundamental rights in the European Union superseded a Security Council counter-terrorism regime that lacked basic guarantees of due process.[12]

Achieving any vision of the rule of law outside the level of a nation-state requires an institutional architecture. But the design of institutions immediately raises questions of the tension between national-level norms of democracy and the rule of law. The law constrains and orders the will of the demos, and is most necessary when that will is attempting to ride unchecked over minorities. Democracy, as has been suggested elsewhere, requires bureaucracy, in particular an administration that can deliver policies on the basis of politically driven choices, and this bureaucracy must follow principles of legality.[13] So, the rule of law is built into democracy as a concept.

[11] *See* Ginsburg, *supra* note 3; Mark Massoud, *International Arbitration and Judicial Politics in Authoritarian States*, 39 L. & SOC. INQUIRY 1 (2014).

[12] Joined Cases C-584/10 P, C-593/10 P & C-595/10 P, Eur. Comm'n v. Kadi, ECLI:EU:C:2013:518 (Mar. 19, 2013).

[13] TOM GINSBURG & AZIZ HUQ, HOW TO SAVE A CONSTITUTIONAL DEMOCRACY (2018).

But the reverse is only partly true. For advocates of a thin, procedural definition of the rule of law, there is no requirement that it be democratically legitimated. Authoritarian states might follow principles of legality and procedural order, which might even constitute "an unqualified human good" in E.P. Thompson's famous phrase.[14] Ideals of global administrative law posit a set of stand-alone technocratic principles of legal process that could be applied against international institutions themselves, but also enforced by those institutions against national democratic majorities.[15] In the former case, the "international" rule of law is a complement to the domestic version; in the latter case, it may be a substitute for it, in the sense that it is most necessary when the domestic version is under threat. But it is also possible that, by undermining the zone of democratic will formation, authorities outside the state can contribute to backlash against the rule of law in its thicker formulation. In short, trans-, supra-, and international institutions can be constitutive of the rule of law, or their antithesis. They can buttress the rule of law at the nation-state level, they can substitute for it, and in some cases their actions will spur backlash against it. For this reason, we are starting to see some scholars concerned with national rule of law and related norms reacting against the transnational rule-of-law complex.[16]

We now turn to several regional institutions to examine their role in protecting the rule of law at the national level – an inquiry especially important in our era of democratic backsliding.

## III Latin America and the Caribbean

The Organization of American States has a long history grounded in the protection of democracy in a region in which it has historically been fragile. The normative architecture includes the American Declaration of the Rights and Duties of Man, the American Convention on Human Rights, the Inter-American Democratic Charter of 2001, and several other instruments. The primary bodies tasked with implementing these norms are the Inter-American Commission on Human Rights

[14] *Cf.* Jothie Rajah, Authoritarian Rule of Law (2015); E.P. Thompson, Whigs and Hunters (1975); Daniel Cole, *"An Unqualified Human Good": E.P. Thompson and the Rule of Law*, 28 J. L. & Soc'y 177 (2001).

[15] Benedict Kingsbury, Nico Krisch, & Richard B. Stewart, *The Emergence of Global Administrative Law*, 68 L. & Contemp. Probs. 15 (2005).

[16] Martin Loughlin, Against Constitutionalism (2022).

(Commission) and the Inter-American Court of Human Rights (IACtHR).

The rule of law received explicit attention as an overarching goal in the Inter-American Democratic Charter, which identified it as an essential element of representative democracy in multiple articles.[17] Even before that, however, the jurisprudence of the Commission and IACtHR addressed rule-of-law issues, particularly through the lens of threats to judicial independence. In *Castillo Páez v. Peru* (judgment on merits of November 2, 1997), the IACtHR defined the content and scope of Article 25 of the Convention, which covers the right to judicial protection. The Court concluded that recourse to courts "is one of the fundamental pillars not only of the American Convention, but of the very rule of law in a democratic society in the terms of the Convention."[18] The Court has also focused on Article 23, which is on the right to political participation, but includes the right and opportunity "to have access, under general conditions of equality, to the public service of his country."[19] While apparently focused on public employment, the provision has provided a hook for protecting judicial independence, particularly against efforts by leftist Bolivarian governments to pack the courts with their own supporters by dismissing judges appointed by prior regimes.[20] Because the rule of law requires respect for legal authorities, and because populists tend to view courts as "the most dangerous branch" requiring control, protecting the integrity of courts is a central task for rule-of-law defenders.[21] This is a good example of a case in which the regional level serves as a backstop and complement to the national level.

[17] Org. of Am. States, Assembly Res. AG/Res. 1 (XXCIII-E/01), Inter-American Democratic Charter art. 2 (2001), https://tinyurl.com/yrs26fte ("The effective exercise of representative democracy is the basis for the rule of law . . . ."); *id.* art. 4 ("The constitutional subordination of all state institutions to the legally constituted civilian authority and respect for the rule of law on the part of all institutions and sectors of society are equally essential to democracy.").

[18] Castillo Páez v. Peru, Merits, Judgment, Inter-Am. Ct. H.R. (ser. C) No. 34, ¶ 82 (Nov. 3, 1997).

[19] Org. of Am. States, American Convention on Human Rights art. 23(1), Nov. 22, 1969, O.A.S.T.S. No. 36, 1144 U.N.T.S. 123.

[20] *See, e.g.*, Apitz Barbera ("First Court of Administrative Disputes") v. Venezuela, Preliminary Objection, Merits, Reparations, and Costs, Judgment, Inter-Am. Ct. HR (ser. C) No. 182 (Aug. 5, 2008); Constitutional Court v. Peru, Merits, Reparations, and Costs, Judgment, Inter-Am. Ct. H.R. (ser. C) No. 71, ¶¶ 56.1–56.5 (Jan. 31, 2001); *see generally* TOM GINSBURG, DEMOCRACIES AND INTERNATIONAL LAW 107–12 (2021).

[21] WOIJIECH SADURSKI, PANDEMIC OF POPULISTS 106 (2022) (describing courts as "most dangerous branch"); AMAL CLOONEY & PHILIPPA WEBB, THE RIGHT TO A FAIR TRIAL IN INTERNATIONAL LAW (2021)

There are other cases, however, in which the two levels are in tension. Take, for example, the IACtHR's doctrine of "conventionality control," announced in 2006 when it declared that all courts in the member states were obligated to review domestic actions for conformity with the Convention, as interpreted in the jurisprudence of the Court.[22] Remarkably, this extended to countries in which the domestic constitution did not automatically incorporate international law or give the Convention higher rank. In this sense, the doctrine both advanced regional rule of law (by pushing for uniform application) and undermined domestic rule of law as conceived within autonomous constitutional orders.[23] This ambitious move led to significant backlash. As Alexandra Huneeus has shown, national courts were leaders in pushing back against the doctrine, raising the issue of exactly whose vision of the rule of law was to be followed.[24] Substituting for a national process raises significant questions of efficacy and invites backlash, and the IACtHR has tempered its approach in recent years.[25]

Another regional body, the Caribbean Court of Justice (CCJ), also has confronted the rule of law through the lens of judicial independence. The CCJ has become a kind of regional constitutional court, able to enforce guarantees from national constitutions against the member states. In *Bisram v. Department of Public Prosecutions*, a Guyanese citizen successfully challenged the procedure used in a murder inquiry.[26] The Public Prosecutions Act allowed the Director of Public Prosecutions to order a magistrate to reopen an inquiry after an initial finding that no prima facie case had been made. Rather than simply address the procedural errors in the instant case, the CCJ relied on the guarantee of judicial independence in Guyana's constitution.[27] Judges at all levels should be

22 Almonacid-Arellano v. Chile, Preliminary Objections, Merits, Reparations, and Costs, Judgment, Inter-Am. Ct. H.R. (ser. C.) No. 154 (Sept. 26, 2006).

23 Ariel E. Dulitzky, *An Inter-American Constitutional Court? The Invention of Conventionality Control by the Inter-American Court of Human Rights*, 50 Tex. Int'l L.J. 45 (2015).

24 Alexandra Huneeus, *Courts Resisting Courts: Lessons from the Inter-American Court's Struggle to Enforce Human Rights*, 44 Cornell Int'l L.J. 493 (2011).

25 Alec Stone Sweet & Wayne Sandholtz, *The Law and Politics of Transnational Rights Protection*, 36 Governance 105 (2023); Wayne Sandholtz & Mariana Rangel Padilla, *Law and Politics in the Inter-American System: The Amnesty Cases*, 8 J.L. & Cts. 151 (2020).

26 Bisram v. Dep't of Pub. Prosecutions, No. GYCR2021/002, Caribbean Court of Justice, [2022] CCJ 7 AJ (GY) (Mar. 15, 2022).

27 Constitution of the Co-operative Republic of Guyana, Feb. 20, 1980, art. 122A.

free from interference by the executive in their decision-making; the CCJ noted that the constitution "expresses the hallowed, overarching principle of judicial independence, which is described by the Bangalore Principles as a prerequisite to the rule of law and a fundamental guarantee of a fair trial."[28]

Finally, we can turn to the international rule of law proper, the application of the principles before international institutions. In at least one case, the IACtHR has conceptualized the state as having an obligation to respond to and appear before the Court itself, as a requirement of the international rule of law. The case concerned Trinidad and Tobago, which had a practice of corporal punishment that was alleged to violate the American Convention on Human Rights. An applicant, Winston Caesar, challenged his punishment as well as significant trial delays in the 1990s.

In response to adverse decisions on the death penalty, Trinidad and Tobago had denounced the Convention in 1998, and refused to participate in the proceedings. The IACtHR, however, took the view that the withdrawal did not affect prior cases, for which it had continuing obligations. In a concurrence, Judge Jackman noted:

> [Trinidad and Tobago's] contumelious refusal to acknowledge its continuing obligations under a treaty that remained in force for it when the violations in this case took place represents a gratuitous attack on the Rule of Law, all the more astonishing in a State that, like other Commonwealth Caribbean states, prides itself on its Common Law traditions, where respect for human rights and for the Rule of Law are deeply embedded in the legal culture.[29]

In his separate opinion, Judge Antônio Cançado Trindade criticized Trinidad and Tobago for repeatedly failing to respond to or appear before the Court.[30] He then discussed the importance of the international rule of law, nonappearance before an international tribunal, and the duty of compliance with its judgment. He noted:

[28] *Bisram*, [2022] CCJ 7 AJ (GY).

[29] Caesar v. Trinidad and Tobago, Merits, Reparations, and Costs, Judgment, Inter-Am. Ct H.R. (ser. C) No. 123 (Mar. 11, 2005) (concurring judgment of J. Jackman), www.corteidh.or.cr/docs/casos/articulos/seriec_123_ing.pdf; *see also* Grace Kim, *Caesar v. Trinidad and Tobago*, 36 LOYOLA L.A. INT'L & COMP. L. REV. 1077 (2014).

[30] Caesar v. Trinidad and Tobago, Merits, Reparations, and Costs, Judgment, Inter-Am. Ct H.R. (ser. C) No. 123 (Mar. 11, 2005) (separate judgment of J. Trindade), www.corteidh.or.cr/docs/casos/articulos/seriec_123_ing.pdf.

> The precedent – among others – set up by the United States, of "withdrawal" and non-appearance before the ICJ, after a Judgment adverse to it on preliminary objections (in 1984) in the *Nicaragua versus United States* case, would be a very bad example for Trinidad and Tobago to follow. On the occasion, the United States earned much criticism from distinct corners of the international community, including from some of its own most distinguished jurists (like the late Keith Highet), for its disservice to the international rule of law.[31]

This places a duty of good faith appearance at the core of the rule of law, and one that applies to states in their international relations with each other. It is a perfect statement of the demands of the international rule of law, but also illustrates how difficult it is to advance those demands against recalcitrant states.

Together, these IACtHR and CCJ cases focus on several discrete aspects of the rule of law: the duty to provide for independent judicial recourse; the tricky question of impunity; and the duty to comply with commands of international courts, without the possibility of escaping international obligations through denunciation of international instruments. These various discrete applications of the rule of law help us to construct a coherent concept, and to understand the institutional dynamics. In the first, the regional body is a complement or backstop to domestic institutions; in the second, it substitutes for them in its judgment about the rule of law; and in the third, it is implementing a truly international rule of law, directed at the institutions of the regional body itself.

## IV Europe

The rule of law is a cornerstone of today's European legal architecture. The European Convention on Human Rights (ECHR), like its counterpart in the Americas, speaks of related values. Article 2(1) of the Treaty on European Union (TEU) cites the rule of law as one of the core values on which the Union is founded. And yet, the rule of law remains one of Europe's most contentious topics, both politically and legally: Poland (for a period of time) and Hungary built what many describe as "illiberal democracies." This has led to a series of responses by various European supranational institutions. These responses show the possibility – and the

[31] *Id.* ¶ 76 (footnote omitted).

limits – of international institutions in backstopping the rule of law in the face of sustained pressure.

The European experience has been central to articulating a core concept of the rule of law. Ideas related to the rule of law emerged in midcentury as something of an overlapping consensus between ordoliberals, who valued transnational protection of property interests, and social democrats, who were concerned with rights more broadly.[32]

At the same time, the European example illustrates why TLO theory emphasizes the networked nature of the legal concepts on the international plane. It is a story of cooperation among supranational actors with different epistemic bases and institutional structures. They include all European Union institutions, as well as the European Court of Human Rights, which is a traditional interstate human rights court. While their respective understandings may differ at the fringes,[33] all the European institutions acknowledge a clear core set of principles, including respect for democratic values, human rights, and an independent judiciary, as part of the rule of law.[34] This understanding emerged as a product of a gradual process that mirrored wider trends: In its early years, the predecessor of what is today the European Union considered itself a trade bloc, without any perceived need or a set of values of its own. But things changed after the Soviet Union fell, when the rule of law became a cornerstone of the legal and political thinking of the time.[35] Equally, the European Union has evolved beyond being a mere trade

[32] QUINN SLOBIDIAN, THE GLOBALISTS (2018).

[33] The Venice Commission's sophisticated rules on corruption and regarding the collection of personal data – Eur. Comm'n for Democracy through L. (Venice Comm'n), *Rule of Law Checklist*, 106th Sess., Study No. 711/2013, CDL-AD(2016) 007-e, at 29–33 (2016) [hereinafter *Rule of Law Checklist*] – feature less prominently elsewhere.

[34] In addition to the *Rule of Law Checklist*, see the definitions in European Commission Communication *Further Strengthening the Rule of Law Within the Union: State of Play and Possible Next Steps*, at 1, COM (2019) 163 final (Apr. 3, 2019), https://eur-lex.europa.eu/legal-content/EN/TXT/?uri=CELEX:52019DC0163; Regulation (EU/Euratom) 2020/2092 of the European Parliament and of the Council of 16 December 2020 on a General Regime of Conditionality for the Protection of the Union Budget, 2020 O.J. (L 433I) 1, recital (3).

[35] For this account, see, for example, Martin Krygier, *The Rule of Law After the Short Twentieth Century: Launching a Global Career*, *in* LAW, SOCIETY AND COMMUNITY: SOCIO-LEGAL ESSAYS IN HONOUR OF ROGER COTTERRELL 327, 336–37 (Richard Nobles & David Schiff eds., 2016); Ronald Janse, *Why Did the Rule of Law Revive?*, 11 HAGUE J. ON RULE LAW 341 (2019).

bloc.[36] What it has evolved into (and how it actually protects its values) is less clear. This of course is the underlying question behind many dynamics in today's rule-of law-discussions.

Finally, the European example shows how difficult it is to operationalize even a robust understanding in light of actual threats to the rule of law. While the European Court of Human Rights has far-reaching powers over the signatory states of the European Convention on Human Rights, it has little leverage to enforce its judgments against a government that is unwilling to abide by its international human rights duties. This is different from the European Union and its institutions, which may be better equipped to handle unwilling member states. But it is much less clear to what extent they can police the member states in areas not expressly governed by the European treaties. European Union involvement therefore adds another layer of complexity when evaluating the supranational response to rule-of-law backsliding: Conflicts about the rule of law are now also domestic constitutional conflicts. They touch on the very nature of the European project.

## 1 *Developing Core Rule-of-Law Principles through the European Courts*

On the EU level, rule-of-law thinking is usually traced to *Les Verts*, a 1987 judgment of the European Court of Justice.[37] The Court explained that the European Community (as it was known as the time) is "based on the rule of law inasmuch as neither its member states nor its institutions can avoid a review of the question whether the measures adopted by them are in conformity with the basic constitutional charter, the Treaty." This implicates what we have called the supranational rule of law.

Even earlier, the Court of Justice had established the principle of legal certainty and protections against retroactive laws in what is now European Union law.[38] In addition, it recognized the principle of

[36] From a specific rule-of-law standpoint, see Ronald Janse, *supra* note 35, and, more generally, Matthias Ruffert, *The EU Institutional Framework*, *in* Oxford Encyclopedia of EU Law paras. 1–4 (Sacha Garben & Laurence Gormley eds., 2022).

[37] Case C-294/83, Les Verts v. Parliament, 1986 E.C.R. 1339, ¶ 23. Note, however, that some would consider Case C-101/78, Granaria BV v. Hoofdproduktschap voor Akkerbouwprodukten, 1979 E.C.R. 623, the first rule-of-law case. *See* Laurent Pech, *Rule of Law*, *in* The Evolution of EU Law 307, 312 (Paul Craig & Gráinne De Búrca eds., 3d. ed. 2021).

[38] See the early cases Case C-98/78, Racke v. Hauptzollamt Mainz, 1979 E.C.R. 69; Case C-99/78, Decker v. Hauptzollamt Landau, 1979 E.C.R. 101, ¶ 8; Joined Cases 212 & 217/

legality – that is, the requirement that rules are set in a transparent, accountable, democratic, and pluralistic process: "In a community governed by the rule of law", the Court said, "adherence to legality must be properly ensured."[39] Similar ideas were to be found in the jurisprudence of the European Court of Human Rights.[40] One by one, the European Court of Justice and the European Court of Human Rights acknowledged the principles that constitute the rule of law. When the European institutions developed today's more comprehensive definitions, they only had to aggregate the courts' jurisprudence on those building blocks.[41]

In 1989, for example, the European Court of Justice acknowledged that in all member states any government intervention needs to have a legal basis and needs to be justified on grounds laid down by law:[42] "The need for such protection must be recognized as a general principle of [what is today European Union] law." This prohibits the arbitrary use of government powers. In keeping with TLO theory's emphasis on the networked nature of the legal concepts on the international plane, the Court's argument mirrored the preamble of the ECHR, which refers to the rule of law as part of the "common heritage" of its signatory states. This is, of course, strikingly different from today's rule-of-law discussions: In this early stage, the rule of law was enshrined in national (constitutional) law and then "borrowed" by the supranational level. The idea that supranational, European rule-of-law principles may need to be enforced *against* a nation-state seemed far-fetched at the time.

Nonetheless, at this early stage the European courts also dealt with what would become today's main battleground: judicial independence. In a Union based on the rule of law, the European Court of Justice ruled, effective judicial review, including respect for fundamental rights, is of

80, Amministrazione delle Finanze dello Stato v. Salumi, 1981 E.C.R. 2735, ¶ 10. See also the early case law cited by Thomas von Danwitz, *The Rule of Law in the Recent Jurisprudence of the ECJ*, 37 Fordham Int'l L.J. 1311 (2014).

39 Case C-496/99 P, CAS Succi di Frutta SpA, ECLI:EU:C:2004:236, ¶ 63 (Apr. 29, 2004).

40 Regarding legality, see, for example, Malone v. United Kingdom, App. No. 8691/79, ¶¶ 67–68 (Aug. 2, 1984), and regarding the requirement to apply the law in a foreseeable and consistent manner, Broniowski v. Poland, App. No. 31443/96, ¶ 184 (June 22, 2004).

41 In fact, most of the following cases were used by the European Commission's in its first extensive rule-of-law study; *see A New EU Framework to Strengthen the Rule of Law*, annex 1, COM (2014) 158 final (Mar. 11, 2014), https://eur-lex.europa.eu/legal-content/EN/ALL/?uri=celex:52014DC0158 [hereinafter *New EU Framework*].

42 Joined Cases C-46/87 & 227/88, Hoechst AG v. Comm'n of the Eur. Cmtys., 1989 E.C.R. 2859, ¶ 19.

central importance.[43] The right to effective judicial protection is again described as "one of the general principles of law stemming from the constitutional traditions common to the Member States."[44] The Court links this idea then to the ECHR and its protection of a fair trial in Article 6 – and to the right to an independent tribunal thereunder.[45] This is yet another example of how the two supranational European courts acted in concert to erect today's rule-of-law edifice.

### 2 *Entrenching and Defining the Rule of Law in Treaty Texts and through Reports by Supranational Institutions*

By the beginning of the 1990s, the European courts had spelled out most of the core principles that fall within the broader concept of the rule of law. While the Council of Europe institutions, in both the Convention preamble and Article 3 of the Statute of the Council of Europe, specifically mention the rule of law, European Community documents did not do so until 1992.[46] But very much in line with a greater focus on democracy and human rights, this marked the beginning of a legal order in which the rule of law is deeply enshrined in all treaty texts. Not only is it a value on which the Union is founded (see Article 2(1) TEU). Respect for and the willingness to promote the rule of law are required to apply for membership in the European Union under Article 49(1) TEU. Also, in its external relations, under Article 21(1) and (2) TEU, rule-of-law considerations are paramount. But one crucial element continued to be missing: No text offered a clear definition of what is meant by the rule of law, let alone one that is actionable in court. Developing such a definition fell to Europe's supranational institutions.

An important first step in this regard was taken by the Venice Commission of the Council of Europe, which conducted an intensive

[43] Case C-50/00 P, Unión de Pequeños Agricultores v. Council of the Eur. Union., ECLI:EU:C:2002:462 (July 25, 2002), ¶¶ 38–39; Case C-550/09, E. and F., ECLI:EU:C:2010:382, ¶ 44 (June 29, 2010); Case C-583/11 P, Inuit Tapiriit Kanatami v. Eur. Parliament, ECLI:EU:C:2013:625, ¶¶ 91–92 (Oct. 3, 2013).

[44] *Unión de Pequeños Agricultores*, ECLI:EU:C:2002:462, ¶ 39.

[45] Case C-185/95 P, Baustahlgewerbe v. Comm'n, ¶ 20 (Dec. 17, 1998); Joined Cases C-174/98 P & C-189/98 P, Netherlands v. Comm'n of the Eur. Comtys., ECLI:EU:C:2000:1, ¶ 17 (Jan. 11, 2000) (citing De Wilde, Ooms and Versyp v. Belgium, App. No. 2832/66; 2835/66; 2899/66, ¶ 78 (Mar. 10, 1972)).

[46] For potential reasons, see Pech, *supra* note 37, at 310–11.

survey of what the rule of law entails.[47] Later, this merged into a *Rule of Law Checklist*.[48] Their contents mostly mirror what the European Commission now considers its core definition of the rule of law, and what eventually made its way into recent European legislation on the "conditionality mechanism" (see Section 3). All in all, there seems to be a rather robust understanding of what the rule of law entails, legality being a core element.[49] It is worth quoting the definition in full:

> [I]t seems that a *consensus* can now be found for the necessary elements of the rule of law as well as those of the Rechtsstaat which are not only formal but also substantial or material (materieller Rechtsstaatsbegriff). These are:
>
> (1) Legality, including a transparent, accountable, and democratic process for enacting law
> (2) Legal certainty
> (3) Prohibition of arbitrariness
> (4) Access to justice before independent and impartial courts, including judicial review of administrative acts
> (5) Respect for human rights
> (6) Non-discrimination and equality before the law.[50]

Under this definition, there is a strong nexus between democratic values, human rights, and the rule of law.[51] The European Court of Human Rights, for example, considers the rule of law inherent in all the articles of the ECHR.[52] The European Commission is of the opinion that "there can be no democracy and respect for fundamental human rights without the rule of law and vice versa."[53] We note in passing that this formulation, unlike the view laid out at the beginning of this chapter, does not contemplate a rule-of-law system without democracy. But it seems to be one very important feature of how supranational institutions

[47] Eur. Comm'n for Democracy through L. (Venice Comm'n), *Report on the Rule of Law*, 86th Sess., Study No. 512/2009, CDL-AD(2011)003rev, at 10 (2011) [hereinafter *Report on the Rule of Law*]. It should be noted that this report relies more heavily on academic writing than the other reports mentioned here.

[48] *Rule of Law Checklist, supra* note 33; Kim Scheppele *The Rule of Law and the Frankenstate: Why Governance Checklists Do Not Work*, 26 GOVERNANCE 559 (2013).

[49] *Rule of Law Checklist, supra* note 33, at 7; *Report on the Rule of Law, supra* note 47, at 10; Regulation (EU/Euratom) 2020/2092, *supra* note 34, recital (3).

[50] *Report on the Rule of Law, supra* note 47, at 10

[51] *See* Chapter 1.

[52] Former King of Greece v. Greece, App. No. 25701/94, ¶ 79 (Nov. 23, 2000); Stafford v. United Kingdom, App. No. 46295/99, ¶ 63 (May 28, 2002); Broniowski v. Poland, App. No. 31443/96, ¶¶ 147, 184 (June 22, 2004).

[53] *New EU Framework, supra* note 41, at 4, https://eur-lex.europa.eu/legal-content/EN/ALL/?uri=celex:52014DC0158.

understand the rule of law today. It is a value-driven approach, developed through the institutional dialogue emphasized by TLO theory. The European Commission, the Venice Commission, and the two European Courts, all relied on each other's work when weaving an ever-stronger understanding of what the rule of law entails. This shared understanding draws strength from the fact that it is anchored in multiple normative systems:[54] the shared traditions of the European nation-states, the ECHR, and the TEU.

## 3 *Values Put to the Test: The Rule-of-Law Crisis in Hungary and Poland, a Multitude of Supranational Responses, and Constitutional Questions*

At a normative level, then, Europe has a robust understanding of what the rule of law entails. But when confronted by the backsliding countries of (at the time) Poland and Hungary, the institutional structures face a new challenge, which has exposed deep tensions in the project. When the European Union was founded, the rule of law in its member states was taken for granted. The new challenge is for European institutions to enforce the rule of law against its own member states. This is where the rule-of-law conflict goes to the very nature of the European project: even if they are appalled by how Hungary and Poland (before the October 2023 elections that ended the rule of the Law and Justice Party) behaved, defenders of the traditional view of member states' sovereignty might, as a matter of principle, feel uneasy when the European level enforces quasi-constitutional norms such as the rule of law.[55]

[54] Armin von Bogdandy et al., *A Potential Constitutional Moment for the European Rule of Law: The Importance of Red Lines*, *in* DEFENDING CHECKS AND BALANCES IN EU MEMBER STATES: TAKING STOCK OF EUROPE'S ACTIONS 388 (Armin von Bogdandy et al., eds., 2021).

[55] For discussions of this sentiment, see Danwitz, *supra* note 38, at 1338–39; M. Bonelli, *From a Community of Law to a Union of Values: Hungary, Poland, and European Constitutionalism*, 13 EUR. CONST. L. REV. 793 (2017); Armin von Bogdandy, *Principles of a Systemic Deficiencies Doctrine: How to Protect Checks and Balances in the Member States*, 57 COMMON MKT. L. REV. 705 (2020); Kim Lane Scheppele et al., *EU Values Are Law, After All: Enforcing EU Values Through Systemic Infringement Actions by the European Commission and the Member States of the European Union*, 39 Y.B. EUR. L. 3 (2021). For a very recent and comprehensive treatment of the issue, arguing in favor of the ECJ's active role, see Armin von Bogdandy & Luke Dimitrios Spieker, Transformative Constitutionalism in Luxembourg: How the Court Can Support Democratic Transitions (MPIL Research Paper No. 2022-14, 2022), https://papers.ssrn.com/sol3/papers.cfm?abstract_id=4146323.

Against this backdrop, the supranational response to the rule-of-law backsliding in Hungary and Poland consisted of three approaches, both politically and legally, of varying novelty. First, the European actors tried to stay very much within the lines of the treaty text. Second, the European Court of Justice opened the door to infringement actions that address one *general* rule-of-law shortcoming: the lack of an independent judiciary. Third, there is the new conditionality mechanism, through which EU funds are conditioned on the member states maintaining the rule of law, more thickly formulated.

### a The Standard Playbook: Specific Infringement Actions and the Process under Article 7 TEU

One way to think about rule-of-law backsliding in the European Union is to consider it a political problem for the member states to solve, with supranational institutions thus playing a limited role. This view seemed to prevail in the European Commission during the first years of the rule-of-law crisis. Under Article 258 of the Treaty on the Functioning of the European Union (TFEU), the European Commission may sue a member state that violates European law. This "infringement action" addresses a specific violation. And in its early response to the developments in Hungary,[56] the Commission did just that: In 2011 and 2012, Viktor Orbán's government lowered the mandatory retirement age for judges, forcing the most senior 10–15 percent of Hungarian judges to leave office.[57] In response, the European Commission brought an infringement action for violations of European law against age discrimination.[58] It did not frame the issue in rule-of-law terms. The same happened when Hungary dismissed its data protection officer despite his independence being guaranteed by European law. The Commission brought an infringement action for violation of this specific provision.[59] Again, the rule of law was not mentioned.[60]

[56] For an overview, see Krista Kovács & Kim Lane Scheppele, *The Fragility of an Independent Judiciary: Lessons from Hungary and Poland – and the European Union*, COMMUNIST & POST-COMMUNIST STUD., Sept. 2018, at 189.

[57] For this part of the Hungarian case, see *id.* at 192.

[58] Case C-268/12, Eur. Comm'n v. Hungary, ECLI:EU:C:2012:687 (Nov. 7, 2012) (retirement age for judges). For a comparison with the ECJ's later cases focused on the rule of law, see Petra Bárd & Anna Sledzinska-Simon, *On the Principle of Irremovability of Judges Beyond Age Discrimination: Commission v. Poland*, 57 COMMON MKT. L. REV. 1555 (2020).

[59] Case C-288/12, Eur. Comm'n v. Hungary, ECLI:EU:C:2014:237 (Apr. 8, 2014) (independence of the data protection "supervisory authority").

[60] Danwitz, *supra* note 38, at 1344, makes it abundantly clear, however, that the ECJconsidered the Hungarian move for what it was – a rule-of-law issue – and that its

It is commonly accepted, however, that the early infringement cases were largely unsuccessful. They failed to restore an independent judiciary, and they failed to deter further backsliding. Acknowledging this, the European Commission introduced a wide range of "soft" devices to tackle rule-of-law issues:[61] Today, the Commission produces a Justice Scoreboard (an annual overview of indicators on the efficiency, quality, and independence of each member state's judiciary), a Rule of Law Framework (a three-step process by which the Commission assesses, addresses, and monitors threats to the rule of law in member states), and an annual Rule of Law Report. In addition, the European Council started its own annual Rule of Law Dialogues.[62] Such "soft" instruments are mirrored by the Venice Commission, which issued "rule-of-law opinions" at almost every step of the Hungarian and Polish cases.

As long as the European Commission limited itself to infringement actions and "soft" instruments, only one tool could address systemic rule-of-law issues: the procedure under Article 7 TEU.[63] Under Article 7(1) TEU, the Council may find by a supermajority that there is a "clear risk" of a "serious breach" of one the Union's core values by one of its member states. Finding the "existence of a serious and persistent breach" requires unanimity in a second vote, reflecting the idea that protecting the European Union's values is for the member states among themselves. And while cases under Article 7 TEU were initiated against both Hungary and Poland,[64] there has been little success, since the two countries can protect each other.[65] (The October 2023 change in power in Poland has changed this dynamic somewhat, but there have not been renewed efforts

technical treatment of the matter should be understood as an attempt to bridge the gap that Hungary would have to overcome in accepting the judgment.

61 For a detailed description of today's tools and their genesis, see Pech, *supra* note 37, at 318–27, 334–37.

62 For harsh criticism of the Council's dialogue, see Peter Oliver & Justine Stefanelli, *Strengthening the Rule of Law in the EU: The Council's Inaction*, 54 J. Common Mkt. Stud. 1075 (2016); Pech, *supra* note 37, at 325–27. For a more general critique of the Council's rule-of-law response, see Laurent Pech et al., *Poland's Rule of Law Breakdown: A Five-Year Assessment of EU's (In)Action*, 13(1) Hague J. on Rule Law 1 (2021).

63 On its genesis, see Wojceich Sadurski, *Adding Bite to a Bark: The Story of Article 7, E.U. Enlargement, and Jorg Haider*, 16 Colum. J. Eur. L. 385 (2010).

64 Eur. Comm'n, Proposal for a Council Decision on the Determination of a Clear Risk of a Serious Breach by the Republic of Poland of the Rule of Law, COM (2017) 835 (Dec. 20, 2017).

65 For a detailed overview of Poland's failure to address the points raised by the European Commission, see Pech et al., *supra* note 62, at 5–17.

to confront Hungary as of this writing.) While politicians often referred to Article 7 TEU as "the nuclear option,"[66] in the end it has turned out to be rather toothless. Criticism focuses on the unanimity requirement, on what is perceived a slow process, and one that is overly politicized.[67] Generally, there seems to be little appetite on the part of the member states to judge their peers. Maybe foreshadowing the European Court of Justice's further involvement, one of its judges spoke of "the inadequacy of the procedure foreseen in article 7 TEU which clearly cannot be considered as an operational or even suitable instrument to ensure the rule of law … and the observance of the values enshrined in article 2 TEU."[68] As in the Inter-American system, a recalcitrant sovereign is difficult to discipline.

### b The ECJ to the Rescue? Article 19(1) TEU and Judicial Independence in Poland.

The legal landscape changed fundamentally in 2018 when the European Court of Justice gave its now famous *Portuguese Judges* judgment.[69] It amounted to a tectonic shift in the European legal landscape. After the global financial crisis, Portugal had mandated pay cuts for all public officials, including judges. Some judges appealed their pay cut, ultimately to the European Court of Justice. By now, the situation in Hungary and Poland was, of course, well known. In its *Portuguese Judges* case, the European Court of Justice ruled that threats to the independent judiciary in a member state were justiciable in the member state's courts, since Article 19(1) TEU requires that member states "provide effective remedies sufficient to ensure effective legal protection in the fields covered by Union law." The European Court of Justice treats this as giving "concrete expression to the value of the rule of law stated in Article 2 TEU."[70] Values suddenly became justiciable: the European Court and the national

[66] Dimitry Kochenov & Laurent Pech, *Better Late than Never? On the European Commission's Rule of Law Framework and its First Activation*, 54 J. COMMON MKT. STUD. 1062 (2016).

[67] *Id.*; Oliver & Stefanelli, *supra* note 62, at 1081. For an overview of political science criticism, see also the works cited by Tom Theuns, *The Need for an EU Expulsion Mechanism: Democratic Backsliding and the Failure of Article 7*, 28 RES PUBLICA 1 (2022).

[68] Danwitz, *supra* note 38, at 1337.

[69] Case C-64/16, Associação Sindical dos Juízes Portugueses v. Tribunal de Contas, ECLI: EU:C:2018:117 (Feb. 27, 2018).

[70] *Id.* ¶¶ 31–32.

courts have a shared duty to ensure that the law is observed. This is then linked to the rule of law: "It follows that every Member State must ensure that the bodies which, as 'courts or tribunals' within the meaning of EU law, come within its judicial system in the fields covered by that law, meet the requirements of effective judicial protection."[71] As all national judges potentially rule on EU law, this last sentence operationalized Article 19(1) TEU to protect an overall independent judiciary in each country. The dynamics of complementarity were in full effect.

This development illustrates a specifically transnational conception of the rule of law, different from the international rule of law that examines procedures before international institutions. The rule of law must be preserved, not for the integrity of the international courts, but because the member states have a system of mutual reliance that European law will be uniformly and fairly applied among them all. The horizontal trust among states is what justifies the international level's scrutiny.

Now, the European Commission could do what it had felt unable to do earlier: it brought a case against Poland for its *systemic* violation of the rule of law by undermining the independence of its judiciary.[72] Essentially, the Polish government had subdued the Constitutional Tribunal, had captured the judicial appointment process, and had established a new "disciplinary regime" to police its judges.[73] The European Commission won all of its infringement cases.[74] And over time the European Court of Justice developed a comprehensive view of an independent judiciary. Under its jurisprudence, Articles 2(1) and 19(1) TEU are invoked if:[75]

> the objective circumstances in which that body was created, the characteristics of that body, and the way in which its members have been appointed are capable of giving rise to reasonable doubts in the minds

[71] *Id.* ¶ 37.

[72] For a critique of its piecemeal approach, see Pech et al., *supra* note 62, at 21–23.

[73] SADURSKI, *supra* note 21.

[74] Case C-619/18 R, Eur. Comm'n v. Poland, ECLI:EU:C:2019:531 (June 24, 2019) (independence of the supreme court); Case C-192/18, Eur. Comm'n v. Poland, ECLI:EU:C:2019:924 (Nov. 5, 2019) (independence of the ordinary courts); Case C-791/19, Eur. Comm'n v. Poland, ECLI:EU:C:2021:596 (July 15, 2021) (disciplinary chamber); Case C-204/21, Eur. Comm'n v. Poland, ECLI:EU:C:2023:442 (June 5, 2023) ("muzzle law"). On the criticism that the Commission brings only "hundred per cent winnable cases," see Pech et al., *supra* note 62.

[75] Case C-791/19, Eur. Comm'n v. Poland, ECLI:EU:C:2021:596, ¶ 86 (July 15, 2021) (disciplinary chamber); *see also* Joined Cases C-585/18, C-624/18 & C-625/18, A. K. v. Najwyższy, ECLI:EU:C:2019:982, ¶ 171 (Nov. 19, 2019); .

of individuals as to the imperviousness of that body to external factors, in particular, as to the direct or indirect influence of the legislature and the executive, and its neutrality with respect to the interests before it.

By relying on Article 19(1) TEU and the rule of law concept, the infringement cases against Poland differed significantly from those brought earlier against Hungary, even though they dealt with similar topics. Both countries, for example, forced large parts of their judiciary to retire.[76] Unlike in the Hungarian case, there has been some early success with such infringement actions against Poland under Article 19(1) TEU. An interim order, for example, after the European Commission's first infringement action, restored some Polish judges to their previous posts.[77]

Operationalizing Article 19(1) TEU, however, opened another avenue for the European Court of Justice to make itself heard: Under Article 267 TFEU, national judges can ask for a preliminary ruling on the interpretation of European law. This deputized national judges to address rule-of-law backsliding. By making a preliminary reference, Polish judges can ask whether they were dealt with in accordance with Article 19(1) TEU.[78] Judges from other member states could ask whether they should treat their Polish colleagues as independent. While Polish judges, for example, asked about the so-called disciplinary chamber,[79] an Irish judge famously asked whether she could still send a detainee to Poland under the European Arrest Warrant scheme.[80] The answer in both cases was similar: the European Court of Justice (ECJ) gave guidance as to what to consider, but the ultimate decision rested with the national court.[81] The ECJ stopped short of declaring the Polish judiciary completely nonindependent.

Polish judges were not the only ones to challenge the Disciplinary Chamber before the ECJ.[82] In addition, the European Commission

[76] *Eur. Comm'n v. Poland*, ECLI:EU:C:2019:531, ¶¶ 71–97; *Eur. Comm'n v. Poland*, ECLI: EU:C:2019:924, ¶¶ 108–35 . On these cases, see Bárd & Sledzinska-Simon, *supra* note 58, at 1564–67, 1569–72; Pech et al., *supra* note 62, at 29–31.

[77] Case C-619/18, Eur. Comm'n v. Poland, ECLI:EU:C:2018:1021 (Dec. 17, 2018) (independence of the supreme court). On this significant point, see Pech et al., *supra* note 62.

[78] For an overview of the many cases brought by Polish judges, see Pech et al., *supra* note 62, at 33.

[79] *A.K. v. Najwyższy*, ECLI:EU:C:2019:982, (Nov. 19, 2019).

[80] On this case, see also Bogdandy et al., *supra* note 54, at 394–99.

[81] For a critique of the ECJ's record in these cases, see Pech et al., *supra* note 62, at 32–38; for a defense of its approach, see Bogdandy et al., *supra* note 54, at 396.

[82] For a timeline of the various cases and the Polish reactions, see Luke Dimitrios Spieker, *The Conflict over the Polish Disciplinary Regime for Judges – an Acid Test for Judicial Independence, Union Values and the Primacy of EU Law: Commission v. Poland*, 59 COMMON MKT. L. REV. 777, 811 (2022).

brought an infringement action. As discussed, Poland lost both cases.[83] But this time, its government did not change course. It chose noncompliance and escalation instead. The Polish Constitutional Tribunal, which had been captured early on,[84] issued a judgment saying that compliance with Article 19(1) TEU violated the Polish constitution. In addition, the Polish government introduced a "muzzle law," which prohibits Polish judges from reviewing whether other judges have been legally appointed (under European law, one might add).[85] In response, the Commission brought yet another infringement case. It also applied for an interim order, which the ECJ granted. When the government refused to comply, Poland was ordered to pay a record-high sum of one million euros for each day it continued to defy the European Court rulings.[86]

At the end of the day, though, a sanction is a price: noncompliance will simply affect the amount of money transferred to Poland, not its ultimate membership of the EU. Poland's reaction to the latest string of rule-of-law cases laid an axe on the foundation of the European Union as a community based on law. In some areas, Poland refused to accept all European law and its supremacy, and Poland had thereby left, at least partially, the European legal space.[87]

Under the logic of *Portuguese Judges* and the European Court of Justice's rule-of-law cases, European values may reign over the member states' constitutions. This might truly be a "constitutional moment" that changes the legal structure of the European Union.[88] It also tells us something about international norms as complementing national law, as substituting for national law, and how the former may turn into the latter. At first, European rule-of-law discourses were clearly aimed to complement and strengthen national constitutional law. This is still true for the *Portuguese Judges* ruling, which Portugal duly

[83] Case C-791/19, Eur. Comm'n v. Poland, ECLI:EU:C:2021:596 (July 15, 2021) (disciplinary chamber).

[84] On the capture, see SADURSKI, *supra* note 21; Oskar Polański, *Poland: Another Episode of "Rule of Law Backsliding" – Judgment P 7/20 and a Threat to the Integrity of the EU Legal Order*, 2022 PUB. L. 153; Oskar Polański, *Poland: Constitutional Tribunal Judgment K 3/21 – a Continued Assault on the Integrity of the EU Legal Order*, 2022 PUB. L. 344; for a broader discussion, see Spieker, *supra* note 82, at 797–805.

[85] *See* Spieker, *supra* note 82.

[86] Case C-204/21 R, Eur. Comm'n v. Poland, Order of the Vice-President of the Court, ECLI:EU:C:2021:878 (Oct. 27, 2021). The sum was later reduced to 500,000 euros; *see* Case C-204/21 R-RAP, Order of the Vice-President of the Court, ECLI:EU:C:2023:334 (Apr. 21, 2023).

[87] Bogdandy et al., *supra* note 54, at 398.

[88] *Id.* at 386–87.

implemented. The picture changed, however, once the Polish government and the Constitutional Tribunal openly defied European law. The European level is substituting its understanding of what the rule entails for what the Polish constitution allegedly says. This is significant. Analyzing this shift as (attempted) substitution rather than as a complementing normative order helps to explain the extraordinary nature of what has happened in *Portuguese Judges*. It helps to conceptualize why the ECJ is so careful to reiterate that it will exercise judicial restraint when asked to apply its new powers.[89] And it explains why, so far, the Court (and the European Commission) have stuck to the now well-trodden paths of judicial independence, rather than using Article 2(1) TEU and the rule of law more broadly to address other shortcomings in certain member states.[90]

In defense of their approach, at least regarding judicial independence, the European actors may point toward a fact that already shaped the genesis of today's rule-of-law definition: Its arguments are tied not only to European Union law. Especially in its cases related to judicial independence, the court relies on the concurrent case law of the European Court of Human Rights[91] and, by extension, the work of the Venice Commission. Of course, this multilayered approach strengthens the argument for substituting for national law. It makes the rule-of-law cases under Article 19(1) TEU look less like overreach by European Union institutions and more like a part of broader development of shared European values. (It is worth noting that Polish voters seemed to agree.[92])

[89] *See generally* Danwitz, *supra* note 38, at 1315, 1340. In the context of the Polish rule-of-law cases, see Bogdandy & Spieker, *supra* note 55, at 12–14; Spieker, *supra* note 82, at 801–03.

[90] This may change, however. In its case against Hungary's "anti LGBTQ law," the Commission, for the first time, relies on Article 2(1) TEU as a stand-alone provision; *see* Lena Kaiser, *A New Chapter in the European Rule of Law Saga*, VERFASSUNGSBLOG (Mar. 4, 2023), https://verfassungsblog.de/a-new-chapter-in-the-european-rule-of-law-saga/. Equally, in its case against Poland's "Lex Tusk," the Commission cites Article 19(1) TEU more broadly, not limiting its scope to cases regarding (the lack of) judicial independence; *see* Nora Visser, *Enforcing Democracy*, VERFASSUNGSBLOG (June 13, 2023), https://verfassungsblog.de/enforcing-democracy/.

[91] *See, e.g.*, Joined Cases C-585/18, C-624/18 & C-625/18, A.K. v. Najwyższy, ECLI:EU:C:2019:982, ¶ 171 (Nov. 19, 2019).

[92] The Polish people, after all, seem to view the interventions of the ECJ as legitimate; see the studies cited by Spieker, *supra* note 82, at 796.

### c The Recent Conditionality Mechanisms

Disobeying the European Court of Justice might come at the hefty price of one million euros a day. But there is a (potentially) even more powerful tool that couples the rule of law and financial pressure: the so-called conditionality mechanism. It makes payments from the general budget as well as payments under the European Union's COVID relief package contingent on abiding by the European rule-of-law standards.[93] The numbers at stake are significant: Poland's share of the COVID recovery fund, for example, is 35.4 billion euros. There is one additional prerequisite, however: the breaches of the rule of law must "affect the sound financial management of the Union budget or the protection of the financial interests of the Union in a sufficiently direct way." In this regard, the final design of the conditionality mechanism marks a notable deviation from earlier ideas by the European Commission (and, in fact, the vision of the European Parliament).[94] The conditionality mechanism is now budget-centered; the rule of law is the means to an end. Not every rule-of-law issue leads to financial consequences, but some nexus between the rule-of-law situation and the EU budget is required.

The conditionality mechanism in its final form marks a compromise. Such an instrument is introduced to protect the rule of law on the European level, but its scope is limited.[95] The conditionality mechanism marks the highly politicized nature of European rule-of-law tools. As in 2014, regarding the first Rule of Law Framework, it was the Council's legal service that considered a more general conditionality unlawful.[96] This time it was heard. The underlying power struggle is, again, as much about protecting the rule of law as it is about the power balance between the European level and its member states.[97] And the lines of conflict are similar to those that have emerged in relation to the jurisprudence of the

[93] *See* Regulation (EU/Euratom) 2020/2092, *supra* note 34, recital (3), arts. 2(a), 3, 4(2).

[94] For an overview of the genesis of today's conditionality mechanism, see Antonia Baraggia & Matteo Bonelli, *Linking Money to Values: The New Rule of Law Conditionality Regulation and Its Constitutional Challenges*, 23 German L.J. 131 (2022).

[95] For defense of this approach, see *id.* at 146–50; Marco Fisicaro, *Protection of the Rule of Law and "Competence Creep" via the Budget: The Court of Justice on the Legality of the Conditionality Regulation*, 18 Eur. Const. L. Rev. 334, 342–43 (2022).

[96] Opinion of the Legal Service of the Council, *Proposal for a Regulation of the European Parliament and of the Council on the Protection of the Union's Budget in Case of Generalised Deficiencies as Regards the Rule of Law in the Member States: Compatibility with the EU Treaties*, 13593/18 (Oct. 25, 2018).

[97] Fisicaro, *supra* note 95.

European Court of Justice under Articles 2 and 19(1) TEU. Far-reaching conditionality mechanisms have a constitutionalizing and federalizing effect.[98] They confer great power on the upper level of government. Of course, the US experience with conditional spending immediately springs to mind.[99] Ultimately, such conditionality mechanisms are yet another tool to incentivize a national legal system to adopt supranational value judgments as substitutes for local ones.

At the same time, for present purposes, the mechanism is rather open about the background against which it was drafted: An independent judiciary features heavily in the legal text.[100] And, as a consequence, the European institutions, initially, approved neither Poland's nor Hungary's application for COVID relief funds. Instead, they set certain "milestones" to be met before any payment would be made. The year 2022 was a story of back-and-forth that highlighted the strengths and weaknesses of the conditionality mechanism and its ultimately political nature:[101] At least on paper, Poland and Hungary seemed willing to compromise. A financial lever and withholding hefty sums proved strong tools. But wielding them requires political will – especially in times of war. Poland – after all, the notorious rule-of-law culprit – came out as one of Ukraine's most reliable allies, while Hungary took a very pro-Russia stance. All this led to initially quite lenient milestones for Poland (many would argue they were too lenient), a later U-turn by the European Commission, and very strict milestones for Hungary. For now, it remains uncertain whether the new conditionality mechanism will restore the rule of law, at least partially. It may well end up as nothing more than an additional bargaining chip on the political table when the next crisis needs addressing.

In terms of substitutes and complements, the European framework is clearly designed to complement local systems in advancing the rule of law. Indeed, the entire European project has depended for decades on national judges as the first line of defense in enforcing European law. Yet, in recent decades populist leaders have leveraged the alleged remoteness

98 Baraggia & Bonelli, *supra* note 94, at 144–45, 154; Fisicaro, *supra* note 95, at 338.

99 South Dakota v. Dole, 483 U.S. 203 (1987); see the discussions by Baraggia & Bonelli, *supra* note 94, at 144–45.

100 *See* Regulation (EU/Euratom) 2020/2092, *supra* note 34, recitals (8)–(10), arts. 2(a), 3(a), 4(d).

101 For the most recent developments, see Jakub Jaraczewski, *Unexpected Complications: The Impact of the Russian Invasion of Ukraine on the Rule of Law Crisis in the EU*, VERFASSUNGSBLOG (Dec. 23, 2022), https://tinyurl.com/2n589ept.

of European institutions to advance their own nationalist projects, many of which seem to undermine the rule of law. One wonders, then, whether the European experience has not been one of substitution rather than complementarity.

## V Africa

African regional institutions have undergone a "good governance" turn in recent decades, in which democracy and the rule of law have been elevated to a high normative position. The African Union (AU), successor to the Organisation of African Unity, has been playing a major role here, and a major first step was the Constitutive Act of the Union, adopted in 2000 at Lomé, Togo, which enshrines the rule of law in its preamble and in the listing of principles in Article 4.[102] Further developing these norms, the AU adopted the African Charter on Democracy, Elections and Governance (ACDEG) in 2007, which at this writing has been signed by forty-six out of fifty-five member states and ratified by thirty-one.[103] The ACDEG mentions the rule of law seven times, as part of its preamble, principles, and as part of the content of good governance. These and other AU norms are enforced in several ways, including monitoring and reports by the African Commission on Human and Peoples' Rights; the African Peer Review Mechanism, a continent-wide mechanism looking at rule of law; and the African Court on Human and Peoples' Rights. In extreme cases, the Peace and Security Council (PSC), an AU organ, can impose sanctions, including suspension, for failure to abide by the policies.

Only a handful of cases of these institutions have referred to the rule of law. In one case, the African Commission found that Cameroon's judicial council, which had the president as chair and the minister of justice as vice-chair, violated judicial independence.[104] This case goes directly to the threat to the rule of law posed by political interference with the

[102] Lome Declaration of July 2000 on the Framework for an OAU Response to Unconstitutional Changes of Government, AHG/Decl.5 (XXXVI), July 12, 2000.

[103] *See generally* Micha Wiebusch et al., *The African Charter on Democracy Elections and Governance*, 63 J. Afr. L. 9, 10 (2019); Christina Murray, Eric Alston & Micha Wiebusch, Presidential Term Limits and the International Community 9 (Inst. of Developmental Pol'y, Working Paper 2018.9, 2018).

[104] Kevin Mgwanga Gunme v. Cameroon, Communication 266/03, African Commission on Human and Peoples' Rts. [Afr. Comm'n H.P.R.] (May 2009). The Commission arrived at similar conclusions in a recent case against the Democratic Republic of Congo (DRC) in which it found that the African Charter guarantees the separation of powers. Jose Alidor

judiciary, and is consistent with standards articulated by the Venice Commission and others. The *appearance* of judicial independence is a common requirement now.

Other cases before the African Court of Human and Peoples' Rights occasionally invoke the rule of law as a kind of freestanding principle that supports particular procedural requirements. For example, in *Kennedy Owino Onyachi v. United Republic of Tanzania*, the Court held that "it is a fundamental rule of law that anyone who alleges a fact must provide evidence to prove it."[105]

There are also important cases in which the rule of law is not specifically mentioned, but is implicitly at issue. In a decision on the extraordinary measures undertaken by President Kais Saeed in 2022, in which he issued emergency decrees suspending the parliament and terminating the government, the Court found the measures to be disproportionate and in violation of the right to be heard, among other norms. It called on the country to establish a constitutional court as well as to repeal the decrees in question.[106]

Subregional trade blocs have also been forceful in dealing with rule of law issues, perhaps because of their explicit mandate to do so. The Treaty for the Establishment of the East African Community entered into force in 2000. Article 6(d) outlines the guiding principles of the Treaty, which include "good governance including adherence to the principles of democracy, the rule of law, accountability, transparency, social justice, equal opportunities, gender equality, as well as the recognition, promotion and protection of human and peoples' rights in accordance with the provisions of the African Charter on Human and Peoples' Rights."[107] Article 3.3(c) includes democracy and the rule of law as criteria for states to take into account in considering new applicants for member-state status. Similarly, the Economic Community of West African States (ECOWAS), founded in 1975, is a regional economic union of fifteen countries.[108]

Kabambi v. DRC, Communication 408/11, Afr. Comm'n H.P.R., ¶¶ 81–90 (Nov. 15, 2016).

105 Kennedy Owino Onyachi v. Tanzania, No. 003/2015, Judgment, African Court on Human and Peoples' Rights [Afr. Ct. H.P.R.], ¶ 142 (Sept. 28, 2017), https://tinyurl.com/yvvm2fr6.

106 Ben Mohamed Ben Ibrahim Belguith v. Tunisia, No. 017/2021, Judgment, Afr. Ct. H.P.R. (Sept. 22, 2022), https://tinyurl.com/yc5cp5hu.

107 Treaty for the Establishment of the East African Community art. 6(d), Nov. 30, 1999, 2144 U.N.T.S. 255.

108 Member states include Benin, Burkina Faso, Cape Verde, Côte d'Ivoire, Gambia, Ghana, Guinea, Guinea-Bissau, Liberia, Mali, Niger, Nigeria, Sierra Leone, Senegal, and Togo.

A Community Court of Justice gives private litigants direct access to the courts and there is no specified catalogue of human rights, although it regularly refers to the African Charter of Human and Peoples' Rights and other such instruments.

A review of the jurisprudence of these bodies shows that the concept of the rule of law arises most often in the context of protecting judicial independence and ensuring the right to a remedy. For example, in a 2004 case, fourteen Ugandan defendants who had been granted bail by the courts were rearrested by security personnel. When national authorities did not intervene, the Uganda Law Society appealed to the East African Court of Justice, which found a violation of the East African Community Treaty.[109] It went on to note that "[a]biding by the court decision is the corner stone of the independence of the judiciary which is one of the principles of the observation of the rule of law."[110]

Africa, as a region, seems like the one in which the dynamic of complementarity is most apparent. National-level judiciaries are relatively weak. Rule-of-law norms are subject to pressure from autocratic governments. In such a context, the regional courts and human rights bodies can restate norms and speak truth to power. How much these interventions achieve in practice is an open question, but they surely do not undermine the efforts of local lawyers and judges.

## VI Conclusion

What does the rule of law look like outside the state? There are multiple institutional settings in which it manifests itself, including on the international plane among states and in the practice of regional supranational institutions; in regional courts and tribunals that seek to discipline the state and provide substitutes or complements to backstop the domestic rule of law; and, in some cases, among states themselves in a directly transnational process. These settings generate various tensions between democratic ideals and those involving the rule of law. Supranational demands for rule of law have been most notable in helping to strengthen judicial independence in the national sphere, providing a kind of complement to domestic principles. In other cases, the rule of law is

ECOWAS has made little progress toward its self-professed goal of regional economic integration.

109 Katabazi v. Sec'y Gen. of the East African Cmty., Ref. No. 1 of 2007, East African Court of Justice (Nov. 1, 2007).

110 *Id.* at 23.

a free-floating principle, used in a procedural manner, largely ensuring consistency across levels.

There are, however, two ways in which there are tensions among levels. First, the insistence of regional bodies that there is only one authoritative interpretation of regional law, and that it is superior to local constitutional orders, has generated some pushback in both Latin America and Europe. Here, the rule of law as pushed from outside comes into direct conflict with the rule of law as locally understood, in a way that has invoked both scholarly criticism and popular backlash. The regional institutions have themselves adjusted, and have not gone away.[111]

A second tension has arisen in the European context. A central characteristic of international law qua international law is that states will ultimately determine the rulings, norms, and requirements with which they will comply. By joining the European Union, however, its member states have accepted the superiority of EU law – as far as the treaties confer power to the European level. Here lies the core problem: The national-level authorities in backsliding states invoke the former rule in their resistance to EU-level efforts to reinforce the rule of law. The European institutions insist on the latter rule. In both Latin America and Europe, rule of law is invoked by both levels of legal order, leading to some confusion and plenty of tension.

Tension, to some extent, is to be expected, especially when international regimes are powerful. The African institutions we looked at have played a part in articulating the rule of law at a normative level, but their decisions have by and large not had a huge impact on the ground. In Europe and Latin America, by contrast, tensions between the two levels are present: the framing of the two levels as complementary has given way to a more tense relationship, in which each seeks to substitute for the other. A harmonious set of interactions sounds appealing in the abstract, but might indicate a situation in which one or the other level is not taking its duties seriously. The tensions we observe may thus be productive ones in terms of protection of rule-of-law values.

The interstate politics at the core of the international order suggest that a true international rule of law, operating on the level of the UN and other interstate bodies, is a distant dream. Nevertheless, much can be done through transnational and supranational processes that advance and complement domestic systems to promote rule-of-law values. Perhaps in our era, transnational rule of law is thus an "unqualified human good."

[111] Stone Sweet & Sandholtz, *supra* note 25.

6

# Transnational Legal Order through Rule of Law?

## Appraising the United Nations Security Council, 1990–2022

JEREMY FARRALL AND TERENCE C. HALLIDAY

## I Introduction

This chapter speaks to the conjunction of two questions that reach to master trends of our time.[1] On the one hand, the UN Security Council (UNSC) stands at the apex of the international political order, the most symbolically powerful political entity in the world beyond the state. The UN Charter empowers the UNSC to make new law, as its decisions are legally binding on all UN member states. Yet the Charter does not set out any clear mechanisms to temper the Council's power. What, then, are the limits on that power? On the other hand, the UNSC has emphasized both the importance of the rule of law (ROL) in international affairs, as well as its own central role in promoting ROL. As ROL is arguably at the forefront of global discursive frames for ordering power in the contemporary world, how might its discursive power be translated into effective means of constraining the UNSC?

Both of these questions may be approached productively through the theoretical lens and empirical scholarship on the theory of transnational legal orders (TLOs). We ask, What do struggles over tempering UNSC power through ROL norms and practice reveal about the properties of transnational legal orders (TLOs)? And, conversely, what can TLO theory illuminate in the natural history of the UN's embrace of ROL as ideology and practice? From the vantagepoint of TLO theory and

An earlier version of this chapter was presented at a conference on international rule of law at the University of California, Irvine, on September 16–17, 2022. We are grateful to all participants in the conference for their comments, and particularly to Anne Peters for her commentary and to Gregory Shaffer and Wayne Sandholtz for their constructive suggestions for revision.

[1] *See* Chapter 1.

research, the ROL beyond the state and the ROL within the UNSC exemplify two distinctives that are associated with a class of TLOs that pose particular challenges for the institutionalization of a legal order that transcends sovereign state boundaries. In contrast to those TLOs where a single global script or law purports to encapsulate a normative consensus, such as the UN Convention on Contracts for the International Carriage of Goods Wholly or Partly by Sea (Rotterdam Rules)[2] or the soft law principles on anti-money laundering propagated by the Financial Action Task Force,[3] there is no single codified script for transnational ROL.[4] And in contrast to TLOs authorized by a single transnational global or regional institution, such as international criminal law, which is codified by the Rome Statute and adjudicated by the International Criminal Court, or European human rights law, which is codified by the European Convention on Human Rights and adjudicated by the European Court of Human Rights, ROL has no single authorizing institution or indeed any single institution responsible for holding states and other actors accountable to ROL.

Here, then, is an empirical curiosity. While there is no single script and no single authorizing institution for a global legal order adhering to ROL norms, the apex institution in the post-WWII political order nonetheless pays rhetorical dues to that rather inchoate body of norms. Yet, in an inherent contradiction, the very body that now discursively champions ROL – the UNSC – has been reluctant to subject itself to either explicit norms or institutional arrangements that would temper its power.[5] Indeed, Scheppele

[2] *See generally* SUSAN BLOCK-LIEB & TERENCE C. HALLIDAY, GLOBAL LAWMAKERS: INTERNATIONAL ORGANIZATIONS IN THE CRAFTING OF WORLD MARKETS (2017) (providing background on the lawmaking of the Rotterdam Rules).

[3] *See* Terence C. Halliday, Michael Levi & Peter Reuter, *Why Do Transnational Legal Orders Persist? The Curious Case of Anti-Money Laundering, in* TRANSNATIONAL LEGAL ORDERING OF CRIMINAL JUSTICE 51 (Gregory Shaffer & Ely Aaronson eds., 2020).

[4] On the developing sociological scholarship on global scripts in international law and governance, see generally Terence C. Halliday, Susan Block-Lieb & Bruce G. Carruthers, *Rhetorical Legitimation: Global Scripts as Strategic Devices of International Organizations*, 8 SOCIO-ECON. REV. 77 (2010); Terence C. Halliday, Shira Zilberstein & Wendy Espeland, *Tempering Unbridled Power: Global Scripts and International Organizations in Struggles for Basic Legal Freedoms*, Paper presented at American Sociological Association Annual Meeting (Aug. 9, 2020); Alexander E. Kentikelenis & Leonard Seabrooke, *The Politics of World Polity: Script-Writing in International Organizations*, 82 AM. SOCIO. REV. 1065 (2017).

[5] JOHN FOSTER DULLES, WAR OR PEACE 194–95 (1950) (arguing that the UNSC's powers effectively place it above the law); 9/11 AND THE RISE OF GLOBAL ANTI-TERRORISM LAW: HOW THE UN SECURITY COUNCIL RULES THE WORLD (Arianna Vedaschi & Kim Lane Scheppele eds., 2021).

proposes that ROL has not only been subordinated to expedient great-power interest in the UNSC but may have been appropriated to ends contrary to its loftiest ideals.[6]

The chapter unfolds in five parts. First, we outline our research design and its empirical sources. Second, we sketch an interpretive narrative of UNSC engagement with ROL from the early 1990s to the present in three areas of UNSC action: peacekeeping, sanctions, and use of force. Third, we offer a schematic framework for ROL in the UNSC insofar as it applies to UNSC mandates for these three areas. We propose that ROL in the UNSC manifests itself in three dimensions: discourse, procedure (or rules), and structures. These dimensions come into play both *internally*, within the UNSC itself, and *externally*, in ROL institution-building in and between states, as well as in post-conflict zones, with a rather gray area between them (e.g., when the UN peacekeeping missions are themselves subject to ROL oversight for the behavior of their personnel). Fourth, we examine the interplay of a so-called meta-TLO for rule of law with three micro-TLOs under construction within the UNSC itself. We conclude with reflections on the capabilities of empowering elected members of the UNSC and weaker states in the UN to press ROL norms on the UNSC as a springboard for ROL global governance via the UNSC.

## II Design

### 1 *An Historical Moment*

The Security Council's engagements with the rule of law can be traced back to its very first meeting, on January 17, 1946, when the French ambassador Vincent Auriol observed: "[W]e are ushering in an epoch of law among peoples and of justice among nations. The UN Security Council's task is a heavy one, but it will be sustained ... by our remembrance of the sufferings of all those who fought and died that the rule of law might prevail."[7] Yet, despite this early appearance in the work of the Security Council, the rule of law featured rarely in the Council's deliberations as the Cold War set in. But it would return with a vengeance following the end of the Cold War, when the concept

6 Kim Lane Scheppele, *The Empire of Security and the Security of Empire*, 27 Temple Int'l & Comp. L.J. 241 (2013).

7 U.N. SCOR, 1st Sess., 1st mtg. at 9, U.N. Doc. S/PV.1 (Jan. 17, 1946).

would become increasingly influential in the UNSC's deliberations and decisions.[8]

Our research pivots on a key moment early in the first decade of the twenty-first century. On September 24, 2003, the Security Council held the inaugural meeting on its new agenda item entitled "Justice and the Rule of Law." The first speaker at that meeting, Secretary-General Kofi Annan, observed that: "This Council has a very heavy responsibility to promote justice and the rule of law in its efforts to maintain international peace and security. This applies both internationally and in rebuilding shattered societies."[9]

Arguably, Secretary-General Kofi Annan's clarion call for a UN rule-of-law agenda in his speech of September 24, 2003, marked a turning point for the UNSC. It was an occasion in which Farrall was informally, even serendipitously, implicated (see Appendix 2). The UNSC sessions on ROL in 2003 and 2004 brought to a head numbers of issues that had been arising in global peace and security since the end of the Cold War and opened up prospects for new normative orders in which variants of ROL might be institutionalized as TLOs. The initial UNSC meeting on the rule of law paved the way for the Council's sustained engagement with the concept, beginning with its consideration, the following year, of a definition proposed by the Secretary-General to guide the UN's work.[10]

We treat the years from 1990 to 2003/2004, and the pivotal moment in the 2003/2004 UNSC sessions on ROL, as a recognition of the dramatic expansion of activity that occurred in the UNSC's use of its powers to maintain international peace and security following the end of the Cold War and the accompanying decades of paralysis in Security Council decision-making caused by ideological antagonism between key permanent members from both the East and the West.

## 2 *A Hard Case*

We acknowledge that it is open to debate whether the ROL does or might serve as a constraint on UNSC activities. The UN's founders unashamedly established the Council as a political body, pairing the

[8] For a discussion of the rule of law's "meteoric" rise in the post-Cold War era, see JEREMY FARRALL, UNITED NATIONS SANCTIONS AND THE RULE OF LAW 18–24 (2007) [hereinafter FARRALL, UNITED NATIONS SANCTIONS AND THE RULE OF LAW].

[9] U.N. Security Council, 58th Sess., 4833 mtg. ¶ 2, U.N. Doc. S/PV.4833 (Sept. 24, 2003).

[10] U.N. Secretary-General, *The Rule of Law and Transitional Justice in Conflict and Post-Conflict Societies*, ¶ 6, U.N. Doc. S/2004/616 (Aug. 23, 2004).

lofty aspirational ideals set out in the UN's principles and purposes, including the promotion of equality and justice, with the pragmatic concession to five great powers (P5) of permanent membership and an accompanying veto power. This marriage of convenience between principle and pragmatism secured the participation of those most capable of destabilizing the new experiment in international organization by granting each of the five permanent members the capacity to prevent the UNSC from taking action by exercising its veto.

This fact, combined with the Charter's vagueness surrounding the limits on the UNSC's exercise of its Chapter VII powers, has led commentators to bemoan both the Council's capacity to do pretty much whatever it wants when the P5 do not disagree, as well as its incapacity, due to the veto, to ensure that it exercises its powers to maintain international peace and security in a consistent, impartial manner.

The UNSC undeniably represents a 'hard' case when it comes to evaluating it as a ROL/TLO case study. Indeed, it struggles to satisfy most of the checks and balances to arbitrariness identified by Shaffer and Sandholtz, such as application of law to rulers; predictability of published rules; available fora for bringing challenges; proportionate link of means to end so that they have some factual grounding; and reason-giving.[11] Yet the fact that the UNSC's decisions are binding upon all UN member states under Article 25 of the Charter reinforces the direct relevance of the ROL to its work: the UNSC relies on member states to implement its decisions in good faith in order to be an effective ROL-creator. This raises the stakes when it comes to the UNSC's performance as a ROL-adherent.

## 3 *A Restricted Focus*

Our research design can be positioned with regard to important scholarly interpretations and interventions on UNSC activities vis-à-vis the ROL and with respect to our own empirical data and methods.

With respect to scholarly framing, there are several studies of the contemporary role and activities of the UNSC in general,[12] yet before 2010 the effect of the concept of the rule of law on UNSC practice had attracted less scholarly attention. While there was already a substantial literature on the general promotion of the rule of law as part of development and

[11] *See* Chapter 1.

[12] David M. Malone, The UN Security Council: From the Cold War to the 21st Century (2004); Vaughan Lowe et al., The United Nations Security Council and War (2008).

peacebuilding,[13] less scholarship had analyzed the particular role of the UNSC in promoting the rule of law or the extent to which the UNSC's activities to maintain international peace and security themselves promote the rule of law. Some legal scholars had explored whether and how the Council's almost unfettered power to take Chapter VII action might be reconciled with the notion of the rule of law.[14] Others had examined the UNSC's relationship with the rule of law in carrying out particular activities, such as imposing sanctions[15] or deploying peacekeeping operations.[16] But prior to Charlesworth and Farrall's Australian Research Council-funded partnership with the Australian Civil Military Centre on the project *Strengthening the Rule of Law through the UN Security Council*, there had been a dearth of systematic studies examining the theory and practice of the UNSC's relationship with the rule of law when employing its most prominent tools to maintain international peace and security: peace operations, sanctions, and the use of force.

An exception is Chesterman's earlier work on UNSC and the rule of law in cooperation with the Austrian government.[17] Using examples from various UNSC activities, his research provides a general analysis of the UNSC in different "modes" of decision-making, such as "legislator,"

[13] THOMAS CAROTHERS, PROMOTING THE RULE OF LAW ABROAD: IN SEARCH OF KNOWLEDGE (2006); Veronica Taylor, *Big Rule of Law (Patent Pending): Branding and Certifying the Business of the Rule of Law, in* STRENGTHENING THE RULE OF LAW THROUGH THE SECURITY COUNCIL 28 (Jeremy Farrall & Hilary Charlesworth eds., 2016); JANE E. STROMSETH, DAVID WIPPMAN & ROSA BROOKS, CAN MIGHT MAKE RIGHTS? BUILDING THE RULE OF LAW AFTER MILITARY INTERVENTIONS (2006); AGNES HURWITZ & REYKO HUANG, CIVIL WAR AND THE RULE OF LAW: SECURITY, DEVELOPMENT, HUMAN RIGHTS (2008).

[14] MOHAMMED BEDJAOUI, THE NEW WORLD ORDER AND THE SECURITY COUNCIL: TESTING THE LEGALITY OF ITS ACTS (1994); DAVID SCHWEIGMAN, THE AUTHORITY OF THE SECURITY COUNCIL UNDER CHAPTER VII OF THE UN CHARTER: LEGAL LIMITS AND THE ROLE OF THE INTERNATIONAL COURT OF JUSTICE (2001); ERIKA DE WET, THE CHAPTER VII POWERS OF THE UNITED NATIONS SECURITY COUNCIL (2004); Simon Chesterman, *'I'll Take Manhattan': The International Rule of Law and the United Nations Security Council*, 1 HAGUE J. ON RULE LAW 67, 67–73 (2009).

[15] FARRALL, UNITED NATIONS SANCTIONS AND THE RULE OF LAW, *supra* note 8.

[16] JESSICA HOWARD & BRUCE OSWALD, THE RULE OF LAW ON PEACE OPERATIONS (2002).

[17] SIMON CHESTERMAN, THE UN SECURITY COUNCIL AND THE RULE OF LAW: THE ROLE OF THE SECURITY COUNCIL IN STRENGTHENING A RULES-BASED INTERNATIONAL SYSTEM: FINAL REPORT AND RECOMMENDATIONS FROM THE AUSTRIAN INITIATIVE, 2004–2008 (2008) [hereinafter CHESTERMAN, THE UN SECURITY COUNCIL] (Also published as Letter dated 18 April 2008 from the Permanent Representative of Austria to the United Nations addressed to the Secretary-General, U.N. Doc. A/63/69–S/2008/270 (May 7, 2008)).

"executive," and "judge." He does not, however, study comprehensively or systematically the theory and practice of the UNSC and ROL in any particular one of the UNSC's mandates, including the now well-defined UNSC spheres of activity in peacekeeping, sanctions, and use of force. Chesterman's policy proposals, moreover, exude more confidence in the prospect of extrapolating the institutional separation of powers model within states to the global domain.

Most recently, Scheppele and her colleagues[18] have offered a powerful critique of the UNSC's adherence to the ROL in its interventions directed at anti-terrorism. Perversely, argues Scheppele, the UNSC in an "imperial mode" subverts the ROL, not only setting itself above these norms but wilfully acting contrary to the very values it preaches to the world. Dominated by the P5,[19] and the common cause found by an otherwise divided P3 (US, UK, France) v. P2 (Russia and China), the UNSC permits, even promotes, the expediency of force, sacrificing the inconvenience of ROL norms for an instrumental goal.

Although both these frames warrant careful engagement on their own terms, we take a more defined and constrained approach. Our exclusive focus on peacekeeping, sanctions, and use of force, which share some overlaps with both Chesterman's and Scheppele's work, nevertheless bounds us more closely to appraise the breadth and depth of UNSC decision-making and behavior vis-à-vis the ROL. By restricting ourselves to these three areas of UNSC action – peacekeeping, sanctions, and force – we attend to the pointy end of Council activity, as they are perhaps the most well-publicized, ambitious, and controversial measures it employs to fulfil its primary responsibility under the UN Charter for the maintenance of international peace and security.[20]

## 4 *Interior Empirical Data*

Our empirical design combines two bodies of data. Like other scholars, we draw heavily on official sources. Unlike most other scholarship, we benefit from the interplay of Farrall's participant observation *internal* to the UNSC operations and his involvement in *external* activism by academics, civil society, the military, and states to reshape ROL practices internal to the UNSC and externally in its operations. Our perspective for

[18] Scheppele, *supra* note 6; 9/11 AND THE RISE OF GLOBAL ANTI-TERRORISM LAW: HOW THE UN SECURITY COUNCIL RULES THE WORLD, *supra* note 5.

[19] The significance of elected members of the UNSC, the E10, do not feature in this account.

[20] U.N. Charter art. 24, ¶ 1.

this narrative overview ranges across insider and outsider roles, encompassing different periods in which Farrall has undertaken stretches of insider and outsider observance, as well as stints in which he has engaged actively as a participant with the intent to strengthen the UNSC's capacity both to promote and to respect the rule of law. Farrall interned at a UN-accredited nongovernmental organization (the Quaker United Nations Office, 1996–97) and was later a UN Secretariat staffer working inside the UNSC and its sanctions committees in New York (2001–04), on the UN Secretary-General's Good Offices Mediation Team in Cyprus (2004, 2008), and for the UN's then biggest peace operation, the UN Mission in Liberia (2004–06). As a scholar, he worked initially on UN sanctions and international law (1998–2004) and subsequently as an Australian Research Council chief investigator on two multiyear research projects analyzing the UNSC and its relationship to the rule of law (2011–22).[21]

Across these roles, he has sought to influence the UNSC's relationship with the ROL in at least three ways. First, his book *United Nations Sanctions and the Rule of Law*[22] presents in an appendix a series of basic policy recommendations to increase the Council's capacity to reinforce the rule of law through its sanctions practice.[23] Second, in March 2016, Hilary Charlesworth and Jeremy Farrall, with accompanying expert commentary by Terence Halliday, presented sixty-six policy proposals for strengthening the ROL through the UNSC to a packed conference room at UN headquarters in New York, following which the document setting out the proposals was published as an official UNSC document.[24] Third, with his colleagues on the E10 Influence Project, he has developed an analytical

[21] The first project was Australian Research Council (ARC) Linkage Project 110100708: *Strengthening the Rule of Law Through the United Nations Security Council* (2011–14). The second was ARC Discovery Project 150100300: *Leveraging Power and Influence on the UN Security Council: The Role of Elected Members* (2015–22).

[22] FARRALL, UNITED NATIONS SANCTIONS AND THE RULE OF LAW, *supra* note 8.

[23] *Id.* at 244–46.

[24] JEREMY FARRALL, HILARY CHARLESWORTH & ALAN RYAN, POLICY PROPOSALS FOR STRENGTHENING THE RULE OF LAW THROUGH THE UN SECURITY COUNCIL (2016). Also published as an official document of the UN Security Council: Letter dated 25 April 2016 from the Permanent Representative of Australia to the United Nations addressed to the President of the Security Council, U.N. Doc. S/2016/397 (Apr. 27, 2016). At the time, Hilary Charlesworth, now a judge at the International Court of Justice, was a professor and director of the Centre for International Governance and Justice, in the Regulatory Institutions Network (RegNet), at the Australian National University. Jeremy Farrall was a research fellow at the same Centre. Dr. Alan Ryan was the executive director of the Australian Civil-Military Centre, the Australian government industry partner with ANU on ARC Linkage Project 110100708.

framework to evaluate and demonstrate instances in which elected members (the so-called E10) have shaped UNSC outputs, despite the fact that they do not possess a veto power.[25] Drawing on empirical studies of E10 influence, the project is advancing proposals to enhance the capacity of the E10 to influence UNSC decision-making.[26]

## III The UNSC and the ROL after the Cold War

### 1 *UNSC Formal Powers to Promote the Rule of Law: A Double-Edged Sword*

The UN Charter grants the Council primary responsibility for the maintenance of international peace and security.[27] The Charter further equips the Council with a wide range of powers to promote the peaceful settlement of international disputes,[28] and to take coercive action, including mandating the application of sanctions and authorizing the use of force, to maintain or restore international peace (Chapter VII).[29] Critically, the Charter also requires all UN member states to give effect to the Council's decisions (Article 25), thus giving those decisions the force of law.

This ability to take legally binding decisions gives the Council substantial capacity to promote the rule of law in international affairs. Ultimately, the Council's effectiveness hinges on the capacity and willingness of UN member states to take the necessary steps to convert its decisions into action.[30] States are more likely to do this if the Council has a reputation for promoting and respecting the rule of law.

### 2 *The UNSC's Expanding Use of Its Powers since the End of the Cold War*

In the UN's first four-and-a-half decades, the ideological divide between East and West severely restricted the UNSC's ability to exercise its powers

25 Jeremy Farrall et al., *Elected Member Influence in the United Nations Security Council*, 33 Leiden J. Int'l L. 101, 101–15 (2020) [hereinafter Farrall et al., *Elected Member Influence in the United National Security Council*].

26 Farrall's insider access, of course, raises the vexing challenges and tensions of the participant–observer acting within, as an advocate, and standing without, as a scholarly observer.

27 U.N. Charter art. 24, ¶ 1.

28 U.N. Charter arts. 33–38.

29 U.N. Charter arts. 39–51.

30 For thoughtful discussion of how UNSC decisions translate into domestic obligations, see Machiko Kanetake, The UN Security Council and Domestic Actors: Distance in International Law (2018).

to promote peaceful settlement and maintain international peace and security, with the consequence that the intervention tools we focus on here – namely, peacekeeping, sanctions, and force – were rarely employed. As a consequence of the infrequency of UNSC action in its first four decades, much of the Cold War era scholarly literature on the Council's powers, including in particular its Chapter VII powers to apply sanctions and authorize the use of force, focused on the question of how to enable the Council to use its powers more regularly.[31] The notion that the Council might exceed its Chapter VII authority was practically unimaginable to the Cold War academy. However, things changed dramatically after the Cold War, with the Council expanding its activities across all three areas.

The development of *peacekeeping* is widely considered to be a Cold War success story. Peacekeeping was an innovation borne of necessity in the UN's early years, when it proved impossible to realize the Charter's vision of UN member states contributing their own military forces to a standing UN army under UN command.[32] Instead, the Secretary-General worked initially with the UN General Assembly, then increasingly with the UNSC, to deploy peacekeepers between hostile forces who had agreed to ceasefires. From 1946 until 1988, the UN established thirteen peacekeeping operations (PKOs). These first-generation operations, premised on three core peacekeeping principles of consent, impartiality, and non-use of force (except in self-defense), were generally tasked with the basic responsibility of monitoring ceasefire lines. Following the end of the Cold War, however, the incidence, scope, and ambition of peace operations expanded significantly. Since 1988, the UNSC has created fifty-eight additional PKOs, deployed around the globe, from Haiti to East Timor and from the Balkans to Mozambique. These post-Cold War operations have been tasked with a broad range of responsibilities. In the case of UN transitional administrations in Kosovo and Timor-Leste, this has even included responsibility for practically all the tasks normally carried out by state institutions. Of particular interest for this chapter, twenty-first-century peace operations have routinely been mandated to strengthen the ROL, with a focus on (re)building police forces, corrections facilities, and judicial systems.

[31] *See* Farrall, United Nations Sanctions and the Rule of Law, *supra* note 8, at 36–37.

[32] U.N. Charter art. 43.

In the area of *sanctions*, between 1946 and 1989 the UNSC was only able to apply two sanctions regimes. In 1966 the Council applied its very first sanctions regime against the illegal white minority government of Ian Smith in Southern Rhodesia.[33] In 1977 the Council applied its second sanctions regime, comprising an arms embargo, against the apartheid administration in South Africa.[34] Since the end of the Cold War, however, the Security Council has been able to achieve the necessary agreement to impose sanctions far more frequently. In the twenty-five years since the Cold War, the Council has created thirty-two additional sanctions regimes, bringing the total number of UN sanctions regimes to thirty-four.[35] The Council has employed its sanctions powers so frequently in the post-Cold War era that the focus of contemporary scholarly literature now tends to be on how to *constrain*, rather than *facilitate*, the Council's use of sanctions.[36]

In the area of *force*, Blokker has observed that during the Cold War it was "inconceivable" that the UNSC would authorize the use of force.[37] However, there was one extraordinary instance during the Cold War. It

33 S.C. Res. 232, ¶ 2 (Dec. 16, 1966) (applying prohibitions against the import from and export to Southern Rhodesia of specific commodities and products, including petroleum and leather goods). Less than two years later, these sanctions were strengthened substantially, making the Southern Rhodesian sanctions regime the first instance of UN comprehensive sanctions, as it sought to prevent the flow to and from Southern Rhodesia of virtually all products and commodities. *See* S.C. Res. 253, ¶¶ 3–6 (May 29, 1968).

34 S.C. Res. 418, ¶¶ 2, 4 (Nov. 4, 1977) (applying an arms embargo).

35 The first twenty-five UN sanctions regimes are charted in the appendices of FARRALL, UNITED NATIONS SANCTIONS AND THE RULE OF LAW, *supra* note 8. The most recent nine sanctions regimes have been: the 1970 (Libya) regime, applied by Resolution 1970 (2011); the 1988 (Taliban) regime, applied by Resolution 1988 (2011); the 1989 (Al Qaida and ISIL) regime, applied by Resolution 1989 (2011); the 1907 (Eritrea) regime, applied by Resolution 1907 (2011); the 2048 (Guinea-Bissau) regime, applied by Resolution 2048 (2011); the 2127 (Central African Republic) sanctions regime, applied by Resolution 2127 (2013); the 2140 (Yemen) regime, applied by Resolution 2140 (2014); the 2206 (South Sudan) regime, applied by Resolution 2206 (2015); and the 2374 (Mali) regime, applied by Resolution 2374 (2017).

36 *See, e.g.*, Larissa van den Herik, *Peripheral Hegemony in the Quest to Ensure Security Council Accountability for Its Individualized Sanctions Regimes*, 19 J. CONFLICT & SEC. L. 427 (2014); ANTONIOS TZANAKOPOULOS, DISOBEYING THE SECURITY COUNCIL: COUNTERMEASURES AGAINST WRONGFUL SANCTIONS (2011); DE WET, *supra* note 14; Erika de Wet, *From Kadi to Nada: Judicial Techniques Favoring Human Rights over United Nations Security Council Sanctions*, 12 CHINESE J. INT'L L. 787 (2013); Alexander Orakhelashvili, *The Impact of Peremptory Norms on Interpretation and Application of the UN Security Council Resolutions*, 16 EUR. J. INT'L L. 1 (2005).

37 Niels Blokker, *Is the Authorization Authorized? Powers and Practice of the UN Security Council to Authorize the Use of Force by "Coalitions of the Able and Willing,"* 11 EUR. J. INT'L L. 541, 543 (2000).

occurred on July 7, 1950, when the Soviet Union made the ill-judged decision to absent itself from a UNSC meeting on the item "Complaint of aggression upon the Republic of Korea," in protest at the alleged misrepresentation of China on the UNSC. However, with the Soviet Union not present to exercise a veto, the UNSC subsequently proceeded to adopt Resolution 84 (1950), in which it determined that an armed attack upon the Republic of Korea by forces from North Korea constituted a breach of the peace,[38] then recommended that UN member states assist the Republic of Korea by making military forces available to a unified command under the United States.[39] As with peacekeeping and sanctions, the UNSC's authorizations of force have increased substantially since the end of the Cold War. Writing in 2000, Blokker identifies twenty-seven resolutions containing authorizations of force – for purposes including the enforcement of sanctions, liberating a country from foreign occupation, and returning to power ousted legitimate authorities – spanning eleven situations on the Council's agenda, ranging from Iraq in 1990 to East Timor in 1999.[40] Bannelier and Christakis trace an additional twenty-one resolutions authorizing the use of force between 2000 and 2014.[41]

## 3 *ROL Challenges in the Areas of Peacekeeping, Sanctions, and Force*

The Security Council has taken important steps since 1990 to strengthen the rule of law through its use of peace operations, sanctions, and force. However, considerable ROL challenges remain.

In the area of *peacekeeping*, while the Council has routinely included the task of strengthening the rule of law in the mandates of its twenty-first-century multidimensional peace operations,[42] inadequate responses to peacekeeping misconduct scandals during this same period, including in the Democratic Republic of Congo and the Central African Republic, revealed that peace operations and peacekeepers were not always held to the same legal standards as those whose peace they were keeping.

38 S.C. Res. 84, pmbl. (July 7, 1950).

39 *Id.* at ¶ 3.

40 Blokker, *supra* note 37, at 543–44.

41 Karine Bannelier & Théodore Christakis, *Between Flexibility and Accountability: How Can the Security Council Strengthen Oversight of Use-of-Force Mandates?*, *in* STRENGTHENING THE RULE OF LAW THROUGH THE UN SECURITY COUNCIL, *supra* note 13, at 209, 209–23.

42 For discussion of the Council's use of peace operations to promote the rule of law during the period 1990–2016, see STRENGTHENING THE RULE OF LAW THROUGH THE UN SECURITY COUNCIL, *supra* note 13, at 87–178.

In the area of *sanctions*, in 2009 the Council made a significant effort to provide greater due process afforded to individuals subject to targeted sanctions under the 1267 (Taliban/Al Qaida) sanctions regime by creating the Office of the Ombudsperson.[43] In 2011, when the Council split that sanctions regime into two separate regimes – the 1988 (Taliban) and 1989 (Al Qaida) sanctions regimes – it empowered the Office of the Ombudsperson, which would now apply only to the 1989 sanctions regime, to investigate the grounds upon which individuals were included in the targeted sanctions list and, when appropriate, to recommend delisting.[44] Moreover, the Council clarified that the Ombudsperson's delisting recommendations must be implemented unless the 1267/1989 sanctions committee as a whole or the Council itself were to decide otherwise.[45] Nevertheless, despite this significant improvement in the due process accorded to individuals on the 1989 Al Qaida sanctions list, those on the other (dozen or so) active targeted sanctions lists do not have recourse to any Ombudsperson process.

In the area of *force*, the endorsement of the "responsibility to protect" doctrine by member states in 2005 recognized the responsibility of all states to protect their own civilians threatened by genocide, crimes against humanity, ethnic cleansing, and war crimes.[46] Where a state was unwilling or unable to meet its responsibility to protect, there was now a responsibility on the international community to intervene to protect those civilians, using force when necessary and acting through the Council. This new doctrine sought to introduce more principled decision-making into the highly politically charged environment surrounding decision-making on the prospective use of force. Yet excesses in the implementation of the Council's authorization to use force to

[43] For the Ombudsperson's initial mandate, see S.C. Res. 1904, ¶¶ 20–21, Annex II (Dec. 17, 2009). For discussion of the role of elected UNSC members and non-UNSC members in the creation and evolution of the Ombudsperson mechanism, including through the activities of the reform-minded group of predominantly small states called "Accountability, Coherence and Transparency," see Jeremy Farrall & Christopher Michaelsen, *Managing the Ebb and Flow of Sanctions Reform: An Important Role for Non-Permanent Security Council Members*, *in* ELECTED MEMBERS OF THE SECURITY COUNCIL: LAME DUCKS OR KEY PLAYERS? 217, 217–36 (Nico J. Schrijver & Niels Blokker eds., 2020).

[44] S.C. Res. 1989, ¶ 23, Annex II (June 17, 2011). For discussion, see Kimberly Prost, *The Office of the Ombudsperson: A Case for Fair Process*, *in* STRENGTHENING THE RULE OF LAW THROUGH THE UN SECURITY COUNCIL, *supra* note 13, at 181, 181–92.

[45] S.C. Res. 1989, ¶ 23, Annex II (June 17, 2011).

[46] G.A. Res. 60/1, ¶¶ 138–39 (Oct. 24, 2005).

protect civilians in Libya under Resolution 1973 (2011) raised concerns about the Council's accountability under the rule of law.[47]

The Council's capacity to serve as an effective promoter of the rule of law and guardian of international peace and security is shaped by its response to these challenges. There is thus a strong need to continue refining the way in which the Council's decisions and activities both promote and respect the rule of law.

## IV ROL and the UNSC: A Conceptual Frame

An overview of the UNSC's encounters with the ROL since the 1990s reveals that ROL manifests itself in three dimensions: discourse, procedures and rules, and structures.[48] Each of these has an internal focus, within the UNSC itself, and an external focus, in the fields of activity in which the UN mounts its missions.

We designate as *internal* those aspects of deliberation and decision-making that occur within the UNSC, whether as an actor or an arena. We designate as *external* those occasions where the UNSC seeks to strengthen ROL because it judges that there has been a breakdown or vacuum of some sort. Thus, peace operations are tasked to strengthen ROL because local ROL authorities and institutions are not able or unwilling to do so. Sanctions are applied against governments and other actors who represent a threat to the peace, which in turn undermines the international ROL. And force is authorized against governments and other actors who represent an even more urgent threat to or breach of international peace and security, and hence to the international ROL.

The relationships between the internal and external locations of the three dimensions align theoretically with Shaffer and Sandholtz's conceptualization of rule of law as both "principle and practice."[49]

[47] For discussion, see the contributions in part IV of STRENGTHENING THE RULE OF LAW THROUGH THE UN SECURITY COUNCIL, *supra* note 13, at 207–84.

[48] We are grateful to Martin Krygier for the comment that a fourth dimension could be added, viz., that of practices. However, insofar as our focus here mirrors that of scholarship on transnational legal orders, we restrict ourselves to the normative elements of an order that may be theoretically distinguishable from the behaviors and practices that stimulate the making of norms or rules or the behavioral outcomes to which a normative order is directed. In any empirical situation, norms and behavior are inextricably interwoven, as, for instance, when norms come to be taken for granted in everyday behavior by actors. Conceptually and theoretically, however, there is value in teasing them apart for more precise scrutiny of their attributes.

[49] *See* Chapter 1.

Table 6.1 *Dimensions of ROL in the UN Security Council*

| Locus of ROL | ROL as discourse | ROL as rules | ROL as structure |
|---|---|---|---|
| Internal | • Secretary-General<br>• UNSC debates<br>• Rhetoric of UN states (P5, E10) | • Four principles expressed as sixty-six recommendations in *Strengthening ROL* (2016) | • Ombudsperson<br>• Subsidiary bodies<br>• UN Sanctions Coordination Committee (R40) |
| External | • Political & legal philosophy<br>• Academic research<br>• Political leaders<br>• Public intellectuals | • Applied to peacekeeping & sanctions in the field<br>• Applied to institution-building in states | • International tribunals<br>• National courts |

The ROL is not unidimensional; it encapsulates both frames of meaning (discourses and rules) and structures that institutionalize that meaning.

It is useful to cross-classify these dimensions and review them systematically (Table 6.1).

## 1 *Discourse*

We designate as "discourse" the bundle of abstract formulations about the rule of law that are expressed through speeches, policy statements, academic writings, and reflective commentary in the public sphere that is brought to bear on the UN in general and the UNSC in particular. These correspond substantially to the "meta-principle" of rule of law identified by Shaffer and Sandholtz.[50] Each discursive form has its own distinctive properties, its own internal logic, rhetorical characteristics, epistemological frames, target audiences, arenas of engagement, and platforms for presentation. While these warrant much more refined empirical analyses in their own right, for present purposes we proceed on the basis of

[50] *See* Chapter 1.

a primary distinction between internal and external forums or arenas in which discourse is situated.

The *internal* rhetoric on ROL is well marked by Secretary-General Kofi Annan's pivotal speech on September 24, 2003. The speech points to the wider phenomenon of rhetorical expression of ROL in pronouncements, statements, and justifications by actors within the UNSC, within the UN, and in the wider international community of nations. In his analysis of UNSC resolutions in the decade before 2005, Farrall observed that its pronouncements on the rule of law were "increasingly frequent," yet "fluid" in meaning, "elusive" and "chameleon-like."[51] At least five clusters of meaning variously pointed to "law and order" or "holding criminals accountable," to "principled governance" or "protection and promotion of human rights," or to "resolving conflicts in accordance with law."[52] Sometimes these complemented each other, sometimes one or another appeared, and sometimes it was unclear which of these adequately captured the vague allusions of a resolution. They functioned as rallying calls for adherence to abstract ideals which might serve as an umbrella for normative consensus and as legitimation for UNSC action. As rhetoric, they valorized an inchoate ideal that arguably had an inner core of commitment to minimizing the "misuse or abuse of political power."[53] We shall observe, however, that between 2003 and 2020 the discourse within the UNSC became more clearly articulated and sharpened as it was expressed in action items and pragmatic recommendations (see Appendix 1).

*External* formulations of ROL of course rest upon the vast scholarly literature on ROL in its historical emergence, comparative and contextual expression, and philosophical and theoretical debates.[54] Our focus, however, adheres more closely to scholarship that holds the UNSC itself to account under ROL norms.[55] Here, we position ourselves more closely to Chesterman's ambitious and optimistic agenda for the UNSC to extrapolate from an institutional configuration within states to a global

51 Farrall, United Nations Sanctions and the Rule of Law, *supra* note 8 at 32, 35.

52 *Id.*

53 *Id.* at 35.

54 Brian Tamanaha, On the Rule of Law: History, Politics, Theory (2004).

55 Chesterman, The UN Security Council, *supra* note 17; Martin Krygier, *The Security Council and the Rule of Law: Some Conceptual Reflections*, *in* Strengthening the Rule of Law Through the Security Council, *supra* note 13, at 13; Scheppele, *supra* note 6; 9/11 and the Rise of Global Anti-Terrorism Law: How the UN Security Council Rules the World, *supra* note 5.

configuration across states, and less closely to Scheppele's pessimistic indictment of the UNSC as a subverter rather than propagator of ROL beyond the UNSC in its anti-terrorism activities following 9/11. Our focus is particular – on use of force, peacekeeping, and sanctions – and limited on what might be possible in the milieux of power within the UNSC.

It is also disciplined by an interior awareness of how the UNSC functions in day-to-day activities and is conditioned by a realism of what is conceivably possible, given that other realism of great-power politics. Here, we find an affinity with Krygier's efforts to valorize ROL as a prevailing value, rhetorically expressed as "tempering unbridled power," yet to undertake research on what means to this end will fit a context "where the institutions typically thought of in connection with the ROL in domestic circumstances don't exist in the international arena."[56]

## 2 *Procedure and Rules*

If the multiple discourses of ROL could arguably be convergent on a generic ideal of checking power, the procedures and rules within the UNSC offer a midlevel of doctrinal specification where empirical research can disclose whether discernible rules or implicit rule-bound actions reflect the higher ideals in ROL discourse.[57] At this midlevel, principles and rules can be layered. In their policy proposals to the UNSC in 2016, Farrall, Charlesworth, and Ryan advance a responsive model of the ROL centered on four basic principles: transparency, consistency, accountability, and engagement.[58] However, they extrapolate directly from these to specific recommendations that might be construed as rules.[59]

For ROL recommendations-cum-rules *internal* to the UNSC, for instance, they propose, under the principle of transparency in peace

[56] Krygier, *supra* note 55, at 19.

[57] In fact, rules within the UNSC are open to a wider socio-legal program of research on the hierarchical ordering of rule types, subsumed under principles, and elaborated for their formal properties as drafting reflects the politics of rulemaking and the objects of rule-governing. *See* BLOCK-LIEB & HALLIDAY, *supra* note 2, at 227–64.

[58] FARRALL, CHARLESWORTH & RYAN, *supra* note 24, at 8–9. Also published as an official document of the UN Security Council: Letter dated 25 April 2016 from the Permanent Representative of Australia to the United Nations addressed to the President of the Security Council, U.N. Doc. S/2016/397 (Apr. 27, 2016). Adapted from the five ROL principles proposed in FARRALL, UNITED NATIONS SANCTIONS AND THE RULE OF LAW, *supra* note 8.

[59] *Id.* at 42–49.

operations, that "[w]hen the Security Council creates or modifies a peace operation mandate that seeks to strengthen the rule of law, the Council should ensure that the mandate clearly identifies the operation's central rule-of-law objectives" (Recommendation 10, p. 43). Under the principle of accountability as it is applied to UNSC use of force, they recommend that the UNSC adopt a practice, or operational rule, whereby "[t]he Security Council should request regular briefings by states and groups of states implementing use of force mandates" (Recommendation 57, p. 48).

For ROL recommendations-cum-rules *external* to the UNSC, on peacekeeping, in adherence to the principle of transparency, they propose that "[t]he Security Council should request the Secretary-General to undertake periodic qualitative and quantitative monitoring and evaluation of each peace operation's rule-of-law objectives (Recommendation 12, p. 43); and in keeping with the principle of accountability, they propose that "[w]hen the Security Council establishes or extends the mandate of a peace operation, it should emphasise the need for troop-contributing countries to ensure accountability for the investigation and prosecution of allegations of serious crimes by their troops" (Recommendation 19, p. 44).

## 3 *Structures*

The ROL as an institutional configuration within states is conventionally understood to require countervailing institutions that divide power and balance it among them. Whether through a separation of powers among executives, legislatures, and judiciaries, or a division of government between federal and subsidiary centers of government, or variants on fracturing power within the state and balancing it with forces outside the state, this structural element of ROL appears integral to its ability to temper power. This, of course, raises the vexing question: Is it empirically, theoretically, or normatively acceptable to extrapolate from institutional configurations within a state to the global order writ large?

Can we treat the UNSC as such an extrapolation? Critics of the UNSC's wide-ranging powers have argued that the Charter permits it to act above the law,[60] even enabling it to engage in imperialism.[61] While the UN's

[60] *See* DULLES, *supra* note 5.

[61] *See* 9/11 AND THE RISE OF GLOBAL ANTI-TERRORISM LAW: HOW THE UN SECURITY COUNCIL RULES THE WORLD, *supra* note 5.

founders might have anticipated that two of the UN's other primary organs – namely, the UN General Assembly and the International Court of Justice – would play the roles of global legislature and judiciary, thus balancing the UNSC's executive mode, the Charter system falls short of a meaningful separation of powers. Indeed, as Chesterman has persuasively argued, the UNSC's practice in the Cold War era reveals instances of the UNSC itself acting in executive, judicial, and legislative modes.[62] Nevertheless, the process of structural differentiation, with a prospect of allocating power to different social entities across different mandates of the UNSC, may open up a line of inquiry to appraise such prospects within the UN itself.

*Internal* to the UNSC we observe minimal and fragile, but discernible, structures that may contribute to UNSC accountability and transparency, among other principles. Eight social entities of one or another kind have been created to advise, enable, and monitor the UNSC's ROL initiatives.[63] To what extent do they perform purely executive functions without any degrees of freedom, or can they exert de facto limits or influences on UNSC actions? For instance, the *sanctions committees* display variations in their adherence to ROL norms in the procedures and working methods they adopt to execute UNSC imposition of sanctions, to administer exemptions, and to evaluate humanitarian impact, among others. For a time, a *Working Group on General Issues of Sanctions* convened to produce recommendations to improve the effectiveness of sanctions. *Bodies of experts* are created for each sanctions regime. Since 2003 on Liberia, and subsequently on Iraq, UNITA, Sierra Leone, Afghanistan/Al Qaida and Sudan, among others, they have become institutionalized and tasked with investigation of implementation and violations of sanctions. The experts are usually based in their home countries and undertake field missions to sanctions sites. Complementing them are *monitoring bodies,* based at UN headquarters in New York, and staffed by UN civil servants. They track implementation of sanctions and report periodically to the relevant sanctions committee. They tend to have a higher status and are more institutionalized than other expert bodies. None are permanent. Their terms and mandates are extended from time to time until the sanctions regime is terminated.

The most important of subsidiary or partially differentiated bodies within the UNSC may be the formation of the Ombudsperson's office in

62 Chesterman, The UN Security Council, *supra* note 17.

63 Farrall, United Nations Sanctions and the Rule of Law, *supra* note 8, at 32–35.

the sanctions regime.[64] Established in 2009, this office was created to deal with applications by individuals and other targeted entities for delisting by the UNSC.[65] Notably, its creation emerged from a series of criticisms after 1999 on the lack of due process in the sanctions regimes. Concerns expressed by many member states obtained legal impetus when the European Court of Justice brought its international juridical authority to bear in the litigation over the *Kadi* case.[66] Here, a global body, the UNSC, hitherto for the most part unchecked by any judicial body of comparable jurisdiction, was prompted to improve the fairness of its sanctions procedures due to a decision by a court with a notable regional, but no global, jurisdiction.

Prost,[67] a serving Ombudsperson for the Security Council Al-Qaida Sanctions Committee, has asserted that the Ombudsperson's office "represents an important step forward in terms of enhancing the rule of law at the international level."[68] In her 2016 stocktaking, she maintains that elements of fairness and due process have been introduced, with varying degrees of success, in four aspects of the Ombudsperson's proceedings: sharing evidence with petitioners of the case against them; giving them an opportunity to answer the charges in that case; seeking to obtain a more independent review of information salient to a case; and undertaking all this in a "fair and timely process." These practices address the third source of arbitrariness identified by Shaffer and Sandholtz[69] – the need for individuals, or states, to question and respond to the way in which power is exercised over them. Nevertheless, Prost also concedes limits to transparency and fairness within proceedings, while confronting the fundamental underlying condition that the UNSC has kept the Ombudsperson's office on a series of temporary extensions rather than giving it any kind of formal continuity and independence.

[64] Prost, *supra* note 44.

[65] Farrall et al., *Elected Member Influence in the United National Security Council*, *supra* note 25, at 109–11.

[66] *See* Joined Cases C-402/05 P & C-415/05, Yassin Abdullah Kadi & Al Barakaat Int'l Found. v. Council of the Eur. Union & Comm'n of the Eur. Cmtys., 2008 E.C.R. I-6351 (Sept. 3, 2008); Joined Cases C-584/10 P, C-593/10 P & C-595/10 P, Eur. Comm'n & the Council of the Eur. Union v. Yassin Abdullah Kadi, ECLI:EU:C:2013:518 (July 18, 2013); *see also* Case T-315/01, Yassin Abdullah Kadi v. Council of the Eur. Union & Comm'n of the Eur. Cmtys., 2005 E.C.R. II-3649 (Sept. 21, 2005); Case T-85/09, Yassin Abdullah Kadi v. Eur. Comm'n, 2010 E.C.R. II-5177 (Sept. 30, 2010).

[67] Prost, *supra* note 44, at 183–87.

[68] *Id.* at 190.

[69] *See* Chapter 1.

*External* structural and institutional tempering of power cannot come from arbiters external to the UNSC. While some international courts have addressed ROL issues in sanctions regimes, these instances are rare and haphazard, as no court exerts systemic or coherent constraints on the UNSC, even if they potentially influence its internal politicking and structural adaptations. Yet external structural expressions of UNSC ROL can be seen in certain issue areas where the UNSC seeks to get beyond itself: to temper power more directly through its peacekeeping forces; to set up or enhance existing structures to ensure that UNSC sanctions regimes, among others, do not abrogate ROL norms that apply to vulnerable populations; and to build ROL institutions within countries. Quite apart from the relative effectiveness of any of these modest extensions of ROL outside UNSC deliberations themselves, they nonetheless may be readily subverted by a perceived lack of adherence by the UNSC to ROL, as we have noted, whether in its internal deliberations or in its wholesale assertion of force by P5 states in seeming disregard for legal processes that would constrain naked power in pursuit of national interest.

## V Transnational Legal Order

The comparative and interdisciplinary project on transnational legal orders seeks to elaborate a systematic framework for building empirically grounded theory on the ordering of law beyond the state. There are increasing indications that TLO theory enables scholars from many disciplines to hold in creative tension the rise and fall of a startling diversity of legal orders beyond the state that purport to solve social problems as unlike as climate change and inhibitions to lending, anti-money laundering and post-conflict resolution, fiduciary relationships and double taxation, constitution-writing and failing businesses, among many others.[70]

The double confounding of rule of law and the UN presents a special challenge. On the one side, the rule of law, a long and amorphous tradition of thought, institutions, rhetoric, and investments, seems constantly to resist encapsulation in theory or practice. On the other side, the sheer vastness of the UN, and its ubiquitous presence or shadow over

[70] Seth Davis & Gregory Shaffer, *Theorizing Transnational Fiduciary Law*, 5 U.C. Irvine J. Int'l Transnat'l & Comp. L. 1, 1–2 (2020); Transnational Legal Orders 3–72 (Terence C. Halliday & Gregory Shaffer eds., 2015).

every international arena, presents a research site so bewilderingly entangled that empirical work invariably falls short. Since ROL, in one or another of its familiar academic formulations, can be found in all the UN's conventions, and no sphere of human behavior falls entirely outside the UN's reach, their conjunction presents a rare challenge to socio-legal scholarship.

For these reasons, as we intimated earlier, we sharply constrict our focus to the apex of the UN as an institution – the UN Security Council – and to ROL in the UNSC's deliberations and three of its mandates. Now we begin to explore whether the lens of TLO theory, and its accumulating evidentiary base, can create some meaning, clarity, or coherence where a universal discourse encounters a universal institution.

Three conceptual aspects of TLO come immediately to the fore. First, whereas much other work on TLOs reaches to regional and global orders on trade or human rights or crime, *transnational* may also be understood as a legal order occurring among nations *within* a given transnational arena such as the UNSC (compare UNCITRAL) – that is, the *order* applies both to the *object* of the lawmaking and the *lawmaking process* itself. Second, the nomenclature that emerged inductively from earlier TLO studies pointed to the merits of imagining, identifying, and researching scales of TLOs. In climate change, for instance, one may point to a meta-TLO (e.g., the Paris Agreement), various mega-TLOs (e.g., within the EU), and micro-TLOs (e.g., agreements on greenhouse gas inventories and maritime transport emissions), as Bodansky notes.[71] Rajah proposes, in fact, that "transnational rule of law discourse may be seen as a meta-TLO that frames and contextualizes all efforts to manage and regulate ... conceptions of legality in the sphere of the transnational."[72] We view the competing visions of ROL in the UNSC as a struggle over the scope and substance of three micro-TLOs on peacekeeping, sanctions, and force, yet each is also nested within a meta-TLO on ROL that presses the UNSC to attain its highest ideals and core principles.

The logic of TLO theory begins with a presenting problem, growing gradually through facilitating circumstances and then sharply through a precipitating event, which energizes social actors to seek a solution

[71] Daniel Bondansky, *Climate Change: Transnational Legal Order or Disorder?*, *in* Transnational Legal Orders, *supra* note 70, at 287. *Cf.* Transnational Legal Orders, *supra* note 70, at 3–72.

[72] Jothie Rajah, *"Rule of Law" as Transnational Legal Order*, *in* Transnational Legal Orders, *supra* note 70, at 340, 343.

through transnational law. That problem is framed in a particular way that lends itself to a particular legal solution. Through a series of recursive moves over months or years, between local, national, and transnational levels of action, and driven by four mechanisms (diagnostic struggles, actor mismatch, inconsistency, and contradictions), an order may emerge that is eventually institutionalized or settled such that a new set of legal norms come to be taken for granted as appropriate bases for action, and they are mutually reinforcing by concordance in transnational, national, and local law. This TLO may be more or less aligned with an underlying problem, or it may overlap, compete, or coexist with other TLOs or forms of order that strive for normative primacy.

The speech to the UNSC by Kofi Annan on September 23, 2003, is a marker for ROL as an explicit normative framing for UN action. It follows fourteen years of post-Cold War reconfigurations in the world geopolitical order with the fall of the Berlin Wall, the dissolution of the Soviet Union, the civil wars in the former Yugoslavia, Iraq's invasion of Kuwait, military and other conflicts in many regions, and a massive enterprise of economic and political development in the 1990s. If collapse of command economies in favor of economic liberalism, the exhaustion of authoritarian regimes in favor of democracies, and the repudiation of rule-by-law regimes in favor of rule of law all heralded, "the end of history", in a now sadly ironic expression of hubris, then the shock of 9/11 and the US and UK invasion of Iraq suddenly precipitated a global reappraisal of military force exercised by the world's hegemon and the questionable status of the UN as a peacekeeper of last resort. While we cannot point definitively to 9/11 and Iraq as the trigger for the Secretary-General's launch of the ROL agenda for the UN, it is striking how widely he throws down a gauntlet and how instantly he restricts it to a narrow strand of UN endeavors: "This Council has a heavy responsibility to promote justice and the rule of law in its efforts to maintain international peace and security. This applies both internationally and in rebuilding shattered societies. It is the latter that I wish to speak about today."[73]

The problem at large confronted by the UNSC just six months after the US invaded Iraq is construed generically as the need "to maintain international peace and security." But Annan instantly retreats to the much safer terrain of "rebuilding shattered societies." If ROL writ large was shunted aside in the extraordinary events that led to the UN's inculpation in the Iraq War, Annan invoked the ROL writ small, seemingly to keep

[73] U.N. SCOR, 58th Sess., 4833 mtg., at 2, U.N. Doc. S/PV.4833 (Sept. 24, 2003).

law, not war, as a prevailing ideal of international conflict resolution, and as a practical tool in very specific domestic trouble spots. From this moment, the ROL agenda writ large radiates across the institutional landscape of the UN in ways far beyond the scope of this study. The UNSC's continuing formal engagement with that agenda is captured by Appendix I, which tabulates the evolution from 2003 to 2020 of the Council's thematic meetings dedicated to ROL issues.

## 1 *Micro-TLOs in the Making?*

A more precise grasp on ROL in the UNSC may be obtained by narrowing attention to the construction of three micro-TLOs – one on each of the UNSC's mandates for peacekeeping, sanctions, and force. Arguably, these micro-TLOs in formation are vehicles for conforming the UNSC's deliberations as a whole, both symbolically and as practice, to the meta-TLO expressed by its discursive proponents within and beyond the UN.

From 2000 to the present, we observe several successive, somewhat interconnected, initiatives to create a legal order in the UNSC that adheres to more explicitly articulated ROL procedural and structural norms. Nevertheless, the respective initiatives differ in their prescriptions. A TLO analysis begins to disentangle some of those convergences and divergences as an incipient episode of TLO-making that has unfolded since 2000.

An initiative, from the years 2004–08, began through cooperation between the government of Austria and NYU's Institute for International Law and Justice (hereafter Austria/NYU). A subsequent initiative, in the years 2010–16 and beyond, was led principally by socio-legal scholars at the Australian National University and the government of Australia (hereafter Australia/ANU). Each resulted in a report delivered to the UN, included in UN proceedings, and delivered to UN forums. Thereafter, a continuing effort has been mounted to influence ROL in the UNSC by mobilizing elected UNSC members to exert their influence in ways not adequately recognized or mobilized until more recently.

The construction of TLOs, small or large, begins with a presenting problem purportedly to be solved by law.[74] Each of the initiatives from below were animated respectively by the research of Chesterman on international humanitarian intervention, UN state-building and global

[74] Terence C. Halliday & Gregory Shaffer, *Researching Transnational Legal Orders*, *in* TRANSNATIONAL LEGAL ORDERS, *supra* note 70, at 473, 495–96.

administrative law,[75] and Farrall's work inside the UN Secretariat and research on UN sanctions and post-conflict peacebuilding.[76] In all cases they observed deficits in UNSC decision-making, which subverted its legitimacy and probable effectiveness, and pathologies in UN practices in the field. In each case they observed manifest deviations from at least the spirit of high ROL ideals, and in each case it appears their initiatives were triggered by the explicit ROL turn in discourse as it was expressed in Kofi Annan's 2003 speech and the UK's effort to put ROL more prominently on the UNSC's agenda. Significantly, in both cases the push for transnational reform came from 'below' and in a partnership of state and nonstate institutions.

Insofar as diagnostic struggles are an integral element of recursive cycles in the rise and fall of TLOs, we observe convergence and divergence. The earlier and later cycles of ROL-making share the view that UNSC-authorized operations fail frequently in their administration of sanctions, their control over peace-keeping forces, and their harms to vulnerable populations, such as women and children. Austria/NYU, however, approaching these problems from a global administrative law frame, diagnoses the problem as a failure of the UN essentially to adopt an institutional and procedural configuration of ROL that is conventional in well-established ROL orders within states. Failures are structural insofar as the UNSC and UN as a whole have not adequately differentiated the legislative, judicial, and executive functions and made the UNSC sufficiently accountable to a global judiciary. The UNSC has insufficient barriers to check what too easily can be abusive power. Australia/ANU, approaching these problems from a more socio-legal and regulatory governance perspective, observes a similar scope of UNSC breaches in the ROL, with particular attention to the deficiencies of sanctions regimes.[77] While Australia/ANU can concur with the Austria/NYU depiction of the global order as deficient in institutional configurations that are morphologically parallel to those within states, it departs from

75 Simon Chesterman, Just War or Just Peace? Humanitarian Intervention and International Law (2006); Simon Chesterman, You, The People: The United Nations, Transitional Administration and State-Building (2004).

76 Farrall, United Nations Sanctions and the Rule of Law, *supra* note 8; Jeremy Farrall, *Impossible Expectations? The UN Security Council's Promotion of the Rule of Law After Conflict, in* The Role of International Law in Rebuilding Societies After Conflict: Great Expectations 134 (2009).

77 Farrall, United Nations Sanctions and the Rule of Law, *supra* note 8.

the Austria/NYU in its appraisal of where the fulcrums of change can be found and in the realism of what prescriptions might follow.

A driver of TLOs in formation or reformation frequently is actor mismatch – those actors who write and promulgate the global norms are not inclusive of all the actors essential for implementation. Those left out use their powers of resistance or noncompliance or governance-skepticism to subvert international norms. It can be noted that in both the Austria/NYU and Australia/ANU proposals for ROL reforms in the UNSC there is an alliance of relative outsiders to the P5 power configuration within the UNSC. Austria used Chesterman's report and the buildup to it to build its legitimacy and case for election to the Council in October 2008, prior to serving on the Council in 2009–10. In Australia's case, its campaign for ROL reforms extended from a similar bid for UNSC elected membership, through the benefits amplified by Australia's UNSC membership in 2013–14, where the Australia/ANU conferences on ROL in New York could profit from greater access to key players in and around the Council, including some P5 diplomats (US, UK), and to follow-through after Australia stepped off the UNSC. Put another way, whereas Austria/NYU rode an electoral bid before membership, Australia/ANU rode a rising wave into the UNSC, a bigger wave during UNSC membership, and then the longer wave of postmembership legacy protection.

Close analysis reveals two further differences. The Austria/NYU initiative is driven by a small state in cooperation with an academic institution. It is true that its many conferences during the years 2004–08 include numerous senior international law scholars, former senior and some serving UN officials, experienced former judges in international tribunals, and numbers of diplomats from small countries, but it is a configuration principally of outsiders to the UNSC and it has none of the force of P5 members. The ANU initiative several years later similarly mobilizes states and nonactors in its series of consultations in Canberra and New York. The Australia/ANU cycle of reform consultations, however, involves actors of a different hue. The ANU alliance with the Australian government is forged through a partnership with a whole-of-government body dedicated to promoting civil–military coordinated responses to natural and man-made disasters in the Asia–Pacific region. By including the military, with areas of expertise essential to peacekeeping and force, there is a legitimating inclusion of an actor integral to UNSC operations. Moreover, from the beginning the ANU project not only aligned itself with Australia's ultimately successful bid to become an elected member of the UNSC for the term 2013–14, but its reformist cycle embraced and ratcheted up the aspirations of that large number of states that aspire to an elected two-year term on the UNSC.[78] Further, the Australia/ANU proposal deliberately sought to translate the balance-of-power asymmetries between the P5 and E10 in the UNSC into a new idiom of UNSC debates, where ROL might present a common ground of discourse, procedure, and structure giving the E10 powers of persuasion that otherwise would be discounted or neglected.

The diagnoses and mix of actors in the Austria/NYU and Australia/ANU led to clear commonalities in principle in their respective sets of norms, but also observable differences. The fact that the Australia/ANU initiative could observe the substance and reception of the Austria/NYU proposals enabled the later cycle of proposed reforms and their propagation to adapt appropriately. To contrast each in broad brush strokes: Whereas the Austria/NYU report derived its recommendations from diffuse ROL norms, the Australia/ANU report explicitly articulated four master norms,[79] themselves revised from an earlier set of five norms.[80] Whereas the NYU ordered its expansive recommendations on the presumption that a state-like separation of powers can be established beyond the state, the Australia/ANU report took a more pragmatic strategy, judging that reforms were only feasible and more probable if they were modest and able to be implemented within the constraints of extant UNSC procedures and structures. Whereas the Austria/NYU report recommended that its diffuse norms be applied to a scattering of UNSC-related operations, the Australia/ANU report tightened its application of its four sets of explicit norms to the three designated areas of sanctions, peacekeeping, and force, thus more

[78] Formally, the relationship between the Australian government and ANU scholars was a little more loose-linked, a structural connection that had benefits for both sides. On the one side, while the partnership with the Civil Military Centre enhanced a de facto relationship with multiple branches of government, the absence of a formal partnership allowed the government to distance itself – as it did on one occasion – from any part of the report presented to the UN that it could not support. On the other side, the underwriting of the academic research by the Australian Research Council assured independence for scholars in their findings and proposals.

[79] These four norms/principles are transparency, consistency, accountability, and engagement. For a description of the way these elements combine to form a responsive model of the ROL, for the purpose of application across UNSC decision-making, peacekeeping, sanctions and force, see FARRALL, CHARLESWORTH & RYAN, *supra* note 24, at 8–9.

[80] In 2007, Farrall constructed a pragmatic model of the ROL for application to the UN sanctions system, comprising the five norms/principles: transparency, consistency, equality, due process, and proportionality. *See* FARRALL, UNITED NATIONS SANCTIONS AND THE RULE OF LAW, *supra* note 8, at 39–41.

sharply linking the application of particular norms to particular spheres of UNSC decision-making and operations. And whereas the 2008 launch of the Austria/NYU norms took place prior to Austria's UNSC term, with the aim of bolstering the legitimacy of its UNSC candidacy, the Australia/ANU ROL recommendations were launched in 2016, with the cosponsorship of Australia, as a recent UNSC member, and Japan, as a current member, supported by the UN Secretariat's ROL unit within the Executive Office of the Secretary-General, in a chamber of 100 or more diplomats and staffers packed into a UN conference room at UN headquarters – a launch explicitly embedded within the motivating frame of increasing the impact of elected members of the UNSC before, during, and after their terms of office.

From Farrall's initial focus on sanctions, to a widening of scope in the Austria/NYU norms, to the tightening and linking of explicit ROL norms to particular UNSC procedures and operations, the iterative process of three cycles both reinforced the pressure for ROL norms and brought the impetus for change more forthrightly into a broader set of impulses in the UN for the vast majority of states to exert greater influence in the UNSC as elected members.

Thus, we should see the succession of the Farrall (2007), Austria/NYU (2004–08) and Australia/ANU (2010–16) initiatives not as independent moments of intervention but as successive recursive cycles of multiple TLO-building efforts, which together constitute an episode to identify and propagate restraining norms that temper inconsistent and arbitrary exercises of unbridled power too often displayed by the UNSC. Focused TLO-building of norms respectively for peacekeeping, sanctions, and force was premised upon and might also lead to an expansive conformity of UNSC deliberations to a meta-TLO on ROL.

In subsequent related work on the E10 Influence Project, a team of scholars from the University of New South Wales, ANU, and the University of Queensland have interrogated a basic assumption underpinning conventional understandings of how the UNSC works – namely, that all of the power and influence on the UNSC resides with the P5 and that the elected members (E10) are just there to make up the numbers.[81] Farrall et al. (2020) identify three examples in which E10 members, working either individually in specific UNSC terms or collectively across

[81] Australian Research Council Discovery Project 150100300: *Leveraging Power and Influence on the UN Security Council: The Role of Elected Members* (2015–22). Jeremy Farrall & Jochen Prantl, *Leveraging Diplomatic Power and Influence on the UN Security Council: the Case of Australia*, 70 AUSTL. J. INT'L AFF. 601, 601–11 (2016).

multiple terms or different members, have been able to shape UNSC decision-making, despite the fact that they do not possess the raw power epitomized by the veto power.[82] All three examples – Brazil and Responsibility While Protecting; Australia and the human rights situation in North Korea; and a broad, sustained coalition comprising successive E10 members and UN member states not on the UNSC for the establishment of the 1267 Ombudsperson[83] – represent attempts to rein in the UNSC's propensity to undermine the ROL and thus to boost its capacity to strengthen the ROL.

The E10 Influence Project, like its predecessor, the Strengthening the ROL Project, has benefited from the engaged support of the Australian mission to the UN. The research team undertook multiple rounds of fieldwork in New York between 2016 and 2019, consulting widely with UN practitioners and diplomatic representatives in order to identify prospective examples of E10 influence. During this fieldwork, the Australian mission provided valuable strategic advice to the team, hosting multiple seminars, bringing the team in close conversation with current and candidate E10 members, on the opportunities and constraints facing the E10 when seeking to shape UNSC decision-making.

How then may we appraise this incipient TLO-making to tighten and sharpen ROL procedures and practices in the UNSC? Insofar as the ROL dimensions in Table 6.1 are salient to the UNSC, there is little doubt that the ROL came to be relatively institutionalized as a discursive frame and a standing agenda item for the UNSC, recurring repeatedly from 2003 to 2022 (Appendix I). The fact that the Austrian/NYU report and, even more, the Australian/ANU policy proposals on ROL could evoke growing attention by some P5 members, many E10 members, and states within the UN General Assembly in itself demonstrated a vibrancy of the ROL discourse in this global diplomatic context. Nonetheless, it is not uncontested. Russia, in particular, has in recent years resisted ROL items on the UNSC agenda. There is some

[82] Farrall et al., *Elected Member Influence in the United National Security Council*, *supra* note 25, at 101–15. For discussion of important E10 contributions to the UNSC, see ELECTED MEMBERS OF THE SECURITY COUNCIL: LAME DUCKS OR KEY PLAYERS?, *supra* note 43.

[83] Farrall et al., *Elected Member Influence in the United National Security Council*, *supra* note 25, at 106–07 (for Brazil and the Responsibility While Protecting); *id.* at 107–09 (for Australia and the human rights situation in North Korea); *id.* at 109–11 (for the 1267 Ombudsperson).

evidence that some states may be adopting a discursive work-around, whereby they reach ROL issues but in the language of "accountability" or "justice," among other less evocative terms.[84]

In terms of the reception by the UNSC of the procedures and rules proposed by the Australian/ANU report, the clearest example relates to the accountability of UN peacekeeping operations. Proposal 20 states that: "When the Security Council establishes or extends the mandate of a peace operation, it should reaffirm that allegations of sexual exploitation and abuse must be investigated and prosecuted by troop-contributing countries."[85] In the months following the distribution of the proposals,[86] the UNSC included a provision requesting troop-contributing countries to ensure full accountability for acts of sexual exploitation and abuse by their troops in eight separate resolutions renewing the mandates of eight different peace operations.[87] While it might be a stretch to claim that the UNSC would not have included this provision in these eight resolutions in the absence of Proposal 20, the fact that the UNSC did so at this moment indicates that the proposal was tapping into currents of change demanding greater ROL adherence by peacekeepers and their countries of origin.

The potentially most significant shift in constraining UNSC arbitrariness on sanctions came with the establishment of the Office of the

[84] For instance, Albania very recently introduced the theme "Strengthening accountability and justice for serious violations of international law" in its one-month role holding the UNSC presidency. For the provisional verbatim record of the meeting, see U.N. SCOR, 77th Sess., 9052nd mtg., U.N. Doc. S/PV.9052 (June 2, 2022). For Albania's concept note setting up the meeting, see U.N. Security Council, Letter dated 24 May 2022 from the Permanent Representative of Albania to the United Nations addressed to the Secretary-General, U.N. Doc. S/2022/418/Rev.1 (May 24, 2022). In diplomatic moves by other states, including Australia, it may be that the toxicity of ROL for Russia requires it to be reached by an alternative linguistic route.

[85] Farrall, Charlesworth, and Ryan, *supra* note 24, at 25.

[86] While the policy proposals were formally launched on 16 March 2016 at UN headquarters, they were distributed electronically to all UN member states the previous month, as an attachment to the formal invitation to the launch.

[87] *See* S.C. Res. 2277, ¶ 39 (Mar. 30, 2016) (extending the mandate of MONUSCO in the Democratic Republic of the Congo); S.C. Res. 2285, ¶ 14 (Apr. 29, 2016) (extending the mandate of MINURSO in Western Sahara); S.C. Res. 2295, ¶ 27 (June 29, 2016) (extending the mandate of MINUSMA in Mali); S.C. Res. 2300, ¶ 13 (July 26, 2016) (extending the mandate of UNFICYP in Cyprus); S.C. Res. 2301, ¶ 48 (July 26, 2016) (extending the mandate of MINUSCA in Central African Republic); S.C. Res. 2305, ¶ 12 (Aug. 30, 2016) (extending the mandate of UNIFIL in Lebanon); S.C. Res. 2313, ¶ 31 (Oct. 13, 2016) (extending the mandate of MINUSTAH in Haiti); S.C. Res. 2330, ¶ 10 (Dec. 19, 2016) (extending the mandate of UNDOF in the Golan).

Ombudsperson. The Australian/ANU report recommended that its temporary status be made permanent and that its restriction to one sanctions regime be expanded to others. De jure permanence has not happened; de facto continuity has taken place as the office has been extended to further terms. And just as a trigger event brought the office into being in the first instance, it is not inconceivable that another trigger event might ensure both its permanence and extension to other sanctions regimes.

## VI Conclusion

We began with a conjunction – the apex of geopolitical power and universality of a legal discourse – and a conundrum: Can an operationalization of the abstract discourse of ROL temper the arbitrary or unbridled power that might be unleashed by the permanent five members of the UNSC? By focusing on three key UNSC mandates, and drawing on empirical observations inside reform initiatives since 2003, we have proposed that question can be constructively approached: first, by developing an analytic frame that more precisely delineates dimensions of ROL in the particular context of the UNSC, and second, by adopting the systematic framework of transnational legal order which draws seemingly discrete or disconnected actions into a temporally sequenced and dynamic account of cumulative action to effect change in a normative order.

We conclude with some provisional observations. First, the discourse of a meta-ROL order can be operationalized in an empirically observable effort at micro-TLO constructions directed inside the UNSC. Those recursive cycles build upon each other to produce a widely accepted frame of lawmaking, which in turn is concretized in specific rules and procedures, being reflected in structures, none highly consequential in themselves, but all cumulatively indicative of momentum toward a now explicit set of norms for decision-making and action by the UNSC. In these senses, the micro-TLO-building represents a tactical shift from what Krygier characterizes as the "emptiness" and "conceptual unclarity" of ROL abstractions to particularities and activities adapted for the singular context represented by the UNSC. Arguably, this momentum reflects a countercurrent to retreats from international rule of law documented elsewhere.[88] Shaffer and Sandholtz ask what might be done to return to a "virtuous transnational

[88] *See* Chapter 1; 9/11 AND THE RISE OF GLOBAL ANTI-TERRORISM LAW: HOW THE UN SECURITY COUNCIL RULES THE WORLD, *supra* note 5.

cycle" that advances the ROL.[89] The reform movements within the UNSC, which we have analyzed through the lens of TLO theory, represent one possible avenue of instigating such a cycle.

Second, there endures a tension between the idealistic view of a classic institutional balancing of powers beyond the state and a pragmatic view that accepts this as a bridge too far. Again, we find Krygier's framing on point. In contrast to the leanings of the Austrian/NYU initiative toward the replication and extrapolation of a within-state institutional separation of powers into the transnational realm, the Australian/ANU iteration of reforms proceeds on the basis of the judgment that a macrocosm of the national in the international would require amendments to the UN Charter – a prospect so unrealistic as to be a nonstarter. The perfect would become the enemy of the good. Why should we expect a global institution to achieve in decades what has taken many countries centuries to accomplish, nations still manifestly confronting the forces that will subvert ROL given the seduction of arbitrary power? An incrementalism *within* the UNSC may parallel the centuries-long struggles among centers of power within states as exceedingly uneven paths to ROL unfolded through revolutions, civil war, and intense political struggles. Hence, the Australian approach adopts a more realist expectation that ROL in the UNSC and its operations will probably be more effective when states themselves, especially the P5, with support or persuasion of some E10 members, draw their own ROL values into the UNSC. This takes the form of internalization rather than exterior pressure or moral suasion.

Third, by extending the ecology of UNSC-engaged actors from the P5 to the E10 and all other UN member states, ROL as an ideology takes on another hue. We postulate that the ROL is an idiom of legalism by which weak states – those outside the P5 – seek to convert their relative political impotence into a force for influence where ROL offers a unifying basis to temper the raw political powers of the P5. In this sense, we agree with Shaffer and Sandholtz that "[d]emocratic participation in the determination of law's substance is . . . a necessary complement to rule-of-law ideals."[90] However, we emphasize the two-way nature of this relation at the transnational level. Not only does participation enhance the ROL, but the ROL provides an avenue through which weaker states can engage in legal rulemaking, using the frame of the ROL to exert influence. Like King John's barons, individually weaker than the Crown, but together strong

[89] *See* Chapter 1.
[90] *See* Chapter 1.

enough to compel the sovereign to yield power, the elected UNSC members, present or future, might wield a moral and legal authority to compel dominant and imperial powers to check their "wild power" and naked national interest in order to maintain some measure of their historical hegemony. Put another way, this raises the question of whether the P5 will find it expedient to make incremental reforms in order to maintain some modicum of their own moral authority. Although the micro-TLOs that have been proposed for the UNSC since 2000 appear far removed from the capacity to restrain imperial propensities of the UNSC, might they constitute small episodes in a long historical trajectory representing moments where the concerted and incremental actions of the relatively weak present modest constraints on the powers of the putatively strong?

## Appendix 1: UNSC Meetings on the ROL, 2003–2022

| UNSC Meeting | Date | Agenda item title | Subitem/agenda document(s) | Decision |
|---|---|---|---|---|
| 4833 | Sept. 24, 2003 | Justice and the Rule of Law: the United Nations Role | | S/PRST/2003/15 |
| 4835 | Sept. 30, 2003 | Justice and the Rule of Law | | |
| 5052 | Oct. 6, 2004 | Justice and the Rule of Law: the United Nations Role | Report of the Secretary-General on the rule of law and transitional justice in conflict and post-conflict societies (S/2004/616) | S/PRST/2004/34 |
| 5474 | June 22, 2006 | Strengthening International Law: Rule of Law and Maintenance of International | S/2006/367 (nonpaper identifying three areas of focus: ROL in conflict and post-conflict situations; | S/PRST/2006/28 |

(*cont.*)

| UNSC Meeting | Date | Agenda item title | Subitem/agenda document(s) | Decision |
|---|---|---|---|---|
| | | Peace and Security | ending impunity for international crimes; and enhancing the efficiency and credibility of sanctions regimes) | |
| 6347 | June 29, 2010 | The Promotion and Strengthening of the Rule of Law in the Maintenance of International Peace and Security | S/2010/322 (concept note identifying three areas of focus: ROL in conflict and post-conflict situations; international justice and peaceful settlement of disputes; and the efficiency and credibility of sanctions regimes) | S/PRST/2010/11 |
| 6705 (and resume 1) | Jan. 19, 2012 | The Promotion and Strengthening of the Rule of Law in the Maintenance of International Peace and Security | Report of the Secretary-General on the rule of law and transitional justice in conflict and post-conflict societies (S/2011/634) | S/PRST/2012/1 |
| 6849 (and resume 1) | Oct. 17, 2012 | The Promotion and Strengthening of | Concept note on peace and justice, with | |

*(cont.)*

| UNSC Meeting | Date | Agenda item title | Subitem/agenda document(s) | Decision |
|---|---|---|---|---|
| | | the Rule of Law in the Maintenance of International Peace and Security: "Peace and Justice, with a Special Focus on the Role of the International Criminal Court" | a special focus on the role of the International Criminal Court (S/2012/731) | |
| 6913 | Jan. 30, 2013 | The Promotion and Strengthening of the Rule of Law in the Maintenance of International Peace and Security | Interim briefing by Deputy Secretary-General on "United Nations system support to the promotion of the rule of law in conflict and post-conflict situations" | |
| 7113 | Feb. 19, 2014 | The Promotion and Strengthening of the Rule of Law in the Maintenance of International Peace and Security | Report of the Secretary-General on measuring the effectiveness of the support provided by the UN system for the promotion of the rule of law in conflict and post-conflict situations (S/2013/341); | |

(*cont.*)

| UNSC Meeting | Date | Agenda item title | Subitem/agenda document(s) | Decision |
|---|---|---|---|---|
| | | | concept note on improving the effectiveness of UN promotion of ROL in conflict and post-conflict situations (S/2014/75) | |
| 7115 | Feb. 19, 2014 | The Promotion and Strengthening of the Rule of Law in the Maintenance of International Peace and Security | Report of the Secretary-General on measuring the effectiveness of the support provided by the UN system for the promotion of the rule of law in conflict and post-conflict situations (S/2013/341); concept note on improving the effectiveness of UN promotion of ROL in conflict and post-conflict situations (S/2014/75) | S/PRST/2014/5 |
| 8262 | May 17, 2018 | Maintenance of International Peace and Security: Upholding International | Concept note on upholding international law within the context of the maintenance of | |

(*cont.*)

| UNSC Meeting | Date | Agenda item title | Subitem/agenda document(s) | Decision |
|---|---|---|---|---|
| | | Law within the Context of the Maintenance of International Peace and Security | international peace and security (S/ 2018/417/Rev.1) | |
| 8499 | Apr. 1, 2019 | The Promotion and Strengthening of the Rule of Law in the Maintenance of International Peace and Security: International Humanitarian Law | | |
| 8596 | Aug. 13, 2019 | The Promotion and Strengthening of the Rule of Law in the Maintenance of International Peace and Security: International Humanitarian Law | | |
| 8599 | Aug. 20, 2019 | The Promotion and Strengthening of the Rule of Law in the Maintenance of International Peace and Security: | Concept note on international humanitarian law (S/ 2019/629) | S/PRST/ 2019/8 |

(*cont.*)

| UNSC Meeting | Date | Agenda item title | Subitem/agenda document(s) | Decision |
|---|---|---|---|---|
| | | International Humanitarian Law | | |
| VTC | Dec. 18, 2020 | The Promotion and Strengthening of the Rule of Law in the Maintenance of International Peace and Security: Strengthening Cooperation between the UNSC and the ICJ | Briefing by president of ICJ to UNSC (S/2020/1286) | |
| VTC | Dec. 21, 2020 | The Promotion and Strengthening of the Rule of Law in the Maintenance of International Peace and Security: Strengthening Cooperation between the UNSC and the ICJ | | S/PRST/2020/13 |
| 9052 | June 2, 2022 | Strengthening Accountability and Justice for Serious Violations of International Law | Concept note on strengthening accountability and justice for serious violations of international law (S/2022/418/Rev.1) | |

## Appendix 2: A Researcher's Serendipity

At a pivotal moment in August 2003, Jeremy was working as a United Nations Secretariat staffer, with responsibility to attend, observe, and report on all of the Security Council's formal and informal meetings for the month, in order to prepare an in-house analysis of key developments in the Council's procedural and substantive practice. Toward the end of the month, during the daily informal consultations of the whole, Jeremy was fascinated to hear the permanent representative of the United Kingdom (which would take its turn as the monthly president of the Council during the following month) announce the scheduling of a meeting on a new agenda item entitled "Justice and the Rule of Law." The inaugural meeting on this agenda item would take place in September, a high-profile time for UNSC activities because the majority of leaders of UN member states are in New York to participate in the UN General Assembly's "Leaders' Week." The Security Council was about to discuss the rule of law at a high level and at a high-stakes moment.

As a UN Secretariat staffer, Jeremy did not participate directly in the Security Council's decision-making process, as that is the privilege of the diplomats who represent the fifteen Council members. However, later on the same day he was presented with a serendipitous opportunity. While waiting for the elevator back to his office, he found himself standing next to one of UN Secretary-General Kofi Annan's speechwriters. As they stepped into the elevator, Jeremy told the colleague he was fascinated that the Council would soon hold a meeting on the rule of law. The colleague said it was uncanny that Jeremy should mention this, as he was about to draft the Secretary-General's comments for that meeting. As Jeremy stepped out onto his floor and the elevator door began to close, the colleague invited him to send any thoughts he might have on what the Secretary-General should say. As soon as he got back to his desk, Jeremy fired off a quick email with half a dozen bullet points on the importance of the Security Council's relationship with the rule of law. On September 24, 2003, the Security Council held the inaugural meeting on its new agenda item entitled "Justice and the Rule of Law." The first speaker at that meeting, Secretary-General Kofi Annan, observed that: "This Council has a heavy responsibility to promote justice and the rule of law in its efforts to maintain international peace and security. This applies both internationally and in rebuilding shattered societies."[91] These words bore an uncanny resemblance to the first bullet point in Jeremy's email!

[91] U.N. SCOR, 58th Sess., 4833 mtg. at ¶ 2, U.N. Doc. S/PV.4833 (Sept. 24, 2003).

# PART III

## National Case Studies in Transnational Context

# 7

# The Rule of Law Writ Large

## The European Union and Its Rogue Member States

KIM LANE SCHEPPELE

## I Introduction

The rule of law has become all things to all people, which is why virtually everyone can agree that the rule of law is a good thing. To some, it stands for rule according to legal standards instead of according to personalistic whim.[1] To others, it stands for purely formal criteria of legality – coherence, noncontradiction, clarity – with the specific content to be sorted out separately.[2] To still others, it stands for predictability and order, a bulwark against the vicissitudes of politics.[3]

This chapter was written while I was a fellow at the Institut für die Wissenschaften vom Menschen (IWM), Vienna, in spring 2023, and it was first presented as a paper at Stanford Law's rule-of-law conference in May 2023. I am grateful to the IWM for material and moral support and to Stanford Law for excellent discussion and feedback on the first draft. I am also grateful to Verfassungsblog, whose symposium on how to move Hungary from autocracy to democracy first made me think hard about these questions in advance of the 2022 Hungarian elections, and to the Max Planck Institute for Comparative Public Law and International Law for the invitation to participate in debates about what Transition 2.0 in Europe should look like in advance of the 2023 Polish elections. Feedback from Gregory Shaffer and Wayne Sandholtz was crucial in linking this piece to the others published in this volume. This chapter was finalized in November 2023, after the Polish elections but before the new government had a chance to reveal its strategy for recovering the rule of law, so events after that date are not included.

1 Identifying the rule of law with the reduction of arbitrariness is the hallmark of the work of Martin Krygier. *See, e.g.*, Martin Krygier, *The Rule of Law: Pasts, Presents and Two Possible Futures*, 12 Ann. Rev. L. & Soc. Sci. 199, 204 (2016); Martin Krygier, *The Rule of Law: Legality, Teleology, Sociology*, *in* Relocating the Rule of Law 45, 60 (Gianluigi Palombella & Neil Walker eds., 2009).

2 Lon L. Fuller, The Morality of Law (rev. ed. 1969).

3 Judith Shklar identified the rule of law with "freedom from fear." Judith Shklar, *Political Theory and the Rule of Law*, *in* Political Thought and Political Thinkers 21, 24 (Stanley Hoffmann ed., 1998).

Philosophical debates have erupted over whether the rule of law should be defined in a "thin" way through primarily procedural requirements or whether the rule of law should include substantive commitments to legal principles that would make the concept "thick."[4] The variations are very nearly endless, especially when one considers the versions that grow from different national histories and that go by the name of the *Rechtsstaat*, *estado de derecho*, *l'État de droit*, *jogállam*, and more.[5]

What most of these diverse conceptions of the rule of law share, however, is the unstated assumption that the rule of law should be understood within the boundaries of national law. The rule of law analyst typically takes the national legal system as if it were the only system in which rule of law had any real purchase and analyzes it in isolation. I will call this nationally focused conception the *rule of law writ small*.

As this volume makes clear, however, the rule of law is no longer properly analyzed as purely national.[6] Not only can one speak of international law as a rule-of-law system of its own (even if flawed),[7] but increasingly transnational law[8] enters into national law itself and

[4] One influential recent handbook on the rule of law has sparring chapters on this distinction: Jorgen Moller, *The Advantages of a Thin View*, *in* HANDBOOK ON THE RULE OF LAW 21 (Christopher May & Adam Winchester eds., 2018); Adriaan Bedner, *The Promise of a Thick View*, *in* HANDBOOK ON THE RULE OF LAW, *supra*, at 34.

[5] A useful review of the way that national conceptions of rule of law vary can be found in THE RULE OF LAW: HISTORY, THEORY AND CRITICISM (Pietro Costa, Danilo Zolo & Emilio Santoro eds., 2007).

[6] As Gregory Shaffer and Wayne Sandholtz argue in Chapter 1: "We … contend that international law is critical for advancing the rule of law in multiple direct and indirect ways that affect individuals and societies." Brian Tamanaha, in Chapter 2, adds that not only individuals but also states themselves are proper subjects of the rule of law.

[7] For an argument that international law is biased in favor of powerful states, see B.S. Chimni, *Legitimating the International Rule of Law*, *in* CAMBRIDGE COMPANION TO INTERNATIONAL LAW 290 (James Crawford & Martti Koskenniemi eds., 2012). For a critique pulling in the opposite direction, which is that powerful states feel free to ignore international law when it suits them, see JACK GOLDSMITH & ERIC POSNER, THE LIMITS OF INTERNATIONAL LAW (2005).

[8] I use the phrase "transnational law" throughout this chapter to include all law above the level of the state. Some of this supranational law is regional or bilateral affecting some states but not others, while some is fully international in the sense of binding all (or even most) countries. Also in Europe, where much of my work is concentrated, European Union law is typically not referred to as international law, because it has primacy and direct effect within national legal systems and thus constitutes part of domestic law as well. So, throughout the chapter, I use "transnational" as the more inclusive term to include all legal norms that have their origins above the level of the individual state.

modifies (or at least is supposed to modify) the operation of what had been imagined by legal philosophers as a hermetically sealed-off space.[9]

This is particularly true in parts of the world in which national legal systems are embedded in increasingly dense webs of transnational legal commitments. The member states of the European Union (EU) as well as the signatory states to the European Convention on Human Rights (ECHR) or the Inter-American Convention on Human Rights or the African Charter on Human and Peoples' Rights are finding an increasingly large number of transnational law incursions on national law as nonoptional parts of their own domestic legal orders. Even more hard law and soft law emerge from international treaty body recommendations, ICRC protocols, WTO rules, bilateral investment treaties, UN Security Council resolutions, or even the UN Charter itself, and these may also constrain what domestic law should do. The United States and the United Kingdom, from which much of the rule-of-law literature in English originates, may be particularly allergic to being (or to admitting to being) encumbered by binding international legal obligations, but that is an increasingly marginal standpoint among the world's democracies and an even more marginal reality in the world as transnational institutions gain more and more reach and enforcement capacity.

As we elaborate what the rule of law requires for any specific country, then, we should consider the national system as it is embedded in its transnational legal commitments. If the transnational legal order requires one set of actions while the national legal order requires another, it may not matter much to the daily life of the law whether each level is consistent and predictable within its own sphere. Legal certainty – the bare-minimum element of the rule of law – can only be obtained if the transnational and national legal orders do not require contradictory things, because otherwise legal subjects will be left wondering which apparently binding rule applies to them. Harmonizing law across transnational and national levels is required for the rule of law to be fully realized, regardless of whether one has a thin or thick conception in mind. Harmonizing across these levels in any given legal space constitutes what I call the *rule of law writ large*.

Why move from thinking about the rule of law writ small to thinking about the rule of law writ large? Thinking of the rule of law as necessarily embracing national and transnational principles helps us to reimagine

9 If transnational law did not have such an effect in national legal systems, aspirational autocrats like Vladimir Putin in Russia and Recep Tayyib Erdoğan in Turkey would not have taken such extraordinary steps to ensure that the national legal system remained impervious to the rulings of transnational courts. *See* Chapters 8 (Russia) and 9 (Turkey).

one of the most important issues of our time: the global crisis of the rule of law. Around the world, once-democratic states are increasingly back-pedaling on their constitutional commitments, as aspirational autocrats compromise the independence of judiciaries, eliminate constraints on executive power, destroy the independence of "fourth branch" good-government institutions, concentrate control of the media in politically friendly hands, restrict the operation of civil society groups, put a political squeeze on universities, and entrench themselves in power for the foreseeable future.[10] But, as we will see, transnational institutions are quickly developing increasingly hard legal standards that make democratic and rule-of-law backsliding ever more clear violations of transnational law.[11]

As long as one does not take into account transnational law, the activities of aspirational autocrats may appear to be perfectly in compliance with the rule of law in the sense of pure legality within the national legal system. In many backsliding democracies, autocrats remove key democratic protections in ways that are perfectly legal. When an aspirational autocrat comes to power with a parliamentary majority and passes laws that compromise the independence of the judiciary, what is wrong with that, especially if the (packed) constitutional court says that it was all constitutional? What is the problem if the parliament delegates unlimited decree power to the executive during a state of emergency, a power that is endlessly extended by continued parliamentary affirmation? These and other examples make clear that formal legality within a national legal system is not the same thing as the rule of law writ large. It may not even be the same thing as the rule of law writ small, but then one gets into the weeds arguing over precisely which definition one has in mind.

Of course, the vast literature on rule of law writ small was in general designed for just this purpose – to provide a critique of formal legality where it fell short of some normative standards.[12] The question is how one generates those standards and whether they can be effectively deployed beyond an academic publication when real-world problems require answers. For most of the academic writing on the subject, the answer comes through political theory – in definitions of democracy,

[10] Kim Lane Scheppele, *Autocratic Legalism*, 85 U. Chi. L. Rev. 545 (2018).

[11] This argument is explained in much greater detail in my 2023 Grotius Lecture: Kim Lane Scheppele, *Restoring Democracy Through International Law*, Am. U. L. Rev. (forthcoming).

[12] Of course, the most famous example is the checklist provided by Fuller, *supra* note 2.

constitutionalism, and even rule of law.[13] But do those standards translate into persuasive public arguments at times of democratic crisis?

Using existing off-the-rack philosophical theories to understand what the rule of law requires often fails to address real-world problems. First, these theories often work by requiring their adherents to use familiar vocabulary in unfamiliar ways, which makes the acceptance of the theories by broader publics difficult. If democracy, for example, is only properly so called when those elected agree to be bound by the laws of their predecessors because that is what the rule of law requires, then what do we make of perfectly reasonable democratic demands for change? If the rule of law smuggles in conceptions of social rights unfamiliar in the particular context in which it will be deployed, then are those who think differently necessarily legal scoundrels? We can solve these problems by defining them away, but democratic publics can be forgiven if they think that definitional sleight of hand is too clever by half.

Second, theories of the rule of law can themselves be manipulated by those who are supposed to be constrained by them. Many autocratic leaders have their own theorists in chief who provide ready-to-hand political-theory answers to complex questions involving the rule of law.[14] In fact, in one of the most famous twentieth-century debates over the rule of law – the debate between Carl Schmitt and Hans Kelsen in interwar Germany[15] – Schmitt's ideas conveniently dovetailed with the interests of the Nazi regime he defended, so it was not surprising that he became their practical theorist of choice. Of course, most academic theorists write about rule of law precisely to oppose dictatorial and genocidal regimes, but nonetheless it is difficult to find good *democratic* – or, for that matter, *rule-of-law* – reasons to defend one academic theory over another without simply arguing from the practical consequences of adopting a particular view. It is easy to see how autocrats can then just say that the academic theorist is simply smuggling a preferred political position into the standards. Autocrats then feel justified in doing the

13 For an excellent review of the options, see BRIAN Z. TAMANAHA, ON THE RULE OF LAW: HISTORY, POLITICS, THEORY 96 (2004).

14 For example, in Hungary, András Lánczi has long provided philosophical cover for the actions of Viktor Orbán. For my analysis of Lánczi's writing, see Kim Lane Scheppele, *The Opportunism of Populists and the Defense of Constitutional Liberalism*, 20 GERMAN L.J. 314 (2019).

15 A useful review of this debate, emphasizing how Schmitt believed that the executive was the "guardian of the constitution" while Kelsen thought the judiciary was the better guardian, can be found in SARA LAGI, *Democracy and Constitution, in* DEMOCRACY IN ITS ESSENCE: HANS KELSEN AS A POLITICAL THINKER 55 (2020).

same – manipulating the choice of theory while accusing those who oppose them of "looking over a crowd and picking out your friends."[16]

Instead, I suggest a less manipulatable and more comprehensible standard: using transnational law to guide transitions back to democracy in rogue states whose resident autocrats have used the law to consolidate power in their hands and attack the rule of law at home. Of course, transnational law is famously incoherent and siloed into different fields that often conflict; hence the calls for "constitutionalization" that have emerged over the years.[17] But an increasing body of transnational law deals directly with questions of democracy and human rights, the typical subjects of constitutionalism within national legal orders. Transnational standards are rapidly emerging in these fields, particularly in regional human rights courts. This new transnational legal scaffolding can support the rebuilding of democracy while it is under reconstruction from within.

By using transnational law as a framework within which to assess and urge changes to national law in states that are declining in their commitments to democracy and the rule of law, we can accomplish three purposes: (a) to elaborate in practice a common baseline of shared

[16] The quotation as a criticism of the selectivity of legal sources appeared in Patricia M. Wald, *Some Observations on the Use of Legislative History in the 1981 Supreme Court Term*, 68 IOWA L. REV. 195, 214 (1983) ("It sometimes seems that citing legislative history is still, as my late colleague [Judge] Harold Leventhal once observed, akin to 'looking over a crowd and picking out your friends.'"). Extended to comparative constitutional law by Justice Stephen Breyer in a debate with Antonin Scalia over whether the US Supreme Court should look to foreign law in making its decision, the same point applies. Breyer argued:

> The criticism is you'll look over the party, the cocktail party – remember Judge Leventhal said this about legislative history: Those who use legislative history, well it's like looking at a cocktail party, you look over the cocktail party to identify your friends. (Laughter.) And I say to that, well then you're not doing your job. . . . I would refer to the cases against me that I come across as much as for me. And the fact that somebody's come out the other way in a foreign court doesn't make it any the less interesting. Maybe it's more interesting. But this is not a major thing. It's not some kind of determinative thing in dozens of cases of constitutional law; it's simply from time to time relevant. And if it becomes more than that, I don't know how it's going to work.

Transcript of discussion between US Supreme Court Justices Antonin Scalia and Stephen Breyer, American University's Washington College of Law (Jan. 13, 2005), www.freerepublic.com/focus/news/1352357/posts.

[17] JAN KLABBERS, ANNE PETERS & GEIR ULFSTEIN, THE CONSTITUTIONALIZATION OF INTERNATIONAL LAW (2009).

standards (thereby eliminating the "double standards" problem); (b) to develop methods for assessing the democratic and rule-of-law *bona fides* of backsliding states that are impossible for domestic parties alone to manipulate (which I will call the "North Star" effect); and (c) to provide a legal justification within national legal systems to make sharp breaks, if need be, with existing domestic autocratic law in order to harmonize national law with transnational democratic law (which I will call the principle of "asymmetric rupture").

## II Tackling Democratic Backsliding within the Rule of Law Writ Small

To show why we need to reach beyond existing national rule-of-law paradigms for democratic restoration, an example will reveal the state of the art. In late 2021, some Hungarian legal scholars tried to crowd-source proposals for a newly elected government to use in restoring democracy to Hungary.[18] Hungary had experienced one of the most spectacular collapses from being a star performer in the postcommunist transitions of the 1990s to being the leader of the democratic backsliders in the region in the 2010s, falling from democracy to autocracy in the space of one decade.[19] After his election in 2010 with a constitutional majority (that is, a majority capable of amending the constitution without partners), Prime Minister Viktor Orbán rewrote the entire legal system, including a new constitution and thousands of pages of laws, to

[18] Verfassungsblog debate *Restoring Constitutionalism* (Dec. 2021–Mar. 2022), https://verfassungsblog.de/category/debates/restoring-constitutionalism/. The debate eventually produced twenty-two contributions.

[19] By 2020, a decade into Prime Minister Viktor Orbán's reign, the key democracy raters agreed. The Varieties of Democracy project, V-Dem, downgraded Hungary to an "electoral autocracy" in 2020, explaining that "Hungary is no longer a democracy, leaving the EU with its first non-democratic Member State." V-Dem Institute, Autocratization Surges – Resistance Grows: Democracy Report 2020 4 (Mar. 2020), https://v-dem.net/documents/14/dr_2020_dqumD5e.pdf. Hungary has remained in the "electoral autocracy" category since. *See* V-Dem Institute, Autocratization Turns Viral: Democracy Report 2021 (Mar. 2021), www.v-dem.net/media/filer_public/c9/3f/c93f8e74-a3fd-4bac-adfd-ee2cfbc0a375/dr_2021.pdf. Freedom House downgraded Hungary from a democracy to a "transitional/hybrid regime" in 2020, explaining that Hungary's decline has been the most precipitous ever tracked in the *Nations in Transit* reports on postcommunist states. Hungary had been one of the three democratic frontrunners as of 2005, but in 2020 it became the first country to descend by two regime categories and leave the group of democracies entirely. Freedom House, Nations in Transit 2020: Dropping the Democratic Façade 2 (2020), https://freedomhouse.org/sites/default/files/2020-04/05062020_FH_NIT2020_vfinal.pdf.

lock power into his inner circle.[20] The parliamentary election in 2022 looked like it would provide the first real chance to defeat Orbán because all of the opposition parties had agreed to work together despite the tilted electoral playing field and their own internal disagreements. The question for them was how they could govern if they won, given that Orbán's constitutional revolution had created a dense thicket of laws that only a two-thirds parliamentary majority could change, while also ensuring that the opposition would almost surely never win even a simple majority in the parliament.[21] The crowdsourcing request asked what a new government could and should do to restore the rule of law, given that, as long as Orbán's party held a mere one-third of the seats in the parliament, it could block virtually all significant changes to the system he had created. How could the opposition, if elected with a bare majority insufficient to alter the "two-thirds laws," restore democracy within the rule of law, given that the national law would be arrayed against them?

Many of the proposals suggested what you would expect constitutional scholars to say. They suggested various ways to convene a constituent assembly to write a new constitution with multiple suggestions as to how to live with bad law in the meantime.[22] Since the European revolutions of 1848, this has been the dominant script of democratic reform.[23] Come to power by revolution or election, convene a constituent assembly, and write (or rewrite) the constitution!

Constituent assemblies have played an important role in history.[24] But they are not the only way that democratic transitions occur. Some of the

[20] For analyses of the new Orbán constitution of 2011–2012, see Miklós Bánkuti, Gábor Halmai & Kim Lane Scheppele, *From Separation of Powers to Government Without Checks: Hungary's Old and New Constitutions*, *in* CONSTITUTION FOR A DIVIDED NATION: HUNGARY'S FUNDAMENTAL LAW (Gábor Attila Tóth ed., 2012); Miklós Bánkuti, Gábor Halmai & Kim Lane Scheppele, *Hungary's Illiberal Turn: Disabling the Constitution*, 23(3) J. DEMOCRACY 138 (July 2012).

[21] On the rigged election law, see Kim Lane Scheppele, *How Orbán Wins*, 33(3) J. DEMOCRACY 45 (July 2022).

[22] For example, Andrew Arato & Gábor Halmai, *So that the Name Hungarian Regain Its Dignity: Strategy for the Making of a New Constitution*, VERFASSUNGSBLOG (July 2, 2021), https://verfassungsblog.de/so-that-the-name-hungarian-regain-its-dignity/; Mark Tushnet, *Restoring Self-Governance: Constitutional Change and the Charge of Illegality*, VERFASSUNGSBLOG (Dec. 14, 2021), https://verfassungsblog.de/restoring-self-governance/.

[23] JOEL COLÓN-RÍOS, CONSTITUENT POWER AND THE LAW (2020); THE PARADOX OF CONSTITUTIONALISM: CONSTITUENT POWER AND CONSTITUTIONAL FORM (Martin Loughlin & Neil Walker eds., 2018).

[24] For a recent symposium on this history, see Joel I. Colón-Ríos et al., *Constituent Power and Its Institutions*, 20 CONTEMP. POL. THEORY 926 (2021), https://doi.org/10.1057/s41296-021-00467-z.

constitutions that have been most successful at creating new stable democracies out of dictatorships – e.g., Germany's and Japan's – were written by experts meeting largely in secret while their respective countries were under foreign occupation. Others have been written under less-than-ideal circumstances in situations of nontransparency, including the 1989 Hungarian constitution itself.[25] Even the much-valorized South African constitution, written with an unprecedented amount of public opportunities for input, turns out to have been written without its drafters taking on board most of the suggestions that arrived on their doorsteps.[26] The recent Chilean constituent assembly, which precisely followed the ideal script, was met with a massive electoral rejection of its proposal.[27] So constituent assemblies, when one looks at them close-up, are complicated and not nearly as participatory, democratic, or successful in action as they are in theory.

More crucially, though, this standard recipe for restoring the rule of law to autocratic countries through constituent assemblies is unlikely to work under present circumstances. In the 1970s–1990s, when first Southern Europe, then Latin America, and then Eastern Europe went through democratic transformations, the antidemocratic forces that were swept aside in these democratic revolutions mostly stood down and did not claim a continued right to rule. Their supporters, if they still had any, faded away quickly. Thus, new constitutions could be written without the dictators or their supporters at the table. Or, if they were there, they quickly vanished in the elections that followed.

In what is sometimes being called "Transition 2.0," focusing on how democracy can be restored now after the autocratic governments have damaged the earlier version,[28] the situation is quite different. By and large, those who destroyed democracy this time did not seize power through coups and military occupation, but instead came to power through elections.[29] These leaders still have support – even if not

[25] Kim Lane Scheppele, *Unconstitutional Constituent Power*, *in* MODERN CONSTITUTIONS (Rogers Smith & Ricard Beeman eds., 2020).

[26] HEINZ KLUG, CONSTITUTING DEMOCRACY: LAW, GLOBALIZATION AND SOUTH AFRICA'S POLITICAL RECONSTRUCTION (2000).

[27] Maria Carrasco, *Why We Failed To Approve The New Chilean Constitution: The Need For A Cultural Transformation*, LSE LATIN AM. & CARIBBEAN BLOG (Sept. 15, 2022), https://tinyurl.com/47mttj2k.

[28] TRANSITION 2.0: RE-ESTABLISHING CONSTITUTIONAL DEMOCRACY IN EU MEMBER STATES (Michal Bobek et al. eds., 2023), www.nomos-elibrary.de/10.5771/9783748914938/transition-2-0.

[29] Scheppele, *supra* note 10.

majority support – among their citizens, and they will demand a role in whatever transition occurs. They and their supporters are not going away. Calling a constitutional convention with the autocrats and their followers at the table is therefore a tricky business. One might well risk a failure to make a democratic transition at all, especially given how adept the autocrats are at rigging the rules for constituent assemblies and how well the autocrats know the systems they designed, which gives them an advantage. Hugo Chávez in Venezuela and Rafael Correa in Ecuador provide two cautionary tales when considering how autocrats can rig constituent assemblies to their own benefit.[30]

If one has a purely national idea of the rule of law and the idea of a constituent assembly fails on practical grounds, then one is left with various unsatisfactory methods for getting out from under the laws created by an autocrat to preserve autocratic rule. Many Hungarian lawyers felt compelled to follow Orbán's laws even as they sought to undermine them, because anything other than obedience to the laws laid down would constitute a violation of the rule of law. When the rule of law is used to justify the continuation of an antidemocratic system, something is wrong with the conception of the rule of law. And what is wrong with standard accounts of the rule of law is their national-only focus. Before explaining how the Hungarian opposition developed a plan to escape Orbán's "constitutional prison"[31] if they had managed to win the election, which I will return to at the end of this chapter, we need to first see how transnational law can be useful in generating rule-of-law alternative paths for restoring constitutional democracy.

## III Addressing Democratic Backsliding with the Rule of Law Writ Large

Transition 2.0, a move away from democratically damaged governments back to democratic health, starts with an important advantage. Across the world, many of the backsliding states are now members of regional bodies that require their members to remain democracies, uphold the rule of law and honor human rights.

30 David Landau, *Constitution-Making Gone Wrong*, 64 Ala. L. Rev. 923 (2013).

31 The solution I elaborate here was first proposed in Kim Lane Scheppele, *Escaping Orbán's Constitutional Prison: How European Law Can Free a New Hungarian Parliament*, Verfassungsblog (Dec. 21, 2021), https://verfassungsblog.de/escaping-orbans-constitutional-prison/.

In Transition 1.0, as democratic waves washed over Southern Europe, then Latin America, and then Eastern Europe, the transnational institutions that might have supported such democratic transitions did not generally include these transitioning states as members, nor did they have robust mechanisms in place to guide a transition to democracy at that time.[32] Southern Europe's last dictatorships democratized in the 1970s mostly outside the Council of Europe (CoE) and what later became the European Union. Latin American dictatorships gave way to democracy in the 1980s, but at the time the regional institutions had not yet developed democratic enforcement tools. For the Eastern Europe states that emerged from the Soviet shadow in the 1990s, joining the CoE was relatively fast but joining the EU took well more than a decade. The EU had never formalized what its membership requirements were until it prepared the "Copenhagen criteria" precisely for the postcommunist states' accession.[33] While in each case full membership in the regional transnational organizations depended on discarding dictatorship, in none of those cases were elaborate democratic and rule-of-law standards well developed to guide these transitions in any detail.

Transition 2.0 starts in a very different place, with many of the problematically backsliding states already inside the tent of the transnational organizations. Before autocrats consolidated power in, for example, Venezuela and Ecuador, Turkey and Russia, or Hungary and Poland, their democratic predecessors had signed onto the jurisdiction of the regional bodies in better times. Now that the aspirational autocrats have come to power and are violating the criteria for admission to the transnational bodies that had membership requirements to get in the door, Transition 2.0 can then start from a different legal foundation. We can take advantage of the fact that many of the now rogue states are still bound by the membership requirements even as their national autocrats have violated these standards through backsliding. The standards of the transnational organizations can now be enforced by restoring the rule of law writ large. Best of all, since the now backsliding states undertook these transnational obligations of their own accord in a not too distant

32 An excellent recent Princeton dissertation traces the history of democracy-strengthening mechanisms in regional organizations: Cassandra Emmons, Regional Organizations as Democracy Enforcers: Designing Effective Toolkits (Jan. 2020) (Ph.D. dissertation, Princeton University), https://dataspace.princeton.edu/handle/88435/dsp01f4752k70w.

33 Dimitry Kochenov, EU Enlargement and the Failure of Conditionality: Pre-Accession Conditionality in the Fields of Democracy and the Rule of Law (2008).

past, enforcing the standards of these transnational organizations simply holds the backsliding states to standards they once committed to follow at a more democratically robust moment.

Enforcement of these transnational standards through the rule of law writ large can occur in three stages. First, the rogue states should comply with transnational law as it applies directly to them. For example, they should honor the decisions of the regional courts and enforcement bodies that have already been made in cases that have arisen during the process of backsliding. They therefore should engage in *direct compliance* by starting with the obvious violations that have already been called out by transnational bodies with binding legal force in their specific country.

Then, Transition 2.0 should build out from there to bring rogue states into compliance with transnational law more generally, not just in the specific matters where the transnational bodies have already ruled directly against them but also in the spirit of the law that applies to all members of these organizations. *Erga omnes compliance* involves working out what the rules of these transnational organizations imply for the domestic governance of all signatory states, including the rogue states, and developing the links between these *erga omnes* standards and the specific offending practices of the rogue states so that they can be corrected.

Finally, rogue states should accept the transnational principles beyond the boundaries strictly required in a binding sense by applying general soft law principles to domestic arrangements that transnational law cannot strictly enforce. *Supererogatory compliance* with transnational values using this strategy would move national law even closer to transnational law but would be doing so without being strictly bound to do so by treaty commitments.

Why consider this strategy of using transnational law to supersede national laws as we think about rule-of-law cures for democratic backsliding? As states go through Transition 2.0 to restore democracy, human rights, and the rule of law, they may find that honoring transnational law now requires breaking national law that was enacted and enforced as states were backsliding. Since the autocrats who are being displaced in Transition 2.0 by new democratic governments have broken the letter and/or the spirit of transnational law in order to create dictatorships, these autocrats and their supporters can (and surely will) say that rupturing national law to restore democratic institutions is simply a political tit-for-tat that is no different from what they did. The autocrats will argue that the democrats are violating the domestic legal order simply to insert their political preferences in order to prioritize transnational standards, just as the democrats once accused the autocrats of having ruptured the legal order by "careening" into a democratically precarious situation in violation of transnational legal standards.[34] Once we accept that the rule of law writ large requires that the national and the transnational be harmonized, the moves of the autocrats and the democrats can be cleanly distinguished. In addition, because it is generally beyond the reach of the national leaders to change the transnational standards, changing national law to create coherence and predictability across all levels of the law no longer looks like just another lawbreaking exercise that could be repeated if the autocratic forces come back into power. Instead, it can be justified as an exercise in honoring the rule of law writ large.

## IV Applying the Rule of Law Writ Large within Europe: The Cases of Hungary and Poland

To make this abstract argument more concrete, we will work through the implications of the rule of law writ large by considering the potential transition of rogue states back to democracy inside a particularly dense web of transnational law. Hungary and Poland are among the leading democratic backsliders in the world, but both are member states of the European Union and signatories to Council of Europe treaties, including the European Convention on Human Rights. European law – particularly EU law and the ECHR – creates one of the most highly developed sets of binding transnational norms in the world, providing transnational standards for democracy, the rule of law, and human rights.

We have already noted that the major democracy-rating organizations now consider Hungary to no longer be a democracy, having fallen from being rated a consolidated democracy when Viktor Orbán first came to power in 2010 to being ranked a "hybrid regime" by 2020.[35] It is almost surely not possible to change the government of Hungary through elections, since the election system has been so distorted that it

[34] Dan Slater has usefully developed the concept of "democratic careening" to cover the situation in which governments engage in "a variety of unpredictable and alarming sudden movements, such as lurching, swerving, swaying, and threatening to tip over. It suggests a bandying back and forth from side to side, with no clear prospect for steadying in sight. It thus captures rather well the sense of endemic unsettledness and rapid ricocheting that characterizes democracies that are struggling but not collapsing." Dan Slater, *Democratic Careening*, 65 WORLD POL. 729 (2013).

[35] *See supra* note 19.

guarantees victory to the governing party almost no matter what its level of public support is.[36] Between being able to change the rules, threaten voters with dire consequences, hand out favors, and generate fake votes through an election machinery that it controls, the governing party in Hungary will almost surely never allow itself to lose an election. The 2022 Hungarian elections, rigged by the Orbán government, certainly confirmed that analysis – and the rule-of-law situation in Hungary deteriorated subsequently with the introduction of a "sovereignty protection law" that cut off all international support (including, by the way, EU support) to the civil sector, independent press, and Hungarian political parties.[37] Nonetheless, given that the Orbán government will have to fall sometime, or at least be suspended from European institutions in the meantime,[38] it is worth considering what compliance with the rule of law writ large would require in order to return Hungary to European good graces.

When the Law and Justice Party (PiS in Polish acronym) captured the presidency and both houses of the Polish parliament in 2015, the new government immediately attacked judicial independence in a particularly brutal and lawless way.[39] Refusing to abide by many European Court of Justice (ECJ) and European Court of Human Rights (ECtHR) decisions, the government simply stonewalled European institutions that were trying to restore the rule of law. Because the PiS government had not completely captured the election law, though it had tilted the playing field in its direction, the 2023 Polish national election was still able to produce a new government in Warsaw, one that had the theoretical possibility of

[36] Scheppele, *supra* note 21.

[37] Lili Bayer, *Orbán Accused of Trying to Silence All Critics in Hungary with New Law*, GUARDIAN (Nov. 23, 2023), https://tinyurl.com/2y2esumb.

[38] The Council of Europe can suspend membership of a signatory state. Nonetheless, it has rarely used this power, not least because, with the rapid expansion of the CoE in the 1990s, many of its states never met the basic standards of the organization and so votes in the Parliamentary Assembly to suspend members are invariably close or fail. It took the Russian invasion of Ukraine in 2022 to cause it to be expelled, despite years of noncompliance with CoE values. For the basic framework, see Kanstantsin Dzehtsiarou & Donal K Coffey, *Suspension and Expulsion of Members of the Council of Europe: Difficult Decisions in Troubled Times*, 68 INT'L & COMP. L.Q. 443 (2019). The EU simply has no way to expel a member state. The most it can do to sideline a member state is to remove its vote in the Council and strip it of its other EU privileges through the invocation of Article 7 TEU, which has such a high threshold for activation that it is for all intents and purposes a dead letter. Dimitry Kochenov, *Article 7: A Commentary on a Much Talked-About "Dead" Provision*, *in* DEFENDING CHECKS AND BALANCES IN EU MEMBER STATES (Armin von Bogdandy et al. eds., 2021).

[39] Kim Lane Scheppele, *The Treaties Without a Guardian: The European Commission and the Rule of Law*, 29 COLUM. J. EUR. L. 93, 124–48 (2023).

actually carrying out a Transition 2.0 to restore the rule of law. How could the new democratic government use transnational law to bring its own legal system back to democratic health?

In this part, then, I will elaborate on how the Hungarian and Polish governments could use the law of the transnational organizations they joined before their episodes of democratic backsliding as a blueprint for democratic reform. In the Polish case, this can even be seen as a practical road map for how to organize a democratic transition.

### 1 *Enforcing Directly Applicable Transnational Law*

In the EU, the principles of direct effect and primacy mean that Union law is already binding inside the national legal orders of its member states so that EU law takes precedence over national law and is directly applicable by national courts.[40] Within the CoE, decisions of the ECtHR are binding, in the narrow sense that the just satisfaction awarded to the petitioners who brought the cases must be paid, and in the broader sense that general measures must be taken by the offending state within its domestic legal order to put an end to the continuing violations found by the Court.[41]

For a new rule-of-law-minded government, the first order of business should be to bring national legal systems into compliance with the law that is already directly binding on their states through court judgments directly applicable to their states that their backsliding governments flouted. Court judgments have already matched the law to the facts, and have produced rulings that explain what it would take to comply given the specific situation. Complying with these decisions should be low-hanging fruit if a new government wants to act quickly, because no further investigation is needed to figure out how national law infringes the transnational standard and what can be done to meet it.

In the cases of Hungary and Poland, there are backlogs of ECJ judgments that are still not honored. Complying with those decisions should be an uncontroversial place to start to restore the rule of law in these countries.

[40] Bruno de Witte, *Direct Effect, Primacy, and the Nature of the Legal Order*, *in* THE EVOLUTION OF EU LAW (Paul Craig & Gráinne de Búrca eds., 3d ed. 2021), https://doi.org/10.1093/oso/9780192846556.003.0007.

[41] EUROPEAN COURT OF HUMAN RIGHTS, GUIDE ON ARTICLE 46 OF THE EUROPEAN CONVENTION ON HUMAN RIGHTS: BINDING FORCE AND EXECUTION OF JUDGMENTS (Aug. 31, 2022), www.echr.coe.int/Documents/Guide_Art_46_ENG.pdf.

In Poland, these judgments primarily concern the structure and independence of the judiciary.[42] For starters, complying with the ECJ judgments would mean replacing the Disciplinary Chamber of the Supreme Court with a truly independent body and reinstating the judges who have been inappropriately disciplined.[43] It should also mean reconfiguring the National Judicial Council, the allegedly self-governing body of the national judiciary that – among other things – selects judges, so that the political influence in the selection of members of this body is reduced.[44] The procedures under which judges are disciplined for making preliminary references to the ECJ must be reformed.[45] And so on, through the growing set of judicial independence cases of the ECJ, comprising both the infringement decisions and the judgments based on preliminary references.

In Hungary, the unenforced ECJ judgments affecting the restoration of the rule of law primarily concern the application of EU asylum rules,[46] measures that must be taken to ensure the free operation of civil society and universities,[47] and ensuring that judges can continue to make preliminary references to the ECJ.[48] And of course, a member state does not have to wait for an ECJ final judgment to rectify specific problems that the Commission has identified through initiating infringement actions. Hungary could get out ahead of the ECJ rulings by addressing the Commission's complaints with regard to the enactment of a discriminatory law against LGBTIQ+

[42] For details about the set of judgments against Poland brought as the result of infringement actions by the European Commission, see Scheppele, *supra* note 39.

[43] Case C-791/19, Comm'n v. Poland (Independence of Judges), ECLI:EU:C:2021:596 (July 15, 2021).

[44] Case C-585/18, A.K. and Others (Independence of the Disciplinary Chamber of the Supreme Court), ECLI:EU:C:2019:982, ¶ 140 (Nov. 19, 2019).

[45] Joined Cases C-558/18 & C-563/18, Miasto Łowicz & Prokurator Generalny, ECLI:EU:C:2020:234, ¶ 58 (Mar. 26, 2020). Because the underlying legal issue before the judge referring the case did not directly invoke EU law, the Court held that the questions sent by the referring judge were inadmissible. But in dicta, the Court made it abundantly clear that threats to punish judges for referring questions to the ECJ were unlawful.

[46] Case C-808/18, Comm'n v. Hungary (Accueil des demandeurs de protection internationale), ECLI:EU:C:2020:1029 (Dec. 17, 2020).

[47] Case C-821/19, Comm'n v. Hungary (Incrimination de l'aide aux demandeurs d'asile), ECLI:EU:C:2021:93 (Nov. 16, 2021); Case C-66/18, Comm'n v. Hungary (Enseignement supérieur), ECLI:EU:C:2020:792 (Oct. 6, 2020).

[48] Case C-564/19, I.S., ECLI:EU:C:2021:949 (Nov. 23, 2021). For a detailed explanation of the judgment and the backstory, see Kim Lane Scheppele, *The Law Requires Translation: The Hungarian Reference Case on Reference Cases, Case C-564/19, I.S., Judgment of the Court of Justice (Grand Chamber), 23 November 2021*, 59 Common Mkt. L. Rev. 1107 (2022).

community members[49] and the refusal to relicense *Klúbrádió,* Hungary's last independent radio station, as independent media in Hungary face extinction,[50] among other infringement actions already in play.

A new set of EU legal regulations that came into effect in 2021 now allows the EU to freeze funds to member states that violate the rule of law. The Conditionality Regulation[51] has been invoked against Hungary because its high levels of corruption mean that the country cannot be counted on to spend EU funds properly. The regulation establishing the Recovery and Resilience Fund[52] has allowed the EU institutions to freeze funds to states that do not heed EU warnings about high levels of corruption and weakening judicial independence. As a result of changes to the Common Provisions Regulation,[53] the EU can also now make the flow of funds allocated under a myriad of other programs conditional on member states honoring the Charter of Fundamental Rights. Now, member states against which these conditionalities have been triggered have an additional set of requirements specifically addressed to them that they must meet before they can receive EU funds.[54] To date, the conditions attached to the receipt of EU funds have included mandatory measures to

49 The Commission decided to refer Hungary to the ECJ in July 2022 over its law to prevent children from having contact with any media portraying gay couples. *July Infringement Package: Key Decisions*, EUR. COMM'N (July 15, 2022), https://ec.europa.eu/commission/presscorner/detail/en/inf_22_3768.

50 The Commission referred Hungary to the ECJ in July 2022 over its denial of a broadcast license to Klubrádió, the country's last remaining independent radio station. *Media Freedom: The Commission Refers Hungary to the Court of Justice of the European Union for Failure to Comply with EU Electronic Communications Rules*, EUR. COMM'N (July 15, 2022), https://ec.europa.eu/commission/presscorner/detail/en/IP_22_2688.

51 Regulation (EU/Euratom) 2020/2092 of the European Parliament and of the Council of 16 December 2020 on a General Regime of Conditionality for the Protection of the Union Budget, 2020 O.J. (L 433I) 1.

52 Regulation (EU) 2021/241 of the European Parliament and of the Council of 12 February 2021 Establishing the Recovery and Resilience Facility, 2021 O.J. (L 57) 17.

53 Regulation (EU) 2021/1060 of the European Parliament and of the Council of 24 June 2021 Laying Down Common Provisions on the European Regional Development Fund, the European Social Fund Plus, the Cohesion Fund, the Just Transition Fund and the European Maritime, Fisheries and Aquaculture Fund and Financial Rules for Those and for the Asylum, Migration and Integration Fund, the Internal Security Fund and the Instrument for Financial Support for Border Management and Visa Policy, 2021 O.J. (L 231) 159.

54 On three legal bases for funding conditionalities and how they were invoked against Hungary and Poland in 2022, see Kim Lane Scheppele & John Morijn, *What Price Rule of Law?*, *in* THE RULE OF LAW IN THE EU: CRISIS AND SOLUTIONS 29 (Anna Södersten & Edwin Hercock, eds., 2013), www.sieps.se/globalassets/publikationer/2023/2023_1op_digital.pdf.

fight corruption (in the case of Hungary),[55] detailed requirements for the restoration of the structural independence of the judiciary (in the case of both Hungary and Poland)[56] and specific changes to domestic law and practice to ensure the realization of rights protected by the Charter of Fundamental Rights, which include gender equality rights (in the case of both Hungary and Poland) as well as asylum rights and academic freedom (in the case of Hungary).[57]

Conditionalities that come with this newly passed set of regulations at EU level are specific to each backsliding country, identify in detail what a member state must do to fix the problems, and come with oversight and enforcement mechanisms to ensure that member states meet their legal obligations. Surely, given the specificity of these diagnoses and remedies, these nationally targeted requirements must also be included among the changes that any new democratic government in a formerly rogue state must enact.

While the Council of Europe has much weaker enforcement powers than does the EU, the decisions of the European Court of Human Rights are binding on signatories to the European Convention on Human Rights. Increasingly, particularly in regard to violations that are likely to produce repeated cases, the CoE Committee of Minister (which is charged with enforcing ECtHR judgments) has been insisting on structural reforms in countries where violations form a pattern. They have opened enhanced supervision procedures against delinquent signatory

[55] Council Implementing Decision (EU) 2022/2506 of 15 December 2022 on Measures for the Protection of the Union Budget against Breaches of the Principles of the Rule of Law in Hungary, 2022 O.J. (L 325) 94, https://eur-lex.europa.eu/legal-content/EN/TXT/PDF/?uri=CELEX:32022D2506.

[56] Council Implementing Decision of 5 December 2022 on the Approval of the Assessment of the Recovery and Resilience Plan for Hungary, Interinstitutional File 2022/0414 (NLE), https://data.consilium.europa.eu/doc/document/ST-15447-2022-INIT/en/pdf; Council Implementing Decision of 14 June 2022 on the Approval of the Assessment of the Recovery and Resilience Plan for Poland, Interinstitutional File 2022/0181 (NLE), https://data.consilium.europa.eu/doc/document/ST-9728-2022-INIT/en/pdf. In the case of Hungary, these requirements for restoring judicial independence go well beyond anything that the ECJ has specified for Hungary, while in the case of Poland the ECJ decisions go beyond what the Commission has required Poland to change to receive EU funds.

[57] Press Release, EU Cohesion Policy 2021–2027: Investing in a Fair Climate and Digital Transition While Strengthening Hungary's Administrative Capacity, Transparency and Prevention of Corruption (2022), https://tinyurl.com/mm6k4xah; Press Release, European Commission, EU Cohesion Policy: Commission Adopts €76.5 Billion Partnership Agreement with Poland for 2021–2027 (June 30, 2022), https://ec.europa.eu/commission/presscorner/detail/en/ip_22_4223.

states to ensure that they do more than simply pay just satisfaction awards to the applicants.

Here, the so far unheeded major ECtHR decisions with regard to Hungary include an open case requiring the protection of judges both from arbitrary dismissal and from violation of their free speech rights,[58] as well as a number of cases with regard to discrimination against Roma, the abuse of pretrial detention, violations of asylum rights, and the creation of an unlimited surveillance system without legal constraints,[59] among others.

Poland has an even worse track record at the ECtHR, compounded by the fact that it gave formal notice in February 2023 that it would refuse to comply with any interim measures ordered by that Court.[60] As of that time, the ECtHR had received 60 requests for interim measures (that is, injunctions) against Poland for matters involving the nonindependence of the judiciary, with 323 cases pending on this issue before the Court.[61]

58 Shortly after the Orbán government was elected in 2010, the then Supreme Court president András Baka was removed from office, three years before the end of his lawful term. His removal occurred through the operation of a new law, which renamed the Supreme Court the Kúria and created a new qualification for serving on this "new" court – namely, that all Kúria judges should have at least five years of judicial experience on the ordinary courts in Hungary. Because President Baka had only three years of judicial experience in Hungary and his seventeen years as a judge on the ECtHR did not count under the law, he was disqualified – the only Supreme Court judge who was removed on the basis of the new qualification. His case at the ECtHR challenging his dismissal confirmed that he had been punished, in violation of his ECHR rights, for having criticized the Hungarian government's changes to the judiciary. Baka v. Hungary, App. No. 0261/12, ECLI:CE:ECHR:2016:0623JUD002026112 (June 23, 2016). This decision has still not been honored by Hungary, which remains under enhanced supervision on the matter. In a hearing in September 2021, the Council of Europe's Committee of Ministers noted "a continuing absence of safeguards in connection with *ad hominem* constitutional-level measures terminating a judicial mandate" and pressed the Hungarian government to adopt "effective and adequate safeguards against abuse when it comes to restrictions on judges' freedom of expression." Committee of Ministers Decision CM/Del/Dec(2021)1411/H46-16, Supervision of the Execution of the European Court's Judgments, H46-16 Baka v. Hungary (App. No. 20261/12), ¶¶ 314–16 (Sept. 16, 2021), https://tinyurl.com/yc4p4xuf.

59 For a list of the major pending cases awaiting execution by Hungary at the Committee of Ministers, see https://rm.coe.int/mi-hungary-eng/1680a23c92.

60 Press Release, European Court of Human Rights, Non-Compliance with Interim Measures in Polish Judiciary Cases, ECHR 053 (2023) (Feb. 16, 2023), https://tinyurl.com/32afd63c.The new government elected in 2023 withdrew this notice to the Court, but cannot easily comply with the decisions given that the national president and the Constitutional Tribunal can block new legislation and both institutions are filled with partisans of the last government.

61 *Id.*

The ECtHR has found, among other things, that the Constitutional Tribunal, the Disciplinary Chamber of the Polish Supreme Court and the Extraordinary Chamber of the Polish Supreme Court are not independent and impartial tribunals established by law due to the presence of judges appointed irregularly either by the parliament (in the case of the Constitutional Tribunal)[62] or by the politically tainted National Judicial Council (in the case of the Supreme Court chambers).[63] Any new Polish government should address these issues by changing the structure and membership of these institutions, guided by decisions of the ECtHR.

Both Poland and Hungary are also now subject to monitoring by the Parliamentary Assembly of the Council of Europe (PACE). In January 2020, PACE voted to put Poland under a monitoring regime, calling for Poland to separate the functions of justice minister and public prosecutor, to reduce the discretionary powers of the justice minister, to reverse political appointments to two new chambers of the Supreme Court, and to establish an independent public inquiry into smear campaigns against judges and prosecutors.[64] In October 2022, PACE voted similarly to put Hungary under monitoring, calling upon the government to reduce the number of laws requiring supermajority votes, to restore a level playing field for elections, to cancel the ongoing state of emergency that had been in effect since 2020, and to carry out a list of seventeen other changes for improve the functioning of democratic institutions.[65]

In considering how Hungary and/or Poland might now bring their domestic legal systems into line with transnational values, compliance with these ECJ and ECtHR decisions as well as the direct requirements under both the conditionality decisions of the EU institutions and the direct recommendations of the PACE would be an important place to start.

62 Xero Flor w Polsce sp. z o.o. v. Poland, App. No. 4907/18 (May 7, 2021), ECLI:CE:ECHR:2021:0507JUD000490718.

63 Advance Pharma v. Poland, App. No. 1469/20 (Feb. 3, 2022), ECLI:CE:ECHR:2022:0203JUD000146920; Reczkowicz v. Poland, App. No. 43447/19 (July 22, 2021), ECLI:CU:ECHR:2021:0722JUD004344719; Dolińska-Ficek & Ozimek v. Poland, App. Nos. 49868/19 & 57511/19 (Feb. 8, 2022), ECLI:CE:ECHR:2021:1108JUD004986819; Wałęsa v. Poland, App. No. 50849/21 (Nov. 23, 2023).

64 *PACE Decides to Open Monitoring of Poland over Rule of Law*, Parliamentary Assembly of the Council of Eur. (Jan. 28, 2020), https://tinyurl.com/3sebc5mf.

65 *PACE Votes to Begin Monitoring of Hungary over Rule of Law and Democracy Issues*, Parliamentary Assembly of the Council of Eur. (Oct. 12, 2022), https://tinyurl.com/2s3jyjrc.

## 2 Erga Omnes *Effects of Transnational Law*

While compliance with the direct decisions of European courts and direct actions taken by the European Commission will begin the process of recovering transnational values in the rogue member states, compliance with only the concrete decisions issued against any particular member state will not be enough for these states to fully restore the rule of law in the domestic legal order. The Commission, in particular, has been very slow to recognize the damage that these rogue governments have done to their constitutional institutions and has therefore not flagged even the major issues that have been responsible for the most serious backsliding.[66] As a result, new governments in these countries do not have a dense and specific case law from the ECJ that would be helpful in precisely guiding them back to the path to harmonizing national law with EU law. In some cases, we have ECtHR decisions that fill some of these gaps in EU law,[67] but the case-by-case way in which the dismantling of constitutional government has been treated in European law means that there is not a complete blueprint of what these rogue states should do to come back into compliance with transnational values, at least not if one looks only at the cases and directions that have the proper names of the particular states attached.

Thus, it will be important for rogue member states that are determined to work their way back into the good graces of European law to consider the way in which European law – both EU law and broader ECHR human rights law – has been applied in respect of other states and to take on board reforms that compliance with this law would necessitate even when the rogue state in question has never been singled out for its violations. Any new government in a formerly rogue state should assess all of its laws against this thick background of European law to see what must be changed to bring the national law into compliance with transnational law. The *erga omnes* effects of all ECJ decisions are well

[66] On the many key issues missed by the Commission just with regard to judicial independence in Hungary and Poland, see Scheppele, *supra* note 39. Of course, the EU does not have jurisdiction over many issues that have contributed to the worsening of the rule of law in Hungary and Poland, but the Commission has been very slow to bring cases against the rogue states even in areas that are squarely within EU law.

[67] The ECtHR can rule on all matters that violate ECHR rights; the EU is limited to considering violations of the Charter of Fundamental Rights only insofar as those violations occur when the member state is acting within the scope of EU law.

documented;[68] the *erga omnes* effects of ECtHR decisions have been persuasively argued to be implied in the ECHR itself.[69]

Of course, this is a huge task because it requires working out not only how the rules should apply within a particular country across the whole range of European law, but also specifically what it is about the rogue country's law that violates transnational law. In this regard, direct compliance with decisions carrying the proper name of the country is much easier because the tough job of fitting rules to facts to see whether compliance has been achieved has already been done in those cases.

Moreover, since the Commission largely ignored the consolidation of power in the hands of the Fidesz governing party over the decade-plus that the Orbán government has been in office, there are as a result no ECJ judgments directly bearing on the most crucial features of Hungarian autocracy, like the capture of formerly independent institutions including the media authority, prosecutor's office, state audit office, election office, data protection office, or the central bank.[70] Nor are there cases about the years of emergency rule that started in 2020, during which the parliament gave the government the power to issue decrees that overwrite statutes. This period extends far longer if one counts the more targeted "migration emergency" that began in 2015. Nor are there cases challenging the way in which markets have been manipulated to reduce pluralism in the media and to stifle competition in state contracts for matters of "strategic national importance." And, perhaps most shockingly, Hungary has compromised the independence of its judiciary in a myriad of ways that the Commission had never criticized until it imposed some limited conditionalities under the Recovery and Resilience Regulation and the Common Provisions Regulation. Moreover, national courts have been cowed into submission by a domestic constitutional provision that puts certain topics off-limits for

[68] *Erga omnes* authority of EU law can be traced to Article 4(3) TEU, which obligates member states to refrain from any measure that would frustrate the realization of EU objectives. *See also* Case 66/80, SpA International Chemical Corporation v. Amministrazione delle finanze dello Stato, ECLI:EU:C:1981:102, ¶¶ 11–13 (May 13, 1981).

[69] Oddný Mjöll Arnardóttir, *Res Interpretata, Erga Omnes Effect and the Role of the Margin of Appreciation in Giving Domestic Effect to the Judgments of the European Court of Human Rights*, 28 EUR. J. INT'L L. 819 (2017).

[70] The Commission was active in some of these areas in 2011 when the takeovers began. Ultimately, the Commission initiated infringement procedures over the independence of the data protection officer who was fired in 2011 and over the independence of the central bank when the Orbán government tried to fire the sitting central bank governor. But in both cases the Commission only challenged treatment of the incumbent occupants of those offices and not the qualifications and structural guarantees of independence of the new occupants of those offices.

preliminary reference questions,[71] and under which judges have already been disciplined.[72] As a result, much of the damage already done to the Hungarian judiciary has not been the subject of any legal proceeding at EU level ordering Hungary to fix it.[73] ECtHR decisions in Hungarian cases fill in some of the gaps, but even they do not even begin to identify all of the ways in which the Hungarian government no longer complies with European standards. Extrapolating requirements for judicial independence that have been established in cases involving other CoE signatory states – particularly Poland – to the Hungarian context would go a long way toward undoing the compromises of judicial independence that have already taken place. But it would take patient work to develop the application of this law to Hungary.

With regard to Poland, the Commission and the ECJ have focused primarily on judicial independence, issuing specific, binding instructions to Poland on how judicial independence can be restored. But there are signs that Poland is also in breach of other important legal obligations, particularly with regard to nontransparent and unjustifiable surveillance of the political opposition using stealthy software that infiltrates cell phones.[74] Pegasus software has been in documented use in both Hungary and Poland, but so far only Hungary is under direct decisions of the ECtHR to bring its legally unlimited surveillance program under

[71] Fundamental Law (Hung.) art. E(2):

> With a view to participating in the European Union as a Member State and on the basis of an international treaty, Hungary may, to the extent necessary to exercise the rights and fulfil the obligations deriving from the Founding Treaties, exercise some of its competences arising from the Fundamental Law jointly with other Member States, through the institutions of the European Union. Exercise of competences under this paragraph shall comply with the fundamental rights and freedoms provided for in the Fundamental Law and *shall not limit the inalienable right of Hungary to determine its territorial unity, population, form of government and state structure.*

English translation issued by Hungarian Ministry of Justice (emphasis added), https://njt.hu/jogszabaly/en/2011-4301-02-00 (last visited Aug. 23, 2024).

The Kúria has interpreted this italicized clause to mean questions touching on those subjects may not be the subject of preliminary references.

[72] For more detail, see Scheppele, *supra* note 48.

[73] The "super milestones" built into the Recovery Plan in order for Hungary to receive the relevant EU funds require judicial reforms, but the list of specific items listed there is not sufficient to restore judicial independence in its entirety.

[74] *Polish Leader Admits Government Bought Spyware*, DW (July 1, 2022), https://tinyurl.com/bdf62wmp.

legal control so that the rights to private life under Article 8 ECHR are respected.[75] If Poland is committing the same violation – using technical tools to spy on the political opposition outside meaningful legal constraints that honor ECHR rights – then it too should modify its laws to comply with the ECtHR's standards, even absent a direct judgment about its own particular practices.

Of course, establishing the *erga omnes* effects of the huge body of EU and ECHR law will not be easy or quick. Among other things, it first involves an analysis of what EU and ECHR law requires with enough specificity to guide lawmaking within a restored democratic government. But requiring changes to domestic law to meet the standards required of other countries by transnational courts would certainly not violate the rule of law and, in my view, would honor the rule of law writ large.

## 3 *Supererogatory Effects of Transnational Law*

Beyond directly applicable binding law exists a web of best practices and general standards – soft law – that could also provide useful guidance for Transition 2.0. Within the Organization for Security and Co-operation in Europe (OSCE), for example, human rights rapporteurs and election monitors make recommendations and assessments that are not binding on governments they examine in the strict legal sense. But since these expert assessments examine the particular track record of particular countries in a nuanced way and provide recommendations for how to

[75] The cases so far decided by the ECtHR predate the discovery of Pegasus in Hungary, but the legal authorizations under which Pegasus was used were already held to have not met ECtHR standards. For the standards, see Szabó & Vissy v. Hungary, App. No. 37138/14 (Jan. 12, 2016), ECLI:CE:ECHR:2016:0112JUD003713814. The European Court of Human Rights again confirmed in September 2022 its finding that the Hungarian government has no meaningful checks on domestic police surveillance, Hüttl v. Hungary, App. No. 58032/16 (Sept. 29, 2022), ECLI:CE:ECHR:2022:0929JUD005803216. More recently, the Hungarian government admitted to using the cellphone infiltration software Pegasus against journalists and government critics, but the data protection officer determined that the use of Pegasus was legal under Hungarian law. NEMZETI ADATVÉDELMI ÉS INFORMÁCIÓSZABADSÁG HATÓSÁG (Hungarian National Authority for Data Protection and Freedom of Information), FINDINGS OF THE INVESTIGATION LAUNCHED EX OFFICIO CONCERNING THE APPLICATION OF THE "PEGASUS" SPYWARE IN HUNGARY (2022), https://tinyurl.com/ywh4cxm3y. Since the initial exposé of the Pegasus surveillance, new investigative reporting has uncovered evidence that the Hungarian government has purchased from foreign sellers a whole range of deep surveillance tools beyond Pegasus. Szabolcs Pányi, *Boosting of Spying Capabilities Stokes Fear Hungary is Building a Surveillance State*, BALKAN INSIGHT (Oct. 13, 2022), https://tinyurl.com/mpdfhhnf.

improve national law on particular subjects, these opinions could also be used as guides for democratic reconstitution.

For example, the Office of Democratic Institutions and Human Rights (ODIHR) at the OSCE routinely engages in election monitoring, writing detailed reports about national election health and recommending specific changes. The report from the 2022 national election in Hungary listed a total of thirty recommended changes to Hungary's election system, eleven of which were priority recommendations to remedy the lack of a level playing field, the weaknesses in the legal framework, the lack of adequate judicial review of election disputes, and unequal access to the media, and to ensure improved election observation and equal treatment of non-resident voters, among other things.[76] In the Polish election of 2023, which the opposition won, the report was more positive, but still identified a number of specific weaknesses in the electoral system, including the undue influence by the governing party over state resources and public media during the campaign as well as the failure to achieve a separation of state and party.[77] These, and the other recommendations made by the ODIHR should be a top priority for changes before the next general election.

The Venice Commission of the Council of Europe, while having no enforcement capacity or even binding force behind its recommendations, assesses particular laws of specific states and makes recommendations grounded in its understanding of transnational legal requirements. Rogue states have already been evaluated under these various rubrics and transnational bodies of neutral experts have found fault with the laws and/or practices of the states in question.[78] Bringing a state into

[76] Office for Democratic Insts. & Human Rights [ODIHR], OSCE, Hungary: Parliamentary Elections and Referendum, 3 April 2022; ODIHR Election Observation Mission Final Report (July 29, 2022), www.osce.org/files/f/documents/2/6/523568.pdf.

[77] Office for Democratic Insts. & Human Rights [ODIHR], OSCE, Poland: Parliamentary Elections, 15 October 2023; Statement of Preliminary Findings and Conclusions (Oct. 15, 2023), www.osce.org/files/f/documents/2/4/555048.pdf. The final report was issued subsequent to this writing; see Office for Democratic Insts. & Human Rights [ODIHR], OSCE, Poland: Parliamentary Elections, 15 October 2023; ODIHR Limited Election Observation Mission Final Report (Mar. 27, 2024), www.osce.org/files/f/documents/b/8/565423_1.pdf.

[78] As of this writing, the Venice Commission has issued twenty-two opinions with regard to Hungary since Viktor Orbán came to power in 2010 and began his constitutional revolution, covering matters from the new constitution to judicial reform, attempts to restrict the civil sector, the election laws, the media laws, educational reform, the

compliance with these reports and recommendations would not strictly be legally required, but such compliance would be a sign that a state was eager to demonstrate its commitment to transnational values.

This *supererogatory* effect of transnational law – supererogatory because the standards so elaborated are the authoritative opinions of bodies that have the power to counsel but not to enforce – would be particularly useful in areas of law that must be changed to ensure that the return to transnational values is robust, but that neither the EU nor the CoE have within their remit to insist upon in a strict legal sense. Election law, for example, is not clearly under the jurisdiction of the EU, save with regard to some general parameters of European parliamentary elections (for example, proportional representation) and with regard to some rules that apply in national elections at local level in which EU citizens have the right to vote (for example, European nondiscrimination principles with regard to citizenship).[79] And while there is a growing body of case law at the ECtHR interpreting ECHR Protocol 1, Article 3, on the right to vote,[80] that jurisprudence has not yet reached the point of giving legally binding guidance on technical questions like the proper constitution of electoral administration bodies,[81] the rules for campaign spending, how

organization of the public prosecutor's office, and various constitutional amendments. The Venice Commission has issued six opinions with regard to Poland since the PiS government came to power in 2015, on topics ranging from attacks on the judiciary to alarming changes in the election law. *See Documents by Opinions and Studies*, Council of Eur. (Venice Comm'n), www.venice.coe.int/webforms/documents/by_opinion.aspx?v=countries.

79 That said, scholars are now starting to argue that Article 10 TEU requires member states of the EU to be democratic across all of its elections rather than just at the time of elections to the European Parliament or in which European citizens can participate outside their countries of citizenship. *See, e.g.*, John Cotter, *To Everything There is a Season: Instrumentalising Article 10 TEU to Exclude Undemocratic Member State Representatives from the European Council and the Council*, 47 Eur. L. Rev. 69 (2022); Luke Dimitry Spieker, *Beyond the Rule of Law How the Court of Justice can Protect Conditions for Democratic Change*, *in* The Rule of Law in the EU: Crisis and Solutions, *supra* note 54, at 72.

80 European Court of Human Rights, Guide on Article 3 of Protocol No. 1 to the European Convention on Human Rights (Aug. 31, 2022), www.echr.coe.int/Documents/Guide_Art_3_Protocol_1_ENG.pdf.

81 The African Court on Human and Peoples' Rights is out ahead on this question. *See* Actions pour la Protection des Droits de l'Homme (APDH) v. Côte d'Ivoire, No. 001/2014, Judgment, African Court on Human and Peoples' Rights (Nov. 18, 2016), https://tinyurl.com/3pn458z3. In this case, the Court found that an election monitoring body composed of eight representatives of government and four of the opposition out of a total of seventeen representatives was not independent or impartial, or compatible with requirements of equal treatment.

to draw legislative districts, what methods are acceptable for counting "lost votes" in proportional representation schemes, and other such issues. By contrast, however, the Venice Commission has elaborated detailed standards for elections[82] and the ODIHR has compiled international standards[83] that it uses as the basis for monitoring elections and issuing recommendations to the specific states it has observed.[84] Taking on board these recommendations would be a good way to move election law away from being tilted in favor of the former governing party and toward a more level playing field.

As a formerly rogue state attempts to restore the rule of law, guidance from transnational institutions on the rule of law itself may be particularly useful in marking out the important parameters of domestic legal change. In particular, the Venice Commission has developed *The Rule of Law Checklist*, which could guide just such an effort.[85] Its definition of the rule of law as "a system of certain and foreseeable law, where everyone has the right to be treated by all decision-makers with dignity, equality and rationality and in accordance with the laws, and to have the opportunity to challenge decisions before independent and impartial courts through fair procedures,"[86] can provide overarching guidance on what a domestic legal system must strive to accomplish. Its more specific benchmarks identify achievable steps on the way to producing such a system. For example – to take one problem that has arisen in a particularly vivid way in Hungary as the country prolongs a series of states of emergency in which the prime minister has the power to override any law by decree – the Venice Commission standards ensure that exceptions to the supremacy of legislation remain limited in time

[82] For a list of the various standards that the Venice Commission has developed in the field of election law, see *Council of Europe Standards in the Electoral Field*, COUNCIL OF EUR. (VENICE COMM'N), www.venice.coe.int/WebForms/pages/?p=01_01_Coe_electoral_standards.

[83] For a list of the international standards for elections of the ODIHR, see *International Standards for Elections*, ORG. FOR SEC. & COOP. IN EUR., www.osce.org/odihr/elections/66040.

[84] The ODIHR has monitored elections in Hungary for decades; *see Elections in Hungary*, ORG. FOR SEC. & COOP. IN EUR., www.osce.org/odihr/elections/hungary. It has also monitored elections in Poland for decades; *see Elections in Poland*, ORG. FOR SEC. & COOP. IN EUR., www.osce.org/odihr/elections/poland. The specific recommendations in each report could be used to improve on the democratic responsiveness of the electoral system.

[85] COUNCIL OF EUR. (VENICE COMM'N), THE RULE OF LAW CHECKLIST (2016), www.venice.coe.int/images/SITE%20IMAGES/Publications/Rule_of_Law_Check_List.pdf.

[86] *Id.* at 10.

and scope and that any delegations of lawmaking power to the executive are explicitly defined.[87] As the Venice Commission says directly: "Unlimited powers of the executive are, de jure or de facto, a central feature of absolutist and dictatorial systems. Modern constitutionalism has been built against such systems and therefore ensures supremacy of the legislature."[88] Extended rule by decree would have to be abolished if these guidelines were followed. And the checklist would help to spot many more offending laws and practices that would have to be changed to restore democratic health.

Supererogatory compliance with transnational standards does not mean that a new government would be simply making up good things to do on its own remit or that a new government is installing its political preferences on a whim. As the examples of election law and the rule-of-law checklist make clear, standards already exist to ensure that democratic, human-rights-respecting, rule-of-law governments can be created and maintained, and they have a definite content that is precise enough to guide domestic lawmaking in very specific directions. These standards gain strength in the process of restoring democratic government precisely because they stand outside the domestic constitutional order and therefore cannot be changed, gamed, or bargained by the parties to the domestic transition.

External standards ensure that there can be no domestically dirty trade-offs in these transitions, in which one side gets to maintain control of the courts in exchange for the other side being able to control the media, for example. Standards must all be met in their entirety and not gamed in the transitions back to democracy. As guidelines external to the process of democratic transition, they maintain their ability to serve as rules of the game that cannot become part of the game itself.

## V Asymmetric Rupture: Breaking the Law to Establish the Rule of Law in Recovering Democracies

As we have seen, the rule of law writ large assesses rule-of-law compliance across multiple legal levels at the same time – both national and transnational – by examining the way that the levels complement and reinforce each other. The rule of law writ large exists when different levels of law do not pull in different directions, putting those who are

[87] *Id.* at 20.
[88] *Id.*

simultaneously bound by those different levels of law into a bind of conflicting legal obligations. The rule of law writ large exists when common values thread through all of the levels at once without contradiction. By contrast, the rule of law writ small considers only the national level, so a domestic legal system can be coherent, consistent, and enforcing rules as written, but nonetheless exist in tension with other levels that remain outside the scope of examination. Autocracy can maintain some highly formal version of the rule of law inside a state as long as the domestic legal system is not required to justify itself externally.[89] When autocracy becomes entrenched through law in this way, however, it may become necessary – and justifiable – to break domestic law to restore democracy again.

Break the law to legitimate a new democratic government? Surely this sounds rather dangerous. From a distance, moves that may be taken by a democracy-restoring government could look just like the moves that were already taken by a democracy-crushing government. After all, didn't the rulers who installed rogue government win elections, change the laws comprehensively, fire incumbents who got in their way, and generally restructure the constitutional system so that the independence of all political and judicial institutions was subordinated to the political ideology of the governing party? A new democratizing government that is winning elections, changing the laws comprehensively, firing incumbents who get in the way, and restructuring independent institutions to match their democratic ideology may appear to be doing the same thing. It may be tit-for-tat, but that doesn't make it right.

But this is where transnational law is crucial to distinguishing the two scenarios. Reconfiguring a legal order, even if done in a formally legal manner, breaks the rule of law writ large when it is done by those who are destroying democracy, when transnational law requires adherence to democratic values. By contrast, those same activities of legal reconfiguration can restore the rule of law writ large when they are done by those who are committed to bringing the national legal system back into harmony with the transnational one. In short, while both kinds of moves produce ruptures in the domestic constitutional order – including sometimes breaking domestic law to achieve change – they do not have the same objective justifications or the same relationship to the rule of law when the rule of law is writ large instead of writ small. The legitimacy of the two ruptures is *asymmetric* in that one direction brings *more* rule of

[89] Scheppele, *supra* note 10.

law across different levels of legality and the other one brings *less*. Asymmetric ruptures to restore the rule of law writ large can therefore be justified in ways that symmetric ruptures to bring about a new rule of law writ small cannot.

But what about the *democratic* legitimation of such a course of action? All of this would be done over the heads of the democratic publics in whose name the new democrats govern, because the principles that would be taking priority – the transnational ones – would not have been voted for in the most recent election that brought the new government to power.

There are two important responses to this objection. First, the transnational obligations that are the sources of direct and *erga omnes* effects were in fact undertaken by previous democratic governments when they ratified treaties and joined the international organizations whose values they are. These principles were not imposed from outside but were undertaken as voluntary commitments to bind the signatory state into the future, much as a domestic constitution commits a government to basic principles beyond the term of a specific government. In fact, both the European Union and Council of Europe have provisions through which their members can quit and therefore bring themselves out from under the legal obligations that would otherwise attach to membership. Honoring international treaties is in many ways like honoring a national constitution. Treaties may not have been adopted by the current government, but they are also a solemn and long-term commitment meant to be carried forward by current and future governments. And, like constitutional revision or amendment, the legal obligations undertaken through treaties can be modified only by a solemn undertaking more complicated than ordinary legal enactments. The tensions between democracy and constitutionalism are well known, and the same tension exists between democracy and treaty commitments. This does not necessarily mean that honoring treaties is antidemocratic, particularly not as long as there is an exit option if a democratic state wants to move in a different direction.

Second, a new democratic government that feels it must break the laws of its predecessor in order to arrive at the rule of law writ large should not destroy more of the domestic rule of law than is absolutely necessary in order to harmonize across levels. A new government with the democratic wind in its sails needs to be both careful and public about what it is doing, maintaining a democratic spirit throughout the process even if it tramples on formal legality along the way. In this regard, parties that joined in a united Hungarian opposition in 2022 can serve as a model for how to do this. They actually put forward their plans to restore democracy by pledging to honor Hungary's European legal commitments and built these plans into their election platform.[90] If they had been elected, they would have taken the election result as a democratic ratification of their approach, including in the specific areas where they noted that they might have to break domestic law to come into compliance with European law.

After the Polish opposition won the 2023 parliamentary election, many of these same questions have arisen there. The Polish opposition did not agree on how to handle these transitional questions before the election, as the Hungarian opposition had, and so an agreement across the three coalition parties in the new government was struck only after the election. The coalition agreement vowed to reverse the damage to the judiciary inflicted by the PiS government and to nullify some decisions of the Polish Constitutional Tribunal holding that the Polish constitution is superior to EU law – a position at odds with EU legal doctrine.[91] That said, the coalition agreement did not say precisely how the parties would fix the damage to the judiciary, and from the start, fissures opened up in the new government's ranks over this. Some advocated that the new government fire all of the judges illegally appointed under the past government, while others advocated that only the unlawfully appointed court presidents, who have the power to control judges in their courts and assign specific cases to specific judges, be replaced. Their disagreements showed that even if, as

[90] The opposition legal transition committee consisted of Zoltán Fleck as chair with Péter Bárándy, Ágota Szentes, Richárd Nagy Szent Péteri, Kinga Surday, Gábor Attila Tóth, and Imre Vörös as members. They produced a nearly 100-page document called the *A jogállam helyreállításának kísérlete* [An Attempt to Restore the Rule of Law] in advance of the election, explaining in detail how the opposition would make changes to the law left behind by the Orbán government if they won. Many of these changes – nearly half of the document – consisted in precisely what I am suggesting here, which is to use EU and ECHR law to guide the transition. I am honored to have played a bit role in this development. *See* Scheppele, *supra* note 31. This was the first proposal along these lines, leaning on the technical fact within Hungarian law that the EU and ECHR treaties were themselves ratified by two-thirds votes of the Hungarian parliament in a system in which many of Orbán's offending laws were buffered from future change by also requiring a two-thirds vote. Because the Hungarian constitution specifies that treaties take precedence over ordinary statutes, the problem of conflicting EU and ECHR norms, on the one hand, and purely domestic norms, on the other, can be treated as a conflict-of-laws problem within Hungarian law and solved in a constitutional fashion, minimizing domestic rule-of-law violations.

[91] Piotr Müller, *Polish Opposition Groups Sign Agreement Setting Out Programme for Future Coalition Government*, NOTES FROM POLAND (Nov. 10, 2023), https://tinyurl.com/2ujrjcxp.

this chapter suggests, it may be possible work out legally what the democratic end-state should look like, there may be many controversies over the methods used to get there. This is not an easy problem, but the rule of law writ large provides a framework for the debate.

If a new government is going to engage in conduct that appears to violate the rule of law writ small in order to achieve the rule of law writ large, then the restoration of democracy should not be done furtively but should remain democratically accountable throughout the process. Law-breaking in the service of the rule of law writ large should be done openly, with clear explanation to democratic publics about why irregular procedures or other legal violations may be required in order to comply with basic principles of democracy, human rights, and the rule of law in the long run. Of course, the new democrats must put themselves before their publics in free, fair, and regular elections to get periodic endorsements (or rejections!) of their approach when their lawful terms end.

The legitimacy of this rule of law writ large strategy for restoring national rule of law is further enhanced by the "North Star" effect of transnational legal standards. Before the days of GPS, and even now among purists, sailors were guided on the open sea by reference to a fixed point of navigation that neither moved as they did nor was within their power to change. The North Star gained its strength as a navigation tool precisely by being fixed and outside the sailors' control, just the way that transnational law operates as a strong point of reference that is (relatively) fixed and outside the reach of change by any of the parties to any particular domestic transition. When democratic transitions are negotiated in constituent assemblies or in pacted transitional bodies, the superior bargaining power of current autocratic incumbents (or even of previous autocratic incumbents who used their incumbency to erect roadblocks to change) means that the new democrats may have to compromise on crucial issues that limit the sort of democracy that they can restore. Tying the debate to transnational standards honoring democracy, the rule of law, and human rights would reduce the power of rogue incumbents in the negotiations while simultaneously not licensing newly elected democrats to do to the prior autocratic incumbents what those aspirational autocrats did to them. When the standard to be achieved is set outside the range of either party's control, it acts like a North Star placing the steady point of navigation back to a safe democratic port outside the reach of those being guided.

By expanding our conception of the rule of law beyond national boundaries to encompass transnational law, particularly in an era when human rights courts and many transnational bodies are busily elaborating standards for democracy, human rights, and rule of law, we can develop a framework for encouraging the restoration of democracy in those places where it has been challenged. The conception of the rule of law writ large provides guidance for new democrats to use in bringing rogue states back into the democratic fold.

# 8

# Russia, the Council of Europe, and the Rule of Law

## Building and Dismantling "Our Common European Home"

JEFFREY KAHN

*In order to develop along the path of progress, the Russian authorities decided to join the Council of Europe. Russia has established the necessary organs and institutions of democratic governance. Perhaps they do not possess all the qualities attributable to truly democratic institutions. But this cannot be achieved in one day. It is only an illusion that Russia was liberal in the 1990s and is authoritarian today.*

—Dmitry Dedov, Russian judge at the European Court of Human Rights, 2013–22[1]

On July 6, 1989, Mikhail Gorbachev spoke before the Parliamentary Assembly of the Council of Europe.[2] At the time, Gorbachev was president of the Supreme Soviet of the Union of Soviet Socialist Republics and secretary-general of the Communist Party of the Soviet Union; eight months later, he would be elected by a new legislative body, the Congress of People's Deputies, as the first (and last) president of the Soviet Union. The Soviet Union was not a member of this international organization, but the newly created status of "special guest" had been conferred on it less than a month before Gorbachev's arrival in Strasbourg.[3]

[1] Dmitry Dedov, *Foreword, in* Russia and the European Court of Human Rights: The Strasbourg Effect xvii, xix (Lauri Mälksoo & Wolfgang Benedek eds., 2018).

[2] Speech by Mr. Mikhail Gorbachev Before the Parliamentary Assembly of the Council of Europe (July 6, 1989), Council of Europe Information Department, D(89)36.

[3] In his memoirs, Gorbachev writes: "The Parliamentary Assembly of the Council of Europe (PACE) decided to give the Soviet Union the status of a 'specially invited state.' The invitation extended to me to speak at the PACE meeting in Strasbourg was the logical result of such a development of events." 2 Михаил Горбачев [Mikhail Gorbachev], Жизнь и реформы [Life and reforms] 194 (1995). (Unless otherwise noted, all

His speech built on the metaphor of constructing a "common European home" for his country with those to its west. Like his twin pursuits of *glasnost'* ("openness" of access to information and tolerance of public criticism) and *perestroika* ("restructuring" of Soviet economic and, later, political systems), both of which ultimately involved substantial legal reforms, this idea of a common European home was not a fully formed or static vision. "I do not claim to carry a finished blueprint of that home in my pocket," he said. "I just wish to tell you what I believe to be most important."[4]

Gorbachev stressed that this common European home should be built on "security issues," viz., nuclear disarmament and conventional force reductions. "The philosophy of the concept of a 'Common European Home' rules out the probability of an armed clash and the very possibility of the use or threat of force, above all military force, by an alliance against another alliance, inside alliances or wherever it may be."[5] But if security concerns were "the foundation of a Common European Home, then all-round cooperation is its bearing frame."[6] The load-bearing beams and lintels that he described spanned a range of economic and political issues across international and domestic lines. And just as reducing the threat of war would be accomplished by the use of international law, cooperation in these other areas implied reforms to core concepts of Soviet domestic law.

Gorbachev spoke of the "economic content" of this Common European Home and endorsed one focused on environmental protection. But he saved his final words for what he called its humanitarian

translations from Russian are by the author of this chapter.) But this gets the sequence backward. The invitation to Gorbachev was extended on June 30, 1988, out of anxiety that the European Parliament, with which the Council of Europe had an unspoken competition, was "also contemplating a similar invitation for the first months of 1989." *See* Report 5937 (1988) on the general policy of the Council of Europe – East-West relations, presented by the Political Affairs Committee, Explanatory memorandum ¶ 35 (Sept. 15, 1988). The resolution to create a special guest status passed on May 11, 1989. *See* Resolution 917 (1989) on Special Guest Status with the Parliamentary Assembly.

4 Gorbachev, *supra* note 2, at 7.

5 *Id.* at 8.

6 *Id.* at 12 (emphasis in original). This all may sound very dreamy, but Gorbachev was quite pragmatic. "In view of the different social systems we are not likely to achieve a complete identity of views." *Id.* at 20. He had no interest in unilaterally adapting to some European norm: "The fact that the states of Europe belong to different social systems is a reality. The recognition of this historical fact and respect for the sovereign right of each people to choose their social system at their own descretion [*sic*] are the most important prerequisite [*sic*] for a normal European process." *Id.* at 3.

content: "A world where military arsenals would be reduced but where human rights would be violated, would not be a safe place."[7] Perhaps it was his legal training that led him to conclude: "We are convinced that the all-European process should rest on a solid legal ground. We are thinking of an all-European home as a community rooted in law." Referencing a resolution passed by the USSR Congress of People's Deputies (which, thanks to Gorbachev's reforms, was a new legislature constituted by the first competitive elections in Soviet history[8]), Gorbachev called for the creation of "an ad hoc working group or a kind of European institute for comparative humanitarian law" and imagined "the possibility of creating a European legal space."[9]

The Soviet Union (and Gorbachev's time in office) did not last long enough to build that space, but the project was taken up by the Russian Federation and its president, Boris Yeltsin. Merely a fortnight after the collapse of the Soviet Union, a letter from Russian Federation foreign minister Andrei Kozyrev was hand-delivered to the secretary-general of the Council of Europe, Catherine Lalumière: "The new Russia wholeheartedly shares the priority principles underlying the action of the Council of Europe – pluralistic democracy, human rights and the rule of law – and has been consistently applying them in its policy during recent years."[10] The

7 *Id.* at 19.

8 These were multicandidate, not multiparty, elections, although not all candidates were members of the Communist Party of the Soviet Union. The resolution of the XIX Party Conference that led to the creation of this body also called, inter alia, for "the establishment of a socialist state committed to the rule of law . . . as a matter of fundamental importance." *On Democratising Soviet Society and Reforming the Political System, in* 19TH ALL-UNION CONFERENCE OF THE CPSU: DOCUMENTS AND MATERIALS 130, 134 (1988).

9 Gorbachev, *supra* note 2, at 20 (emphasis in original). The Congress's resolution, as noted by Gorbachev in his remarks, stated: "Guided by international rules and principles, including those in the Universal Declaration of Human Rights, the Helsinki accords and agreements, and bringing its domestic legislation in line with the above, the USSR will seek to contribute to the establishment of a world community of states rooted in law." *Id.*

10 Secretariat Discussion Paper on the Former Soviet Union, Misc(92)9, app. I (Jan. 20, 1992) (letter from Andrei Kozyrev to Catherine Lalumière, Jan. 7, 1992). The letter also noted that the Russian Federation "has announced its firm intention to conform to all the international obligations of the former USSR, as well as its decision to be the successor State to the USSR in international affairs as a whole." On March 27, the Committee of Ministers agreed "that the Russian Federation is a Contracting Party to the seven Conventions of the Council of Europe to which the Soviet Union had acceded" and that the Secretariat would "continue, notably through contact groups set up on both sides at senior official level with the co-operation and assistance programmes which had been developed with the Soviet Union since 1989." Communication of the Activities of the Committee of Ministers (Jan.–Apr. 1992), Statutory Report, CM(92)96, Doc. 6602, at 3, § I.1.e (May 4, 1992).

empirical claim was a gross exaggeration, but Russia asserted a foreign policy goal that seemed genuine: "the aim of becoming a full member of the Council of Europe."[11] The letter was followed by a meeting in February with the president of the Supreme Soviet, Ruslan Khasbulatov, and a personal visit to Strasbourg by Kozyrev in May.[12] In between, the Constitutional Committee of the Supreme Soviet requested an examination of its draft constitution by the European Commission on Democracy through Law (the Venice Commission).[13]

Thus began a four-year process of assessment, negotiation, reform, and promises of future reform, all focused on joining an international organization established to promote democracy, human rights, and the rule of law.[14] To use the language of transnational legal order theory adopted by Shaffer and Sandholtz, this was nothing less than a concerted effort to apply "normative orders that implicate law and legal practice across and within multiple national boundaries," so as to adopt a "transnational framing and understanding of a social problem, which catalyzes actors to seek a resolution through law."[15] The decision to admit Russia as a member was reached in 1996; Russia ratified the European Convention on Human Rights in 1998. As the millennium drew to a close, there seemed cause for genuine hope for a successful, if gradual, transition from the authoritarianism that was a hallmark of Russian and Soviet history toward a more embedded respect for the rule of law.

Roughly a quarter century later, all such hope had vanished as Russia began its full-scale invasion of Ukraine, a fellow member state in the Council. Twenty-seven days after the Russian army began its advance on Kyiv, the Committee of Ministers (the Council's decision-making body composed of the foreign ministers of all member states) decided that Russia ceased to be a member.[16] In the words of the Statute of the Council

[11] Secretariat Discussion Paper Misc(92)9, *supra* note 10, app. I.

[12] Note for the File: Exchange of Views with the Minister for Foreign Affairs of the Russian Federation, Misc(92)35, § 2 (May 4, 1992); Minutes of the 90th Session of the Committee of Ministers, CM(92)PV1, PV2 & PV3 (May 7, 1992).

[13] Communication CM(92)96, *supra* note 10, § IV.7.

[14] Statute of the Council of Europe, pmbl., May 5, 1949, Eur. T.S. No. 1.

[15] *See* Chapter 1.

[16] The Council suspended Russia's rights to representation in the organization the day after the invasion began. *See* Decision, *Situation in Ukraine: Measures to Be Taken, Including under Article 8 of the Statute of the Council of Europe*, CM/Del/Dec(2022)1426ter/2.3 (Feb. 25, 2022). Russia was expelled three weeks later. *See* Resolution CM/Res (2022)2 on the Cessation of the Membership of the Russian Federation to the Council of Europe (Mar. 16, 2022). Sitting in plenary session, the European Court of Human Rights resolved that Russia would cease to be a High Contracting Party to the European

Europe, Russia had "seriously violated" the Council's core principles "of the rule of law and of the enjoyment by all persons within its jurisdiction of human rights and fundamental freedoms."[17] The idea of a common European home – at least one that included Russia – had gone up in flames. Russia's leaders were the arsonists.

Though this war of aggression had lit the match on Russia's relationship with the Council of Europe, Russia's incendiary actions had been threatening the organization's inner workings as well as its members for some time. Inside the organization, for example, Russia blocked efforts to pursue procedural reforms in the European Court of Human Rights for more than three years, the only holdout among forty-six other member states between 2006 and 2010.[18] These reforms were needed in no small part because of the huge volume of violations of the Convention coming from Russia – between 23.2 and 28.9 percent of all applications pending before a decision body of the Court during this same time period.[19] Meanwhile, Russia engaged in violent disputes with fellow member states. In 2008, Russia created statelets in Abkhazia and South Ossetia, recognized by virtually no one, following its war with Georgia. In 2014, Russia first occupied and then annexed Crimea. These actions repudiated the customary international law principle of *uti possidetis* and flagrantly disregarded Article 2(4) of the United Nations Charter.

As this volume notes, "international law is critical for advancing the rule of law in multiple direct and indirect ways that affect individuals and societies."[20] So it should not be surprising that, during roughly the same time period, Russia also weakened the load-bearing structures within the Council of Europe's key institutions, particularly its highly respected court of human rights. Increasingly resistant to the Strasbourg Court's

Convention on Human Rights in six months. *See* Resolution of the European Court of Human Rights on the Consequences of the Cessation of Membership of the Russian Federation to the Council of Europe in Light of Article 58 of the European Convention on Human Rights (Mar. 22, 2022).

17 Statute, *supra* note 14, arts. 8, 3.

18 By October 2006, forty-six member states had ratified Protocol 14, proposed in 2004. The Russian State Duma voted against ratification in December 2006. Bill Bowring, *The Russian Federation, Protocol No. 14 (and 14bis), and the Battle for the Soul of the ECHR*, 2 Goettingen J. Int'l L. 589, 605 (2010). Russia ratified it in January 2010. *See* Chart of Signature and Ratifications of Protocol No. 14 to the Convention for the Protection of Human Rights and Fundamental Freedoms, Amending the Control System of the Convention (CETS No. 194), Council of Europe Treaty Office.

19 *See* European Court of Human Rights Analysis of Statistics 17 (for 2006); *id.* at 7 (for 2007); *id.* at 8 (for 2008, 2009, and 2010).

20 *See* Chapter 1.

jurisdiction over claims that Russian law or official conduct violated the European Convention on Human Rights, Russia challenged and then repudiated that jurisdiction.[21] Simultaneously, President Vladimir Putin abandoned legal reforms initiated by his predecessor, Boris Yeltsin, as he saw less and less value to membership in the organization.[22] Changes to Russian law occurring in this period, some subtle and some quite brazen, moved from "rule of law" to "rule by law" as the Russian state reverted to past Soviet and even imperial Russian practices.[23] This, too, fully bears out the observation made by Shaffer and Sandholtz that "[a]lthough political actors increasingly deploy rule-of-law discourse, they frequently abuse it to legitimate authoritarian rule, often in the name of law and order."[24] Notwithstanding continuing obligations under the European Convention on Human Rights, Russian officials turned the law and courts into weapons to assault regime opponents, silence dissenters, and privilege commercial interests valued by the state. This had repercussions for the international organization Russia had joined as much as it facilitated Russia's retrograde descent into authoritarianism.

Russia has now revised its history of past eagerness to join the Council of Europe and other international organizations, now claiming this all to have been chimerical and built on false premises. "To tell the truth," Foreign Minister Sergei Lavrov wrote in March 2023, "we no longer have any illusions about converging with Europe, being accepted as part of the 'common European home,' or creating a 'common space' with the EU. All these declarations made in European capitals have turned out to be a myth and a false-flag operation."[25] One by one, Russia abandoned security agreements central to Gorbachev's earlier vision.[26] The fact

[21] *See* Jeffrey Kahn, *The Relationship Between the European Court of Human Rights and the Constitutional Court of the Russian Federation: Conflicting Conceptions of Sovereignty in Strasbourg and St. Petersburg* 30 Eur. J. Int'l L. 933 (2019).

[22] Irina Busygina & Jeffrey Kahn, *Russia, the Council of Europe, and "Ruxit," or, Why Illiberal Regimes Join International Organizations*, 67 Probs. Post-Communism 64 (2020).

[23] Jeffrey Kahn, *The Rule of Law Under Pressure: Russia and the European Human Rights System*, 44 Rev. Cent. & E. Eur. L. 275 (2019).

[24] *See* Chapter 1.

[25] Сергей Лавров, *Российская дипломатия в меняющемся мире* [Russian diplomacy in a changing world], Разведчик [Intelligence agent] 3, 5 (Mar. 2023) (translation corresponds to "Russian Government News," March 24, 2023, published by SeeNews).

[26] In December 2022, Russia suspended participation in the new Strategic Arms Reduction Treaty. *See* Ben Aris, *New START Missile Treaty Suspended as Tensions Escalate Between Russia and US*, BNE Intellinews (Dec. 4, 2022), https://tinyurl.com/yeyw5863. In May 2023, President Putin signed an order to begin the process of denunciation of

that the metaphor of a common European home originated with the last Soviet leader was cast into a memory hole.[27] "There will be no 'business as usual' again," Lavrov announced. "We will not knock on the closed door, let alone make unilateral concessions."[28]

Thus, Russia's relationship with the Council of Europe now has a beginning, a middle, and an end. Through an examination of primary sources, and with a particular focus on the rule of law, this chapter explores how the dynamics of Russia's pursuit of membership in the Council of Europe affected both the Russian state and the international organization asked to admit it as a member. The chapter contributes a case study on how this international organization translated its rule-of-law values into measurable metrics for success and failure in seeking to establish the rule of law in Russia. And how, after roughly a decade of concrete advances, the effort foundered and then collapsed.

This study has more than academic or historical value. The policy questions that led to Russia's hasty application to, and inclusion in, the Council of Europe have not changed. They will be the same questions in need of answer when, to quote Gorbachev again, the opportunity reemerges to ask "about the architecture of our 'common home', on how it should be built and even on how it should be 'furnished.'"[29]

## I Ambitions

Shaffer and Sandholtz note that "[u]ltimately, for the rule of law to become effective, it must be institutionalized as part of a culture of conduct."[30] Among those most influenced by Gorbachev's thinking, there was considerable ambition to build up legal institutions and establish that culture.

In June 1987, Gorbachev reported to the plenum of the Party Central Committee the basic principle behind his economic reforms: "The approach is simple," he announced. "One is allowed to do everything that is not prohibited by law."[31] (Considering his position as the leader of

Russia's commitments under the Treaty on Conventional Armed Forces in Europe. *See* Распоряжение Президента Российской Федерации, № 140-РП, 10 мая 2023 г. [Order of the president of the Russian Federation, No. 140-RP, May 10, 2023], http://publication.pravo.gov.ru/Document/View/0001202305100001.

27 George Orwell, 1984, at 38 (Houghton Mifflin Harcourt 2008) (1949).

28 Лавров, *supra* note 25, at 5.

29 Gorbachev, *supra* note 2, at 7.

30 *See* Chapter 1.

31 "Разрешается делать все, что не запрещено законам." 5 М.С. Горбачев [M.S. Gorbachev], Избранные речи и статьи [Selected speeches and articles] 183 (1988).

a post-totalitarian authoritarian regime, such a view of law must count as apostasy.) At the XIX Party Conference held in 1988, a turning point for Gorbachev's reforms, it was resolved that:

> the forthcoming reform of the political system must tackle the following tasks: . . . to radically strengthen socialist legality and law and order so as to rule out usurpation or abuses of power, effectively combat bureaucratic and formalistic attitudes, and ensure reliable guarantees for the protection of the people's constitutional rights and freedoms and for the performance by citizens of their obligations before society and the state.[32]

Increasingly, Gorbachev referred to a rule-of-law state and law-governed civil society ("правовое государство" and "правовое гражданское общество") to describe what he insisted to be the key to his reforms, "a legal revolution."[33] This implied a state subordinated to law, a notion simply anathema to long-standing Soviet legal practice and the shifting influence of various Marxist-Leninist theories of law.[34]

This new thinking had practical implications. Soviet judges, long accustomed to "low status and few rewards," were given heightened protections through a new appointments process, longer terms of service, and expanded jurisdiction to review the legality of state action.[35] New laws on state enterprises and cooperatives expanded property and contracting rights of businesses, including an emerging class of entrepreneurs.[36] And a 1989 law, also for the first time, "provided a mechanism for the direct incorporation of various international rules in the Soviet domestic legal system."[37] By that

Gorbachev was repeating, with conviction, the idea published in *Pravda* by Vladimir Kudryavtsev, the director of the Institute of State and Law, six months before: "Of the two possible principles, 'You may do only what is permitted' and 'You may do everything that is not forbidden', priority should be given to the latter inasmuch as it unleashes the initiative and activism of people." ARCHIE BROWN, THE GORBACHEV FACTOR 145–46 (1996).

32 *On Democratising Soviet Society and Reforming the Political System*, *supra* note 8, at 130.

33 Интервью М.С. Горбачева журналу «Шпигел» (ФРГ), Правда (Москва), Окт. 24, 1988 г., стр. 1 [Interview of M.S. Gorbachev to the magazine "Spiegel" (FRG), *Pravda* (Moscow), Oct. 24, 1998, at 1]; *see also* BROWN, *supra* note 31, at 145–46, 176.

34 W.E. BUTLER, RUSSIAN LAW 70–79 (2d ed. 2003).

35 PETER H. SOLOMON, JR. & TODD S. FOGLESONG, COURTS AND TRANSITION IN RUSSIA: THE CHALLENGE OF JUDICIAL REFORM 6, 8–9 (2000).

36 MARIA YEFREMOVA, SVETLANA YAKOVLEVA & JANE HENDERSON, CONTRACT LAW IN RUSSIA 11 (2014); WILLIAM POMERANZ, LAW AND THE RUSSIAN STATE: RUSSIA'S LEGAL EVOLUTION FROM PETER THE GREAT TO VLADIMIR PUTIN 108–09 (2019).

37 Gennady M. Danilenko, *International Law and the Future of Rechtstaat in Russia*, in LAW AND DEMOCRACY IN THE NEW RUSSIA 96, 98 (Bruce L.R. Smith & Gennady M. Danilenko eds., 1993).

time, more than a third of the 1977 USSR Constitution – a document that had been amended just once before 1988 – had been subject to amendment.[38] And in 1990, the constitution was further amended to eliminate the Communist Party's monopoly and create the office of president of the Soviet Union. As Robert Sharlet notes, "In most Western constitutional systems, these systemic changes alone would represent an extraordinary development, nearly the equivalent of the constitutional transition from the Fourth to the Fifth French Republic under De Gaulle in 1958."[39] In the words of the late Bernard Rudden, "During the last years of its life the Soviet Union turned to law like a dying monarch to his withered God. . . . enact[ing] and amend[ing] statutes with the fervour of one who sees in legislation the path to paradise."[40]

But institutionalizing the rule of law "as part of a culture of conduct" must extend beyond the leadership circle, whose consensus on its value is necessary but not sufficient to establish it. Even beyond institutions such as the legislature, judiciary, police, and administrative bodies (which are fed by, as much as generating, that "culture of conduct"),

> the rule of law in a modern state also requires a variety of non-state institutions: organised legal education, a professional bar, and a myriad of supporting professions (accountants, investigators, etc.) and organisations (newspapers, public registries, credit bureaus, etc.). The rule of law affects the development of mass attitudes and commercial behaviour. It imbeds itself in a country's political culture and in its civil society. It entrenches expectations about the role and limits of a state bureaucracy, and the limits of commercial freedom and individual autonomy. Finally, but most importantly, the rule of law requires some level of shared expectations by political elites, lawyers, and laypersons about what *counts* as law, about what are the limits of judicial power, and about the spheres of life into which the law should *not* be permitted to intrude.[41]

The failure to entrench that culture can be seen as a fundamental factor in what can now be seen as the limited lasting effect of legal reforms attempted in the first decade after the collapse of the Soviet Union. No such rule-of-law institutions or culture had existed ever before in any

[38] ROBERT SHARLET , SOVIET CONSTITUTIONAL CRISIS: FROM DE-STALINIZATION TO DISINTEGRATION 86 (1992).

[39] *Id.*

[40] Bernard Rudden, *Civil Law, Civil Society, and the Russian Constitution*, 110 L.Q. REV. 56 (1994).

[41] Jeffrey Kahn, *The Rule-of-Law Factor, in* INSTITUTIONS, IDEAS AND LEADERSHIP IN RUSSIAN POLITICS 163 (Julie Newton & William Tompson eds., 2010).

space governed from St. Petersburg or Moscow.[42] The Russian Empire had no tradition of "law-boundedness."[43] It was "the 'autocratic and unlimited' ruler (to borrow tsarist terminology) who [] consistently set both the tempo and the tone of Russian law."[44] The starting point of Soviet legal thinking was the initial Marxist–Leninist belief in the withering away of law and state in their entirety – an idea (coupled with the Red Terror) that extinguished the spark of judicial and legal reforms imposed by Alexander II and weak constitutional reform coerced out of Nicholas II.[45] And although the first Bolshevik decrees abolishing laws, courts, and lawyers were eventually found to be unworkable, the laws and legal institutions that built the Soviet system were conceived entirely in the service of the state – ironically, a theme of Russian history dating to the first Romanovs.[46] No one put their purpose better than the first Soviet commissar of justice, Nikolai Krylenko:

> The court is, and still remains, the only thing it can be by its nature as an organ of the government power – a weapon for the safeguarding of the interests of a given ruling class ... A club is a primitive weapon, a rifle is a more efficient one, the most efficient is the court ... The court is an organ of state administration and as such does not differ in its nature from any other organs of administration which are designed, as the court is, to carry out one and the same governmental policy ....[47]

Through multiple constitutions and shifting approaches to governance, ranging from the nihilistic vision of the early Bolsheviks to the ossification of a massive, centralized bureaucracy, Soviet law never withered away.

[42] For more detailed discussions of legal history, see BUTLER, *supra* note 34; F.J.M. FELDBRUGGE, RUSSIAN LAW: THE END OF THE SOVIET SYSTEM AND THE ROLE OF LAW (1993) JOHN N. HAZARD, WILLIAM E. BUTLER & PETER B. MAGGS, THE SOVIET LEGAL SYSTEM (3d ed. 1977); Jeffrey Kahn, *The Search for the Rule of Law in Russia*, 37 GEO. J. INT'L L. 353 (2006); Jeffrey Kahn, *Vladimir Putin and the Rule of Law in Russia*, 36 GEORGIA J. INT'L & COMP. L. 511 (2008); POMERANZ, *supra* note 36.

[43] 3 S.E. FINER, THE HISTORY OF GOVERNMENT: EMPIRES, MONARCHIES, AND THE MODERN STATE 1407 (1999) ("In effect, until as late as the mid-nineteenth century, Russia did without systematized laws, a legal profession, and the law-boundedness that was the essential characteristic of the western state tradition.").

[44] POMERANZ, *supra* note 36, at 4.

[45] In the words of Pyotr Stuchka, first president of the USSR Supreme Court, "Communism means not the victory of socialist law, but the victory of socialism over any law, since with the abolition of classes with their antagonistic interests, law will die out altogether." HAROLD J. BERMAN, JUSTICE IN THE USSR: AN INTERPRETATION OF SOVIET LAW 26 (1966).

[46] POMERANZ, *supra* note 36, at 4–7.

[47] 1 VLADIMIR GSOVSKI, SOVIET CIVIL LAW 241 (1948).

Nor, at least until Gorbachev's preliminary efforts, was there ever any sustained interest in the rule-of-law goal of opposing arbitrary power. In that context, Gorbachev's efforts both stood out from this history and faced substantial obstacles to overcome it. For, as Alexander Lukin observed, "while arguing for the rule of law or a law-based state, 'democrats' saw law as a means of toppling the regime, as a tool that should have been directed mainly against their Communist opponents, while they themselves did not feel bound by what they considered to be outdated and unjust Communist laws."[48]

Nevertheless, Gorbachev's ambitious reforms seized the attention of Strasbourg, which had its own institutional ambitions. The Soviet Union had been an obstacle to the Council of Europe's efforts to build democracy and the rule of law in a unified Europe since the Council's founding in 1949.[49] But Gorbachev increasingly appeared to open an opportunity: he was younger than his immediate predecessors (aged fifty-four in 1985, compared to Brezhnev (dead at seventy-five), Andropov (sixty-nine), and Chernenko (seventy-three)), comparatively much better traveled, and trained in law (the first such leader since Lenin).[50] As his reforms began, though ever evolving throughout his leadership, there was significant debate among Western observers over whether this amounted to cosmetic repairs to the system or more systematic change.[51]

Sharp-eyed observers in the top echelons of the Council of Europe perceived in his early efforts an opportunity to promote the core, unifying mission of the Council: human rights, democracy, and the rule of law. Among those observers was Catherine Lalumière, a deputy in the

[48] Alexander Lukin, Democratic Groups in Soviet Russia (1985–1991): A Study in Political Culture 323 (1997) (D.Phil. thesis, University of Oxford). For a critical examination of the use of metaphors concerning the rule of law in Russia, see Jeffrey Kahn, *The Law Is a Causeway: Metaphor and the Rule of Law in Russia*, *in* THE LEGAL DOCTRINES OF THE RULE OF LAW AND THE LEGAL STATE (RECHTSSTAAT), IUS GENTIUM: COMPARATIVE PERSPECTIVES ON LAW AND JUSTICE 38, 229 (J.R. Silkenat et al. eds., 2014).

[49] *See, e.g.*, Parliamentary Assembly Resolution 22 (1952), *Reaffirming Once More the Assembly's Faith in the Unity of the Whole of Europe* (Sept. 29, 1952); Report of the Committee on Political Affairs and Democracy, *Common European Policy at Future East-West Conferences*, Doc. 419 (1955), ¶¶ 7, 26–27 (Oct. 14, 1955); Parliamentary Assembly Resolution 588 (1975), *Security and Co-operation in Europe (General Policy of the Council of Europe)* (Jan. 28, 1975); Declaration CM(89) on the Future Role of the Council of Europe in European Construction (May 5, 1989).

[50] BROWN, *supra* note 31, at 29.

[51] ARCHIE BROWN, SEVEN YEARS THAT CHANGED THE WORLD: PERESTROIKA IN PERSPECTIVE xv (2007).

Parliamentary Assembly, rapporteur for its influential Political Affairs Committee, and the soon-to-be head of the organization. As will be seen, after having catalyzed Gorbachev's invitation as rapporteur in 1988, she would preside as secretary-general at his speech in July 1989. Lalumière recognized the nineteenth Party conference as "an historic event."[52]

She was right. Lalumière also recognized that this opportunity came at a time when her institution felt the need to reinvigorate itself. The Council confronted the accelerating success of competing international organizations. The European Community that would shortly become the European Union was one of them. It was clear that the EU – pursuing a single monetary union and open trade across national borders – would outpace the Council of Europe in economic (and therefore political) power. Another was the Conference on Security and Co-operation in Europe, which concluded the Helsinki Final Act of 1975. Principle VII and the "Third Basket" of the Final Act subjected a bevy of human rights issues to monitoring and rounds of follow-up meetings, overlapping with much of the Council's *raison d'être*. Lalumière's predecessor as rapporteur, Harold Lied, put the matter bluntly: "The crucial question for us is: who is to take the initiative in this European process?"[53] As one high-ranking Council of Europe insider described his sense of the priorities at a time when the European Community "was starting to move into the Council's own spheres of excellence":

> [T]he most important and pressing need was to explore ways in which the Council might open up towards eastern Europe through relations with those countries involved in implementing the Helsinki Accords which seemed willing to co-operate with our Organisation. In our view this was the best way of opening up new avenues of development for the Council and ensuring that it remained in control of its destiny, at a time when the European Community was growing in influence, following the Fontainebleau Summit of June 1984. But arguments were needed in support of our position, which was not yet widely shared within the Organisation.[54]

Lalumière made those arguments, keen to thread a needle between "the two pitfalls of over-enthusiasm and frosty caution."[55] On the one hand, she urged her colleagues against "displaying excessive caution" in responding

[52] Report 5937 (1988), *supra* note 3, Explanatory Memorandum ¶ 7 (Sept. 15, 1988).
[53] Parliamentary Assembly, Official Report of Debates, Sept. 27, 1985, at 386.
[54] Bruno Haller, *"Ostpolitik" Makes Its Appearance*, *in* EUROPE: A HUMAN ENTERPRISE 53 (Denis Huber ed., 2019). From 1984 to 1989, Bruno Haller was director of the private office of Secretary-General Marcelino Oreja.
[55] Report 5937 (1988), *supra* note 3, Explanatory Memorandum ¶¶ 3, 34.

to Gorbachev's reforms, all the more so since, "[i]f we are to believe another resolution [of the 1988 Party Conference,] the Soviet Union is aspiring to become a state based on the rule of law . . . ."[56] On the other hand, she recognized the need for the Council of Europe to stay true to its own principles: hastily engaging with countries unable to meet its high standards would be self-defeating and risk being "suspected of betraying the principles of democracy and human rights which our organization defends."[57] Still, one can sense her look-over-the-shoulder awareness that the rival European Parliament had already begun to contemplate inviting Gorbachev to visit in early 1989 and her concern that "the Committee of Ministers would be displaying excessive caution" if it waited for the CSCE's Vienna follow-up meeting to conclude before inviting an aspiring Eastern European country to engage with the Council.[58]

These aspirations, as will be seen, could cloud judgment on both sides. This had an impact on Russia's negotiated path to membership and, consequently, the strength of its legal reforms.[59] Russian promises of various reforms – made to reassure the Council that its criteria for membership would be satisfied – sometimes were disconnected from practical realities. And decision-makers at the Council of Europe began to see Russia's difficulties in satisfying those membership criteria as all the more reason to admit Russia into an organization that could help it achieve its professed goals. The most prominent critic of this approach referred to it as the policy of "therapeutic admission."[60]

As Part II suggests, institutional pressures on the Council to renew its mission affected how the Council's decision-makers perceived the strength of its applicants' cases for membership, particularly the Russian case. That

[56] *Id.* ¶ 8.

[57] *Id.* ¶ 33.

[58] *Id.* ¶¶ 35, 32.

[59] Not everyone shared Lalumière's eagerness. The rapporteur for the Committee on Relations with European Non-Member Countries, Loyola de Palacio Vallelersundi, countered: "If we are not to be the protagonists of an 'overly enthusiastic attitude or frosty caution,' as our Rapporteur said, it seems essential for us to keep past experience in mind and contemplate the development of Soviet society cautiously, which does not boil down to transmitting public speeches but also to observe the profound behaviour of a nation which, according to some sources, is probably not strictly unanimous in backing up the Gorbachev reforms." Opinion on the General Policy of the Council of Europe – East-West Relations Presented by the Committee on Relations with European Non-Member Countries, Doc. 5958, ¶ 7 (Oct. 5, 1988).

[60] Peter Leuprecht, *Innovations in the European System of Human Rights Protection: Is Enlargement Compatible with Reinforcement*, 8 TRANSNAT'L L. & CONTEMP. PROBS. 313, 332 (1998).

fact was not lost on the Russian side, which took advantage of those pressures as it pursued spirited negotiations for a place in the organization whose criteria for membership it struggled to meet.

## II Negotiation

By the time of Russia's application, the Council of Europe had an established process for admitting new members.[61] Article 4 of the Statute provided that "[a]ny European State which is deemed to be able and willing to fulfil the provisions of Article 3 may be invited to become a member of the Council of Europe by the Committee of Ministers." Article 3, in turn, required that every member "must accept the principles of the rule of law and of the enjoyment by all persons within its jurisdiction of human rights and fundamental freedoms, and collaborate sincerely and effectively" to pursue the Council's aim to realize those ideals and principles.

By composition and institutional position, the Committee of Ministers is a political body. And Article 4 makes clear that a decision to admit a new member state requires a subjective political judgment, viz., that the applicant be "deemed to be able and willing" to comply with rule-of-law and other criteria. That these criteria are capable of more objective measurement, as well as the accretion of precedent about what "counts" to satisfy them, generates some constraints on decision-making but does not remove policy considerations from the final decision. This mix of law and politics in the decision-making process would emerge as particularly important in the Russian case.

Although the Committee of Ministers had the legal authority, an important consultative role had devolved on the Parliamentary Assembly, from which the Committee always requested an opinion in advance of its decision. This injected politics into the mix, too, but it also offered the opportunity for careful appraisal of an application by distinguished legal experts and rapporteurs for the Assembly's committees:

> They have the opportunity to discuss matters relevant to the admission to the CoE with all leading personalities, including representatives of opposition groups, national minorities, trade unions, religious groups, etc., so as

[61] Eckart Klein, *Membership and Observer Status*, *in* The Council of Europe: Its Law and Policies §§ 3.34, 3.37–3.38 (Stefanie Schmahl & Marten Breuer eds., 2017).

> to enable them to obtain a complete and objective picture of the country. . . . They have discharged their tasks with an objectivity and thoroughness that has earned them respect even from governments they severely criticized.[62]

Importantly, this work was not only an assessment of eligibility, but also a tool to leverage legal reforms satisfactory to the Council. As noted by Peter Leuprecht (who would rise to be deputy secretary-general of the Council before resigning in protest at the decision to admit Russia and Croatia as members): "Experience has shown that it is at the pre-accession stage that the Council's representatives have the most leverage and can press for the reforms needed to bring the applicant country into line with the Council's standards."[63]

Ironically, that statement exposed a certain schizophrenia that developed in the organization as the Iron Curtain began to fall. Its original ten members could credibly assert (in the words of the preamble to the Statute) their "common heritage" of shared principles and values as "like-minded countries of Europe."[64] But the Council also aspired to grow "to create an organisation which will bring European States into closer association."[65] Growing eastward, that like-mindedness was more difficult to perceive and those values (especially concerning the rule of law) less firmly in place. What to do? This was the dilemma of "therapeutic admission": Why should like-minded states sharing such a common heritage need to be leveraged and pressed for such reforms in the first place?

In Russia's case, the Committee of Ministers invited the Parliamentary Assembly to express its opinion but put a heavy thumb on the scales right from the start:

> First of all, the Committee of Ministers wishes to inform the Assembly that there is consensus among its members in favour of the Russian Federation's joining the Organisation as soon as the conditions laid down in the Statute, that is implementation of the principles of pluralist parliamentary democracy, respect for human rights and the rule of law, have been satisfied. This implies that the legislative and judicial systems of the Federation as well as its component entities would have to conform to the principles of the rule of law.[66]

[62] Hans Winkler, *Democracy and Human Rights in Europe: A Survey of the Admission Practice of the Council of Europe*, 47 Austrian J. Pub. Int'l L. 47, 160–61 (1995).

[63] Leuprecht, *supra* note 60, at 328.

[64] Statute, *supra* note 14.

[65] *Id.*

[66] Resolution (92) 27 on the Russian Federation (June 25, 1992).

Lest there remain doubt that this was a case of therapeutic admission, the Committee took note of Russia's size and "the diversity of its cultural and administrative traditions" to acknowledge that "it will take time to translate theoretical freedoms into actual practice, and more especially to improve conditions for their respect in Russian administration and society."[67] Whether that translation from theory to practice and the improvement of conditions was a *sine qua non* for admission, or a desired consequence of it, was left diplomatically vague.

As in the past, the Assembly sought guidance from its Committee on Political Affairs, which in turn was informed by opinions from the Committee on Legal Affairs and Human Rights and the Committee on Relations with European Non-Member Countries.[68] In addition, the Assembly requested a report from six "eminent lawyers," three chosen from the then-existing European Commission on Human Rights and three from the European Court of Human Rights (all serving in their personal capacities).[69] Each group wrote reports generated through visits to Russia, spot inspections, interviews, and meetings.[70] This slightly confusing procedure is depicted in graphic form in Figure 8.1.

Russia's admission to the Council of Europe did not occur in a vacuum. After the fall of the Berlin Wall, the states once behind the Iron Curtain all began to seek membership. Hungary (November 1990), Poland (November 1991), and Bulgaria (May 1992) were followed by a rapid expansion in 1993: Estonia and Lithuania (May), the Czech and Slovak republics

67 *Id.*

68 The committees' chairmen were Ernst Mühlemann (Political Affairs), Ole Espersen followed by Rudolf Bindig (Legal Affairs), and David Atkinson (Non-Member Countries).

69 Six jurists were selected, three each from the then existing European Commission of Human Rights and the European Court of Human Rights: Rudolf Bernhardt (vice president of the Court), Stefan Trechsel (Commission chamber president), Albert Weitzel (Commission chamber president), Felix Ermacora (Commission member), Franz Matscher (Austrian judge at the Court), and Luzius Wildhaber (Swiss judge at the Court). Matscher and Wildhaber, for personal reasons, did not participate. Report on the Conformity of the Legal Order of the Russian Federation with Council of Europe Standards, Doc. AS/Bur/Russia (1994), at 7 (Sept. 28, 1994), *reprinted in* 15 HUMAN RIGHTS LAW JOURNAL 249 (1994) (hereafter Eminent Lawyers Report). *See also Present State of Relations with the Russian Federation*, Secretariat Information Paper SG/INF(94) 12, at 2 (May 6, 1994). Ordinarily, two "eminent lawyers," – one from the Commission and one from the Court – were thought sufficient. *See* Winkler, *supra* note 62, at 160; Klein, *supra* note 61, § 3.37.

70 Simultaneously, numerous contact groups, delegations, and other joint activities took Russian officials to Strasbourg and Council of Europe officials to (almost exclusively) Moscow.

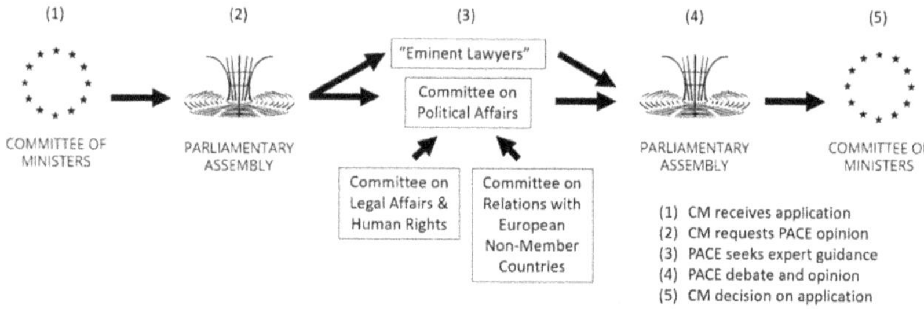


**Figure 8.1** Council of Europe deliberative process on Russia's application for membership.

(readmitted separately in June following Czechoslovakia's dissolution), and then, most controversially, Romania (October). Pressure built to allow accession despite deficiencies identified in committee reports. Thus, for example, Poland was granted conditional admission contingent on holding free and fair elections, which occurred more than a year later.[71] Estonia only partially fulfilled a commitment to protect the political rights of national minorities.[72] Romania, which rapporteurs concluded did not satisfy numerous membership requirements concerning the rule of law (including, for example, an independent judiciary), was admitted with a new monitoring procedure soon to be entrenched for all new members.[73] Each change was precedent for more flexibility for the next applicant because, as was argued in the Romanian debates, "to close the door would deprive us of a means of exerting pressure on Romania to introduce democracy."[74]

The Committee of Ministers adopted the resolution to admit Romania on October 4, 1993.[75] This was the day before an important summit in Vienna of the heads of state and government of member states of the Council of Europe, at which the organization declared itself to be "the pre-eminent European political institution capable of welcoming, on an

[71] *See* Winkler, *supra* note 62, at 156, n.13.

[72] Opinion 170 (1993) of the Parliamentary Assembly on the Application of the Republic of Estonia for Membership of the Council of Europe, ¶ 5 (May 13, 1993); Winkler, *supra* note 62, at 158–59.

[73] Opinion 176 (1993) of the Parliamentary Assembly on the Application by Romania for Membership of the Council of Europe (Sept. 28, 1993); *see also* Winkler, *supra* note 62, at 164; Philip Leach, *The Parliamentary Assembly of the Council of Europe*, *in* The Council of Europe: Its Law and Policies, *supra* note 61, § 7.38. The new mechanism, the "Halonen Order," is Order 488 (1993), *Honouring of Commitments Entered into by New Member States* (June 29, 1993).

[74] Leach, *supra* note 73, § 7.39.

[75] Resolution (93) 37, *Invitation to Romania to Become a Member of the Council of Europe.*

equal footing and in permanent structures, the democracies of Europe freed from communist oppression."[76] But it also coincided with the violent culmination of a constitutional crisis in Russia as President Yeltsin ordered tanks to shell the parliament building. Among his opponents there sat the chairman of the legislature, Ruslan Khasbulatov, who had met with Council of Europe officials in February 1992 as Russia began its application. European leaders gathered in Vienna expressed their "deep concern" and commitment to support "the message from the President of the Russian Federation reaffirming the irreversible policy of reforms and democratic transformation, conducive to the approachment of Russia with the Council of Europe."[77]

Despite Yeltsin's clear support for reforms to prevent a return to the Soviet past, and his rivals' opposition to those efforts, this crisis and its aftermath were not a ringing endorsement of the rule of law in Russia. Yeltsin had ordered the legislature disbanded at the start of the crisis and, by its conclusion, had also suspended the operation of the Constitutional Court (which had held that dissolution order unconstitutional). Vice President Alexander Rutskoi (who sided with the opposition), Khasbulatov, and many of their supporters were imprisoned for months. Yeltsin removed from office the Constitutional Court's chairman, Valery Zorkin, though neither he nor his fellow judges lost their liberty. A new, strongly presidential constitution and a weaker legislature were established through elections in December. Russia's application was not off to a good start.

The report of the eminent lawyers was submitted in late September 1994.[78] This could be said to have set the baseline for assessing how much must change in Russia for membership to become a reality. The report was the product of visits by four experts to Russia over twelve days in May and June for a tightly structured program of high-level meetings with executive, legislative, and judicial officials, journalists, lawyers, and civil society leaders, and inspection visits to jails and penal colonies in Moscow, Petersburg, and Krasnoyarsk.[79]

Rudolf Bernhardt, vice president of the Strasbourg Court, provided a general introduction to the report. He concluded that the detailed list

[76] Vienna Declaration, Oct. 9, 1993.

[77] Declaration on Russia, Vienna, Oct. 8, 1993.

[78] *See* Eminent Lawyers Report, *supra* note 69.

[79] This program is at Appendix I. Although most meetings were arranged long in advance, several surprise visits to detention facilities were accommodated. *Id.* at 266. A March meeting in Moscow occurred between two of the experts and Russian government officials. *Id.* app. II.

of human rights in the new Russian constitution, like the institutional mechanisms for their enforcement, remained parchment promises: "[T]his seems to be more theory than practice. Nearly all officials and private individuals we have met concede and confirm that the implementation of the human rights guarantees in actual State practice has many deficiencies or is even non-existent."[80] This was not to discount significant advances, especially concerning a free press and media space, but in many more subject areas there was no recognizable advance from Soviet times. A new code of criminal procedure, for example, was held essential to "eliminate practices which are incompatible with several provisions in the European Convention on Human Rights."[81] A particular concern was a culture of executive impunity: "the old ways of authoritarian thinking are still dominant in public administration. This seems to be a wide-spread 'disease' which might be understandable after so many decades of an authoritarian regime which led to deep-rooted patterns of behaviour."[82]

The eminent lawyers also focused on discrete issues, many of which are foundational to a rule-of-law system. The preliminary conclusions (repeatedly acknowledging the limits of experts to gain firm understandings while working under such tight time and space constraints) were not optimistic:

> The practical implementation of human rights by the authorities cannot but be affected by the state of the legislation which does not encourage a favourable perception of the principle of the rule of law. Even where the practice is relatively liberal, such as seems to be the case in the fields of freedom of expression, freedom of association, freedom of assembly and freedom of religion, such a liberal approach is not ensured by the law itself and the population may even have the feeling that the more restrictive laws in force are being twisted.[83]

This general view was shared by the expert charged with assessing conditions of confinement and respect for fundamental human rights in pretrial and postconviction detention facilities, Stefan Trechsel, chamber president of the then existing European Commission of Human Rights:

> Finally, it cannot be said that, at the present time, the Russian Federation presents the features of a State based upon the rule of law. The activities of public authorities are mainly decided upon according to general policy

[80] Eminent Lawyers Report, *supra* note 69, at 250.
[81] *Id.* at 251.
[82] *Id.*
[83] *Id.* at 266. The rights of national minorities and rights concerning detention (pretrial and postconviction) were also significant sections of the report.

> choices, personal allegiance and the effective power structure. In the areas I have examined it cannot, therefore, be said that the Russian Federation fulfils the requirements for membership of the Council of Europe.[84]

The findings by individual experts were reflected and emphasized in the conclusions of the four experts as a group. Keeping firmly in mind their charge ("whether the Russian Federation fulfils the prerequisite of being a genuine democracy showing respect for the rule of law and human rights"), they could identify discrete avenues of improvement in all three areas but concluded that Russia did not meet Council of Europe standards in any of them.[85] Their conclusion concerning the mentality of officialdom was Cassandra-like: "The traditional authoritarian thinking still seems to be dominant in the field of public administration. . . . The courts can now be considered structurally independent from the executive, but the concept that it should in the first place be for the judiciary to protect the individuals has not yet become a reality in Russia."[86]

The work of the Parliamentary Assembly's committees, which had begun undertaking their own visits to Russia, was derailed almost before it began, when Yeltsin launched a full-scale air and ground assault on the non-Russian ethnic republic of Chechnya in December 1994. The horror that followed constituted "a grave violation of the Council of Europe's most elementary human rights principles, which Russia, by requesting membership in the Organisation, pledged to uphold", and the Assembly suspended indefinitely procedures concerning its opinion on Russia's request for membership.[87] As with the October 1993 constitutional crisis, the war in Chechnya exposed deep pathologies stemming from Russia's Soviet and imperial pasts. Many of these were described in subsequent reports by the Legal Affairs and Human Rights Committee in late June 1995, which detailed humanitarian and human rights violations in Chechnya, and the disintegration of the rule of law there in a word picture worthy of Hieronymous Bosch's imagination of Hell.[88]

[84] *Id.* at 287.

[85] *Id.*

[86] *Id.*

[87] Resolution 1055 (1995), *Russia's Request for Membership in the Light of the Situation in Chechnya* (Feb. 2, 1995). The Legal Affairs and Human Rights Committee was instructed to send its subcommittee on human rights to Chechnya after cessation of hostilities. Order 506 (1995), *Russia's Request for Membership in Light of the Situation in Chechnya* (Feb. 2, 1995).

[88] Committee on Legal Affairs and Human Rights, *Report on the Human Rights Situation in Chechnya*, AS/Jur (1995)22 (June 29, 1995).

As 1995 began, the Assembly's president and its three committee rapporteurs received a letter signed by President Yeltsin, Prime Minister Chernomyrdin, and the chairs of both houses of the Russian legislature, Shumeyko and Rybkin. With the leveling of Grozny still underway, its assertions seemed incongruous: "Our desire to gain full membership of the Council of Europe is a logical consequence of our current policy aimed at establishing the rule of law, strengthening democracy and genuinely securing human rights in Russia." Perhaps more encouraging was their admission that "we are aware that we still have a long way to go," their promise to accede to the European Convention on Human Rights, and an attached list of concrete plans to improve the Russian legal system.[89] This was followed in August by an updated list of legislative accomplishments and further reforms planned for the future.[90]

Bindig and Atkinson, at least, both mention this letter as crucially important to the process.[91] And there is no gainsaying the substantial and high-quality legislative efforts by which many of the promises in that letter were kept, including new codes of civil law (1994), criminal law (1996), and a law regulating the procuracy.[92] Others were promised for the near future, including new codes of criminal procedure (2001), civil procedure (2002), laws creating a commissioner of human rights (1997) and a professional bar (2002), and laws further protecting the rights of religious (1997) and ethnic (1999) minorities – all these came to fruition.[93] These efforts often involved the assistance of experts from the Council of Europe, the US Department of Justice, and states with robust rule-of-law traditions. To take just one example, the new 2001 Criminal Procedure Code (a body of law identified by the eminent lawyers as needing substantial reform) was likened by many participants in its drafting to the "legendary" 1864 legal reforms of Alexander II.[94] The

[89] Report, *Russia's Request for Membership of the Council of Europe*, Doc. 7443, app. III, at 26–27 (Jan. 2, 1996).

[90] *Id.* app. VI.

[91] Rudolf Bindig, *Russia's Accession to the Council of Europe and the Fulfilment of Its Obligations and Commitments*, *in* Russia and the Council of Europe: Ten Years After 36–37 (Katlijn Malfliet & Stephan Parmentiereds., 2010); David Atkinson, *20 Years on the Council of Europe: A Personal Retrospective*, *in* Law in Greater Europe: Towards a Common Legal Area 281 (Bruno Haller, Hans Krüger & Herbert Pezold eds., 2000).

[92] Kahn, *supra* note 23, at 284.

[93] *Id.*

[94] *See* Christopher Lehman, *Introduction*, *in* The Russian Federation Code of Criminal Procedure ii (U.S. Department of Justice trans., 2004).

Code shifted responsibility for pretrial detention from prosecutors to judges, strengthening core rule-of-law issues concerning the separation of powers and opportunities for the arbitrary use of power.[95]

The Parliamentary Assembly restarted its consideration of Russia's application in September 1995, two months after what it called a "fragile" peace agreement in Chechnya under which "violations may continue."[96] A split had emerged between the Assembly's committees. The Legal Affairs and Human Rights Committee, chaired at the relevant time by Rudolf Bindig, accepted that the peace agreement might allow the process to continue, but was quite pessimistic about outcomes: "development in the area of protection of human rights and the rule of law seems to have gone backwards, if anything."[97] The Political Affairs Committee, chaired by Ernst Mühlemann, on the other hand, resignedly accepted that future conflicts within Russia were possible ("Such is the heritage of dictatorships," he wrote) but asserted that "[r]eform in Russia appears to be irreversible."[98] The Assembly resolution resuming the process reflected more the thinking of this latter committee:

> Russia is in a state of radical transition. The timescale of this transition is in quinquennia, even decades. Its pace will vary. Policies of the state authorities will fluctuate. This is because of immense social and economic difficulties, including the fight against organised crime. Tragic errors of policy in dealing with the Chechnya conflict have been recognised. Accordingly, the Assembly has no wish to throw in doubt the long-term direction of this transition: towards democracy, the rule of law, and human (including social) rights and freedoms.[99]

But this perspective turned the membership process upside down. The reason to extend membership – a decision, as it turned out, just months away – now sharply discounted Russia's present inability to satisfy the membership requirements. More important seemed to be the prospect of continuing dialogue, using the process to bring attainment of those goals within reach in the future. The reference to the "long-term direction" of transition made this sound predetermined and impliedly unidirectional.

95 *See* William Burnham & Jeffrey Kahn, *Russia's Criminal Procedure Code Five Years Out*, 33 Rev. Cent. & E. Eur. L. 1, 11–12 (2008).

96 Resolution 1065 (1995), *Procedure for an Opinion on Russia's Request for Membership of the Council of Europe*, ¶ 4 (Sept. 26, 1995).

97 Opinion, *Procedure for an Opinion on Russia's Request for Membership of the Council of Europe*, Doc. 7384, ¶ 8 (Sept. 15, 1995).

98 Report, *Procedure for an Opinion on Russia's Request for Membership of the Council of Europe*, Doc. 7372, ¶ 16 and Conclusion ix (Sept. 11, 1995).

99 Resolution 1065, *supra* note 96, ¶ 8.

As Mühlemann would conclude in his report for the influential Political Affairs Committee, it was clear that "Russia does not yet meet all Council of Europe standards. However, integration is better than isolation; co-operation is better than confrontation."[100]

This was the full-blown process and effects of "therapeutic admission" expanding eastward that so concerned Deputy Secretary-General Peter Leuprecht, leading to an overreliance on the goodwill of leaders and bureaucracies barely distanced from decades of repressive rule: "Some of the countries concerned suffer from serious evils and will have to go through a long healing process, but success in therapy presupposes the consent of the 'patient.'"[101] The rapid admission of these states was seen as part of the "new purpose" of the Council of Europe traceable to Gorbachev's "common European home" speech. Among those holding this view was David Atkinson, the chair of the Committee for Relations with European Non-Member Countries, the third PACE committee involved in the process.[102] The shift in purpose that worried Leuprecht was of far less concern to Atkinson:

> It was always clear that Russia, given its seventy years of Communist denial of freedom and democracy, its chronic economic problems as well as its size and ethnic composition, would not fully satisfy our standards of membership for a great many years, perhaps a generation. However, given its importance it was vital to encourage and assist the forces of reform by the earliest possible accession without ridiculing our standards. This had a particular urgency in view of the forthcoming presidential elections.[103]

Atkinson's reference to the Russian presidential elections (which occurred in June 1996) points to an important factor in this process: the Russian side's awareness of the Council's institutional anxieties and flexibility over previously firm requirements. Fear of undercutting an ally like Yeltsin pervaded the debates on Russian admission because in January 1996, when the PACE vote occurred, "few analysts or politicians predicted that Boris Yeltsin would win reelection as Russia's President."[104] It was lost on no one that the alternative to progressive-minded reformers could be communists, nationalists, or worse, who had met startling success in the December 1995 parliamentary elections.

[100] Report 7443, *supra* note 89, § II.6.103.xii.
[101] Leuprecht, *supra* note 60, at 332.
[102] Atkinson, *supra* note 91, at 277.
[103] *Id.* at 281.
[104] Michael McFaul, Russia's 1996 Presidential Election: The End of Polarized Politics ix (1997).

Another source of empowerment for Russian negotiators – without concrete evidence, it is hard to conclusively call it a negotiating tactic – were rumors circulated about the creation of a regional human rights convention for states of the former Soviet Union. In such a body the Council of Europe perceived many perils. It was very unlikely to be as effective as the Strasbourg system, thus diminishing the likelihood of lasting rule-of-law and human rights reforms. Its very existence would threaten the ability of the Council of Europe to satisfy its unifying ambitions. These twin anxieties were fed from the beginning. When the eminent lawyers asked "during a meeting in the Institute of State and Law of the Russian Academy of Science, for information on the relationship between such new Euro-Asian organs and the organs under the European Convention on Human Rights, we were told that an individual complaint should at first be submitted to the new system and only thereafter, if necessary, to the institution(s) in Strasbourg."[105] The prospect of conflicting positions by different regional human rights bodies with jurisdiction over the same space was chilling enough that renunciation of this plan was explicitly included in the list of commitments Russia promised to undertake in exchange for membership.[106]

By the time of the Assembly's vote, two conclusions seemed inescapable. First, the shift to therapeutic admission (replacing benchmark prerequisites) was complete. The Political Affairs Committee, by a vote of 24–4–6, recommended Russia be invited to join the Council because "Russia is making progress towards becoming a state based on the rule of law."[107] (Put more bluntly by the Legal Affairs Committee, "the Russian Federation cannot be regarded as a State based on the rule of law."[108]) Second, the Council of Europe took this action fully aware of the most threatening of Russia's rule-of-law problems:

> [T]he mentality towards the law has not changed. In Soviet times, laws could be completely disregarded – party politics and "telephone justice" reigned supreme. While it cannot be said that laws are ignored as a matter of course in present times, they are disregarded if a "better" solution to

105 Eminent Lawyers Report, *supra* note 69, at 252 (recounting "obvious" dangers beyond multiple institutions creating "more confusion than protection," and warning that the Strasbourg system would "necessarily lose its unifying effect and force" and become "of secondary importance").

106 Opinion 193 (1996), *Russia's Request for Membership of the Council of Europe*, § 10.16 (Jan. 25, 1996).

107 Report 7443, *supra* note 89, § II.6.103.i.

108 Committee Opinion, *Russia's Application for Membership of the Council of Europe*, Doc. 7463, at VIII (Committee on Legal Affairs and Human Rights, Jan. 18, 1996).

> a particular problem seems to present itself. This assertion is valid for every echelon of the Russian state administration, from the President of the Federation . . . down to local officials . . . .[109]

Thus, the Assembly debate opened with the unchallenged admission of the "first, primordial concern" of arbitrariness that Shaffer and Sandholtz identify with the absence of the rule of law: "where the wielder of power is not subject, in practice, to the law, its controls and limits."[110]

On January 25, 1996, the Parliamentary Assembly voted 164–35 to recommend membership.[111] It identified twenty-five concrete commitments to be undertaken by the Russian Federation in exchange. These needed to be done to satisfy the interpretive gloss the Assembly gave to the admission requirements stated categorically in Articles 3 and 4 of the Statute but expressed now in a future conditional, noting "the Assembly believes that Russia – in the sense of Article 4 of the Statute – is clearly willing and will be able in the near future to fulfil the provisions for membership of the Council of Europe as set forth in Article 3 . . . ."[112] The Committee of Ministers extended this invitation a fortnight later, declaring that "the Russian Federation complies with the conditions" for membership.[113]

## III Participation

At least for a while, the decision to admit Russia continued to produce positive results: modernized codes of law, increased procedural regularity in a judiciary with greater insulation from political forces, and the gradual, concomitant development of stability and predictability in relations between state and citizen that are hallmarks of the rule of law. Nor did accession end the process of legal reform, although Leuprecht proved to be right that the Council had the most leverage at the pre-accession stage. In significant ways, the Council of Europe's institutions kept a close eye and a guiding hand on Russian developments.[114]

But as time passed, Russian officials cared less and less about this relationship. With the resignation of President Boris Yeltsin, a sharp

109 *Id.* at II.
110 *See* Chapter 1.
111 Caroline Southey, *Council of Europe Votes Russia In*, Financial Times (UK) (Jan. 26, 1996).
112 Opinion 193 (1996), ¶ 7.
113 CM Resolution (96) 2, *Invitation to the Russian Federation to Become a Member of the Council of Europe* (Feb. 8, 1996).
114 Bindig, *supra* note 91, at 34.

break was created in Russia's relationship with the Council of Europe. Vladimir Putin was appointed to the office of prime minister in August 1999 as a wave of terrorist attacks swept Russia. He had not participated in any part of the accession process or presided over Russia's first years as a member. Yet it would fall to him to bring the idea of a common European home and the promises of the lengthy accession process to reality.

Putin responded to those attacks by launching a second, brutal war in Chechnya. Council of Europe observers condemned widespread violations of human rights and humanitarian law.[115] In 2005, Atkinson and Bindig, serving as monitors of Russia's past promises, used variations on the phrase "climate of impunity" more than ten times in their report, mostly about violations of human rights in Chechnya.[116] This was the third such report, following those in June 1998 and April 2002. Even the rapporteurs acknowledged that the ordinary biennial reporting requirement for a monitored country had proven impossible in Russia. It was becoming clear that Russia was in little hurry to make good on many of its commitments, even as it struggled to abide by others.

One commitment kept, however, was ratification of the European Convention on Human Rights. Russia ceded jurisdiction to the European Court to interpret and apply the Convention and agreed "to abide by the final judgment of the Court in any case" in which it was a party.[117] This provides useful metrics to measure both the Court's effects on the development of the rule of law in Russia and Russia's effect on the operation of the Court.

The first data point worth considering is the rapid rise of merits judgments found against Russia. These are tabulated in Figure 8.2.[118]

The number of judgments finding no violation of Convention obligations remains consistently small, while findings of violations rise precipitously over time (depressed only slightly by reforms Russia itself stalled). Judgments

[115] For a review of these reports, see Kahn, *Vladimir Putin and the Rule of Law*, *supra* note 42, at 528 n.69.

[116] Report, *Honouring of Obligations and Commitments by the Russian Federation*, Doc. 10568 (June 3, 2005).

[117] Федеральний закон № 54-ФЗ "О ратификации Конвенции о защите прав человека и основных свобод и Протоколов к ней," [Federal Law No. 54-FZ "On the ratification of the Convention for the Protection of Human Rights and Fundamental Freedoms and Protocols to it"], Собр. Законод. РФ [Collected Legislation of the Russian Federation], 1998, No. 14, Art. No. 1514, at 2939–40.

[118] Data from the Court's *Annual Report*, 2001 through 2022. There are small discrepancies among the Court's reports for total judgments in 2001–2006. *Annual Report 2016* is used here.

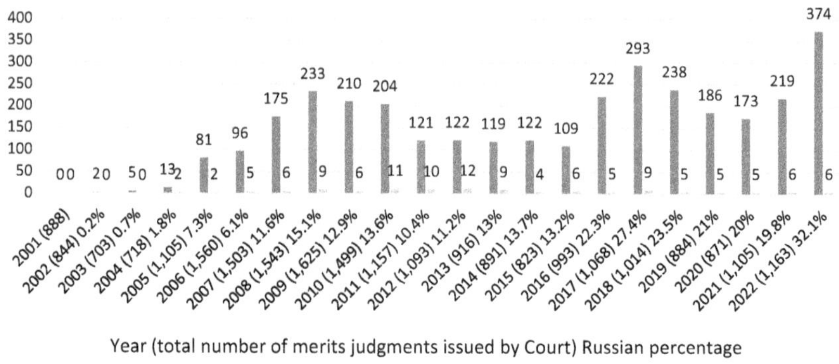


Figure 8.2 Judgments on the merits by the ECtHR concerning Russia, 2001–22.

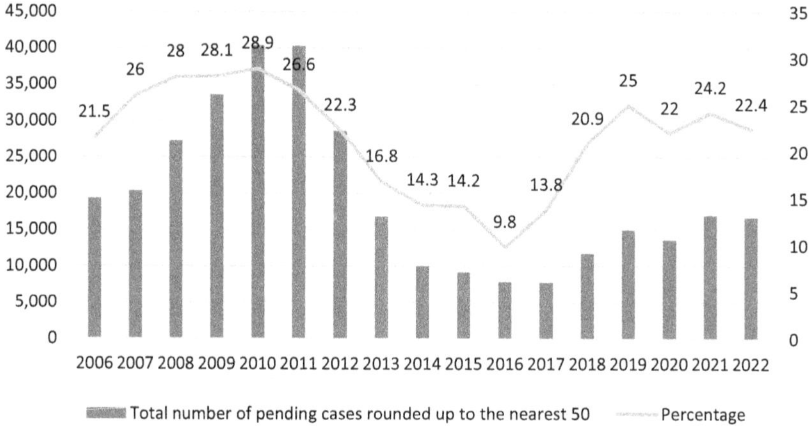


Figure 8.3 Pending Russian cases allocated to judicial formations of the ECtHR, 2006–22.

against Russia as a percentage of all merits judgments across member states also rises, from single digits to an astonishing 32.1 percent in 2022. After 2016, Russia accounted for nearly a fifth of all judgments every year.

These statistics correlate with a consistently large and disproportionate share of pending cases awaiting the Court's assessment. Figure 8.3 shows this effect in absolute and percentage terms.[119] Only during a short period in which the Court's procedural reforms helped dispense with many cases

[119] *Id.*

(again catalyzed in no small part by Russia's volume) did Russia account for less than a fifth of all pending cases. Many have commented on the effects on the entire Strasbourg system of such a backlog clogging the Court's docket.

Most telling of all, however, are the nature of violations. Figure 8.4 identifies Russia's four most numerous types of violations each year.[120] Every single year, Russia violated the Article 5 right to liberty and security, which protects various fundamental interests during arrest, pre- and post-trial detention, and other forms of deprivation of physical freedom. For fourteen of twenty years, this was the leading violation. Russia violated the Article 6 right to a fair trial in all but two reporting years. Similar violations for the excessive length of judicial proceedings or for the absence of effective state investigation into loss of life, torture, or inhuman treatment are ubiquitous, as is the substantive violation of the prohibition in Article 3 against torture and inhuman or degrading treatment or punishment.

The steadily rising number of cases concerning these various rights suggests the dismantling of the Council's therapeutic efforts in Russia. The very first case concerning Russia was brought by pensioner Burdov seeking payment due for work at the Chernobyl nuclear disaster. Despite repeatedly suing the state, Burdov could not enforce his favorable judgments. A unanimous court held that Russia violated both Burdov's property rights and his Article 6 right to a fair trial since "that right would be illusory if a Contracting State's domestic legal system allowed a final, binding judicial decision to remain inoperative to the detriment of one party."[121]

The emergence of increasingly effective courts able to enforce property rights within a reasonable time would seem a strong indicator of the strengthening of the rule of law in a state. But not only does this chart show Russia's regression from that very first judgment, seven years later, the same Burdov succeeded with the same claims in *Burdov v. Russia (No. 2)*, in which the Court *sua sponte* also found a violation of the Article 13 right to an effective remedy.[122] Likewise, the second case decided against Russia concerned egregiously inhuman and degrading (and lengthy) conditions of pretrial confinement.[123] As Figure 8.4 shows, these violations increased over the duration of Russia's membership.

[120] *Id.*

[121] Burdov v. Russia, App. No. 59498/00 (May 7, 2002), https://hudoc.echr.coe.int/eng?i=002-5350.

[122] Burdov v. Russia No. 2, App. No. 33509/04 (Jan. 15, 2009), https://hudoc.echr.coe.int/eng?i=001-90671.

[123] Kalashnikov v. Russia, App. No. 47095/99 (July 15, 2002), https://hudoc.echr.coe.int/?i=001-60606.

| YEAR | SUBJECT OF VIOLATION (NUMBER OF VIOLATIONS) |
|---|---|
| 2003 | Liberty (4); Fair Trial (3); Length of proceedings (1); Respect priv'y/fam'y (1); Property (1) |
| 2004 | Liberty (7); Length of proceedings (6); **TORTURE** (4); **INHUMAN TREATMENT** (4); ***Effective Remedy*** (4) |
| 2005 | Property (48); Fair Trial (45); Length of proceedings (21); Liberty (11) |
| 2006 | Fair Trial (64); Property (49); Liberty (19); Length of proceedings (18) |
| 2007 | Fair Trial (127); Property (114); Liberty (47); **INHUMAN TREATMENT** (25) |
| 2008 | Fair Trial (159); Property (122); Liberty (67); **INHUMAN TREATMENT** (63) |
| 2009 | Liberty (109); **INHUMAN TREATMENT** (84); Fair Trial (74); ***Effective Remedy*** (73) |
| 2010 | **INHUMAN TREATMENT** (102); Liberty (89); Fair Trial (55); ***Effective Remedy*** (55) |
| 2011 | Liberty (68); **INHUMAN TREATMENT** (62); Lack eff. inv. A-2 (58); ***Effective Remedy*** (58) |
| 2012 | Liberty (64); **INHUMAN TREATMENT** (48); Fair Trial (36); Lack eff. inv. A-3 (25) |
| 2013 | Liberty (63); **INHUMAN TREATMENT** (49); ***Effective Remedy*** (30); Fair trial (25) |
| 2014 | Liberty (56); **INHUMAN TREATMENT** (50); ***Effective Remedy*** (30); Fair trial (24) |
| 2015 | Liberty (58); **INHUMAN TREATMENT** (44); ***Effective Remedy*** (22); Lack eff. inv. A-2 (20); Lack eff. inv. A-3 (20) |
| 2016 | Liberty (153); **INHUMAN TREATMENT** (64); ***Effective Remedy*** (50); Fair trial (41) |
| 2017 | Liberty (116); **INHUMAN TREATMENT** (107); ***Effective Remedy*** (83); Fair trial (59) |
| 2018 | Liberty (99); **INHUMAN TREATMENT** (99); ***Effective Remedy*** (67); Fair trail (46) |
| 2019 | Liberty (90); Fair trial (61); **INHUMAN TREATMENT** (57); ***Effective Remedy*** (43) |
| 2020 | Liberty (82); Fair trail (54); **INHUMAN TREATMENT** (41); ***Effective Remedy*** (27); Lack eff. inv. A-2 (27) |
| 2021 | Liberty (96); **INHUMAN TREATMENT** (76); Fair trial (53); Respect Priv'y/Fam'y (53) |
| 2022 | Inhuman treatment (198); Liberty (195); ***Effective Remedy*** (119); Respect Priv'y/Fam'y (98) |

**Key:**

| | |
|---|---|
| Liberty | Article 5 Right to liberty and security |
| Fair Trial | Article 6 Right to a fair trial |
| **INHUMAN TREATMENT** | Article 3 Prohibition of inhuman or degrading treatment or punishment |
| ***Effective Remedy*** | Article 13 Right to an effective remedy for violation of Convention rights |
| **TORTURE** | Article 3 Prohibition of torture, inhuman or degrading treatment/punishment |
| Property | Protocol 1, Article 1 Right to the peaceful enjoyment of property |
| Length of proceedings | Article 6 Right to a fair and public hearing within a reasonable time |
| Respect Priv'y/Fam'y | Article 8 Right to respect for private and family life |
| Lack eff. inv. A-2 | Article 2 State's positive obligation to effectively investigate fatal incidents |
| Lack eff. inv. A-3 | Article 3 State's positive obligation to effectively investigate torture, etc. |

**Figure 8.4** Leading violations of the Convention by Russia by year, 2003–22.

Starting in 2009, violation of the right to an effective remedy was a leading (and increasingly frequent) violation every year save two. Violations of the prohibition against torture, inhuman and degrading treatment or punishment, and lack of effective investigation of such matters remained prominent and increased. Such cases of mistreatment, ineffective mechanisms of judicial control, and indifference to holding state officials accountable strongly suggest the "five sources of arbitrariness to which different rule-of-law prescriptions respond."[124]

With hindsight, discrete cases now seem akin to canaries in a coal mine. Vladimir Gusinskiy was detained at the notorious Butyrka prison and compelled by an acting minister for press and mass communications to sell his media holdings to a state company (at that company's price) in exchange for his freedom – an abuse of power in which the Strasbourg Court had little difficulty finding a pretextual use of law.[125] With remarkable understatement, the Court noted that "it is not the purpose of such public-law matters as criminal proceedings and detention on remand to be used as part of commercial bargaining strategies."[126]

The arrest and separate convictions of another oligarch, Mikhail Khodorkovsky, and the nationalization of his Yukos Oil Company led to the Court's largest-ever award of damages (€1.8 billion).[127] Khodorkovsky's second conviction prompted analysis by experts selected by the Russian Presidential Council on the Development of Civil Society and Human Rights.[128] The experts' reports led the Council to recommend, inter alia, review of the verdict with a view to its repeal due to fundamental errors and violations of law at trial.[129] These reports and recommendations were submitted to President Medvedev shortly before Vladimir Putin's return to the presidency, following which there began a criminal investigation and harassment of the Russian experts.[130]

124 *See* Chapter 1.

125 Gusinskiy v. Russia, App. No. 70276/01 (May 19, 2004), https://hudoc.echr.coe.int/fre?i=001-61767.

126 *Id.* ¶ 76.

127 OAO Neftyanaya Kompaniya Yukos v. Russia, App. No. 14902/04 (July 31, 2014), https://hudoc.echr.coe.int/fre?i=001-145730.

128 The author was one of those experts. *See* Jeffrey Kahn, *Introduction to the Report*, 4 J. Eurasian L. 321, 327–28 (2011).

129 *Id.*

130 Jeffrey Kahn, *The Richelieu Effect: The Khodorkovsky Case and Political Interference with Justice*, *in* A Sociology of Justice in Russia 231 (Marina Kurkchiyan & Agnieszka Kubal eds., 2018); Jeffrey Kahn, *In Putin's Russia, Shooting the Messenger*, N.Y. Times (Feb. 25, 2013), www.nytimes.com/2013/02/26/opinion/in-putins-russia-shooting-the-messenger.html.

A short time later, the Yukos case was the second of only two cases selected by the Russian Constitutional Court to employ a 2015 law that gave the Court responsibility (not the mere discretion) to prohibit compliance with ECtHR judgments found contrary to the Russian Federation's constitution. There is reason to think the law was promulgated with this arbitrary purpose in mind.[131] The Russian Court applied this law to hold that Russia could not pay the Strasbourg Court's massive award.[132] For the first time, a member state's highest court had directly challenged the authority of the European Court and flatly refused to permit execution of its judgment.[133]

One can add other names now also recalling abuses of power that could reach individuals both abroad and within Russia: Alexander Litvinenko, assassinated with polonium-210 in London in 2006; Boris Nemtsov, assassinated outside the Kremlin in 2015; Vladimir Kara-Murza, twice poisoned, in 2015 and 2017, and imprisoned; Alexei Navalnyy, poisoned with novichok in 2020 and imprisoned (where he died in 2024 under suspicious circumstances). More could also be said about the deconstruction of legal protections that meant little without the institutionalization of a mindset that had been recognized as missing from the start. Unlike a statute, such an ethos could not simply be promulgated.

## IV Conclusion

Russia presented the Council of Europe with a devilish problem of practical definition: How much rule-of-law reform was enough to join an international organization for which the rule of law is a prerequisite? This question arrived when the organization, uncertain about its future, was presented with opportunities to aid in legal and democratic reforms sought by states emerging from behind the Iron Curtain. The momentum

[131] Kahn, *supra* note 21, at 934.

[132] Постановление № 1-П/2017 от 19 января 2017 г. по делу о разрешении вопроса о возможности исполнения в соответствии с Конституцией Российской Федерации постановления Европейского Суда по правам человека от 31 июля 2014 года по делу «ОАО «Нефтяная компания «ЮКОС» против России» в связи с запросом Министерства юстиции Российской Федерации [Judgment No. 1-P/2017 (Jan. 19, 2017) in the case on the resolution of the issue of the possibility of executing, in conformity with the Constitution of the Russian Federation, the judgment of the European Court of Human Rights of July 31, 2014 in the case of "OAO Oil Company 'Yukos' against Russia" in connection with the request of the Ministry of Justice of the Russian Federation].

[133] Kahn, *supra* note 21, at 958.

that built in the Council's accession process enveloped nearly half of Europe in a well-intentioned effort to foster the rule of law and other values in countries with histories revealing varying levels of experience with them. This led to a process the deputy secretary-general of the organization called therapeutic admission that was full of risk, Russia's admission especially so.

Russian leaders who took no part in imagining or attempting to build a common European home presided over the dismantling of its limited success. In that destruction, what was a liability for reformers like Gorbachev and Yeltsin served as a means of control for Putin. Amending slightly the words of the Committee on Legal Affairs and Human Rights, the mentality toward law had not changed, at least not enough.[134] No amount of legislating or adjudicating could speed up that change in time. "Such is the heritage of dictatorships," Mühlemann acknowledged, and Russia had been one for centuries.

It can only be hoped that the experience of nearly thirty years that spanned this relationship from start to finish offers a better start to the next opportunity Russians and Europeans may have to attempt to build that home again.

134 *See* Opinion 7463, *supra* at note 108, at II.

9

# Authoritarian Rule by Law

## Erdoğan and the European Court of Human Rights

DILEK KURBAN

In the early to mid 2000s, the 'new' Turkey under the leadership of the Justice and Development Party (Adalet ve Kalkınma Partisi, or AKP) was seen by the international community as a beacon of light in the Middle East. Within a decade, Turkey has turned from a country in democratic transition whose reforms earned it European Union (EU) accession status and victories at the European Court of Human Rights (ECtHR) to one engaged in systematic rule-of-law violations, state violence, and legal repression. A decade later, Turkey is an autocratic country under the one-man rule of Recep Tayyip Erdoğan, who has eroded any remnants of rule of law and democracy. Yet, none of the human rights and rule-of-law transnational legal orders (TLOs)[1] of which Turkey formally is a part has sanctioned this country.

From one perspective, this is nothing new. Turkey has never been a democracy, despite its decades-long engagement with European institutions. Its frequent military interventions have all taken place since Turkey joined the Council of Europe (CoE) and ratified the European Convention on Human Rights (ECHR) in 1954. As far as the EU is concerned, with the exception of the first, all of these interventions took place after the signing of the 1963 Association Agreement. Throughout, European institutions repeatedly upheld their security interests, in preference to human rights in support of the rule of law, by failing to sanction Turkey.[2]

The research underlying this chapter forms part of the Human Rights Nudge project, which has received funding from the European Research Council (ERC) under the European Union's Horizon 2020 research and innovation programme (Grant Agreement No. 803981).

1 Terence C. Halliday & Gregory Shaffer, *Transnational Legal Orders, in* Transnational Legal Orders 3 (Terence C. Halliday & Gregory Shaffer eds., 2015).

2 Jon C. Pevehouse, Democracy From Above: Regional Organisations And Democratization (2005).

Nonetheless, there is something truly puzzling in the current situation. The worst instances of state violence have occurred since Turkey recognized the ECtHR's compulsory jurisdiction in 1990. By the mid-1990s, when violations in the Kurdish region had reached the level of atrocities, the ECtHR had evolved into a powerful regional court.[3] One decade later, it was the world's "most effective court,"[4] operating under the world's "most effective human rights regime."[5] Yet, despite hundreds of adverse ECtHR judgments, Turkey did not change course. Under Erdoğan, the country evolved into a full-blown autocratic regime despite its EU accession status, ordinarily reserved for adherents to the rule of law.

In light of all of this, European institutions' failure to sanction Turkey is perplexing. As Turkey's systemic rule-of-law violations intensified, the ECtHR became increasingly inaccessible for their victims. Contrary to Tom Ginsburg's assessment of the CoE as a regional organization where liberal member states stand up for "the defense of democracy,"[6] none of them brought an interstate case against Turkey nor sought its suspension from membership. Similarly, the EU and its liberal members continue to let Turkey reap the political, financial, and reputational benefits of its accession-country status. Even more, they have taken steps to deepen relations with Turkey in some areas, most notably through the 2015 refugee agreement.[7]

Is the Turkish case a singular story of democratic transition gone wrong, or does it speak to broader issues concerning the ways in which human-rights and rule-of-law TLOs interact with authoritarian regimes? Claiming the latter, this chapter puts forth theoretical insights based on an empirical analysis of Turkey's relationship with European institutions. Going beyond conventional analyses that characterize interactions between international institutions and nation-states as one-way relationships where norms flow (or not) from the top down, it looks into what

[3] Mikael Rask Madsen, *From Cold War Instrument to Supreme European Court: The European Court of Human Rights at the Crossroads of International and National Law and Politics*, 32 L. & Soc. Inquiry 137 (2007).

[4] Laurence R. Helfer, *Redesigning the European Court of Human Rights: Embeddedness as a Deep Structural Principle of the European Human Rights Regime*, 19 Eur. J. Int'l L. 125, 126 (2008).

[5] Alec Stone Sweet & Helen Keller, *Introduction: The Reception of the ECHR in National Legal Orders, in* A Europe of Rights: The Impact of the ECHR on National Legal Systems 3, 3 (Helen Keller & Alec Stone Sweet eds., 2008).

[6] Tom Ginsburg, Democracies and International Law 288 (2021).

[7] Josef Janning, *Germany's Gambit: Turkey and the Refugee Crisis*, Eur. Council on Foreign Rels. (Jan. 28, 2016), https://ecfr.eu/article/commentary_germanys_gambit_turkey_and_the_refugee_crisis5080/.

Gregory Shaffer and Wayne Sandholtz call the "enmeshment of national and international trends."[8] Doing so, however, it does not solely ask whether and how human rights norms are applied in authoritarian contexts, but also how international organizations tasked with upholding the rule of law not only permit illiberal states to violate those norms but also themselves undermine such norms.

While I also analyze the EU in this regard elsewhere,[9] in this chapter I focus on the CoE, more specifically the ECtHR, for several reasons. First, since Turkey is not a member state, quasi-judicial and judicial EU sanctioning mechanisms are not available against this country; the EU's toolbox is limited to suspending/ending the accession negotiations and cutting down/freezing preaccession funds. In contrast, as a CoE member, Turkey is under obligation to uphold the rule of law, democracy, and human rights and to comply with ECtHR judgments. Second, contrary to the EU, which has received a fair amount of criticism for its inadequate action vis-à-vis democratic backsliding in Hungary and Poland, the ECtHR has not been sufficiently held accountable for its failure in Russia, Turkey, Azerbaijan, and beyond; its ineffectiveness has been mainly attributed to compliance failure. In reality, as the Turkish case illustrates, the ECtHR has never made full use of its powers to expose systemic rule-of-law and rights violations in authoritarian regimes.

## I Conceptualizing the Rule of Law

As Martin Krygier has put it, the rule of law "has become an unavoidable cliché of international organizations of every kind."[10] Virtually all international and regional institutions require actual and prospective member states to adhere to the rule of law without specifying what that actually means.[11] Scholarship has not provided much clarity either;[12] the rule of law remains an "essentially contested"[13] and "elusive"[14]

[8] *See* Chapter 1.

[9] Dilek Kurban, *Rethinking Enmeshment and the Rule of Law in Authoritarian Contexts*, 8 U.C. Irvine J. Int'l Transnat'l & Comp. L. 107 (2023).

[10] Martin Krygier, *The Rule of Law: Pasts, Presents, and Two Possible Futures*, 12 Ann. Rev. L. & Soc. Sci. 199, 200 (2016).

[11] *See* Chapter 4.

[12] Brian Z. Tamanaha, On The Rule Of Law: History, Politics, Theory (2004).

[13] Jeremy Waldron, *Is the Rule of Law an Essentially Contested Concept (in Florida)?*, 21 L. & Phil. 137 (2002).

[14] Brian Z. Tamanaha, *The History and Elements of the Rule of Law*, Sing. J. Legal Stud. 232, 232 (2012).

concept. For some, it refers to a mode of governance where rules abide by procedural criteria such as generality, foreseeability, applicability, certainty, and nondiscrimination.[15] Proponents of a thick formulation argue that there can be no rule of law without individual rights, democracy, and justice.[16] Accordingly, what distinguishes the substantive conception of the rule of law is that it is designed by democratically accountable officials and institutions with the goal of advancing and upholding fundamental rights and individual justice.

Another way in which legal theorists and philosophers approach conceptualizing the rule of law is, instead of listing its institutional elements "as though they were ingredients in a recipe,"[17] to ask what it seeks to achieve. In Brian Tamanaha's functionalist approach, the rule of law exists when law provides security and trust, social order, individual liberty, and economic development; restrains officials; gives prominence to legal professionals; and, most controversially, reflects and maintains power structures in society.[18] For Terry Nardin, the rule of law is first and foremost "a moral idea," which limits the exercise of power[19] – in contrast to rule by law, where powerholders "make and enforce legal norms . . . to regulate and control the population."[20] In Krygier's end-oriented approach, while "never the only thing we want,"[21] what is distinctive about the rule of law is that it aims at the "institutionalized tempering"[22] of power. Power is arbitrary when it is uncontrolled, unpredictable, unrespectful, and ungrounded.[23] Where a reason is provided, its pursuit must be proportionate to that goal. A goal-oriented approach cautions against the authoritarian capture of the rule-of-law rhetoric, where law functions "as an instrument of power" rather than "a constraint on the exercise of power."[24]

[15] Ron L. Fuller, The Morality of Law (rev. ed. 1969); Joseph Raz, The Authority of Law: Essays on Law and Morality (1979).
[16] Ronald Dworkin, A Matter of Principle (1986).
[17] Krygier, *supra* note 10, at 212.
[18] Brian Z. Tamanaha, *Functions of the Rule of Law*, *in* The Cambridge Companion to the Rule of Law 221 (Jens Meierhenrich & Martin Loughlin eds., 2021).
[19] Terry Nardin, *Theorising the International Rule of Law*, 34 Rev. Int'l Stud. 385, 385 (2008).
[20] *See* Chapter 1.
[21] Krygier, *supra* note 10, at 205.
[22] *Id.* at 199.
[23] Martin Krygier, *Poder atemperado: Cómo pensar, y no pensar, sobre el Estado de Derecho* [Tempering power: How to think, and not to think, about the rule of law], 25 Eunomía: Revista en Cultura de la Legalidad 22, 34–36 (2023).
[24] Nardin, *supra* note 19, at 385.

But what is the rule of law's relationship to democracy and human rights? As distinct as these concepts are, can they exist in isolation or are they *sine qua non* elements of each other? If the goal is to ensure the nonarbitrary exercise of power, can that be achieved without democratic accountability and representation? How can power be tamed in the absence of the free exercise of civil and political rights? Gregory Shaffer and Wayne Sandholtz point out that when those governed by the law have no input in its substance, "adherence to rules is less a matter of choice and more a reflection of power relations."[25] Thus, democratic participation in lawmaking processes is a *sine qua non* of the rule of law, even by its thin conceptualization. Similarly, the nonarbitrary exercise of power can be possible only in contexts where rulers adhere to fundamental human rights norms, such as the right to due process. So, the thin/thick distinction is not conceptually sound nor practically attainable.[26]

Socio-legal research has demonstrated that the rule of law and rule by law do not represent a binary, but rather, as Jens Meierhenrich has put it, "a continuum of legality"; there are variations of both ends of the spectrum and countries may fall in different points along the continuum at different times.[27] The rule of law (a normative state) and rule by law (a prerogative state) may even coexist in "hybrid authoritarian regimes"[28] – a truth verified in contexts ranging from the military dictatorship in Chile to the single-party rule in China.[29] Whereas the dual states in Nazi Germany and apartheid South Africa operated along racial lines, much of empirical scholarship concerns hybrid cases, where the rule-of-law bit applies to the economic sphere to attract foreign investment, whereas the political sphere is ruled by law to suppress the opposition. In reality,

[25] *See* Chapter 1.

[26] *See* Chapter 1; Krygier, *supra* note 10.

[27] Jens Meierhenrich, Is the Authoritarian Rule of Law an Oxymoron? Paper presented at the Rule of Law in Transnational Context symposium, U.C. Irvine Law Sch., Sept.16–17, 2022 (unpublished manuscript).

[28] JENS MEIERHENRICH, THE REMNANTS OF THE RECHTSTAAT: AN ETHNOGRAPHY OF NAZI LAW (2018).

[29] JOTHIE RAJAH, AUTHORITARIAN RULE OF LAW: LEGISLATION, DISCOURSE, AND LEGITIMACY IN SINGAPORE (2012); TAMIR MOUSTAFA, THE STRUGGLE FOR CONSTITUTIONAL POWER: LAW, POLITICS, AND ECONOMIC DEVELOPMENT IN EGYPT (2007); LISA HILBINK, JUDGES BEYOND POLITICS IN DEMOCRACY AND DICTATORSHIP: LESSONS FROM CHILE (2007); JENS MEIERHENRICH, THE LEGACIES OF LAW: LONG-RUN CONSEQUENCES OF LEGAL DEVELOPMENT IN SOUTH AFRICA, 1652–2000 (2008); Kanishka Jayasuriya, *The Exception Becomes the Norm: Law and Regimes of Exception in East Asia*, 2 ASIAN-PAC. L. & POL'Y J. 108 (2001).

authoritarian regimes often go beyond that and blend rule by law with lawlessness by simultaneously operating inside and outside the law. China under Xi Jinping turns both to law "as a tool of governance" in the economic sphere[30] and to lawlessness to engage in what has been argued to constitute genocide[31] or crimes against humanity[32] against the Uyghur minority. Nor is the dual state limited to antidemocratic contexts. As Michael McCann and Filiz Kahraman show, the binary of liberal democracies of the Global North and authoritarian regimes of the Global South as regime types respectively representing the rule of law and rule by law does not match reality. Legal hybridity is much more common and the (racialized) dual state also exists in countries where certain parts of the population have systematically been denied their core liberties, albeit in varying degrees over time.[33]

Where we stand, many things remain unresolved. One concerns the use of violence. Much of socio-legal research on rule by law is limited to repression as a form of governance. What to do with instances where the state turns to violence toward certain (racialized) segments of the population in utter lawlessness? Examples are plenty – dictatorships in the Southern Cone of Latin America, Russia in the Northern Caucasus, Turkey in the Kurdish region, China in Xinjiang, and so forth. This goes far beyond the arbitrary exercise of power, which McCann and Kahraman label as authoritarianism, and speaks to a mode of governance, which is illiberal[34] or antiliberal[35] in the sense that it denies core civil liberties to specific groups within the populace. Thus, if we are to agree that the rule of law stands on one end of the spectrum, the far end seems to be lawlessness, not rule by law, and the dual state or "authoritarian legalism"[36] stands somewhere in between. The dual state's

[30] GINSBURG, *supra* note 6, at 257.

[31] *The Uyghur Genocide: An Examination of China's Breaches of the 1948 Genocide Convention*, NEWLINES INST. FOR STRATEGY & POL'Y (Mar. 8, 2021), https://tinyurl.com/38m3u34v.

[32] *"Like We Were Enemies in a War": China's Mass Internment, Torture and Persecution of Muslims in Xinjiang*, AMNESTY INT'L (June 10, 2021), www.amnesty.org/en/documents/asa17/4137/2021/en/.

[33] Michael McCann & Filiz Kahraman, *On the Interdependence of Liberal and Illiberal/Authoritarian Legal Forms in Racial Capitalist Regimes . . . The Case of the United States*, 17 ANN. REV. L. & SOC. SCI. 483 (2021).

[34] *Id.*

[35] Martin Krygier, at the Rule of Law in Transnational Context symposium, U.C. Irvine Law Sch., Sept.16–17, 2022.

[36] MEIERHENRICH, *supra* note 28, at 245.

prerogative half need not only refer to the sovereign's violation of its own laws but also extends to institutionalized lawlessness.[37]

Another outstanding question concerns the object of our inquiry. Scholarship predominantly focuses on the nation-state and to the extent that it turns its lens on international institutions, the analysis is limited to their impact, or lack thereof. The relationship is defined in unidimensional terms where norms flow (or not) from the supranational to the domestic level. Certainly, this dualist perspective has faced formidable challenges recently. Halliday and Shaffer adopt an empirically based theoretical approach which integrates top-down and bottom-up analyses to understand the variable ways in which legal norms and practices are "developed, conveyed, and settled" transnationally through a "dynamic tension" between the local, national, international, and transnational levels.[38] Similarly, Shaffer and Sandholtz argue that the interaction between national and international laws and practices is recursive, in that the erosion in the former implicates the latter, cyclical, in that it alternates between positive and negative cycles, and variable, in that it changes within and across regions.[39] Tom Ginsburg provides a global, empirical overview of the rising authoritarian threat to the international order, documenting the ways in which illiberal norms and practices are competing with their liberal counterparts – an international rule by law, so to speak.[40] Kim Scheppele documents how "autocratic legalists" not only defy the EU's founding norms and rules but also seek to undermine its capability to respond to the illiberal challenge.[41]

Yet, we lack comparable empirical work on the performance of other international institutions facing authoritarian backlash to their rules and norms. Nowhere is the gap between scholarly assessments and empirical reality as wide as in the practice of the ECtHR. A growing body of scholarship places this court on the receiving end of backlash without sufficiently inquiring into its own role in the rule-of-law crisis in Europe.[42] While the European Commission and, to some extent, the

[37] *Id.* at 237–38.

[38] Halliday & Shaffer, *supra* note 1, at 1.

[39] *See* Chapter 1.

[40] GINSBURG, *supra* note 6.

[41] Kim Lane Scheppele, *Autocratic Legalism*, 85 U. CHI. L. REV. 545, 548 (2018).

[42] Basak Cali, *Coping with Crisis: Whither the Variable Geometry in the Jurisprudence of the European Court of Human Rights*, 35 WIS. INT'L L.J. 237 (2017); Øyvind Stiansen & Erik Voeten, *Backlash and Judicial Restraint: Evidence from the European Court of Human Rights*, 64 INT'L STUD. Q. 770 (2020); Mikael Rask Madsen, *Rebalancing European Human Rights: Has the Brighton Declaration Engendered a New Deal on*

European Court of Justice received considerable critical attention by scholars of rule-of-law backsliding within the EU,[43] the ECtHR enjoys scholarly praise as the bastion of liberal democratic order in Europe.[44]

What lies beneath this skewed depiction of the ECtHR is a methodological bias. With the exception of a few,[45] scholars base their empirical analyses solely on judgments – where the ECtHR addresses the merits of the case.[46] Yet, such rulings constitute a tiny fraction of the ECtHR's jurisprudence – only 9 percent. Of the cases reaching Strasbourg, 84 percent are rejected as inadmissible, while 6 percent are struck out on grounds of friendly settlements and 1 percent on grounds of unilateral declarations.[47] It is this giant bottom of the iceberg where most of the "enmeshment" of ECtHR norms, national rules, and practices occur. What this publicly invisible interaction reveals is not a "trustee court" holding states accountable for their violations,[48] but an international institution enabling the consolidation of authoritarian legalism.

To address these gaps in rule-of-law scholarship, this chapter focuses on the ECtHR's interaction with Turkey to inquire how human rights courts do and should react to authoritarian challenge to the rule of law. Conceptually, it analyzes the Court's case law concerning both Turkey's resort to law to consolidate its power (rule by law) and disregard of rules,

*Human Rights in Europe?*, 9 J. Int'l Disp. Settlement 199 (2018); Laurence R. Helfer & Erik Voeten, *Walking Back Rights in Europe?*, 31 Eur. J. Int'l L. 797 (2020).

43 R. Daniel Kelemen & Kim Lane Scheppele, *How to Stop Funding Autocracy in the EU*, Verfassungsblog (Sept. 10, 2018), https://verfassungsblog.de/how-to-stop-funding-autocracy-in-the-eu/; Laurent Pech, Patryk Wachowiec & Dariusz Mazur, *Poland's Rule of Law Breakdown: A Five-Year Assessment of the EU's (In)Action*, 13 Hague J. on Rule L. 1 (2021).

44 *See, e.g.*, Kim Lane Scheppele, *The Treaties Without a Guardian: The European Commission and the Rule of Law*, 29 Col. J. Eur. L. 93 (2023); Cali, *supra* note 42. *But see* Mikael Rask Madsen, *The Narrowing of the European Court of Human Rights? Legal Diplomacy, Situational Self-Restraint, and the New Vision for the Court*, 2 Eur. Convention Hum. Rts. L. Rev. 180 (2021).

45 Helen Keller, Magdalena Forowicz & Lorenz Engi, Friendly Settlements Before the European Court of Human Rights: Theory and Practice 10 (2010); Veronika Fikfak, *Against Settlement Before the European Court of Human Rights*, 20 Int'l J. Const. L. 942 (2022).

46 Stiansen & Voeten, *supra* note 42; Helfer & Voeten, *supra* note 42.

47 Eur. Ct. of Hum. Rts., Analysis of Statistics 2021, at 11 (2022), www.echr.coe.int/Documents/Stats_analysis_2021_ENG.pdf.

48 Alec Stone Sweet & Clare Ryan, A Cosmopolitan Legal Order: Kant, Constitutional Justice, and the European Convention on Human Rights (2018).

including its own, in engaging in repression and violence (lawlessness). Methodologically, it goes beyond judgments and takes a close look at inadmissibility decisions and strike-out rulings.

## II Turkey under Erdoğan: Between Rule by Law and Lawlessness

An analysis of authoritarianism embedded in Turkey's politico-juridical regime, which I have done elsewhere,[49] is beyond the scope of this chapter. Suffice here to say that exceptional legal regimes, special criminal tribunals, and anti-terror laws have been constant during military *and* civilian rule in Turkey. At the same time, the current period cannot be explained by domestic historical continuities alone. The particularity of the AKP rule stems from the quick succession, and at times overlap, of unprecedented EU-induced rule-of-law reforms with rule by law and, more recently, lawlessness – the timing, duration, and intensity of which were closely related to the fluctuations of Turkey's relations with European institutions. What renders the AKP rule striking is Erdoğan's ability to pull this off at a time when Turkey was enjoying the deepest integration with human rights and rule-of-law TLOs in its history.

### *1 Continuity: Rule by Law with Strategic Rule-of-Law Reforms*

Any assessment of the rule of/by law under Erdoğan needs to start from the elections that brought him to power in 2002. Erdoğan claimed democratic legitimacy based on the strong mandate he claimed to have received from the electorate, which enabled him to form a single-party government. Yet, this legitimacy rested on a fallacy. Of the eighteen parties that took part in the elections, only two could enter the parliament, leaving 45 percent of the electorate without representation. One of these two parties was the AKP, which acquired 65 percent of the parliamentary seats with only 34 percent of the votes.

Such an antidemocratic outcome was possible thanks to the highest electoral threshold in Europe for parliamentary representation – 10 percent. What's more, the threshold was introduced by the military regime months before it stepped down in November 1983. Fearing that a future pro-Kurdish party would receive high support in the southeast where the Kurds are the majority, the junta introduced a *national* threshold to deny

[49] *See* Dilek Kurban, Limits of Supranational Justice: The European Court of Human Rights and Turkey's Kurdish Conflict (2020).

them political representation.[50] The generals were right in their projections. In 2002, the pro-Kurdish Democratic People's Party (Demokratik Halk Partisi, or DEHAP) could not enter the parliament because its nationwide votes remained at 6.2 percent – although it received up to 56 percent of the votes in the Kurdish region. In Diyarbakır, the largest Kurdish city, DEHAP received 56 percent of the votes, whereas the AKP a mere 16 percent. Had the threshold been 5 percent as in Germany, DEHAP would have gained eight of the ten parlıamentary seats allocated to Diyarbakir – and AKP none. Instead, six seats were allocated to the AKP and four to independent candidates.

Once in power, Erdoğan needed the EU's support to consolidate his rule against the military, and yet the accession status he desperately sought hinged on rule-of-law reforms. Initially, he continued the reforms initiated by the preceding government. Among others, his government adopted relatively progressive laws and established the constitutional supremacy of international human rights treaties over domestic law.[51] Caught between the need to acknowledge this progress and the resistance in some member states to Turkey's accession, the European Council concluded in December 2004 that "Turkey *sufficiently* fulfils the Copenhagen political criteria" and decided to commence the accession process the following year.[52] Never before had the EU made such an exception to its accession conditionality – nor has it since.

Almost immediately after they started, accession negotiations halted due to two mutually reinforcing developments. Domestic debates in several member states linked discussions over the EU's future with Turkey's accession, leading to the European Council's announcement that negotiations would be "an open-ended process."[53] Meanwhile, Cyprus's EU accession and acquisition of veto power over further enlargement turned the Cyprus conflict into a stumbling block for Turkey's membership. When Turkey refused to open its ports and airports to the vessels and flights of Cyprus, the EU froze negotiations

[50] Milletvekili Seçim Kanunu [Law on the Election of Members of the Parliament], No. 2839, June 10, 1983, OFFICIAL GAZETTE, No. 18076 (June 10, 1983) art. 33 [hereinafter Law No. 2839].

[51] *2004 Regular Report on Turkey's Progress Towards Accession*, at 50, COM (2004) 656 final (Oct. 6, 2004), www.ab.gov.tr/siteimages/birimler/kpb/tr_rep_20061998/2004_tr_rap.pdf.

[52] Presidency Conclusions, Brussels European Council (Feb. 1, 2005), www.consilium.europa.eu/ueDocs/cms_Data/docs/pressData/en/ec/83201.pdf (emphasis added).

[53] Council, Enlargement: Accession Negotiations with Turkey: General EU Position, Annex II: *Negotiating Framework*, 12823/1/05 REV 1 (Oct. 12, 2005).

of eight chapters in 2006, followed by similar unilateral decisions by France and Cyprus.

Turkey's diminishing prospects for EU membership enabled the AKP to pursue its own 'reform' agenda, which sought two goals. The first was to diminish the number of adverse ECtHR judgments by creating domestic remedies which, if found effective by the Court, would lead to inadmissibility decisions in pending cases and lower the number of new applications. The most consequential measure was the introduction of the individual right to constitutional complaint.[54] That the right was granted with an eye on Strasbourg was evident in legislative intent: achieving "a considerable decrease in the number of files against Turkey."[55] It was further evident in the intense backdoor diplomacy carried out by CoE secretary-general Thorbjørn Jagland, who later referred to this mechanism as a "system [that Turkey and the CoE] have built together" and "a source of immense pride."[56]

The second, and predominant, goal was to expand Erdoğan's control over the military and the judiciary, in response to their coordinated efforts to preclude the election of the AKP's candidate as president[57] and the legalization of headscarfs at universities,[58] and to dissolve the AKP.[59] Erdoğan's immediate response was to go to the people. He submitted to a national referendum a constitutional reform package seeking to increase his influence over the composition of the Constitutional Court (Anayasa Mahkemesi, or AYM) and the High Council of Judges and Prosecutors (Hakimler ve Savcilar Yüksek Kurulu, or HSYK).[60]

These amendments would have tremendous implications for Turkey's political future, which became evident to most observers only retrospectively.

[54] Türkiye Cumhuriyeti Anayasasının Bazı Maddelerinde Değişiklik Yapılması Hakkında Kanun [Law on the Amendment of Certain Provisions of the Constitution of the Republic of Turkey], No. 5982, May 7, 2010, OFFICIAL GAZETTE, No. 27580 (May 13, 2010).

[55] Venice Comm'n, *Opinion on the Law on the Establishment and Rules of Procedure of the Constitutional Court of Turkey*, CDL-AD(2011)040, at 3 (Oct. 18, 2011), www.venice.coe.int/webforms/documents/default.aspx?pdffile=CDL-AD(2011)040-e.

[56] Esra Demir-Gürsel, *The Former Secretary-General of the Council of Europe Confronting Russia's Annexation of the Crimea and Turkey's State of Emergency*, 2 EUR. CONVENTION HUM. RTS. L. REV. 303, 329–30 (2021).

[57] Asli Bâli, *Courts and Constitutional Transition: Lessons from the Turkish Case*, 11 INT'L J. CONST. L. 666 (2013).

[58] The Constitutional Court (Anayasa Mahkemesi, or AYM) annulled a constitutional amendment abolishing the ban on headscarf at universities. AYM, E. 2008/16, K. 2008/116 (June 5, 2008).

[59] The AKP escaped dissolution by one vote. AYM, E. 2008/1, K. 2008/2, (July 30, 2008).

[60] Ozan Erözden et al., *A Judicial Conundrum: Opinions and Recommendations on Constitutional Reform on Turkey*, TESEV (May 6, 2010), https://tinyurl.com/4tcnents.

The first indication was the 2010 HSYK elections, resulting in the victory of candidates endorsed by the AKP.[61] At the time, dissenting voices within the judiciary contended that the government supported candidates affiliated with the Fethullah Gülen movement,[62] enabling it to dominate the HSYK.[63] Soon after, the AKP and the Gülenists had a public fallout, culminating in a 2013 corruption case implicating the family members of Erdoğan and his ministers.[64] Erdoğan declared war against his former ally, the battleground of which would be the judiciary. From 2014 onward, the AKP "has asserted an unprecedented degree of control over the judiciary" by reestablishing its control over the HSYK and purging alleged Gülenist judges and prosecutors.[65] In December 2015, it classified the Gülen movement as a terrorist organization. The dramatic events of summer 2016, when Erdoğan survived a coup attempt, would show that the war was not over.

## 2 *Rupture: From Rule by Law to Lawlessness*

Since his election to presidency in 2014, Erdoğan had incrementally usurped the constitutional powers belonging to the parliament and the prime minister. As he declared in August 2015, Turkey's system of government had effectively changed and what needed to be done now was "to give a legal framework to this de-facto state with a new constitution."[66]

61 Venice Comm'n, Interim Opinion on the Draft Law on the High Council for Judges and Prosecutors (of 27 September 2010) of Turkey, CDL-AD(2010)042, ¶ 37 (Dec. 20, 2010) www.venice.coe.int/webforms/documents/default.aspx?pdffile=CDL-AD(2010)042-e. Erdoğan publicly acknowledged the government's meddling in the HSYK elections. INT'L COMM'N OF JURISTS, TURKEY: JUDICIAL SYSTEM IN PERIL; A BRIEFING PAPER 3 (June 2, 2016), https://tinyurl.com/5c9mw9xh.

62 An Islamic preacher, Fethullah Gülen is the leader of a transnational religious movement whose members gained increasing power and influence in the education, judiciary, business, and police fields thanks to its political alliance with the AKP.

63 AHMET İNSEL, ALI BAYRAMOĞLU, İBRAHIM OKUR, KORAY ÖZDIL, LEYLA KÖKSAL TARHAN, MITHAT SANCAR, UĞUR YIĞIT & YÜCEL SAYMAN, THE HIGH COUNCIL OF JUDGES AND PROSECUTORS IN TURKEY: ROUNDTABLE DISCUSSION ON ITS NEW STRUCTURE AND OPERATIONS (Ferda Balancar & Belgin Çınar eds., Fethi Keleş trans, Jan. 10, 2013), https://tinyurl.com/5ec8ntyt.

64 Günter Seufert, *Is the Fethullah Gülen Movement Overstretching Itself? A Turkish Religious Community as a National and International Player*, STIFTUNG WISSENSCHAFT UND POLITIK (SWP) (Jan. 13, 2014), www.swp-berlin.org/en/publication/turkey-the-fethullah-guelen-movement/.

65 INT'L COMM'N OF JURISTS, *supra* note 61, at 10.

66 Agence France Presse, *Defiant Erdogan Vows to Press for New Turkey Constitution*, GUARDIAN (Aug. 14, 2015), https://guardian.ng/news/defiant-erdogan-vows-to-press-for-new-turkey-constitution.

The principal hurdle was the presence in the parliament of the pro-Kurdish Peoples' Democratic Party (Halkların Demokratik Partisi, or HDP). For decades, the Kurdish movement had circumvented the electoral system by entering in preelection coalitions with social democratic parties or running with independent candidates, for whom the threshold does not apply. In June 2015, the Kurds dared, for the first time, to participate in the elections under the rubric of their own party. Running on a platform to bar Erdoğan from introducing a presidential regime, the HDP won 13.1 percent of the votes – corresponding to eighty parliamentary seats. The HDP's victory created a hung parliament, depriving the AKP not only of the two-thirds majority it needed to change the constitution or at least the three-fifths majority to call a referendum to establish a presidential system, but even the simple majority to continue its single-party government.[67]

Having faced the first electoral defeat of his career, Erdogan took a decisive turn to rule by lawlessness. He used the hung parliament's inability to produce a government as a pretext to hold repeat elections in November. He resumed war with the PKK to attract the nationalist votes he needed to regain a parliamentary majority.[68] In July, the military went into densely populated towns with combat-ready troops, tanks, and heavy artillery, allegedly to remove the barricades and trenches the PKK had built in residential areas. From August onward, local authorities declared round-the-clock, open-ended curfews in over thirty towns.[69] Civilians were trapped in curfew zones, without access to food, water, power, and health services during long winter months. No one, including children, the sick, the wounded, the elderly, and the disabled, was allowed to leave without authorization, while parliamentarians, aid workers, and human rights observers were denied access. Journalists who tried to enter were threatened, arrested, and, in at least one case, shot.[70] Witnesses "painted an

67 Alberto Nardelli, *Turkey Election Results: What You Need to Know*, GUARDIAN (June 8, 2015), www.theguardian.com/news/datablog/2015/jun/08/turkey-election-results-what-you-need-to-know.

68 Ümit Cizre, *Introduction: The Politics of Redressing Grievances – The AK Party and its Leader*, *in* THE TURKISH AK PARTY AND ITS LEADER: CRITICISM, OPPOSITION AND DISSENT 1 (Ümit Cizre ed., 2016).

69 Eur. Parl. Ass., The Functioning of Democratic Institutions in Turkey, 24th Sess., para. 10 (June 22, 2016).

70 U.N. Off. of the High Comm'r for Hum. Rts. (OHCHR), Report on the Human Rights Situation in South-East Turkey, July 2015 to December 2016 (Feb. 2017); Comm'r for Hum. Rts. of the Council of Eur., Memorandum on the Human Rights Implications of Anti-Terrorism Operations in South-Eastern Turkey, CommDH(2016)39 (Dec. 2, 2016).

apocalyptic picture of the wholesale destruction of neighbourhoods."[71] By December 2016, some 2,000 people, including 1,200 civilians, were killed.[72]

As noted by the CoE Commissioner for Human Rights[73] and the Venice Commission,[74] the operation was unequivocally against Turkish law, which authorizes executive curfews only under a state of emergency, which the government had not declared. Lawlessness was also evident in the absence of any proportionality between the curfews and the counter-terrorism operations accompanying them and the security goals they allegedly pursued. There was a "big contrast" between the number of affected (1.6 million) and displaced (355,000) civilians and the official number of terrorists killed, injured, or captured (873, 196, and 718, respectively) and the "tremendous" destruction of residential areas.[75]

Though still short of the two-thirds majority to call for a referendum on its own, the AKP gained its fourth single-party rule as a result of snap elections held in November 2015. Yet, the HDP still passed the threshold, though now with 10.7 percent, and was still the third-largest party in the parliament. Erdogan turned to the HDP's nemesis, the Nationalist Movement Party (Milliyetçi Hareket Partisi, or MHP), which demanded the Kurdish deputies' ousting from the parliament in return for helping Erdoğan hold a referendum. On April 2, 2016, the AKP presented to the parliament a draft law introducing a one-time exception to the constitutional immunity regime by allowing a blanket vote on all dossiers awaiting legislative authorization.[76] The draft bypassed the constitutionally required regular procedure whereby the plenary reviews the dossiers before the vote and grants affected deputies the right to defend themselves.[77] Any dossier to reach the parliament after May 20 would be subject to the regular immunity regime.

While the amendments seemingly affected all similarly situated parliamentarians, the real target was the HDP deputies, as evident from Erdoğan's concerted campaign after the June 2015 elections. He had

[71] U.N. Off. of the High Comm'r for Hum. Rts. (OHCHR), *supra* note 70, at 7–8.

[72] *Id.* at 10.

[73] Comm'r for Hum. Rights of the Council of Eur., *supra* note 70.

[74] Venice Comm'n, Turkey: Opinion on the Legal Framework Governing Curfews, CDL-AD(2016)010, ¶ 86 (June 13, 2016).

[75] Comm'r for Hum. Rights of the Council of Eur., *supra* note 70, ¶¶ 28–29.

[76] Türkiye Cumhuriyeti Anayasasinda Değişiklik Yapilmasina Dair Kanun [Law on the amendment of the Constitution of the Republic of Turkey], No. 6718, May 20, 2016, Official Gazette, No. 29736 (June 8, 2016).

[77] Venice Comm'n, *Turkey: Opinion on the Suspension of the Second Paragraph of Article 83 of the Constitution (Parliamentary Inviolability)*, CDL-AD(2016)027 (Oct. 14, 2016).

called on the parliament to strip HDP deputies of their immunity to make them "pay the price one by one" for supporting terrorism.[78] He claimed that HDP cochairs Selahattin Demirtaş and Figen Yüksekdağ engaged in "constitutional crimes" by calling for democratic autonomy and appealed to the parliament to lift their immunities "in the name of counter-terrorism."[79] In May 2016, hours before the vote in the parliament, Erdoğan noted that the highest number of dossiers concerned deputies from "the party supported by the separatist terrorist organization" and expressed his hope for a favorable outcome to enable their immediate prosecution.[80] Prosecutors hastily prepared new dossiers to ensure the prosecution of the highest number of HDP deputies in the greatest number of cases. Of the 468 new immunity dossiers sent to the parliament between Erdoğan's call on January 2 and the law's entry into force on June 8, 368 were against the HDP deputies, 154 of which were prepared between April 21 and May 20 alone.[81] In the end, 55 out of the 59 HDP parliamentarians lost their immunities.[82]

The HDP deputies sought constitutional review, arguing that the law was a parliamentary decision subject to AYM's oversight rather than a constitutional amendment falling outside the AYM's review powers.[83] They further argued that the law violated the nonviolability and nonliability of parliamentarians by enabling their prosecution for constitutionally protected acts and statements; deprived the deputies of their constitutional right to defend themselves; and stripped the immunities on a collective instead of the constitutionally prescribed individual basis. Denying review in a unanimous ruling, the AYM reasoned that while it is authorized to review parliamentary decisions concerning immunities, what was at issue here was a "special process" that had all the formal elements of a constitutional

[78] *Turkey's Erdoğan Demands Lifting of HDP Deputies' Immunity*, Hürriyet Daily News (July 29, 2015), www.hurriyetdailynews.com/turkeys-erdogan-demands-lifting-of-hdp-deputies-immunity-86038.

[79] *Cumhurbaşkanı Erdoğan'dan HDPliler için "Dokunulmazlık" Çağrısı* [President Erdoğan makes an "immunity call" regarding the HDP deputies], Ajans Haber (Jan. 2, 2016), https://bedirhaber.com/erdogandan-hdplilere-dokunulmazlik-mesaji-bedelini-odemeliler/.

[80] *Erdoğan'a göre HDP'liler Zaten Yargılanacak: Bu İşten Kaçış Yok* [According to Erdoğan, the HDP deputies will be prosecuted anyhow: There is no way out], Diken (May 20, 2016), www.diken.com.tr/cumhurbaskani-dokunulmazliklari-kaldirdi-bile-bu-isten-kacis-yok/.

[81] Peoples' Democratic Party (HDP), The Lifting of Legislative Immunities at the Parliament of Turkey: An Assessment Report 5 (2016).

[82] *Id.* at 7–14.

[83] AYM, E. 2016/54, K. 2016/117 (June 3, 2016).

amendment and gave rise to "special legal consequences."[84] Thus, by inventing a new rule, the AYM refrained from fulfilling its constitutional duties and endorsed Turkey's transition into rule by lawlessness.

Then came the coup attempt of July 15, 2016. Almost immediately, Erdoğan declared Fethullah Gülen as the culprit, leading to the arrest, purge, and blacklisting of anyone remotely linked to his movement. On July 16 alone, roughly 3,000 judges and prosecutors, including two AYM judges, were arrested.[85] Erdoğan declared emergency rule and adopted thirty-seven executive decrees, only five of which were approved by the parliament despite the constitutional requirement of prompt ex post facto approval. Although several of these decrees introduced permanent measures, the AYM declined to annul them on grounds of ultra vires[86] – despite a 1991 precedent where it had granted itself the power to review whether emergency decrees are temporally, geographically, and substantively limited to the respective boundaries of emergency rule. The decrees bestowed upon the government powers to dismiss civil servants collectively, close civil society organizations, and arrest individuals without a shred of due process. By December 2018, 57,000 individuals were held in pretrial detention, amounting to 20 percent of the total prison population in Turkey.[87] By the end of 2021, over 125,000 civil servants were dismissed and their pensions, properties, savings, and passports were confiscated; and 2,761 associations, foundations, trade unions, media organizations, companies, hospitals, schools, and dormitories were closed.[88] Many of these measures remain in force, even though the emergency rule was lifted two years after its proclamation.[89]

[84] *Id.* ¶ 11.

[85] Alparslan Altan v. Turkey, App. No. 12778/17, ¶ 14 (Apr. 16, 2019), https://hudoc.echr.coe.int/fre?i=001-192804. A further 1,393 were dismissed in the following months. Turan v. Turkey, App. No. 75805/16 and 426 others, ¶ 18 (Nov. 23, 2021), https://hudoc.echr.coe.int/fre?i=001-213369.

[86] AYM, E. 2016/166, K. 2016/159 (Oct. 12, 2016).

[87] AMNESTY INT'L, TURKEY: AMNESTY INTERNATIONAL'S BRIEF ON THE HUMAN RIGHTS SITUATION 2 (Feb. 1, 2019), Index No. EUR 44/9747/2019, www.amnesty.org/en/documents/eur44/9747/2019/en/.

[88] STATE OF EMERGENCY INQUIRY COMMISSION, ACTIVITIES REPORT 2021, at 27, https://ohalkomisyonu.tccb.gov.tr/docs/OHAL_FaaliyetRaporu_2021.pdf [hereinafter ACTIVITIES REPORT 2021].

[89] Bazı Kanun ve Kanun Hükmünde Kararnamelerde Değişiklik Yapılmasına Dair Kanun [Law on the Amendment of Certain Laws and Legislative Decrees], No. 7145, July 25, 2018, OFFICIAL GAZETTE, July 31, 2018.

Erdoğan regarded the coup attempt as "a gift from God"[90] and used it to complete his unfinished business with Kurdish politicians. Without a trace of evidence, he accused the HDP cadres of having collaborated with the Gülenists. On November 4, 2016, thirteen deimmunized HDP deputies, including the cochairs Demirtaş and Yüksekdağ, were placed in pretrial detention. The list has since grown, enabled by the AYM's reluctance to exercise review.[91] Erdoğan's next target was the HDP mayors. An executive decree adopted in September 2016 authorized the government to dismiss, arrest, or ban from public office mayors and municipal officials accused of terrorism and to replace them with bureaucrats ("trustees").[92] The AKP thus grasped by executive force the governance of Kurdish towns it had been unable to win in local elections, where an electoral threshold is not applicable. This policy, too, remains in effect nearly eight years later. By April 2022, the number of municipalities the HDP had won in the 2019 local elections had gone down from sixty-five to six. At the time of this writing, a closure case against the HDP is pending before the AYM.

Erdoğan then turned to his other unfinished project: consolidating his one-man rule. Only several weeks after the arrest of HDP deputies, the AKP and the MHP jointly submitted to the parliament constitutional amendments introducing a "Turkish-style" presidency.[93] The changes were adopted by the parliament on January 21, 2017, signed by Erdoğan on February 10, and approved in a referendum on April 16. Throughout this period Turkey was governed under emergency, and the imprisoned HDP deputies were not allowed to participate in the parliamentary process. The changes gave Erdoğan exclusive powers to appoint and dismiss ministers and high state officials, dissolve the parliament on any ground, issue decrees exempt from constitutional review, and declare a state of emergency – changes interpreted by the

[90] Marc Champion, *Coup Was "Gift from God" for Erdogan Planning a New Turkey*, Bloomberg, (July 17, 2016, 11:00 PM), https://tinyurl.com/43d7m9ad.

[91] AYM, Gülser Yıldırım (2), App. No. 2016/40170 (Nov. 16, 2017), https://kararlarbilgibankasi.anayasa.gov.tr/BB/2016/40170; AYM, Selahattin Demirtaş, App. No. 2016/25189 (Dec. 21, 2017), https://kararlarbilgibankasi.anayasa.gov.tr/BB/2016/25189.

[92] Olağanüstü Hal Kapsaminda Bazi Düzenlemeler Yapilmasi Hakkinda Kanun Hükmünde Kararname [Decree with the force of law concerning certain regulations in the context of state of emergency], No. 674, Official Gazette, No. 29818 (Sept. 1, 2016), arts. 38, 39.

[93] *See* Hilal Köylü, *5 Points on Turkish Constitutional Reform*, DW (Jan. 21, 2017), www.dw.com/en/turkish-constitutional-reform-5-important-points/a-37221685.

Venice Commission as a decisive move "towards an authoritarian and personal regime."[94]

The personal nature of the new regime became abundantly clear in March 2021. Without obtaining the constitutionally required parliamentary approval, Erdoğan singlehandedly withdrew Turkey from the Council of Europe Convention on Preventing and Combating Violence against Women and Domestic Violence, known as the Istanbul Convention.[95] One man, without giving any reason, deprived the female population of an entire country of the human rights vested on them through a unanimous vote of the Turkish parliament in 2011.[96] This was an arbitrary exercise of power par excellence, as defined by Shaffer, Sandholtz, and Krygier.[97]

## III The ECtHR's Dual Role in Authoritarian Rule

Certainly, the ECtHR has enabled domestic groups to make rights claims and empowered victims in their pursuit of justice across Europe.[98] And yet, in the last two decades, the Strasbourg Court has had a dual impact on human rights, democracy, and the rule of law in Turkey – an impact that has increasingly tilted on the negative side. The rest of this chapter focuses on the dark side of this dual role.

### 1 *"Excessive" but Suitable for Turkey: Europe's Highest Electoral Threshold*

The ECtHR delivered one of its most important judgments on democracy in a case concerning Turkey's electoral threshold.[99] The case was brought under Article 3 of Protocol No. 1, which protects the electorate's free expression of its opinion in the choice of the legislature. The applicants were two Kurdish politicians who had received 45.95 percent of the votes

94 Venice Comm'n, *Opinion on the Amendments to the Constitution Adopted by the Grand National Assembly on 21 January 2017 and to Be Submitted to a National Referendum on 16 April 2017*, CDL-AD(2017)005 (Mar. 13, 2017), ¶ 133.

95 I thank Anne Peters for reminding me of this particular instance of lawlessness.

96 Ayşegül Kula, *An Unconstitutional Setback: Turkey's Withdrawal from the Istanbul Convention*, VERFASSUNGSBLOG (Mar. 22, 2021), https://verfassungsblog.de/erdogan-istanbul-convention/.

97 *See* Chapter 1; Krygier, *supra* note 10.

98 KURBAN, *supra* note 49.

99 Yumak v. Turkey, App. No. 10226/03, at 439 (July 8, 2008), https://hudoc.echr.coe.int/?i=001-87363.

in the Kurdish province of Şırnak, but could not enter the parliament because their party, the Democratic People's Party (Demokratik Halk Partisi, or DEHAP), received 6.2 percent of the votes in the 2002 elections and could not pass the national threshold. Two of the three parliamentary seats allocated to Şırnak were given to the AKP, which polled only 14 percent, and the third to an independent candidate who polled 9.69 percent.[100]

While considering "in general" a 10 percent threshold to be "excessive," the ECtHR did not find a violation in this case "in the light of the specific political context of the elections in question."[101] The law sought to avoid excessive political fragmentation and strengthen stability, the threshold applied to all parties, and the electoral system was based on the "context of a unitary State,"[102] which requires parliamentarians to represent the whole nation and not a particular region. The electoral system had "correctives … to counterbalance the threshold's negative effects":[103] the possibility to run as an independent candidate or to join the list of another party likely to pass the threshold. There were past examples of both of these correctives; the candidates of pro-Kurdish parties had been elected to the parliament from the lists of another party in 1991 and as independent candidates in 2007.[104]

In unquestionably deferring to Turkey's argument regarding the unique context of social and political instability in which elections were held, which rendered the risk of fragmentation too costly, the Grand Chamber overlooked the fact that the threshold was introduced in 1983, and it applied to all elections before and after 2002. The emphasis on the principle of unity not only suggests that the Court approves an electoral system which renders the representation of regional minority parties impossible, but also ignores how the same principle had led to the dissolution of successive Kurdish parties – which the ECtHR had found to be in violation of the Convention.[105]

[100] On the democratic deficit nationwide, see *id.* ¶ 82.
[101] *Id.* ¶ 147.
[102] *Id.* ¶ 124.
[103] *Id.* ¶ 133.
[104] *Id.* ¶ 97–99.
[105] Freedom and Democracy Party (ÖZDEP) v. Turkey, App. No. 23885/94 (Dec. 8, 1999), https://tinyurl.com/yj523a3t; Yazar v. Turkey, App. No. 22723/93, 22724/93 & 22725/93 (Apr. 9, 2002), https://hudoc.echr.coe.int/?i=001-60416; Dicle for the Democracy Party (DEP) of Turkey v. Turkey, App. No. 25141/94 (Dec. 10, 2002), https://hudoc.echr.coe.int/eng#;{%22itemid%22:[%22001-65370%22]}.

As the dissent noted, the Grand Chamber's endorsement of "stratagems" not only encourages candidates into "playing 'hide and seek' with the voters" and raises "an obvious problem of political morality"[106] but also rests on a distorted reading of the domestic context, where the competition between political parties and independent candidates is structurally unfair. The latter cannot receive votes from constituents abroad,[107] must individually bear a very high financial cost to stand for elections,[108] cannot make electoral broadcasts,[109] and need more votes than a party to gain the same parliamentary seat. Moreover, in assuming that the Kurds could easily form alliances with mainstream Turkish parties, the Grand Chamber was oblivious to the fact that Kurdish deputies, who had indeed formed a preelection coalition with a social democratic party in 1991, were expelled within months of their election upon the nationalistic frenzy caused by their presence in the parliament.

Thus, the Grand Chamber effectively condoned depriving the majority of the electorate in the Kurdish region of representation in Turkey's parliament. It moreover disregarded the essential and unique role of political parties in democracies, which the ECtHR had emphasized since its 1998 decision in *United Communist Party*.[110]

### 2 *On the Disenfranchisement of a Minority*

Although the cases of HDP parliamentarians qualified for priority treatment, it took the ECtHR twenty-one months to issue a ruling. When it finally spoke, it did so selectively – only with respect to HDP cochair Demirtaş, leaving out the remaining eleven deputies for no apparent reason.[111] The crux of Demirtaş's Article 5 claim concerned the illegality of his detention. The government crackdown on his party intensified after the HDP's electoral gains in 2015. The number of investigations against HDP deputies over a period of eight years almost tripled in the six months following Erdoğan's speech calling on the parliament to lift their

[106] Yumak v. Turkey, App. No. 10226/03, at 439, ¶ 4 (July 8, 2008) (Tulkens, J., Vajic, J., Jaeger, J., & Sikuta, J., dissenting), https://hudoc.echr.coe.int/?i=001-87363.

[107] Sinan Alkin, *Underrepresentative Democracy: Why Turkey Should Abandon Europe's Highest Electoral Threshold*, 10 Wash. U. Glob. Stud. L. Rev. 347, 356 (2011).

[108] Law No. 2839, *supra* note 50, at Art. 21(2).

[109] Alkin, *supra* note 107, at 356.

[110] United Communist Party of Turkey v. Turkey, App. No. 133/1996/752/951 (Jan. 30, 1998), https://tinyurl.com/3sae5ut6.

[111] Selahattin Demirtaş v. Turkey (No. 2), App. No. 14305/17 (Nov. 20, 2018), https://tinyurl.com/2c4f7w42.

immunities. The prolonged nature of his detention was intended to prevent his participation in the referendum concerning the transition to a presidential system and the presidential elections thereafter.

While noting the temporal link between Erdoğan's speeches and the acceleration of criminal investigations against Demirtaş, the ECtHR was reluctant to conclude that Turkish courts acted as government pawns. Deferring to the AYM, and disregarding the Venice Commission, the ECtHR concluded that lower courts had shown sufficient evidence to demonstrate a reasonable suspicion that Demirtaş had committed a criminal offence. The problem was in the continuation of the detention, which "pursued the predominant ulterior purpose of stifling pluralism and limiting political debate" in violation of Article 18.[112] Thus, bad faith was *not* in Demirtaş's detention, but in its prolonged nature.[113]

The implications for the regime were clear; as long as Turkish courts showed *some* justification for arrests and kept pretrial detention periods reasonably short, Kurdish deputies were fair game. Upon instructions from Erdoğan to "finish the job"[114] and fourteen days after the ECtHR ruling calling for Demirtaş's immediate release, a lower court sentenced Demirtaş to four years and eight months of imprisonment relating to a speech he had made five years earlier. By September 2019, twenty-two HDP deputies had been convicted and sentenced to up to sixteen years and eight months of imprisonment.[115] Certainly, the Grand Chamber rectified the Chamber's Article 5(1) judgment, finding that neither the initial nor the continued pretrial detention was based on a reasonable suspicion that Demirtaş had committed a crime. By extension, it found an Article 18 violation in conjunction with not only the third but also the first, clause of Article 5.[116] But it was too late; Demirtaş was no longer a detainee, but a convicted felon.

Despite its significance, not least as the first Article 18 judgment against Turkey, *Selahattin Demirtaş* is symptomatic of the Court's decontextualized and case-by-case approach. While Demirtaş is an important political symbol in Turkey, jurisprudentially speaking, there was no

112 *Id.* ¶ 273.

113 The Chamber also found a violation of Article 3 of Protocol No. 1 on account of Demirtaş's inability to take part in parliamentary activities.

114 *Erdoğan: AIHM'nin Kararları bizi Bağlamaz* [Erdoğan: We are not bound by the ECtHR rulings], DEUTSCHE WELLE (Nov. 20, 2018), https://tinyurl.com/ms3fb38v.

115 HDP, undated and untitled document (on file with the author).

116 Selahattin Demirtaş v. Turkey (No. 2), App. No. 14305/17 (Dec. 22, 2020), https://hudoc.echr.coe.int/fre?i=001-207173.

justifiable reason to exclude the remaining deputies. If the reason was Demirtaş's status as a leader of the opposition, then at the very least his cochair Yüksekdağ should have been included. If it was rather that Demirtaş had run in the presidential elections and the concern was his inability to run on equal terms with the other candidates, the Chamber should not have waited until five months after these elections. All twelve HDP deputies were stripped of their immunities and placed in pretrial detention under the same circumstances and at around the same time as Demirtaş. So similar were the cases that the Court itself had joined them in June 2017. And yet, it treated Demirtaş's case in isolation from cases of the remaining deputies and from Turkey's history of suppressing Kurdish electoral representation.

## 3 *Cases Not Heard*

The "constitutive capacity of the law" is not limited to social movements; it also extends to governments.[117] By the early 2000s it had become much more difficult for Kurdish lawyers to mobilize the ECtHR.[118] While the Kurds had become "repeat players" in Strasbourg,[119] so had their adversary. The government had understood the reputational, financial, and political costs of denial and noncooperation. The authoritarian outlook had become all the more costly when, in 1999, the EU granted Turkey candidacy for membership, but made accession contingent on its execution of ECtHR rulings.

Turkey's initial strategy was to minimize the number of ECtHR judgments in admitted cases by extending friendly settlement offers to applicants and, when refused, submitting to the Court unilateral declarations to win strike-out rulings. In these declarations, the government partially acknowledged that gross violations occurred but did not accept responsibility or promise to carry out investigations – flying in the face of established ECtHR jurisprudence. Yet, the strategy worked – at least initially. The ECtHR struck out several right-to-life cases, effectively penalizing applicants for refusing to settle their claims with the

[117] Michael McCann, *Reform Litigation on Trial*, 17 L. & Soc. Inquiry 715, 733 (1992).

[118] Kurban, *supra* note 49; Dilek Kurban, *Mobilizing Supranational Courts Against Authoritarian Regimes*, *in* Research Handbook on Law, Movements, and Social Change 197 (Steve Boutcher, Corey Shdaimah & Michael Yarbrough eds., 2023).

[119] Marc Galanter, *Why the "Haves" Come Out Ahead: Speculations on the Limits of Legal Change*, 9 L. & Soc. Rev. 95 (1974).

government.[120] While the Grand Chamber interrupted this process in 2003 due to substantial factual disputes between the parties and the government's failure to acknowledge responsibility or to undertake an investigation,[121] the ECtHR resumed this practice in 2021.[122]

When the AKP came to power, it pursued a more proactive strategy by developing new domestic remedies which, if found effective by the Court, would trigger inadmissibility decisions in pending cases, save money in compensation, and bring Turkey down in the list of worst offenders. When the context became all the more useful for Turkey with the introduction of the ECtHR's pilot judgment mechanism,[123] the government adopted laws tailored for three groups of cases pending in Strasbourg concerning property rights in Turkish-occupied northern Cyprus,[124] forced displacement of Kurdish civilians during the 1990s,[125] and excessively lengthy proceedings.[126]

As it familiarized itself with the ECtHR's growing propensity to invoke subsidiarity to alleviate its docket, the AKP perfected its counter-reform strategy. The goal now was to prevent the ECtHR from admitting new cases, or to at least further prolong the already long path to Strasbourg. The most effective means to achieve this was to create a constitutional complaint mechanism, which would introduce a new layer of domestic remedy that needs to be exhausted by all ECtHR applicants. The remainder of this section addresses this particular measure.

### a Rule by Law

The AKP's most successful and consequential counter-reform strategy was the constitutional complaint mechanism, which entered into force in 2012. Responding expeditiously (only seven months after commencement), the

[120] *See, e.g.*, Akman v. Turkey, App. No. 37453/97, at 69 (June 26, 2001), https://tinyurl.com/wad3ctuf

[121] Tahsin Acar v. Turkey, App. No. 26307/95 (May 6, 2003), https://tinyurl.com/5buzp3xv.

[122] Erdem v. Turkey, App. No. 64727/11 (Mar. 30, 2021), https://tinyurl.com/2usjjjbu.

[123] Committee of Ministers, Resolution Res(2004)3 on Judgments Revealing an Underlying Systemic Problem; Recommendation Rec(2004)6 to Member States on the Improvement of Domestic Remedies. Both adopted on 12 May 2004.

[124] Katselli Proukaki, *The Right of Displaced Persons to Property and to Return Home after Demopoulos*, 14 Hum. Rts. L. Rev. 701 (2014).

[125] Dilek Kurban, *Forsaking Individual Justice: The Implications of the European Court of Human Rights' Pilot Judgment Procedure for Victims of Gross and Systematic Violations*, 16 Hum. Rts. L. Rev. 731, 736–37 (2016).

[126] Committee of Ministers, Communication from Turkey Concerning the *Ormanci and Others* Group of Cases Against Turkey, at 30, COM (2014) 1468 final, ¶ 106 (Dec. 2, 2014).

ECtHR rejected a case on the ground that the applicant had not applied to the AYM – without assessing whether the new remedy was effective.[127]

The ECtHR did not change its stance in response to the AKP's postcoup crackdown. Zeynep Mercan was a judge dismissed and arrested two days after the coup attempt. In justifying skipping the constitutional complaint process, Mercan cited special circumstances – the AYM's dismissal of its own two members.[128] For the ECtHR, this fact did not "cast doubt" on the effectiveness of the mechanism and Mercan's "fears" of the AYM's impartiality did not relieve her of the obligation to exhaust it.[129] After all, the AYM had proven its effectiveness in finding the pretrial detention of two journalists to be unconstitutional.[130] The ECtHR was telling the applicant to seek justice at a court that had dismissed its own members without a hint of due process – based on similar accusations and on the grounds of the same decree. Moreover, it was giving assurances based on the AYM's judgments *before* the coup attempt. In the postcoup phase, the AYM had made it very clear that it would not look for evidence linking its dismissed members with Gülenists, let alone with the coup attempt; the "conviction" of remaining judges was sufficient.[131] As the Venice Commission noted, once the AYM confirmed the validity of an emergency decree dismissing thousands of judges, there would be "little chance of success" for challenging mass dismissals of judges and prosecutors before Turkish courts.[132] There was another sticking point that the ECtHR disregarded: dismissals via emergency decrees (as opposed to by administrative bodies) cannot be contested before Turkish courts.[133]

CoE institutions called for Turkey to establish a mechanism to resolve the postcoup dismissals at the national level.[134] In January 2017, Turkey passed a law establishing the State of Emergency Inquiry Commission.[135] The ECtHR lost little time in rejecting the application of a dismissed

[127] Uzun v. Turkey, App. No. 10755/13 (Apr. 30, 2013), https://tinyurl.com/54ybdmwb.

[128] Mercan v. Turkey, App. No. 56511/16, ¶ 18 (Nov. 8, 2016), https://tinyurl.com/33s7msha.

[129] *Id.* ¶ 26.

[130] AYM, Erdem Gül and Can Dündar, App. No. 2015/18567 (Feb. 25, 2016), https://kararlarbilgibankasi.anayasa.gov.tr/BB/2015/18567?Dil=en.

[131] AYM, E. 2016/6, K. 2016/12, ¶ 84, (July 4, 2016) https://siyasipartikararlar.anayasa.gov.tr/Dosyalar/Kararlar/KararPDF/2016-12-spdi.pdf.

[132] Venice Comm'n, *Turkey: Emergency Decree Laws No. 667–676 Adopted Following the Failed Coup of 15 July 2016*, CDL-AD(2016)037, ¶ 186 (Dec. 12, 2016).

[133] *Id.* ¶¶ 200–01.

[134] Demir-Gürsel, *supra* note 56.

[135] Olağanüstü Hal İşlemleri İnceleme Komisyonu Kurulması Hakkında Kanun Hükmünde Kararname [Decree on the establishment of the State of Emergency Procedures Investigation Commission], No. 685, OFFICIAL GAZETTE, No. 29957, January 23, 2017.

teacher for failure to exhaust this remedy.[136] It did not matter that the Commission had been established only one month earlier, was not yet operational, and the applicant had unsuccessfully petitioned the AYM before taking the case to Strasbourg. Thereafter, the ECtHR sent repeated warnings to Ankara that it would start reviewing the remaining dismissal cases unless the new mechanism became functional immediately. Two days after the Commission began accepting applications,[137] the ECtHR rejected 12,600 petitions.[138] The consequences were dire; by the end of 2021, the Commission had reviewed 120,703 of the 126,783 submitted applications, rejecting 100,000.[139] It reinstated to their jobs only 3,733 of the 125,678 dismissed civil servants.[140]

Finally addressing the effectiveness of the constitutional complaint mechanism in March 2018, the ECtHR did not see a reason to depart from its (precoup) finding that the AYM was an effective remedy for individuals deprived of their right to liberty.[141] It has not changed its stance since. Even in cases where it found violations in the pretrial detentions of a former AYM judge,[142] several journalists,[143] and over 400 judges and prosecutors,[144] the ECtHR evaded the issue – glossing over the fact that in these very cases the AYM had either found no violation[145] or dismissed the applications.[146] Effectively, the ECtHR gave the AYM a blank check, the bankability of which became evident two months later.

[136] Köksal v. Turkey, App. No. 70478/16 (June 6, 2017), https://tinyurl.com/bdfpm54w.
[137] *Jagland Calls Turkey for Release of Hunger Strikers Gülmen and Özakca*, Stockholm Ctr. for Freedom (June 26, 2017), https://stockholmcf.org/jagland-calls-turkey-for-release-of-hunger-strikers-gulmen-and-ozakca/.
[138] Turkish Ministry of Justice, *OHAL Komisyonu Kurulmasıyla AİHM Binlerce Dosyayı Düşürdü* [AIHM dismissed thousands of cases with the establishment of the State of Emergency Commission] (July 14, 2017), www.inhak.adalet.gov.tr/duyurular/faaliyet_duyurular/2017/Temmuz/basin-ilani.pdf.
[139] Activities Report 2021, *supra* note 88, at 25.
[140] *Id.* at 7.
[141] Mehmet Hasan Altan, App. No. 13237/17, ¶ 142 (Mar. 20, 2018), https://tinyurl.com/mrpdau5y; Şahin Alpay, App. No. 16538/17, ¶ 121 (Mar. 20, 2018), https://tinyurl.com/y23xbb7a.
[142] *E.g.*, Alparslan Altan v. Turkey, App. No. 12778/17 (Apr. 16, 2019), https://hudoc.echr.coe.int/fre?i=001-192804.
[143] Sabuncu v. Turkey, App. No. 23199/17 (Nov. 10, 2020), https://tinyurl.com/4bndsvap.
[144] Turan v. Turkey, App. Nos. 75805/16 and 426 others, ¶ 18 (Nov. 23, 2021), https://hudoc.echr.coe.int/fre?i=001-213369.
[145] *E.g.*, Ahmet Hüsrev Altan v. Turkey, App. No. 13252/17 (Apr. 13, 2021), https://hudoc.echr.coe.int/fre?i=001-209444.
[146] *E.g.*, Alparslan Altan v. Turkey, App. No. 12778/17.

### b Lawlessness

On December 28, 2011, Turkish military jets killed thirty-four Kurdish civilians, including seventeen minors, who were crossing the Iraqi border back into Turkey, smuggling goods with the knowledge and implicit consent of local authorities.[147] A military court investigation found that the military had carried out the aerial bombardment upon the general staff's approval and presumably with the government's consent. Yet, the military prosecutor dismissed the case, concluding that the victims were mistaken as PKK militants.

From the moment the families filed their complaint, the case was a hot potato for the AYM. As the first serious human rights case that it was asked to review, this was not a residue of the 1990s for which the current government bore no responsibility. To the contrary, in addition to authorizing the bombardment, the government covered up parliamentary and judicial investigations into it. At the same time, the ECtHR's recent judgment, in a similar case, that the killing of Kurdish civilians in a 1994 aerial bombardment was a substantive violation of Article 2 left the AYM no room for the kind of ruling it ought to give.[148]

What rescued the AYM from this dilemma was the lead lawyer's submission of the requested additional information with two days' delay. Finding the lawyer's medically certified illness not to be grave enough, the AYM rejected the case.[149] A dissenting judge reminded the majority of ECtHR case law establishing that very short time periods, unreasonable bureaucratic hurdles, and formalistic procedural requirements are disproportionate restrictions on access to justice. He noted that (1) the AYM could have easily obtained the information itself; (2) the remoteness of the villages where the applicants lived and the security situation might have reasonably delayed the completion of the process; and (3) rules of procedure on constitutional complaints did not give guidance as to which illnesses constitute valid excuses for delays.[150] The ECtHR dismissed the case on the same grounds as the AYM.[151] Displaying extreme procedural

[147] *Jetler Sivilleri Vurdu* [The jets struck civilians], CUMHURIYET, Dec. 30, 2011.

[148] Benzer v. Turkey, App. No. 23502/06 (Nov. 12, 2013), https://tinyurl.com/4nj7fyrf.

[149] AYM, Mehmet Encü, App. No. 2014/11864 (Feb. 24, 2016), https://kararlarbilgibankasi.anayasa.gov.tr/BB/2014/11864.

[150] AYM, Mehmet Encü, App. No. 2014/11864 (Feb. 24, 2016) (Osman Alifeyyaz Paksüt, J. dissenting), https://kararlarbilgibankasi.anayasa.gov.tr/BB/2014/11864.

[151] Selahattin Encü v. Turkey, App. No. 49976/16 (May 7, 2018), https://tinyurl.com/we2ubtmj.

rigidity, it went against its own jurisprudence and refused to pass judgment in arguably the most critical case filed against Turkey in decades.

## IV The Authoritarian Threat to the Rule of Law

The Turkish case confirms the overall theme of this volume: while authoritarians make increasing use of rule-of-law norms and practices, they do so to consolidate their power and not to pursue rule-of-law goals. At the same time, it illustrates the need for broadening our conceptualizations of the rule of law to account for the "enmeshment" of national and international law in authoritarian contexts.[152] This is necessary in two respects.

First, if the rule of law is at one end of the analytical spectrum on the arbitrary exercise of power, what lies at the other end is lawless rule, not rule by law. Certainly, lawlessness is not inevitable. Whether, and if so when, countries end up in this situation hinges on endogenous and exogenous factors. The longer and deeper a country has been ruled by authoritarian legalism, the more likely it will revert to lawlessness. It is essential to see the gray areas along this continuum, where different conceptual categories can coexist and vary across time and space. One would be hard-pressed to find examples where the entirety of a country is governed through the rule by law at all times. Rather, governance can fall across different dimensions over time depending on the strength of internal and external liberal forces. There may be "rule-of-law pockets to rule by law"[153] or, by extension, rule-by-law pockets to lawlessness. As far as authoritarian regimes are concerned, the longer and deeper they are subject to viable external pressure for democratic change, the better their chances are to move toward the rule-of-law end of the continuum. Regime survival is another factor; when autocrats feel secure in their seats, they may be more willing to adopt rule-of-law reforms to provide some space for the expression and representation of dissent. Where they face a formidable domestic rival, in the form of a civil society movement on the streets or a political party on the ballot, they would have self-interest in shifting the pendulum toward lawlessness. A further factor is the decline in the moral authority, institutional strength, or bargaining power of the international community. Where they perceive weakness,

[152] *See* Chapter 1.

[153] I am thankful to Greg Shaffer and Wayne Sandholtz for this nice formulation.

hesitation, or confusion on the part of international institutions in upholding their own norms and practices, autocrats do not shy from abusing their bargaining positions to undermine the global security, legal, and economic order. Thus, where a country falls on the arbitrary-exercise-of-power spectrum varies across time in accordance with internal and external push and pull factors.

TLO theory underscores the recursive interaction of domestic and international levels. Indeed, Turkey's swings along the pendulum were shaped by (1) the ups and downs of its EU accession process; (2) its engagement with the ECtHR; (3) actual (HDP and the Gülen movement) and perceived (Gezi protests[154]) internal threats to Erdoğan's authoritarian rule; and (4) broader geopolitical developments (the end of the Cold War, migration crisis in Europe, and Russia's invasion of Ukraine). Turkey came closest to its democratic transition moment between 2002 and the middle of that decade, when the EU accession carrot was most viable, Erdoğan's AKP desperately needed the support of the international order, and the ECtHR's docket was not yet experiencing the adverse impact of post-Cold War enlargement. This progress toward the rule of law was the direct outcome of TLOs' conversation with, responsiveness to, and support for, domestic civil society groups, amplifying their voices and giving them an international platform to experience their grievances. Adversely, when the EU and the CoE were grappling with the institutional overload caused by their eastward enlargements, causing the former to effectively end Turkey's accession prospects and the latter to adopt radical reforms to ease the ECtHR's workload, and Erdoğan was enjoying international endorsement as the reform-minded leader of the new Turkey, the pendulum started to quickly shift toward rule by law. The diminished international support for human rights activists and victims, such as the ECtHR's inadmissibility decisions and strike-out rulings, helped Erdoğan consolidate his power. By the 2010s, the EU was distracted by internal (rule-of-law backsliding in new member states) and external (uncontrolled mass migration from conflict zones and poor countries) crises, the ECtHR was institutionally paralyzed with an unmanageable docket, and Erdoğan's one-man rule was under increasing threat by external (the Arab Spring) and internal (the HDP appealing to non-Kurdish liberal votes and the AKP falling out with Gülenists) developments. For Erdoğan, the longevity of his power lay not in rule-of law-reforms, but in combining rule by law (replacing the ECtHR's

[154] Özge Zihnioğlu, *The Legacy of the Gezi Protests in Turkey, in* After Protest: Pathways Beyond Mass Mobilization 11 (Richard Youngs ed., 2019).

oversight with that of captured domestic courts) with lawlessness (disregarding the outcome of elections, terrorizing Kurdish towns through unlawful curfews, locking up elected Kurdish politicians, and taking over the local governance of Kurdish towns with executive fiat). By the 2020s, internal (a failed coup against the AKP) and external (the global rise of illiberalism and Russia's and China's growing threats to the international order) dynamics had emboldened Erdoğan to rule by lawlessness. This time, his disregard of rules extended to foreign policy by blocking Sweden's (and initially Finland's) NATO accession and thus undermining European security amidst the growing Russian threat. Erdoğan was mirroring Hungary's Orban (who has been obstructing EU efforts to sanction Russia) in abusing his veto powers within an international organization for his domestic political purposes.

Second, the arbitrary-exercise-of-power spectrum applies not only to governments interacting with TLOs but also to those orders themselves. As Shaffer and Sandholtz point out, the rule of law and democracy are interdependent; we can only speak of the rule of law if the substance of rules is determined by democratic participation.[155] As substantively antidemocratic as it is, Turkey's electoral threshold does not even meet the basic procedural requirements of democracy; it was introduced by a military regime. Yet, European institutions have not problematized this democratic deficit, which has enabled the AKP's single-party rule for a long time. The embrace of a thin notion of democracy and the rule of law has also permeated the ECtHR's jurisprudence on Turkey. In a striking factual mistake, the ECtHR treated the threshold as the "choice of the legislature" and granted Turkey the wide margin of appreciation it affords member states on electoral issues.[156] Just as the election system that enabled and sustained Erdogan's single-party rule lacked minimal procedural safeguards, so did the referendum that changed the regime type to a presidential system. The amendments were adopted by the parliament, where the detained HDP deputies were not allowed to participate, and submitted to a referendum conducted under emergency rule. Yet, the international community recognized the referendum results without question.

According to Shaffer and Sandholtz, a central reason for adopting a goal-oriented definition of the rule of law is "the risk of creating

[155] *See* Chapter 1.

[156] Yumak v. Turkey, App. No. 10226/03, at 439 (July 8, 2008), https://hudoc.echr.coe.int/?i=001-87363.

formulaic checklists based on specified, formal characteristics."[157] The performance of European institutions pursuant to this conceptualization does not hold either. Take the constitutional complaint mechanism, treated by the EU and the CoE as a *sine qua non* for the rule of law. Neither Brussels nor Strasbourg considered whether the AYM, which has long been complicit with authoritarianism in Turkey, would be able and willing to conduct a rights-oriented review in accordance with European human norms.

Nor does the ECtHR withstand the arbitrariness scrutiny developed by Shaffer, Sandholtz, and Krygier. It has been striking out cases from its list where applicants did not accept Turkey's unilateral declarations and pressuring applicants to accept the government's settlement offers. These policies, resulting from a self-interest to eliminate as many cases as possible, went against the right of individual petition – the core of the European human rights regime. Similarly, in rejecting justiciable claims concerning gross violations on grounds of an ineffective domestic remedy, the ECtHR has denied victims their only chance for a day in court. Nor has the ECtHR met the requirements for "reason-giving"; it has given either no reason, since it is not required to do so in inadmissibility decisions, or an unjustifiable one. The pursuit of subsidiarity is not proportionate to the rejection of tens of thousands of applicants due to their nonexhaustion of a domestic remedy that has proven to be ineffective.

As Ginsburg notes, liberal democracy "can be promoted, defended or undermined by international legal institutions."[158] The ECHR system has not only failed to defend, but has undermined, liberal democracy in Turkey at critical points. It is difficult to make a counter-factual argument as to whether Erdoğan would have complied with an ECtHR judgment against Turkey's electoral threshold. Coming at a time when Erdoğan still needed European support to consolidate his power against the military, such a ruling could have pushed for rule-of-law reform. At the very least, it would have drawn international attention to the anti-democratic nature of Turkey's electoral regime and undermined Erdoğan's claim to majoritarian democracy. Similarly, had the CoE's Committee of Ministers started infringement proceedings for nonexecution of the ECtHR's *Demirtaş* judgment and moved expeditiously thereafter toward suspending Turkey for its noncompliance, it could have

[157] *See* Chapter 1.

[158] GINSBURG, *supra* note 6, at 290.

forced Erdoğan to change course by, for example, releasing Kurdish parliamentarians held in captivity. At the very least, it would have drawn international attention to the antidemocratic nature of Turkey's electoral regime and undermined Erdoğan's claim to majoritarian democracy. Even if such an outcome did not materialize, the ECHR regime would have demonstrated commitment to its principles in relation to authoritarian regimes. This, in itself, would have been a remarkable outcome, particularly in light of the proven failure of restraint and appeasement policies in taming antiliberal governments.

# 10

# The Rule-of-Law Crisis as a Testing Ground for Latin American Constitutionalism

## A View from Mexico under López Obrador

FRANCISCA POU GIMÉNEZ

## I Introduction

Recent debates on public law have been analyzing developments that were difficult to imagine two decades ago, when democratic constitutionalism was expanding and reigned undisputed at the level of normative ideals. As the literature has underscored, the world has been a pasture for leaders that engage in anti-pluralist, polarizing, illiberal politics in recent years. On the basis of often massive electoral victories, populist politicians deploy policies that are against migration, globalization, environmental sustainability, and equality. They pose a distinctive challenge to democracy because, far from denouncing democratic rule, they claim to represent a more perfect instantiation of it. They pose a distinctive challenge to constitutionalism because, in contrast to the authoritarian leaders of the past, they do not set aside constitutions but rather use – and abuse – them, gradually emptying them of their substance. They pose a distinctive challenge to the rule of law because they extensively draw on legal means to advance their policies. They practice government *per lege* in an effort to mask performances ever more distant from government *sub lege*.

Latin America partakes in these familiar trends challenging the rule of law. We find paradigmatic examples in Brazil, El Salvador, and Mexico. In Brazil, Jair Bolsonaro was elected on an "anti-politics" platform that

I thank Erick Moreno Zúñiga and Jesús Figueroa Velasco for excellent research assistance. I also thank the organizers and participants at the rule-of-law symposium held at the University of California, Irvine, in September 2022 for their very insightful comments, carefully curated by Gregory Shaffer and Wayne Sandholtz.

openly advocated hatred against indigenous populations, Afro-Brazilians, and civil society organizations.[1] His government brought together military officers, neoliberal tycoons, and religious activists; despite scarce support for his policies in Congress and significant judicial drawbacks, he partly advanced his agenda.[2] Mimicking Donald Trump, Bolsonaro spent months aggressively attacking the electoral authorities, proclaiming that he would not accept the results of the November 2022 election (which he lost), and urging the army and his supporters to resist the results – something they actually did, blocking the roads in many parts of the country and mounting a physical assault on Congress and the Supreme Court.[3]

In El Salvador, Nayib Bukele similarly gained office by portraying himself as the alternative to traditional corrupt political parties, using new styles of political communication and promising to meet effectively the needs of the population.[4] His administration has been marked by gross abuse of the state of exception, nullification of presidential term limits, destruction of judicial independence, and plain irrationality – including its decision to make Bitcoin legal tender and undertake investments in this cryptocurrency that have been ruinous for the country.[5]

In Mexico, Andrés Manuel López Obrador (popularly known as AMLO) ran on a leftist platform, only to deploy, once in office, policies contrary to progressivism: militarization, anti-migration, efforts to control the judiciary and eliminate independent agencies, defunding of public services, strict fiscal policy, and daily broadcast attacks on all

[1] Pedro Henrique Leal, *Bolsonaro and the Brazilian far right*, Open Democracy (Apr. 24, 2017), www.opendemocracy.net/en/democraciaabierta/bolsonaro-and-brazilian-far-right/.

[2] Suely Mara Vaz Guimaraes de Araujo, *Environmental Policy in the Bolsonaro Government: The Response of Environmentalists on the Legislative Arena*, 14 Brazilian Pol. Sci. Rev. (2020); Carolina Moehlecke, *Businessmen Support Amidst the Turmoil: The Second Year of Bolsonaro's Presidency in Brazil*, 41 Rev. cienc. polít. (Santiago) 239 (2021); Bertelsmann Stiftung, BTI 2022 Country Report: Brazil (2022), https://tinyurl.com/446vv3b2.

[3] Diego Werneck Arguelhes, *Weak, but (Very) Dangerous: The Bolsonaro Paradox*, Verfassungsblog (July 22, 2022), https://verfassungsblog.de/weak-but-very-dangerous/.

[4] Ricardo Roque Baldovinos, *Nayib Bukele: Populismo e implosión democrática en El Salvador*, 18 Andamios 233 (2021), www.scielo.org.mx/pdf/anda/v18n46/1870-0063-anda-18-46-233.pdf.

[5] *El Salvador: President Bukele Engulfs the Country in a Human Rights Crisis After Three Years in Government*, Amnesty Int'l (June 2, 2022), https://tinyurl.com/mry6cy7f; *El Salvador: State of Emergency Has Created a Perfect Storm of Human Rights Violations*, Amnesty Int'l (Apr. 25, 2022), https://tinyurl.com/365sxn2a.

sectors of society, including feminists, academics, scientists, the press, and civil society organizations.[6] His policies are far from not only progressive liberal democratic politics but also left-wing populism as practiced in the past in Latin America by leaders such as Juan Domingo Perón or Getulio Vargas. Although authoritarian, such populism was state-friendly and inclusive of industrial workers and popular masses, unlike the state-shrinking drive and almost exclusive reliance on cash transfers (as opposed to structural redistribution) that marked López Obrador's policies.[7]

A focus on Latin America, however, invites us to unsettle and refine prevailing narratives of constitutional retrogression. In Latin America, many of the current trends are not unprecedented. The region has long dealt with challenges to the "constitutional trinity" of human rights, democracy, and the rule of law,[8] including problems that derive not from direct violations but from abuse and covert undermining of these goals. Sure, these problems were until recently framed as temporary problems, to be overcome through the process of progressive consolidation of democracy – a linear, happy-ending frame – whereas now, in parallel to challenges elsewhere, they are portrayed as chapters in a narrative of retrogression running in the opposite direction. Nonetheless, as a result of Latin America's long-standing familiarity with these challenges, regional constitutions include a wealth of innovations intended to counter them. While countries that perceive themselves as mature democracies are wondering what sort of reforms could help contain or reverse current developments, in Latin America those reforms have already been attempted, and the relevant contemporary agenda is therefore to inquire what has worked, and what has not, and why.

[6] Carlos Elizondo Mayer-Serra, Y mi palabra es la ley: AMLO en Palacio Nacional [And my word is the law: AMLO at National Palace] 87–169 (2021).

[7] On Latin American left-wing populism, see Alejandro Rodiles, *Is There a Populist International Law (in Latin America)?*, 49 Neth. Y.B. Int'l L. 69 (2018); Carlos de la Torre & Cynthia Arnson , Latin American populism in the Twenty-First Century (2013); Juan F. González Bertomeu & María Paula Saffon, *The Mix of Latin American Populist Constitutionalism*, 16 L. Ethics Hum. Rts. 137 (2022). On López Obrador's neoliberalism, see Rosa Albina Garavito Elías, *El continuismo neoliberal de AMLO* [AMLO's neoliberal continuity], Proceso (Mar. 5, 2022), https://tinyurl.com/yc3c3bsc; Roger Bartra, *López Obrador es un populista de derecha de manual* [López Obrador is a textbook right-wing populist], El País (Mar. 28, 2021), https://tinyurl.com/mrw645nt.

[8] Mattias Kumm, Anthony Lang, James Tully & Antje Wiener, *How Large Is the World of Global Constitutionalism?* 3 Glob. Const. 1 (2014).

This chapter's aim is to introduce and further invite assessments of whether the institutional solutions typically embraced by contemporary Latin American constitutions make a difference in fighting contemporary patterns of rule-of-law violations and what sort of difference they make.

The chapter advances the preliminary hypothesis that Latin American last-wave constitutions make a positive difference. Many features of constitutional design are arguably helping to sustain democracy and the rule of law in the region in times of authoritarian, neopopulist onslaught, setting the ground for the middle-term reinvigoration of democracies and rule-of-law guarantees. The analysis suggests, however, that these features help fight erosion in a relatively ineffective way because most of them are reactive, ex post defenses, and overcharge the judiciary. A more effective, systemic prevention of rule-of-law erosion would require the design or reinforcement of preemptive solutions, both in the domain of rights and in the domain of the organization of powers.[9]

There are grounds for confirming this hypothesis in various countries – such as Brazil, Ecuador, Colombia, or Bolivia – where periods of hyper-presidential rule have been reversed. The focus of this chapter, however, will be exclusively on Mexico, in order to more fully ground the analysis. Among the many patterns of rule-of-law undermining currently underway, this chapter concentrates on two episodes and the reactions to them on the basis of Mexico's Constitution—the onslaught against the National Electoral Institute as the arbiter of electoral fairness and the enhancement of the military's role in society, particularly in relation to public security and the economy.

In pursuing this analysis, the chapter first recalls historic trends with regard to democracy and the rule of law in Latin America. Second, it provides an overview of the standard institutional tools contained in Latin American constitutions that can be put at the service of the rule of law and other normative ideals. Third, it describes rule-of-law undermining patterns that illustrate the current situation in Mexico and explores how the Constitution is used to resist them. Throughout, the chapter draws inspiration from Shaffer and Sandholtz's five-dimensional conception of the rule of law, which assesses whether (1) power is ex ante

[9] For an interesting survey of different mechanisms (including elections, separation of powers, constitutional rights, and administrative law) for the control of executive policy-making in Latin America, and an argument about their insufficiency, see Susan Rose-Ackerman & Edgar Andrès Melgar, *Hyper-Presidential Administration: Executive Policymaking in Latin America*, 64 Ariz. L. Rev. 1097 (2022).

subject to limits and accountability mechanisms; (2) individuals have a degree of predictability as to how power is exercised; (3) individuals can question and respond to the exercise of power; (4) authorities engage in reason-giving; and (5) there is proportionality in a set of distinct state responses.[10] These dimensions provide a background grammar for assessing current challenges and the strengths and weaknesses of available constitutional responses.

## II The Long Quest for the Rule of Law in Latin America

In the countries that experienced the "third wave of democratization" – those in Latin America and Central and Eastern Europe – constitutional democracy has a contorted history. The first Latin American constitutions were passed in the early years of the nineteenth century, after independence revolutions similar to those that had taken place shortly before in the United States and France. As Roberto Gargarella has observed, these first regional constitutions alternate or combine designs that embody three distinct understandings of individual autonomy and collective self-rule – liberal, conservative, and radical.[11] The second half of the nineteenth century saw the stabilization of a "constitutionalism of fusion" based on a long-lasting liberal-conservative pact. This pact supported checks and balances, but it tilted in favor of executive power; federal states with very strong centers; religious tolerance, though without depriving the Catholic Church of its privileges; and bills of individual rights, without any social precommitments, at a time of increasing social unrest.[12]

While for some time constitutions embraced French-inspired systems of political review of legislation, in the second half of the nineteenth century most countries established systems of decentralized judicial review allowing for the nonapplication of statutes in individual cases – with additions, like the *amparo* writ in Mexico or certain modalities of abstract review in Colombia and Venezuela. The hybrid legal traditions

[10] *See* Chapter 1.

[11] Roberto Gargarella, The legal foundations of inequality: Constitutionalism in the Americas, 1770–1860 (2010); Roberto Gargarella, Latin American Constitutionalism 1810–2010: The Engine Room of the Constitution 1–20 (2014) [hereinafter Gargarella, Latin American Constitutionalism].

[12] Gargarella, Latin American Constitutionalism, *supra* note 11, at 20–43. Constitutions representative of this period include those of Argentina (1853), México (1857), Peru (1860), Uruguay (1830), Colombia (1886), and Paraguay (1870).

of Latin America thus progressively developed, with bodies of civil, criminal, commercial, and procedural law codified and applied within structures typical of the civil law tradition, and constitutions featuring presidentialism, federalism, and decentralized review, much in the style of the United States.[13]

However, as in other countries, constitutions had long been operating more as political documents than as legally enforceable ones. The historical dockets of Latin American supreme courts contained some important constitutional cases, but law enforcement consisted for the most part in enforcing codified legislation. Constitutional rule was seriously compromised in most countries through abuse in the form of emergency states, civil wars, and military coups.[14] As reflected in popular sayings, academic literature, and literary works, overt or covert noncompliance with the law has been widespread and often normalized in Latin America.[15] As García Villegas remarks, for some, these attitudes can be ultimately traced back to colonial times, during which the formula *se acata pero no se cumple* (complied with but not fulfilled) served as a means to adapt the law that came from the Iberian peninsula to the very different conditions of the colonies; others associate it with the influence of iusnaturalism, which makes the validity of the law conditional on its moral weight – an attitude similar to the perspective of those who find no reason to obey the law under conditions of gross socioeconomic injustice, where the state is authoritarian or itself disobeys the law.[16] Constitutions and laws were, therefore, not irrelevant, but existed in a medium where flexibility and negotiation were common, in constant interaction with rules of other sorts.

In the twentieth century, a diversified political and constitutional setting coexisted with widespread ambivalence about the cause of liberal democracy.[17] As Javier Couso has explained, until the decades of the

[13] Francisca Pou Giménez, *Hybridity and Constitutional Taxonomy in Latin America*, 16 L. & Ethics Hum. Rts. 245 (2022).

[14] Between 1949 and 1991, Colombia was under a state of exception for more than thirty years. Between 1970 and 1991, it lasted for 206 months (equivalent to 17 years, or 82 percent of the time). Mauricio García Villegas, Normas de papel: La cultura del incumplimiento de reglas [Paper rules: The culture of normative noncompliance] 227–28 (2009). On the abuse of emergency powers in Mexico, *see* José Antonio Aguilar Rivera, El manto liberal: Los poderes de emergencia en México, 1821–1876 (2001).

[15] Villegas, *supra* note 14, at 15–35.

[16] *Id.* at 283–302.

[17] Gargarella, Latin American Constitutionalism, *supra* note 11, at 105–31, posits that between 1930 and 1980 Latin American countries explored five different "exit doors" to the social question that dominated the zeitgeist: the authoritarian,

1970s and 1980s, both the Right and the Left in Latin America held constitutional democracy in considerable disdain.[18] For the Left, highly influenced by Marxism and the Cuban Revolution, little was to be gained from the establishment of liberal constitutions and political democracy unaccompanied by economic transformation:[19] constitutional limits on democratically elected governments – such as the right to property – were benefits for the conservatives.[20] For the latter, in turn, "order and progress," and a concern for the preservation of public and national security, were always paramount, which often translated into support for military coups and strong presidents.[21]

## III Contemporary Latin American Constitutionalism and the Exercise of Power

Everything changed in the 1980s and 1990s. Couso remarks that, at that time, both the Left and the Right changed their views on liberal democracy and the rule of law. In the case of the Left, the atrocities suffered at the hands of the military dictatorships led to an appreciation of legal institutions such as habeas corpus and due process guarantees.[22] In the case of the Right, free-market ideology was important; from the 1980s onward, the idea that the rule of law, well-defined property rights, judicial independence, and effective state apparatuses were indispensable for economic growth became central to Latin American conservatism.[23]

In this environment, emerging from different circumstances but all in need of relegitimation, the countries of the region underwent a wave of

endorsed by "order and progress" regimes, military and civil dictatorships, and hegemonic party regimes; the reformist, based on the introduction of social rights in the constitution and the moderation of presidentialism (formulas that can be found in the constitutions of Bolivia (1938), Cuba (1940), Guatemala (1945), Costa Rica (1949), Uruguay (1942), and Brazil (1946)); the populist, practiced by Perón and Vargas (combining anti-communism, anti-liberalism, and authoritarianism with social commitment); the exclusionary democratic pact exit, practiced in Colombia and Venezuela when the Left and the Right accorded alternations in power; and the socialist, assayed in Cuba, Nicaragua, and, briefly, in Chile.

18 Javier Couso, *Los desafíos de la democracia constitucional en América Latina: Entre la tentación populista y la utopía neoconstitucional* [The challenges of constitutional democracy in Latin America: Between the populist temptation and the neoconstitutional utopia], 6 Anuario De Derechos Humanos 33 (2010).

19 *Id.*

20 *Id.* at 35.

21 *Id.*

22 *Id.* at 38.

23 *Id.* at 39.

political transformation, regularly accompanied by the making of new constitutions (Brazil in 1988, Colombia in 1991, Paraguay in 1992, Peru in 1993, Argentina in 1994, Venezuela in 1999, Bolivia in 1994 and 2009, Ecuador in 1998 and 2008) or the reform of existing ones (Costa Rica in 1989, and Mexico on many occasions over the last three decades).

The new and reformed Latin American constitutions have a significant collection of common traits and generally evince a commitment to organize the exercise of power within new parameters. While commentators have pointed out that the degree of innovation in the domain of power structures is smaller than what we find in declarations of rights – to the detriment of the underlying transformative project – historical designs have not survived untouched.[24]

A first area of (modest) innovation implicating power structures is the regulation of the relations between the executive and legislative branches: all countries retain a presidential system of government, but adjustments have been made to reinforce the legislative branch, and many executive attributions have been transferred to independent agencies and fourth-branch institutions.[25] Moreover, constitutions introduce mechanisms of direct or participatory democracy (popular consultation, presidential recall, popular legislative initiative, and sometimes participatory budgeting).[26] A second area where more robust changes have occurred is the design of the judiciary, which now enjoys a system of self-government under Judiciary Councils; a broad menu of responsibilities that diversifies citizens' channels for accessing justice; and, in some countries, an architecture that features several apex courts, including electoral courts.[27] The granting of constitutional status to international human rights, moreover, gives the doctrines of the Inter-American Court

[24] *See* GARGARELLA, LATIN AMERICAN CONSTITUTIONALISM, *supra* note 11, 148–71; *see also* Roberto Gargarella, *Una maquinaria exhausta: Constitucionalismo y alienación legal en América Latina* [Exhausted Machinery: Constitutionalism and legal alienation in Latin America], 33 ISONOMÍA 7 (2010).

[25] *See, e.g.*, Eric Magar, *Los contados cambios al equilibrio de poderes* [The few changes to the equilibrium of powers], *in* REFORMAR SIN MAYORÍAS [Amending without majorities] (M.A. Casar & Ignacio Marván eds., 2012); Ana María Bejarano & Renata Segura, *The Difference Power Diffusion Makes: Explaining Divergent Outcomes in Colombia (1990-1991) and Venezuela (1998-1999)*, *in* REDRAFTING CONSTITUTIONS IN DEMOCRATIC REGIMES (Gabriel Negretto ed., 2020).

[26] For a mostly skeptical view, see Tom Ginsburg, *"The Economy, Stupid": Notes on a Continuing Conversation*, 49 REVISTA DERECHO DEL ESTADO 15 (2021).

[27] Patricio Navia & Julio Ríos-Figueroa, *The Constitutional Adjudication Mosaic of Latin America*, 38 COMP. POL. STUD. 189 (2005); Francisca Pou Giménez, *Supreme and Constitutional Courts: Directions in Constitutional Justice*, *in* HANDBOOK OF LAW AND

of Human Rights (IACtHR) a permanent role in day-to-day constitutional dynamics within Latin American countries, implicating rule-of-law practices.

Innovation is even greater when it comes to fundamental rights. In his portrayal of last-wave regional constitutions, Rodrigo Uprimny identifies ten major changes: redefinition of national unity, replacing traditional homogenization drives with recognition of diversity and the foundational status of indigenous peoples; elimination of the residues of religious establishment and guarantee of religious freedom; protection of disadvantaged and discriminated groups, including indigenous and black communities, which are often granted special rights or jurisdiction; generous recognition of rights, including social rights, and new categories of rights-holders, like nature, groups, or communities; great openness to international human rights law, which often operates as a block in conjunction with the constitution; transformation of the system of legal sources, resulting in statutory law now coexisting with other sources of normativity; strong commitment to equality, including affirmative action; introduction of umbrella clauses that synthesize the foundations of the constitutional project, like the "Social and Democratic State" clause or varieties that go beyond European postwar models; inclusion of principles and tools that evince deep concern for the efficacy of rights; and references to the economy, even if heterogenous and irreducible to a single message.[28]

## IV Undermining of the Rule of Law in Contemporary Mexico

The fact that democracy has for three decades remained the only road to political and legal authority in Latin America is in itself an immense, historic watershed.[29] In general, civil society has been revitalized, there is widespread public recognition of social and cultural pluralism, and the constitutionalism of rights has given the law a centrality it had never enjoyed before in the region.[30] There has been an abundance of developments around new vindications (social rights, equality, environmental,

Society in Latin America (Rachel Sieder, Karina Ansolabehere & Tatiana Alfonso eds., 2019).

28 Rodrigo Uprimny, *The Recent Transformation of Constitutional Law in Latin America: Trends and Challenges*, *in* Law and Society in Latin America: A New Map 111–17 (César Rodríguez Garavito ed., 2015).

29 Couso, *supra* note 18.

30 *See* Handbook of Law and Society in Latin America, *supra* note 27.

and indigenous rights), which have supported new forms of adjudication, including structural rulings, innovative remedial practices, and continuous interaction between national courts and the IACtHR.[31] Political dynamics have embraced a wider assortment of legitimate social claims, often outside the frame of traditional party politics.[32]

However, numerous problems remain. In recent times, the persistence of unacceptable levels of inequality,[33] public and private violence,[34] inappropriate coverage of basic needs,[35] and the ineffectiveness and corruption of many institutions have eroded the status that constitutional democracy and the rule of law had gained in the region.[36] New political trends have developed in response. The political projects of presidents Rafael Correa in Ecuador (2007–17) and Evo Morales in Bolivia (2006–19) had an egalitarian thrust along with the strong personalism that dominated their administrations. The political projects of presidents Bolsonaro in Brazil and Nayib Bukele in El Salvador, by contrast, cater to the worst instincts of electorates that are now prepared to support an anti-politics style and policies that sacrifice liberties and the rule of law for the benefit of security as an act of revenge against the so-called traditional political class.

What these projects all have in common is the expansion of presidential powers, and the consequent distaste for constitutionalism understood as the ideal of limited government and protection of the rule of law.

[31] *See* Handbook of Constitutional Law in Latin America (Conrado Hübner-Mendes, Roberto Gargarella & Sebastián Guidi eds. 2022).

[32] *See generally* Diana Kapiszewski, Steven Levitsky & Deborah Yashar, The Inclusionary Turn in Latin American Democracies (2021).

[33] *See* Matías Busso & Julián Messina, The Inequality Crisis: Latin America and the Caribbean at the Crossroads (2020).

[34] Press Release, CEPAL, Al menos 4.473 mujeres fueron víctimas de feminicidio en América Latina y el Caribe en 2021 [At least 4,473 women were victims of feminicide in Latin America and the Caribbean in 2021] (Nov. 24, 2020), https://tinyurl.com/2tdxxmdj; Editorial, *Violencia en Latinoamérica*, El País (Apr. 9, 2023), https://elpais.com/opinion/2023-04-10/violencia-en-latinoamerica.html.

[35] Press Release, CEPAL, CEPAL insta a fomentar las inversiones en servicios hídricos para mejorar el bienestar, la calidad de vida y reactivar la economía de la región [CEPAL invites investment in hydric services to improve well-being and quality of life, and to reactivate regional economy] (Feb. 1, 2023), https://tinyurl.com/h2h8ej89; CEPAL, Panorama Social de América Latina y el Caribe (2022), https://tinyurl.com/4cnxy882.

[36] Javier Couso, *Las democracias liberales y el nuevo constitucionalismo latinoamericano* [Liberal democracies and new radical Latin American constitutionalism], *in* Derechos Humanos: Posibilidades Teóricas y Desafíos Prácticos 196, 197 (2014); *see also* Javier Couso, *A Tale of Two Cities*, *in* Handbook of Constitutional Law in Latin America, *supra* note 31.

While they do not reject the constitution per se, since upholding a permanent electoral style is crucial to them, they relativize the division of powers, the idea that the rulers must strictly abide by the rules that define the contours of their powers, and the idea that government must give appropriate reasons for actions – all of which are central to the rule of law. Because of their style of governance, which pits groups of people against each other, these administrations erode respect for pluralism and civil liberties. Because of their personalistic quest for concentrating power, they undermine the rule of law.

In what follows, this chapter focuses on some of the developments underway in Mexico, which provide a paradigmatic illustration of such neo-authoritarian dynamics. Mexico has traced a singular path of constitutional evolution. It transitioned to democracy while maintaining its 1917 Constitution, which has nonetheless undergone more than 800 amendments, especially from the 1990s onward. While the Mexican patterns of accelerated reform pose important problems, they have also brought the country in line with the common features of contemporary constitutionalism in the region.[37] Thus, Mexico has a generous declaration of rights, which includes international human rights and enforceable social rights; a sophisticated model of division of powers, with an assortment of fourth-branch institutions; emphatic constitutional recognition of indigenous nations and a model of moderate legal pluralism; channels of participatory democracy; and a reinforced judicial branch, even if the traditional *amparo* complaint procedure is hardly sufficient in ensuring equal access to justice for all.

Within this framework, Mexico has held indisputably reliable elections.[38] Yet, important wider problems persist. They include massive deadly violence, which, following state responses to drug trafficking, has increased dramatically since the presidency of Felipe Calderón, who launched a "war against drugs" at incalculable human, political, and legal cost – a policy that has been continued, with less energy, by his successors.[39] Other problems include a problematic Gini coefficient; a vitiated political class; very weak provision of public services; and

[37] *See* Francisca Pou Giménez, *The Constitution of Mexico*, *in* HANDBOOK OF CONSTITUTIONAL LAW IN LATIN AMERICA, *supra* note 31.

[38] JOSÉ WOLDENBERG, HISTORIA MÍNIMA DE LA TRANSICIÓN DEMOCRÁTICA EN MÉXICO [Minimal history of the democratic transition in Mexico] (2012).

[39] Nina Lakhani & Erubiel Tirado, *Mexico's war on drugs. What has it achieved and how is the US involved?*, THE GUARDIAN (Dec. 8, 2016), www.theguardian.com/news/2016/dec/08/mexico-war-on-drugs-cost-achievements-us-billions.

patterns of judicialization that, despite being progressive, do not benefit the majority of the population.

Against this background, in the 2018 election Mexicans gave the presidential seat to Andrés Manuel López Obrador, an old-style politician who was once a member of the Partido Revolucionario Institucional (PRI) and held office as mayor of Mexico City at the turn of the century. He ran twice for the presidency (in 2006 and 2012) under the party that he founded after leaving the PRI (named MORENA). He finally won by a massive vote in 2018, supported by millions who, fed up with the frustrations of standard politics, gave their confidence to the only candidate that seemed to promise real change. In the campaign, he famously promised "*abrazos, no balazos*" (hugs, not bullets), which sounded like a commitment to find a durable solution to the problem of violence in the country.[40]

On gaining office, however, López Obrador took a completely different route. He has applied a strictly populist rulebook and has deployed a large number of reforms that are at odds with progressive politics. His policies and daily gestures are problematic for fundamental rights and respect for the rule of law.

President López Obrador's distaste for pluralism is visible in his continuous criticisms of civil society organizations, scholars, scientists, journalists, lawyers, judges, feminists, and even the entire middle class (whom he disparages as selfish and "aspirationist").[41] His daily morning shows (*las mañaneras*) are an occasion to name and shame an unending succession of individuals and groups. The promotion of an insurmountable divide between "them" and "us" – between "our enemies," "the conservatives," "the corrupts," on the one hand, and "the people," on the other – is explicit and repeated incessantly every day.[42] These attacks

[40] José Antonio Belmont, *Con "abrazos, no balazos," AMLO promete reducir violencia* [With "hugs, not bullets," AMLO promises a reduction of violence], Milenio (Apr. 12, 2018), www.milenio.com/politica/abrazos-balazos-amlo-promete-reducir-violencia; Jannet López Ponce, *En mi gobierno habrá abrazos, no balazos: AMLO* [In my government there will be hugs, not bullets], Milenio (July 7, 2018), www.milenio.com/politica/en-mi-gobierno-habra-abrazos-no-balazos-amlo; Maria Abi-Habib & Oscar López, AMLO prometió "abrazos no balazos," pero la violencia continúa [AMLO promised "hugs, not bullets," but violence persists], N.Y. Times (Aug. 31, 2022), www.nytimes.com/es/2022/08/31/espanol/mexico-violencia-amlo.html.

[41] Jorge Monroy, *López Obrador reitera que la clase media es de "aspiracionistas sin escrúpulos morales"* [López Obrador reiterates that the middle class is "aspirationist without moral qualms"], El Economista (June 14, 2021), https://tinyurl.com/mr3enj5f.

[42] Lidia Arista, *Mañaneras: cuatro años de ataques, agenda y propaganda en el gobierno de AMLO* [The morning show: Four years of attacks, agenda, and propaganda in AMLO's

have not remained at the level of words but have been accompanied by police reform. The public research centers that were not legally autonomous, for instance, have lost their main sources of funding and have seen partisan individuals appointed as directors.[43] The National Research Council has suppressed several scholarship programs,[44] cut research stimulus to private university researchers, reformed applicable regulations several times, and denounced scientists on criminal grounds merely for being critical.[45] Civil society organizations, for their part, have endured a reform in their accounting duties that makes it extremely difficult for them to receive donations and other sources of funding on which they are heavily dependent.[46]

In addition, AMLO has pursued a policy of radically shrinking state capacities, with serious consequences in several domains, most notably health and education. Under the banner of austerity, the president has cut back on the funding of research and science, educational programs, health and daycare, and ordinary expenses throughout the entire administration, leaving many departments without the means to fulfill their basic responsibilities and generally nurturing state arbitrariness.[47] In the

government], Expansión Política (Dec. 23, 2022), https://politica.expansion.mx/amlo-mananeras-cuantas-van-cuatro-anos.

[43] Nelly Toche, *Conacyt sufre recorte en el PPEF 2023* [Conacyt suffers cuts in the 2023 federal budget], El Economista (Sept. 9, 2022), https://tinyurl.com/5n77f6u2; Juan Ortiz, *Confirman irregularidades en designación de Romero Tellaeche al frente del CIDE* [Irregularities in the appointment of Romero Tellaeche at CIDE are confirmed], La Silla Rota (Dec. 2, 2023), https://tinyurl.com/47zswa9z.

[44] *Comunidad científica pide a Conacyt no eliminar becas de posgrado en el extranjero* [Scientific community asks Conacyt not to eliminate scholarships for graduate programs abroad], El Universal (Mar. 4, 2021), https://tinyurl.com/udatdnum; *Los planes de López Obrador para el Conacyt: Austeridad y menos poder para las empresas* [López Obrador's plans for Conacyt: Austerity and less power], El País (Dec. 16, 2022), https://tinyurl.com/muawbyn2.

[45] Emilia López Pérez, *CIDE entrará en "economía de guerra" por recorte del 75% de su gasto operativo* [CIDE will enter war economy mode after 75% cut in its operative funding], El Financiero (May 27, 2020), https://tinyurl.com/454jshxu; Dalila Sarabia, *Comisión de Ética del CIDE resuelve que Romero Tellaeche sí plagió, pero no alcanzan votos para sancionarlo* [CIDE's Ethics Commission concludes Romero Tellaeche is a plagiarist, but votes are insufficient to impose a sanction on him], Animal Político (Sept. 7, 2022), www.animalpolitico.com/sociedad/romero-tellaeche-cide-plagio-votos.

[46] Unidad de Investigación Aplicada, *Gobierno federal amenaza el funcionamiento de sociedad civil* [Federal government places the operation of civil society under threat], Mexicanos contra la Corrupción y la Impunidad (Oct. 18, 2021), https://contralacorrupcion.mx/gobierno-federal-amenaza-funcionamiento-de-sociedad-civil.

[47] Montserrat Antúnez Estrada, *Las estancias infantiles cumplen un año sin subsidio: Unas cierran y otras suben las colegiaturas* [Daycare without subsidies for one year: Some units close and other raise their fees], Sin Embargo (Mar. 1, 2020), www.sinembargo.mx/01-

domain of health, the creation of the INSABI *(Instituto de Salud para el Bienestar)* to replace the Seguro Popular (a program for which people outside the other social security subsystems could self-enroll) did not succeed, leaving millions without coverage.[48] The president decided to rescind existing contracts with pharmaceutical suppliers, yet the inability to secure new ones left the health system in a state of chronic shortage of medicines.[49] The conflict this caused with the parents of children suffering from cancer, who were left without medicines, is only one visible manifestation of the seriousness of the situation.[50] In the field of education, the devastating effects of the pandemics were not addressed, twenty-two programs have been suppressed,[51] and the education secretary has been placed under the direction of two people with no expertise.[52]

True, the president has raised the minimum salary and expanded cash transfer programs – approximately 30 percent of the population

03-2020/3739422; *Los recortes presupuestarios en México amenazan la salud y la igualdad de las mujeres* [Budgetary cuts in Mexico endanger women's health and equality], United Nations (Oct. 16, 2020), https://news.un.org/es/story/2020/10/1482492.

48 Three years later, in 2022, the government recognized the INSABI failure and announced people would start to be covered by IMSS-Bienestar. *See* Andrea Vega, *Arranca plan B del gobierno para dar atención en salud a población sin seguridad social, tras fracaso del Insabi* [Governmental Plan B to provide health services to uninsured population starts off, following Insabi's failure], Animal Político (Apr. 1, 2022), www.animalpolitico.com/salud/plan-b-salud-tras-fracaso-del-insabi.

49 Eduardo Esquivel Ancona, *Gobierno de México cancela contrato con UNOPS para compra de medicamentos* [Mexican government cancels medicine provision contract with UNOPS], SDP Noticias (Oct. 18, 2022), https://tinyurl.com/24vrfm7h; Beatríz Guillén, *El Gobierno mexicano inhabilita a la farmacéutica Pisa tras meses de tensión* [Mexican government disqualifies PISA Pharmaceutics after three months of tension], El País (Oct. 21, 2020), https://tinyurl.com/muw8y2uu.

50 Fabiola Martínez, *Acusa AMLO a opositores de protestas de padres de niños con cáncer* [AMLO blames opponents for the protests of the parents of children with cancer], La Jornada (Nov. 11, 2021), https://tinyurl.com/yc8k6wyy.

51 Information from a study by Mexicanos Primero, unpublished document on file with the author. *See also* Felipe J. Hevia et al., *Estimation of the Fundamental Learning Loss and Learning Poverty Related to COVID-19 Pandemic in Mexico*, 88 Int'l J. Educ. Dev. 102515 (2022).

52 *Leticia Ramírez, titular de SEP, no sabe cómo un niño de segundo de primaria aprenderá matemáticas* [ Leticia Ramírez, education secretary, does not know how second-grade children will learn math] SDP Noticias (Sept. 5, 2022), https://tinyurl.com/mvdytjz9; Arturo Contreras Camero, *Leticia Ramírez: De la "primavera magisterial" a la Secretaría de Educación Pública* [Leticia Ramírez: From the "teachers' spring" to public education secretariat], Pie de Página (Aug. 16, 2022), https://tinyurl.com/4bjnfv6y; Marco Antonio Martínez, *Delfina Gómez en la SEP, sin logros y muchos pendientes: Experto* [Delfina Gómez at the public education secretariat: No achievements and many pending issues, expert says], La Silla Rota (Aug. 9, 2022), https://tinyurl.com/usvad4c7.

receive some kind of direct, nonconditional cash benefit.[53] Aside from these transfers, however, and the ever-growing sums assigned to the army,[54] an immense amount of public funds go to Pemex and other projects associated with fossil fuel (like the construction of a refinery in Dos Bocas and the acquisition of another one in Texas) and to flagship works of infrastructure like the Maya Train (traversing ecosystems of great environmental value) or the Felipe Ángeles Airport, not to mention the cancellation of the already half-built Texcoco Airport at a cost of close to USD 5,700 million.[55] Under his administration poverty has stabilized,[56] despite a context of relative economic normalcy: the country accumulates gains from nearshoring; the money transfers sent by the US Mexican diaspora have grown; and the currency has not depreciated, thanks to the orthodox monetary policy followed by the government.[57]

[53] Stefano Pozzebon, *Aumenta el salario mínimo en México un 20% para 2023: ¿Cuánto será la cantidad y cuándo entra en vigor?* [Minimum salary 20% increase in Mexico for 2023: How much is it and when will it be effective?], CNN Latinoamérica (Jan. 4, 2023), https://tinyurl.com/yzbjuu4f; Luis Miguel González, *¿Por qué no cuadran las cifras de beneficiarios de programas sociales?* [Why do figures for social program recipients not square?], El Economista (Aug. 11, 2021), https://tinyurl.com/2kxsevv7; Dulce Soto, *Transferencias monetarias de AMLO aumentan, pero llegan menos a los más pobres* [AMLO money transfers increase but reach fewer of the poorest], Expansión Política (Feb. 16, 2023), https://tinyurl.com/mrcw2fny.

[54] Alfredo Fuentes, *Sedena gastó 49 mil mdp de más en dos años: MUCD* [Sedena overspends by 49,000 million pesos in two years], El Sol de México (Oct. 1, 2022), https://tinyurl.com/mu3pe3zs.

[55] Agencia EFE, *Cancelar el aeropuerto de Texcoco en México costó 5.692 millones de dólares* [Cancellation of Texcoco Airport cost 5,692 dollars], SWI swissinfo.ch (May 1, 2021), https://tinyurl.com/3zp9cj24 ; Karol García, *ASF: Pemex gastó 2.6 veces lo programado para Dos Bocas* [Pemex overspent Dos Bocas budget by 2.6 times], El Economista (Feb. 20, 2023), https://tinyurl.com/4cm962jh; Emmanuel Carrillo, *Refinería de Dos Bocas lleva inversión de 233 mil mdp: AMLO* [Dos Bocas refinery absorbs 223,000 million pesos investment: AMLO], Forbes (Oct. 7, 2022), www.forbes.com.mx/refineria-de-dos-bocas-lleva-inversion-de-233-mil-mdp-amlo/; Karol García, *Pemex pagaría hasta 1,000 mdd más por Deer Park* [AMLO would pay up to 1,000 million pesos more for Deer Park], El Economista (Dec. 9, 2021), https://tinyurl.com/4stx5nn9.

[56] Consejo Nacional de Evaluación de la Política de Desarrollo Social, Informe de Evaluación de la Política de Desarrollo Social 2022 (Feb. 2023), www.coneval.org.mx/Evaluacion/Documents/Informes/IEPDS_2022_Presentacion.pdf (showing the proportion of the population below the poverty level has gone from 41.9 percent in 2018 to 43.9 percent in 2020; and levels of absolute poverty from 34.9 percent in 2018 to 35.4 percent in 2020).

[57] Orlando Delgado Selley, *Decisión monetaria* [Monetary decision], La Jornada (Feb. 16, 2023), www.jornada.com.mx/2023/02/16/opinion/020a1eco.

Overall, AMLO's challenges to the rule of law are numerous, as the following two sections illustrate. The president has repeatedly expressed a deep distaste for all things legal. He has portrayed the law as an instrument of the *ancien régime* and legal requirements as hurdles in the way of attaining the "Fourth Transformation of Mexico."[58] A painful, paradigmatic illustration of this approach to the law is the executive decree that declared public works of infrastructure (such as the construction of the Maya Train) to be "national security" issues, obliging all administrative units to issue the corresponding permits notwithstanding any statutory norm to the contrary.[59]

An abundance of developments reveal tensions along the five dimensions that Shaffer and Sandholtz identify as defining a goal-oriented understanding of the rule of law. To illustrate some of them, this chapter focuses on two clusters of developments. The first is the frontal attack on the National Electoral Institute, the independent agency that remains the key guarantor of electoral regularity. The second is the militarization of state functions – first, public security, and later a much wider set of state responsibilities, including the provisions of public services and the construction of public works.

All of them reveal a willingness to eliminate checks and balances; a general disregard for the idea of reason-giving; a decline in the predictability of public action since many measures are processed speedily (with or without the intervention of a dominated legislature), often in open violation of legal requirements. As in other situations of autocratic legalism, the pattern is gradual, with the overall impact being greater than the sum of its parts. Intertwined with that pattern, however, is degree of legal contestation that has no precedent in Mexico. In the face of inaction on the part of the political opposition, many agents are

[58] Diego Badillo, *Para AMLO, el derecho es un estorbo: Juristas* [For AMLO law is an annoyance, say lawyers], El Economista (Dec. 1, 2020), https://tinyurl.com/3ztck7wf; *Que AMLO demerite la ley afecta al estado de derecho en México* [AMLO's downplaying of the law damages the rule of law in Mexico], El Financiero (May 29, 2022), https://tinyurl.com/36u6mv7t.

[59] Acuerdo por el que se instruye a las dependencias y entidades de la Administración Pública Federal a realizar acciones que se indican, en relación con los proyectos y obras del Gobierno de México considerados de interés público y seguridad nacional, así como prioritarios y estratégicos para el desarrollo nacional [Agreement instructing the agencies and entities of the Federal Public Administration to carry out the actions indicated in relation to the projects and works of the Government of Mexico considered of public interest and national security, as well as priority and strategic for national development] (Nov. 22, 2021), www.dof.gob.mx/nota_detalle.php?codigo=5635985&fecha=22/11/2021#gsc.tab=0.

using instruments and spaces that were unavailable in previous historical instantiations of rule-of-law disregard.

## V The Quest against Electoral Reliability

The construction of a strong independent authority capable of organizing clean elections and the reform of the electoral system based on administrative rule of law was the keystone of the Mexican transition.[60] The country was not emerging from a military dictatorship and it had never formally abolished elections. However, under the political system progressively installed by the PRI, elections were rigged and won by the person designated by the president. The PRI was to a certain extent inclusive of various social groups and provided a system of elite rotation.[61] It also provided peace and stability in a country that had endured significant turmoil during the nineteenth century.[62] But it was not a democracy: there were formal elections, but no actual rule-of-law preconditions to ensure free voting and political competition.

When it ultimately became impossible to maintain the system without changes, several constitutional reforms introduced electoral competition and progressively built independent electoral authorities.[63] An institution called IFE (Instituto Federal Electoral) was created in 1990, together with parallel institutions at state level. In 1996, the IFE gained complete independence from the executive, and in 2013 a constitutional reform renamed the institution INE (Instituto Nacional Electoral) and gave it more powers over the organization and monitoring of elections at state level. The institution soon established itself as one marked by professionalization (its employees are career officials) and a model of election organization and supervision that included extensive input from the citizenry and was grounded in administrative rule of law. Thus, the voting booths in Mexico are managed by citizens who are selected on the basis of their birth month, trained before the elections by the INE, and

60 Tom Ginsburg defines the rule of law in the administration of elections as a key component of democracy. TOM GINSBURG, DEMOCRACIES AND INTERNATIONAL LAW 21 (2021).

61 *See* Philip Paolino, *The PRI's Position in Mexican Politics*, 16 POLÍTICA Y GOBIERNO 321, 348 (2009).

62 *See* Lucía Álvarez Mosso, *"Estabilidad": Un logro de la coalición priista* [Stability: An achievement of the Priistas coalition] (Review of ROGER D. HANSEN, LA POLÍTICA DEL DESARROLLO MEXICANOy), 11 PROBLEMAS DEL DESARROLLO 163, 165 (1972).

63 For an overview of the Mexican electoral transition to democracy, see WOLDENBERG, *supra* note 38.

who count the votes and make the results public before taking them personally to the INE offices. The INE General Council's members do not need to be lawyers.

The INE is a huge institution responsible for many tasks: it issues voter ID; it organizes the elections and trains the citizens who run the voting and do the counting; it reviews whether candidates satisfy the conditions of eligibility and monitors observance of legal requirements concerning access to and use of funding and access to mass media space and time during campaigns and precampaigns; and it supervises certain aspects of political party life outside electoral processes.

Despite winning 53.19 percent of the vote in an election that, by all accounts, was impeccable, AMLO soon leveled fierce criticism at the INE – initially, as part of a broader campaign against all independent agencies as well as the judiciary. The attacks on INE, however, continued to grow and, over time, reached astounding levels. (The 2006 election had been narrowly won by Felipe Calderón, and from that moment AMLO became disillusioned with the INE, despite the great credibility of the system and the political alternation in the presidency.) One of the more worrying episodes occurred in April 2021, when the INE, applying existing law, cancelled the candidacy of Félix Salgado Macedonio in the Guerrero gubernatorial election because he failed to report on his precampaign expenditures (paid in Mexico with public money).[64] Salgado then mounted a demonstration in front of the INE, which included the presentation of a huge coffin and the issuing of assassination threats against the INE president; threats were also made against INE counsellors, whose home addresses Salgado urged his followers to locate. Salgado (who had also been denounced for several instances of sexual abuse) was the candidate AMLO wanted to win in Guerrero, and the president did not abandon him. He rather defended Salgado, saying that the INE should have imposed a fine but not prevented him from running.[65] In the end, MORENA selected the daughter of Salgado Macedonio as the candidate – and she won the election. The incident gave the impression that the president was happy to validate the most egregious attacks on

[64] *See* Ley General de Instituciones y Procedimientos Electorales [LGIPE], as amended, art. 229, Diario Oficial de la Federación [DOF], May 5, 2014.

[65] Almudena Barragán, *López Obrador defiende a Salgado Macedonio frente al INE: "Sanciónenlo, pero no le quiten el derecho de participar"* [López Obrador defends Salgado Macedonio against INE: "Sanction him, but let him run"], El País (Apr. 13, 2021), https://tinyurl.com/2p9zpru9.

institutions (and persons) if there were political gains in return, in violation of basic rule-of-law norms.

In November 2021, the MORENA-controlled Congress approved the budget for the year 2022, and it did not assign to INE the funds that it had precalculated. In particular, the INE was not given the funds necessary to organize the presidential recall consultation that the president had already scheduled for August 2022 to forecast his popular support. The INE then filed two constitutional claims before the Supreme Court: one to protect its counselors from incurring administrative or criminal liability if they organized the recall in disregard of legal parameters for lack of money to comply with them; and the other denouncing the unconstitutionality of the budgetary cut.[66] In February 3, 2022, the Supreme Court declared that the INE could and should organize the presidential recall as best it could with existing funds and the reduced budget passed by Congress,[67] and on June 1, 2022, it declared the budget cut to be invalid.[68]

At the time, President López Obrador had already decided to submit the proposal of a constitutional amendment to change the existing architecture of the electoral system. The reform proposed five main changes: the transformation of INE into a National Institute of Consultations and Elections, headed by counselors elected by popular vote from candidates selected by Congress, the executive, and the Supreme Court; a reduction in the amount of public funds received by political parties; electronic voting; a reduction in the number of members of Congress, state legislatures, and municipal councils; and changes in the size of the electoral districts for the election of deputies by proportional representation.[69] While some of these

[66] Suprema Corte de Justicia de la Nación [SCJN] [Supreme Court], Press Release No. 396/2021 (Dec. 22, 2021), www.internet2.scjn.gob.mx/red2/comunicados/noticia.asp?id=6704.

[67] SCJN, Feb. 3, 2022, Controversia Constitucional 209/2021; *see* Jorge Monroy, *Avalan que INE organice consulta con los recursos que tiene* [Organization of consultation with the resources INE enjoys is authorized], El Economista (Feb. 3, 2022), https://tinyurl.com/e3ypzesv.

[68] SCJN, June 1, 2023, Controversia Constitucional 244/2021. The Court ordered the Chamber of Deputies to reanalyze the INE proposal for allocations in the 2022 budget and authorize or reject the resources asked for following a process of "reinforced motivation." The Chamber, however, simply announced in the Official Gazette (DOF, October 4, 2022) that it was reiterating the same allocation of resources, without developing any "reinforced motivation." *See* Jorge Monroy, *INE presenta queja ante la SCJN por recorte presupuestal en 2022* [INE complains before SCJN over 2022 budget cut], El Economista (Nov. 16, 2022), https://tinyurl.com/5d4wv6bw.

[69] Belén Zapata, *¿Cómo es la reforma electoral de México? ¿Qué propone y qué causa controversia?* [What is Mexico's electoral reform like? What are the proposals and what

changes were reasonable and not particularly dangerous in rule-of-law terms, they were packaged with the first proposal, the risks of which unbalanced any other potential gains. The proposal to elect counselors by popular vote would have allowed the government to remove all existing counselors and bring ordinary party politics into an institution that should operate as a neutral electoral arbiter. It would have generated an "adverse selection" effect, in view of the trouble associated with the need to launch a political campaign to be an electoral counselor, after being included on a short list largely rigged by the executive (given its control of the legislative branch, and its unpredictable future influence on the Supreme Court).[70]

In November 2022, this reform was discussed in Congress against a background of high political contestation. A popular demonstration in support of the INE, called by a heterogenous assembly of civil society groups, took place on November 13, and its success surpassed everyone's expectations. The streets of Mexico City around the Monument to the Revolution and Reform Avenue were filled by an organized throng of thousands of families and groups of citizens, and the same occurred in the main cities outside the capital.[71] A few days before, the president had asked his followers to "allow" the demonstration, while qualifying those planning to attend as "racist" and "classist."[72] The day after the march, clearly upset, he summoned his followers to attend a "response" demonstration on November 27 "to celebrate the gains of four years of Transformation" – which also was a success.[73]

The constitutional reform did not pass, however. Having lost the capacity to amend the constitution alone after the results of the intermediate 2021 election, MORENA was unable to secure the necessary

is controversial?], CNN LATINOAMÉRICA (Nov. 15, 2022), https://tinyurl.com/5n6mh5b7.

70 Erika Hernández, *Los riesgos de la reforma electoral, según el INE* [The risks of the electoral reform, in INE's opinion], REFORMA (Jan. 28, 2023), https://tinyurl.com/5b4tmwkk.

71 Ricardo Raphael, *La marcha a favor del INE y las razones de la retórica polarizante de AMLO* [The march in favor of INE and the reasons for AMLO's polarizing rhetoric], WASH. POST (Nov. 16, 2022), https://tinyurl.com/kzhjwa6h.

72 *AMLO pide a sus simpatizantes permitir marcha a favor del INE, aunque la descalifica* [AMLO asks followers to permit the pro-INE march, but discredits it], ANIMAL POLÍTICO (Nov. 7, 2022), www.animalpolitico.com/politica/amlo-ine-marcha-provocaciones.

73 Zedryk Raziel, *López Obrador encabezará una manifestación para mostrar el apoyo a su Gobierno tras la marcha contra su reforma electoral*, EL PAÍS (Nov. 16, 2022), https://tinyurl.com/2hwk8szp.

support by negotiating with the other political parties, which felt the pressure of the popular march.[74] A few days later, however, on December 13, 2022, with the holiday season about to start, the president made a surprising move and submitted to Congress the so-called Plan B electoral reform. This contained a proposal to amend six statutes (something MORENA could do by a simple majority vote). At its core, it involved a radical shrinking and weakening of INE as an institution, to the point of compromising its ability to organize and supervise elections under the rule of law.[75]

Several parts of the project are perfectly acceptable, even to be welcomed, such as the overdue guarantee of the right for people in prison to vote, the regulation of online trials, the simplification of complaint procedures, the need to implement gender parity in elections for state governors, and the restructuring of the calendar for federal and state elections. Yet other proposals are sensitive, and some deeply troubling. In this last category are the elimination of the rule that had so far prevented individuals holding public office (and in receipt of a salary paid with public money) from engaging in political advocacy in electoral campaigns; the elimination of the INE administrative apparatus across the country, endangering electoral IDs and the training of citizens who serve on election day; the reorganization of the INE's internal units, with the immediate removal of the executive secretary, the dissolution of the trusts guaranteeing the salaries of INE employees (which would now depend on annual budgetary allocations); and the provision (tailored to "save" a future Salgado Macedonio) that being sanctioned by the INE for violating electoral law is no impediment to run for elections (only a criminal conviction is).

Plan B was published in two steps. After the publication of a first package, more than one hundred constitutional *controversias* were filed by municipalities, which maintained that their powers of self-organization

[74] Noticias del Congreso, *Desechan en San Lázaro reforma constitucional en materia electoral*, CANAL DEL CONGRESO (Dec. 6, 2022), https://tinyurl.com/bdsyw5sd.

[75] *See* JAVIER MARTÍN REYES & MARÍA MARVÁN LABORDE, RADIOGRAFIA DEL PLAN B: LA REFORMA ELECTORAL DE 2023 A EXAMEN [Plan B: Electoral reform under scrutiny] (2023); *see also* Instituto Nacional Electoral, *Plan B de reforma electoral pone en riesgo derechos político-electorales de personas históricamente discriminadas* [[Plan B of electoral reform endangers political rights of historically discriminated people], CENTRAL ELECTORAL (Feb. 8, 2023), https://tinyurl.com/bddn75n7; Samedi Aguirre, *Presupuesto del INE: Cuánto es para elecciones y cuánto más para los partidos* [INE budget: How much for elections and how much more for political parties], ANIMAL POLÍTICO (June 4, 2021), https://tinyurl.com/2s49tj3c.

were curtailed, and by actors, who argued that the reform affected electoral processes already underway, thus disregarding the prohibition on making amendments to electoral rules in the ninety days preceding an election.[76] Before the publication of the remaining package of reforms, civil society organizations summoned a new march in defense of the vote on February 26, 2023, with great success. This time, people gathered at the Zócalo, the tectonic power center in Mexico, and available estimates put the attendance in Mexico City and other cities across the country at approximately 700,000.[77]

On March 4, 2023, however, the second package of Plan B was published. A few days later, the INE filed two *controversias* against the reform and two groups of Congress members filed *acciones de inconstitucionalidad.*[78] As the demonstrators in the February march made clear through their banners and chants, protection of democracy and the rule of law would depend on the Supreme Court.

AMLO has striven to undermine the Court using all means. He has taken advantage of the opportunity to appoint four justices, two of whom are unconditional supporters, while the other two have proven to be fairly independent. Yet, for a statute to be declared void in abstract review in Mexico, and disappear from the books, there must be a qualified majority of eight votes – a threshold difficult to pass in any scenario, but specially so in the current climate. Further, for four years the presidency of the Court was held by Arturo Zaldívar, who was quickly criticized for cultivating an excessive closeness to the government. Under his presidency, the Court delayed decisions in many politically sensitive cases.

In the electoral domain, however, the Court's decision-making is subject to time limits. And its performance as regards Plan B has been admirably solid, even in the face of all imaginable kinds of pressure. In admitting the cases, the Court thus precautionarily suspended the effects of the reforms,[79] to which MORENA "responded" the next day by filing

[76] Eduardo Murillo, *Admite SCJN 17 controversias contra primera fase de "Plan B"* [Supreme Court admits 17 *controversias* against first phase of "Plan B"], La Jornada (Mar. 9, 2023), https://tinyurl.com/mtxtfrk8.

[77] Alejandra Lisette, *Marcha INE: decenas de miles de mexicanos protestaron contra el Plan B de López Obrador* [Tens of thousands of Mexicans protest against López Obrador's Plan B], Infobae (Feb. 26, 2023), https://tinyurl.com/yckazah7.

[78] SCJN, Acciones de Inconstitucionalidad 29/2023, 30/2023, 31/2023, 37/2023, 38/2023, 43/2023, 47/2023.

[79] SCJN, Feb. 20, 2023, Incidente de suspensión en la Acción de Inconstitucionalidad 29/2023 y sus acumuladas 30/2023, 31/2023, 37/2023, 38/2023, 43/2023 y 47/2023. *See also* Instituto Nacional Electoral, *Suspende INE implementación de Reforma Electoral 2023*

a bill of constitutional amendment for the entire judiciary to be selected by popular vote.[80] And in May and June 2023, applying precedents developed and regularly enforced since 2005, the Court invalidated the two segments of Plan B for reasons everyone in Mexico had witnessed in the media: the flagrant disregard of the requirements safeguarding legislative procedure,[81] without any need to assess the content of the statutes. This came as a relief to many, but the government again responded by redoubling its attacks on the judges.[82]

## VI The Militarization of Public Life and State Functions

From the 1940s and throughout the rest of the twentieth century, in contrast to the situation in other countries in the region, the Mexican army was securely subordinated to civil authorities. It was in this subordinated quality that the army was involved in the dark episodes of the "dirty war" of the 1970s.[83] Yet, during the gradual transition to democracy of the 1980s and 1990s, the military was generally held in high regard by the population – which would associate it with assistance during natural disasters, among other tasks of that sort.

The situation changed when Felipe Calderón won the presidency in 2006. Some two years later, although the matter had been mentioned during his campaign, Calderón decided to launch a "war against drugs" that put the army on the streets in several parts of the country without any legal basis for doing so. In December 2017, during the presidency of Enrique Peña Nieto, and partly responding to demands from the army

*y operará con normatividad anterior* [INE suspends the 2023 electoral reform and will operate under the previous regulation], CENTRAL ELECTORAL (Mar. 28, 2023), https://tinyurl.com/yc2cy963.

[80] Beatriz Guillén, *Morena propone modificar un artículo para que los jueces sean elegidos por voto popular* [Morena proposes modification of an article to have all judges elected by popular vote], EL PAÍS (Mar. 24, 2023), https://tinyurl.com/59z7hxsn.

[81] Zewdryk Raziel, *El Supremo invalida la primera parte del Plan B de López Obrador* [Supreme invalidates first part of López Obrador's Plan B], EL PAÍS (May 8, 2023), https://tinyurl.com/4dwtxbvt.

[82] José Ramón Cossío, *Drama constitucional en tres actos: ¿Por qué culpar a otros de la propia arrogancia o impericia?* [Constitutional drama in three acts: Why blame others for one's own arrogance or lack of skill?], EL PAÍS (June 27, 2023), https://tinyurl.com/re26tmbz.

[83] During the so-called Dirty War (extending from the 1960s until the 1990s), the Mexican army deployed irregular operations against individuals and guerilla groups in Guerrero, Oaxaca, Hidalgo, Morelia, Chiapas, and other states, engaging in forced disappearance, sexual abuse, torture, and illegal detention. *See* Jorge Mendoza García, *Torture in the context of Mexico's "Guerra Sucia": An exercise of collective memory*, 7 POLIS 139 (2011).

itself, aware of the absence of legal grounds for its street-level operations, Congress enacted the Interior Security Act (*Ley de Seguridad Interior*), which enabled military personnel to participate alongside the police in ordinary tasks of maintaining public security in the country's public spaces.[84]

The national ombudsperson and several state counterparts filed challenges against the Interior Security Act before the Supreme Court, which declared it invalid in November 2018.[85] The Court found a violation of Article 21 of the Constitution, which allowed for army participation only in tasks associated with national security; the statute wrongfully allowed for army participation in ordinary daily tasks of public security, which had to be fulfilled by ordinary political forces.[86]

By the time AMLO became president, the degree of damage caused in the country by the "war against drugs" was already incalculable.[87] Everybody expected a change of strategy from López Obrador, who during the campaign had advocated for the massive problems of violence to be managed "with hugs, not bullets" (*abrazos, no balazos*). Soon after taking office, however, in March 2019, with the cooperation of the inoperative "opposition" parties, he submitted an amendment to Article 21 of the Constitution to create the National Guard.[88] Congress approved fast-tracking this reform and four complementary statutes: the Law of the National Guard, the Law on the National Registry of Detentions, the National Law on the Use of Force, and the General Law of the Public Security System,[89] all of them raising frontal challenges to controls over the arbitrary exercise of power under the rule of law.[90]

84 Jaime Cárdenas Gracia, *Ley de seguridad interior y* militarización [Homeland security law and militarization] 40 CUESTIONES CONSTITUCIONALES 277 (2019).

85 SCJN, Nov. 15, 2018, Acciones de inconstitucionalidad 6/2018, 8/2018, 9/2018, 10/2018, 11/2018.

86 *Id.* §§ 117–61.

87 Francisca Pou Giménez & Catalina Pérez Correa, *Prohibitionist Drug Policy in Mexico: A Systemic Constitutional Underminer*, 31 WASH. INT'L L.J. 58 (2021).

88 Decreto por el que se reforman, adicionan y derogan disposiciones de la Constitución Política de los Estados Unidos Mexicanos en materia de Guardia Nacional [Decree amending, supplementing, and repealing the provisions of the Constitution concerning the National Guard], DOF, Mar. 26, 2019, www.diputados.gob.mx/LeyesBiblio/proceso/docleg/64/235_DOF_26mar19.pdf.

89 Decreto por el que se expide la Ley de la Guardía Nacional [Decree enacting the National Guard Law], DOF, May 27, 2019, www.dof.gob.mx/nota_detalle.php?codigo=5561285&fecha=27/05/2019#gsc.tab=0.

90 In 2019, several crimes were added to those punished by automatic pretrial imprisonment: use of social programs for electoral purposes; corruption in connection with illicit enrichment and abusive exercise of functions; cargo theft in any modality; theft of

A month later, Article 19 of the Constitution also was reformed and the range of cases in which judges are obligated to order automatic pretrial imprisonment (an institution incompatible with standard due process guarantees) was greatly expanded.

Many in civil society, wary of the president's militarized conception of the National Guard and knowing how lethal the army's record was, organized the platform "*Seguridad sin guerra*" (security without war).[91] The great efforts they made before Congress resulted in the Constitution providing that the National Guard remains ultimately subordinated to civil authorities – specifically, the Secretary of Public Security.[92] However, the decree creating the National Guard included a transitory provision that few noticed at the time, allowing the army to "perform tasks of public security in an extraordinary, regulated, supervised, subordinated, and complementary manner" for a period of five years. These were the exact words that the IACtHR had used when condemning Mexico in its *Alvarado Espinoza* ruling[93] concerning a woman whom the army forcibly abducted while deploying tasks of ordinary security. The IACtHR declared that the army's involvement in these tasks was inadmissible; only in an extraordinary, regulated, supervised, subordinated, and complementary manner could the army be involved in them.[94]

The statutes relating to the National Guard were deeply troubling and were soon challenged before the Supreme Court by the national ombudsperson (still directed by a person appointed during the former administration).[95] The Law on the National Guard, for instance, defines the functions of the National Guard in a most open-ended way, paving the way to clearly unconstitutional action. It empowers the National Guard to investigate ordinary crimes and to supervise and check migrant people, but fails to define torture and forced disappearance as serious

petrochemicals, petroleum, or oil and gas; crimes related to forced disappearance of persons committed by private parties; and crimes committed by violent means such as weapons and explosives.

91 Colectivo Seguridad sin Guerra, *Elementos para la construcción de una política de seguridad pública* [Elements for the construction of a public security policy] (Jan. 2019), www.seguridadsinguerra.org/#block-10549.

92 Constitución Política de los Estados Unidos Mexicanos [Const.], as amended, art. 21, DOF, Feb. 5, 1917: "The institutions of public security, including the National Guard, shall be civil, disciplined, and professional in nature. . . ."

93 Alvarado Espinoza v. Mexico, Merits, Reparations, and Costs, Judgment, Inter-Am. Ct. H.R. (ser. C) No. 370 (Nov. 28, 2018).

94 *Id.* ¶¶ 177–85.

95 SCJN, Apr. 25, 2023, Acciones de inconstitucionalidad 62/2019, 63/2019, 64/2019, 66/2019. *See also* Amparo en revisió 24/2022.

crimes.[96] The Law on the National Registry of Detentions, for its part, leaves out essential elements required by the Constitution. It does not indicate what action is to be taken when events occur that put the detentions database at risk, and it is ambiguous regarding the obligations of the army when participating in tasks of public security, since it can be interpreted to mean that the army is not subject to the constitutional obligation to immediately communicate any detention to the police and provide the information necessary for it to be properly registered, and thereby allow oversight of rule-of-law protections.[97]

The National Law on the Use of Force similarly fails to regulate the minimum elements required by the constitutional amendment that created the National Guard and fails to specify the scope of crucial notions such as *fuerza epiletal*. Another provision could be interpreted as authorizing deadly use force from the moment operations are planned, as opposed to being a last-resort response to an actual or imminent aggression. Moreover, the law is unclear about the possibility of using force in demonstrations; interpreted *contrario sensu*, it opens the door to the use of all levels and means of force, including firearms and deadly weapons, in "illicit" demonstrations – a notion that is left undefined – or demonstrations that become violent.[98] The General Law of the Public Security System, for its part, violates the right of access to public information by authorizing total ex ante withholding of all information in the national public security information system and national registries, preventing public access to this information to defend rule-of-law guarantees.[99]

While these cases were at the Supreme Court, the army was given an ever-growing number of responsibilities: the administration of the main ports,[100] the administration of customs,[101] and the construction of a wide range of

[96] These problems were identified and denounced by the National Commission of Human Rights in its claims before the Supreme Court, *in* CDHN, Informe Especial sobre Acciones de Inconstitucionalidad 48–51 (2019), https://tinyurl.com/4bmae5pn.

[97] *Id.* at 51.

[98] *Id.* at 52.

[99] *Id.* at 52.

[100] Elías Camhaje, *López Obrador anuncia la militarización de puertos y aduanas para frenar el contrabando y el narcotráfico* [López Obrador announces militarization of ports and customs to stop smuggling and drug trafficking], El País (July 17, 2020), https://tinyurl.com/4kytsdb8.

[101] Alberto López, *López Obrador militariza las 50 aduanas de México* [López Obrador militarizes Mexico's 50 customs authorities], Infodefensa (June 2, 2022), https://tinyurl.com/mt496p4s.

public works, including 1,500 branch offices of Banco del Bienestar, the Maya Train and the Felipe Ángeles Airport.[102] This means that the army has immense economic power at the moment.[103] The so-called Guacamaya leaks demonstrated the army's ubiquity (both legal and illegal) in all areas of public life in Mexico.[104] As of June 2023, the marines have been given the administration of the main Mexico City airport and the government continues negotiations to buy Mexicana de Aviación – one of Mexico's first commercial airlines, which went into insolvency in 2010 – for it to be run by the army.[105]

The army manages the training of the National Guard, 75 percent of whose members are former soldiers.[106] In May 2020, the president, taking advantage of the window opened by the transitory constitutional provision,[107] issued an executive decree providing that the army would assist the National Guard in performing public security tasks for a period of five years. In a surreal turn, the heading of the decree (known in Mexico as *Acuerdo militarista*) reads: "Decree providing for the

102 Jacobo García, *El Ejército mexicano aumenta su poder con la construcción y explotación del nuevo aeropuerto* [Mexican army increases its power with construction and operation of new airport], El País (Mar. 20, 2020), https://tinyurl.com/2ybs8ytd; Yulia Bonilla, *Diputados alistan reforma para que ganancias del AIFA, Tren Maya y otras obras vayan a pensiones de militares* [Deputies prepare reform to transfer profits from AIFA, Maya Train, and other public works to military pension funds], Razón (Feb. 22, 2023), https://tinyurl.com/2ffp48r6.

103 Raul Trejo Delarbe, *El Ejército hace política y hace negocios* [Army is doing politics and business], Crónica (Nov. 21, 2021), www.cronica.com.mx/opinion/ejercito-politica-negocios.html.

104 Press Release, Comisión Nacional de Derechos Humanos, CNDH manifiesta preocupación por espionaje a periodistas y defensores de DDHH [National Commission of Human Rights expresses concern over spying of journalists and human rights defenders], No. DGC/195/2021 (July 21, 2021); *¿Qué se sabe del espionaje a periodistas durante el gobierno de AMLO?* [What do we know about spying of journalists during AMLO's government?], Expansión Política (Oct. 4, 2022), https://politica.expansion.mx/mexico/2022/10/04/claves-espionaje-amlo-sedena-periodistas; Jacobo García, *Una masiva filtración expone el poder del ejército mexicano en la vida pública* [Massive leak shows power of Mexican army in public life], El País (Oct. 1, 2022), https://tinyurl.com/9ywa4rpc.

105 *AMLO plantea que aerolínea del Ejército se llame Mexicana de Aviación; utilidades se usarán en pensiones de soldados, dice* [AMLO suggests the army airline be called Mexicana de Aviación and says profits will go to soldier's pensions], Animal Político (Oct. 5, 2022), www.animalpolitico.com/politica/amlo-aerolinea-sedena-mexicana-aviacion-pensiones.

106 INEGI, Censo Nacional de Seguridad Pública Federal [National Federal Public Security Census], www.inegi.org.mx/contenidos/programas/cnspf/2021/doc/cnspf_2021_resultados.pdf.

107 *See* Part IV.

participation of the Army in public security tasks in an extraordinary, regulated, supervised, subordinated, and complementary manner." Yet these adjectives do not appear in the body of the text; on the contrary, the text of the decree fails to place any conditions on the participation of the army,[108] thus disregarding IACtHR doctrine and the fact that the Constitution's reference to those limitations meant that they had to be observed and taken up by the legislative branch.

The *Acuerdo militarista*, too, was challenged before the Supreme Court. Three municipalities filed *controversias* denouncing infringement of jurisdiction, and the Chamber of Deputies filed another one arguing that the president had bypassed Congress in addressing the matter by way of a decree, without prior enabling legislation.[109] This time, the National Commission of Human Rights, now under the direction of a close ally of the president, did not react.[110]

To complete the circle, at the request of the president, the Law on the National Guard was amended in September 2022, so as to place its operation more fully under military command.[111] The law was fast-tracked and, after being passed in the Chamber of Deputies without discussion by commissions, was approved by the Senate within twelve hours of receipt.[112] As Estefanía Vela and Nuria Valenzuela observe, the

[108] Acuerdo por el que se dispone de la Fuerza Armada permanente para llevar a cabo tareas de seguridad pública de manera extraordinaria, regulada, fiscalizada, subordinada y complementaria [Agreement whereby the permanent armed forces are available to carry out public security tasks in an extraordinary, regulated, supervised, subordinate, and complementary manner], DOF, May 11, 2020, https://dof.gob.mx/nota_detalle.php?codigo=5593105&fecha=11/05/2020#gsc.tab=0.

[109] Poder Ejecutivo del Estado de Michoacán, 17 de junio de 2020, CC 87/2020; Municipio de Colima, Colima, 7 de julio de 2020, 85/2020; Alcaldía de Pabellón de Arteaga, Aguascalientes el 26 de junio de 2020, CC 91/2020; Cámara de Diputados, CC 90/2020.

[110] Gloria Leticia Díaz, *La CNDH traiciona a la gente, acusan consejeros* [Counselors accuse CNDH of letting people down], PROCESO (Nov. 22, 2022), https://tinyurl.com/mryrff7j; Víctor Ballinas & Andrea Becerril, *Rosario Piedra Ibarra enfrenta las críticas de la oposición* [Rosario Piedra confronts criticism from opposition], LA JORNADA (Dec. 8, 2022), https://tinyurl.com/mrxvs3vr.

[111] Sonia Corona, *La Cámara de Diputados aprueba las reformas para que la Guardia Nacional pertenezca al Ejército* [Chamber of Deputies approves amendments that make National Guard belong to army], EL PAÍS (Sept. 3, 2022), https://tinyurl.com/yc46c2mf.

[112] Maritza Pérez, *Morena impone una discusión "fast track" de la iniciativa para pasar la Guardia Nacional a la Sedena* [Morena forces a fast-track debate on bill to transfer National Guard to Sedena], EL ECONOMISTA (Sept. 3, 2022), https://tinyurl.com/mstfbhpx.

"civil" National Guard is now an empty shell.[113] The reforms do not comply with the conditions put forward in the Constitution and entrust the SEDENA (the Secretary of National Defense) with full financial, administrative, and operative control of the National Guard.[114] A formal mention of the Secretary of Public Security means nothing in a detailed regulation that places the body under the leadership of a person designated by the president on the basis of criteria that only high-ranking military officers can meet, and which situates operation and infrastructure under military control.[115] A group of senators again challenged the law before the Supreme Court.

A Supreme Court under siege has dealt unevenly with these cases, often in a miminalist way, but also refraining from acknowledging the legitimacy of the militarist onslaught. On November 29, 2022, the Court declared the "Militarist Decree" valid on the basis of the purely formal argument that it did not contradict the literal text of the Constitution,[116] ignoring IACtHR decisions. Yet on April 20, 2023, on the basis of a draft prepared by one of AMLO's appointees, the Supreme Court declared the transfer of the National Guard to the military branch invalid and ordered civilian control of this body from January 1, 2024.[117] Given the amount of political pressure the judges had endured – including insertions in national newspapers paid by MORENA governors requiring the Court to certify the validity of the reform – this was seen as an immense victory by the law's opponents.

The Court also discussed the question of automatic pretrial preventive imprisonment, but there was no consensus over declaring it invalid. The fact that it features in the Constitution, and not just in statutes, posed a great problem for a Court that has never declared the unconstitutionality of a constitutional amendment. Shortly afterward, in any case, the IACtHR decided the cases *Tzompaxtle Tecpile v. Mexico* and

[113] Nuria Valenzuela & Estefanía Vela, *Ahora sí, guardia militar* [Now it is really here: military guard], Animal Político (Sept. 8, 2022), www.animalpolitico.com/blog-de-intersecta/ahora-si-la-guardia-militar/.

[114] *Id.*

[115] Santiago Aguirre, *La iniciativa sobre Guardia Nacional: Cambiar la ley para evadir la Constitución* [National Guard bill: Changing the law to evade the Constitution], Nexos (Sept. 1, 2022), https://tinyurl.com/49jjcrxd; Lidia Arista, *Guardia Nacional: 41 meses de operar bajo mandos y protocolos militares* [National Guard: 41 months to operate under military commands and protocols], Expansión Política (Nov. 19, 2022), https://tinyurl.com/mrx9pcb4.

[116] Haydeé Gómez & Regina Isabel Medina, *Los (des)tiempos de la Suprema Corte frente a la militarización* [(Mis)timings of Supreme Court with regard to militarization process], Nexos (July 5, 2021), https://tinyurl.com/33b8vcsn.

[117] SCJN, Apr. 20, 2023, Acción de Inconstitucionalidad 137/2022.

*García Rodríguez v. Mexico*, declaring that *arraigo* (pretrial unsupervised house arrest by the prosecutor) and automatic preventive imprisonment were incompatible with the American Convention.[118] The IACtHR has directed Mexico to enact the necessary changes in national law – that is, the Constitution.[119] Again, this was experienced by many in civil society as an immense triumph of rights in defense of the rule of law. The day after *Tzompaxtle* came out, the home affairs secretary (*Secretario de Gobernación*), an individual close to the president and prospective candidate in the next presidential election, declared that the ruling was not to be complied with. In the buildup to the 2024 election, we will see how this saga and the many dozens of others underway unfold for the future of the rule of law in Mexico.

## VII Concluding Considerations: A War of Attrition, and the Difference the Constitution Makes

This chapter's account, while providing overwhelming evidence of challenges to the rule of law in Mexico, is based on only a few paradigmatic examples of current dynamics. The AMLO administration in Mexico viewed basic rule-of-law requirements as daily obstacles to the fulfillment of its political program. In contrast to other autocratic legalists, who have tried to conceal contortions of the law or bypass, rather than openly disregard, constitutional requirements, President López Obrador has not hidden his distaste for legal "barriers." He has defied them, among other reasons because he knows that the law is something people can be polarized about in countries where compliance with the law has not historically been an unconditional good, and where constitutional democracy has not brought about the material progress expected.[120]

[118] Tzompaxtle Tecpile et al. v. Mexico, Merits, Reparations, and Costs, Judgment, Inter-Am. Ct. H.R. (ser. C) No. 470, ¶ 173 (Nov. 7, 2022), https://corteidh.or.cr/docs/casos/articulos/seriec_470_ing.pdf; García Rodríguez et al. v. Mexico, Merits, Reparations, and Costs, Judgment, Inter-Am. Ct. H.R. (ser. C) No. 482, ¶ 298 (Jan. 25, 2023), https://corteidh.or.cr/docs/casos/articulos/seriec_482_ing.pdf.

[119] See *Tzompaxte*, operative provisions 7 and 8; *García Rodríguez*, operative provisions 13 and 14 ("13. The State shall repeal in its domestic legislation the provisions relating to pre-procedural *arraigo*, pursuant to paragraphs 292 to 294, 298 to 300, and 302 to 303. 14. The State shall adapt its domestic legal system in relation to mandatory pretrial detention, pursuant to paragraphs 292 and 293, 295 to 299 and 301 to 30. . . .").

[120] Ugo Mattei & Laura Nader, Plunder: When the Rule of Law is Illegal (2008).

The Mexican president has substantially progressed in his quest to weaken the checks and balances that the other branches apply to the executive. He has striven to suppress, defund, or leave unstaffed the independent agencies that in Mexico underpin the constitutional division of powers. He has tried to neutralize the judiciary through a mixture of partisan appointments to the Supreme Court, personal public attacks on judges, efforts to negotiate with the former president of the Court, and continual threats of radical reform. He has engaged in fast-track maneuvers to push through the enactment of core political measures, without opening them to public debate and deliberation. Day after day, he has trashed the individuals and groups that shape public opinion and watch over the exercise of power, like the press, the scientific and academic community, civil society organizations, and a varied assortment of other groups. He has structurally changed the nature of public (and economic) power in Mexico by putting the military on an equal footing with the executive. The number of problematic initiatives and actions that he and his parliamentary allies promote every week is astounding. And added to that, López Obrador has engaged in a strategy of attrition–, consisting in uninterrupted legal defiance that leaves political and social actors overwhelmed, without time and energy to react.

We have nonetheless seen that several decades of democratic constitutionalism have placed significant hurdles to this project of personalistic rule that violates core aspects of the rule of law. Concentrating all power has not been ultimately as smooth as imagined for López Obrador, even after a massive electoral victory that left him without any meaningful opposition in Congress. The existence of a highly detailed constitution, as well as fourth-branch institutions with constitutional status, has been crucial in slowing down (and until now preventing) the destruction of the electoral arbiter. Had the INE not been regulated in the Constitution, had it not been designed the way it was, and had it lacked standing to defend its jurisdiction before the Supreme Court, electoral credibility in Mexico might now be something of the past. The results of the intermediate election – which, importantly, diffused power by leaving MORENA as the majority party but unable to amend the Constitution alone – could not have happened without an independent electoral authority.

The presence of reinforced judicial structures with a wide menu of responsibilities and diversified channels of access, has maintained the engagement of the Supreme Court and lower-ranked judges, propelling procedural innovations that will help supervise power in the future, no matter who holds public office. If the national ombudsperson, a body with constitutional status, had not been designed to be appointed on a six-year basis, the militarist statutes enacted at the beginning of AMLO's term would not have been challenged before the Supreme Court. The Inter-American regional system of rights protection has been equally crucial in aiding national judges under severe pressure. Public criticism of regressive pieces of public policy and regulation would have been impossible without the human rights reforms that have fortified civil society.

Latin America has been able to halt several neo-authoritarian processes. Even if the ups and downs of the political landscape signal a great need for political redirection in ways that genuinely benefit the people, they also show that the sustained, unbridled exercise of presidential power could be something of the past. The dangers of hyperpresidentialism are still here, but the evolution of the region gives some cause for hope. In Ecuador, Lenin Moreno ran for office as a close ally of former president Rafael Correa, but soon became a moderate, and the Council of Social Accountability and Participation provided an appropriate framework for a reappointment process that reversed the presidential capture of state institutions. Colombia lived for eight years under a right-wing populist president, Álvaro Uribe, whom the Constitutional Court stopped from reforming the Constitution so he could run for a third term. Respect for institutions was restored under Juan Manuel Santos, and in 2021, Gustavo Petro won the presidential election with a leftist program committed to reform in crucial areas like land tenure, social policy, and the environment. In Brazil, Bolsonaro deployed policies with immense cost in terms of social justice, pluralism, and democracy. But he lost the election to Lula da Silva and had to leave office, even with his supporters using force in an effort to prevent it.

The hypothesis proposed in this chapter regarding the case of Mexico is that these signs of contestation and recovery in response to challenges to the rule of law by populist leaders have been critically supported by the regional human rights regime as accompanied by broader constitutional developments. The analysis illustrates how important have been features such as the creation of new independent constitutional agencies underpinning the division of powers and the diversification and strengthening of the judiciary, which together have multiplied spaces and occasions for public mobilization. It also suggests, however, that most constitutional resources are activated ex post and place an immense burden on the courts. More effective, systemic prevention of rule-of-law erosion would require the enhancement and use of preemptive solutions, both in the domain of rights and in the domain of the organization of powers. Constitutions in the region are being seriously tested. Nonetheless, carefully pondering their positive contributions in times of crisis gives us reason to continue using the resources they provide in defense of the rule of law, offering resistance to the neo-authoritarian onslaught, and hopefully paving the way to a better future.

# 11

# The Challenge to the Rule of Law and Democracy in Contemporary West and Central Africa

OLABISI D. AKINKUGBE

## I Introduction

Over the last decade, the democratic wave of the 1990s in sub-Saharan Africa, the accompanying constitutional reforms, and the cautious optimism about the possibility of entrenching the rule of law have come under significant stress.[1] A thriving democracy is characterized by a cycle of electoral process, free and fair elections, respect for the institutional legitimacy and independence of the judiciary, legislature, and executive and is constrained by the primacy of the fundamental rights of the citizens.[2] After a moment that was characterized by

A version of this chapter was presented as part of the late-breaking panel "International Law As a Tool Against Democratic Backsliding" at the 2023 annual conference of the American Society of International Law. As a cautionary note, the heterogeneity of African states requires avoiding tropes that generalize the decline of the rule of law in Africa if the analysis is not backed up by empirical data from all the states concerned. This chapter avoids the temptation to project the experiences of a handful of states across the continent as a whole.

[1] *See generally* Makau Mutua, *Africa and the Rule of Law*, 13 SUR REVISTA INTERNACIONAL DE DIREITOS HUMAN 159 (2016) (arguing for a conception of the rule of law that accounts for the cultural, geographic, and economic peculiarities of each state and offering seven core values that must be reflected in the rule of law in order to achieve sustainable development across Africa); Tom Ginsburg, *Democracies and International Law: An Update*, 23 CHI. J. INT'L L. 1 (2022); TOM GINSBURG, DEMOCRACIES AND INTERNATIONAL LAW (2021).

[2] This definition is akin to Ginsburg's "relatively minimalist understanding of democracy ... a system of electoral competition, underpinned by freedoms of speech, association, and other rights closely tied to elections. It is also underpinned by a bureaucracy that administers the elections in a neutral way, bound by the rule of law." Ginsburg, *supra* note 1. *See generally* TOM GINSBURG & AZIZ Z. HUQ, HOW TO SAVE A CONSTITUTIONAL DEMOCRACY (2018).

a flurry of constitutional reforms and elections, coups have returned to Africa.[3]

The stress that threatens democratic regimes in contemporary Africa is not unique to the region. Globally, there is a decline in the rule of law and democracies.[4] Democracy and the rule of law are under challenge in the Global North and Global South. Imperial Western countries, like the United States and countries in Europe hitherto regarded as the prime examples of *stable* democratic governance are today confronted with the fragility of their claims and democratic experiences.[5] In Latin America, recent democratic elections illustrate the decline and erosion of democratic norms and institutions.[6] In Africa, a confluence of events – colonial legacies[7], uprisings, regional conflicts, term elongations, challenges to the dynastic style of leadership, and the rising incidence of coups – challenge the entrenchment of the rule of law in contemporary Africa. After six decades of independence in many African countries, the governance outlook is to a lesser degree democratic.

The judicialization of election disputes before national[8] and regional courts[9] in Africa has added a further layer to analysis of the rule of law

[3] *See generally* AJLabs, *Mapping Africa's Coups d'État Across the Years*, AL JAZEERA (Aug. 30, 2023), www.aljazeera.com/news/2023/8/30/mapping-africas-coups-detat-across-the-years ("Out of the 486 attempted or successful military coups carried globally since 1950, Africa accounts for the largest number with 214, of which at least 106 have been successful.").

[4] Michelle Bachelet, UN High Comm'r for Hum. Rts., Crisis and Fragility of Democracy in the World, Opening Workshop for the International Association of Jesuit Universities, Boston College (Aug. 2, 2022), www.ohchr.org/en/statements-and-speeches/2022/08/crisis-and-fragility-democracy-world.

[5] *See generally* Naja Bentzen, *Democracy in America 2022: Current Challenges to US Democracy and First Lessons for Europe*, EUR. PARLIAMENTARY RES. SERV. (Nov. 2022), www.europarl.europa.eu/RegData/etudes/BRIE/2022/738199/EPRS_BRI(2022)738199_EN.pdf.

[6] *See generally* Jorge G. Castañeda, *Latin America's Beleaguered Democracies*, PROJECT SYNDICATE (July 12, 2023), https://tinyurl.com/3cze3v6j. As Castañeda aptly notes: "For years now, polls have shown diminishing support for democratic rule in Latin America. Fragile economic conditions, new post-pandemic social demands, and polarized, distrustful electorates are fueling a politics of backlash that is likely to intensify threats to democracy in the region in the coming years."

[7] *See generally* Salmon A. Shomade, *Colonial Legacies Endure in Africa's Legal Systems – Undermining Rule of Law*, WASH. POST (Mar. 18, 2022), https://tinyurl.com/4dvbce2d.

[8] O'Brien Kaaba & Charles M. Fombad, *Adjudication of Disputed Presidential Elections in Africa*, *in* DEMOCRACY, ELECTIONS, AND CONSTITUTIONALISM IN AFRICA 361 (Charles M. Fombad & Nico Steytler eds., 2021).

[9] For analyses of the election disputes before the ECOWAS Community Court of Justice, see Olabisi D. Akinkugbe, *Towards an Analysis of the Mega-Politics Jurisprudence of the ECOWAS Community Court of Justice*, *in* THE PERFORMANCE OF AFRICA'S INTERNATIONAL COURTS: USING INTERNATIONAL LITIGATION FOR POLITICAL,

and its implementation on the continent. The motivations for the pursuit of election disputes before national and regional courts in Africa differ. At the national level, the basis for triggering an election dispute process is circumscribed by the relevant electoral laws as a means of seeking redress. The objective is to overturn the outcome of the election in favor of the election petitioner. The approach is different before regional courts in Africa. Litigants engage the regional courts in Africa as alternative forums to center public debate "about policy choices and as a platform to campaign for desired political, social, and legal change."[10] Although the disputes before regional courts in Africa are couched in the language of alleged human rights violations, this chapter argues that they are as much about the rule of law, which is often foreclosed in disputes before national courts. Despite increased judicialization of election disputes before regional courts in Africa, the transnational rule-of-law aspect of these cases has received less scholarly inquiry.[11]

This chapter reimagines contemporary Africa as a theatre for the national, regional, and transnational mutation and contestation of the rule of law and democracy. Focusing on the geographical, socio-cultural, economic, legal, and political landscape between 2020 and 2023 in selected states in sub-Saharan Africa, this chapter critically analyzes the challenge of upholding the rule of law and democratic governance in contemporary Africa.[12] Between 2020 and 2023, at least nine military coups have occurred in West Africa, Central Africa, and the Sahel region.[13] The chapter envisions the phenomenon of the rule of law as a continuum, with ruptures occasioned by various factors. The chapter asks: Against the background of recent coups, how should we analyze the

LEGAL, AND SOCIAL CHANGE 149 (James Thuo Gathii ed., 2020); James Thuo Gathii & Olabisi D. Akinkugbe, *Judicialization of Election Disputes in Africa's International Courts*, 84 L. & CONTEMP. PROBS. 181 (2021).

10 THE PERFORMANCE OF AFRICA'S INTERNATIONAL COURTS: USING INTERNATIONAL LITIGATION FOR POLITICAL, LEGAL, AND SOCIAL CHANGE, *supra* note 9, at 23.

11 Although Mihreteab Tsighe Taye picks up the rule of law and human rights in his article, he comes at this issue from a different line of inquiry that does not necessarily focus on the possibility of the emergent transnational rule of law in Africa. *See* Mihreteab Tsighe Taye, *Human Rights, The Rule of Law, and the East African Court of Justice: Lawyers and the Emergence of a Weak Regional Field*, 34 TEMP. INT'L & COMP. L.J. 340 (2020).

12 In this sense, this chapter undertakes a more granular analysis of the challenges to the rule of law in contemporary Africa and as such both differs from but also complements the contribution by Tom Ginsburg and Christoph Schoppe in Chapter 5.

13 Mali, Guinea, Sudan, Chad, Burkina Faso, Niger, and Gabon are some of the countries where coups have occurred. Failed coup attempts have also taken place in the Gambia, Guinea-Bissau, and Sao Tome and Principe.

rule of law in contemporary Africa? Is the decline of the rule of law and democratic governance in sub-Saharan Africa as a region overstated, given that the coups are concentrated in Francophone West and Central Africa? How should we think of the role of geopolitical contestations and colonial linkages and legacies in unsettling democratic regimes and eroding the rule of law in Africa?

The chapter argues that the answer to the foregoing is at best murky. In sub-Saharan Africa, the factors that lead to episodes of rupture in the rule of law and democracy have overlapping roots in historical, geopolitical, national, and colonial legacies. Consequently, analyses of the decline of the rule of law and democratic governance in contemporary Africa that omit to center the overlapping contributions of these factors to the rupture we see in the rule of law offer an incomplete narrative. To unpack what the chapter describes as the murky narratives of the challenge of the rule of law in Africa, I focus on three frontiers: first, the rise of military coups, elongation of constitutional terms while in office, and the decline of the rule of law in Africa (2020–23). This section draws on experiences in Gabon, Niger, Burkina Faso, and Guinea. Second, the chapter examines entrenchment of the rule of law in terms of a successful transition of power. This section draws on the 2023 presidential elections in Nigeria and Liberia. Third, the chapter assesses the judicialization of election disputes before national courts and an emerging crisis of legitimacy. The judicialization of election disputes in national courts may have two implications for the entrenchment or weakening of the rule of law. On the one hand, the judicialization of election disputes and emergence of a winner as declared by the courts is an affirmation of a core tenet of the rule of law enshrined in the role of the courts. On the other hand, the incessant judicialization of election disputes risks weakening the authority of the concerned national court. To illustrate the enmeshment or nonenmeshment of the rule of law and the challenges this poses for the legitimacy of the judiciary, I draw on contemporary experiences in Nigeria.

Methodologically, this chapter engages in socio-legal analysis. The analysis draws on the contemporary practices, debates, and national – and where relevant, international – factors to analyze the interconnectedness and confluence of factors that should underpin analyses of the rule of law and democracy in Africa. Analyses of the rule of law in the African context are laden in the contested discourse of the creation of African states and the continued power relations that they encounter. Put differently, as a form of social thought, without cultural and historical contexts, Eurocentrism is fully expressed in the rule of law. Consequently, an analysis of the rule of law to be seen as non-Eurocentric, and thus not a mere transplant of ideas, must be narrated through the understanding of the peoples concerned.[14] The chapter foregrounds the understanding of the principles of, and challenges to, the rule of law as they manifest in different African states, in contrast to a universally valid idea of the rule of law. Consequently, the analysis in this chapter sidesteps the critique of "normative incompleteness, cultural blindness, Anglo-Saxon imperial complicity and historical context"[15] by weaving in the unique confluence of social, economic, political, socio-cultural, and geopolitical contexts that overlap in its analysis of the rule of law in Africa.

## II The Rule of Law in Contemporary Africa in Context

Democratic experiences in Africa remain relatively young and fragile.[16] Since the democratic turn of the 1990s and early 2000s that birthed modern constitutionalism and democratic governance in different African states, the challenge of the rule of law has ignited various kinds of debates. But what, exactly, is the rule of law? Undoubtedly, the rule of law and democracy are contested concepts.[17] In their introduction, Gregory Shaffer and Wayne Sandholtz conceptualize the rule of law in terms of ideals and goals. In terms of goals, the rule of law serves to "protect individuals from arbitrary power through legal rules and institutionalized practices, while providing channels for cooperative and coordinative activities."[18] As an ideal, the rule of law presupposes that "individuals are not to be subject to the arbitrary exercise of power."[19]

[14] *See generally* JOTHIE RAJA, AUTHORITARIAN RULE OF LAW: LEGISLATION, DISCOURSE AND LEGITIMACY IN SINGAPORE (2012). Nick Cheesman has also called for "ethnographically informed research on the rule of law." Nick Cheesman, *Rule-of-Law Ethnography*, 14 ANN. REV. L. & SOC. SCI. 167 (2018).

[15] Mutua, *supra* note 1, at 160.

[16] On fragile democracies generally, see MARK FATHI MASSOUD, LAW'S FRAGILE STATE: COLONIAL, AUTHORITARIAN, AND HUMANITARIAN LEGACIES IN SUDAN (2013); GRETCHEN CASPER, FRAGILE DEMOCRACIES: THE LEGACIES OF AUTHORITARIAN RULE (1995); SAMUEL ISSACHAROFF, FRAGILE DEMOCRACIES: CONTESTED POWER IN THE ERA OF CONSTITUTIONAL COURTS (2015).

[17] Martin Krygier, *Democracy and the Rule of Law*, *in* THE CAMBRIDGE COMPANION TO THE RULE OF LAW 406 (Jens Meierhenrich & Martin Loughlin eds., 2021); W.B. Gallie, *Essentially Contested Concepts*, 56 PROC. ARISTOTELIAN SOC'Y 167 (1956).

[18] *See* Chapter 1.

[19] *Id.*

The rule of law, they argue, is "a normative ideal that should be viewed teleologically in terms of its ends."[20] For Shaffer and Sandholtz therefore, the rule of law is most effectively entrenched in democratic regimes as a result of its becoming "institutionalized . . . a habit or routine."[21] Their analysis of the rule of law differs from the parochial checklists that some Western scholars develop from their own legal traditions and universalize. In this regard, Shaffer and Sandholtz argue, and I agree, that: "Countries can produce quite different sets of rules for regulating social life in furtherance of rule-of-law principles."[22]

Across African states, the rule of law is envisioned as a vehicle for the transformation of states into liberal democracies and for the protection of individual rights and the promotion of freedom. Despite contestations with respect to its evolving and pluralized contours, the rule of law remains the cornerstone of any legitimate democratic society.[23] Adherence and fidelity to the rule of law is fundamental to meaningful democracy. At the same time, law constitutes and reconstitutes unequal social relations. As a result, a continent like Africa, uniquely characterized by its contested histories and challenging contemporary realities that differ from state to state, must be placed in context.

The discourse, permutations, and understandings of the rule of law vary and are keenly contested by and among states. A conventional approach to understanding the rule of law is based on the ethos of good governance, accountability, and democracy that are prescribed by Global North countries for their Global South counterparts. Contemporary democratic practices and backsliding of the rule of law differ and do not fit strictly into the conventional framework of top-down diffusion of ideas from the West.[24] In a sense, they are counterintuitive. Hence, metrics – qualitative and quantitative – that have been developed

20 *Id. See generally* Martin Krygier, *The Rule of Law: Legality, Teleology, Sociology, in* RELOCATING THE RULE OF LAW 45, 60 (Gianluigi Palombella & Neil Walker eds., 2009).

21 *See* Chapter 1.

22 *See* Chapter 1. Cheesman notes that "[c]ounterhegemonic work on the rule of law also involves counterintuitive findings, which go against accepted wisdom about what the rule of law is and why it might or might not matter to people in a particular place. Counterintuitive findings are sometimes anticipated, sometimes not." Cheesman, *supra* note 14, at 176.

23 *See generally* Anne Orford, *A Global Rule of Law, in* THE CAMBRIDGE COMPANION TO THE RULE OF LAW, *supra* note 17, at 538.

24 MAAME EFUA ADDADZI-KOOM, MICHAEL ADDANEY & LYDIA A. NKANSAH, DEMOCRATIC GOVERNANCE, LAW, AND DEVELOPMENT IN AFRICA: PRAGMATISM, EXPERIMENTS, AND PROSPECTS (2022).

to measure the rule of law have not been as helpful in the African context, as the spectrum on which various indicators exist differs from state to state.[25]

Postcolonial realities, dictatorships, democratic turns and setbacks, state capture by national elites, rise of populism, coups, and the rising incidence of fake news and disinformation all test the limits of the rule of law in Africa. In historical and contemporary African societies, the legal, social, historical, political, cultural, geographical, and other circumstances differ; consequently, they place a limit not only on a rigid conceptualization of the rule of law but also on its practices.[26] Whether we think of the phenomenon of the rule of law as thick or thin, as procedural or substantive, as modern constitutional law, or as norms of cultural behavior or democratic governance, the manifestations of the rule of law in Africa buttress the assertion that it is an essentially contested concept.[27] Africa is thus a theatre for the national, regional, and transnational mutation and contestation of the rule of law and democracy. Accordingly, the study of Africa and the rule of law must be done on its own terms. In essence, there is no singular idea of the rule of law, nor is it determinate without context. It is in this context that I agree with Shaffer and Sandholtz that, to avoid the temptation of "formulaic checklists based on specified, formal characteristics," the rule of rule should be defined "in terms of goals and practices."[28]

Notwithstanding its contested nature, a core function of the rule of law is that it offers an assurance to the citizens about the steps and standards to which electoral processes will be held as well as the remedies that are available in the event of default or noncompliance. The rise of multiparty elections in Africa heralded an era of potential consolidation of democratic governance and the ethos of rule of law. The rule of law is critical

[25] In this regard, I agree with Shaffer and Sandholtz when they note: "How to measure these shifts is a challenge given the variety of institutional means to advance or undermine the rule of law, yet both qualitative and quantitative analyses indicate overall declines in rule-of-law protections transnationally, which are essential for individuals to lead lives not subject to domination." *See* Chapter 1.

[26] *See generally* SALMON A. SHOMADE, COLONIAL LEGACIES AND THE RULE OF LAW IN AFRICA: GHANA, KENYA, NIGERIA, SOUTH AFRICA, AND ZIMBABWE (2022).

[27] On the rule of law as an essentially contested concept, see the influential works of Jeremy Waldron, *Is the Rule of Law an Essentially Contested Concept (in Florida)?*, 21 L. & PHIL. 137 (2002); Jeremy Waldron, *The Rule of Law as an Essentially Contested Concept*, *in* THE CAMBRIDGE COMPANION TO THE RULE OF LAW, *supra* note 17, at 121; BRIAN Z. TAMANAHA, ON THE RULE OF LAW: HISTORY, POLITICS, THEORY (2004).

[28] *See* Chapter 1.

for the conduct of elections in democratic regimes.[29] Electoral laws regulate the conduct of elections and the challenging of outcomes and offer general guidance on how political office holders are to be elected across local, state, and federal elections. The consistent conduct of elections in many Africa states has seen growth in opposition candidate victories in many countries.[30] These outcomes are increasingly contested before Africa's national and regional courts.[31] Africans are more aware of their civil and political rights in the context of elections as well as the role courts play in the adjudication of disputes emerging from the conduct of elections. Yet, these gains in election consolidation have not completely dispelled the view relating to the precarity of the rule of law in the region. Elections and the disputes that follow are therefore an important terrain where the practice of the rule of law must be analyzed.

The rhetoric of the protection of the rule of law is consistently weaponized by both democratic and authoritarian governments. For many years in postcolonial Africa, authoritarian regimes characterized the landscape of the continent.[32] The continuum of colonialism, colonial legacies, state capture by national elites, and weaponization of the institutions of liberal democratic states to legitimize elite interests must be viewed in a wholistic way – not in isolation. Likewise, the ongoing effects of geopolitical contestations by powerful Western states with economic and military interests in Africa has a direct connection to the entrenchment or weakening of the rule of law in African states. Yet, it must be noted that "a system governed by the rule of law . . . may not address

[29] *See generally* Brian Z. Tamanaha, *Functions of the Rule of Law*, *in* The Cambridge Companion to the Rule of Law, *supra* note 17, at 221.

[30] The presidential election in Liberia, in October with runoff in November, which saw the emergence of an opposition candidate and peaceful transfer of power, offers an important example. *See* Carielle Doe & Alphonso Toweh, *Liberia President George Weah Concedes Election Defeat to Joseph Boakai*, Reuters (Nov. 18, 2023), https://tinyurl.com/24ab4nf9.

[31] Akinkugbe, *supra* note 9; Gathii & Akinkugbe, *supra* note 9; Karen J. Alter & Mikael Rask Madsen, *The International Adjudication of Mega-Politics*, 84 L. & Contemp. Probs. 1 (2022)

[32] As John Mukum Mbkau argues, the threats to the rule of law in Africa include, but are not limited to, "government impunity, military intervention in governance, manipulation of national constitutions by presidents in order to remain in power indefinitely, political interference with the judiciary or lack of judicial independence, failure of the majority of citizens in each African country to understand and appreciate the constitution and its role in their lives, failure to domesticate international human rights instruments, and extreme poverty and political and economic exclusion." John Mukum Mbaku, *Threats to the Rule of Law in Africa*, 48 Ga. J. Int'l & Compar. L. 293, 384–85 (2020).

deeply embedded inequities. It may provide procedural justice but deny substantive social justice."[33]

Shaffer and Sandholtz's conceptualization acknowledges the plurality of legal orders and traditions that would generate one's understanding of the rule of law. In the peculiar context of Africa, several legal orders coexist within a state and across the continent. As such, rather than undertake a definition of the rule of law, I agree with Shaffer and Sandholtz's argument that "any meaningful understanding of the rule of law must be based on cultures of practice embedded in rule-governed institutions."[34]

Accordingly, the chapter conceives of the rule of law as a bulwark against the arbitrary exercise of power. Attempts by political leaders at any level of government to curtail the rights of the individual can be resisted by seeking redress within the institutions of a democracy. A system of government that denies the existence of such rights would not entrench the rule of law. The rule of law is a means to achieve several public goods and serves to address shortcomings in a society.[35] Analyses of the challenges – strengthening or declining – of the rule of law in Africa must be embedded in the particular socio-cultural, legal, political, and historical contexts in question. At the same time, scholarly analysis that is not enmeshed in the transnational context of the interactions and reinforcing nature of the factors that trigger the breakdown of law and order which aggravate the likelihood of human rights violations would fail to capture the wider factors at play in Africa – particularly as they relate to the role of former colonial metropoles in disrupting democratic governance in African states.

This chapter foregrounds a bottom-up approach to the analysis of the challenges to the rule of law in Africa. It differs from a priori measurement standards, often Western-centric, that become the tool for the assessment of the rule of law. The rule of law's legitimacy crisis has not weakened its importance in every society. The promises of the rule of law, even in its weakened state, trump any authoritarian or military ideal. Authoritarianism, and particularly military dictatorship as many African states have experienced, proscribes the fundamental human rights of peoples, leaving them in a vulnerable state. Likewise, national courts are placed in a precarious position with respect to their capacity to

[33] Mutua, *supra* note 1, at 160.

[34] *Id.*

[35] *See generally* STEPHEN HUMPHREYS, THEATRE OF THE RULE OF LAW: TRANSNATIONAL LEGAL INTERVENTION IN THEORY AND PRACTICE (2010).

adjudicate cases that involve the violation of human rights. My conceptualization of the rule of law in the African context foregrounds the value of historical and socio-cultural practices, and the heterogeneity of states and regions as essential to understanding the rule of law in Africa.[36] Pluralized conceptualizations of the rule of law "lay the conditions for each conception to be enriched by elements that are not initially part of its content."[37] In Part III, I turn to the three narratives through which I analyze the challenges to the rule of law in contemporary Africa.

## III Murky Narratives of the Strengthening or Decline of the Rule of Law in Africa

Rule of law is a convenient alibi for various actors in the governance of African states.[38] Incumbent and opposition political parties deploy the rule of law to justify different narratives that suit their pursuit of, or entrenchment in, power. In many cases, when the rule of law comes under scrutiny in Africa, it becomes apparent that the interests of the people and the state are not the drivers of actions. With eight presidential and overlapping legislative elections spread across the length and breadth of the continent, 2023 has been described as Africa's election year.[39]

This section analyzes the contemporary practices and developments of selected African states along three major themes. First, it assesses the rise of military coups, elongation of constitutional terms while in office, and the decline of the rule of law in Africa (2020–23), drawing on experiences in Gabon, Niger, Burkina Faso, and Guinea. Second, it examines cases of the entrenchment of the rule of law in terms of successful and peaceful

36 As Shaffer and Sandholtz note: "Pragmatically, we know the value of the rule of law through historical and contemporary experiences of the arbitrary exercise of power." *See* Chapter 1.

37 Waldron, *The Rule of Law as an Essentially Contested Concept*, *supra* note 27, at 136.

38 *See generally* DEMOCRACY AND THE RULE OF LAW (José María Maravall & Adam Przeworski eds., 2023); John C. Mubangizi, *Democracy and the Rule of Law: Comparative Lessons Between Uganda and South Africa*, 27 L. DEMOCRACY & DEV. 468 (2023).

39 "From 2011 to 2022, 42 new African leaders took office after an election. Of these, 17 were successors from an incumbent party. The other 25 were opposition politicians, a higher number than in any of the three preceding decades. Such transitions have recently taken place in Kenya, Malawi and Zambia, among other places." John McDermott, *2023 Will Be a Busy Year for Elections in Africa*, ECONOMIST (Nov. 18, 2022), https://tinyurl.com/umerta43; Joseph Siegle & Candace Cook, *Africa's 2023 Elections: Democratic Resiliency in the Face of Trials*, AFRICAN CTR. FOR STRATEGIC STUD. (Nov. 9, 2023), https://tinyurl.com/ytvf5fx5.

transition of power, drawing on the 2023 presidential elections in Nigeria and Liberia. Third, it analyzes the judicialization of electoral disputes before national courts, drawing on Nigeria to illustrate the challenges it poses for the legitimacy of the judiciary, thus implicating broader rule-of-law concerns.

## 1 *Narrative I: Military Coups, Elongation of Constitutional Terms while in Office, and the Decline of the Rule of Law in West Africa (2020–2023)*

The rise of outright military coups in West Africa (and particularly in Francophone Africa) offers the first case for the decline of the rule of law. Between 2020 and 2023, Africa witnessed seven military coups.[40] As of August 2023, it was reported that of the "486 attempted or successful military coups carried out globally since 1950, Africa accounts for the largest number with 216, of which at least 106 have been successful."[41] Coups dash the dimmest possibility for the practice of the rule of law and democratization.[42] Coups epitomize the complete failure of the possibility of the nurturing of the rule of law. While they last, coups trump the ethos of constitutional democracy and portend irreparable damage for the rights of citizens. Coups and the ensuing military governments epitomize unbridled and arbitrary exercise of power.

An essential imperative that would ensure that the rule of law thrives is the existence of a democratic or liberal legal order. The nonexistence of a democratic state portends a significant danger not only for the protection and enforcement of the human rights of the citizens but also for the capacity of the of other institutions of the state to function effectively. Thus, on the face of it, the rise of military coups provides preliminary and uncontested evidence of the decline of the rule of law. Although it does not impact the substantive analysis, I draw a distinction between what I call outright military coups in contrast to military interventions that were reportedly motivated by attempts by elected leaders to enlarge their term in office through constitutional amendments.[43] The elongation of constitutional

[40] Gabon (August 2023); Niger (July 2023); Burkina Faso (2022); Chad, Guinea, and Sudan (2021); and Mali (2020).

[41] AJLabs, *supra* note 3.

[42] Clayton L. Thyne & Jonathan M. Powell, *Coup d'État or Coup d'Autocracy? How Coups Impact Democratization, 1950–2008*, 12 FOREIGN POL'Y ANALYSIS 192 (2016).

[43] On term limits, see generally Kennedy Kariseb, *State Sovereignty and Presidential Term Limits in Africa, in* THE PALGRAVE HANDBOOK OF DEMOCRACY, GOVERNANCE AND

term limits by sitting presidents who seek to entrench themselves in office and the refusal of democratically elected political leaders to cede power and conduct elections is another arena where the decline of the rule of law is manifesting.[44] The repressive and oppressive conduct of the sitting democratically elected president becomes the catalyst for the taking over of power. Often lacking in credibility, the military capitalizes on this as the rationale for its intervention. Between 2020 and 2023, coups in Niger, Gabon, Burkina Faso, and Guinea offer examples.

In **Niger**, on July 26, 2023, President Mohamed Bazoum was overthrown by the military. Citing the deteriorating security situation and bad governance in the country as the basis for its intervention, the military declared it had taken over power from the civilian administration in this Francophone West African country.[45] President Bazoum had assumed office amid a historic presidential election runoff on February 21, 2021.[46] Pertinent facts go to the heart of the argument advanced in this section. First, the election that birthed the short-lived tenure of President Bazoum was Niger's first civilian handover between elected leaders since independence in 1960. Second, President Bazoum's assumption of office followed a voluntary stepping down of his predecessor, President Mohamadou Issoufou, who had governed for two five-year terms and oversaw the first civilian to civilian democratic transition since Niger's independence.[47] Rather than entrench himself in power through constitutional changes that would extend his time in office, President Issoufou's democratic credentials and good governance were enhanced by the choice of peace and avoidance of violent protests, leading him, among other reasons, to win the much coveted Mo Ibrahim prize for leading Niger "on a path of progress."[48] Third, despite its

Justice in Africa 61 (Adeola Aderomola & Matua W. Makau eds., 2022). On the murky overlap between "third-termism" and the role of the military in Africa, see Trésor Muhindo Makunya & Kwadwo Appiagyei-Atua, *Soldiers in Civilian Uniforms: The Role of the Military in the Pursuit of Third-Termism*, *in* The Palgrave Handbook of Democracy, Governance and Justice in Africa, *supra*, at 75.

44 John Mukum Mbaku, *Constitutional Coups as a Threat to Democratic Governance in Africa*, 2 Int'l Comp. Pol'y & Ethics L. Rev. 77, 90 (2018).

45 *See generally* Morgane Le Cam, *Niger: Junta is Fueled by Anger Against a "Sick Democracy,"* Le Monde (Aug. 9, 2023), https://tinyurl.com/3uhj8z4a.

46 *Niger Election Set for February Runoff*, DW (Jan. 2, 2021), www.dw.com/en/nigers-presidential-election-heads-to-february-runoff/a-56114951.

47 Fred Muvunyi, *Niger Set for First-Ever Peaceful Transition of Power*, DW (Feb. 19, 2021), www.dw.com/en/niger-set-for-first-ever-peaceful-transition-of-power/a-56627959.

48 *See President Mahamadou Issoufou: 2020 Laureate*, Mo Ibrahim Foundation, https://tinyurl.com/mr48uz3c (last visited Aug. 24, 2024).

significance, the gains of the first peaceful democratic transfer of power in Niger lasted only two years.

One may question whether this is a temporary setback, and perhaps there lies an opportunity for Niger to return to the path of democratic governance in a similar turn of events that brought in President Issoufou.[49] While a possibility, that consideration is beyond this chapter's analysis of the decline or strengthening of the rule of law in Africa. Yet, our understanding of the intricacies of the back and forth of military coups that civilian administrations are sandwiched between in today's Niger is enriched by an analysis of the rule of law that centers important overlapping economic, historical, and geopolitical contexts in Niger.

The military coup in Niger has three important points of confluence that contribute to the rupture of democratic governance and the rule of law: first, economic in the context of uranium mining; second, historical as it relates to the role of France, a former colonizer meddling in the politics of a sovereign state; third, geopolitical in the context of military solidarity within the Francophone West African states and the role of China and Russia. These factors are overlapping and no individual one exclusively explains this coup and consequential decline in democracy. First, economic interest lies at the heart of the postcoup analysis and complicates the path to the return of a democratic regime in Niger given the extraction of uranium by corporations from France.[50] Uranium mined from Niger has been critical to the operation of French nuclear power plants for many years.[51] Second, although mining of uranium by

[49] The circumstances leading to President Issoufou's election in 2011 were linked to the conduct of his predecessor:

> President Mamadou Tandja had refused to step down after two terms, as stipulated in the country's constitution. He first took office in 1999 and was reelected in 2004. Instead of obeying the constitution, he then went on to dissolve parliament and the constitutional court, simultaneously organizing a referendum on the possibility of a third term for himself. But he had not expected the reaction of the civil society and the Nigerien opposition, who boycotted the referendum and parliamentary elections and denounced Tandja's actions as illegal. In the end, the military intervened and ousted Tandja.

Antonio Cascais, *Niger's Chance for a Democratic Change of Power*, DW (Feb. 18, 2020), www.dw.com/en/nigers-chance-for-a-democratic-transition-of-power/a-52413783.

[50] *See* Assma Maad, *How Dependent Is France on Niger's Uranium?*, Le Monde (Aug. 4, 2023), https://tinyurl.com/byxykb4v.

[51] Giorgio Leali, *Niger Coup Sparks Concerns About French, EU Uranium Dependency*, Politico (July 31, 2023), www.politico.eu/article/niger-coup-spark-concerns-france-uranium-dependency/.

French corporations has continued, it has raised questions around the neocolonial nature of this relationship. This factor assumes a different undertone because Niger was a colony of France. In turn, this has prompted allegations of the crumbling of a quasi-empire of France, which may open the door to other rich powers like Russia.[52] Third, the geopolitics have both an international and a regional dimension. At the regional level, Mali and Burkina Faso issued a joint statement warning that intervention by the Economic Community of West African States (ECOWAS) could lead to a military response from them.[53] Internationally, the coup has heightened questions around the military presence of Russia, France, and the United States of America in Niger and the Sahel. As an editorial of the *Review of African Political Economy* observes: "The dominant framing of Western media reporting about the recent coups is indeed a geopolitical one, classifying African politics within the current remake of the East–West bloc confrontation."[54] The geopolitics of military presence in Africa and their contribution to unsettling democratic regimes has been underanalyzed in the discourse of the rule of law. As Jubril Ibrahim rightly observes:

> The Nigeriens are screaming at the top of their voices that this historical juncture is for the dismantling of French neo-colonialism in their country, and not democracy. There is a rising campaign, significantly facilitated by the Russian Wagner Group, that opposition to military rule is tantamount to supporting French and American imperialism. The narrative is presenting ECOWAS and Nigeria as the new lap dogs of French and American imperialism.[55]

Niger's coup therefore exemplifies the confluence of the murky nature of how factors – national, regional, and international – with contested

[52] *See generally* Michael M. Philips, Benoit Faucon & Drew Hinshaw, *Niger Coup Upends U.S. Security Plans in West Africa, Handing Russia an Opportunity*, Wall St. J. (July 27, 2023), https://tinyurl.com/5datc437; Nabila Ramdani, *The Niger Crisis Shows France's Quasi-Empire in Africa Is Finally Crumbling*, Guardian (Aug. 5, 2023), https://tinyurl.com/2kytrk5m.

[53] *Burkina Faso, Mali Warn Against Military Intervention in Niger*, Al Jazeera (Aug. 1, 2023), https://tinyurl.com/4y56w7rc ("The transitional governments of Burkina Faso and Mali express their fraternal solidarity . . . to the people of Niger, who have decided with full responsibility to take their destiny in hand and assume the fullness of their sovereignty before history," the military governments of the two countries said. "Any military intervention against Niger would be tantamount to a declaration of war against Burkina Faso and Mali," they warned, adding that such a move could result in "disastrous consequences" that "could destabilise the entire region.").

[54] Bettina Engels, Editorial, *Coups and Neo-colonialism*, 50 Rev. African Pol. Econ. 147, 147 (2023).

[55] Jibrin Ibrahim, *Niger Coup: Defending Democracy or Combating French Neo-colonialism*, Premium Times Nigeria (Aug. 11, 2023), https://tinyurl.com/5x645nbw.

economic and political dimensions and actors add complexity to contemporary analysis of the rule of law and democratic decline.

**Burkina Faso**, since its independence in 1960, illustrates a deep history of military rule, coups, and social and religious conflict.[56] Accordingly, Burkina Faso is viewed as the epicenter of conflict in the Sahel. More recently, President Blaise Compaoré, who took power in 1983, was ousted in a popular uprising in 2014 after attempting to amend the constitution to extend his rule.[57] In what some describe as a momentous victory for the rule of law and democratic consolidation in Africa, President Compaoré was later tried in absentia and convicted for his part in the assassination of Thomas Sankara.[58] Subsequently, elections were conducted in 2015 and in 2020, when President March Roch Christian Kaboré was returned for a second term.[59] This reelection ended prematurely two years later. In 2022, Burkina Faso experienced two military coups: first, in January 2022, Burkina Faso's army removed President Roch Kaboré, blaming him for failing to contain violence by Islamist militants.[60] Second, in September 2022, there was a second coup by army captain Ibrahim Traoré, who forcibly removed Paul Henri-Damiba.[61] Admittedly, the latest Burkina Faso coups were staged against a background of a preexisting weak democratic institution with a concerning humanitarian crisis. Yet, a noncontextual and historical analysis of the Burkina Faso military coups of 2022 fails to appreciate the limitations of traditional measurement of rule-of-law compliance. Beyond the abhorrent practice of military juntas and the cleavages that characterize the national context for the coups, the coup was also about

[56] Folahanmi Aina, *Jihadism and Military Takeovers in West Africa: Burkina Faso Coup Highlights the Links*, CONVERSATION (Nov. 8, 2022), https://tinyurl.com/3w7avck4.

[57] Mathieu Bonkoungou & Joe Penney, *Protests Force Out Burkina President, Soldiers Vie for Power*, REUTERS (Oct. 30, 2014), www.reuters.com/article/us-burkina-politics-idUSKBN0IJ0NZ20141031.

[58] Ebenezer Obadare, *Blaise Compaore's Conviction Is a Momentous Victory for the Rule of Law and Citizen Power in Africa*, COUNCIL ON FOREIGN RELS. (Apr. 6, 2022), https://tinyurl.com/bdhknrw5.

[59] Sam Mednick, *Burkina Faso President Roch March Christian Kabore Re-elected*, TORONTO STAR (Nov. 26, 2020), https://tinyurl.com/4ym7m4zf.

[60] *Burkina Faso: Coup Puts Rights at Risk – Uphold Basic Protections, Restore Civilian Democratic Rule*, HUM. RTS. WATCH (Jan. 27, 2022), www.hrw.org/news/2022/01/27/burkina-faso-coup-puts-rights-risk.

[61] *Understanding Burkina Faso's Latest Coup*, AFR. CTR. FOR STRATEGIC STUD. (Oct. 28, 2022), https://africacenter.org/spotlight/understanding-burkina-faso-latest-coup/; *see also* Louisa Brooke-Holland, *Burkina Faso: Second Coup of 2022*, HOUSE OF COMMONS LIBR. (Oct. 19, 2022), https://commonslibrary.parliament.uk/research-briefings/cbp-9633/.

geopolitical struggles between powerful Western countries such as France, the United States of America, and Russia. Western influence, though diminished, remains considerable for historical reasons, and because many African countries still look to the West for aid, investment, and sympathy in international lending bodies. In turn, powerful Western governments have been accused of supporting rival factions in states where their economic and military interests exist. Like Niger, Burkina Faso is caught amidst the geopolitical struggle for influence by countries such as France, Russia, and the United States, which have military and transnational economic interests in Burkina Faso's extractive industry. The coup in Burkina Faso is a manifestation of dissatisfaction, schisms, and power struggles at the national level, often linked to questions about the role of external actors with interests.[62] In turn, external support through funding, weapons, and training as part of security and regional conflict management unwittingly lay the groundwork for military coups.[63]

As for **Gabon**, in August 2023, the now ousted president Ali Bongo Ondimba was declared the winner of the national election that would have returned him for a third term. The election was strongly disputed. President Ondimba had ruled the country since 2009 and seemed destined to follow in his father's footsteps. Omar Bongo – Ali Bongo's father – had ruled Gabon between 1967 and 2009. In Ali Bongo's case, the military argued that the elections were rigged and designed to entrench the former president and his close supporters in power. In turn, they promised to return power to civilians through elections at the end of a transition period. This was Gabon's first successful coup. On August 30, 2023, the military announced that the election that returned Ali Bongo as president for the third term lacked credibility and was therefore annulled. If all goes to plan, the military authorities in Gabon have announced elections for August 2025.[64]

Likewise, in **Guinea**, in September 2021, special forces commander Colonel Mamady Doumbouya overthrew President Alpha Conde.[65]

[62] *See* Emma Heywood et al., *Burkina Faso Coup Raises Questions About Growing Russian Involvement in West Africa*, CONVERSATION (Oct. 11, 2022), https://tinyurl.com/96jt4kkp.

[63] Stephanie Savell, *U.S. Security Assistance to Burkina Faso Laid the Groundwork for a Coup*, FOREIGN POL'Y (Feb. 3, 2022), https://tinyurl.com/42367vsu.

[64] *Gabon: Military Authorities Announce Elections for August 2025*, AFRICANEWS (Nov. 13, 2023), https://tinyurl.com/45fswbdj.

[65] *Guinea Coup: Who Is Col Mamady Doumbouya*, BBC (Oct. 1, 2021), www.bbc.com/news/world-africa-58461971.

A year earlier, President Conde spearheaded a change of the constitution to circumvent the two-term limit that would have prevented him from standing for a third term. While the constitutional change was described by opposition leaders as an abuse of power and Conde was accused of becoming an authoritarian, he argued that it would modernize the country, and citizens overwhelmingly voted in favour of the amendment in a controversial referendum.[66] Although the constitutional amendment would limit presidential terms to two, its effect would have reset the timetable to allow President Conde to contest for another two terms of six years each. A critical point to highlight is that President Conde, who first assumed office in 2010, was Guinea's first democratically elected president.[67] Conde, a former opposition leader who was sentenced to death by a former authoritarian, has taken on the full character of entrenching himself in office forcefully.

One major implication that arises from the foregoing analysis is the interconnectedness of the rule of law developments with internal and external geopolitical struggles.[68] In an interconnected global order, the decline of regions such as Europe and powerful Western countries like the United States and the negative transnational diffusion to other regions of the world is an important factor. In Africa, this decline empowers would-be authoritarians to undermine the liberal democratic order either through term elongation or other repressive and oppressive measures that limit opposition. Mutua frames this challenge as "Africa's relationship with the international legal, political, and economic order. International institutions, hegemonic states, and the culture of international law have at best been negligent, and destructive at worst."[69]

Mutua centers the challenge on the nature of the African state. According to him: "The African state is reflexively repressive and generally disdainful of civil society. It has trouble performing the basic functions of statehood. Its proclivity for corruption is well known. These problems stand at the centre of the crisis."[70] From the foregoing, the motivation for the resurgence of military interventions between 2020

[66] *Guinea President Alpha Conde Enacts New Constitution*, Al Jazeera (Apr. 7, 2020), www.aljazeera.com/news/2020/4/7/guinean-president-alpha-conde-enacts-new-constitution.

[67] James André, *Alpha Conde Declared Winner in Guinea Presidential Run-off*, France 24 (Nov. 16, 2010), https://tinyurl.com/ytku49tf.

[68] *See* Alexis Arieff, *Burkina Faso: Conflict and Military Rule*, Cong. Res. Serv. (Sept. 28, 2023), https://sgp.fas.org/crs/row/IF10434.pdf.

[69] Mutua, *supra note* 1, at 165.

[70] *Id.*

and 2023 is attributable in part to the greedy desires of elected leaders. The nature and circumstances of the coups differ from the first generation of coups after many African states attained independence in that more recent coups were precipitated by unpopular and controversial amendments to constitutional term limits, as the cases of Niger, Guinea, and Gabon illustrate. Likewise, it appears that the military juntas are more amendable to setting an agenda for the transition back to civilian administration rather than entrenching themselves in office. Nevertheless, the resurgence of military coups demonstrates a clear decline of democratic values that undermines the possibility of rule-of law-values becoming entrenched.

Lastly, there is a Francophone and neocolonial resistance pattern that emerges from the incidences of military coups in West, Central, and Sahel regions of Africa.[71] Virtually all of the states that have experienced coups between 2020 and 2023 are former French colonies.[72] As such, the decline of the rule of law, in the context of democratic governance, should not be rendered solely as a product of national struggles. In some cases, coups disrupt the capture of the state by elites that have dominated the rulership of the nation for a long time – even if they are replaced by another elite. For example, in Gabon, while the ousted president Ali Bongo took over power following his father's death in 2009, the military government's new leader is in fact a cousin of the former president Ali Bongo.[73]

[71] In the words of Kent Mensah:

> But it is not easy for West Africa and the Sahel to forget France's long history in their regions, say analysts. France has historically prioritised order within the borders of its African partners, supporting leaders who rely on dubious elections and wield the military to prevent challenges to their power. France has also turned a blind eye to the impoverishment of African people by their governments, which have successfully laundered billions of dollars of public funds through European and French institutions. Only in recent years, under pressure from African anticorruption campaigners, has France begun to probe some of the allegations of corruption, such as against Denis Sassou Nguesso, president of the Democratic Republic of the Congo (DRC), in 2015.Kent Mensah, *Africa's Coup Epidemic: Has Democracy Failed the Continent?*, AL JAZEERA (Sept. 22, 2023), https://tinyurl.com/ye238hrc.

[72] Folahanmi Aina, *French Mistakes Helped Create Africa's Coup Belt*, ALJAZEERA OPINIONS (Aug. 17, 2023), www.aljazeera.com/opinions/2023/8/17/french-mistakes-helped-create-africas-coup-belt.

[73] Nosmot Gbadamosi, *Has Gabon's "All-Powerful" Bongo Dynasty Really Lost Its 55-Year Grip?*, AL JAZEERA (Sept. 1, 2023), https://tinyurl.com/2yv4747k.

## 2 Narrative II: A Tale of Two Presidential Elections: Entrenchment of the Rule of Law – Successful Transition of Power in West Africa

The transition of power from one civilian administration to another is important for the consolidation of democracy and the ultimate expression of the rule of law.[74] In this second narrative, I examine the situations where elected African states have successfully conducted elections and transitioned from one civilian government to another as an example of the deepening of democracy and the rule of law. Nigeria and Liberia, two countries that conducted their presidential elections in 2023 and transitioned to new administrations, contrast with the experiences in Francophone countries like Gabon and Burkina Faso analyzed in Narrative I. Whereas the election in Nigeria saw the transfer of power from a ruling party to another candidate of the same party, the election in Liberia was more consequential as the transfer of power was to the opposition. In addition, whereas the perception was that the Nigerian election was not free and fair, reports so far have praised the Liberian election as free and fair. Attributes such as transparency, responsiveness, equity and inclusiveness, and democracy are interconnected with the socio-economic development of any nation. Entrenchment of the rule of law enhances the likelihood that the voices of the most vulnerable in society are heard in decision-making.

Whereas the national incumbents in the Democratic Republic of Congo, Zimbabwe, Liberia, Madagascar, and Sierra Leone were seeking a second term, Nigeria was an outright contest for vacancy in the office of the presidency following a two-term presidency. I now turn to the two countries.

The presidential election in **Nigeria** offers a compelling case of the entrenchment of democratic governance in Africa's most populous country. Nigeria returned to democracy in 1999 after three decades of almost uninterrupted military rule.[75] Since its return to democratic governance, accusations of ballot rigging and fraud have followed its electoral cycles.[76] The 2023 contest was well contested between four candidates for the first time in Nigeria's recent history. President Bola Ahmed Tinubu was the candidate of the ruling party, All Progressive

[74] In 2020, the limits of this sacred constitutional practice were tested in the United States of America as well. *See* Daniel L. Weiner & Tim Lau, *Why the Presidential Transition Process Matters*, Brennan Ctr. (Nov. 13, 2020), https://tinyurl.com/e6rhy5xx.

[75] *See generally* Salmon A. Shomade, *Nigeria: History, Colonial Legacy, and the Rule of Law*, *in* Colonial Legacies and the Rule of Law in Africa (2023)

[76] Mark A. Green & Johnnie Carson, *The Pursuit of Democracy: The Importance of Nigeria's Elections*, Wilson Ctr. (Mar. 8, 2023), www.wilsoncenter.org/article/pursuit-democracy-importance-nigerias-election.

Congress (APC); a former vice president, Alhaji Atiku Abubakar, for the People's Democratic Party (PDP); a former governor from the South-Eastern region of Nigeria, Mr. Peter Obi, for Labour Party (LP); and another former governor, senator, and former federal minister of defense, Mr. Rabiu Musa Kwankwaso, for the New Nigeria Peoples Party (NNPP). Nigeria's presidential election of February 29 returned the APC's candidate as the president-elect.

Unexpectedly, complaints centered around conventional allegations of challenges to the rule of law and newer ones driven by technology. The election was alleged to have been marked by traditional challenges such as voter suppression in some regions, vote buying, violence, and by new challenges posed by developments in technology.[77] The promise of digital technology as a panacea to manual procedural challenges in elections in Africa has generated a different genre of dilemmas for African elections.[78] The challenges raise questions around democratic credibility, conduct of the elections, and the legitimacy of the winning candidate.[79] Undoubtedly, Nigeria's democratic experience with cyclical elections is consolidating. Yet even though Nigeria's presidential elections successfully consolidated the formal aspects of the transfer of power from one civilian administration to another, the electoral process raised many questions that were heard before Nigerian courts. I return to this point in my analysis of Narrative III. Regardless of its weaknesses, Nigeria's 2023 presidential election yielded at least two important lessons that bode well for the consolidation of democracy in Africa's most populous country. First, since Nigeria's independence, it is the first time that a third-party presidential candidate made a serious showing.[80] Second, since the end of military rule in 1999, it was also significant in that the recycling of former military generals as civilian leaders may have halted as there was none on the ballot.

[77] Abiodun Fatai, *Nigeria's Election Was Nearly Derailed by Technology – but Biometric Devices Weren't the Problem*, CONVERSATION (Mar. 2, 2023), https://tinyurl.com/2nxwr7fs; *see also* Marystella Simiyu, *Election Technology as a Means of Enhancing Democratic Legitimacy: A Case of Kenya*, *in* THE PALGRAVE HANDBOOK OF DEMOCRACY, GOVERNANCE AND JUSTICE IN AFRICA, *supra* note 43, at 114; Rhoda Osei-Affu, *Solutions or Problems? The Increasing Role of Technology in African Elections*, WILSON CTR., AFR. UP CLOSE (Dec. 11, 2017), https://tinyurl.com/3dfs3cy7.

[78] Nic Cheeseman, Gabrielle Lynch & Justin Willis. *Digital Dilemmas: The Unintended Consequences of Election Technology*, 25 DEMOCRATIZATION 1397 (2018).

[79] James Rupert, *Nigeria's Vote Signals Risks: How Its Partners Can Support Democracy*, U.S. INST. OF PEACE (Mar. 9, 2023), https://tinyurl.com/mprs9ree.

[80] Macdonald Dzirutwe & Temilade Adelaja, *How Nigeria's Presidential Election Is Galvanizing Young Voters*, REUTERS (Feb. 20, 2023), https://tinyurl.com/ya9zst2z.

**Liberia**, a small African state unlike Nigeria, is the second example that illustrates the entrenchment and consolidation of democratic regimes in Africa. Under the current leadership of President George Weah, Liberia's presidential election initially held on October 10, 2023,[81] headed for a runoff election between the incumbent and the opposition candidate, a former vice president, Mr. Joseph Boakai. Neither candidate met the threshold to be declared outright winner.[82] As Liberia's fourth postwar presidential election, the trend is again headed toward a consolidation of democratic governance. The significance of the election lies not only in what so far appears to be a free and fair conduct of the elections like in 2019,[83] but also the fact that it is the first presidential election in Liberia without the presence of the United Nations mission that previously supported Liberia's elections commission.[84] The runoff election resulted in the opposition candidate, Mr. Joseph Boakai, as the winner.[85] Unlike the trend in some other African states, outgoing president Weah did not attempt to extend his term in office unconstitutionally, nor has Liberia deteriorated into anarchy on account of the loss by the incumbent, who conceded defeat despite the closeness of the vote.[86]

While the elections in Nigeria and Liberia at least formally entrenched democratic processes, perceptions about them differ. The manipulation of electoral processes and constitutional rules to extend presidential terms undermines citizens' trust in democratic institutions.[87] Whereas Nigeria's election ended up in court, Liberia's incumbent president conceded defeat, dispensing with the likelihood of judicial involvement. Flawed elections engender a democratic backslide.[88] Nigeria and Liberia illustrate two different tales: it is not just about the outcome. The process

[81] *What to Know About Liberia's Presidential Election*, AL JAZEERA (Oct. 10, 2023), www.aljazeera.com/news/2023/10/10/what-to-know-about-liberias-upcoming-elections.

[82] *Liberians Vote for President in Tightly Contested Run-Off Election*, AL JAZEERA (Nov 14, 2023), https://tinyurl.com/mr2n66hv.

[83] *Free and Fair Elections "Confirm Liberia's Steady March Towards Lasting Peace," Says UN Chief*, UN PEACEKEEPING (Dec. 29, 2017), https://tinyurl.com/2s3p5xmt.

[84] Press Release, ECOWAS Comm'n, ECOWAS Preliminary Declaration: 2023 Run-Off Presidential Election in Liberia (Nov. 16, 2023), https://tinyurl.com/3dkzth6p.

[85] Press Release, ECOWAS Comm'n, *ECOWAS Congratulates the Republic of Liberia* (NOV. 18, 2023), https://ecowas.int/ecowas-congratulates-the-republic-of-liberia/.

[86] *Liberia's George Weah Concedes to Joseph Boakai in Presidential Polls*, AL JAZEERA (Nov. 18, 2023), https://tinyurl.com/uuw9m2x9.

[87] Oge Onubogu, *African's Reactions to Disputed Elections and Coups Show Discontent with Democracy*, WILSON CTR. (Sept. 5, 2023), https://tinyurl.com/y8khr8nj.

[88] Mark Green, Derek Mitchell & Daniel Twining, *Nigeria's Flawed Election Risks a Democratic Backslide*, FOREIGN POL'Y (Mar. 14, 2023), https://tinyurl.com/57x6x2x3.

is where accountability, transparency, and fairness that are germane to the rule of law matter: formal consolidation of democracy with procedural challenges that go to the root rule of law is not enough. Consequently, while elections have become more popular and sustained in Africa, citizens increasingly have less faith in their capacity to deliver free and fair outcomes.[89] As I argue in the previous section, the formal consolidation of democracy with procedural challenges that go to the root rule of law portend greater danger when judicialized, especially in the age of disinformation and social media. They risk delegitimizing or weakening the legitimacy of the institutions that uphold the rule of law.

### 3 *Narrative III: Judicialization of Disputes before National Courts and Legitimacy Crises*

In contemporary Africa, the judicialization of presidential elections between incumbents and challengers in courts is on the rise.[90] The judicialization of election disputes is mostly analyzed because of their potential to influence the trajectory of the concerned state. Nullification of election results as a result of judicialization is not a common phenomenon in Africa. The role of the judiciary is critical in safeguarding the ongoing democratization in Africa by ensuring credibility in the adjudication of electoral disputes. National, regional, and international courts play significant roles in the entrenchment of the rule of law.[91] Although

[89] Fredline M'Cormack-Hale & Mavis Zupork Dome, *Support for Elections Weakens Among Africans; Many See Them as Ineffective in Holding Leaders Accountable*, Afrobarometer Dispatch, No. 551 (Sept. 16, 2022), https://tinyurl.com/ykt36mnp.

[90] The increased judicialization should be understood against a background of a judiciary that is struggling for legitimacy in many African countries. Makau Mutua puts this succinctly:

> The Africanisation and indigenization of the judiciary failed to transform the justice sector from a colonially racist, anti-people, and oppressive instrumentality. Judges became extensions of the executive and served at its whim. Instead of becoming fountains of justice, courts were used to instill fear in the populace at the behest of the executive. The courts were used to crush political dissent and curtail civil society . . . Judges were viewed with disdain, contempt, or fear in most African states. This is why today the law, courts, and the legal sector are viewed with suspicion by most Africans. Judiciaries are not perceived to be the guardians of legality or impartiality. To be sure, the illegitimacy of the justice sector extended to all the other arms of the state.
>
> Mutua, *supra* note 1, at 161–62.

[91] The Performance of Africa's International Courts, *supra* note 9; Tom Ginsburg & Tamir Moustafa, Rule of Law: The Politics of Courts in Authoritarian Regimes (2008).

the decisions are outside the purview of the period that this chapter analyzes, in the recent past courts in Kenya[92] and Malawi[93] have risen to the occasion in standing up for free and fair electoral processes. In nullifying the 2017 presidential election, the Supreme Court of Kenya noted that "[t]he greatness of a nation lies in its fidelity to the Constitution and the strict adherence to the rule of law."[94] The decisions in Kenya and Malawi offered a potent display of judicial independence where courts often come under intense pressure from political leaders.

Yet, judicialization of **high-profile** elections before national courts has implications for the ongoing legitimacy of the courts. These election disputes include cases relating to good governance and the rule of law, constitutional and electoral law amendments, and regime changes. The disputes attain a higher level of socio-economic and cultural undertone because of the national profile of the wealthy political elites involved in them.[95] For example, in the 2023 Nigerian presidential elections, many Nigerians viewed leading candidates through the lens of national geopolitical divisions with deep-seated histories and complexities. Indeed, a newspaper editorial described the election as one of:

> the most divisive electoral contests ever held in the country since the advent of self-governance. They were ethnically-charged and deeply polarising along religious lines. The political elite, their "influencers," as well as a section of the religious elite pushed Nigeria close to the brink of national collapse yet again through their actions and utterances.[96]

With the foregoing context, the judicialization of the election outcome not only heightened the socio-political division in the country and activated beliefs about the marginalization of a region but also exposed the limits of formal rules and the rule of law in addressing far-reaching social justice issues.

High-profile judicialization of election disputes before national courts weakens the legitimacy of the judiciary. The judicialization of high-profile

[92] Kimiko de Freytas-Tamura, *Kenya Supreme Court Nullifies Presidential Election*, N.Y. Times (Sept. 1, 2017), www.nytimes.com/2017/09/01/world/africa/kenya-election-kenyatta-odinga.html.

[93] Michael Wahman, *Will Bold Landmark Election Ruling Improve Malawian Democracy?*, Conversation (Feb. 10, 2020), https://tinyurl.com/mr224dha.

[94] Raila Amolo Odinga & Another v. Independent Electoral and Boundaries Commission & 2 Others [2017] EKLR, ¶ 394.

[95] *See* Akinkugbe, *supra* note 9.

[96] Editorial, *2023 Elections, Divisive, Politics, and National Reconciliation*, Premium Times Nigeria (Mar. 27, 2023), https://tinyurl.com/yc5vyppa.

disputes with complex socio-cultural and geopolitical implications can increase distrust of the adjudication of electoral disputes, leading in turn to a lack of confidence in the national courts.[97] The judicialization of election disputes before national courts when results go against the claims of the opposition in high-profile disputes weakens the trust of citizens in the judiciary. In such situations, allegations of compromise and state capture (among others) are levied against the judiciary. Nigeria's 2023 presidential elections offer a compelling example of this. Both the major opposition (PDP) and third-party (Labour Party) presidential candidates challenged the election of President Tinubu of the APC.[98] The Nigerian Court of Appeal and subsequently the Supreme Court of Nigeria affirmed the victory of the ruling party candidate, leading to polarizing analyses about the courts and their role.[99]

The point is not so much about the technicalities of the courts' analyses and reasoning as it is about the aspersion and shadow of bias that is cast on Nigeria's judiciary because of the judicialization of high-profile election disputes, prompting allegations of judicial capture and co-optation.[100] To illustrate, so great was the pressure on the third arm of the government that there were billboards, rallies, and social media trends with "#All Eyes on The Judiciary" as their hashtag. As one newspaper wrote: "Their purpose was clear – to exert pressure on the esteemed judges of the panel, with a view to ensuring that they do not compromise the integrity of the case at hand."[101] As another commentator noted:

> In Nigeria's history, the judiciary has never been faced with mounting pressure as it is facing currently. Since after the general election when the battle for the validity of the results of the elections shifted to the various Election Petitions Tribunals, many Nigerians have turned their focus on the judiciary, insisting that it should deliver substantial justice without fear and favour.[102]

[97] Gathii & Akinkugbe, *supra* note 9.

[98] Camillus Eboh, *Nigeria's Obi, Atiku Challenge Presidential Election Results*, Reuters (Mar. 21, 2023), https://tinyurl.com/3yae8sb5.

[99] *See, e.g.*, Sonala Olumhense, *Nigeria Court Didn't Want Contested Election Case. It Just Defended the Winner*, Open Democracy (Sept. 15, 2023), https://tinyurl.com/y79n32mn; Camillus Eboh, *Nigeria Opposition's Obi Slams Court Ruling Confirming Tinubu Election*, Reuters (Nov. 6, 2023), https://tinyurl.com/2vcp9ye8.

[100] Shaffer and Sandholtz caution that "any institutional means can be co-opted, abused, and subverted in practice." *See* Chapter 1.

[101] *Mounting Undue Pressure on the Judiciary*, This Day, www.thisdaylive.com/index.php/2023/08/20/mounting-undue-pressure-on-the-judiciary (last visited Jan. 4, 2024).

[102] *Id.*

The expectation from these opposition candidates is that they want the Nigerian courts to be brave and annul the election if it is indeed found to be deeply flawed, as their counterparts in Kenya and Malawi did.[103] The view that the judiciary is the last line of defense for the liberal democratic constitutional order therefore leaves two possibilities: while it heralds the possibility of entrenching democratic norms and the rule of law, it simultaneously weakens the trust of the public in the judiciary and its legitimacy. Put differently, given the low level of judicial rejection of election results in Africa, the unabating judicialization of election disputes in national courts may lead to two contrasting developments with direct implications for the strengthening or weakening of the rule of law. On the one hand, the judicialization of election disputes and emergence of a winner as declared by the courts is an affirmation of a core tenet of the rule of law enshrined in the role of the courts. Where there is no distrust in the judiciary, notwithstanding the high-profile nature of the election dispute, such an outcome will enhance citizens' belief in the rule of law. On the other hand, keenly contested election disputes, such as presidential elections, risk delegitimizing the judiciary as they are not viewed as impartial arbiters. For example, Nigeria's 2023 presidential election was conducted against a background of sharp division along geopolitical, religious, and tribal lines. The subsequent judicialization of the election disputes before the tribunal and courts manifested suspicion and mistrust in the judiciary's capacity to arbitrate in an unbiased manner.[104] Consequently, distrust of the independence and impartiality of the judiciary casts a negative shadow on the efficacy of the rule of law.

Furthermore, the overwhelming attitude of African national judiciaries to abstain from overruling presidential elections inadvertently empowers would-be authoritarians who see the courts as tools to support the outcome of flawed elections, or to pursue constitutional change. Particularly, the practice not to overturn presidential elections conversely operates to legitimize "regime actions that helped actors consolidate power, undermine the opposition, and tilt the electoral playing field

[103] *See* Olabisi D. Akinkugbe & James Thuo Gathii, *Judicial Nullification of Presidential Elections in Africa: Peter Mutharika v. Lazarus Chakera and Saulos Chilima in Context*, Afronomicslaw Blog (July 3, 2020), https://tinyurl.com/mtfbn4ma.

[104] Ahead of the release of the judgments on the election disputes arising from Nigeria's 2023 presidential elections, there was a social media campaign dubbed "All Eyes on the Judiciary." *See generally* Funmilayo Odude, *What's Wrong with All Eyes on the Judiciary*, Financial Nigeria (Sept. 11, 2023), www.financialnigeria.com/what-s-wrong-with-all-eyes-on-the-judiciary-blog-813.html.

heavily in their favour. *Regimes turn to courts to carry out their dirty work because, in doing so, they benefit from the associations that judicial review has with democratic constitutional traditions and the rule of law.*"[105]

The rising practice of judicializing presidential elections by political actors is thus strategic and not simply about establishing the rule of law. While the finality of the decision of the courts as the source of legitimacy for contested elections remains germane, high-profile election disputes reveal the limits of formal rules of elections in addressing social inequities and the marginalization of candidates, raise allegations of judicial capture, and unwittingly weaken the legitimacy of the courts. This does not bode well for the rule of law.

These three narratives of the rule of law in contemporary Africa illustrate deeply contradictory practices. The concept is equally deployed by liberal and illiberal regimes to defend and legitimize their actions. The rule of law falls short of addressing any of the deep-seated hierarchies that characterize the African continent. As such, the extent to which a consistent appeal to the virtues of the rule of law alleviates the challenges facing African states remains murky.

## IV In Lieu of Conclusion: Emerging Transnational Rule of Law and Good Governance in Africa?

This chapter would be incomplete without some reflection on the evolving transnational practice of the rule of law as championed by Africa's regional and subregional courts. The transnational context of the rule of law is equally gaining ground in Africa. In Africa, where national courts have struggled, as the previous section on judicialization illustrates, Africa's international – regional and subregional – courts increasingly provide an alternative forum for litigation to advance protections against alleged arbitrary exercises of power by the national ruling party. The emerging jurisprudence and legal order that Africa's regional courts offer is transnational in nature.

The concept of Transnational Legal Orders (TLOs) advanced by Terrence C. Halliday and Gregory Shaffer "provide[s] new theoretical tools to integrate transnational, national, and local lawmaking and

[105] *See* David Landau & Rosalind Dixon, *Abusive Judicial Review: Courts Against Democracy*, 53 U.C. Davis L. Rev. 1315 (2020) (emphasis added).

practice into a coherent framework to capture the dynamic changes in legal ordering taking place today."[106] The allure of coherence in the transnational legal order, however, belies the fluidity, complexity, and ambivalence of the rule of law practices before Africa's regional courts. The disputes that are judicialized before Africa's regional courts emerge from different legal regimes, contexts, and facts, and the motives for their judicialization differ. As such, the case for coherence in the rules of the legal order that Africa's regional courts are developing is less persuasive. In engaging the rule of law as a transnational legal order, Jothie Rajah makes a similar observation. For Rajah, "the regulatory precision implied by the order is paradoxically undermined by the shifting meanings of the rule of law."[107]

Most importantly, as Shaffer and Sandholtz note in their contribution to this book, TLOs "are normative orders that implicate law and legal practice across and within multiple national boundaries."[108] For them, "transnational legal processes provide normative resources to protect human rights, uphold democratic processes, and safeguard the rule of law."[109] Shaffer and Sandholtz also assess the role of international law and institutions in entrenching the rule of law from a transnational perspective.[110] Still, the emerging transnational rule of law in Africa, as

[106] Transnational Legal Orders 63–64 (Terrence C. Halliday & Gregory Shaffer eds., 2015). According to the authors, the project on TLOs comprises three aspects:

> First, it seeks to explain the origins, formation, and change of TLOs through different facilitating and precipitating conditions and through the dynamic, recursive, processes between law formation and implementation of the transnational, national, and subnational levels. Second, it aims to observe and theorize the development of different configurations of TLOs in terms of the settlement of transnational legal norms and variations in the alignment of one or more TLOs with an issue. Third, it aims to understand the variable impacts of different TLOs on international organizations and nation-states, national policy-makers and officials, private-markets and occupations, civil society, and individuals.

[107] Jothie Rajah, *"Rule of Law" as Transnational Legal Order*, *in* Transnational Legal Orders, *supra* note 106, at 340, 342.

[108] *See* Chapter 1.

[109] Gregory Shaffer & Wayne Sandholtz, *The Rule of Law in Transnational Context: Introduction to the Symposium*, 8 U.C. Irvine J. Int'l Transnat'l & Comp. L. 1 (2023).

[110] *Id.* at 16 ("From a transnational perspective, we contend that international norms and institutions are important for protecting individuals from the arbitrary exercise of power. In practice, international law and institutions can contribute to the rule of law, although (as we will see) they also can advance the rule of the powerful by and through law.").

opined by Africa's regional courts, does not presuppose a coherent and single narrative about legal principles and legal orders.

Africa's regional courts have been at the forefront of mega-political disputes. The impact of Africa's regional and subregional courts as actors in transnational normative processes, in the context of high-profile elections, and how they contribute to the strengthening of transnational public discourse have been documented by scholars. While transnational judicial dialogue[111] between African, European, and Latin-American regional judicial legal orders is trending upward, the extent to which the transnational judicial dialogue is happening between regional and national legal orders in Africa remains very low.

The strategic litigation of the rule of law in Africa's regional courts, which foregrounds the socio-political, legal, economic, and cultural contexts of the disputes, bypasses national challenges and pushes back on "elite agreement at transnational level."[112] In turn, the growing judicialization before Africa's regional courts opens the door for a more transnational articulation of the rule of law in Africa. Increasingly, Africa's regional courts monitor states' "behind the border adherence to international commitments such as human rights treaties, ... [and] rule of law."[113] Africa's regional and subregional legal orders that guarantee rights for individuals and civil societies (as norm developers to access their courts) have transnational effect.[114] Strategic human rights litigation, with express overlap on the rule of law, has been judicialized before Africa's regional and subregional courts. These disputes, arising from various national contexts, are anchored on the importance of the rule of law and consolidation of democratic governance in Africa.[115]

[111] *See* Knut Traisbach, *A Transnational Judicial Public Sphere as an Idea and Ideology: Critical Reflections on Judicial Dialogue and its Legitimizing Potential*, 10 GLOB. CONSTITUTIONALISM 186 (2021).

[112] STEPHEN HUMPHREYS, THEATRE OF THE RULE OF LAW: TRANSNATIONAL LEGAL INTERVENTION IN THEORY AND PRACTICE 224 (2010).

[113] Alter & Madsen, *supra* note 31.

[114] *See generally* Theresa Squatrito, *The Democratizing Effects of Transnational Actors' Access to International Courts*, 24 GLOB. GOVERNANCE 595 (2018).

[115] As Shaffer and Sandholtz observe in Chapter 1:

> International law and institutions implicate rule-of-law protections for individuals in the following three ways. First, from a minimalist perspective, international law and institutions can help to secure international peace, which ultimately affects individuals and societies. Second, international law and institutions can indirectly affect domestic rule-of-law

Litigants before regional courts frame disputes in a transnational way.[116] Africa's regional courts are in essence invited by litigants to adjudicate over processes and outcomes that in many cases have been the subject of votes by the citizens. If, as Shaffer and Sandholtz argue, "in an interconnected world, the rule of law should be viewed as a normative social order that involves the horizontal, vertical, and transversal interaction of domestic and international law, which, in turn, reciprocally affect each other,"[117] there is more to be thought about and written on the transnational rule of law aspects of the disputes before Africa's regional courts.

Africa's regional courts are transnational venues that welcome litigants – individuals, civil society, multinational corporations – as transnational entrepreneurs.[118] Africa's regional courts are nonstatic in the generation, affirmation, and protection of the rule of law. Normatively, then, the courts are agents for the generation, affirmation, and protection of a transnational rule of law in Africa. Under their watch, transnational litigation, naming and shaming, and cases initiated for the purpose of accountability and for social engineering are accepted to push back on the decline of the transnational rule of law in Africa. Notably, there are lingering signs of a decline of the rule of law where member states limit the opportunities for individuals and civil society to pursue cases against them in the regional courts. In the context of the African Court on Human and Peoples' Rights, some states have tried to shield themselves from scrutiny by withdrawing the declaration that allows citizens and relevant nongovernmental organizations direct access to the African Court. In a similar vein, other subregional courts also have faced backlash from their member states.[119] The emergent body of

practices in relation to individuals. National law often incorporates international law; national courts and other bodies may reference it; and national actors may otherwise harness it, including to protect rule-of-law concerns. Third, international law and institutions can directly provide rights to individuals and impose duties on national governments, international institutions, and private actors.

[116] Olabisi D. Akinkugbe, *Houngue Éric Noudehouenou v. Republic of Benin*, 115 AM. J. INT'L L. 281 (2021).

[117] *See* Chapter 1.

[118] As Shaffer and Sandholtz note: "Private actors, such as multinational companies, also harness rule-of-law rhetoric to advance their material interests." *See* Chapter 1.

[119] Karen J. Alter, James T. Gathii & Laurence R. Helfer, *Backlash Against International Courts in West, East and Southern Africa: Causes and Consequences*, 27 EUR. J. INT'L L. 293 (2016).

transnational rule of law from Africa's regional and subregional courts should not be restricted to judicialization of high-profile election disputes alone. Future research can explore the evolving transnational legal ordering of environmental law,[120] climate policies, and mutinational corporations before regional courts, among other issues.

[120] *See generally* Yusra Suedi & Marie Fall, *Climate Change Litigation Before the African Human Rights System: Prospects and Pitfalls*, J. Hum. Rts. Prac. (2023); Sonja Kahl, *Environmental Litigation Before Regional Economic Courts in Africa and Latin America*, *in* The Future of Environmental Law (Stefan E. Weishaar & Kars J. de Graaf eds., 2023); James Thuo Gathii, *Saving the Serengeti: Africa's New International Judicial Environmentalism*, 16 Chi. J. Int'l L. 386 (2016); Eghosa O. Ekhator, *International Environmental Governance: A Case for Sub-regional Judiciaries in Africa*, *in* Human Rights and the Environment under African Union Law 209 (Michael Addaney & Ademola Oluborode Jegede eds., 2020).

# 12

## The Criminalization of Dissent

### Challenges to the Rule of Law in Thailand

TYRELL HABERKORN

In June 2020, people took to the streets calling for democratic and legal reform in Thailand. The National Council for Peace and Order (NCPO) had installed a military government on May 22, 2014, the thirteenth coup since the transition from absolute to constitutional monarchy in 1932. Though the junta had officially exited from power following a general election in March 2019, its leader, General Prayuth Chan-ocha, remained prime minister and many laws and policies put in place by the military regime remained in place. The protests coalesced around three initial demands: the prime minister must resign, a new constitution must be drafted, and the state must stop threatening dissidents. In August 2020, the fourth demand was added: the monarchy must be reformed. Despite the nominal status of Thailand as a constitutional monarchy for over ninety years, the position of the monarchy in the polity, which formally is to be a democracy with the king as head of state, remains unclear.[1] Increasingly large protests in September, October, and November 2020 supported the demand for reform of the monarchy. The government responded with police violence and prosecutions, particularly under Article 112 of the Criminal Code. Article 112, often referred to simply as Thailand's lese majesty provision, stipulates an outsize punishment of three to fifteen years' imprisonment per count of defamation, insult, or threat to the king, queen, heir apparent, or regent. The second postcoup general election, held in May 2023, resulted in an overwhelming victory for opposition parties and a strong mandate for both the military to exit from power and the constitution to be revised. But the Move Forward Party, which secured the most votes and included reform of Article 112 as one of its key policy provisions, faced social and legal accusations of disloyalty to the monarchy for daring to do so.

[1] The very meaning of "rule by democracy with the king as head of state" also remains unclear.

On the surface, Thailand may appear to be a particularly egregious illustration of the rule by law, of the thin rule of law, or of law-and-order regimes favored by autocrats.[2] But examination of the criminalization of calls for reform around the monarchy indicates that a deeper, and more concerning, development may be underway. The law is being used to criminalize peaceful dissent over, or even mere questioning of, how power is apportioned and exercised in the polity, so as to preserve the monarchy. Procedure is being interpreted to restrict and twist fundamental concepts, including innocence and guilt. The interpretation and implementation of the law are being deployed in an attempt to transform the political and legal system.

The recent movement for reform of the monarchy can be understood as being in the service of what Gregory Shaffer and Wayne Sandholtz define as "the rule of law as an ideal – or meta-principle – under which individuals are not to be subject to the arbitrary exercise of power."[3] The movement aims to clarify and limit the ambiguous institutions behind the arbitrary exercise of power (i.e., the monarchy and its allies – namely, the military and the judiciary) and create space for the voices and desires of the people to be meaningful in governing the polity.[4] The backlash should be understood as an attack on the rule of law that aims to expand and entrench the arbitrary exercise of power within and in relation to the law and judicial process. The primary tool of repression is the law itself (i.e., the use of Article 112 and related constitutional provisions), which obscures the violence contained within it. After all, those who hold power are only enforcing the law against those who violate it.

Motivated by concern with both the immediate effects on the lives of those who dare to dissent and the long-term changes in law and politics, I examine the movement for democracy and reform of the monarchy and the backlash in 2020–23 through Shaffer and Sandholtz's framework. I focus on the five sources of arbitrariness within regimes that present themselves as pro–rule of law but act to weaken or destroy it. The specificity of the framework makes it possible to apprehend the

[2] Tom Ginsburg & Tamir Moustafa, Rule by Law: The Politics of Courts in Authoritarian Regimes (2008); Jothie Rajah, Authoritarian Rule of Law Legislation, Discourse and Legitimacy in Singapore (2012); Nick Cheesman, Opposing the Rule of Law: How Myanmar's Courts Make Law and Order (2015).

[3] *See* Chapter 1.

[4] Eugenie Merieau, Constitutional Bricolage: Thailand's Sacred Monarchy vs. the Rule of Law (2021).

operations and entrenchment of the arbitrary in the law, the significance of challenging it, and the tremendous courage of those who risk doing so. I proceed by first offering a brief recent history of the rule of law and Article 112, highlighting the entry of the five sources of arbitrariness into the judicial process. Second, I analyze the movement in 2020–23 as a response and challenge to this history and the obstacles to the rule of law it entrenched. Third, I examine the backlash as both an attempt to halt transformation and evidence of how far the monarchy and their allies are willing to go to preserve their power. Finally, I conclude with preliminary reflections on ongoing developments at the time of this chapter's completion. Ten years and two elections after the May 2014 coup, it is time for a transition to democracy in Thailand, but dangers to the rule of law remain strong. This demands scholarship capable of both comprehending those dangers and identifying strategies to challenge them.

## I A Recent History of the Rule of Law and Article 112

On June 24, 1932, when the People's Party, a civilian–military coalition, fomented the transformation from absolute monarchy to a constitutional regime, their goal was to "change from the system of government in which the king is above the law to the system of government in which the king is under the law."[5] Making everyone in the polity subject to the same law should have been a foundational step to establish the rule of law and stem the arbitrary exercise of power. Yet the political and legal history of the last ninety years in Thailand demonstrates the challenges in doing so. The challenges are most evident in the series of periodic coups and the difficulty of bringing the king – and his close allies in the military – under the law. Prior to 1932, the military was the army of the king and this has changed little, and even intensified during the Cold War, with their interests and resources linked.

Beginning with a military coup in 1933, only a year after the end of absolute monarchy, there began a cycle consisting of a coup and the abrogation of the constitution, drafting of a new constitution and elections, and then another coup once democracy becomes too unruly. Since 1932, there have been twelve coups, twenty constitutions, and thirty

[5] Pridi Banomyong, Pridi by Pridi: Selected Writings on Life, Politics, and Economy 124–25 (Chris Baker & Pasuk Phongpaichit trans., 2000).

prime ministers.[6] Part of this cycle is impunity for those who launch coups, with each coup followed by an amnesty law. Legal scholar Somchai Preechasinlapakun argues that this provides an incentive for would-be coup-makers to overturn the system. Rather than the rule of law, he explains that a "rule of coups" is present.[7] Accompanying the rule of coups, Thongchai Winichakul argues that the rule of law is royalist, meaning that "the king is above law and justice (not the constitution or parliament that are held to be universal norms)."[8] From the very beginning, citizens have pushed back against both the rule of coups and the royalist rule of law, but it has been difficult for them to gain traction against both ingrained practices.

Yet, as the Cold War wound down by the early 1990s, democracy seemed possible and coups seemed to perhaps be a phenomenon of the past in Thailand. In 1997, the seventeenth constitution, dubbed the "People's Constitution" due to the participatory process through which it was drafted, seemed like it might be permanent.[9] But as parliamentary politics and political parties without strong allegiance to either the monarchy or the military grew too strong and unruly, the rule of coups returned. On September 19, 2006, the twelfth coup ousted the elected prime minister, Thaksin Shinawatra, and set in motion a sustained attack on democracy and the rule of law, which continues today. This included both a brutal state crackdown on protestors calling for the return of elections in April–May 2010 and then the May 22, 2014, coup, which is the primary subject of this chapter.

The May 22, 2014, coup by the NCPO ushered in the most repressive regime in Thailand since the counterinsurgency regimes of the Cold War. The regime promised to "return happiness to the people" after nearly ten years of polarized political contention beginning in the period prior to the previous coup, which took place on September 19, 2006. The 2006 coup was instigated by those who perceived that the government of democratically elected prime minister Thaksin Shinawatra – and, in

[6] The total number of coups in Thailand is thirteen, with the transformation from absolute to constitutional monarchy on June 24, 1932, being the first.

[7] Somchai Preechasinlapakun, *The Coup Rule of Law*, *in* THE 19 SEPTEMBER COUP: COUP FOR DEMOCRACY WITH THE KING AS HEAD OF STATE 192 (Thanapol Eawsakul ed., 2007).

[8] Thongchai Winichakul, The Legal Privileged State and Royalist Rule of Law: History of the Genealogy of Thai-style Rule by Law, 17th Puey Ungpakorn Special Lecture (Mar. 9, 2020), *in* WAY MAG. 79 (2020).

[9] Erik Martinez Kuhonta, *The Paradox of Thailand's 1997 "People's Constitution": Be Careful What You Wish For*, 48 ASIAN SURV. 373 (2008).

particular, its widespread popular support – was a threat to the monarchy.[10] Rather than resolving it, the coup only deepened the conflict between the royalist–nationalists who called for it and the democratic–populists who opposed it. While review of the contention between 2006 and 2014 is beyond my analysis here, the choice of a coup to attempt to resolve it set the stage for the entrenchment of the violation of the rule of law.

Article 112 has been part of the Criminal Code since its last revision in 1957, but it was rarely used until after the September 19, 2006, coup.[11] Anyone can walk into a police station to make an accusation of lese majesty against another, and the police are then obliged to investigate it. Cases began emerging following the 2006 coup, with dissident activists, writers, and netizens being prosecuted. Then, following the 2014 coup, Article 112 became one of the NCPO's key tools to remake society, and cases quickly spiked and far exceeded previous records. The increase in cases paralleled the advancing age of King Bhumipol, who was the longest-reigning monarch in the world at the time of his death on October 13, 2016, and concern over the transition to his son, Vajiralongkorn, who was surrounded by unsavory rumors about his personal life and his fitness for kingship.[12] The NCPO most frequently opted to use the law and prosecution, rather than extrajudicial violence, as its tool to suppress and silence its critics. The NCPO also sought to stifle dissent by revoking the passports of Thai citizens who resided abroad and declined to return.[13]

[10] Good Coup Gone Bad: Thailand's Political Developments Since Thaksin's Downfall (Pavin Chachavalpongpun ed., 2014).

[11] On the history of Article 112 and related defamation laws, see David Streckfuss, Truth on Trial in Thailand (2010).

[12] Although extensive discussion of the monarchy is beyond the scope of this chapter, it is worth noting that Bhumipol became an outsize, god-like figure over the course of his lifetime. After falling into irrelevance following the end of absolute monarchy through World War II and the unexpected death of King Ananda, Bhumibol's older brother, in 1946, the combined efforts of the institution of the monarchy, the military, and the US government created new social, cultural, and political significance for Bhumipol and the monarchy during the Cold War. *See* Paul Handley, The King Never Smiles: A Biography of Thailand's Bhumipol Adulyadej (2006); Thongchai Winichakul, Thailand's Hyper-royalism: Its Past Success and Present Predicament (ISEAS Trends in Southeast Asia No. 7, 2016).

[13] Dissidents summoned for "attitude adjustment" shortly after the coup who were out of the country and did not return, such as Pavin Chachavalpongpun, had their passports revoked. *See* Pavin Chachavalpongpun, *The Case of Thailand's Disappearing Dissidents*, N.Y. Times (Oct. 14, 2019), www.nytimes.com/2019/10/14/opinion/thailand-dissidents-disappearance-murder.html.

According to Thai Lawyers for Human Rights (TLHR), formed in the first days after the coup to document rights violations and defend those targeted, at least 162 were prosecuted for violation of Article 112 during the NCPO's five-year regime.[14] People were prosecuted under Article 112 for performing plays, writing graffiti in bathrooms, having conversations in taxis, and – representing the largest number of cases – making social media posts. The longest known punishment was handed down to Wichai (family name withheld), who was sentenced to thirty-five years' imprisonment for ten Facebook posts deemed to violate the law in June 2017; Wichai's sentence was reduced from seventy years as he confessed.[15] After King Bhumibol's death in October 2016, there was initially a rapid decline in new Article 112 cases. After a decade of increasing accusations and prosecutions, this seemed like a hopeful sign of decriminalization of speech critical of the monarchy. Upon closer examination, however, it soon became clear that the lack of prosecution did not mean that critics of the monarchy were now free to criticize the king, but rather signaled a new kind of danger for dissidents and the Thai polity.[16] The murder or disappearance of at least nine republican critics in exile illustrated the gravity of this danger.

Unjust prosecutions of dissidents and extrajudicial killing of them is part of a continuum of violence. These actions, as well as the difficulty of halting the prosecutions or holding the assassins to account, exemplify the crisis of the rule of law in Thailand. Shaffer and Sandholtz's five sources of arbitrariness highlight the dangers to both individuals and the polity.

The five sources of arbitrariness point to a range of moments, sites, and actors involved in the unjust exercise of power detrimental to the rule of law. The first source of arbitrariness is based on the radical inequality of those within the polity, in which "the wielder of power is not subject, in practice, to the law, its controls and limits."[17] Accompanying Article 112, which provides special protection for the king, queen, heir apparent, or

14 THAI LAWYERS FOR HUM. RTS., COLLAPSED RULE OF LAW: THE CONSEQUENCES OF FOUR YEARS UNDER THE NATIONAL COUNCIL FOR PEACE AND ORDER FOR HUMAN RIGHTS AND THAI SOCIETY 26–32 (2018).

15 *Man Jailed for 35 Years in Thailand for Insulting Monarchy on Facebook*, GUARDIAN (June 9, 2017), https://tinyurl.com/hs2uweps.

16 I have written elsewhere about two Article 112 cases involving alleged defamation of King Vajiralongkorn that made it to court and their irregularities. Tyrell Haberkorn, *Dictatorship, Monarchy and Freedom of Expression in Thailand*, 77 J. ASIAN STUD. 935 (2018). Both punishment and leniency were arbitrary and without legal basis.

17 *See* Chapter 1.

regent, Article 6 of the 2017 Constitution further stipulates that: "The king shall be enthroned in a position of revered worship and shall not be violated. No person shall expose the king to any sort of accusation or action." This means that the king cannot himself face prosecution and exists above the law.

Compounding the inequality between the rulers and the ruled in the polity, it is impossible for citizens to guess when they will or will not be charged under Article 112. Once the surge in prosecutions began after the 2014 coup, many people were concerned that they would be arrested for articles they had written, social media comments they had posted, and other actions. Some were, but many were not. Many were also concerned that they might be killed, and, again, some were. This reflects the second source of arbitrariness, in which "individuals are unable to know and predict how power will be wielded over them."[18] The condition of not knowing what violence one will experience for expressing one's view generates fear that limits public discussion about the monarchy and power generally in Thailand.

The third and fourth sources of arbitrariness further structure the relationships between those who hold power and those subject to its operations by distinguishing between those who are not permitted to explain their actions and, conversely, those who can act without having to offer any explanation. Shaffer and Sandholtz explain that the third source of arbitrariness "is where individuals have no place to be heard, inform, question, or respond to how power is exercised over them."[19] Many Article 112 cases arise precisely from questioning or responding to the exercise of power by the monarchy, not from anything clearly recognizable as defamation, insult, or threat. Yet judges interpret the very questioning of the king's power as all three. Defendants in Article 112 cases who choose to plead innocent and fight their cases are further punished with a nearly certain guilty verdict, while those who confess are rewarded with a halving of their sentence. The fourth source of arbitrariness intersects closely with the third and is "where authorities do not engage in public reason-giving in issuing their decisions, which reasons then can be contested, including before judicial, political, and administrative processes."[20] The courts frequently cite the long-standing presence of the monarchy and a presumed universal love for the king as the reasons

[18] *See* Chapter 1.
[19] *See* Chapter 1.
[20] *See* Chapter 1.

for their harsh punishment of those who dissent. No arrests have been made in the cases of the nine disappeared or extrajudicially killed republican exiles; the ability to kill one's critics with impunity further reflects and consolidates the power of the monarchy and its allies.

The fifth source of arbitrariness is "the proportionality of any measure in terms of the reasonable relationship of means and ends."[21] The minimum punishment per violation of Article 112 is three years and the maximum is fifteen years. There are no standard sentencing guidelines, but several examples illustrate the outsized punishments meted out to those who dissent. Daranee Charnchoengsilpakul, prosecuted in the first wave following the September 19, 2006, coup, was initially sentenced to eighteen years' imprisonment for three counts of violation of the law in relation to roughly fifty-five minutes of speech. Her sentence was reduced on appeal to fifteen years' imprisonment or roughly one year for each four minutes of speech.[22] Wichai, mentioned above as receiving the longest sentence during the NCPO regime, was initially sentenced to seventy years' imprisonment for ten Facebook posts, or seven years per post; his sentence was reduced to thirty-years once he confessed. These sentences cannot be understood as anything other than disproportionate.

Activists, lawyers, journalists, academics, and others kept up a steady challenge against the abuse of Article 112 and the accompanying forms of the arbitrary exercise of power that began with the September 2006 coup. Some defendants, like Daranee Charnchoengsilpakul, chose to fight their cases as a further form of protest even though they knew it would likely result in a harsher punishment. Lawyers provided pro bono defense for those accused and a few brave journalists reported on the cases. During the relatively open period of 2012, while Yingluck Shinawatra was prime minister, a coalition of academics, journalists, and others formed the Campaign Committee for the Amendment of Article 112 (CCAA112) to advocate for the amendment of the law so as to limit who could make accusations of violation of the law and reduce the possible punishment. CCAA112 used a constitutional provision enabling any citizen group that gathered enough signatures of support to propose the draft of a law for parliament to review, but parliament refused to even consider the draft on the basis of national security. Then, in the first few days following the May 22, 2014, coup, when the likely depth of the NCPO's repression

[21] *See* Chapter 1.

[22] Tyrell Haberkorn, *Engendering Sedition: Ethel Rosenberg, Daranee Charnchoengsilpakul, and the Courage of Refusal*, 24 Positions: E. Asia Cultures Critique 621 (2016).

became clear, lawyers and activists, many active during the preceding decade, joined together to establish TLHR, which became the primary documentary and advocacy organization defending dissidents. But while those active in challenging the arbitrary exercise of power were committed, their numbers remained small until 2020, when a movement emerged to name and directly counter the forms of arbitrariness and clarify the place of the monarchy in law and politics in defense of the rule of law.

## II A Movement Emerges

The disappearance of the ninth exiled republican critic, Wanchalearm Satsaksit, in Phnom Penh on June 4, 2020, catalyzed a wave of protests.[23] In June 2020, there had been no domestic transmission of the coronavirus for over two months, and while the emergency law prohibiting mass gatherings was still in place, activists began to assemble, initially to call for justice for Wanchalearm and the other disappeared and murdered republican exiles, and then to make broader demands for democracy. By July, regular protests were taking place in Bangkok and provinces around the country, organized by different groups of youth activists. Initially, the protests had three main demands. First, the current prime minister, General Prayuth Chan-ocha, must resign. General Prayuth governed for five years as head of the NCPO and then retained his position following the March 2019 general election through a series of antidemocratic maneuvers. The election was meant to mark the end of military dictatorship but instead signaled a new era of authoritarian repression cloaked in the form of electoral democracy.[24] Second, a new constitution must be drafted. The 2017 Constitution, Thailand's twentieth, was drafted by a junta-appointed body and expanded the authority of the state and king while dispossessing the people of rights.[25] Third, the state must stop threatening dissidents through both excessive legal prosecution and extrajudicial intimidation and violence.

[23] These nine are Ittiphol Sukphaen, Wuthipong Kachathamakal, Surachai Sae Daen, Chatcharn Buppawan, Kraidej Luelert, Chucheep Chiwasut, Sayam Theerawut, Krisana Thapthai, and Wanchalearm Satsaksit. To date, no arrests of possible perpetrators have been made and the investigations are stalled.

[24] Prajak Kongkirati, *Overview: Political Earthquakes*, 41 Contemp. Se. Asia 163 (2019).

[25] Khemthong Tonsakulrungruang, *Thailand: The State of Liberal Democracy*, 16 Int'l J. Const. L. 643 (2018).

In August 2020, a fourth demand was added: the institution of the monarchy must be reformed. The demand for reform of the institution of the monarchy was first publicly introduced by Arnon Nampa, a human rights lawyer at TLHR and poet, during a speech at a Hogwarts-themed protest on August 3, 2020. Dressed as Harry Potter, Arnon promised that he would speak openly about the institution of the monarchy from that day forward and called on others to do so. Arnon argued that without speaking openly about the monarchy, the other three demands of the protestors were meaningless and could not result in change. Speaking openly about the monarchy is both the first step and essential to curtailing the sources of arbitrariness in the polity. Foreseeing the impending backlash, he said that speaking about the monarchy.

> Is not the toppling of the monarchy. But it is talking about it so that the monarchy will exist in Thai society in manner that is correct and legitimate for a democracy with the king as head of state. All of the students who came out to protest after the new year are aware of this . . . . Do not leave it to those on the margins to have to talk about the monarchy and then face threats and harassment all alone. Do not leave it to the political exiles to talk about the monarchy and then be brutally murdered and disappeared. From now on, this is not going to happen anymore. From now on, no one who comes out to talk about the monarchy will be accused of being crazy or insane and scooped up and put in the hospital even though they spoke the truth.[26]

To make visible the forces behind the arbitrary exercise of power in the polity is threatening to those who benefit from such power.

A week later, on August 10, 2020, the United Front of Thammasat and Demonstration (UFTD), a new student organization based at Thammasat University, the historic center of student protest in Thailand, held a protest in which it unveiled a ten-point proposal that elaborated how to carry out the reform of the institution of the monarchy. The proposal, read by Panusaya Sitthijirawattanakul, a sociology and anthropology student at Thammasat and one of the leaders of the UFTD, included calls for restraints to be placed on the king's authority – importantly, including an end to royal endorsement of coups; for the personal, private assets of the king to be separated from the public assets of the crown financed by the people; for military units the king had placed under his own command to be transferred back to the usual chain of

[26] Arnon Nampa, The Monarchy and Thai Society 21 (2021). For the original Thai version, see อานนท์ นำภา, สถาบันพระมหากษัตริย์กับสังคมไทย (2020), https://tinyurl.com/3vvacz8y.

military command; for Article 112 to be abolished; and for justice to be secured in the cases of the disappeared and murdered republican exiles.[27] While the institution of the monarchy developed strong links to the military and the financial, landholding, industrial, and other forms of capital under Bhumipol, Maha Vajiralongkorn transferred public crown assets to his personal control and placed military units under his direct command.[28] The palace is not legally required to provide full financial transparency nor does it do so voluntarily. But *Al Jazeera* reported in January 2021 that King Vajiralongkorn was the world's wealthiest monarch, with a fortune of at least USD 30 billion and perhaps up to USD 70 billion.[29]

The UFTD's ten demands for reform became a staple of protests in the next months. They aimed to counter arbitrariness in the Thai polity by bringing the wielder of power under the law, ceasing the unpredictable exercise of power upon dissidents, and ending disproportionate punishment, or any punishment, for the peaceful expression of dissenting opinions. Most significantly, the demands and the broader movement were a direct claim to question and counter the arbitrary exercise of power.

## III A Backlash Ensues

After the August 3 and August 10, 2020, protests, many observers were concerned that speaking so frankly about the monarchy would frighten the majority of the people and end the budding democracy movement. Instead, the movement "shattered the ceiling" ("ทะลุเพดาน") of what could be said about the monarchy in public discussions in Thailand. For a time, Thailand seemed poised on the brink of tremendous change in terms of a transition to democracy, reform of the monarchy, and strengthening of the rule of law. But then a backlash began, marked by entrenchment of existing sources of arbitrariness.

Parit Chiwarak, another Thammasat University student and member of the UFTD, concluded a speech he gave in Khon Kaen province in

[27] For the full statement, see *The Demonstration at Thammasat Proposes Monarchy Reform*, PRACHATAI ENG (Aug. 11, 2020), https://prachatai.com/english/node/8709.

[28] On Bhumipol's links to capital, see PUANGCHON UNCHANAM, ROYAL CAPITALISM: WEALTH CLASS AND MONARCHY IN THAILAND (2020).

[29] *Thailand Protests: How Much Is the King Worth?*, AL JAZEERA (Jan. 30, 2021), https://tinyurl.com/2dsjnxtw.

northeastern Thailand on how the king's endorsement of coups had harmed society by noting that:

> Finally, as we are well aware of how our country works, I don't know that I will have another opportunity to say the things that I have said here in Khon Kaen. I don't know what will happen to me when I come down from the stage and leave. For those who do not think well of me, who think of using methods outside the law to harm me, do whatever you are going to do. But we have unmasked our struggle. If you do anything to us, if you do anything to me, we have only one enemy. We will all know who ordered it. Let me take this opportunity, before I do not have any more opportunities, to affirm to my brothers and sisters that as long as I am still breathing, I will struggle with you for our enduring ideals. If I have blundered, been careless, erred, or ever been offensive, I ask for forgiveness here.[30]

Parit's comments reflected his awareness of the nine disappeared and murdered republican exiles and the risk that those who speak about the monarchy incur. His choice of words – "We all will know who ordered it" – is both a critique of the king's power and a challenge to it in the form of speaking about it openly. Parit remains alive, but has twenty-four pending Article 112 cases against him. Were he to be convicted in even only a handful of these cases, this would result in a de facto life sentence. Beginning in November 2020, criminal cases began to be brought against activists who participated in demonstrations, particularly those who called for the reform of the monarchy, with many cases against Parit, Arnon, Panusaya, and other leaders and activists.[31] According to a TLHR report, between November 24, 2020, and June 26, 2023, at least 252 individuals have been arrested and charged with violation of Article 112.[32] The majority of these charges stem from peaceful, unarmed expression of opinion about the monarchy and its place in the Thai polity. Periods of denial of bail prior to trial have

[30] My translation. Parit Chiwarak, *Down With Feudalism, Long Live the People* [In Thai: พริษฐ์ ชิวารักษ์, ศักดินาจงพินาศ ประชาราษฎร์จงเจริญ], Demonstration organized by Khon Kaen Has Had Enough, Khon Kaen (Aug. 20, 2020).

[31] Parit is the activist facing the largest number of Article 112 cases. Arnon is currently facing fourteen; Panusaya is facing ten; and Panupong Jadnok, a Ramkhamhaeng University student and also UFTD activist, is currently facing nine. Although all four are currently released on bail, it could be revoked at any time. In addition, they are subject to extensive restrictions, including having to wear electronic monitoring anklets at all times.

[32] These numbers were last updated on June 26, 2023. For regular updates, see สถิติผู้ถูกดำเนินคดีมาตรา *112* [Statistics of those prosecuted in Article 112 cases], TLHR, https://tlhr2014.com/archives/23983.

become routine for those accused, and adherence to stringent bail conditions is required for those released. One of these conditions is to not participate in any further protest or do anything that might damage the monarchy, which is left unspecified in the release orders.

Alongside the criminal proceedings under Article 112, another judicial process related to the August 3 and 10, 2020, demonstrations illustrates the dwindling of the rule of law and the expansion of arbitrariness in Thailand. Article 49 of the 2017 Constitution permits anyone who believes that others are engaged in efforts to overthrow rule by democracy with the king as head of state to request that the Constitutional Court examine their actions, and for the cessation of such efforts to be ordered if found to constitute overthrow. Like the courts of justice as a whole, the Constitutional Court is closely linked to the institution of the monarchy.[33] First established following the promulgation of the 1997 Constitution, it comprises nine justices royally appointed following suggestion by royally connected institutions. The nine justices of the current court include three Supreme Court justices appointed by the Supreme Court, two Supreme Administrative Court justices appointed by the Supreme Administrative Court, and two legal experts and two political science experts appointed by the Senate, whose current members were appointed by the NCPO leaving office in 2019.

Article 49, which first appeared in the 1997 Constitution, was intended to protect against future coups. But in September 2020, Nattaporn Toprayoon, a royalist lawyer, submitted a petition to the Constitutional Court arguing that Arnon's speech on August 3 and the peaceful, unarmed demonstration by the UFTD at Thammasat University on August 10 and its ten-point proposal constituted an overthrow of

[33] Article 49 states:

> No person shall exercise the rights or liberties to overthrow the democratic regime of government with the king as head of state.
>
> Any person who has knowledge of an act under paragraph one shall have the right to petition to the attorney general to submit a motion to the Constitutional Court for an order to cease such act.
>
> In the case where the attorney general orders a refusal to proceed as petitioned or fails to proceed within fifteen days as from the date of receiving the petition, the person making the petition may submit the petition directly to the Constitutional Court.
>
> The action under this section shall not prejudice the criminal prosecution against the person committing an act under paragraph one.

democracy with the king as head of state.[34] In sloppy prose and with unclear logic, Nattaporn advanced a series of arguments aiming to discredit and vilify the activists. He denied the activists' claim that they aimed to reform the institution of the monarchy and instead argued that they aimed to create disorder and division.

There were two key slippages in his argument. The first is that he did not define the meaning of a system of rule by democracy with the king as head of state and instead argued that the activists disrespected and wished to overthrow the monarchy. While Article 49 of the Constitution applies specifically to the system of rule, accusing the activists of aiming to overthrow the monarchy is a much stronger, and (for the activists) more dangerous, argument to make. Nattaporn's second slippage is complementary. He collapsed the meaning of opposition and overthrow into one another.[35] This move fails to recognize the role of peaceful opposition in building and sustaining democracy. Rather than a clear argument as to how the activists' peaceful speeches constituted, or would even lead to or prompt, overthrow of rule by democracy with the

[34] The Constitutional Court has been involved in many highly politicized cases since September 19, 2006, coup. *See* Andrew Harding & Peter Leyland, THE CONSTITUTIONAL SYSTEM OF THAILAND: A CONTEXTUAL ANALYSIS (2011); Eugénie Mérieau, *Thailand's Deep State, Royal Power and the Constitutional Court (1997–2015)*, 46 J. CONTEMP. ASIA 445 (2016); Khemthong Tongsakulrungruang, *The Constitutional Court of Thailand: From Activism to Arbitrariness*, *in* CONSTITUTIONAL COURTS IN ASIA: A COMPARATIVE ANALYSIS 184 (Albert H.Y. Chen & Andrew Harding eds., 2018); DUNCAN MCCARGO, FIGHTING FOR VIRTUE: JUSTICE AND POLITICS IN THAILAND (2020) (especially ch. 8, *Courting Constitutionalism*, 184–210).

[35] He wrote:

> The words "overthrow" and "opponent" are not defined in law. But these two words are ordinary words in the Thai language that have commonly used and known meanings. Therefore, the court itself knows that overthrow refers to actions with the intention to destroy or devastate in order to cause to cease to exist, to not be preserved, or to no longer have. Regarding the word opponent, it does not have to have to be violent to the degree of having the intention to overthrow and destroy until it no longer exists. It does not have to be to the degree of positioning oneself as the enemy or the opposite side only. It is simply action characterized by the characteristic of being obstructive or blocking to keep from progressing. Or actions that cause there to be the impact of erosion, sabotage until it falls into disrepair and decay, or becomes weaker. This falls within the category of acting as an opponent already.

Petition for Constitutional Court to Rule According to Article 49, *in* JUST. IN SE. ASIA LAB, UNIV. OF WIS.-MADISON CTR. FOR SE. ASIAN STUD., CONSTITUTIONAL COURT RULING NO. 19/2564: A SELECTION OF DOCUMENTS 9, 45 (Tyrell Haberkorn trans., Dec. 2021) [hereinafter CONSTITUTIONAL COURT RULING].

king as head of state, Nattaporn instead repeatedly claimed that the speeches made him and others who loved the king uneasy.[36] Nattaporn included extensive quotes from the activists' speeches in his complaint, but the quotations called his argument into question.

The three activists named in the petition – Arnon, Panusaya, and Panupong Jadnok, a student at Ramkhamhaeng University and member of the UFTD – were limited to submitting a written response to his petition. They explained that they were calling for reform, not overthrow, of the institution of the monarchy; challenged the vagueness of his argument; and indicated their willingness to provide verbal testimony to the Constitutional Court if needed.[37] Despite the gravity and complexity of the case, neither the three activists nor the academics and other

[36] *E.g.*, *id.* at 44, 45:

> The aforementioned speeches at the times, dates, and locations contain content that gravely distorts, encroaches upon, ridicules, and defames the institution of the monarchy such as has never occurred. The actions of the aforementioned group of people have caused the Thai people who love the nation, religion, and king to be aware and see the images and actions of the overconfident daring of the protestors. They are gravely concerned and worried that this group of youth of the nation have this attitude and expression that is an overconfident ridiculing like this. It is action that has the intention to overthrow rule by democracy with the king as head of state.
>
> The Petitioner, as a Thai person, feels very disappointed and uneasy about the aforementioned expression of this group of people, along with the students, professors, politicians, former politicians, as in Document No. 8 who claim that the aforementioned actions are the exercise of fundamental rights according to democracy and are not against the law. In addition, they claim that these demands are not a proposal to overthrow the institution of the monarchy, but are a proposal with good intentions so that the institution of the monarchy can continue to be idolized by the people under a democracy.

[37] Their response to the accusation of overthrow is particularly important:

> The petition submitted by the Petitioner is ambiguous and unclear. That is, Article 49 of the 2017 Constitution of the Kingdom of Thailand stipulates that no person shall exercise their rights or freedoms to overthrow rule by democracy with the king as head of state. But the Petitioner's petition does not clarify how the three Respondents exercised their rights or freedoms to overthrow rule. Namely, from the content of the petition, the Petitioner does not describe the meaning, essence, and constituent elements of rule by democracy with the king as head of state. The facts and accusations that the Petitioner describes are vague and the Petitioner does not specify which rights or freedoms the three Respondents exercised, or what actions were the overthrow of rule by democracy with the king as head of state. For example, the Petitioner describes the facts about the "Thammasat Won't Stand For It"

experts they prepared as witnesses were allowed by the Constitutional Court to provide verbal testimony. When arbitrariness reigns, those who hold power are seen as beyond question and those who challenge it beyond reason.

The Constitutional Court spent over a full year considering the petition. In November 2021, the Constitutional Court ruled that the activists' actions constituted overthrow of rule by democracy with the king as head of state and ordered them to cease their activities immediately. An abbreviated version was read on November 10, 2021, and the full ruling was released on November 29, 2021. The Constitutional Court framed its ruling by recounting the facts and describing the context of the case in a way that favored Nattaporn. The Constitutional Court discounted any need to protect human rights by emphasizing the performance of duty and maintenance of good morals rather than freedom of expression. The Court placed duty in relation to a narrative of Thai history that centered the king as an unchanging, central figure in the polity, whose role was unaffected by the events of June 24, 1932. Like Nattaporn, the Constitutional Court opted not to believe the activists when they said that their intention was to reform the institution of the monarchy in order to preserve it. Relying on an unusual definition of overthrow, the Constitutional Court therefore concluded that the activists were engaged in overthrow of rule by democracy with the king as head of state and ordered them to immediately cease their activities.[38] The ruling rendered by the Constitutional Court was one in which the Constitution was

> demonstration on August 10, 2020, by recounting the event, but does not specify which actions or words of the three Respondents are overthrow of democracy with the king as head of state. In addition, on page 22 of the petition, the Petitioner describes Constitutional Court Ruling No. 3/2562 that provides the meanings of the words "overthrow" and "opponent," which have different meanings. Then the Petitioner discusses the expression of opinions by Mr. Piyabutr Saengkanokkul, Mr. Parit Chiwarak, and Mr. Jatuporn Prompan in which they mentioned the institution of the monarchy. This is neither an action by the three Respondents nor related to the actions of the three Respondents in any way. In addition, the petition does not describe how the ten proposed demands to address the problems about the institution of the monarchy are overthrow of rule by democracy with the king as head of state. The Petitioner merely describes his own feelings and opinions.

Counter Statement by Respondents, *in* CONSTITUTIONAL COURT RULING, *supra* note 35, at 59, 59–60.

[38] Constitutional Court Ruling No. 19/2564, *in* CONSTITUTIONAL COURT RULING., *supra* note 35, at 80, 113–14:

interpreted in such a way as to further unquestioning valorization of the monarchy as the only perspective possible, at the expense of the protection of rights and freedom of expression.

One of the initial concerns when the Constitutional Court's ruling was announced was whether Arnon, Panusaya, Panupong, and other activists already facing numerous Article 112 cases would also be charged with violation of Article 113, or treason, which carries a maximum penalty of life imprisonment or death. This has not happened. But the potential impacts, both short-term and long-term, of the Constitutional Court ruling on the provision of justice, the rule of law, and the visions of a democratic future that dissidents imagine remain unclear.

> The exercise of rights and freedoms of Respondents No. 1, No. 2, and No. 3 is not in line with the principles of democracy. The actions of Respondents No. 1, No. 2, and No. 3 are the claiming of rights and freedoms without taking equality and fraternity into consideration. Respondents No. 1, No. 2, and No. 3 exercised their freedom of expression and did not listen to the opinions of other people. They did not accept views that were different and violated the rights of other people by reviling them, invading their personal space, and agitating and inciting using facts that distorted reality. Facts and eyewitness evidence show that Respondents No. 1, No. 2, and No. 3 have organized groups in the form of a network to use violence continuously. In some instances, Respondents No. 1, No. 2, and No. 3 have used provocative parts of their speeches to stir up violence and create disharmony among the people in the nation. This has created division among the people in the nation and is the destruction of the principles of equality and fraternity. The effect of the actions of Respondents No. 1, No. 2, and No. 3 will be to ultimately overthrow democracy. In addition, the facts show that in many demonstrations there was destruction of portraits of the king. There was the removal of the blue sections from the national flag, which means the removal of the institution of the monarchy from the national flag. The ten demands of Respondents No. 1, No. 2, and No. 3, such as the revoking of Article 6 of the Constitution, the abolishing of the giving and receiving of donations by royal charity funds, the abolishing of the royal prerogative to express political opinions in public, are demands to cause the status of the institution of the monarchy to not be as it is in the tradition of democratic rule to which the Thai nation has always adhered. The continuous conduct and actions of Respondents No. 1, No. 2, and No. 3 illustrate that Respondents No. 1, No. 2, and No. 3 had the ulterior motive to exercise their rights and freedoms to overthrow rule by democracy with the king as head of state. It is not reform.

## IV Working against Arbitrariness and toward the Rule of Law

The ongoing arrests and prosecutions under Article 112 have heightened the risks of questioning power and its unjust exercise in Thailand. While the majority of those accused have ultimately been granted bail, including the leaders discussed earlier – Arnon, Panusaya, Panupong, and Parit – their release has carried the condition of nonparticipation in political protest or other activities that might damage the monarchy. The frequency of protests declined as arrests took place throughout 2021 and 2022, but did not stop completely.

One of the most compelling new groups to emerge is Shattering the Palace (ทะลุวัง), whose primary protest action is to carry out public polls. Activists go to shopping malls, train stations, and selected public events armed with posterboards and small stickers for respondents to indicate their views on various topics about the monarchy. For daring to ask these questions, members of the group have been arrested, charged with violation of Article 112, and subjected to long periods of pretrial detention. One stark example is the case of Tantawan Tuatulanon, released on May 26, 2022, after thirty-seven days of pretrial detention following accusation of violation of Article 112 for live broadcasting and peacefully asking the police questions about the monarchy prior to a royal motorcade. She was on hunger strike for the entire period of her detention in protest at the denial of bail. Her lawyers made four applications for bail for her before the Criminal Court finally assented. She is confined to her home for twenty-four hours per day, must wear an electronic monitoring anklet, and is forbidden from participating in protests or damaging the monarchy.

Two additional members of Thaluwang, Bung and Bai Por, were held for ninety-one days of pretrial detention, including sixty-four days on hunger strike, after carrying out a poll at a shopping mall on whether or not royal motorcades caused inconvenience. They made seven bail requests before it was finally granted; each denial order noted that their lives were not yet in danger from their hunger strike and they were flight risks and would likely continue to engage in similar actions were bail to be granted. During one bail hearing, after being on hunger strike for fifty-four days, the two young women were so weakened by the trip from the Central Women's Prison where they are being detained that they collapsed and were rushed to the nearest hospital for treatment; the physician on duty reported to the court that they were in "normal" condition. Pretrial bail has long been denied in a majority of Article 112 cases, but the Thaluwang cases are different, both due to the nature of the action deemed to potentially constitute lese majesty and the court's lack of concern about the health of the detainees. To be clear, while individuals accused of violent crime are routinely granted bail in Thailand, all three Thaluwang activists were subject to denial of bail and arbitrary detention for asking questions and carrying out a poll about royal motorcades.

In the May 2023 general election, the second since the May 2014 coup, the liberal democratic Move Forward Party secured the largest number of votes and a clear popular mandate to form a government. They ran on a platform of policies that included legalization of same-sex marriage, the end of compulsory military conscription, and amendment of Article 112 to reduce the punishment. But very soon after the election it became clear that the monarchy and military-aligned forces would not allow Move Forward Party to form a government. One of the legacies of the NCPO period is that the parliament is composed of 500 elected members and 250 senators who were appointed by the junta. A petition was submitted to the Constitutional Court in late June 2023, alleging that Move Forward Party's proposal to amend Article 112 constituted overthrow of the government. Like the Constitutional Court petition brought against Arnon, Panusaya, and Panupong, this one verges on the absurd: How could a policy proposal conceivably constitute overthrow? Yet the possible effects of the petition are potentially profound. The petition was brought a week before the planned election of the prime minister in the parliament, and many neutral members of parliament and even some senators who had previously indicated they would vote for Pita Limjaroenrat, the Move Forward Party candidate, opted to abstain, likely out of concern of being perceived to support an anti-monarchy party. Instead, in August 2023, a coalition made up of parties loyal to the military and monarchy, which secured few votes, formed a government and selected a prime minister whose party did not win the popular vote. A year later, in August 2024, the Constitutional Court ruled that the Move Forward Party's proposal of an amendment to Article 112 constituted overthrow. The party was dissolved and its executive banned from holding political office for ten years.

## V Conclusion: Toward a Future Rule of Law

The rise in arbitrariness and attacks on the rule of law in Thailand come at a time when authoritarianism is on the rise across Asia. A military court in Myanmar on February 1, 2021, ended the cautious transition to democracy and brought a sharp crackdown. Dissidents are subject to arbitrary arrest and summary sentencing in secret trials.[39] Since the presidential election of Rodrigo Duterte in 2016 and with little change following the election of Bongbong Marcos, Ferdinand Marcos's son, in 2022, extrajudicial killings, attacks on press and academic freedom, and a general climate deleterious to the rule of law have become entrenched in the Philippines.[40] The rule of law in Hong Kong has declined precipitously as China has claimed legal and political control far in advance of 2047, the previously agreed-upon date of incorporation into China. Activists, journalists, and academics are facing increasing prosecutions under the draconian National Security Law for engaging in basic expression of opinion and political rights.[41] Compounding the difficulty in stopping the rise of arbitrariness and the violation of human rights is that, unlike the Americas, Europe, or Africa, there are no regional or subregional human rights mechanisms. The governments in the region make it a practice to cite the inviolability of sovereignty whenever they are called upon to criticize their neighbors. While the region remains safe for capital, as Ji Li notes regarding China in this volume (in Chapter 13), it is increasingly unsafe for dissidents.

Writing in the context of Putin's Russia, Masha Gessen argues that: "In functioning democracies the contradictions between avowed ideals and reality can be and often are called out, causing social and political change. That does not eliminate the built-in gap, but it has a way of making societies a little more democratic and a little less unequal, in spurts. Totalitarian ideology allows no such correction."[42] The fine-grained framework to examine the rule of law developed in this book by Shaffer and Sandholtz is a key tool to discover and call out gaps between ideals and reality in disparate contexts. Rather than seeing a possible trajectory in which challenges to the rule of law in Thailand, which have been particularly grave since the May 22, 2014, coup, are reversed, the situation remains challenging despite some elements that seem to signal

[39] Assistance Ass'n for Pol. Prisoners (Burma), The Flow of Injustice (July 2023), https://tinyurl.com/47hxs2m9.

[40] For an account of the human rights situation from the perspective of a journalist who has documented and fought against it, see Maria Ressa, How to Stand Up to a Dictator: Fighting for Our Future (2022).

[41] Thomas E. Kellogg & Eric Yan-Ho Lai, *The Tong Ying-Kit NSL Verdict: An International and Comparative Law Analysis* (GCAL Briefing Paper, Oct. 20, 2021), https://tinyurl.com/mrxmn3mn.

[42] Masha Gessen, The Future is History: How Totalitarianism Reclaimed Russia 97–98 (2017).

positive developments, such as elections. The Constitutional Court of Thailand's characterization of peaceful dissent and policy proposals as overthrow, with correspondingly harsh consequences, is an expression of the arbitrary exercise of power par excellence. Our job as scholars is to track, analyze, and criticize the means and methods by which such undermining of the rule of law takes place, as part of our contribution to strengthening it.

13

# The Evolving Rule of Law with Chinese Characteristics and Its Impacts on the International Legal Order

JI LI

## I The Evolving Rule of Law with Chinese Characteristics

The development of the Chinese legal system and discourse on law and governance have in the past four decades undergone major shifts[1] that have spawned a great deal of insightful research.[2] However, much of the accumulated scholarship has adopted a state-centered approach,

For valuable comments, the author thanks Greg Shaffer, Wayne Sandholtz, Martin Krygier, Tom Ginsburg, Anne Peters, Terry Halliday, Alejandro Ponce, Jens Meierhenrich, Tyrell Haberkorn, and other participants and attendants at the University of Caliornia, Irvine School of Law symposium on the rule of law in transnational context. The author also thanks Kangdi Cheng, Ryan Riedmueller, Miranda Tafoya, Jacob Greenstein, Haley Trudell, Yiching Yang, Veronica Ying, and Megan Qiyu Wang.

1 The focus on elite discourse is not to deny that the Chinese masses may have incongruent interests and that the popular narratives of domestic and international legal order may "diverge in certain ways from the official and academic discourses," or to deny that the divergence matters in an increasingly populist political climate. But given the ability of the Chinese government to manipulate public opinion, its effect, if any, would be largely endogenous and better left for future research. Pitman B Potter, *China and the International Legal System: Challenges of Participation*, 191 China Q. 701 (2007).

2 *See, e.g.*, Ruiping Ye, *Shifting Meanings of Fazhi and China's Journey Toward Socialist Rule of Law*, 19 Int'l J. Const. L. 1859 (2021); Zhang Wenxian (张文显), *Fazhi Yu Guojia Zhili Xiandaihua* (法治与国家治理现代化) [The rule of law and modernization of national governance], Zhongguo Faxue (Wen Zhai) (中国法学(文摘)) [China Legal Sci. (Dig.)], no. 4, 2014,at 5; Benjamin L. Liebman, *Legal Reform: China's Law-Stability Paradox*, 143 Daedalus 96 (2014); Qianfan Zhang, *The Communist Party Leadership and Rule of Law: A Tale of Two Reforms*, 30 J. Contemp. China 578 (2021); Taisu Zhang & Tom Ginsburg, *China's Turn Toward Law*, 59 Va. J. Int'l L. 306 (2019); Albert H.Y. Chen, *China's Long March Towards Rule of Law or China's Turn Against Law?*, 4 Chinese J. Comp. L. 1 (2016); Carl Minzner, *China's Turn Against Law*, 59 Am. J. Comp. L. 935 (2011); Jianfu Chen, Chinese law: context and transformation 39–75 (2008); Stanley B. Lubman, Bird in a Cage: Legal Reform in China After Mao 1–39 (1999); Randall Peerenboom, *The Battle over*

neglecting interest and normative divisions within the regime[3] and underappreciating the influence of China's international context. Authoritarian states are neither monolithic nor static.[4] Shifting dynamics of domestic elite politics change policy priorities and modify the official perceptions and preferences about law and governance, as well as the academic debates. Meanwhile, as in other countries, scholarly debates in China also have direct impacts on the legal reforms and subtle effects on the official narratives about the rule of law.[5] Moreover, post-Cultural Revolution China increasingly interacts with the rest of the world, and the interactions have led to domestic realignment of power and facilitated exchanges of ideas.[6] Thus, the following analytical survey of Chinese legal reform and rule of law discourse incorporates three interwoven aspects: political contestations among Chinese ruling elites, academic debates about law and governance, and China's interactions with the outside world.

Soon after taking power in 1949, the Chinese Communist Party (CCP) formed an alliance with the Soviet Union and imported its model of legal institutions and legal education. Though the alliance collapsed,[7] the inchoate Chinese legal institutions continued to operate according to the Soviet design, and Soviet-trained teachers dominated Chinese law schools,

*Legal Reforms in China: Has There Been a Turn Against Law?*, 2 Chinese J. Comp. L. 188 (2014).

3 The divisions within the authoritarian state have been well documented elsewhere. *See, e.g.*, Jessica Chen Weiss & Jeremy L. Wallace, *Domestic Politics, China's Rise, and the Future of the Liberal International Order*, 75 Int'l Org. 636, 651 (2021); Andrew Mertha, *"Fragmented Authoritarianism 2.0": Political Pluralization in the Chinese Policy Process*, 200 China Q. 995 (2009); Min Ye, *Fragmentation and Mobilization: Domestic Politics of the Belt and Road in China*, 28 J. Contemp. China 696 (2019); Kenneth Lieberthal & Michel Oksenberg, Policy Making in China: Leaders, Structures, and Processes 137–49 (1988).

4 Weiss & Wallace, *supra* note 3, at 643.

5 Chris Alden & Daniel Large, *On Becoming a Norms Maker: Chinese Foreign Policy, Norms Evolution and the Challenges of Security in Africa*, 221 China Q. 123 (2015).

6 Weiss & Wallace, *supra* note 3, at 643.

7 Cai Dingjian (蔡定剑), *Guanyu Qiansulianfa Dui Zhongguo Fazhi Jianshe de Yingxiang: Jianguo Yilai Faxuejie Zhongda Shijian Yanjiu (22)* (关于前苏联法对中国法制建设的影响: 建国以来法学界重大事件研究 (22)) [On the influence of the laws of the former Soviet Union on the construction of China's legal system: Research on major events in the legal circle since the founding of the People's Republic of China (22)], Faxue (法学) [Legal Sci. Monthly], no. 5, 1999, at 2; Sun Guangyan (孙光妍) & Yu Yisheng (于逸生), Sulianfa Yingxiang Zhongguo Fazhi Fazhan Jincheng zhi Huigu (苏联法影响中国法制发展进程之回顾) [A Review of the Soviet Influence on the Development of the Legal System in China], Faxue Yanjiu (法学研究) [Chinese J.L.], no. 1, 2003, at 139.

indoctrinating students with the Marxist and Leninist view of courts as a tool for social ordering and class oppression.[8] The basic institutional structure for socialist rule by law, however, suffered severe damages during the Cultural Revolution (1966–76), which paralyzed much of the state apparatus. At the time, all Chinese law schools were shut down, along with any meaningful academic debate about law and governance.[9]

Mao's death in 1976 paved the way for the ascent of Deng Xiaoping and his allies, who ended the "legal nihilism" and ushered in an era of reform.[10] Having personally suffered the chaotic and arbitrary rule of Mao's totalitarian dictatorship, the reformers deemed rule of man to be "very dangerous, not reliable"[11] and were determined to reestablish basic legal institutions. For instance, the first order issued in 1979 by the resurrected Standing Committee of the National People's Congress (SCNPC) amended the Regulations of the People's Republic of China on Arrest and Detention, which provided better legal protection for individual freedom and imposed more stringent procedural requirements for its deprivation.[12] Meanwhile, Chinese courts and procuratorates reclaimed their authority, enforcing a growing number of statutes aimed at preserving political, social, and economic order. This period between the end of the Cultural Revolution and Deng's Southern Tour in 1992 featured pragmatic institutional experiments, policy uncertainties, and intense political debates. While a faction of the ruling elites advocated political reforms that would create a more liberal and democratic state relatively separated from the CCP,[13] the conservative faction strongly opposed the "corrosive influence of bourgeois ideas."[14]

This same period witnessed a sea change in Chinese academic discourse on law, as law schools and departments reopened and law professors were reinstated. While many of them received direct or indirect Soviet-style

[8] Gu Peidong (顾培东), *Dangdai Zhongguo Fazhi Huayu Tixi de Goujian* (当代中国法治话语体系的构建) [Construction of Chinese discourse system of rule of law], FAXUE YANJIU (法学研究) [Chinese J.L.], no. 3, 2012, at 3, 5.

[9] Carl F. Minzner, *The Rise and Fall of Chinese Legal Education*, 36 FORDHAM INT'L L.J. 334 (2013).

[10] Carlos Wing-Hung Lo, *Socialist Legal Theory in Deng Xiaoping's China*, 11 COLUM. J. ASIAN L. 469 (1997).

[11] Zhang Wenxian, *supra* note 2, at 14.

[12] Zhonghua Renmin Gongheguo Daibu Juliu Tiaoli (中华人民共和国逮捕拘留条例) [Regulations of People's Republic of China on arrest and detention] (promulgated by the Standing Comm. Nat'l People's Cong., Feb. 23, 1979, effective Feb. 23, 1979, abolished Mar. 17, 1996), https://pkulaw.com/chl/503.html?tiao=0.

[13] Zhang Wenxian, *supra* note 2, at 582.

[14] Kalpana Misra, *Neo-left and Neo-right in Post-Tiananmen China*, 43 ASIAN SURV. 717, 720 (2003).

legal training,[15] China's opening-up policy allowed legal scholars access to Western political and legal thought. Having personally suffered the lawless atrocities of the Cultural Revolution, many became highly receptive to core tenets of liberalism and the rule of law.[16] For them, the ultimate objective of legal reform in China should be to achieve legal constraint over state power. In that regard, their voice resonated with a cohort of reformers among the CCP leaders. For instance, Peng Zhen, then chairman of the Legal Committee of SCNPC, insisted that "the law be superior to the Party."[17] The normative tensions among the ruling elites manifest in the drafting and promulgation of the Administrative Litigation Law of the People's Republic of China in 1989, which for the first time in Chinese history codified a rather comprehensive statutory procedure for victims of governmental mistreatment to seek legal remedy,[18] yet at the same time exempted actions taken by the CCP from such challenges.

Deng's Southern Tour in 1992 moved the factional balance decisively in favor of the reformers, who undertook a series of structural reforms.[19] To establish a "Socialist market economy," a wide range of enabling institutions were put in place that embodied major attributes of their Western equivalents. To expedite and consolidate the reform, the pro-market faction negotiated China's entry into the WTO.[20] Its subsequent integration into the global economy further strengthened the reformers and facilitated the implementation of their policy agenda.[21] Meanwhile, the official narrative on law shifted from enacting laws and reestablishing basic legal institutions

[15] *See* Gu, *supra* note 8, at 4–5; William Partlett & Eric C. Ip, *Is Socialist Law Really Dead*, 48 NYU J. INT'L L. & POL. 463, 465–66 (2015).

[16] Zhang Wenxian, *supra* note 2, at 581; Xie Libin & Haig Patapan, *Schmitt Fever: The Use and Abuse of Carl Schmitt in Contemporary China*, 18 INT'L J. CONST. L. 141 (2020).

[17] Zhang Wen, Shen Xinwang Wen & Shu Lin (章文, 申欣旺 & 文舒琳), *Lifa Liu Jin Suiyue* (立法流金岁月) [Golden Times of Legislation], ZHONGGUO XINWENZHOUKAN (中国新闻周刊) [Chinese News Wkly.], no. 2010044 (Nov. 30, 2010).

[18] The General Principles of the Civil Law also contained language that allowed citizens to sue government officials in certain circumstances. Ji Li, *Suing the Leviathan: An Empirical Analysis of the Changing Rate of Administrative Litigation in China*, 10 J. EMPIRICAL LEGAL STUD. 815 (2013).

[19] Ji Li, *A Chinese Model for Tax Reforms in Developing Countries?*, *in* THE BEIJING CONSENSUS? HOW CHINA HAS CHANGED THE WESTERN IDEAS OF LAW AND ECONOMIC DEVELOPMENT AND GLOBAL LEGAL PRACTICES 189 (Weitseng Chen ed., 2017); *see* Misra, *supra* note 14.

[20] Ka Zeng, *Domestic Politics and the US-China WTO Agreement*, 37 ISSUES & STUD. 105 (2001).

[21] Julia Ya Qin, *The Impact of WTO Accession on China's Legal System*, 2 SUNGKYUNKWAN J. SCI. & TECH. L. 253 (2008).

to promoting the "rule of law,"[22] and considerable efforts were made to professionalize the judiciary and elevate its status.[23] For instance, the Judges Law of the People's Republic of China was enacted in 1995 and established merit-based staffing of Chinese courts, which used to recruit from retired military officers without any formal legal training.[24] Also, as shown in Figures 13.1 and 13.2, the number of civil and administrative lawsuits surged in the first half of this period. However, the official narrative of legal reform no longer contemplated the separation of the CCP from the state organs, including the judiciary. Without major reform of the political–legal structure, Chinese courts, subject to various institutional constraints such as personnel and resource control by local CCP leadership and other government bodies, proved less effective in resolving disputes than expected or portrayed by the reformers. And, the number of civil and administrative cases plateaued in the second half of this period (see Figures 13.1 and 13.2).

The contemporaneous debates in the legal academy largely continued the liberal trajectory.[25] Growing interactions with international actors socialized

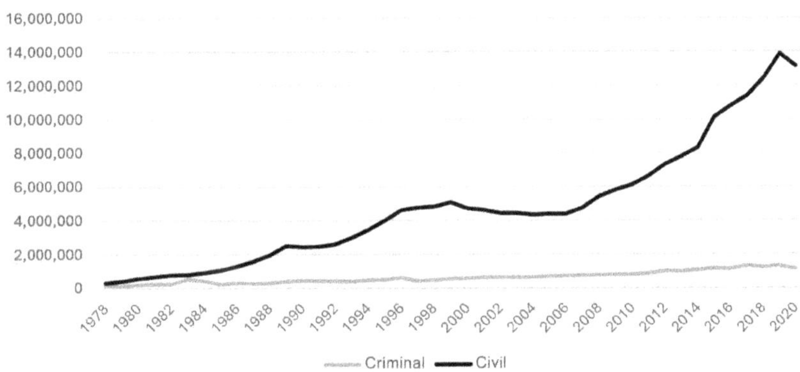


**Figure 13.1** Number of first instance civil and criminal cases in China (1978–2020). Source: *China Statistical Yearbook 2021* [Table 24-18], www.stats.gov.cn/tjsj/ndsj/2021/indexch.htm

22 Susan Trevaskes, *A Law unto Itself: Chinese Communist Party Leadership and Yifa Zhiguo in the Xi Era*, 44 MOD. CHINA 347, 348 (2018).

23 Zhang Wenxian, *supra* note 2, at 579.

24 Zhonghua Renmin Gongheguo Faguan Fa (中华人民共和国法官法) [Judges law of China] (promulgated by the Standing Comm. of the Nat'l People's Cong., Feb. 28, 1995), www.npc.gov.cn/zgrdw/npc/xinwen/2019-04/23/content_2086082.htm.

25 Yang Jianjun (杨建军), *Zhongguo Fazhi Fazhan: Yibanxing yu Teshuxing zhi Jianrong* (中国法治发展：一般性与特殊性之兼容) [The development of China's rule of law:

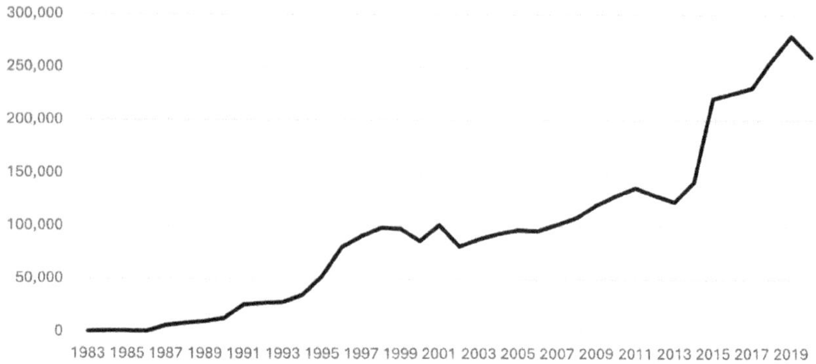


**Figure 13.2** Number of first instance administrative cases in China (1983–2020). Source: *China Statistical Yearbook 2021* [Table 24-18], www.stats.gov.cn/tjsj/ndsj/2021/indexch.htm

Chinese officials, scholars, and practitioners in varying degrees to core liberal norms.[26] At one point, Western legal theories so dominated the jurisprudential discourse in China that a prominent legal scholar expressed grave concerns about his colleagues' collective "cultural aphasia."[27] However, this marked shift in discourse and massive institutional transplantation also sparked backlashes. The tensions peaked and triggered nationwide debates in 2005 and 2006 when the reformers' plan to enact a property law based on German law principles was temporarily shelved after a legal scholar trained in the former Yugoslavia published an open letter alleging the protection of private property ownership would undermine the socialist nature of the Chinese political system as enshrined in the Constitution,[28] galvanizing fierce resistance from the conservative faction. While the national legislature eventually adopted the property law as proposed, Chinese socio-legal scholars have since

Compatibility of generality and particularity], BIJIAOFA YANJIU (比较法研究) [Comp. L.], no. 4, 2017, at 155, 170; Libin & Patapan, *supra* note 16, at 139.

[26] Scott Wilson, *Seeking One's Day in Court: Chinese Regime Responsiveness to International Legal Norms on AIDS Carriers' and Pollution Victims' Rights*, 21 J. CONTEMP. CHINA 863 (2012).

[27] Xia Yong (夏勇), *Fazhi Shi Shenme? Yuanyuan, Guijie yu Jiazhi* (法治是什么? 渊源, 规诫与价值) [What is rule of law? Origin, admonitions and values], ZHONGGUO SHEHUI KEXUE (中国社会科学) [Soc. Sci. Chi.], no. 4, 1999, at 142.

[28] Andreas Møller Mulvad, *China's Ideological Spectrum: A Two-Dimensional Model of Elite Intellectuals' Visions*, 47 THEORY & SOC'Y 635 (2018); Joseph Fewsmith, *China in 2007: The Politics of Leadership Transition*, 48 ASIAN SURV. 82 (2008).

demonstrated more interest in value-neutral comparisons with foreign legal systems,[29] as well as in rediscovering the values of China's domestic institutions for resolving disputes and delivering substantive justice.[30] Interestingly, as shown in Figure 13.3(a), the rule-of-law discourse outside China also reached a turning point around the year 2006. Given how tightly China had been integrated in the global system at the time, the rebalancing of the rule-of-law debate in China might have simply reflected the global trend.

The power dynamics within the Chinese ruling elites tilted further in favor of the conservatives after 2008, when the global financial crisis severely eroded the normative appeal of free market capitalism and its enabling institutions, and the massive stimulus program implemented by the Chinese government to salvage the economy materially empowered the state sector. A systematic "turn against law" ensued.[31] The leadership began to emphasize the role of Chinese courts to construct a "harmonious society."[32] Remarkably, an official without any formal legal training was appointed president of the Supreme People's Court in 2008 and promoted a "Three Supremes" doctrine: "in enforcing the law, judges should take into account first the supremacy of the Party's undertaking, second the supremacy of the popular interest, and only third the supremacy of the law."[33] During this period, the academic discourse on law and governance also intensified.[34] While the "legally trained elites" continued to favor "more expansive, liberal and state-constraining conceptions of law,"[35]

[29] *See, e.g.*, Zheng Chengliang (郑成良) & Zhang Yingxia (张英霞), *Zhongmei Liangguo Sifa Linian de Bijiao* (中美两国司法理念的比较) [Comparative analysis on judicial notion in China and the United States], FAZHI YU SHEHUI FAZHAN (法制与社会发展) [L. & Soc. Dev.], no. 2, 2003, at 3, 9.

[30] Su Li (苏力), *Bianfa, Fazhi Jianshe Jiqi Bentu Ziyuan* (变法, 法治建设及其本土资源) [Reform, rule of law, and its local resources], ZHONGWAI FAXUE (中外法学) [Peking U. L.J.], no. 5, 1995, at 1; SU LI (苏立), SONG FA XIAXIANG: ZHONGGUO JICENG SIFA ZHIDU YANJIU (送法下乡: 中国基层司法制度研究) [Sending law to the countryside: A study on the grassroot-level judicial system in China] (2000).

[31] Minzner, *supra* note 2; Benjamin L. Liebman, *A Return to Populist Legality? Historical Legacies and Legal Reform, in* MAO'S INVISIBLE HAND: THE POLITICAL FOUNDATIONS OF ADAPTIVE GOVERNANCE IN CHINA 165 (Sebastian Heilmann & Elizabeth J. Perry eds., 2011).

[32] Liebman, *supra* note 2.

[33] Rogier Creemers, *Party Ideology and Chinese Law, in* LAW AND THE PARTY IN CHINA: IDEOLOGY AND ORGANISATION 31 (Rogier Creemers & Susan Trevaskes eds., 2020).

[34] He Li, *Chinese Discourse on Constitutionalism and Its Impact on Reforms*, 22 J. CHINESE POL. SCI. 407, 413 (2017).

[35] Jacques deLisle, *Law in the China Model 2.0: Legality, Developmentalism and Leninism Under Xi Jinping*, 26 J. CONTEMP. CHINA 68, 82 (2017).

**Figure 13.3(a)** Google NGram search result by “rule of law” from 1949 to 2019: frequency with which the term appeared in English publications during the search period.

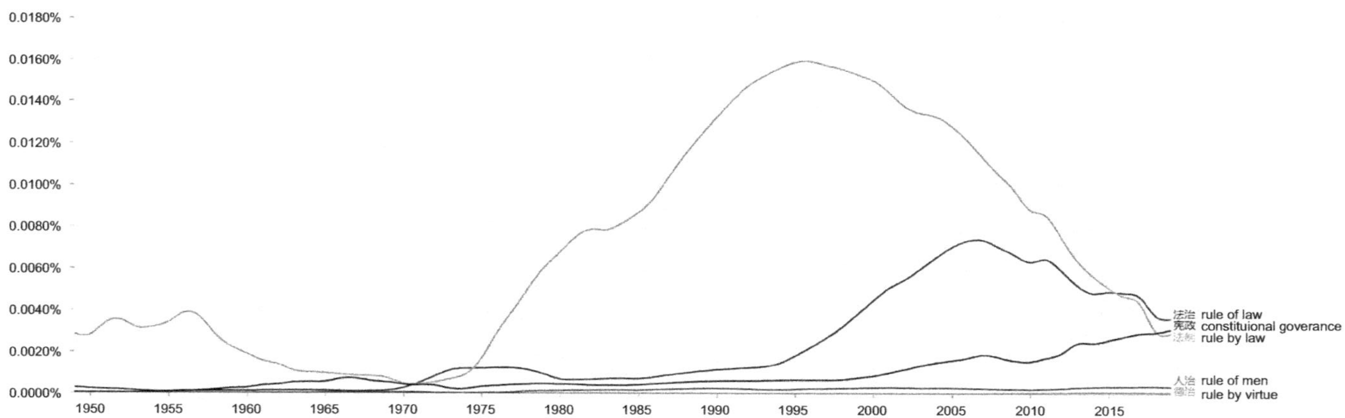


**Figure 13.3(b)** Google NGram search by various Chinese terms relating to rule of law, 1949–2019: frequencies with which the terms appeared in Chinese publications during the search period.

critiques of the liberal legal order began to enjoy a larger audience. The critiques also became more sophisticated, frequently quoting and referencing works by prominent US legal realists and critical legal theorists.[36] After decades of searching for ideal institutional models elsewhere, first in the Soviet bloc, then the Western world, a growing number of Chinese legal scholars started to look inward for theoretical inspiration.[37]

After 2012, when Xi Jinping assumed top Party leadership, the CCP embarked on a multiyear campaign to build "socialist rule of law with Chinese characteristics."[38] Having managed to consolidate and expand his power to a level comparable to that of Mao,[39] Xi advocated for a "comprehensive rule of law" (or, in Xi's words, "containing power in the cage of institutions"[40]) and constitutional governance.[41] However, the "rule of law" so propagated deviates from the liberal concept,[42] as it is "predominantly about fortifying and legitimizing the CCP's leadership through law over state institutions,"[43] constituting a form of rule by law. The campaign aimed to have the Party "lead all rule of law activities including legislation, law enforcement, administration of justice and law observance."[44] The CCP supremacy was finally enshrined in the Constitution.[45] And the official rhetoric publicly denounced the "erroneous" Western legal models.[46] In 2020, during the first central CCP conference on work related to "overall law-based governance," Xi summarized his thought on the rule of law in "eleven upholds," the top three of which were "upholding CCP leadership," "taking

[36] Gu, *supra* note 8, at 7–8.

[37] He Li, *supra* note 34; Gu, *supra* note 8; Yang, *supra* note 25; John W. Head, *Feeling the Stones When Crossing the River: The Rule of Law in China*, 7 Santa Clara J. Int'l L. 25, 69 (2010).

[38] Ling Li, *Chinese Characteristics of the "Socialist Rule of Law": Will the Fourth Plenum Cure the Problems of the Chinese Judicial System?*, 20 Asia Pol'y 17 (2015).

[39] Susan L Shirk, *China in Xi's "New Era": The Return to Personalistic Rule*, 29 J. Democracy 22, 24 (2018).

[40] DeLisle, *supra* note 35.

[41] Wu Changchang, *Debates on Constitutionalism and the Legacies of the Cultural Revolution*, 227 China Q. 674 (2016).

[42] DeLisle, *supra* note 35.

[43] Trevaskes, *supra* note 22.

[44] *Id.* at 350.

[45] Ling Li & Wenzhang Zhou, *Governing the "Constitutional Vacuum": Federalism, Rule of Law, and Politburo Politics in China*, 4 China L. & Soc'y Rev. 1 (2019); He Li, *supra* note 34.

[46] He Li, *supra* note 34, at 408.

a people-centered approach," and "staying on the path of the socialist rule of law."[47] Meanwhile, the official narrative began to integrate the socialist rule of law with "rule by moral virtue."[48] Some scholars view this moralistic turn in the official rhetoric as nothing but a revival of traditional Chinese philosophies on governance – that is, the coexistence of legalism, which emphasizes governance with legal instruments, and Confucianism, which stresses governance through moral guidance and rites,[49] repackaged by sleight with esoteric Marxist concepts such as the dialectical unity of two terms with conflicting meanings.[50]

All these attributes of the Chinese legal reform under Xi's leadership suggest that China is moving away from the rule-of-law concept defined as imposing legal constraints over powerholders.[51] The power of Xi and his allies, wielded through the CCP decision-making mechanism, is free from any legal restraint.[52] Nonetheless, the CCP is increasingly relying on legal institutions to govern,[53] and, in the process, Xi's campaign has shown positive effects,[54] as it provides more accessible forums for challenging low-level exercise of power, enhances predictability of published rules, and promotes reason-giving.[55] These effects are, for instance, the centralization of the court system, to shield judicial decisions from local politics;[56] rendering judges individually accountable, arguably to enhance independent adjudication and reduce shirking and corruption;[57] mitigating substantive review for case registration, to enable easier access to justice; and a broadened scope for legal challenges of government malfeasance, to rein in abusive officials.[58] As a result, the arbitrary exercise of power may have

[47] *Xi Focus: Xi Jinping Thought on the Rule of Law Guides Law-Based Governance in China*, XINHUANET (Dec. 10, 2020), www.xinhuanet.com/english/2020-12/10/c_139578646.htm.

[48] Trevaskes, *supra* note 22, at 357–58.

[49] Ye, *supra* note 2, at 14.

[50] Trevaskes, *supra* note 22, at 361.

[51] *See* Chapter 1.

[52] Other types of restraints such as factional checks and external pressure, especially from the United States, may modify how Xi exercises his power.

[53] Taisu Zhang & Tom Ginsburg, *China's Turn Toward Law*, 59 VA. J. INT'L L. 278, 315–16 (2019).

[54] *Id.*

[55] *See* Chapter 1.

[56] Yueduan Wang, *"Detaching" Courts from Local Politics? Assessing the Judicial Centralization Reforms in China*, 246 CHINA Q. 545, 547 (2021).

[57] Benjamin L. Liebman, *China's Courts: Restricted Reform*, 191 CHINA Q. 620, 620 (2007).

[58] Zhang & Ginsburg, *supra* note 53, at 306, 309.

abated in certain issue areas that do not pose a threat to the regime. Routine civil cases, for instance, may receive neutral and fair treatment in Chinese courts, especially when the litigants are similarly situated in the power hierarchy.[59] The same is true for lawsuits against local government actors, the number of which surged in 2015, when the case registration reform took effect (see Figure 13.2).

Meanwhile, however, cases of significant social, economic, or political consequences continue to be avoided or "harmonized."[60] For instance, the implementation of the zero-COVID policies has upended the lives of millions of people in China, yet courts have been largely silent. Businesses can be shut down and individuals locked up without minimal due process or any legal remedy. Moreover, the prosecution of activists in China has been growing, often with charges based on the ambiguous crime of "picking quarrels and provoking trouble."[61] In short, the "comprehensive rule of law" campaign remains contested in terms of its impacts,[62] with many considering its effects to be "partial,"[63] "uneven,"[64] or "dualist."[65] That being said, scholars generally agree that the campaign's ultimate goal is no more than instrumentalist governance by law and regime preservation.

In parallel, partially due to the resurrection of personalistic authoritarianism under Xi and the disrupted factional power balance,[66] the space for academic debates shrank considerably.[67] The state tightened its control over views inconsistent with the government's rhetoric, and the escalating geopolitical rivalry with the United States alienated Chinese legal scholars more receptive to liberal values or leaning toward normative pluralism. Nonetheless, rule-of-law debates continued among

[59] Ji Li, *The Power Logic of Justice in China*, 65 Am. J. Comp. L. 95, 95 (2017).

[60] Qianfan Zhang, *supra* note 2, at 593; Ji Li, *supra* note 59, at 21; Xin He, *A Tale of Two Chinese Courts: Economic Development and Contract Enforcement*, 39 J.L. & Soc. 384, 388 (2012); Ying Sun & Hualing Fu, *Of Judge Quota and Judicial Autonomy: An Enduring Professionalization Project in China*, 251 China Q. 866, 867 (2022).

[61] Guo Rui, *"Picking Quarrels and Provoking Trouble": How China's Catch-All Crime Muzzles Dissent*, S. China Morning Post (Aug. 25, 2021), https://tinyurl.com/mryy97kj.

[62] Wang, *supra* note 56, at 22; Qianfan Zhang, *supra* note 2, at 587.

[63] Chen, *supra* note 2, at 35.

[64] DeLisle, *supra* note 35, at 79.

[65] Qianfan Zhang, *supra* note 2, at 594.

[66] Björn Alexander Düben, *Xi Jinping and the End of Chinese Exceptionalism*, 67 Probs. Post-Communism 111, 116 (2020).

[67] He Li, *supra* note 34, at 421; Qianfan Zhang, *supra* note 2, at 586.

Chinese scholars who have become well versed in relevant Western literature on law and governance.[68] The liberal voice has been subdued, but not extinguished.[69] And more scholars have joined in the search for novel alternative theories.[70]

Finally, China's interactions with the outside world also have altered its state ideology. Granted, the components of orthodox Marxism advocating class struggles have lost practical relevance and been largely abandoned,[71] hence the widely accepted claim that China has "entered a post-ideological age."[72] However, basic causal beliefs and worldviews integral to dialectical materialism and historical materialism still offer the most salient cognitive framework for Chinese ruling elites in interpreting complex and ambiguous social and political phenomena such as law's role in, or relationship with, governance.[73] Briefly, political institutions, as a category of the societal superstructure, are determined by the mode of production, and legal institutions are regarded as tools of oppression and regime preservation employed by the ruling class. Because members of the Chinese ruling elites must demonstrate mastery of the state ideology in order to advance in the fiercely competitive political system,[74] they have internalized the core ideological remnants, which, I argue, gives rise

[68] He Zhipeng (何志鹏), *"Liangfa" yu "Shanzhi" he yi Tongyang Zhongyao: Guoji Fazhi Biaozhun de Shensi* ("良法" 与 "善治" 何以同样重要: 国际法治标准的审思) [Why sound law and good governance are equally important: The criteria of international rule of law revisited], ZHEJIANG DAXUE XUEBAO (RENWEN SHEHUI KEXUEBAN) (浙江大学学报 (人文社会科学版)) [J. Zhejiang U. (Humanities & Soc. Sci.)], vol. 44, no. 3, 2014, at 131; Yang, *supra* note 26; He Zhipeng (何志鹏), *Guoji Fazhi: Yige Gainian de Jieding* (国际法治: 一个概念的界定) [International rule of law: defining a concept], ZHENGFA LUNTAN: ZHONGGUO ZHENGFA DAXUE XUEBAO (政法论坛: 中国政法大学学报) [Trib. Pol. Sci. & L.] vol. 27, no. 4, 2009, at 63, 78; Qiang Shigong (强世功), *"Fazhi Zhongguo" de Daolu Xuanze: Cong Falu Diguo dao Duoyuan Zhuyi Fazhi Gongheguo* ("法治中国" 的道路选择: 从法律帝国到多元主义法治共和国) [The path choice of "China with rule of law": From a legal empire to a pluralistic republic with rule of law], WENHUA ZONGHENG (文化纵横) [Beijing Cultural Rev.], no. 4, 2014, at 38.

[69] He Li, *supra* note 34, at 411; Qianfan Zhang, *supra* note 2, at 583; DeLisle, *supra* note 35, at 82–83.

[70] Samuli Seppänen, *Ideological Renewal and Nostalgia in China's "Avant-Garde" Legal Scholarship*, 13 WASH. U. GLOB. STUD. L. REV. 83, 84 (2014); Zhang Wenxian, *supra* note 2, at 23.

[71] For instance, the dictatorship of the proletariat has been dropped from the official rhetoric. He Li, *supra* note 34, at 421.

[72] Creemers, *supra* note 33, at 31.

[73] *Id.* at 41.

[74] David Shambaugh, *Training China's Political Elite: The Party School System*, 196 CHINA Q. 827 (2008).

to three shared perceptions of law and legal institutions: legal instrumentalism, economic determinism, and linearity of institutional changes.

To be concrete, the Chinese ruling elites have generally perceived law and legal institutions as a means to achieve other objectives,[75] be it political oppression,[76] reducing corruption,[77] facilitating an efficient market economy,[78] maintaining social order and stability,[79] sustaining regime legitimacy,[80] enhancing the government's international reputation,[81] enabling modernization,[82] or symbolizing social and cultural progress.[83] Teleologically conceptualized,[84] the rule of law has never acquired the same normative appeal in China as in the West.[85] Additionally, the shared view of economic determinism underlies Chinese government policies and the official narrative about law and governance. Reformers and conservatives alike contend that the characteristics of economic relations in China necessitate a more professional and independent judiciary or, on the contrary, justify preserving the institutional status quo, or even reverting to Mao-era practices.[86] Moreover, prior studies in China have either concluded, or adopted the assumption, that modes of production determine legal institutions in a linear fashion, so economically developed regions and countries will feature professional and independent courts, whereas developing ones will be characterized by dysfunctional courts and incompetent judges.[87] As will be demonstrated, these ideology-shaped perceptions also modify China's interactions with the international legal order.

To summarize, this first part of the chapter has offered a nuanced recounting of Chinese legal reform and its evolving rule-of-law discourse

[75] DeLisle, *supra* note 35, at 79; Head, *supra* note 37, at 34–35.
[76] Partlett & Ip, *supra* note 15, at 470–71.
[77] Jennifer R. Wilking & Gregory J. Love, *Why the Rule of Law? Experimental Evidence from China*, 41 Just. Sys. J. 360 (2020).
[78] DeLisle, *supra* note 35, at 68.
[79] Liebman, *supra* note 2, at 96.
[80] Susan H. Whiting, *Authoritarian "Rule of Law" and Regime Legitimacy*, 50 Comp. Pol. Stud. 1907 (2017).
[81] Zhang Wenxian, *supra* note 2, at 586.
[82] Trevaskes, *supra* note 22, at 353.
[83] *Id.* at 353.
[84] Ewan Smith, *The Rule of Law Doctrine of the Politburo*, 79 China J. 40 (2018).
[85] Chen, *supra* note 2, at 20.
[86] Minzner, *supra* note 2, at 939.
[87] Yuhua Wang, When Do Authoritarian Rulers Tie Their Hands: The Rise of Limited Rule of Law in Sub-National China (2011) (Ph.D. dissertation, University of Michigan) (on file with University of Michigan Library); Xin He, *supra* note 60, at 395–401.

by examining the contestations among China's ruling elites and the influence of external normative and geopolitical environments. Xi's assumption of CCP leadership ushered in a new era of legal reform marked by greatly tightened CCP control and centralization of judicial power. Meanwhile, the CCP has exhorted Chinese officials and scholars to "vigorously participate in the formulation of international norms[,] . . . strengthen [China's] discourse power and influence in international legal affairs[,] . . . [and] use legal methods to safeguard [China's] sovereignty, security and development interests."[88] And empirical data indicates that in 2012, when Xi became the party secretary, the Chinese rule-of-law discourse clearly diverged from that of the Western world.[89] All these changes render it timely and important to analyze China's actual or potential impacts on the international legal order.

## II Impacts on the International Rule of Law

During the Cultural Revolution, China was largely isolated from the rest of the world, and the ruling elites were deeply skeptical and inimical toward both the US-led Western international order and the Soviet-dominated rules governing relations between states within the Communist bloc.[90] Running an autarky, the Chinese government saw little need for international rules to facilitate cross-border transactions. Moreover, the CCP leaders, steeped in orthodox Marxism, regarded the existing international laws as primarily a hegemonic instrument of oppression.[91] As noted, the post-Cultural Revolution reforms reconnected China with the international community, giving rise to functional needs for international agreements. While some members of the ruling elites continued to view international institutions as favoring the United States and its allies,[92] and rejected the rules of the game as they were made

[88] Quoted in Isaac B. Kardon, *China Can Say "No": Analyzing China's Rejection of the South China Sea Arbitration; Toward a New Era of International Law with Chinese Characteristics*, 13 U. PA. ASIAN L. REV., 1, 2 (2018), https://scholarship.law.upenn.edu/alr/vol13/iss2/1.

[89] The NGram data may be greatly impacted by government censorship in China. Censorship very likely has been enhanced since 2012, which is another reason why rule-of-law discourses in China and in the English-speaking world diverged thereafter.

[90] Youcheer Kim, *Is China Spoiling the Rules-Based Liberal International Order? Examining China's Rising Institutional Power in a Multiplex World Through Competing Theories*, 56 ISSUES & STUD. (2020).

[91] Phil C.W. Chan, *China's Approaches to International Law Since the Opium War*, 27 LEIDEN J. INT'L L. 859, 879 (2014).

[92] Graham Allison, *China vs. America: Managing the Next Clash of Civilizations*, 96 FOREIGN AFFS. 80, 85 (2017).

when China was "absent from the world stage,"[93] others, realizing the necessity and benefits of accommodating the US hegemon, began to socialize with the international legal community. After Deng's Southern Tour, the Chinese government, then dominated by reformers, stepped up its efforts to integrate into the global economy by, among other steps, joining the WTO.[94] Today, China is a party to hundreds of bilateral and multilateral treaties in a broad range of subject-matter areas, such as anti-corruption, arms control, environmental protection, and avoidance of double taxation.[95] The Chinese government also has assumed a more prominent role in drafting and amending international agreements[96] and aspired to profoundly reshape the international legal order.[97]

China's rise and its actual or potential impacts on international law and institutions have stimulated heated debates. Some contend that China's growing influence will have significant, detrimental effects on the liberal international legal order.[98] Others view China as a manageable threat.[99] By contrast, some scholars emphasize the positive effects of China's participation in making and reforming international law.[100] Still others have taken an empirical approach, documenting China's evolving and varying policies regarding international law and international institutions.[101] Still others consider international law largely irrelevant in the China-driven shift of global geopolitics.[102]

93 *Id.* at 86.

94 Gregory Shaffer, Emerging Powers and the World Trading System: The Past and Future of International Economic Law 174 (2021).

95 Robert D. Williams, Brookings Inst., International Law with Chinese Characteristics: Beijing and the "Rules-Based" Global Order 3 (2020).

96 *Id.*

97 Kardon, *supra* note 88.

98 *See* Ingrid Wuerth, *International Law in the Post-Human Rights Era*, 96 Tex. L. Rev. 279 (2017); Tom Ginsburg, *Authoritarian International Law?*, 114 Am. J. Int'l L. 221 (2020); Timothy Webster, *Retooling Sanctions: China's Challenge to the Liberal International Order*, 23 Chi. J. Int'l L. 178 (2022); Gregory Shaffer & Henry Gao, *A New Chinese Economic Order?*, 23 J. Int'l Econ. L. 607 (2020).

99 *See, e.g.*, G. John Ikenberry, *The Rise of China and the Future of the West: Can the Liberal System Survive?*, 87 Foreign Affs. 23 (2008).

100 *See* Congyan Cai, The Rise of China and International Law: Taking Chinese Exceptionalism Seriously (2019); William W. Burke-White, *Power Shifts in International Law: Structural Realignment and Substantive Pluralism*, 56 Harv. Int'l L.J. 1 (2015).

101 *See, e.g.*, Kong Qingjiang, *Beyond the Love–Hate Approach? International Law and International Institutions and the Rising China*, 15 China: Int'l J. 41 (2017); Potter, *supra* note 1; Shaffer, *supra* note 94.

102 *See* Eric A. Posner & John Yoo, *International Law and the Rise of China*, 7 Chi. J. Int'l L. 1 (2006).

While consensus is lacking, the bulk of the literature features a shared methodological approach – treating the sovereign state as the unit of analysis.[103] Such a simplified conceptualization, commonly adopted by realists in international relations, makes the corresponding analytical model too blunt a tool to explicate the heterogeneity of the interactions between multiple relevant Chinese actors and non-Chinese actors in various international legal fields. Again, applying the analytical frame of transnational legal ordering,[104] this chapter contends that China's impacts are more nuanced and varied, and researchers will gain more insights by penetrating the sovereign facade and focusing on different cohorts of key Chinese international law actors. Given the subject matter of the field, lawyers, legal scholars, and legally trained government officials often play important roles. Moreover, depending on the specific issue area, conservative state actors lacking any formal legal training and two types of organizational actors – business organizations (i.e., domestic and multinational firms) and civil society organizations (e.g., NGOs) – may also occupy the interfaces between China and international law. These Chinese actors differ in their interests, internalized norms, ideologies, and causal beliefs, which shape their interactions with and impacts on international law.

Let me begin with interests. At the risk of overgeneralizing, Chinese lawyers seek higher income and professional status, which are intimately interconnected; Chinese legal scholars desire status and prestige associated with their academic and policy impacts and, to a lesser extent, higher income; Chinese government officials, much like their US counterparts, typically crave power and status and avoid risk; business organizations in China maximize profits, though state-owned firms often prioritize government policy objectives; Chinese civil society organizations, heavily state-dependent and systematically subdued, seek to make issue-specific impacts in areas tolerated by the authoritarian government.

Additionally, embedded in the Chinese institutional context, these actors naturally adopt its dominant normative framework,[105] which enables them to define, interpret, and appropriately carry out interactions with foreign

[103] *See, e.g.*, CAI, *supra* note 100; Simon Chesterman, *Asia's Ambivalence About International Law and Institutions: Past, Present and Futures*, 27 EUR. J. INT'L L. 945 (2016); Posner & Yoo, *supra* note 102.

[104] *See, e.g.*, Gregory Shaffer, *Theorizing Transnational Legal Ordering*, 12 ANN. REV. L. & SOC. SCI. 231 (2016); Harold Hongju Koh, *Transnational Legal Process*, 75 NEB. L. REV. 181 (1996).

[105] The general framework consists of key elements of Sinicized Marxism and Confucianism.

international law parties. However, the actors may deviate from the default set of schemas and norms because of extensive socialization with outside or subcultural groups. Among these key groups of Chinese actors, lawyers and legal scholars tend to be more socialized in the global legal community. As alluded to earlier, the post-Cultural Revolution Chinese legal ecosystem evolved along with expansive statutory and theoretical transplantation from Western countries, and in the past few decades a growing number of Chinese law students and practitioners have received advanced legal education in European and US law schools. After years of intensive socialization, many among these two groups have internalized the core elements of international legal norms.

The exposure of Chinese government actors to the outside world varies widely. Reformers tend to dominate in some functional areas (e.g., trade, foreign affairs, and finance), where senior government officials are legally trained, globe-trotting career bureaucrats; some have even received degrees from prominent foreign universities.[106] In other state organs (e.g., security and defense), the conservative faction reigns, and the high-ranking officials rarely engage extensively with foreign peers, let alone with members of the international legal community. Thus, their internalized domestic normative framework remains largely intact.

The exponential growth of the Chinese economy in the past few decades has projected numerous Chinese firms onto the global stage for trade and investment, exposing them to different business and societal norms. The extent of their normative adaptation, however, turns on multiple factors, including, among others, the degree of exposure, the importance of the foreign market, and the institutional distance they must traverse.[107] Nonetheless, most Chinese non-state-owned firms have proved highly pragmatic and adaptable in finding efficient solutions to their cross-border business problems.[108]

Along with China's reform and opening-up, civil society organizations with tight, extensive international connections mushroomed from bare existence. Many such organizations are clan-based and historically have

[106] For decades, the Chinese government has been sending officials, mostly from economy-related departments, to US and European universities for training and education.

[107] *See* Ji Li, The Clash of Capitalisms? Chinese Companies in the United States 48–50 (2018).

[108] *See* Deborah Brautigam, The Dragon's Gift: The Real Story of China in Africa (2009); Ji Li, *I Came, I Saw, I ... Adapted: An Empirical Study of Chinese Business Expansion in the United States. and Its Legal and Policy Implications*, 36 Nw. J. Int'l L. & Bus. 143 (2016).

played a key role in attracting foreign direct investment. In the past three decades, civil society organizations also emerged to push for various legal reforms, and before Xi consolidated his power, US and European NGOs (e.g., the Ford Foundation and the American Bar Foundation) used to fund rule-of-law-themed programs in China, many of which were implemented in close collaboration with China's domestic organizations.[109] In short, before the Chinese government tightened its control over foreign NGOs, they maintained broad and close contacts with social legal organizations in China, immersing them in the global legal community.

## 1 *Actors, Organizations, and Issue-Specific Norms*

A heterogeneity of interests and normative frameworks guide various groups of Chinese actors populating the interfaces between China and international law. As international legal issues vary, so do the coalitions of the actors. I propose that the varying combinations of interests the actors pursue and norms they have internalized offer a new theoretical angle that helps to explain the variations in China's approaches to, and impacts on, the international legal orders governing different issue areas.

Take international commercial arbitration as an example. In this issue area, a variety of Chinese actors occupy the field, including Chinese firms, lawyers, domestic arbitration commissions, scholars, judges, and reform-minded government officials immersed in international legal norms. For reasons such as cultural affinity and cost concerns, China-based businesses prefer to resolve their international commercial disputes before Chinese arbitral tribunals.[110] This demand has spurred an explosive growth in China's arbitration service market. To maximize revenue, Chinese lawyers and law firms compete fiercely for a larger share of the growing business, as do more than two hundred local arbitration commissions. Market pressure motivates nonstate Chinese actors to adopt international best practices. While the field of international commercial arbitration used to be dominated by a "small cadre of elite arbitrators,"[111] who were mostly

[109] *See* Ronald C Keith, Zhiqui Lin & Huang Lie, *The Making of a Chinese NGO: The Research and Intervention Project on Domestic Violence*, 50 PROBS. POST-COMMUNISM 38 (2003); Chongyi Feng, *The NGO Law in China and Its Impact on Overseas Funded NGOs*, 9 COSMOPOLITAN CIV. SOCIETIES: INTERDISC. J. 96 (2017).

[110] *See* Matthew S Erie & Monika Prusinowska, *The Future of Foreign Arbitration in the People's Republic of China: Current Developments and Challenges Ahead*, 28 ASIA PAC. L. REV. 259 (2020).

[111] ALEC STONE SWEET & FLORIAN GRISEL, The Evolution of International Arbitration: Judicialization, Governance, Legitimacy 45 (2017).

US and European lawyers, the expansion of China-related arbitration business will inevitably give Chinese elite lawyers more voice and influence in the international community. Likewise, Chinese arbitration institutions will see their influence grow. Meanwhile, reform-minded state actors, by virtue of extended socialization in the international legal community, have adopted policies and reforms that reflect a mixture of domestic normative preferences and international norms governing commercial arbitration. For instance, the Chinese government was among the first to sign the Singapore Mediation Convention.[112] Also, the government has created international commercial courts as alternatives to commercial arbitration, and the courts were designed to be one-stop-shops for cross-border dispute resolution, reflecting the instrumentalist view of law commonly shared among the Chinese ruling elites.[113]

By contrast, China's approach toward, and impact on, international law governing territorial disputes is dramatically different, as illustrated by its handling of the South China Sea arbitration with the Philippines government under the United Nations Convention on the Law of the Sea. Nonstate actors were largely absent in this issue area. While multiple state actors historically played a part in the issue area, Xi consolidated the decision-making power and elevated the role of the Chinese military. Thereafter, powerful conservative constituencies in the defense and national security sectors reacted to the arbitration in a way that reflected their internalized normative contempt for judicial dispute resolution. They adopted a position of "Four Nos": "no participation, no acceptance, no recognition and no enforcement."[114] This attitude led to China's attack against both the Permanent Court of Arbitration and its decisions, which were widely regarded as "an overwhelming victory for the Philippines and a heavy defeat for China."[115] Since then, the Chinese government has made repeated efforts to modify the international norm regarding the jurisdiction of international tribunals to adjudicate territorial disputes.

To summarize, the rise of China has certainly brought more actors onto the global legal stage in certain issues areas, especially those pertinent to

[112] *China Signs the United Nations Convention on International Settlement Agreements Resulting from Mediation*, MINISTRY OF COM. (Aug. 8, 2019), https://tinyurl.com/4xxnc9zw.

[113] *See* Weixia Gu, *China's Law and Development: A Case Study of the China International Commercial Court*, 62 HARV. INT'L L.J. 67 (2021).

[114] Feng Zhang, *Assessing China's Response to the South China Sea Arbitration Ruling*, 71 AUSTRALIAN J. INT'L AFFS. 440, 440–41 (2017).

[115] *Id.* at 440.

cross-border commerce and investment. China's growing go-it-alone power also has boosted its capacity to establish new international organizations "in which its political power is more commensurate with its economic power."[116] Moreover, in some issue areas, Chinese actors have been striving to alter the existing international law norms, with varying degrees of success. However, as will be discussed below, China has not mounted any systematic challenge against the fundamental norms on which the liberal international legal order is premised.

## 2 *Fundamental Norms Underlying the International Legal Order*

The rest of this chapter concentrates on China's impact on the fundamental norms and worldviews undergirding the international legal order, which enable international actors to form their identities, preferences, and objectives and formulate legitimate means to achieve them. As noted in Part I, Chinese ruling elites share three basic causal beliefs about law and legal institutions: legal instrumentalism, economic determinism, and linearity of institutional changes. Because of these perceptions, the Chinese government has approached international law with mainly its instrumental value in mind.[117] Echoing the shared ideological view, Deng, in the late 1980s, remarked that the core values of liberalism were "designed only to safeguard the interests of the strong, rich countries, which take advantage of their strength to bully weak countries, and which pursue hegemony and practice power politics."[118] Government officials were urged to be "adept at using international law as a 'weapon' to defend the interests of our state and maintain national pride," and to "strengthen China's 'discourse power and influence' in international legal affairs."[119] The instrumentalist approach explains the shift in the government's position with regard to investment treaties. When China was a net capital importer, its investment treaties with other countries curtailed foreign investors' recourse.[120] But as soon as the country turned into a net capital exporter, the government negotiated broader investor protection in its bilateral investment treaties to safeguard

116 James F. Paradise, *The Role of "Parallel Institutions" in China's Growing Participation in Global Economic Governance*, 21 J. Chinese Pol. Sci. 149, 169 (2016).

117 Creemers, *supra* note 33.

118 Allison, *supra* note 92.

119 Williams, *supra* note 95.

120 Justin Carter, *The Protracted Bargain: Negotiating the Canada–China Foreign Investment Promotion and Protection Agreement*, 47 Can. Y.B. Int'l L. (Annuaire canadien de Droit international) 197, 210–11 (2010).

the interests of Chinese outbound investors.[121] Following the same instrumentalist logic, in issue areas where the Chinese government anticipates to win some and lose some, it has been an active participant. China's engagement with the WTO dispute settlement mechanism serves as a good example.[122]

Of course, the instrumentalism is not narrowly material. Much of China's engagement with international law (e.g., human rights treaties[123]) is driven by concerns about building the regime's legitimacy[124] or intentions to facilitate domestic reforms.[125] Even the Chinese academic discourse on international law stresses the value of safeguarding the core interests of China,[126] including, among others, "maintaining the fundamental institutions, sovereign and territorial integrity, and social and economic stability and development,"[127] or more broadly facilitating China's modernization, improving its international image, and enhancing the welfare of the global community.[128] Because instrumentalism is inherently issue-specific and

[121] *Id.* at 210–13.

[122] Shaffer & Gao, *supra* note 98.

[123] Potter, *supra* note 1, at 708–09.

[124] *Id.* at 702; WILLIAMS, *supra* note 95, at 10.

[125] Qin, *supra* note 21.

[126] Li Lin (李林), *Xin Shidai Zhongguo Fazhi Lilun Chuangxin Fazhan de Liu Ge Xiangdu* (新时代中国法治理论创新发展的六个向度) [Six important dimensions in the innovative development of China's rule of law in the new era], FAXUE YANJIU (法学研究) [Chinese J.L.], vol. 41, no. 4, at 3 (2019).

[127] Zeng Lingliang (曾令良), *Zhongguo Guoji Faxue Huayu Tixi de Dangdai Goujian* (中国国际法学话语体系的当代构建) [The contemporary construction of the Chinese discourse system on international law], ZHONGGUO SHEHUI KEXUE (中国社会科学) [Soc. Sci. Chi.], no. 2, 2011, at 35; Zhao Jun (赵骏), *Quanqiu Zhili Shiye Xia de Guoji Fazhi yu Guonei Fazhi* (全球治理视野下的国际法治与国内法治) [International and domestic rule of law from the perspective of global governance], ZHONGGUO SHEHUI KEXUE (中国社会科学) [Soc. Sci. Chi.], no. 10, 2014, at 79.

[128] Zeng Lingliang (曾令良), *Guoji Fazhi yu Zhongguo Fazhi Jianshe* (国际法治与中国法治建设) [International rule of law and the development of the rule of law in China], ZHONGGUO SHEHUI KEXUE (中国社会科学) [Soc. Sci. Chi.], no. 10, 2015, at 135; Han Yonghong (韩永红), *Guojifa Heyi Dedao Zunshou: Guowai Yanjiu Shuping yu Zhongguo Shijiao Fansi* (国际法何以得到遵守: 国外研究述评与中国视角反思) [The compliance theory of international law: Review and reflection], HUANQIU FALV PINGLUN (环球法律评论) [Glob. L. Rev.], no. 4, 2014, at 167, 183–84; He Zhipeng (何志鹏), *Guoji Fazhi de Zhongguo Biaoda* (国际法治的中国表达) [China's voice in international rule of law], ZHONGGUO SHEHUI KEXUE (中国社会科学) [Soc. Sci. Chi.], no. 10, 2015, at 159, 167; Pan Wei (潘维), *Fazhi yu Weilai Zhongguo Zhengti* (法治与未来中国政体) [The rule of law and China's political regime in the future], ZHANLVE YU GUANLI (战略与管理) [Strategy & Mgmt.], no. 5, 1999, at 30, 36; Zhang Wenxian, *supra* note 2, at 10.

nonstatic, this shared perception undermines any effort to formulate systematic contestation of fundamental international legal norms.

Moreover, economic determinism, rooted in historical materialism, also shapes the international law strategies of the Chinese government. Under this doctrine, major shifts in the international economic order will bring about a new international legal order.[129] In other words, international law will inevitably evolve in China's favor as long as the Chinese economy continues to grow. The causality belief partially explains the willingness of the Chinese government in the early stage of the reform period to accept much of the existing international legal order, "bide its time,"[130] and be content with incremental changes of international law. The shared belief in economic determinism also partially explains the relative passivity of the Chinese ruling elites in proposing comprehensive reforms of the existing international legal order and their demonstrated preferences for incremental changes.

The state ideology has also cast an enormous shadow over Chinese academic debates about international law.[131] Largely in line with the official narrative, Chinese scholars have considered the international legal order as an institutional instrument that embodies and preserves the values and interests of the West.[132] With that ontological postulation, a great deal of the Chinese scholarship on international law has been either thematically critical or substantively doctrinal.[133] Motivated by the need to "garner state patronage, which is a prerequisite for funding, publishing, and policy impact,"[134] many Chinese international law scholars have oriented their research toward policy questions dovetailing with the governmental agenda, such as law's role in preserving the

[129] Zeng, *supra* note 128, at 146.

[130] Gregory Chin & Ramesh Thakur, *Will China Change the Rules of Global Order?*, 33 WASH. Q. 119, 121–22 (2010).

[131] Though Marx and Engels themselves said little about international law. Bill Bowring, *Marxist International Law Methodology?*, in RESEARCH METHODS IN INTERNATIONAL LAW 161 (Rossana Deplano ed., 2021).

[132] He Zhipeng, *The Chinese Expression of the International Rule of Law*, 38 SOC. SCI. IN CHI. 175, 178–79 (2017); He Zhipeng (何志鹏), *Guojifa de Xifang Chuantong yu Zhongguo Guannian* (国际法的西方传统与中国观念) [International law: Western tradition and Chinese concept], FAXUE ZAZHI (法学杂志) [L. Sci. Mag.], no. 2, 2018, at 63; Matthew S. Erie, *China and Comparative International Law: Between Social Science and Critique*, 22 CHI. J. INT'L L. 59, 64 (2021).

[133] Erie, *supra* note 132.

[134] *Id.* at 64.

hegemonic world order and how to expand China's discourse power in the epistemic community of international law.[135]

In sum, China in the near future will have no more than marginal impacts on the fundamental norms underlying the international legal order. For reasons noted above, China has failed to provide a coherent and novel alternative ideology.[136] Sinicized Marxism now furnishes mainly a set of causal beliefs and worldviews linking the material world with metapolitical institutions such as the international legal order.[137] Much of the Chinese academic discourse on international law has been in line with the relevant official narrative and has not yet articulated any alternative model of international legal ordering unmoored from selected concepts and values of ancient Chinese philosophies.[138] Hence, Chinese international law scholarship has added marginal theoretical value beyond neo-Marxism, legal realism, and other branches of critical legal theories.[139] A keen observer of Chinese international law scholarship recently lamented the field's theoretical impoverishment.[140]

Additionally, neo-authoritarianism, a term often used to label the Chinese political system taking shape in the past two decades along with China's rise,[141] arguably offers an alternative model (also known as the

[135] *Id.* at 68–69; Yang Zewei (杨泽伟), *Gaige Kaifang 30 Nian Lai Zhongguo Guoji Faxue Yanjiu de Huigu yu Qianzhan* (改革开放 30 年来中国国际法学研究的回顾与前瞻) [Review and prospect of China's study of international law science in the 30 years of reform and opening], Waijiao Pinglun (Waijiao Xueyuan Xuebao) (外交评论(外交学院学报)) [Foreign Affs. Rev.], no. 3, 2008, at 74; He Zhipeng (何志鹏), *Zhongguo Guoji Faxue de Shuangwei Zhuliuhua* (中国国际法学的双维主流化) [Two-dimensional mainstreaming of China's international law], Zhengfa Luntan (政法论坛) [Trib. Pol. Sci. & L.], vol. 36, no. 5, 2018, at 173; Zeng, *supra* note 127, at 39; Yang, *supra* note 25.

[136] Jessica Chen Weiss, *A World Safe for Autocracy: China's Rise and the Future of Global Politics*, 98 Foreign Affs. 92 (2019); Randall L. Schweller & Xiaoyu Pu, *After Unipolarity: China's Visions of International Order in an Era of US Decline*, 36 Int'l Sec. 41, 54 (2011).

[137] Erie, *supra* note 132, at 64–65.

[138] Xuetong Yan, *Chinese Values vs. Liberalism: What Ideology Will Shape the International Normative Order?*, 11 Chinese J. Int'l Pol. 1 (2018); He Zhipeng, *The Chinese Expression of the International Rule of Law*, *supra* note 132, at 181–82; Tokujin Matsudaira, *Tianxia, or Another Grossraum? US–China Competition and Paradigm Change in the International Legal Order*, 23 Chi. J. Int'l L. 130 (2022).

[139] Erie, *supra* note 132, at 68.

[140] *Id.* at 66.

[141] Stephan Ortmann & Mark R. Thompson, *Introduction: The "Singapore Model" and China's Neo-authoritarian Dream*, 236 China Q. 930 (2018); Elizabeth J. Perry, *China in 1992: An Experiment in Neo-authoritarianism*, 33 Asian Surv. 12 (1993).

China model, or the Beijing Consensus[142]) for some states to resist liberal democracy,[143] which might indirectly erode key international legal norms.[144] However, China under Xi's leadership has been steadily reverting to prototypical authoritarianism and cult politics,[145] and as such the China model, for its lack of long-term stability and resilience, is losing its credibility and persuasive power.[146] The plummeting public opinion toward China around the world serves as a good illustration.[147]

In short, Sinicized Marxism, or China exceptionalism, has guided Chinese interactions with the international legal community,[148] and, as a result, it has had very limited impact on the international legal order at the fundamental normative level.[149] Of course, the Chinese government has taken proactive measures to shape certain international law discourses, "strengthening its control and influence,"[150] especially those concerning its legitimacy. For instance, for years the government has tried to "articulate and justify new standards for human rights that comport with its own policy

[142] Weitseng Chen, The Beijing Consensus?: How China has Changed Western Ideas of Law and Economic Development (2017); Scott Kennedy, *The Myth of the Beijing Consensus*, 19 J. Contemp. China 461 (2010).

[143] Weiss, *supra* note 136, at 95.

[144] Ginsburg, *supra* note 98, at 259.

[145] Düben, *supra* note 66, at 122–23.

[146] Steve Tsang, *Has Xi Jinping Made China's Political System More Resilient and Enduring?*, 43 Third World Q. 225, 237 (2022).

[147] *See* Laura Silver, Kat Devlin & Christine Huang, Unfavorable Views of China Reach Historic Highs in Many Countries (Oct. 2020), https://tinyurl.com/44ess33d.

[148] *See, e.g.*, Gu Zuxue (古祖雪), *Guoji Zaofa: Jiben Yuanze Jiqi dui Guojifa de Yiyi* (国际造法: 基本原则及其对国际法的意义) [International law-making: Basic principles and implications for international law], Zhongguo Shehui Kexue (中国社会科学) [Soc. Sci. Chi.], no. 2, 2012, at 127, 128; He Zhipeng, *The Chinese Expression of the International Rule of Law*, *supra* note 132, at 181–82; Song Yunbo (宋云博), *Renlei Mingyun Gongtongti Jiangou xia "Guoji Dezhi" yu "Guoji Fazhi" de Ronghe Hudong* (人类命运共同体建构下 "国际德治" 与 "国际法治" 的融合互动) [On integration and interaction of "international rule of morality" and "international rule of law" under the construction background of community of shared future for mankind], Zhengfa Luncong (政法论丛) [J. Pol. Sci. & L.], no. 6, 2018, at 58, 64; He Zhipeng (何志鹏), Guoji Jingji Fazhi Geju de Yanpan yu Yingdui: Jianlun TPP de Zhongguo Lichang (国际经济法治格局的研判与应对: 兼论 TPP 的中国立场) [Analysis and response to the rule of international economic law: Also on China's standpoint regarding TPP], Dangdai Faxue (当代法学) [Contemp. L. Rev.], no. 1, 2016, at 43, 50–51.

[149] Han, *supra* note 128, at 182.

[150] Shi Jingxia (石静霞), *Guoji Maoyi Touzi Guize de Zaigoujian ji Zhongguo de Yinying* (国际贸易投资规则的再构建及中国的因应) [The reconstruction of investment rules in international trade and the Chinese response], Zhongguo Shehui Kexue (中国社会科学) [Soc. Sci. Chi.], no. 9, 2015, at 128, 129.

priorities."[151] The government also implements socialization and training programs to spread its knowledge and norms to Global South states,[152] where it has found "generally positive reception" among the ruling elites.[153] And since the 19th Party Congress in 2017, the CCP has "sent international propaganda delegations abroad to introduce its programmes and opinions."[154] It is likely that the Chinese government's "norm entrepreneurship" will continue and be more impactful.[155] Yet, given the way the government has framed its arguments, the efforts appear to be primarily "normative resistance" against international criticism rooted in liberal values,[156] rather than a coordinated offense that formulates a coherent normative alternative.[157] Recent research confirms the lack of zeal for the Chinese government to export its legal institutions absent such threat or criticism.[158] The passive approach to international law renders China underprepared when it faces the pressure to be more engaged, as it lacks "the courage, keenness and self-confidence required to participate in the international rule of law."[159] The diffusion of Chinese norms is limited outside certain subject-matter areas and a number of developing countries sharing similar political structures. In other words, until very recently China sought "a gradual modification of Pax Americana, not a direct challenge to it."[160] Moving beyond that poses a daunting challenge, at the core of which is formulating coherent ontological and epistemological systems (as the foundation of a new international legal order) that are not anchored to China's idiosyncratic social, political attributes. China's reversion to totalitarian

[151] Potter, *supra* note 1, at 710.
[152] Lina Benabdallah, *Contesting the International Order by Integrating it: The Case of China's Belt and Road Initiative*, 40 Third World Q. 92 (2019).
[153] Ilaria Carrozza, *Legitimizing China's Growing Engagement in African Security: Change Within Continuity of Official Discourse*, 248 China Q. 1174 (2021).
[154] Yan, *supra* note 138, at 6.
[155] Cai, *supra* note 100, at 10.
[156] Courtney J. Fung, *Rhetorical Adaptation, Normative Resistance and International Order-Making: China's Advancement of the Responsibility to Protect*, 55 Cooperation & Conflict 193 (2020).
[157] Potter, *supra* note 1, at 714; Weiss & Wallace, *supra* note 3; Chih-yu Shih & Chiung-Chiu Huang, *Preaching Self-Responsibility: The Chinese Style of Global Governance*, 22 J. Contemp. China 351 (2013).
[158] *See, e.g.*, Matthew S. Erie & Do Hai Ha, *Law and Development Minus Legal Transplants: The Example of China in Vietnam*, 8 Asian J.L. & Soc. 372 (2021); Kim, *supra* note 90.
[159] He Zhipeng, *The Chinese Expression of the International Rule of Law*, *supra* note 132, at 176.
[160] Schweller & Pu, *supra* note 136, at 54.

dictatorship in the past decade and stringent government censorship add to the challenge of that task.[161]

To summarize, given its economic expansion and growing geopolitical influence, China will supply more international law actors (e.g., Chinese lawyers acting as international commercial arbitrators and Chinese judges sitting on international tribunals); create, or participate in the creation of, new international organizations and agreements (e.g., the Asian Infrastructure Investment Bank and the Regional Comprehensive Economic Partnership); and push for incremental reforms of existing international organizations. In some issue areas, the Chinese government has engaged in normative interpretation and contestation to serve its interests and policy preferences. Yet, for reasons elaborated in this chapter, China will have a marginal influence on the fundamental norms undergirding the existing international legal order. Put differently, in issue areas concerning trade and investment, China is expected to "champion the established rule and the international order based on it"[162] or propose incremental reforms; in other areas, it will likely embrace the Westphalian principles coalescing around sovereign supremacy.[163]

161 Erie, *supra* note 132, at 69.

162 Muthucumaraswamy Sornarajah & Wang Jiangyu, *China, India, and International Law: A Justice Based Vision Between the Romantic and Realist Perceptions*, 9 ASIAN J. INT'L L. 217, 243–44 (2019).

163 *Id.*; Weiss & Wallace, *supra* note 3, at 657.

# PART IV

# Conclusion

# 14

## Pressures Old and New

MARTIN KRYGIER

The rule of law is not a natural state of affairs. Nor is it simple to contrive, particularly when, as so often, unruly power comes to be concentrated in the big grasping hands of small numbers. Often despotism is simpler,[1] unruliness easier still,[2] the latter often leads to the former,[3] and the two frequently coexist.[4]

Almost everywhere and everywhen, the rule of law, where it can be said to exist at all, is bound to come under pressure. For power is at stake. Often those whose power matters most, and to whom power matters most, simply cannot imagine that theirs should or could be tempered.[5] Others understand the idea but reject it.[6] Successes occur and some have endured,[7] but they are

[1] *See* Montesquieu, The Spirit of the Laws 63 (Cambridge Univ. Press 1992) (1748).

[2] *See* Thomas Hobbes, *Of the Natural Condition of Mankind as Concerning Their Felicity and Misery*, in Leviathan (C.B. Macpherson ed., Penguin 1968) (1651).

[3] *See* John Locke, *Second Treatise*, *in* Two Treatises of Government (Peter Laslett ed., Cambridge Univ. Press 1988) (1689); Philippe Nonet & Philip Selznick, Law and Society in Transition: Toward Responsive Law 36–37, 39, 44 (Transaction 1978).

[4] *See* Daron Acemoglu & James A. Robinson, The Narrow Corridor: How Nations Struggle for Liberty 341 (2020) (on "paper Leviathans").

[5] "For my friends everything. For my enemies the law," attributed to Oscar R. Benavides, president of Peru 1933–39 (among others). *See also* Richard Pipes, Russia under the Old Regime (1974); Fernanda Pirie, *Chinese Emperors: Codes, Punishments, and Bureaucracy*, *in* The Rule of Laws: A 4,000-Year Quest to Order the World (2022) (on Imperial China).

[6] *See* Nick Cheesman, Opposing the Rule of Law: How Myanmar's Courts Make Law and Order (2015); Nick Cheesman, *Law and Order as Asymmetrical Opposite to the Rule of Law*, 6 Hague J. on Rule L. 96 (2014); Donald C. Clarke, *Order and Law in China* (Geo. Wash. L. Sch. Pub. L. & Legal Theory Paper No. 2020-52, 2020), https://papers.ssrn.com/sol3/papers.cfm?abstract_id=3682794; Moritz Rudolf, *Xi Jinping Thought on the Rule of Law* (SWP Comment No. 28, 2021), www.swp-berlin.org/publications/products/comments/2021C28_Jinping_RuleOfLaw.pdf.

[7] *See* 1 Harold Berman, Law and Revolution: The Formation of the Western Legal Tradition (1983); 2 Harold Berman, Law and Revolution: The Impact of the Protestant Reformations on the Western Legal Tradition 2006); Fernanda Pirie, The Rule of Laws: A 4,000-Year Quest to Order the World (2022).

historically rare[8] and typically unstable. So pressure is not an anomalous contemporary defect but a historically standard default. That has been a perennial challenge to admirers of well-tempered power.

The rule of law is not hostile to power, but it makes demands on how it can be exercised. Indeed, taming power takes a lot of power, and not everyone has it or can arrange and deploy it to good effect. In development literature, after all, "fragile state" is a sad term of art.[9] Well-tempered power needs resources; institutions; social and political supporting structures; norms and habits; effective technologies; incentives for good acts and protections against bad ones; and typically time and good fortune. Historically, these have come together rarely.[10] So, worldwide, a sturdy regime of rule of law has always been exceptional. Where realized in reasonable measure, something significant has been accomplished, arguably against the grain of human affairs.

However, from the early 1990s many people came to think things might be different. The rule of law came to be unprecedentedly exalted and optimistically proposed for an indefinite, sometimes almost infinite, range of problems. The phrase circumnavigated the globe, acquiring a kind of omnipresent rhetorical aura, up there with long-established and still unassailable icons such as justice, liberty, democracy, equality, constitutionalism, due process, legality, and the Rolling Stones.

In particular, in the last decade of the twentieth century and the first of the twenty-first, the rule of law came to be lauded as an indispensable condition for economic development, relief of poverty, democracy, human rights, security, peace, stability, and many other good things. Rule-of-law packages for export became standard, central, and pricey elements of international aid for benighted countries thought to lack it. Indeed, more and more international aid and financial packages became conditional upon various approved measures being undertaken to achieve the rule of law.

Asked what was the central failure of failed states, a stock answer came to be: absence of the rule of law. What was wrong with dictatorships?: same. Rule-of-law promotion boomed; states and agencies "programmed"

[8] *See* Douglass C. North, John Joseph Wallis & Barry R. Weingast, Violence and Social Orders (2009); Acemoglu & Robinson, *supra* note 4.

[9] *See* Fragile States Index, https://fragilestatesindex.org/ (last visited Feb. 20, 2024); Org. for Econ. Co-operation & Dev., States of Fragility 2022 (2022), www.oecd.org/publications/states-of-fragility-fa5a6770-en.htm.

[10] *See* Heinrich Popitz, Phenomena of Power. Authority, Domination, and Violence 41–42 (2017).

it;[11] thousands were employed to develop it; billions of dollars have been spent on it. Rule-of-law programs were implemented at vast expense in countries from, literally, Afghanistan to Zambia. As Brian Tamanaha observed at the peak of this recent resurgence: "This apparent unanimity in support of the rule of law is a feat unparalleled in history. No other single political ideal has ever achieved global endorsement."[12]

This new ambitiousness quickly came to have a transnational character. It was borne by a variety of transnational actors, proposed in relation to more and more transnational activities, recommended to – indeed required of – nations themselves, by transnational organizations. Indeed, rule of law (ROL) promotion became a transnational *project*. It rose to be near the top of the declared agendas of organizations such as the UN, the EU, the World Bank, the IMF, OSCE, EUPol, bar associations, and financial institutions around the world, with dedicated departments charged with developing the rule of law internationally. Transnational corporations, mining companies, and investors came to demand it. This spawned many of the ventures that form the subject of this book.

The book is the work of many hands and has many parts. However, two distinctive themes are central and recur frequently throughout. The first is a distinctive approach to understanding the rule of law that, unlike most writing on the subject, begins by seeking to identify its central aspiration or goal rather than by postulating any particular checklist of legal rules and institutions taken to constitute its necessary institutional elements. It starts with the end, the point of the enterprise, as it were, rather than enumeration of any particular assemblage of purported institutional means. The point the editors identify, and most of the book's authors endorse, is reduction of the possibilities of arbitrary use and abuse of power.

The second distinctive feature of the collection is its geopolitical frame. Both the threats and the promises to and of the rule of law are discussed in a transnational, not merely domestic-national, context. As several authors stress, this framing is uncommon and uncommonly significant. Let us take these two features in turn.

[11] *See* Balakrishnan Rajagopal, *Invoking the Rule of Law in Post-Conflict Rebuilding: A Critical Examination*, 49 Wm. & Mary L. Rev. 1347 (2008).

[12] Brian Z. Tamanaha, On the Rule of Law 3 (2004).

## I What's the Point?

"The rule of law" is not a simple descriptive term, with obvious empirical instantiations, like "stick" or "stone." It is rather a conceptual placeholder for a range of concerns. Ideas about what we now seek to capture with this phrase can be plausibly identified in many traditions of thought, in many civilizations, over long periods of time.[13] The traditions differ in many ways, of course, and so too, many of the terms and ideas, but there are common concerns and themes that overlap and recur, over time and in many places.

Similar concerns have been expressed in various terms, in many languages, over centuries. In English, phrases such as "the supremacy of law," "government of [or "according to"] laws," and the "rule of laws and not men"[14] have long histories. Many other languages have overlapping, though not necessarily identical, concepts and traditions of concern, expressed in various ways. There are literatures devoted to the *Rechtsstaat, l'État de droit, lo Statto di diritto, praworządność*, etc.,[15] which, like so many of our most important contemporary ideas and ideals – indeed, as the sources of many of them – can already be found deeply considered among the ancient Greeks,[16] in Rome, in Jewish, Christian and Muslim writings, in medieval Europe, thirteenth and seventeenth-century England, and in many places at many times before and between then and now.[17]

The use of one particular phrase, "the rule of law," to express some of these ideas – globally – is, by contrast, relatively recent.[18] Indeed, the current ubiquity of the term is itself a transnational phenomenon. In the

[13] Fernanda Pirie's *The Rule of Laws* documents a "4,000-Year Quest to Order the World."

[14] *See* J.A. Sempill, *Ruler's Sword, Citizen's Shield: The Rule of Law and the Constitution of Power*, 31 J.L. & Pol. 333, 336–37 (2016).

[15] *See* Martin Krygier, *Rule of Law (and Rechtsstaat)*, in XX International Encyclopedia of the Social & Behavioral Sciences 780 (James D. Wright ed., 2d ed. 2015); Gianluigi Palombella, È possibile una legalità globale? Il Rule of law e la governance del mondo (2012).

[16] Mirko Canevaro, *The Rule of Law as the Measure of Political Legitimacy in the Greek City States*, 9 Hague J. on Rule L. 211 (2017); J.A. Sempill, *The Rule of Law and the Rule of Men: History, Legacy, Obscurity*, 12 Hague J. on Rule L. 511 (2020).

[17] *See* Pirie, *supra* note 7.

[18] Dicey famously discussed the rule of law in his *Introduction to the Law of the Constitution* of 1885, but the phrase appears earlier ("The precise issue we raise is this – that throughout our empire the British rule shall be the rule of law . . ."), *in* Frederic Harrison, Martial Law: Six Letters to "The Daily News" 4 (1867), *quoted in* Dylan Lino, *The Rule of Law and the Rule of Empire: A.V. Dicey in Imperial Context*, 81 Mod. L. Rev. 739 (2018). And central elements of Dicey's ideas – but, so far as I know, not the phrase – were prefigured by W.E. Hearn, the first dean of the law faculty law at the University of Melbourne. *See* H.

late nineteenth century, Albert Venn Dicey, Vinerian Professor of the Laws of England at Oxford, chose to deploy this phrase to explore, adapt, and appropriate for England (indeed, as peculiarly English), some of these very old (and frequently encountered) problems, concerns, and hopes. He did not coin the phrase[19] but launched it on a huge Anglophone career. His brief three-point distillation of the concept, usually torn from his larger discussion, was drummed into generations of Anglophone law students for much of the twentieth century: inability of authorities to exercise "wide, arbitrary, or discretionary powers of constraint"; subjection of all citizens, whatever their "rank or condition," to the same, ordinary, law administered by the same ordinary courts – no special courts for special purposes or people (as found in France, which was therefore *sans* the rule of law); and constitutional principles that flowed up from court judgments in particular cases rather than down from general written constitutional documents. Dicey had other and more interesting things to say, but this capsule account dominated discussion so much that Judith Shklar, who was not fond of Dicey's account, nevertheless acknowledged it as "the most influential restatement of the Rule of Law since the eighteenth century."[20]

But outside the law, and outside England, no one used this phrase much. Not every lawyer, particularly if they spoke French or German, had reason to be persuaded by "Dicey's unfortunate outburst of Anglo-Saxon parochialism . . . [whereby] the Rule of Law was thus both trivialized as the peculiar patrimony of one and only one national order, and formalized, by the insistence that only one set of inherited procedures and court practices could sustain it."[21] Nevertheless, the fortuitous coincidence of English becoming the "default language"[22] of the contemporary world with the (quickly waxing and perhaps already waning) moment of Western international and transnational hegemony after 1989 has given this phrase remarkable global reach in recent decades.

Indeed, the phrase has now so solidified that even one tiny change – "a" rule instead of "the"; "by" law instead of "of" – can be taken to suggest

W. Arndt, *The Origins of Dicey's Concept of the "Rule of Law"*, 31 AUSTRALIAN L.J. 117 (1957).

19 ALBERT VENN DICEY, INTRODUCTION TO THE LAW OF THE CONSTITUTION (1885).

20 JUDITH N. SHKLAR, *Political Theory and the Rule of Law*, *in* POLITICAL THEORY AND POLITICAL THINKERS 21, 26 (Stanley Hoffman ed., 1998).

21 *Id.*

22 *See* ANNA WIERZBICKA, IMPRISONED IN ENGLISH: THE HAZARDS OF ENGLISH AS A DEFAULT LANGUAGE (2013).

very different things. On their own, however, the words do not tell you much. You won't get to the heart of the matter just by looking them up, individually or together. The ideas, not the words, are the thing. And some of them are not bad ideas.

Notoriously, understandings of this pivotal phrase and ideas that have been associated with it are many, various, and contested.[23] That is true in the world, and to a lesser extent it is also true in this collection. There is variety in the volume, and also some disagreement. However, the framing conception that is introduced by the editors, and adopted by many though not all of our contributors, follows a distinctive approach and embodies a particular substantive core.

The approach Shaffer and Sandholtz favor is what they and I call "teleological,"[24] in contrast to the "anatomical" ways in which the rule of law is commonly understood. Legal anatomists (who dominate the field) typically begin by stipulating one or other or several lists of legal-institutional components – rules,[25] procedures,[26] institutions,[27] content[28] of particular forms and character – that purportedly make up, and so are taken to define, the thing we call the rule of law.

On the account favored here, by contrast, we should instead move to any detailed specification of the ingredients necessary for the rule of law only in the light of, and therefore *after*, we have reached a view as to the *telos,* the purpose or good we invoke and seek its help to achieve. Only then, goal in view, does it make sense to try to stipulate what might be necessary to attain or approach it. That, in turn, will vary with time and context, so that what might be required to attain the goal of the rule of law cannot be specified in detail in advance, least of all in "formulaic check-lists based on specified, formal characteristics."[29] Understood in this way, the rule of law is what Jeremy Waldron has called a "solution concept."[30]

[23] *See* Jeremy Waldron, *Is the Rule of Law an Essentially Contested Concept (in Florida)?*, 21 L. & Phil. 137 (2002).

[24] Martin Krygier, *The Rule of Law: Legality, Teleology, Sociology*, *in* Relocating the Rule of Law 44 (Gianluigi Palombella & Neil Walker eds., 2008); Martin Krygier, *Four Puzzles about the Rule of Law: Why, What, Where? And Who Cares?*, *in* Getting to the Rule of Law 64 (James E. Fleming ed., 2011).

[25] Lon L. Fuller, The Morality of Law (2d ed. 1969); Joseph Raz, *The Rule of Law and Its Virtue*, *in* The Authority of the Law 210 (1979).

[26] Jeremy Waldron, The Rule of Law and the Importance of Procedure, *in* Getting to the Rule of Law, *supra* note 24, at 3.

[27] Dicey, *supra* note 19.

[28] Tom Bingham, The Rule of Law (2010).

[29] *See* Chapter 1.

[30] Waldron, *supra* note 23, at 158.

If so, as with any postulated solution, we need to begin with the problem it is meant to solve.

The substantive problem Shaffer and Sandholtz identify for the rule of law is arbitrary exercise of power. Appeal to the rule of law signals the hope that there may be ways, and that the rule of law might be among them, to diminish the kinds and levels of arbitrary sway available to those who exercise (substantial)[31] power. The ambition, to use a term found in many traditions of thinking about these matters, is to reduce the chances of arbitrariness by "tempering"[32] the ways in which substantial power can be exercised. These are very old and widespread concerns, as well as ways of expressing them.[33]

Few people would deny that the rule of law has arbitrary power in its sights, and several authors in this collection adopt this approach explicitly. However, in Chapter 2, Brian Tamanaha questions the sense of starting this way, and more generally of narrowing the ends of the rule of law to just this one, or indeed any *one*. While not doubting that arbitrary power is among the targets of the rule of law, he points out that there are plenty of others, and a focus on each will stress different things from a focus on any of those others. Why give priority just to one? All the more, given that:

> the assertion that the rule of law serves a specific purpose (*telos*) that explains its existence (*raison d'être*) fits uneasily with how the rule of law has come about. The rule of law (whatever it means) was not designed or created by anyone for a particular purpose, but rather evolved over centuries owing to a confluence of beliefs, motivations, circumstances, and institutional developments in connection with cultural, religious, economic, political, legal, and other factors. Every rule-of-law society has a unique history, institutional arrangement, and set of consequences. Assertions about *the* purpose is a projection by given theorists based on their particular priorities.[34]

[31] *De minibus non curat lex* (the law is not concerned with trifles).

[32] *See* Martin Krygier, *Tempering Power*, *in* BRIDGING IDEALISM AND REALISM IN CONSTITUTIONALISM AND THE RULE OF LAW 34 (Maurice Adams et al. eds., 2016); Martin Krygier, *Poder atemperado: Cómo pensar, y no pensar, sobre el Estado de Derecho* [Tempering power: How to think, and not to think, about the rule of law], 25 EUNOMÍA: REVISTA EN CULTURA DE LA LEGALIDAD 22 (2023).

[33] *See* John Philip Reid, *In Legitimate Stirps: The Concept of "Arbitrary," the Supremacy of Parliament, and the Coming of the American Revolution*, 5 HOFSTRA L. REV. 459 (1977); Sempill, *supra* note 14; DAVID M. BEATTY, FAITH, FORCE AND REASON: AN ARMCHAIR HISTORY OF THE RULE OF LAW (2022); PIRIE, *supra* note 7; GERALD POSTEMA, LAW'S RULE: THE NATURE, VALUE, AND VIABILITY OF THE RULE OF LAW (2023).

[34] *See* Chapter 2.

Tamanaha prefers to say that "*the rule of law exists in a society when government officials and legal subjects are bound by and abide by law.*" Such a "legally ordered community" might serve a variety of "functions" – among them, reduction of arbitrariness in the exercise of power, but that is just one among a number of others that include supporting freedom and dignity, security and trust, construction and institution of institutions, enhancement of economic development, and likely, he allows, others as well.[35]

It is impossible to legislate in these matters, given the currency of the term and the contending confusion, or confusing contention, about what it means. One can only propose and commend. In support of the approach and focus that the editors (and I) commend, I would offer two considerations. First of all, reduction of arbitrary power is distinctive in Tamanaha's list of "functions." This flows from its instrumental and foundational character. Whereas we might hope that a "legally constituted community" will support freedom, dignity, security, trust, etc., it is unlikely to do so if wielders of power are free (whether outside law or, as often occurs, authorized by it) to exercise power arbitrarily in the ways Shaffer and Sandholtz enumerate.

Law is *essentially* a vehicle and channel for the exercise and communication of power. That is what it does. There are many ways to exercise power, and different ways enable different functions to be performed. Power – whether legal or not – can support freedom, dignity, trust, and so on, but it can deny them as well, and often does. Frequently it does so by means of law, as chapters in this book show plentifully. What Haberkorn shows of Thailand – "[t]he primary tool of repression is the law itself"[36] – is true of many contemporary regimes and arguably transnational organizations of other kinds as well. It does the former more readily when it is reliably tempered, and the latter more easily when its wielders are free to exercise it arbitrarily. The hope of partisans of the rule of law is that power might be reliably, routinely tempered, in ways that both help guard against abusive uses and enable it to be channeled in fruitful ways and directions.

The ways that power can be exercised are, then, a specific, immanent concern of the rule of law. Tempering power to reduce the chances of its arbitrary exercise is a specific internal ambition. That achieved, many other possibilities flow, functions are enabled, that would otherwise be at

35 See Chapter 2.
36 *See* Chapter 12.

risk or more difficult to attain. These include various moral, political, economic, and other goals, ideals, and functions, often larger than 'mere' tempering of power – among them, those Tamanaha suggests. Such tempering is not necessarily ultimately more important than other goals, but it is normatively prior in a different sense. It has a specific, immediate, instrumental importance not reducible to other things, commonly a condition for the best of them, and often not separately considered. Wheels perform many important functions, but they do most of them better if they are round. Unfortunately, what goes to reduce arbitrary power is more complicated and variable than a wheel.

Ways of exercising power, including nonarbitrary and nondominating ways, are in other words closely tied up with the concept of the rule of law, immanent in the idea. They are a *feature* (and certainly not a bug) of the ideal, not just a function it might serve or a consequence that might follow its observance. Other goods – say, freedom, dignity, security, trust, economic development, or democracy – may, as has in recent times commonly been claimed, flow from the rule of law (and are the only reasons many people today are interested in it[37]), but they are not immanent in this way. If the rule of law enables them, these are, as it were, external and contingent benefits that might flow from a well-constituted "legally ordered community," that is, one in which the likelihood that power will be exercised arbitrarily has been reduced. But legal communities are often not well constituted, and never so when arbitrary power is rife. For unfortunately, as we have seen frequently in recent years, and as the discussions of "rule *by* law" in several chapters in this book attest, a "legally ordered community" full of laws in appropriate forms, yet awash with arbitrary power, is no oxymoron or empirical oddity.[38] And where it occurs, the functions that Tamanaha attributes to such a community are unlikely to be well performed.

According to the view recommended here, then, one starts by thinking about how arbitrariness in the exercise of power might be reduced. This is because arrangements – deliberate or not, legal or other, intended for this purpose or not – that reduce the ability of power-holders to wield power

[37] *See* Martin Krygier, *Transformations of the Rule of Law: Legal, Liberal, Neo*, *in* The Politics of Legality in a Neoliberal Age 19 (Ben Golder & Daniel McLoughlin eds., 2017).

[38] *See* Martin Krygier, *Domestic Abuse: Populists and the Rule of Law*, 130 IWMpost 3 (2022), www.iwm.at/publication/iwmpost-article/domestic-abuse-populists-and-the-rule-of-law; András Sajó, *The Rule of Law as Legal Despotism: Concerned Remarks on the Use of "Rule of Law" in Illiberal Democracies*, 11 Hague J. on Rule L. 371 (2019).

arbitrarily, and constitute, frame, and channel ways of nonarbitrary exercise of power, are foundational for the achievement of many other things we might value, not least those we might value more. Well-tempered power is less an alternative to any of them than a condition for them; at least for many of them, less an intrinsic value that should compete in some ultimate social ideal with, say, liberty, equality, security, or whatever, than a foundational achievement, necessary for the attainment of many other values unlikely to be attained when power is left to its holders' own devices. It operates at a different, earlier, foundational level. Ceilings are often more attractive than foundations, but the former are precarious unless the latter are secure.

The ideal of the rule of law – well-tempered power – is a relative and variable achievement, not all-or-nothing. But one can say it exists in good shape or repair insofar as a certain sort of valued state of affairs, to which law contributes in particular and variable ways, exists. According to this conception, the ideal is well served insofar as the exercise of political, social, and economic power in a society (or an "order") is effectively tempered, constrained, constituted, and channelled so that nonarbitrary exercises of such powers are relatively routine, while arbitrary ones are not.

Well-tempered power is, then, a complex, practical, and instrumental ideal. It is complex because a lot is needed even to approximate it and that lot varies and changes depending on the nature of specific problems, circumstances, and available responses. That is why Shaffer and Sandholtz, and several other authors here, such as Akinkugbe and Farrall and Halliday, are right to distrust "formulaic checklists."[39] The ideal is practical because it is neither a natural fact nor a Utopian fantasy we might only dream of, but a goal intended to be made good (even if only partially, to varying degrees) in the real world. It is instrumental since it is rarely anyone's ultimate passion, but rather is understood as a means to help solve a problem that threatens the attainment of other goals. And it is a normative-descriptive goal and ideal rather than a simple description. The concept is normative, the condition supposed to be valuable.

It is also important. Circumstances in which some are able to exercise significant power arbitrarily over others are at once pernicious and pervasive. As I have argued at greater length elsewhere, they threaten

[39] *See* Chapters 1 and 11. See also the discussion of TLO (nonformulaic) theory by Jeremy Farrall & Terence C. Halliday in Chapter 6.

human dignity,[40] equality,[41] and liberty;[42] are liable to lead to domination[43] and fear;[44] imperil trust and social coordination;[45] and generate solipsistic short-sightedness and stupidity among the powerful, who foolishly fancy they benefit from being blocked from contestation and free flows of judgment and information.[46] More can be said about all of these values and the contribution of tempered power to them, but enough for now. Thought of this way, then, well-tempered power is not one among other good things that might flow from the existence of a "legally ordered community." It is, as it were, an ecumenical resource that the rule of law helps provide for such a community. That good secured, many other goods might flow.

Thus understood, the notion of "tempering" power has two implications, not always reflected in the rule-of-law literature. First, though it is common to believe otherwise, one does not temper power simply by *limiting* it, as writers on the rule of law often presume. Rather, well-*tempered* power is modified (and in Montesquieu's conception, "moderated") in various ways – mixed and balanced, refined, blended, separated, but also distributed, connected, and so in many ways *strengthened* – in order at the same time to make power available, disciplined, directed, and channeled, and thus better equipped to support the effective exercise of power for good purposes rather than bad. Weakness is not a virtue of the rule of law. Failed and fragile states exhibit the former and never the latter. If you slam a door, hope that the glass is tempered rather than not; tempered steel, too, is immensely stronger than its untempered elements. Both have been refined, and their elements blended and mixed, to be fitter for purpose. A society where the rule of law is strong is one where

[40] *See* FULLER, *supra* note 25, at 162–63; Waldron, *supra* note 26.

[41] *See* PAUL GOWDER, THE RULE OF LAW IN THE REAL WORLD (2016).

[42] *See* Charles Larmore, *Liberal and Republican Conceptions of Freedom*, 6 CRIT. REV. INT'L SOC. & POL. PHIL. 96 (2003); Christian List, *Republican Freedom and the Rule of Law*, 5 PHIL POL. & ECON. 201 (2006).

[43] Philip Pettit, Republicanism (1997); Gianluigi Palombella, *The Rule of Law as an Institutional Ideal, in* RULE OF LAW AND DEMOCRACY: INQUIRY INTO INTERNAL AND EXTERNAL ISSUES 3 (Gianluigi Palombella & Leonardo Morlino eds., 2010).

[44] *See* JUDITH N. SHKLAR, *The Liberalism of Fear, in* POLITICAL THEORY AND POLITICAL THINKERS, *supra* note 20, at 3; SHKLAR, *Political Theory and the Rule of Law, in* POLITICAL THEORY AND POLITICAL THINKERS, *supra* note 20, at 21.

[45] On the key importance of which in modern societies, see ADAM SMITH, AN INQUIRY INTO THE NATURE AND CAUSES OF THE WEALTH OF NATIONS 26 (Liberty Classics 1981) (1776).

[46] Stephen Holmes, *In Case of Emergency: Misunderstanding Tradeoffs in the War on Terror*, 97 CAL. L. REV. 301 (2009).

power is also strong but balanced by other powers, internal and external, and well-tempered, neither weak nor ill-tempered.[47]

Another misleading commonplace in the literature, several times referred to in this volume, is a forced choice between "thin" and "thick" conceptions of the rule of law. That distinction has spawned a hackneyed debate among writers on the rule of law over whether it is enough to adopt the forms and restrict oneself to characteristics of institutions and rules thought to add up to the rule of law ("thin"), or whether that is not enough and one needs to take account of the moral purposes and content of the law as well. There are problems with lurching too far in either direction.

Arbitrary ways of exercising power are objectionable in themselves, even when the institutions seem to conform to rule-of-law checklists, and not merely when they are yoked to bad purposes. So this concern straddles that old divide. On the one hand, it cannot be restricted to any list of rules and institutions since not they themselves but whether they actually turn out to reduce arbitrary power is what matters. And often they don't, even when well formed. As several contributors to this collection emphasize, modern authoritarians are well-versed in ways of generating traditional legal rules and institutions in order to enable rule *by*, rather than *of*, law. So much so, that a new form of legal scholarship has emerged in recent years. It investigates what has variously been called "abusive constitutionalism," "stealth authoritarianism," "constitutional coups," "autocratic legalism," "abuse of the constitution," or "twisting and turning of the rule of law."[48] So, "thin" is not enough.

On the other hand, as the legal philosopher Joseph Raz long ago warned, if we equate the rule of law with "the rule of the good law then to explain its nature is to propound a complete social philosophy. But if so the term lacks any useful function. We have no need to be converted to the rule of law just in order to discover that to believe in it is to believe

[47] *See further* JOHN BRAITHWAITE, MACROCRIMINOLOGY AND FREEDOM (2021).

[48] David Landau, *Abusive Constitutionalism*, 47 U.C. DAVIS L. REV. 189 (2013); Ozan Varol, *Stealth Authoritarianism*, 100 IOWA L. REV. 1673 (2015); Kim Lane Scheppele, *Constitutional Coups in EU Law, in* CONSTITUTIONALISM AND THE RULE OF LAW: BRIDGING IDEALISM AND REALISM 446 (Maurice Adams, Ernst Hirsch Ballin & Anne Meuwese eds., 2017); Kim Lane Scheppele, *Autocratic Legalism*, 85 U. CHI. L. REV. 545 (2018); Grażyna Skąpska, *The Decline of Liberal Constitutionalism in East Central Europe, in* ROUTLEDGE INTERNATIONAL HANDBOOK OF EUROPEAN SOCIAL TRANSFORMATION 130 (Peeter Vihalemm, Anu Masso & Signe Opermann eds., 2018); András Sajó & Juha Tuovinen, *The Rule of Law and Legitimacy in Emerging Illiberal Democracies*, 64 OSTEUROPA RECHT 506 (2019).

that good should triumph."[49] So, although the rule of law's recent iconic status has tended to move ambitions for it in such all-encompassing directions, that is not a good idea. The goal of the rule of law, as distinct from other goals one might seek, is to accomplish an immediate, specific, if complex, task, the achievement of which has the virtue of spawning or underpinning many other virtues, but it is not the same as them. That task is to reduce arbitrariness in the exercise of power. And so, the rule of law extends to matters of content, but only insofar as they affect the ability of power-holders to exercise arbitrary power. As legal autocrats in many countries today have demonstrated, that is many places. A common contemporary strategy is to do whatever they can by means of conventional legal institutions and rules, using the law to expand central power, reduce independence of institutions of adjudication and governance (in sometimes more and sometimes less subtle ways), and cement loyal incumbents in key positions so that they thereby open the already uneven playing field to only one team (as was frequently attempted by the former Polish government before losing the 2023 election), even after that team has ostensibly lost the power to govern.

To sum up, the rule of law is an *achievement,* at once modest and precious. It is modest because it will never be all we want, and it might conflict with other things we might want. If so, accommodations might be necessary. Nevertheless, it is precious because it is a condition for avoiding many things we should never want, indeed some of the worst things that can be done to us. Equally valuable, it enables many things that we do and should wish for.

So, we can maintain a teleological approach to the rule of law while acknowledging, as we must, Tamanaha's point that the rule of law has developed – where it has – in various ways, for various motives, conscious and unconscious, as a result of good and bad fortune, and so forth. Well-tempered power is the *telos* of the rule of law, not in the sense that whoever benefits from it must have had it in mind, still less because some canonical institutional checklist has been followed. Reduction of arbitrary power is an achievement to be valued, not a historical explanation of how or why it came about. There are, of course, many ways of getting there, or some way there, or not at all, or somewhere else, as Tamanaha says. Postulating what we find valuable in it is not to say this is what people have intended (though sometimes they have), but that it is a valuable kind of achievement, however attained, an ideal that might

[49] Raz, *supra* note 25, at 211.

orient some of our practices and hopes, serve as a source of critique when they are denied, and help us attain others.

Indeed – and my second consideration in support of the approach recommended in this book – it is precisely because, as Tamanaha rightly observes, the ideal of the rule of law might be attained (and undone) in many ways and to many degrees that we should not begin with some purported institutional identikit checklist of elements of the *thing* supposed to help in attainment of the ideal. As the rule-of-law promotion industry has learnt at cost, there is no such one thing.

If one begins with the end of well-tempered power, the next step is to ask how to get there in the contexts one seeks to do so. The answer to that question must be contingent on facts and circumstances, and an implication of this way of proceeding is not simply that anatomy comes second, but that it cannot be assumed always to take any specific form that conventional rule-of-law promoters promote, nor indeed that it is to be found where they typically look for it. We need things in the world to achieve it, but what we need will depend on what we want to achieve as well as on the conditions and circumstances in which we seek to achieve it. Given that times, problems, institutions, imaginations, technologies, and social, political, legal and economic contexts differ and change, the specific answers to that second question will necessarily vary. So institutional checklists should come not second but third: goal, circumstances, institutional design. This is simply to generalize Akinkugbe's suspicion of "the parochial checklists that some Western scholars develop from their own legal traditions and universalize."[50]

Instead, the rule of law has too often been treated – in fact, even if not in rhetoric – as the product of some legal-institutional package or portfolio of packages, available for export all around the world. But it has become abundantly clear that in many contexts the conventional packages that the rule-of-law industry provides, or indeed that law provides, will not do the trick. First of all, particular rules and institutions are unlikely to be universally transferable since they depend on so much else where they come from (which is not packageable for export), like old traditions of thinking and behaving (*manières d'agir et de penser* in Durkheim's terms), and they enter into contexts with so much else that has not been developed for or with these transplants in mind. And yet there is the fundamental point, stressed by Shaffer and Sandholtz, that even if institutional templates were well designed by those who developed

[50] *See* Chapter 11.

them, "[u]ltimately, for the rule of law to become effective, it must be institutionalized as part of a culture of conduct. It must become a *practice*."[51] That will not happen in a day, and standard rule-of-law legal-institutional packages on their own are unable to make it happen. For effective tempering of power is a complex cultural, social, and political, *as well as* legal achievement. It will not spring fully formed from any institutional fix. Conversely, as we have seen and as modern populists contrive to display every day, many hallowed 'rule of law' institutions appear to be readily available to be subverted without needing to be eliminated. And they can help in the subversion of the very values that were thought to underpin them.[52]

Notwithstanding these salutary lessons, as several chapters in this book make clear, many attempts to transplant such packages have repeatedly exhibited a quaint combination of confidence and cluelessness. As one, somewhat chastened, rule-of-law promoter observed at the height of rule-of-law promotional activity: "we know how to do a lot of things, but deep down we don't really know what we're doing."[53] The results have not often been glorious, and that should be no surprise.

## II Transnational Rule of Law?

The second distinctive feature of this collection is its transnational focus. For, traditionally, when anyone discussed the rule of law it was with domestic models in mind. As Scheppele remarks of what she calls "the rule of law writ small," "[w]hat most . . . conceptions of the rule of law share . . . is the unstated assumption that the rule of law should be understood within the boundaries of national law. The rule of law analyst typically takes the national legal system as if it were the only system in which rule of law has any real purchase and analyzes it in isolation."[54] Even when, less commonly, discussion was extended to "the international rule of law," that was about relations *between* such states, and the first question typically asked was whether there could ever really be such a thing.[55] The rule of law was regarded as paradigmatically an

[51] *See* Chapter 1.

[52] *See* Krygier, *supra* note 38.

[53] Quoted in Thomas Carothers, Promoting the Rule of Law Abroad: In Search of Knowledge 15 (2006). *See also* Deval Desai, Expert Ignorance: The Law and Politics of Rule of Law Reform (2023).

[54] *See* Chapter 7.

[55] *See* Chapter 1.

attribute or product of domestic state legal orders replete with institutions able to issue, interpret, and enforce "commands" in respect of subjects who, in the phrase of arch-positivist John Austin, were "habitually obedient or submissive to a certain and common superior."[56] These latter would be in luck, protected by the rule of law, when those laws took particular forms, were issued, interpreted, and enforced by particular types of legal institutions, especially courts, acting in particular types of ways. What then was to be said of a realm where the familiar institutions of the domestic rule of law were lacking, and where what institutions there were bore a very different relationship to their "subjects"?

Hence numerous hackneyed debates among lawyers, philosophers, and students of international relations about whether international law is law at all, given the absence, or at least paucity, of centralized and hierarchical institutional structures, serviced by legislatures, courts, and officials with powers of enforcement, that bear plausible analogies to those found within states themselves. And even if we can call it law, can such an institutionally impoverished setting support the rule of law?

The *trans*national domain – "transnational legal orders" and actors themselves, whether in their interactions with other organizations and actors or in the whole complex of multilevel interactions described in this book's introduction and throughout – might be considered in even worse shape. For they mix *everything* up: state/nonstate/transstate/interstate/intrastate; public/private; hard/soft; top-down/bottom-up; vertical/horizontal. All this generated by state and suprastate regulators, nonstate businesses, civil society actors, and other players, bearing few preformed hierarchical relationships and few regular institutions with generalized interpretive authority or powers to enforce. Multitudes of levels, legal (and nonlegal and quasi-legal) orders, actors, domains, problems, and attempts to solve them are, to use Shaffer and Sandholtz's word, thoroughly "enmeshed" in the transnational legal world. As Ginsburg and Schoppe stress, "[w]e thus have an ideal, operating at multiple levels of law that interact in complex ways. Enmeshment can take various forms."[57]

Domestic institutional analogies with all this color and movement are unlikely to be readily apparent. And yet, as cases discussed in this volume make clear again and again, arbitrary power is no less likely to be

[56] John Austin, The Province of Jurisprudence Determined 179 (Wilfrid E. Rumble ed., 1995).
[57] *See* Chapter 5.

a problem within and between transnational organizations and arrangements and in their relationships with other orders, including states, than within national settings themselves. As our editors argue forcefully, the fates of the rule of law in domestic, transnational, and international settings are increasingly and often inextricably intertwined.

One "vexing question" all this enmeshment raises for conventional understandings of the rule of law, as Farrall and Halliday observe, is whether it is "empirically, theoretically, or normatively acceptable to extrapolate from institutional configurations within a state to the global order writ large?"[58] The implication of Part I of this chapter, and indeed of all the chapters in this book, is "no." As we have seen, legal-institutional "extrapolations" are frequently perilous even between different domestic contexts. Little reason, then, to believe that they can be relied upon to illuminate more brightly in the multifarious contexts and activities of transnational orders as their 'models' (are thought to) do at home.

This truism has two divergent implications. On the one hand, for the reasons already rehearsed, the transnational adoption of complexes of legal rules, institutions, procedures, etc. developed in particular domestic contexts cannot without more (and sometimes without less) be relied upon to enhance the rule of law, as understood here, in the very various and different circumstances of transnational arrangements.

This is all the more the case in circumstances (not rare) where such arrangements involve deployment of conventional rule-of-law standards and institutions to extract advantages for powerful transnational players at the expense of arbitrary interferences with the choices of governments and peoples dependent upon them or their activities. This can be a fraught aspect of transnational invocation of rule of law "guarantees." Thus, Jennifer Lander observes that:

> Virtually all "national" economic strategies now revolve around becoming *globally* competitive, whether in relation to financial services, agriculture and manufacturing, extractive and energy industries, technology and telecommunication, health and education ... All of these economic sectors are governed by legal rules and norms that are increasingly *trans*national in their scope, meaning that a body of legality has achieved regulatory resonance and effectiveness across scales of jurisdiction (international, regional, national, sub-national).[59]

[58] *See* Chapter 6.

[59] JENNIFER LANDER, TRANSNATIONAL LAW AND STATE TRANSFORMATION: THE CASE OF EXTRACTIVE DEVELOPMENT IN MONGOLIA 5 (2019).

As she documents in the case of Mongolia, international mining companies, financial institutions, foreign investors, and multinational corporations negotiate multiple conditions and demand guarantees (some of them indeed necessary to make investment secure) to be enforced by the state in which they offer to invest. Such states, keen to capture the investment, have strong incentives – pressure, indeed – to comply and require citizens to comply with conditions they might otherwise reject. The transnational legal ordering that results distorts local politics, governance, democracy, and economic and social options in ways not dreamt of by Alfred Dicey. All in the name of the rule of law. As Lander observes and documents in uncomfortable detail:

> In Mongolia we can see the influence of a distinctly *global* rule of law discourse in shaping expectations of state behaviour, promoted by both internal policy elites and external actors.[60]
>
> … Where previously the Mongolian government promoted legal change in relation to the mining sector whilst maintaining a national conception of the rule of law, the post-2014 reforms implicitly presume the *stability* of the legal environment as a new criterion for the rule of law. In this sense, a version of the rule of law that privileges the stability of the investment environment functions as the new basic norm upon which the new extractive order rests.[61]

Akinkugbe's chapter suggests African parallels, as when he writes that:

> a noncontextual and historical analysis of the Burkina Faso military coups of 2022 fails to appreciate the limitations of traditional measurement of rule-of-law compliance. Beyond the abhorrent practice of military juntas and the cleavages that characterize the national context for the coups, the coup was also about geopolitical struggles between powerful Western countries such as France, the United States of America, and Russia. Western influence, though diminished, remains considerable for historical reasons, and because many African countries still look to the West for aid, investment, and sympathy in international lending bodies. In turn, powerful Western governments have been accused of supporting rival factions in states where their economic and military interests exist.[62]

[60] *Id.* at 228.

[61] *Id.* at 229; *see also* Kinnari I. Bhatt, Concessionaires, Financiers and Communities: Implementing Indigenous Peoples' Rights to Land in Transnational Development Projects (2020); Kinnari Bhat, *Review Symposium: The Rule of Law in Transnational Development Projects – Private Actors and Public Chokeholds*, 17 Int'l J.L. Context 99 (2021).

[62] *See* Chapter 11.

And the point is made at large by Stephen Humphreys:

> Versions of what Thomas Carothers once called (with deliberate irony) the rule of law "standard menu" have played an important role in concretising a vision of law and its institutions stripped of historical, local, cultural or social peculiarities: an easy universalism is instead constructed in these visions (laws are known and internally consistent, they are applied to all equally by independent judiciaries, and so on), which in turn translates quickly, when we look abroad, into a register of presence and absence, without needing to open questions of cultural specificity or historical cause.[63]

Secondly and conversely, however, it is not all bad news. For there is no reason – at least, the limitations of the "standard menu" by itself are not the reason – to deny the possibility of the rule of law in transnational contexts. For, viewed teleologically, the end, not the means, is the thing. Other than conventional legal arrangements are certainly likely to be necessary, and they might work. This, for example, is the burden of explorations of transnational "societal constitutionalism" by Gunther Teubner and others in his orbit and influenced by him, which "exceed the borders of the nation state in two ways. Constitutionalism beyond the nation state means two different things: constitutional problems arising outside the borders of the nation state in transnational political processes, and at the same time outside the institutionalized political sector, in the 'private' sectors of society."[64]

As Teubner argues, institutional experimentation and creativity are unavoidable in the many *different* settings *and sorts of settings* where needs and demands for new forms of "constitutionalization" emerge. He argues that such experimentation is plentiful and often successful, but it takes many different forms in the many transnational settings, where one might not be "blessed" with what Malinowski, after all, long ago found Trobriand Islanders did without – "central authority, codes, courts, and constables"[65] – and where often political power is not the currency of

63 Stephen Humphreys, The Theatre of the Rule of Law. Transnational Legal Intervention in Theory and Practice 220–21 (2010).

64 *See* Gunther Teubner, Constitutional Fragments. Societal Constitutionalism and Globalization 1–2 (2012); *see also* Angelo Golia & Gunther Teubner, *Societal Constitutionalism: Background, Theory, Debates, Debates*, 15 Vienna J. on Const. L. 357 (2021); David Sciulli, Theory of Societal Constitutionalism (1992); Chris Thornhill, A Sociology of Transnational Constitutions: Social Foundations of the Post-National Legal Structure (2016).

65 Bronisław Malinowski, Crime and Custom in Savage Society 37 (Routledge, 2017) (1926).

exchange. Old-school "formulaic checklists" might have no foothold, and yet power might be tempered and arbitrary exercise of it resisted in other ways. Rule-of-law anatomists might find that hard to accommodate, but teleologists are concerned with making a point rather than sticking to a script. And as theorists of transnational legal orders (TLOs) have tracked and shown,[66] there are many ways to make, and fail to make, that point, and these ways can differ and change.

Which is a good thing, too, since there are many transnational domains which raise just such rule-of-law issues, but for which it makes little sense to search for some national institutional model to "extrapolate." TLOs are of all sorts and do all sorts of things. What might or might not make sense within the UN Security Council is unlikely to have a close bearing on the World Trade Organization. And are we talking about tempering the power of and within transnational organizations themselves, or about their efforts to generate the rule of law elsewhere, including nation-states? What questions of feasibility and appropriateness arise in these different domains? Each context is likely to have different modalities of the exercise of power, and those hoping to temper power will need to address the specifics. Strategies, tactics, means, and ends will all vary.

Given what can be at stake where substantial powers are involved, and the variety of contexts, arrangements, means, and ends where attempts to temper them might be made, it would seem wise to combine modesty of the intellect with keenness of the will[67] – a combination that seems exemplified in Farrall and Halliday's account of how, in light of TLO theory, one might think of tempering the power of "the most symbolically powerful political entity in the world beyond the state":[68] the United Nations Security Council.

Comparing the recommendations of one group from the Austrian government and New York University's Institute for International Law and Justice (Austria/NYU) with another from the Australian government and the Australian National University (Australia/ANU), they emphasize the difference between the highly ambitious institutional assessment of

[66] *See* Chapter 1; Terence C. Halliday & Gregory Shaffer, *Transnational Legal Orders*, *in* TRANSNATIONAL LEGAL ORDERS 3 (Terence C. Halliday & Gregory Shaffer eds., 2015).

[67] This is, of course, a riff on the phrase "pessimism of the intellect, optimism of the will," commonly attributed to Antonio Gramsci, who took it from Romain Rolland. *See* Francesca Antonini, *Pessimism of the Intellect, Optimism of the Will: Gramsci's Political Thought in the Last Miscellaneous Notebooks*, 31 RETHINKING MARXISM 42 (2019).

[68] *See* Chapter 6.

the former and a more "pragmatic" approach of the latter. Austria/NYU "diagnoses the problem as a failure of the UN essentially to adopt an institutional and procedural configuration of ROL that is conventional in well-established ROL orders within states";[69] Australia/ANU, by contrast, "took a more pragmatic strategy, judging that reforms were only feasible and more probable if they were modest and able to be implemented within the constraints of extant UNSC procedures and structures."[70] Farrall and Halliday argue that:

> there endures a tension between the idealistic view of a classic institutional balancing of powers beyond the state and a pragmatic view that accepts this as a bridge too far. . . . In contrast to the leanings of the Austrian/NYU initiative towards the replication and extrapolation of a within-state institutional separation of powers into the transnational realm, the Australian/ANU iteration of reforms proceeds on the basis of the judgment that a macrocosm of the national in the international would require amendments to the UN Charter – a prospect so unrealistic as to be a nonstarter. The perfect would become the enemy of the good. Why should we expect a global institution to achieve in decades what has taken many countries centuries to accomplish . . .?[71]

The difference pointed to here might not be simply between perfectionism and pragmatism, however, but a deeper contrast of both principle and expectations between anatomical and teleological approaches to reform. Why imagine that institutional models plucked out of domestic settings, embedded in particular social and cultural histories and forms and functions and everything else that goes with governing a long-existing state, will even in principle be transplantable to a constructed organization of completely different character, functions, membership, challenges, and background? Nothing much in the history of international relations or transnational rule-of-law promotion gives warrant to anatomical adventurism in these matters. That is a truth not confined to the UNSC. It is general, perhaps universal.

Apart from the internal workings of transnational organizations themselves, half of the chapters of this book[72] are concerned with interactions between organizations purporting specifically to embody and promote the rule of law and nation-states. How have they fared? And should they have fared differently?

[69] *See* Chapter 6.
[70] *See* Chapter 6.
[71] *See* Chapter 6.
[72] Chapters 1, 4, 5, 7, 8, 9, and 10.

One would be more confident about these matters if one could point to a healthy dose of experiments that actually worked. The scorecard, however, while not blank, is not hugely encouraging. Montoya and Ponce and Shaffer and Sandholtz track a steady decline in rule-of-law scores globally. Ginsburg and Schoppe emphasize the range of available outcomes. Strong regional ROL TLOs can come into tension with nation-states notionally part of them, but weak ones can buy harmony at the price of effectiveness. Regional TLOs might *complement* the rule of law within states, but then again they might *substitute* for it and then lead to anti-TLO and anti-RoL backlash. In Latin America, Pou Giménez finds that while the regional human rights regime had "critically supported" responses to "challenges to the rule of law by populist leaders . . . most constitutional resources are activated ex post and place an immense burden on the courts."[73] From her panoramic discussion of transnational organizations that seek to further the rule of law, Peters concludes that "both in Europe and in the Global South, the external constitutional assistance lent by international organizations has produced only moderate positive effects – if any at all – for the functioning of the rule of law."[74]

It appears, and might indeed be, that you're damned if you do and damned if you don't. Starting with the latter option, Kahn and Kurban point to dramatic failures in relation to Russia (Council of Europe) and Turkey (European Court of Human Rights), respectively, where the relevant "supervisory" transnational organizations seemed to bend over backward to encourage "therapeutic admission,"[75] avoiding close scrutiny of actually existing practices, in the hope that admission might soften and conciliate the recalcitrant leaders of those states. That their backs were bent, according to our authors, is pretty clear; that any therapy or conciliation occurred is doubtful.

The question Kurban raises is key: "Is the Turkish case a singular story of democratic transition gone wrong, or does it speak to broader issues concerning the ways in which human-rights and rule-of-law TLOs interact with authoritarian regimes?"[76] From the Turkish case, she concludes that the European Court of Human Rights specifically, with parallels

[73] See Chapter 10.
[74] *See* Chapter 4.
[75] This wonderful term was coined by Peter Leuprecht, *Innovations in the European System of Human Rights Protection: Is Enlargement Compatible with Reinforcement*, 8 Transnat'l L. & Contemp. Probs. 313, 332 (1998), and is quoted by Jeffrey Kahn in Chapter 8.
[76] *See* Chapter 9.

among rule-of-law-promoting TLOs more generally, "not only permit illiberal states to violate those norms but also themselves undermine such norms."[77]

Kahn restricts his discussion to the Russian case, but his meticulous account of the mutual courtship of the Council of Europe and postcommunist Russia, proceeding through "therapeutic admission," accelerating violations that caused damage not only to Russia but to the "load-bearing structures" of the Council itself, to the point of eventual and perhaps eternal breakdown of the relationship, does not give cause for comfort.

After a slow start, by contrast, the European Union has in recent years become more assertive – at least against Poland and Hungary – in attempting to promote and sustain the rule of law among its member states, in particular by beginning to call out domestic regime rule-of-law "backsliding." Ten new states were admitted to the EU in 2004, when "end of history" optimism had not yet disappeared. Others followed. As Ginsburg and Schoppe point out, "[t]he idea that supranational, European rule-of-law principles may need to be enforced *against* a nation-state seemed far-fetched at the time."[78] So far-fetched, indeed, that it appears to have been thought possible that *at the moment of accession* candidates could satisfy the EU that, after bringing their laws and institutions in line with the 80,000 pages of the *acquis communautaire*, they had achieved "stability of institutions guaranteeing democracy, the *rule of law*, human rights and respect for and protection of minorities … Membership presupposes the candidate's ability to take on the obligations of membership … "[79] The sentence is an anatomists' parody gone wild: "have achieved"? "stability"? "institutions guaranteeing"? Where could any of that have ever been imagined to come from, fifteen years after the collapse of a multinational political order that had systematically denied all those values, had none of those institutions, and rested on the back of long histories where these were rarely among the rules of any of the games played in any local town?[80]

And now things have changed – in some cases, such as Poland (at least until 2023) and Hungary, for the worse. Other acceders (e.g., Bulgaria,

[77] See Chapter 9.

[78] *See* Chapter 5.

[79] Conclusion of the Presidency, European Council in Copenhagen (June 21–22, 1993) at 13, quoted by Peters in Chapter 4.

[80] *See* Martin Krygier, *Introduction*, *in* SPREADING DEMOCRACY AND THE RULE OF LAW? THE IMPACT OF EU ENLARGEMENT FOR THE RULE OF LAW, DEMOCRACY AND CONSTITUTIONALISM IN POST-COMMUNIST LEGAL ORDERS 1 (Wojciech Sadurski, Adam Czarnota & Martin Krygier eds., 2006).

Romania, Slovakia, and Slovenia) wobble this way and that. The jury is out on whether regional organizations such as the EU can do much to further the rule of law in member states once the authoritarian genie has, as it were, made it back into the bottle. Certainly, Polish and Hungarian "backsliding" in recent years has shocked the system, though the EU has in recent years tried harder and harder to toughen several vertebrae in its own spine.

The picture remains mixed. In her report of volatility, backsliding, and worse in Latin America, Pou Giménez nevertheless rightly insists that

> The fact that democracy has for three decades remained the only road to political and legal authority in Latin America is in itself an immense historical watershed. In general, civil society has been revitalized, there is widespread public recognition of social and cultural pluralism, and the constitutionalism of rights has given the law a centrality it had never enjoyed before in the region.[81]

Ginsburg and Schoppe show that the least tensions occur between TLOs and states within their orbit when the former ask for least. But then their effects are unlikely to be great either. Perhaps all the tension in the EU will prove worthwhile. After all, where the EU has been most active, member states have not done the worst things they might have and indeed not so long ago actually did. Though opponents of the government might be sued and sacked in Poland, no one is killed or jailed. Elections are held and they are free, if not fair. And in Poland, though not Hungary, the government lost an election (an event whose consequences they are vainly trying to undo as I write). Critics come and go. Part of this chapter was written in Budapest, capital of an undemocratic country where the EU is having great difficulty restoring semblances of the rule of law. Its ruler has proclaimed Hungary under his regime an "illiberal state," and he has been true to his word. However, while the Central European University, the parent teaching body of the institute with which I am affiliated, has been kicked out of the country, the members of the CEU Democracy [research] Institute go about their business, which has a lot to do with investigating and criticizing the unruly and undemocratic acts of the local government (and others). This does not happen in Russia, China, Venezuela, and many other rule-of-law miscreant states, unpoliced, or policed by weak regional organizations. There have been no coups in the EU.

[81] *See* Chapter 10.

But then Poland and Hungary, for all their huffing and puffing, are keen to stay in the club. They abuse it (after the Polish elections of October 2023 one might have to say "abused," though it is too soon to tell), if only because they have drawn heaps of money from it, and hope to get more. Moreover, even though the inveterately abusive Kaczyński might compare the EU to Russia, given the Poles' eons-old (and well-grounded) distrust of Russia, he knew there was a difference, and anyway the Poles have nowhere else to go. His successors don't abuse and don't want to go anywhere else. Orbán hopes to play both sides, as he performs his "peacock dances" at the EU, plays hard to get on Ukraine, but eventually backs down at crucial moments. And the EU slowly, cumbersomely, and uncertainly makes occasional (small) advances. What should we expect, however, as Carlos Closa recently asked,[82] if real heavyweights, such as Germany or France, the largest contributors to EU budgets, were to go rogue, as they might yet do? What pressures would or could the EU apply?

Whatever the answers to such questions turn out to be, a normative question remains: Apart from what rule-of-law-leaning transnational organizations should *expect*, what should they *do*? Is the fate of the rule of law within states any business of anyone outside those states? Tamanaha argues that "it is not acceptable to penetrate state sovereignty for other than the most blatant violations of human rights."[83] It is not clear whether he thinks that, say, the EU's demand that Poland and Hungary honor agreements to observe the rule of law, which they made to enter the organization in the first place, amounts to such an unacceptable penetration of state sovereignty. However, it is clear that several states would find his argument welcome, brandishing not only their sovereignty but their "constitutional identity"[84] as shields against transnational intervention. As Ginsburg and Schoffe point out, "even if they are appalled by how Poland and Hungary . . . behaved, defenders of the traditional view of member states' sovereignty might, as a matter of principle, feel uneasy when the European level enforces quasi-constitutional norms such as the rule of law."[85] And Anne Peters surveys

[82] At the "From Rule of Law Backsliding to A Sustainable Rule of Law" conference, September 21–23, 2023, Radboud University, Nijmegen, The Netherlands.

[83] *See* Chapter 2.

[84] *See* JULIAN SCHOLTES, THE ABUSE OF CONSTITUTIONAL IDENTITY IN THE EUROPEAN UNION (2023); ANTI-CONSTITUTIONAL POPULISM pt. IV: EU Responses (Martin Krygier, Adam Czarnota & Wojciech Sadurski eds., 2022); *see also* Chapter 4.

[85] *See* Chapter 5.

the efforts of international and regional organizations around the world, to supervise constitutional developments in states within their orbits. She reports (presumably local) sentiment "that the international organizations' various techniques of cajoling, persuading, and motivating states to adopt constitutions that embody the rule of law constitute an unlawful intervention into the domestic affairs of the receiving states, a risk of infringement of state sovereignty and national self-determination, or simply unfairness and normative inappropriateness, due inter alia to selectivity and hypocrisy."[86] Peters responds thoughtfully and with nuanced care to such accusations, allowing that there might be something in them but certainly not everything. However, and of course, populist leaders seize upon them as evidence of the malign insensitivity of new transnational "imperialists."

Scheppele disagrees. Transnational law now "increasingly . . . enters into national law itself and modifies (or at least is supposed to modify) the operation of what had been imagined by legal philosophers as a hermetically sealed-off space."[87] Given that national, transnational, and international are inextricably enmeshed, they must be harmonized, lest "legal subjects will be left wondering which apparently binding rule applies to them."[88] The resultant harmonized order Scheppele calls the "rule of law writ large." If nation-states legally subject to such orders seek to object, they are, as it were, hoist by their own petard:

> We can take advantage of the fact that many of the now rogue states are still bound by the membership requirements [of the transnational organizations to which they belong] even as their national autocrats have violated these standards through backsliding. The standards of the transnational organizations can now be enforced by restoring the rule of law writ large. Best of all, since the now backsliding states undertook these transnational obligations of their own accord in a not too distant past, enforcing the standards of these transnational organizations simply holds the backsliding states to standards they once committed to follow at a more democratically robust moment.[89]

Enforcing such standards might even include countenancing "asymmetric rupture: breaking the law to establish the rule of law in recovering democracies."[90]

[86] *See* Chapter 4.
[87] *See* Chapter 7.
[88] *See* Chapter 7. Under PiS, Polish courts and subjects were already in exactly that position in several spheres.
[89] *See* Chapter 7.
[90] *See* Chapter 7.

I have much sympathy with Scheppele's position, particularly in relation to the European countries we both know best and which have committed to, and benefited hugely from, the agreements they have made. However, I think that to be persuasive the argument needs some more *normative* support (which includes legal support) than mere membership and numbers of entities involved. Certainly (nor is this Scheppele's argument), that support will not come simply from the discovery that "rogue states" deviate from the "formulaic checklists" of old, and of some transnational, bodies. To them, Viktor Orbán already has a well-rehearsed and superficially effective response: "cultures are different, constitutional traditions are different, so there is no single European definition and no single European standard. And if you create a case without these, the result will be not 'the rule of law' but the 'rule of man.'"[91] As we have seen, there is something in the argument. The idea that different constitutional traditions have generated different ways of doing things, and might be driven by different concerns, is both true and the reason why legalistic checklists so often fail to take in inhospitable climes. However, constitutional identity is a concept that can be, and is, easily abused. Blurring the difference between a plausible "margin of appreciation" that allows that cultures are not identical, on the one hand, and a wall of "constitutional solipsism,"[92] on the other, simply enables, and is often intended to enable, authoritarians to do their own thing, whatever be the values to which they claim to adhere. That is why, as Keleman and Pech have argued, "autocrats love constitutional identity"[93] and are actually fond of battling on the terrain of forms and checklists. On the one hand, recent authoritarian-populist regimes around the world have contrived to undermine the ideal of the rule of law with the assistance of hallowed legal forms.[94] It turns out it's not so hard. But if it is, they can play the "constitutional identity" card: "That's not the way we do things here."

Forms of chicanery multiply, whereby one pretends fidelity to formal rules in order to achieve purposes alien to the underlying (and often

[91] Balázs Orbán (@BalazsOrban_HU), X (Jan. 7, 2023, 11:30 AM), https://twitter.com/BalazsOrban_HU/status/1611671705101176833.

[92] SCHOLTES, *supra* note 84.

[93] R. Daniel Kelemen & Laurent Pech, *Why Autocrats Love Constitutional Identity and Constitutional Pluralism: Lessons from Hungary and Poland* (RECONNECT, Working Paper No. 2, 2018), https://tinyurl.com/a6wuppk8.

[94] *See* Gianluigi Palombella, *The Abuse of the Rule of Law*, 12 HAGUE J. ON RULE L. 387 (2020).

unwritten) aims, values, practices, and institutions on which the substance of the rule of law was supposed to rest.[95] Moreover, because those aims and values have no weight with these leaders, they can be constitutionally pedantic when it serves their ends,[96] and "constitutionally shameless"[97] when pedantry does not work for them. Given the often-sophisticated legalistic pretences that accompany these subversive practices, conventional partisans of the rule of law have difficulty knowing how to respond. Thus, as Scheppele has observed of Orbán's mock objection quoted above: "Here is Viktor Orbán's approach to the rule of law – making every requirement so detailed that the forest is lost in the trees. He loves checklists because they can always be gamed. But he hates general principles because he violates them all."[98]

But if the rule of law requires that power be tempered so as not to be arbitrary, these gambits are less persuasive. Though particular ways of achieving this result might vary greatly, the rule of law calls for key powers to be checked, balanced, and separated (and then connected). Instead, anti-rule-of-law populists seek to consolidate and concentrate power in their own hands. Where well-tempered power depends on substantial independence of power-adjudicators from power-wielders, such populists increase their dependence. Where one mediates power and calls for a patient filtering of decisions through institutions, the other seeks to make it all personal, unmediated, and unconstrained: it endorses an instantaneous quasi- or pseudodemocracy in which a decision by the leader may become law the next day.

Rule-of-law backsliding should be rejected, not because some item or other in a checklist goes unticked but to the extent it can be shown that the practices in question violate the *point* of the enterprise, which is the reduction of the possibility of arbitrary exercise of power. Among regimes that have undertaken to support the rule of law, legalistic tricks that aid arbitrary power are not sacrosanct elements of "constitutional identity" but violations of it. Indeed, there is point in Scheppele's argument that successor governments might be justified in breaking the law to restore the possibility of the rule of law where it has been

[95] *See* ANDRÁS SAJÓ, RULING BY CHEATING (2022).

[96] *See* Kim Lane Scheppele (@KimLaneLaw), X (Jan. 8, 2023, 2:56 PM), https://tinyurl.com/ye22ywdn.

[97] Tarunabh Khaitan, *Killing a Constitution with a Thousand Cuts: Executive Aggrandizement and Party-State Fusion in India*, 14 L. & ETHICS HUM. RTS. 49 (2020).

[98] Kim Lane Scheppele (@KimLaneLaw), X (Jan. 8, 2023, 2:56 PM), https://tinyurl.com/ye22ywdn.

significantly abused and undermined. However, there is a significant step short of that which it would be wise to try first. This is what András Sajó calls "militant rule of law":

> the aggressive use of tried-and-tested rule of law standards and rules tailored to specific circumstances. Militant rule of law allows for exceptions to the rule of law which are already recognized in rule of law standards and a principled reinterpretation of rule of law precepts. When it comes to reliance on the recognized exceptions of the rule of law, it is vital that these exceptions be temporary, subject to proportionality and independent control.[99]

Standards that Sajó has in mind include intent analysis, reasonableness review, abuse, bad faith, and others in a similar vein. He is expanding his analysis as I write.[100] There's plenty of material to work on in backsliding nation-states.

## III The Geopolitical Dimension

Still, however much we tinker with the law, ultimately we must recognize that pressures that both support the rule of law and those that deny it are never all legal. That is a general truth,[101] but particularly in the transnational context there are specific circumstances and pressures quite beyond the powers, intentions, and even domains of concern of the specific actors engaged. One is geopolitics. We would not be discussing this subject but for them.

It has already been stressed in this book and this chapter, and it is worth stressing again, how new all this is. In world-historical terms, the global apotheosis of the rule of law began virtually a moment ago. As Farrall and Halliday point out,[102] though lip service was occasionally paid to it earlier, the rule of law became an agenda item in the UN General Assembly only in 1992.[103] By 2012, it was, also for the first time, the

[99] András Sajó, *Militant Rule of Law*, Verfassungsblog (Dec. 23, 2023), https://verfassungsblog.de/author/andras-sajo/.

[100] *See* András Sajó, *Militant Democracy and Not-So-Bad Law* (Democracy Inst. Working Paper No. 2024/21, 2024), https://tinyurl.com/2psw89j6.

[101] *See* Martin Krygier, *Why Rule of Law Promotion is Too Important to Be Left to Lawyers*, *in* Who's Afraid of International Law 133 (Raimond Gaita & Gerry Simpson eds., 2017); Martin Krygier, *The Ideal of the Rule of Law and Private Power*, *in* Research Handbook on the Politics of Constitutional Law 14 (Mark Tushnet & Dimitry Kochenov eds., 2023).

[102] *See* Chapter 6.

[103] *See United Nations and the Rule of Law*, United Nations, www.un.org/en/ruleoflaw/ (last visited Feb. 20, 2024).

exclusive subject of a "high-level meeting" of the Assembly, which, in its "declaration on the rule of law at the national and international levels," affirmed "that human rights, the rule of law and democracy are interlinked and mutually reinforcing and that they belong to the universal and indivisible core values and principles of the United Nations" (even though the Assembly had explicitly begun to register the place of the rule of law in this pantheon only twenty years before, in its forty-sixth year of existence). Over the same period, as Farrall has noted elsewhere, there occurred a

> transformation of the rule of law from curiosity to familiar friend [] in the term's increasing appearance in the Council's resolutions. During the Cold War, rule of law featured in Security Council resolutions a mere handful of times. By contrast, in the nine years from the beginning of 1998 until the end of 2006, the phrase "rule of law" appeared in no fewer than sixty-nine Council resolutions.[104]

Moreover, as we have seen throughout this book, this recent eruption of concern for the rule of law was not confined to the United Nations; it was standard. Whereas in earlier decades, it would be hard to underestimate its global rhetorical significance, from the 1990s and in the first decade of this century it would be hard to exaggerate it. At least at the level of transnational rhetorical endorsement, by the beginning of this century "rule of law" quickly scooped the pool.

So much so, that transnational supply often outpaced domestic demand, indeed stimulated much of it, even took on a life of its own. Of course, the rule of law is notably absent from many of the places and predicaments the UN and TLOs more generally encounter, so there was reason for demand to have been high in any event, but then that absence was already evident for decades before the UN began to talk about the rule of law. There must have been other reasons for its invocation than the need for it, given that that need has been perennial but rule of law only became such an omnipresent hurrah phrase yesterday. And, as many of the chapters in this volume attest, a similar acceleration of interest at the end of the last century can be observed among scores of other international and transnational organizations concerned with scores of different subjects and places and peoples.

Why this occurred just when it did is an intriguing story, including several novel trends that converged around the 1980s: in theories of

[104] Jeremy Matam Farrall, United Nations Sanctions and the Rule of Law 22 (2007).

development,[105] democratization,[106] economics,[107] and regional governance.[108] These ideas might have stayed in the academy, however, were it not for one world-historical geopolitical development that moved them from theory to practice. Though some general impulse came from the "third wave" of democratization[109] in Latin America and Southeast Asia in the 1980s, the burst of the rule of law into dramatic prominence only came on the unanticipated crest of that "wave": the collapse of European communism.[110]

For none of this occurred in a geopolitical vacuum. Indeed, it is far from clear that it was the irresistible charms of the rule of law that accounted for the recent transnational vogue for it. It was carried along by geopolitical changes that, in the first instance, had nothing particularly to do with it. During the Cold War, the rule of law played no part in the glorifying myths and narratives of one of the two grand competitors, and no role in what Eric Hobsbawm described as "the special house-style [communism] imposed on its successors."[111] And while in the West, by contrast, law and the rule of law were indeed vaunted, sometimes even

[105] *See* F. Charles Sherman, *Law and Development Today: The New Developmentalism*, 10 German L.J. 1264 (2009); Jane Stromseth, David Wippman & Rosa Brooks, Can Might Make Rights? Building the Rule of Law after Military Interventions (2006); Deval Desai & Michael Woolcock, *The Politics of Rule of Law Systems in Developmental States: "Political Settlements" as a Basis for Promoting Effective Justice Institutions for Marginalized Groups* 5 (Effective States & Inclusive Dev., Working Paper No. 8, July 2012), https://tinyurl.com/y23p99x4; Kevin Davis & Michael Trebilcock, *The Relationship Between Law and Development: Optimists Versus Skeptics*, 56 Am. J. Comp. L. 895, 945–46 (2008).

[106] Guillermo O'Donnell, *The Quality of Democracy: Why the Rule of Law Matters*, 15 J. Democracy 32 (2004).

[107] *See* Douglass North, Institutions, Institutional Change and Economic Performance (1990); The New Law and Economic Development: A Critical Appraisal (David M. Trubek & Alvaro Santos eds., 2006); Stephen Haggard & Lydia Tiede, *The Rule of Law and Economic Growth, Where Are We?*, 39 World Dev. 673 (2011).

[108] *See* Ronald Janse, *Why did the Rule of Law Revive?*, 11 Hague J. on Rule L. 341 (2019).

[109] *See, e.g.*, Samuel Huntington, The Third Wave: Democratization in the Late Twentieth Century (1991).

[110] I have sought to explain why this explosion of the global promotion of the rule of law began in the 1990s and could not have occurred earlier, in Martin Krygier, *The Rule of Law After the Short Twentieth Century: Launching a Global Career, in* Law, Society and Community: Essays in Honour of Roger Cotterrell 327 (Richard Nobles & David Schiff eds., 2014); revised and updated version published in The Long 1989: Decades of Global Revolution 161 (Piotr H. Kosicki & Kyril Kunakhovich eds., 2019).

[111] Eric Hobsbawm, The Age of Extremes: The Short Twentieth Century 1914–1991, at 4 (1994).

considered national treasures, there were hefty barriers to export since "we" only owned a part of things, and no one thought that was going to change in a hurry. As Farrall and Halliday point out, just as Security Council peacekeeping operations awaited the end of the Cold War,[112] so too, given the competitive struggling and posturing that dominated the world, the rule of law could never be part of any inter and transnational lingua franca. There was no room then for a global career, for the rule of law to be invoked with reverence by international agencies and the great and the good of all types around the globe.

The collapse of European communism, and with it the world-historical communist mission, quite literally changed the "conceptual geography"[113] of the world. In a moment, it appeared to many that the twentieth century's great ideological and systemic struggles were over. And there was a winner. To put it crudely, of the two contestants that had survived World War Two, one of which denied and denounced the rule of law, while the other boasted of it, the former collapsed and the other was left standing. One was out the window; the other came confidently through the door, keen to fill the room and rearrange (and replace) much of the furniture with its own styles and brands. Prominent in all models for refurbishment was the rule of law (with, if the mangled metaphor be allowed, its two partners – democracy and human rights – all rhetorically attached at the hip). As we have seen, the idea, if not the achievement, quickly attained unprecedented global prominence and was proclaimed to have well-nigh universal salience. For once and for a moment it seemed to lack rivals and gained apparently eager constituencies: some because they believed in it; some because it was a condition for other things they wanted, such as admission to hitherto exclusive clubs like the European Union or Council of Europe; some because there was a buck in it; and some for the whole cascade of reasons. Many constituents were happy in every way. For a while.

The career prospects of the rule of law, then, were transformed by the same historical transformations that prompted Francis Fukuyama to ask whether the world had reached or might be approaching the end of history. Around the world, countries were encouraged to join the winning team and adopt its models of democracy, human rights, and rule of law – the last now claimed as central to the others. For some time, the enthusiasms of promoters were reciprocated by promotees as "the rule of

[112] *See* Chapter 6.

[113] Tony Judt, *The Rediscovery of Central Europe*, 119 DAEDALUS 1, 25 (1990).

law became the big tent for social, economic, and political change generally."[114] The question mark[115] that followed the four words in Fukuyama's famous/notorious provocation was little noticed at the time and did not make its way into his subsequent book.[116] It should have, since the answer seems to be "no." Still, for a while many key liberal notions, central among them the rule of law, seemed, if not at the end, then at least high on the wave, of history.

It was not always so, and it might pass; I am tempted to say it must pass. Indeed, it might well be passing as I write and you read.[117] If geopolitical and transnational forces accounted for the rule-of-law moment, they might also come to account for its passing. The future global career of the rule of law, within nations and among them, might turn out to depend less on people's attachment, or lack of it, to the ideal of the rule of law itself than on what is thought, for whatever reason, of its avatars and homes. The prestige of "the West" was high for a moment after 1989. All sorts of features, real or imagined, attributed to the available option were considered valuable and important to emulate, just because of their provenance, associations, and apparent success appeal. This assumption of virtue by association is unlikely to continue, after these once hallowed sources of influence and prestige have seen their lustre dim in so many aspects – internal, external; national, transnational – justifiably or not.[118] Given all these challenges, one should expect them to be reflected in the future career prospects of the rule of law, both as a cliché with which everyone seeks to be associated and, far more important, as embodying or serving ideals that all should value. Today, after all, it is not only Xi Jinping who believes that "the East is rising and the West is declining."

Quite apart from those transnational actors that might be thought to have their hearts in the right place on this issue, even if their heads wobble about, there are others, and other actors within them, whose hearts appear to be in a different place. The bad news from many sources in this book and elsewhere is that the climate for the rule of law appears –

[114] Agnès Hurwitz, *Towards Enhanced Legitimacy of Rule of Law Programs in Multidimensional Peace Operations*, *in* AGNÈS HURWITZ & KAYSIE STUDDARD, RULE OF LAW PROGRAMS IN PEACE OPERATIONS 1, 4 (2005).

[115] Francis Fukuyama, *The End of History?*, 16 NAT'L INT. 3 (1989).

[116] FRANCIS FUKUYAMA, THE END OF HISTORY AND THE LAST MAN (1992).

[117] See the bracing data in Chapter 1.

[118] *See Discrediting Democracy in "Sharp Power" Battle of Ideas*, DEMOCRACY DIG. (Nov. 1, 2021), www.demdigest.org/discrediting-democracy-in-sharp-power-battle-of-ideas/.

nationally and transnationally, and not coincidentally but enmeshedly – increasingly to be turning sour.

Thus, as we have seen, several countries around the world – many of them prominent "beneficiaries" of rule of law programs in the Global North, South, East, and West – are now ruled by illiberal populists who have little time for the traditional *ideals* of the rule of law, even if for many reasons they still claim to be implementing it, albeit in their own way, infused with their own "national characteristics."[119] Indeed, such populists have come to form transnational ambitions and organizations of their own.[120] Politically, they routinely connect the likes of Steve Bannon, Viktor Orbán, Marine Le Pen, Giorgia Meloni, former Australian prime minister (and, I confess, my former student) Tony Abbott, and many other populist worthies, cronies, and supporters. They build transnational organizations, such as the Danube Institute, and exchange illiberal advice. Legally, they indulge in routine "abusive constitutional borrowing," to borrow the title of an excellent recent study.[121]

On the one hand, while these regimes typically flout the ideals and assault the institutions associated with the rule of law – deliberately, systematically, and often together – they vehemently deny that is what they are doing and invest a good deal of effort to pretend they are doing otherwise. They might cheat to do so, but, like hypocrisy, this is still some sort of tribute, for "legal cheating is pretending to be faithful while violating underlying principles. It is not a defiant gesture."[122] Part of the reason for such pretence, as discussed in several chapters in this book, is that these regimes are trying to persuade various transnational promoters (and policers) of the rule of law that their impostures should be taken literally.

On the other hand, those illiberal regimes that pretend to observe the rule of law do not seem much embarrassed when they are caught out and, notwithstanding heaps of rule-of-law-based critique, that does not seem

119 *See* ANTI-CONSTITUTIONAL POPULISM (Martin Krygier, Wojciech Sadurski & Adam Czarnota eds., 2022).

120 *See* Jonathan Kuyper & Benjamin Moffitt, *Transnational Populism, Democracy, and Representation: Pitfalls and Potentialities*, 12 GLOB. JUST.: THEORY PRAC. RHETORIC 27 (2020); THORSTEN WOJCZEWSKI, THE INTER- AND TRANSNATIONAL POLITICS OF POPULISM, FOREIGN POLICY, IDENTITY AND POPULAR SOVEREIGNTY (2023).

121 ROSALIND DIXON & DAVID LANDAU, ABUSIVE CONSTITUTIONAL BORROWING: LEGAL GLOBALIZATION AND THE SUBVERSION OF LIBERAL DEMOCRACY (2021).

122 ANDRÁS SAJÓ, RULING BY CHEATING: GOVERNANCE IN ILLIBERAL DEMOCRACY 285 (2023).

likely to change. For the rhetorical power of the rule of law and professed attachment to its animating values have undoubtedly waned considerably in the last few years. Some of its putative exemplars have let it down, its opponents have muscled up, and its real prospects and significance in the life of nations are coming under varied, sustained, and imminent threats from many familiar and some quite novel quarters.

We are, then, in an ambiguous – one might say, fraught – moment. Even though the term is still everywhere, it's hard to say we see more rule of law in the world. Certainly, inhabitants of Myanmar or Belarus or Afghanistan or Russia or Ukraine or any of the countries discussed in Chapters 7 to 13 of this book have seen little of it recently. In Hong Kong, it is a fast-disappearing memory. In China itself, the term has not disappeared but is embraced within sinister qualifiers like "socialist rule of law with Chinese characteristics."[123] That term is not empty of significant content, but if it has anything to do with tempering power, it is not the power of those who propagate the term. More generally, Anne Peters is right to speak in this volume of "[t]he current backlash against the 'international liberal order' with the rule of law at its core."[124] One might add, following Shaffer and Sandholtz, that this is not merely an international but also, and not coincidentally, a transnational and national phenomenon at the same time.

On the other hand, while the momentum of rule-of-law enthusiasm is already slowing down or at least facing some stiff pressures, its end is not yet in sight or inevitable. The expression still has global presence and rhetorical force. The UN, World Bank, EU, the American Bar Association, and other international organizations still laud the rule of law and expend much sweat and treasure, and sometimes blood, in efforts to bring it about. The programs generated in those times of enthusiasm have not evaporated, though their promoters today appear less confident – a confidence perhaps always unfounded – that they know what they are doing.[125] At least in the West and its appendages, rule of law still remains in the foreground of publicly professed political and legal ideals, with such others as justice, democracy, and human rights, where not so long ago it stood in their shadows.

Whatever settles from all the shocks, challenges, and disappointments will be different from what seemed possible, even likely to some, at the

[123] *See* Rudolph, *supra* note 6; Taisu Zhang & Tom Ginsburg, *China's Turn Toward Law*, 58 VA. J. INT'L L. 306 (2019); *see also* Chapter 13.

[124] *See* Chapter 4.

[125] *See* DESAI, *supra* note 53.

end of the twentieth century. If these are signs that we might be moving from the end of history to "no one's world"[126] (or to someone else's world), this is certain to be reflected in the international and transnational popularity and career prospects of the rule of law, and the ideals associated with it.

## IV Conclusions: Take Your Time

As Yogi Berra sagely cautioned, it is hard to make predictions, especially about the future. Only time will tell, or perhaps more bleakly, "Time will say nothing but I told you so."[127] So many unpredictable factors are involved that the longer-term results must remain uncertain. All the more is this the case when the transnational enters the domain. It is all so vast and so new. Just as it was folly to imagine initial institutional enthusiasms would be quickly vindicated, so we should not be too quick to abandon worthy projects – if that is what we judge them to be – because they have run into predictable, if often unpredicted, bumps in the road.

Time makes a difference in another sense as well, and one that we should take more into account than we typically do. It encapsulates the magnitude of the challenges facing friends of the rule of law, but it might offer some consolation/explanation for the many immediate difficulties their activities have faced. For, apart from institutions and goals, time is an under-understood, or even thought-about, ingredient and variable in all these experiments. Expectations for "growing" and "grafting" the rule of law (metaphors of cultivation are altogether more apt than ever optimistic, can-do ones of "construction" and "building") need to take account of the time one might expect one's seedlings to sprout, even in the best of all possible worlds. For, as Michael Woolcock has observed, development professionals, among them ROL development professionals, always need to ponder whether they are in the sunflower or the oak tree business. It makes a difference:

> If one wants to grow an oak tree, it helps to have both an acorn and a working knowledge of the conditions under which an acorn is most likely to become an oak tree. One also needs to know how long the

[126] Charles Kupchan, No One's World: The West, the Rising Rest, and the Coming Global Turn (2012).

[127] W. H. Auden, *But I Can't, in* Selected Poems 119 (Edward Mendelson ed., rev. ed. 2009).

> germination process is likely to take – in the case of the red oak, upwards of two years from flowering to acorn to sapling. Absent such knowledge, one might reasonably (but incorrectly) infer that, upon seeing no outward signs of life six months after planting the acorn, one's efforts had been in vain. It is only assessment against informed expectations at any given point after planting the acorn that allows one to make accurate inferences regarding success or failure. Needless to say, if one wanted to grow sunflowers instead – which have a wildly different growth trajectory to that of oak trees – one would need knowledge of that trajectory in order to accurately assess the effectiveness of one's horticultural skills.[128]

If one is seeking reliable, institutionalized, well-tempered power – the priceless goal of the rule of law, and not merely within particular nations but throughout the transnational world – it's oak trees all the way down.

[128] *See Guest Post: Michael Woolcock on the Importance of Time and Trajectories in Understanding Project Effectiveness*, DEV. IMPACT (2011), https://tinyurl.com/2f7cfx6j.

# INDEX

www.ingramcontent.com/pod-product-compliance
Lightning Source LLC
Chambersburg PA
CBHW072137080125
20113CB00004B/70